COSTA RICA GUIDE

YOUR PASSPORT TO GREAT TRAVEL!

CRITICAL ACCLAIM FOR OPEN ROAD PUBLISHING'S CENTRAL AMERICA TRAVEL GUIDES

"If a visiting tourist had to limit himself to one book, the **Costa Rica Guide** would certainly be my recommendation... As accurate, detailed and practically oriented as any I have seen...this book is a pleasure to read."
The Tico Times (Costa Rica's weekly English language newspaper)

"If you have to choose one guidebook, Paul Glassman's **Costa Rica Guide** provides a wealth of practical information, with a sharp eye and a sense of humor."
Travel and Leisure

"Belize Guide is *the* book you need. Don't leave home without it. Invaluable."
- International Travel News

"... full of well-researched information on hotels, restaurants, sightseeing, history, and culture ... Selections for lodging and food cover a wide range of prices with plenty of inexpensive and moderate choices. Glassman's practical information tips are worth the price of the book alone ... definitely recommended." *-
Series Reviews (Reviews of Travel Guide Series)*

Guatemala Guide is "filled with useful information ... thoroughly explores the territory and subject."
Booklist

ABOUT THE AUTHOR

Paul Glassman is the foremost authority on Central America travel, and has been writing the best-selling travel guides to the area since 1975. His **Costa Rica Guide, Belize Guide, Guatemala Guide**, and **Honduras Guide** are the best sources for accurate, comprehensive, inside travel information to these beautiful and exciting lands. His research and attention to detail is unsurpassed, his style lively and literate.

Glassman's books are widely considered to be the classic guides to Central America.

COSTA RICA
GUIDE

PAUL GLASSMAN

OPEN ROAD PUBLISHING
PASSPORT PRESS

5th Edition

ACKNOWLEDGMENTS
MANY THANKS to Edgar and Eleicsa Zamora, Mike and Sue Kalmbach, Tom Douglas, Natalie Ewing and Francisco Calderón, Paul Vigneault, Jean Harvey, and many, many others for assistance during my research for this latest edition.

Library of Congress Catalog Card No. 93-85357
ISBN 1-883323-03-7

Front cover photo courtesy of Calypso Tours
Back cover photo of toucan courtesy of ER Publishing
Back cover photo of waterfall and all interior photos by Ron Charles

TABLE OF CONTENTS

MAPS AND SIDEBARS

MAPS

SIDEBARS

1. INTRODUCTION

Costa Rica is a Caribbean vacation destination without Caribbean prices!

It's nature's wonderland, with more bird species than in all of North America, more butterfly species than in all of Africa - all within an easy day's round trip from the capital, San José. There are cruises to unpopulated tropical isles, ascents to the craters of smoking volcanoes, and superb accommodations, from all-inclusive beach resorts to youth hostels to inns that recall the days when travel was not for the masses.

The booze is cheap, the sun is reliable. And to top it off, Costa Rica is Latin America's longest-running democracy, and the Costa Ricans are the continent's friendliest people. Gone are the days when people thought of Costa Rica as some little-known Caribbean island or confused it with its war-torn neighbors. A Nobel Peace Prize has brought prominence, and has caused the world to take another look at this tropical oasis.

Do you want to see the whole country in a week or two? It's eminently possible. Do you want to look into the possibilities of moving to Costa Rica? You'll be tempted. Perhaps a spa vacation, or a week of fishing in *two* oceans, or diving among schools of fish that number in the hundreds or even *thousands*, or a hike to enjoy and discover the fascinating treasures of the tropical forests.

Or maybe your jungle adventure involves floating down a lazy river, or paddling furiously through rapids, or enjoying cocktails and an ocean view, while howler monkeys roar and bicker, and macaws flitter silently through the air in unearthly beauty.

Maybe you'll ponder all the possibilities while you relax at the beach, and leaf through the pages of this book.

All the information you need for a great trip is right in your hands!

Note from the First Edition

COSTA RICA has in the past been covered briefly in guidebooks for all of Central America, and for Costa Rican tourism today, this is too bad. Interest in seeing all of Central America has waned. But facilities in Costa Rica have continued to expand, and curiosity about the country is on the rise.

I hope to help remedy the lack of detailed, current information about travel and living in Costa Rica with this book. History, culture and geography are covered. But this book is also about places and how to visit them; about the capital city of San José and how to live well there at modest expense; about beaches and fishing villages and small towns, and the buses and chugging trains and canal boats that take you to them; about what to take along in your travels and where (and whether) you will find a comfortable place to sleep.

Read this book all the way through if you wish, or consult the table of contents and index to find what you need to know. And if there's something missing, or if you discover in your travels something that you want to share with others, please write to me in care of my publisher.

I hope that you enjoy your visit to Costa Rica.

WITH THIS LATEST EDITION, I've tried to keep up with the hectic but uneven growth of facilities for visitors to Costa Rica. I've taken into account hotels that have opened in the last few years; non-traditional activities and unconventional ways to explore them; new roads, and better transportation on old ones. Maps have been added, and others have been improved. Some of the material has been reorganized into what I hope will be a more logical and practical format.

I am grateful for the suggestions, comments, and leads that I have received from readers of previous editions, and for the hospitality that I have been privileged to enjoy on my repeated visits to Costa Rica.

WHAT'S NEW?

New hotels are opening all over Costa Rica, relieving a severe room shortage. And the quality of lodging is rising rapidly.

Among the best new hotels are **Casa Turire**, a superb plantation hotel; **Lapa Ríos**, a luxurious rain forest lodge; **El Jardín del Edén**, a first-rate intimate beach hotel at Tamarindo; and **Playa Tambor**, a world-class all-inclusive beach resort.

Theft is up. Theft from cars is taken for granted. But you can protect yourself.

Tour operators are offering nature-oriented excursions with ever-escalating price tags in popular spots such as **Manuel Antonio National Park**. But low-priced travel shops are mushrooming in places like **Fortuna** and **Puerto Viejo de Talamanca**, offering comparable adventures at a fraction of the rates charged by outfits in San José.

You can now dial toll-free to numerous hotels and travel services in Costa Rica from the United States and from Canada. And there are other ways to bypass the scandalous Costa Rican mail system.

All telephone numbers are changing. Look for the extra digit after April 1, 1994.

Prices are up . . . and up. Room rates have risen by as much as 50 percent in the last two years in certain hot spots. . . but bargains still abound away from where the package tours go.

There are new cruises . . . horseback tours . . . bicycling trips . . . visits with indigenous families . . . float trips down lazy tropical rivers . . . language schools . . . and more.

Turn the page and read all about it!

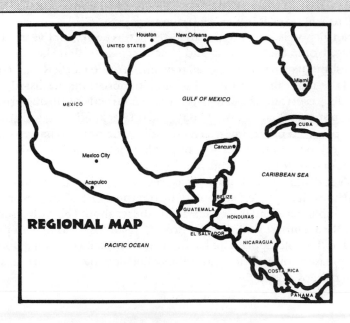

REGIONAL MAP

HOW TO USE THIS BOOK

The pages that follow cover the major towns, national parks, beaches and other points of interest in Costa Rica; how to get to them and what you'll find; where to stay, and what you should keep in mind before you go. Of course, not all appropriate travel advice can be repeated for every destination, so you'll also want to review part of the chapter of practical information before you set out for any place.

Prices are quoted in U.S. dollars, and, in the case of hotels, include sales and room taxes totalling about 16%. These are subject to change, and should be taken as approximate. You can easily check the latest hotel rates through a travel agent, or by calling toll-free telephone numbers, where these are given. Restaurant prices include tax and service charge, and indicate the approximate tab for a meal appropriate to the establishment.

Bus, railroad, and airplane schedules are, of course, also subject to change. I've given recent schedules to show the ease or difficulty of getting around by public transportation, and to help you plan your time. The tourist office in San José has the latest schedules for public transportation from the capital, or will get them for you. For travel from intermediate points (say, from Nicoya to one of the Pacific beaches), call the hotel where you plan to stay, in order to confirm the latest timetables.

For additional information and directions, the tourist office on the Plaza of Culture in San José is your best bet. Elsewhere, simply ask any handy Costa Rican. I do not know of another country where so many people will drop whatever they are doing, and take you, practically by the hand, to wherever it is you are trying to get to.

Not all hotels in Costa Rica are listed in this book, but I've tried to give a range, from basic *pensiones* and beach *cabinas* to first-class and luxury establishments. In general, when traveling around Costa Rica, I'd plan to spend the night in towns for which accommodations are listed. Phone ahead for reservations when you can, either directly or through someone else who speaks Spanish. At holidays and on weekends, this will guarantee you a room. At other times, a call will allow the hotel to have your room ready and to lay in supplies — an important factor at some of the beaches where food is not easily available.

Most distances and other measures are given in the metric system. Population figures are extrapolated from the latest official estimates.

Complaints about prices, service or abuses should be addressed to the **Costa Rica Tourist Board**, P. O. Box 777, San José, along with proof, if available. I would appreciate having your complaints as well, along with more pleasant discoveries and tidbits of advice that you care to send to me, in care of my publisher.

2. EXCITING COSTA RICA!
- OVERVIEW -

Natural wonders and opportunities for sport, adventure, and relaxation abound in Costa Rica. Volcanoes are at hand for rugged ascent by foot, or in the comfort of a car or bus. Within sixty miles of the capital are cloud forests, dense jungles sandy beaches, tropical savannah and piney highlands with rushing rivers and white waterfalls. Birds from humdrum sparrow to exotic macaw, beasts from deer to jaguar to monkey, are equally at home. Experienced sportsmen find fishing on two coasts that is unsurpassed in the hemisphere.

Comfortable lodging, civilized dining, and excellent transportation are all widely available at reasonable prices in a tropical setting that has yet to be heavily traveled. A self-confident people welcomes visitors as equals, not adversaries. All the surprises here are pleasant ones – which is the best surprise of all.

Here's a quick preview of what Costa Rica has in store for you:

SAN JOSÉ

In San José, the capital of Costa Rica, the hotels, country clubs, fine dining, recreational opportunities and measured pace invite the visitor to linger, especially when the weather at home is unpleasantly cold or oppressively hot. The city is low-key, a pleasant place in which to live, and therefore a nice place to visit.

Travelers use San José as a takeoff point for excursions to the many beaches and natural wonders of Costa Rica.

THE CENTRAL VALLEY

In almost every way, the Central Valley is the heart and soul of Costa Rica. The relatively advanced development of the Central Valley makes it easy for the visitor to explore. Roads go everywhere, and on most of them, you'll find buses both comfortable and frequent.

In the Central Valley, man and nature appear for all the world to live in beauteous harmony. All of man's intrusions might have been placed with a sense of how things look, how they interrelate, and how they are kept up. It is this machine-in-the-garden aspect of the Central Valley that is especially attractive, and unique in this part of the world.

THE WILD EAST

The trip to Limón is a descent from highlands to jungle through varied zones of vegetation. The Caribbean coastline is one nearly continuous sweep of white beach, most of it deserted. Wildlife treasures abound, including green turtles in their protected nesting area at Tortuguero. Fishing, especially for tarpon, is world-class.

Spurred by new road and canal construction, settlements are today spreading through much of the formerly empty Caribbean region. Forests are being cut down and converted to pasture, or tilled for crops. And the once-moribund banana industry is reviving.

PACIFIC COSTA RICA

Pacific Costa Rica covers a vast sweep of territory along the wide side of the country, from Nicaragua down to the Panamanian border. Overlooking a complicated, varied terrain are the volcanoes and mountain peaks of the Guanacaste, Tilarán, and Talamanca mountain ranges.

Travel to the main towns in the northern part of the Pacific coastal region — Puntarenas, Cañas, Liberia — is made easy by an excellent highway and frequent bus service. Most of the main attractions — notably the best beaches, such as those on the Nicoya Peninsula — are off this route, however, and are reached by plane, or with difficulty on poor roads.

The southern Pacific beaches of Costa Rica are every bit as inviting and pleasing to the eye as those along the Nicoya Peninsula, though they differ in character. Most are more open, sweeping and exposed, with fewer bordering outcrops of rocks. The farther south you go, the more humid and rainy is the climate, and the more lush and exuberant the vegetation that runs up to the sand. The mugginess is always relieved and attenuated, however, by breezes blowing off the water.

AROUND THE VOLCANOES

North of San José, over and beyond the volcanoes Irazú and Poás, is an area that includes gently rolling pastured hillsides often shrouded in fog; high montane tropical forest barely touched by human exploitation; hot springs gurgling up from the interior of the earth; jungle dripping with heat and wet; homesteads hacked out of the forest by modern pioneers; and banana lands that have been cultivated for more than 100 years. All this is within just 60 kilometers of San José in a straight line.

But until recently, mountains, rivers, jungle, and traditional trade routes that ran elsewhere, kept most of this triangle off the beaten track for visitors and Costa Ricans alike. Now, with the completion of a few strategic stretches of highway, it's possible to make a circular trip through this varied area in a matter of hours, even by bus. But for the lack of beaches, it's almost like seeing all of Costa Rica, and every era of its development, in just one day.

ECO-TOURIST MECCA

No doubt about it, Costa Rica is the world's eco-tourism mecca. There are hundreds of bird species, thousands of plants, and insects numbering in the tens of thousands, in habitats ranging from steaming lowland jungle to cloud forest to frosty peaks. Several worlds are crowded into a land of modest size, and visitors can appreciate them all, with not a few aches and mud puddles in the process.

But for most visitors, eco-tourism is a theme, the modern folklore of travel to Costa Rica that corresponds to Mayan culture in Guatemala and schnitzel in Vienna. It involves rafting trips and hikes to hot springs, but largely, it is pattering guides, bus rides, hotels with good and bad restaurants (with or without cable television), and friendly management.

DIVING

When you think of spectacular diving in Central America, you usually think of Belize or the Bay Islands of Honduras. But – surprise of surprises – Costa Rica holds its own in undersea as well as on-shore natural attractions. There are morays, jewfish, octopus, manta rays, grunts, snappers, and occasionally sharks, in schools that number in the hundreds. There are also rock formations, rather than intricate coral reef, though there are some undersea caves and coral clusters.

TAKING THE KIDS

Is Costa Rica kid-friendly? For most kids and parents, probably yes. Health and sanitary standards are acceptable, and few people give you funny looks if you take children to restaurants, museums, or anywhere else. But there sure is a lot to choose from: the zoo in San José, and private mini-zoos elsewhere; beaches; hotel-resort complexes with kiddie-size pools and even child care; jungle boat rides and monkey-watching expeditions.

FISHING

There's great sport fishing in Costa Rica, not only along both coasts, but in mountain streams and lakes as well. Plenty of world records have been broken.

COSTA RICA AWAITS YOU!

CRUISING A TROPICAL RIVER SYSTEM

Now you can board a bus in San José, drive past the La Paz falls between Barva and Poás volcanoes, and embark on a river boat at Puerto Viejo on the Sarapiquí. Downriver, past stands of bananas and still-uncut forest, the craft navigates the San Juan, along the northern limit of the Barra del Colorado Wildlife Refuge. Joining you at various times are toucans, crocodiles, sloths, monkeys and butterflies. The delta branch of the San Juan called the Colorado leads into Costa Rican territory, through palms and a network of man-made and jungle canals, to the Caribbean at the village of Barra del Colorado.

RAFTING THE RAPIDS

There's plenty of water in Costa Rica's rivers. You can go rafting somewhere in the country at almost any time of year, the sights along the way — exotic macaws, flocks of monkeys, sugarcane fields, dense rain forest trailing vines into the water — are available on comparable trips nowhere else, and, maybe best of all, the water is warm.

KAYAKING COSTA RICA

River kayaking trips most often are an easy float down the Bebedero River through the marshy and jungly Palo Verde Reserve in the northwestern lowlands, or along the Sarapiquí in the northern lowlands. More ambitious trips take you paddling from beach to beach along the rocky Pacific coast.

RIDING BIKES

Ascend to the top of a volcano, look around, and start down! Or set out from San José . . . it's all downhill, to the east and west. Take your bike along from home, with proper precautions for packing, or rent one when you get to San José.

GETTING A BIRD'S EYE VIEW

Flightseeing, that staple of scenic viewing in Alaska, has come to Costa Rica. And in a country where so many vistas and topographies are packed into a small area, viewing it all from above is both practical and priceworthy.

HORSEBACK RIDING

Horses are available almost anywhere in Costa Rica. Knowledgeable folk are not put off by the small, local animals, known as *criollos* (which are bred to get a job done without consuming excess feed), though larger, more well known breeds — Arabians, Morgans — will also be found.

RIDING THE WIND

Get set for takeoff! World-class windsurfing attracts more and more Costa Ricans and foreigners to Lake Arenal. Winds are steady out of the east at 20 to 30 knots, and water temperature is about 70 degrees Fahrenheit.

VISITING THE NATIONAL PARKS

Costa Rica is one of the leaders in Latin America in preserving its natural treasures. More than a quarter of the country's land area is protected in some way in national parks, national monuments, nature reserves, biological reserves and recreation areas. Park planners have attempted to protect a sample of each climate and ecosystem in the country.

WATCHING THE FIREWORKS OF NATURE

Much of the backbone of Costa Rica, the mountainous spine of the country, was formed in fire and brimstone, as the molten underworld spewed up in the eruptions that formed today's volcanoes, and enriched the soil of the Central Valley.

The most reliable performer these days is Arenal, the perfect volcanic cone that lies about three hours' traveling time to the northwest of San José.

On most nights, clouds of iridescent gas cling to the summit. The earth rumbles, and boulders the size of a house explode a thousand feet into the air, to a resounding orchestral accompaniment of pops and crackles and booms, to bounce and shatter their way down. Lava in red, orange, and yellow spews and slithers along the slopes.

MANY CUISINES

Gourmet restaurants in San José and nearby cook tender meats to order and serve them in delicate sauces along with crisp vegetables. Chinese, German, French, Italian, Swiss and even the better "international" restaurants produce superb results with foods that are fresh and abundant throughout the year. Costa Rica's excellent coffee, of course, is enjoyed with all meals.

PEACEFUL COSTA RICA

In a region where the watchwords are rebellion, repression, corruption, and suffering, Costa Rica can be described almost endlessly by what it is not. There is no long tradition of military takeovers. Indeed, there is not even an army, and elections have been free and fair for longer than in many European countries. No caste has been placed at the margin of society, toiling to enrich a small class of landowners, and the social tensions of neighboring lands are lacking.

Typical street scenes reveal few beggars or hustlers, refugees are not the most current export, and almost all people can read and write. Hardly anything happens to attract attention from far away, and no visions of dark, unofficial doings need trouble a traveler to the country.

COSTA RICA IN A NUTSHELL	
Population:	3,000,000 (approximate)
Government:	Constitutional, with separately elected executive (president and two vice presidents) and Legislative Assembly, appointed judiciary. Regional officials are appointed.
Languages:	Spanish; English in Caribbean region; Indian languages throughout.
Highest point:	Mount Chirripó
Coastline:	Caribbean, 132 miles; Pacific, 635 miles
Diversity:	850 bird species, 35,000 insect species, 9000 plant species, 208 mammalian species, 220 reptilian species, 160 amphibian species; habitat from steaming lowland jungle to beaches to temperate forest to frosty bare peaks.

3. THE LAND & PEOPLE

Costa Rica stretches from sea to sea. Sandy beaches fringed by palms, grassy savannahs, warm inland valleys, temperate plateaus, smoking volcanoes, frosty peaks, forested slopes and steamy jungles succeed each other across the landscape. Twice as many species of tree are native to the many regions of the country as to the continental United States. More than a thousand types of orchids flourish. The national wildlife treasures are still being discovered and inventoried.

Yet, by most standards, Costa Rica is small. From north to south or east to west, the country runs only 200 miles. The shortest distance between oceans is only 75 miles. With an area of 19,575 square miles (50,700 square kilometers), Costa Rica compares to Vermont and New Hampshire combined, or to the province of Nova Scotia. But the influences of two seas and seasonal tropical winds, earthquakes, volcanic eruptions that have enriched the soil, and altitudes that vary from sea level to nearly 4,000 meters, make of Costa Rica a continent in miniature.

Costa Rica drapes itself upon a jagged, mountainous spine that runs from northwest to southeast, part of the great intercontinental Sierra Madre-Andes chain. The volcanic Guanacaste, Tilarán, and Central ranges, separated from each other by relatively low passes and valleys, rise successively higher down the northern two-thirds of the country. Traversing the south of Costa Rica and continuing into Panama is the Talamanca range, which encompasses the highest points in the country. Cool and even frigid, the mountain slopes remain in part in their natural, breathtaking condition, but are more and more being deforested and exploited as pasture.

THE CENTRAL VALLEY

South of the volcanoes of the Central Range is the Meseta Central, or Valle Central – the Central Plateau, or Central Valley – in every sense the heart of Costa Rica. Measuring only about 20 by 50 miles, the Central Valley covers an area roughly equivalent to that of metropolitan Los Angeles. Yet packed into it are not only the capital city and most of the major population centers, but the richest farmland. Ranging from about

3,000 to 5,000 feet above sea level, with rolling, forested, and farmed terrain, the valley also abounds in natural beauty.

For centuries from the arrival of the Spaniards, virtually the only organized settlement in Costa Rica was in the Central Valley. Even today, this small area is a virtual city-state, dominating every aspect of national life. It claims well over 60 percent of the nation's population, concentrated in the capital, San José, and in the nearby cities of Cartago, Heredia, and Alajuela, and in dozens of small towns. Almost all industry clusters around the capital. Small farms crowd all cultivable land, producing vegetables for home use, as well as most of the nation's main export crop, coffee.

VALLEY OF THE GENERAL RIVER

East of the Central Valley, between the Talamanca Range and the Pacific, is the valley of the General River, which was isolated from the rest of the country until the construction of the Pan American Highway in the 1950s. Here, at elevations lower and warmer than those of the Central Valley, is Costa Rica's fastest-growing concentration of family farms, many operated by migrants from the more crowded core of the country.

THE PACIFIC COAST

Toward the Pacific, Costa Rica tilts precipitously down a slope broken by fast-flowing rivers, some of them harnessed to provide electrical power. In the northwest, on the edge of the hilly Nicoya Peninsula, are miles of sandy beach where Costa Rica's new resort industry is concentrating. Just inland are the savannahs of Guanacaste, populated mostly by fat, grazing cattle. Opposite Nicoya on the mainland is Puntarenas, once the nation's major port. Near Panama, to the south, are stretches of fertile lowland — once important banana-producing areas — as well as the hilly Osa Peninsula. The remainder of the Pacific coastal area consists of low hills, with a narrow, flat, fertile strip along the water. Temperatures all along the coast are regularly in the eighties and nineties (Fahrenheit), in contrast to the comfortable seventies of the Central Valley.

With its multiple bays, inlets, peninsulas, and hills that plunge into the sea, the Pacific coastline measures more than a thousand kilometers (630 miles), though a straight line from border to border is only half that length. The less broken Caribbean coastline runs only about 212 kilometers (133 miles).

THE EAST AND NORTHEAST

To the northeast of Costa Rica's mountainous spine, the land slopes down to a broad, low-lying triangle of hardwood forest and jungle, with two sides formed by the Caribbean Sea and the 300-kilometer (186-mile) border with Nicaragua. This is the land of eternal rainfall, where coastal storms can blow in at any time of the year. Elsewhere in Costa Rica, the central mountains block Caribbean storms, and it rains only from May to November, when the winds are from the Pacific.

For many years, the eastern lowlands were the impenetrable Costa Rica. Heat, disease, swamps and apparent lack of resources kept the first European explorers even from crossing the area, and the highlands were settled from the Pacific coast. It was only with the construction of a railroad to the sea at the end of the last century, and the immigration of workers from Jamaica, that permanent settlements were established. Even today, communication is difficult and population sparse. Few roads disturb the landscape in the forests along the border with Nicaragua, and most transport is by riverboat and canoe.

THE GOOD EARTH

With its varied climates, the Costa Rican earth can and does produce all the fruits and vegetables of the temperate zones, along with tropical plants, from mangoes, papayas, pineapples and oranges to *chayote, anona, pacaya, zapote* and many others whose names in English are either non-existent, or so unfamiliar as to be meaningless.

But for all the diversity of the land, Costa Rica has always relied mostly on a handful of crops. Corn and beans dominated the subsistence scratched from the earth for centuries as a colony, and are still the staples of most Costa Ricans' diet, along with rice. Coffee, grown in and around the Central Valley, and bananas, grown along both coasts, turned Costa Rica from a poor backwater into one of the better-off nations of Latin America. Sugar, in the lower elevations, and cotton, from the Pacific lowlands, are newer exports, along with beef from the grazing lands of Guanacaste. On these few products, with their rising and falling prices and years of lean and bountiful harvests, the prosperity of the nation depends.

FLORA AND FAUNA

Costa Rican flora and fauna, and tropical flora and fauna in general, are too varied to be treated justly in a small section of this book, or even in a few books devoted exclusively to the subject. Botanists refer to the natural exuberance of the tropics as "species richness." An area that supports two or three types of trees in the temperate zones might lodge dozens or even hundreds of plant species from ground level to forest canopy in the tropics. Some dimensions of this natural abundance in Costa Rica: more than 2,000 species of tree have so far been catalogued, twice as many as in the continental United States. Two-thirds of all known seed plants are found in Costa Rica. And there are over 1,000 orchids, ranging from the *guaria morada*, the purple national flower, down to those with blossoms too tiny to be casually noticed; more than 800 species of fern; and so on, and so on.

One explanation of this variety takes into account the poverty of many tropical soils, which might encourage plants to adapt and compete for nourishment at all levels, up to the tops of the tallest trees. Some draw nutrients from the soil, others feed themselves by sending roots into neighboring plants as parasites, or by capturing dust and decay washed down by rain. All nutrients are continually recycled. Abundant water helps to make this many-tiered world possible. Plants take moisture from the earth, the rain, from pools in large leaves, and from the very humidity of the air around them.

This general tropical description applies to much of the Caribbean lowlands of Costa Rica, and to cloud forest at high elevations. The temperate central valley, with its grassy meadows, pine forests, and rich volcanic soil, will not appear exotic to most visitors. But even here, a number of trees flourish that are so unfamiliar as to be without names in English. The Pacific lowlands, also with rich soil, support their own varieties of forest, which vary according to rainfall.

Random Sample of Wild and Cultivated Trees and Plants
Sea level to 2,000 feet: Palms (coconut, African oil, American oil, etc.), mangrove, mahogany, cedar, laurel, quinine, banana, rubber, walnut, guanacaste earpod, silk cotton (ceiba), cotton, cacao, sugarcane, rice, bamboo.
2,000 to 6,000 feet: coffee, corn, beans, pasture grass, wild fig (*higuerón*, *amate*), orchids and bromeliads, citrus, avocado, mango, cactus, pomegranate, papaya.
6,000 feet and higher: pine, fir (silvertree, etc.), cypress, alder, madrone, potato, peach, apple.

Many of the plant species of Costa Rica are described in *The National Parks of Costa Rica*, available in San José. Additional species are mentioned in the coverage of national parks in this book.

As a bridge between two continents, Costa Rica is home to animal forms both familiar and exotic. More than 750 species of bird inhabit Costa Rica, as many as in all of the United States. These range from common jays and orioles to large-beaked toucans and macaws, and the exquisite and elusive long-tailed quetzals of the trogon family. The national list includes 50 species of hummingbird, 45 tanagers and 72 flycatchers. A checklist of birds of Costa Rica is available for $2 from Natural History Tours, Box 1089, Lake Helen, FL 32744.

As for mammals, monkeys abound, among them howler, spider, white-faced, and the tiny marmoset. White-tailed deer, raccoons, and rattlesnakes, all common in North America, live alongside their South American cousins, the brocket deer, coatimundi, and bushmaster. Sea turtles — six of the world's eight species — nest on Costa Rica's shores. Alligators, peccaries (hatchback versions of the domestic pig), tepezcuintles (pacas), jaguars, ocelots, pumas and many other "exotic" species are still not uncommon in parts of the country.

Paradoxically, many of these species are difficult to sight. In settled areas, native animals and plants have been wiped out by hunting, land-clearing and poaching. In less-settled areas, the lack of roads and trails keeps out the interested visitor. Fortunately, however, many species can be seen in Costa Rica's national parks.

A MYSTERY OF NATIONAL CHARACTER

The Switzerland of Central America . . . more teachers than policemen . . . peaceful and idealistic . . . no sharp class distinctions . . . Costa Rica sometimes sounds like an earthly version of heaven, where all live in peace, and the cares of a less civilized age have been transcended.

No nation could live up to such a billing, however, and the facts bear sorting out. The relative lack of beggars and street urchins indicates that in at least *this* Central American country, there is a minimal social justice. Citizens do, indeed, respect authority and national institutions, rather than fear them.

But there are also elements of more fallible societies. Most Costa Ricans are moderately poor, though poverty is buffered by social services. The bloodiest war in the nation's history occurred only 40 years ago; political exiles have attempted, unsuccessfully, to invade and stir general uprising; and terrorist incidents, attributed to foreigners, have occasionally taken place. There is no army, but the police forces are organized along military lines. As in other parts of Latin America (and in many "advanced" countries), though to a much lesser degree, corruption is part of the way things work.

Still, in its usual state of social peace, in its profession of and adherence to democratic values, Costa Rica is more like nations in North America or Europe than its seething neighbors. It is the social democracy, rather than the Switzerland, of Latin America. That this is so is the primary mystery of the place to many first-time visitors.

There are no easy explanations, no easy descriptions of this regional anomaly. Costa Ricans are Latins, like most of their neighbors to the north and south. But they are a paler shade of Latin. Literally this is so, for though Costa Ricans come in all colors and mixtures of European, native American and African, the European strain predominates. But also in their ways, Costa Ricans are just like their neighbors, only — to turn an ethnic punch-line around — less so. Costa Ricans profess the sanctity

SHOOTING THE BREEZE

of the family as much as other Latins, and social life centers on the home, but the family is not quite the unassailable bastion of elsewhere. Catholicism is ingrained in national life, but public displays of religious fervor are relatively restrained. A Costa Rican male will maintain as strongly as any Latin that sex is a major occupation or preoccupation, but unbridled machismo is not the norm.

Why are the Costa Ricans a little bit different? Relative prosperity, inevitably, has something to do with it. But a few American nations have had fortune and circumstances comparable to those of Costa Rica. Argentina comes to mind immediately as a country that is fairly well off, even more European-descended than Costa Rica, and mostly middle class. Yet Argentine politics has been so fractious that many in that country consider dictatorship a necessity to sort themselves out. Costa Rica does not have this problem.

Costa Ricans themselves usually find the explanation in their history. The national myth that informs the way Costa Rica looks at itself arises out of the hardships of the colonial period. In that time, all were small farmers, equally poor and equally proud; all had to labor to sustain themselves. There were no slaves, no social classes, no wealth for anyone to accumulate, nor differences of race or privilege. No man could hold himself to be the better of another. Colonial Costa Rica was a natural democracy.

The national myth is, indeed, only a myth today. Costa Ricans are no longer equally poor. Opportunities to advance did finally present themselves in the era of coffee expansion, and there were no barriers to getting ahead other than those of talent and will. Most Costa Ricans now aspire to be part of the middle class, and a few are wealthy. But they still uphold equality of opportunity, independence, self-reliance and hard work, concepts converted from everyday facts of colonial life into generally accepted values. The heritage of social tensions of other Latin American countries — race against race, class against class — is not ingrained in Costa Rica. Individually, and as a nation, Costa Ricans erect few barriers against each other, and against outsiders.

The Ticos

Not everything about the Costa Rican character, however, is unique, different, or even positive. Some of the shadings of variation from neighboring lands are rather delicate, and easily over-emphasized.

Nobody who visits Costa Rica has any doubts about what region of the world he is in. Attitudes about time are relaxed, bureaucracy is stifling, and logic sometimes follows a non-western course. But few fail to notice, as well, a fresh air of difference. To themselves, and to those who know them, Costa Ricans are *Ticos*. The nickname derives from the way they speak. Diminutives are common in the language of Latin America. A moment becomes a "little moment," a *momentito*, to indicate "in a little while." But in Costa Rica, the word is *momentico*, and the peculiar ending is applied to the people who use it.

Like their Spanish language, which was locked away for centuries from the outside world by mountains, jungles, and seas, Costa Ricans are gracious, courteous, traditional, even a bit archaic. The *retreta* — that circling of boys and girls in the central square on weekend evenings, with shy glances that could, just could, lead to romance — hung on in Costa Rica even as it was disappearing from elsewhere in Latin America and Spain. Now, dating is the norm. But old-fashioned prudishness survives in public. Movies, for one, are heavily censored.

The sense of tradition and what is proper extends to marriage, of course. Most couples are married in church, and the common-law unions that elsewhere in Latin America may outnumber legal marriages are in Costa Rica the small minority. Marriage is usually life-long. Divorce is technically legal, but scandalous. If a marriage fails, the family stays together, though a husband sometimes spends his nights away from home. And even in successful marriages, the sexual wanderings of men are said to be tolerated, while women's are limited by social pressures and home duties; though how this can be is, of course, a great statistical mystery.

MINORITY GROUPS

Two minority groups – blacks and Indians – maintain ways different from those of the vast majority of Costa Ricans.

Blacks

Blacks were present in early colonial Costa Rica in small numbers as slaves, but those who survived the harsh conditions and ill treatment of that era merged into the general population. A later generation of blacks arrived in Costa Rica at the close of the nineteenth century, from Jamaica and elsewhere in the West Indies, to construct the railroad from San José to the Atlantic, and remained to labor on the banana plantations established by Minor Keith.

The newcomers were not welcomed with open arms. Blacks were confined to the coast by a prohibition against spending a night in the Central Valley. But in the lowlands they prospered, taking the best jobs on the plantations, and in commerce in the port of Limón. When Panama disease forced the relocation of the banana industry to the Pacific lowlands in the thirties, many blacks became small farmers, or labored on cacao plantations.

The 30,000 blacks in the country today more and more consider themselves Costa Ricans. All legal discrimination ended with the constitution of 1949. Most blacks who attended school since that time learned Spanish as well as English. Bilingualism has earned some good jobs in commerce and the travel industry in the Central Valley, though, as Protestants, they stand apart from other Costa Ricans.

Indians

Indians, or native Americans, are Costa Rica's forgotten minority. Their numbers are few – 20,000, perhaps even less – and they live in small groups away from the centers of population.

The original Indian tribes of Costa Rica fragmented and regrouped as a result of war, disease, and exile. The Indians of today range from those whose ways are indistinguishable from those of other Costa Ricans, to jungle groups who have only recently made contact with the outside world.

The Indians of the Talamanca group live in the forested valleys north of the Talamanca mountain range, and in the adjacent Caribbean lowlands. Their ancestors were forced into the area from central Costa Rica and from the Caribbean coast, and there they have remained, except for some who have migrated to the Pacific region. Two tribes survive, the **Cabécar** and the **Bribri**, composed of the remnants of a number of pre-Conquest tribes.

For many years, the Talamancan Indians were ruled only nominally from San José, through a native king. As banana operations pushed into their territory, many Talamancans came into regular contact with outsiders; but some of the inland groups remain steadfastly isolated and hostile even to Indians not of their own clan.

The most traditional Talamancan clans are dominated by women, and maintain peculiar customs that include relocating a corpse after a year's burial, isolation of a woman at birth, and native healing rituals.

The **Borucas** of the southern Pacific coastal area, near Panama, still live largely where they did before the Conquest. Aside from working their land communally, they live like other rural Costa Ricans. But by their racial heritage, their particular devotion to the celebration of the Immaculate Conception, and through pre-Columbian ritual that survives as superstition, the Borucas maintain a separate identity.

Other Indian groups are the **Chorotegas** of the Nicoya peninsula, who lost the use of their separate language years ago, and are almost indistinguishable from the mestizo, or mixed-blood, Costa Ricans of the area; and a few **Guatusos**, who live in the northern border lowlands east of the Guanacaste mountains.

RELIGION

The overwhelming majority of Costa Ricans is Catholic. The government contributes money to the Church, and religious education is part of the public-school curriculum, though technically optional. Catholicism is somewhat taken for granted. Men especially are lax in their practice, and for many persons, baptisms, weddings, and funerals are the only occasions for seeing the inside of a church. Religious holidays dot the calendar, and the saints' days of the towns and villages are regularly celebrated. But mystical devotion that transcends the hardships of everyday life is simply not part of the Costa Rican national experience. Fiesta processions pale before those of other Latin American countries. The country is short of priests, and most of the clergy is Spanish, Italian, Irish or American, rather than Costa Rican.

For many years, the missionary Protestant evangelism that had spread to Latin America from the United States had little impact in Costa Rica. Sudden modernization, disruption of isolated village life, prolonged warfare, natural disasters, and the hopeless poverty that elsewhere loosened ties with the traditional church exist to a lesser degree or not at all in Costa Rica. Some Protestant sects made their headquarters in San José not because Costa Rica was a fertile field, but because of its central location for their Caribbean and Central American efforts, and because life in San José is pleasant.

But in recent years, as Costa Rica has become a more mobile society, where jobs and residences change more than once in a lifetime, the bastions of Catholicism have begun to yield. Protestantism has now spread well beyond the West Indians who were the first to establish a non-Catholic foothold in Costa Rica. Evangelical churches are found in all the major towns, and in lowland areas that have received migrants from the Central Valley.

Civic pride is said to be the second great religion of many Costa Ricans. The *fiestas cívicas* — the year-end celebrations—bring out more parades, floats, dancing, puppeteers and music than any church commemoration. And national elections — when the peaceful governmental tradition is most evident— are the occasion for the largest celebrations. Costa Ricans are conscious that their national traditions and values differ from those of their neighbors, and are protective of their separateness. To outsiders, they may be Latin Americans. And a Guatemalan or a Honduran, when outside his homeland, may allow himself to be called a Central American. But a Costa Rican is always a Costa Rican.

EDUCATION AND CULTURE

Education and culture are national icons. A sense of what is proper and of the importance of being a well-mannered person are part of the way people live, not merely lessons taught in school. The high rates of literacy and school attendance are facts of life sometimes repeated ad nauseam. Culture in the highbrow sense is a near-mania.

The reason why is one of Costa Rica's mysteries. Only 150 years ago, as the coffee era began, Costa Ricans were just emerging from the era of barefoot, dirt-poor, ignorant backwardness. Not only was there no widespread literacy at the time, there was no national culture, no music, nothing but hard work to survive. Costa Rica's present love of the finer things traces back to the frontier days not at all, except, perhaps, as overcompensation, an obsession with what was once out of reach, and with being a people worthy of relative prosperity.

And how the Costa Ricans have tried to catch up! Long before oil sheiks gave out contracts to raise universities in the desert, Costa Rica invested coffee wealth in crash programs to expand primary education. When opera companies invited from afar had no place to perform, the coffee growers taxed themselves to finance the construction of a national theater to rival any hall in Latin America. When local folk traditions were found to be somewhat pale or even non-existent, the dances and music that were imported with the annexation of Guanacaste province were adopted by all Costa Ricans; the *punto guanacasteco*, performed to the accompaniment of guitar and the xylophone like gourd marimba, became the national dance, and the national folk music became what was played on the *quijongo*, ocarina and *chirimía*, wind instruments of pre-Columbian origin.

Most recently, when President Figueres cast his glance about, and saw that classical music was good, but that Costa Ricans were not adept, he arranged for the importation, whole, of a national orchestra and music school, to be staffed, eventually, by national counterparts in training.

Unlike some notorious opera houses that stand empty in jungles and deserts, the imported elements in the case of Costa Rica were brought to fertile ground, and have taken root. A respectable literature includes novels of social realism about exploitation on the banana plantations, and of *costumbrismo*, depicting the everyday happenings and ways of the cities and small towns. Modern and classical composers are appreciated on a broad scale. The best of the visual artists, such as engraver Francisco Amighetti Ruiz, have reached audiences outside of Costa Rica.

Strangely, for a people that has grabbed hold of its destiny and managed it fairly well, Costa Ricans have a strain of fatalism. This is said to come from their Hispanic heritage, and the churchly lessons of submission and obedience. It also comes out of hundreds of years of poverty that could not be transcended until relatively recently. The values of working hard and bettering oneself predominate, but these don't necessarily go along with planning ahead and being prudent. Costa Ricans are poor savers, and some big-ticket public investments were financed by foreign loans that are now burdensome. But with a sense of limited control over the future, and a past of deprivation, they are consumers par excellence. Those who can afford it, and those who can't, eat, drink, and dress well, buy all the consumer gadgets they can get their hands on, and enjoy life while they can.

4. A SHORT HISTORY

Here are some paradoxes:
Hardly a building survives in Costa Rica from the colonial era, though such relics abound elsewhere in Central America. There are few public historical monuments. Yet Costa Ricans, unlike their neighbors, refer almost constantly to the past to explain why they are the way they are; hardly a visitor escapes acquaintance with the country's post-Conquest history.

In museums and shops, exquisite ceramics and wrought gold recall pre-Columbian Indian cultures. Yet virtually no Costa Rican feels a link to the first inhabitants of the land.

The proudest moment in Costa Rica's history was a military intervention in a neighboring country. Yet Costa Rica claims a peaceful tradition of non-interference that sets it apart from other Latin American nations.

PRE-COLUMBIAN COSTA RICA

Even before the first Spaniards arrived, what was to become Costa Rica differed from neighboring lands. To the north, in what are now Mexico, Belize, Guatemala, Honduras and El Salvador, and to the south, in mainland South America, civilizations arose based on the cultivation and harvest of bountiful crops of corn by large groups of settled people. Some societies were so powerful and complex that they altered the landscape with great cities, subjugated peoples for hundreds of miles around, traded regularly with distant lands, wrote histories, and made complex astronomical calculations.

But the Costa Rica of that time was off civilization's beaten track. Armies and traders moved south from Mexico and Guatemala, and north from Peru. Some left their influences in Costa Rica. But none succeeded in dominating the land. Costa Rica was for both cultural regions a distant backwater, removed from the main communication routes. Mountains and swamps impeded passage. Population was sparse. Abundant food and water allowed the native groups to move easily from place to place, which made them difficult targets for conquest. As well, there were few riches to arouse long-term interest by outsiders. Contacts existed between north and south — Peruvian gold and seashells have been found in Mayan tombs — but the path of least resistance was by sea.

The peoples living in Costa Rica when the Spanish arrived belonged to five major cultural groups. **Caribs**, of South American and Antillean origin, inhabited the Atlantic region. **Borucas**, related to peoples of Colombia, lived in the lower Pacific coastal area. The **Corobicís**, the oldest of the native groups, lived in small bands in the valleys of the north. There were also a few **Nahuatl-speaking Indians** recently arrived from Mexico. The **Chorotegas**, the most numerous, lived in the Nicoya Peninsula, which was not to become part of Costa Rica until the end of the colonial period. More advanced and settled than the other groups, they cultivated corn and beans for subsistence, and cacao for trade.

In all, about 25,000 persons inhabited Costa Rica at the beginning of the sixteenth century, mostly in groups isolated from each other by rivers and mountains and jungles. Even related bands spoke mutually unintelligible languages. They made war on each other, and sacrificed or ate captured enemies.

Archaeologists have been able to trace a shadowy cultural history of the first peoples of Costa Rica, using the objects they left behind. Pottery from Nicoya from before the time of Christ shows similarities to Mesoamerican styles of the period, with red coloring on a buff background. Elsewhere in Costa Rica, pottery was made in a single color, as in South America. A few hundred years later, jade appeared in Nicoya and central Costa Rica, probably imported from Guatemala.

The northern influence is evident also in the appearance at the same time of the Mexican god Tlaloc on pottery in Guanacaste, in the northwest. In the sixth century, gold from South America began to appear in southern Costa Rica, possibly following the fall of the empire of Teotihuacán in Mexico, and the disruption of maritime trade routes.

By 1000 A.D., multicolored pottery was the norm in Guanacaste and Nicoya, and houses were built in rectangular shapes, all attributes of cultures to the north. Elsewhere in Costa Rica, houses were circular, while pottery featured appliquéd decoration, both characteristics of areas to the south. But while some of the influences of north and south are evident, the dividing line between the two in Costa Rica was generally faint and meandering.

SPANISH OCCUPATION

In densely settled parts of the Americas, the Spanish conquest followed a set pattern. The Spaniards made hesitant contacts with the natives of the coast, learned of a ruling civilization inland, marched to the interior, made war and alliances along the way, and finally subjugated the capital of the native empire, along with everything it ruled. Gold was sought by adventurers, souls by the Church, and glory by both. A new order was imposed, as Indians were parceled out to Spaniards to be converted, resettled, and put to work. Slaves were imported as necessary to replace those who did not survive war, disease, abuse and outrage. Spaniard married native, and a new set of classes, with the native-born Spaniard clearly on top, replaced in a few decades what had existed before.

In Costa Rica, events took a somewhat different turn, though not for want of effort on the part of the Spaniards. Indian battled Spaniard, but there was no empire to be subdued, and usually no surrender. Riches were elusive, and few slaves were imported. Soldiers and fortune-hunters gave way to subsistence farmers. With the passage of time, the settlement came to have more in common with English and French colonies in North America than with other Spanish dominions.

It was Christopher Columbus himself who discovered Costa Rica, and whose sailors were the first Europeans to be discovered by the natives of Costa Rica. The encounter took place on or soon after September 18, 1502, when Columbus, on his fourth voyage to the New World, took shelter from a storm at what is now Uvita Island, just off the port of Limón.

No account survives of the impression that the intruders, with their white skins and huge ships, made upon the natives. But the Spaniards noted straight off the golden disks and animal-form decorations worn by the inhabitants, and acquired some of them in exchange for junk jewelry. And through native playfulness or cunning, or faulty interpretation, or wishful thinking on the part of the newcomers, the Spaniards departed with the impression that there were treasures aplenty in all landward directions. Thus, and with similar exchanges on succeeding expeditions, did the nickname of Costa Rica — the Rich Coast — become applied to the land that the Spaniards officially called Veragua.

Attempts to subdue the land and its peoples, and appropriate its reputed treasures, however, faltered. A party led by Diego de Nicuesa in 1506 explored the Atlantic coast of present-day Costa Rica and Panama. But the close-knit native bands viewed all outsiders with mistrust, and none made the fatal mistake, so common elsewhere, of allying itself with the newcomers against traditional enemies. Attacked by Indians who vanished into the jungle, ravaged by heat, diarrhea, yellow fever and assorted diseases to which they had no resistance, tormented by clouds of mosquitoes, drenched by seemingly inexhaustible rains, bogged down in mud, unable to replenish supplies, the men of the Nicuesa party departed without founding a permanent settlement, and later expeditions likewise came to grief.

Frustrated on the Atlantic side, the Spaniards turned their efforts to the Pacific shore. Here the terrain was less of a morass, the vegetation less impenetrable, the inhabitants more permanently settled and less intractable. Spanish attempts to conquer were less of a failure. The expedition of Gil González Dávila in 1522 succeeded in peacefully converting many Chorotega Indians under Chief Nicoya to Catholicism. Quantities of gold were carried off as well. The price was over a thousand men dead from the familiar trio of hunger, disease, and raids. Francisco Fernández de Córdova later founded a town called Bruselas near present-day Puntarenas, but infighting among Spaniards led to its abandonment.

Short-lived settlements were established on both coasts, but for more than half a century from the arrival of Columbus, there was no permanent Spanish foothold. Finally, in 1561, Juan de Cavallón, with a party of Spaniards and domestic animals, founded the successful settlement of Garcimuñoz in the Pacific lowlands. For lack of finding gold, however, Cavallón himself withdrew.

It was under Juan Vásquez de Coronado, Cavallón's successor as governor, that Costa Rica's course began to differ from that of the other Spanish provinces. Vásquez moved the main settlement from the lowlands to the temperate Central Valley, and renamed it Cartago, or Carthage. The search for gold was abandoned, and Vásquez attempted to deal with the natives in friendship. Spaniards cultivated crops for their own consumption, lived mostly in peace, but achieved no great prosperity. Cartago was not the sort of outpost that attracted adventurers, but at least it survived. The luck of Costa Rica in being governed by Vásquez, however, did not extend to him personally: he was lost at sea after a voyage to Spain to seek financial aid for the colony.

COLONY AND NATION

Despite the initial peaceful settlement of the valley, conflict with the natives was inevitable, and the Spaniards dealt with them in characteristically harsh fashion. A few were subjected, and came to live peacefully alongside the Spaniards, to serve them and eventually to intermarry with them. Others were conquered and removed to areas where they could be easily watched over. By far the largest numbers refused to submit. Some simply moved on to remote areas of the lightly populated country. Most either died violently or succumbed to the diseases brought by the Spaniards, to which they had no resistance. There was no Indian problem in the parts of Costa Rica settled by Spaniards simply because there were soon few Indians.

Without native labor to exploit, without crops to grow for export on a large scale, restricted in trade by Spanish mercantile policy, hemmed into a small valley by hostile environments, Costa Rica stagnated, and the very name of the colony must at times have seemed a cruel hoax. No great public buildings were erected. Little moved out of the province but small amounts of meat, cacao, honey and potatoes. Traders faced a journey to port made hazardous by Indians. Sea traffic was ravaged by pirates. Manufactured goods were in short supply. Costa Rica was virtually isolated from Nicaragua, and communication with Panama existed only by a mule trail that was often impassable.

Spain responded to piracy by closing the ports in 1665. Trade plummeted, though smuggling to Panama and illegal contacts with Dutch and English merchants continued. The shortage of money forced the colonists to revert to the traditional Indian medium of exchange, cacao beans. Cloth was so scarce that tree bark and goat hair were used to make clothing. Even the governor had to grow his own food.

The forlorn colonists remained isolated on their farms, not even coming to town to attend church, not least because they had nothing to wear. Family life was disorganized, and church officials complained of the licentiousness of the populace. A few immigrants drifted in, but the colony hardly grew; more than a hundred years after its founding, Cartago, the capital, was barely more than a village, with fewer than a hundred houses, and a single church. It was destroyed almost entirely by the eruption of the volcano Irazú in 1723.

Costa Rica's last century as a colony saw some improvement in the standard of living, and even a modicum of prosperity. Religious authorities, alarmed at the depths of poverty and ignorance, the low level of morality, and their declining influence, in the late eighteenth century ordered the populace to resettle and concentrate around the churches. Trade with the other colonies was officially re-opened toward the beginning of the eighteenth century. Cacao plantations near the Caribbean expanded as the coastal area was fortified, and by the end of the eighteenth century, Costa Rica was exporting tobacco, sugar, wheat and flour, as well as cacao. To the first towns of Cartago and Aranjuez were added Heredia, San José, Alajuela, and Escazú, all organized in the eighteenth century as agriculture and settlement pushed westward from Cartago.

But progress was relative. In comparison with neighboring colonies, Costa Rica still remained poor, isolated, sparsely populated, a social misfit in its lack of a class structure. There were probably no more than 20,000 persons in Costa Rica at the opening of the nineteenth century, most descended from the few score families that had first settled the colony. Less than one-eighteenth of the land had any significant settlement.

INDEPENDENCE

Independence, when it came, had little initial effect on Costa Rica. Spain had administered the five Central American provinces from

Guatemala; toward the end of the colonial period, Costa Rica was reduced to the status of a dependency of Nicaragua. In practice, however, Costa Rica had long gone its own way. Without the ambitions and class conflicts of the other colonies, living at subsistence, Costa Rica required only minimal government.

News of the independence of Central America, declared in Guatemala on September 15, 1821, reached Costa Rica at the end of the year. A provincial government was hastily formed, and soon acceded to annexation to Mexico. Opinion on the association was divided, however, and a short civil war was fought. The forces of the town of San José, rejecting Mexico, gained the upper hand. In the end, the Mexican empire collapsed in 1823, and Costa Rica joined the United Provinces of Central America, with full autonomy in its internal affairs. The most important result of independence was the elimination of Spanish trading restrictions, but since the world was not beating a path to Costa Rica's door, even this freedom was of limited value.

With little administrative heritage from Spain, Costa Rica's form of government varied over the years. At times it was frankly experimental, as the legislature changed from bicameral to unicameral and back again, and the capital was rotated between towns on a trial basis. Internal strife also came with independence, though to a lesser degree than elsewhere in the region.

Costa Rica's first elected president, Juan Mora Fernández, held office until 1833, and began the policy of encouraging coffee cultivation. Civil war broke out toward the end of his term over the location of the capital. Braulio Carrillo, chosen for the presidency by congress in 1835, succeeded in stabilizing the country politically and financially, and planted the capital firmly in San José. Carrillo extended his term by coup d'etat, and ruled as a benevolent dictator until overthrown in 1842 by Francisco Morazán, a Honduran and Central American federalist. Morazán's extranational ambitions led to his own overthrow and execution in 1843.

Costa Rica made do with a weak central government after Morazán, and even abolished its army for a short time. In 1848, all connections with the moribund Central American federation were severed. A strong leader emerged once again in 1849 with the election to the presidency of Juan Rafael Mora, a representative of the new coffee aristocracy.

Mora's term saw the one glorious military episode in Costa Rica's history. The American adventurer William Walker had taken control of Nicaragua, and Mora responded to the challenge by raising an army to oppose him. Aided by Britain and by American business interests, Costa Rica played the major role in ousting Walker from the isthmus.

Following the Nicaraguan adventure, Mora was overthrown, and was subsequently executed when he attempted a comeback. A military

government gave way to a series of constitutional presidents who represented the aristocracy. In 1879, Tomás Guardia overthrew the government, and ruled as a military strongman until his death in 1882. The
presidency then passed in turn to two of Guardia's relatives.

DEVELOPMENT AND EXPANSION

The topsy-turvy politics of Costa Rica in the nineteenth century were
only a sideshow to the economic changes that were taking place. Costa
Rica was transformed, as coffee came to be cultivated on a large scale.

Coffee was first grown in Costa Rica toward the end of the colonial
period. The plant was so eminently suited to the highland volcanic soil
and held such obvious promise that the newly independent republic
granted it exemption from a number of taxes. By 1829, coffee was Costa
Rica's most important product. In 1831, the government began to give
away land on which to plant the crop. Production grew from 50,000
pounds in 1832 to 9 million pounds in 1841, and by the 1880s, annual
harvests approached 100 million pounds.

Inevitably, the rewards of coffee cultivation were not distributed
evenly. Some families acquired large expanses of land, transformed their
wealth into political power, and developed tastes for culture and the finer
things in life that the nation had done without for so long. But despite
the emergence of a class structure, there appeared to be land and profit
enough for all, and no sector of society failed to advance.

Although he was autocratic, Tomás Guardia saw himself as a benefactor of his people. Under his government and those of his two successors,
roads were built and improved, public buildings erected, capital punish-
ment abolished, and primary education made free and compulsory, and
independent of the church. Coffee earnings, and borrowings against
future earnings, financed the expenditures.

The problems of shipping coffee led indirectly to the development of
a second major export crop. Coffee was sent by oxcart to the Pacific port
of Puntarenas, then on a long voyage around South America to markets
in the eastern United States and Europe. To shorten the journey,
President Guardia ordered the construction of a railroad line to the
Atlantic. Bananas were planted as a stop-gap measure to provide revenue
for the financially troubled project. The new crop proved immensely
profitable, and large areas were soon planted in the fruit.

DEMOCRATIC COSTA RICA

Costa Rica's modern, democratic tradition started with the election
of 1889, the first that was honest, open, and direct. No violent revolution-
aries clamored for reform at the time. In a typically Costa Rican way,
President Bernardo Soto, in response to demonstrations, called for the

free election whose time, apparently, had come. José Joaquín Rodríguez, a candidate opposed by Soto, won the election and, against expectations, took office. The course of democracy was to have its ups and downs thereafter. Presidents attempted to amend the constitution in order to succeed themselves, and dismissed uncooperative legislatures. But peaceful transitions of power, and more active participation in politics by all sectors of the population, characterized the years that followed.

The major challenge to the democratic trend came in 1917. Claiming that the government was corrupt, Minister of War Federico Tinoco Granados seized power and ruled as a dictator. Opposition by the United States helped force his resignation after two years, and elections were held for a successor.

In the 1930s, Costa Rica began to show signs of social unrest. Many of the benefits of coffee wealth had gone to relatively few families. An extraordinarily high rate of population growth had led to repeated division of the smaller landholdings, and many workers owned no land at all. A strike in the banana plantations succeeded in obtaining higher pay, and agitation was threatened elsewhere.

The response of those in power was to take the lead in distributing wealth more evenly and improving the security of workers. President Ricardo Jiménez Oreamuno organized a government insurance company, and in 1935 began the distribution of United Fruit Company land to farmers, in small plots. Under Rafael Angel Calderón Guardia, a physician who became president in 1940, the measured pace of reform continued as the first social security legislation was enacted.

Calderón was to be one of the more controversial figures in modern Costa Rica. His social programs – including paid vacations, unemployment compensation and an income tax – and his early declaration of war on Germany, offended many of his original conservative supporters. Calderón sought to broaden his political base by allying himself with the Communist-influenced Popular Vanguard party. The polarization of the country continued under Calderón's successor, Teodoro Picado. Conservatives considered the government radical, while liberals, led by José Figueres Ferrer, felt reform programs were ineffective.

In 1948, Calderón ran again for the presidency, and lost to Otilio Ulate. But the government claimed fraud, and the legislature annulled the results. Tensions rose, and finally broke out into an open rebellion led by José Figueres. Armed by the governments of Guatemala and Cuba, the rebels prevailed in a few weeks over the army. The short civil war was the bloodiest in Costa Rica's history, with more than 2000 killed.

MODERN COSTA RICA
    José Figueres led an interim administration that attempted to restore

order to a disrupted nation. Banks were nationalized and taxes restructured. Most curiously following a civil war, and amid threats from domestic plotters and opponents in exile, Figueres and his allies chose not to purge and restructure the army, but to abolish it altogether, retaining only those elements of the old security forces that they considered appropriate in the Costa Rican context: a national police force, and the military bands.

A constituent assembly proceeded to write a constitution that re jected some of Figueres' proposals, but extended social welfare programs, gave the vote to women, ended discrimination against blacks, and established an electoral tribunal with broad powers to ensure the honesty of elections. Following the legislative elections of 1949, Figueres stepped aside, and Otilio Ulate, the victor of the disputed 1948 vote, assumed office as president.

Despite the bitterness of the civil war, politics in Costa Rica since 1948 have been remarkably peaceful and democratic. Exiles have threatened invasions on two occasions, but have found no internal support, and their movements have fizzled. José Figueres himself twice served as president, from 1953 to 1957 and from 1970 to 1974, and his National Liberation Party has dominated electoral politics. But it has only twice held the presidency for more than a single term.

Social and economic progress since 1948 has contributed to stability. With revenues growing as a result of high coffee prices and expanded cultivation, the government acted to improve living conditions and modernize agriculture and industry. Social legislation was implemented without the heavy-handed opposition by business interests that plagued Costa Rica's neighbors.

By 1981, social security programs — medical care, health services and income maintenance — served 90% of the population, took 40% of the national budget, and were the largest employer in Costa Rica. Education accounted for 30% of the budget, and basic schooling was widespread. Government clinics and private agencies have provided birth-control information to a people concerned not with surviving but with maintaining its standard of living.

A population growth rate that was one of the highest in the world at mid-century was reduced from over 4% to well under three percent. Life expectancy has meanwhile risen to 75 years, the longest in Latin America, and a respectable figure for any country.

GOVERNMENT

The national government is divided into legislative, judicial and executive branches, each with substantial independence guaranteed by the 1949 constitution.

The president and two vice presidents are elected every four years. To control personal power, the constitution prohibits a president from succeeding himself, and bars certain high officials and close relatives of an incumbent from seeking the office. Incumbents may not take an active part in presidential campaigns, and control of the Civil Guard is turned over at election time to the Supreme Electoral Tribunal, which has broad powers to ensure the fairness of voting.

The Legislative Assembly consists of a single chamber whose deputies are elected for terms of four years by proportional representation. There is one deputy for approximately every 30,000 inhabitants in each province.

The judicial system consists of a Supreme Court and lower courts. Judges are appointed by the legislature. Minor matters in small towns are taken before the mayor or local police agent.

Administratively, Costa Rica is divided into provinces, cantons, and districts. The seven provinces, most with boundaries radiating from the Central Valley, are divisions of the national government, with appointed governors. The 80 cantons are local governmental units administered by elected councils. Districts are subdivisions of cantons.

Public order is maintained by civil guards, rural guards, and municipal police. Some units of the civil guard are, in fact, quite military, with helmets, battle fatigues, and anti-infiltration training, while a rural guardsman's daily uniform might consist of Acapulco tourist shirt, sunglasses, and blue jeans with pistol stuffed in the waistband.

ECONOMIC GROWTH

Economically, Costa Rica has diversified considerably. Industry expanded at phenomenal annual rates of over 10% in the sixties, as manufactured goods were exported to the new Central American Common Market. Exports to other areas remained largely agricultural, but expanded to include meat, lumber, sugar, cacao, and flower seeds, along with coffee and bananas.

Massive public works have helped to improve living standards. Hydroelectric projects have brought power to most homes in the Central Valley. An intracoastal canal along the Atlantic has improved access to parts of the lowlands. The highway system has been extended even to the once-forbidding Caribbean region. Government land continues to be available to those who are willing to work it. Foreigners and foreign investment have been equally welcome, and tourism has grown to become the second source of foreign exchange, after bananas.

But not everything has been rosy for Costa Rica. Through the 1980s, unstable coffee prices, oil bills, disruptions of trade in the Central American Common Market, the arrival of refugees from Nicaragua, the shutdown of banana plantations in the face of higher taxes and labor strife, and the costs of social programs all gave the society and economy a jolt. The government has at times been hard-pressed to meet payments on loans from abroad, which take up most export earnings, and the currency has been regularly devalued. National income has fallen in some years, and unemployment has risen.

Attempts have been made to stimulate a stagnating economy through diversification of agriculture and development of new sources of revenue, such as manufacturing and distribution in duty-free zones, but results have been illusory. Unofficially, money laundering and transit of controlled substances have have helped balance the books. And grantsmanship has helped to see the country through difficulties: on a per-capita basis, Costa Rica has at times ranked second only to Israel as a recipient of U.S. aid, though assistance has declined markedly since 1985.

Elsewhere in the region, economic crises of these proportions have led to turmoil and bloodshed. In Costa Rica, administrations that have failed to stabilize the economy have been turned out of office democratically. But while Costa Ricans are proud of their stability, it has provided little consolation when they have had to make do with less.

PEACEFUL COSTA RICA

Internationally, Costa Rica has continued to exert a strong moral influence as a nation that has officially renounced the use of arms. Administrations have generally been pro-Western, and some have given more than passive support to armed movements in neighboring countries.

Most recently, reconciliation between all parties in conflict in Central America has been actively promoted. For his key role in putting together a regional peace plan, president Oscar Arias was awarded the 1987 Nobel Peace Prize.

The successor to Arias is Rafael Angel Calderón Fournier, son of former president Rafael Angel Calderón Guardia. Calderón took office in 1990 with strong business support, coming back after a string of electoral defeats. He has promised to streamline Costa Rica's bureaucracy and pay more attention to domestic problems than his predecessor. But under heavy pressure from the International Monetary Fund, his first actions included unpopular increases in sales taxes and fees for government services.

5. PLANNING YOUR TRIP

As Latin American countries go, Costa Rica can be rated a relatively carefree destination. Clean hotels are available almost everywhere, the food is generally safe to eat and sometimes of gourmet quality, and service is competent, even gracious. Transportation is well-developed and comfortable in many parts of the country. Officials generally do not expect to be bribed. Even "roughing it" can be accomplished in style and without hassle, on fully inclusive soft-adventure jungle trips, and white-water rafting and kayaking excursions arranged by experienced travel companies. There is plenty to appeal to personal interests — fishing, birding, spelunking, Spanish-language study, and much more — and you'll find plenty of information about these activities throughout this book.

Of course, it's still possible to muck things up. Though Costa Rica is eminently suited to independent travel, there *are* a few spots where accommodations are limited. Some places just can't be reached easily by public transportation. There are times of year when everything is full, and some hotel owners won't resist the temptation to raise rates beyond authorized levels. You just might come fishing in the wrong season. I hope that the remainder of this book will help you to decide your strategy and avoid pitfalls.

BEFORE YOU GO . . .
Planning Basics

Even at the budget level, hotel space is extremely tight in Costa Rica from December through April, when most foreign visitors arrive, when Costa Ricans themselves take their holidays, and when the roads in outlying regions are most easily passable. At the very least, to avoid disappointment, you should reserve hotel space for the beginning of your trip, either by contacting a hotel directly by fax or letter (to the hotel's post office box, or *apartado*), or through a travel agency. If you have difficulty getting around, or have small children, you should consider reserving all of your accommodations, either by booking directly, or by purchasing a package trip from a travel agency familiar with Costa Rica.

Outside the periods of heavy travel, reservations are not indispensable, except for locales that are not easily accessible, such as Tortuguero National Park and some of the jungle lodges.

Of course, rain can be a damper on travel from May through November, the so-called "green season." But if you look at the climate section below, you'll see that in parts of the country, there isn't *that* much of a difference between June and January. Many hotels lower their rates or are willing to strike a deal during periods when their occupancy rates drop.

WHEN TO GO — CLIMATE AND WEATHER
Dry and "Green" Seasons

Most visitors arrive in Costa Rica during the northern winter and spring, and for obvious reasons. This is when it's best to get away from the cold, of course. But it also coincides with the dry season, from about November through April, when the western side of Costa Rica receives hardly any rain, and when temperatures are usually most pleasant.

But there are a few good words to be said for the rainy times, which promoters have taken to calling the "green season" — and not without reason. On the western side of the country, the annual drought is broken in May, and the fields turn green and exuberant. Facing the Caribbean, where the rains take no annual vacation, the downpours are heavier and last longer. For rafters, the rivers are full of water. And for wise travelers, hotel occupancy drops, and so do rates.

And, though it's the rainy season, it never (well, hardly ever), rains all day. That's because weather forms in a different way than in the temperate latitudes, where a mass of clouds could stay in one place for days. In Costa Rica, a rainstorm is usually a daily phenomenon in season, blowing up from the coast on winds that follow the warming of the day, and dispersing after a few hours.

Then there are differences in climate between the temperate zones and Costa Rica. In the United States, latitude largely determines climate — Florida is warm, Georgia is pleasant, Minnesota is frigid in winter. In Costa Rica, despite "tropical" latitudes, mountain barriers, altitude and prevailing winds create zones that vary from chilly to humid and sweltering, throughout the year. These zones are right next to each other, and you can change your climate according to your mood. If you're feeling cold and damp in Monteverde in February, hop on a bus, and in a couple of hours you can get to a dry and sun-baked beach on the Gulf of Nicoya — and pass through a continent's worth of climates in the process.

Here is a general picture of the climatic zones of Costa Rica.

Highland Weather

The highland climate of the major cities – San José, Cartago, Heredia and Alajuela – is often called "eternal spring," a term that is not used merely to attract tourists. Temperatures are in the low seventies Fahrenheit (about 22 Centigrade) during the day throughout the year. High mountains and volcanoes to the north of San José block the clouds that blow in from the Atlantic, and it rains only from April to November or December, when winds are from the Pacific. But a long rainy day is a rarity in the Central Valley.

Mornings are generally clear, followed by a few hours of heavy downpour in the afternoon. Sometimes the rain can last into the night. Clouds hold in the heat of the day, and nights are generally warm. The rainy season is called *invierno* (winter), even though Costa Rica is in the northern hemisphere. In the dry times, or *verano* (summer), not even the thought of rain occurs. Days are uniformly warm and sunny. Nights are clear, and the temperature can sometimes drop into the fifties (about 10 Centigrade).

Pacific Coast Weather

Down toward the Pacific coast, the climate is hotter. In Puntarenas, daytime temperatures are in the nineties (above 32 degrees Centigrade) throughout the year. But at the beaches, refreshing breezes moderate the heat. The rainy season is the same as in the Central Valley, but precipitation is heavier. The exceptions are the extreme north and extreme south. The Guanacaste plain suffers periodic droughts, which bother farmers more than visitors. And around Golfito, near Panama, peculiarities in the mountains and winds bring rains throughout the year.

Atlantic Coast Weather

On the Atlantic slope of Costa Rica, storms may blow in at any time, though rainfall is lightest from February through April and in September. Precipitation is over ten feet at Limón in most years, and even higher to the north. Storms appear suddenly and with a frightening fury, but they are usually quickly gone. Temperatures are generally as hot on the Caribbean as on the Pacific, and the humidity is more enervating.

Higher Altitude Weather

The higher altitudes are cooler. Frosts occur above 2,150 meters (7,000 feet) during the dry season. And atop volcanoes and in the Talamanca mountains, temperatures can plunge from warm to below freezing in a few hours.

NATIONAL HOLIDAYS

Some Costa Rican holidays, such as Christmas and Easter, will be known to most visitors. But you can't be expected to be aware of a favorite saint's special day. Take a quick look at the list of public holidays below. If any occur while you're in Costa Rica, don't plan to get anything done on that day except relaxing.

January 1	New Year's Day
March 19	Day of St. Joseph (San José)
Moveable	Holy Thursday
Moveable	Good Friday
	(Many businesses close all Holy Week)

On Good Friday, processions reenact the Passion of Christ, in San José and in villages throughout the country, often with scores of participants in full Roman regalia.

April 11	Battle of Rivas
May 1	Labor Day
Moveable	Corpus Christi
June 29	Day of Saints Peter and Paul
July 25	Annexation of Guanacaste
August 2	Day of Our Lady of the Angels
	(specially celebrated in Cartago)
August 15	Assumption Day
September 15	Independence Day
October 12	Columbus Day (Día de la Raza)
December 8	Immaculate Conception
December 24, 25	Christmas Eve and Christmas
December 31	New Year's Eve

LOCAL CELEBRATIONS

In addition to the national holidays, all towns celebrate the feast day of their patron saint – San Marcos (St. Mark) on April 25, Santiago (St. James the Apostle) on July 25, etc. Images of the patron saint are borne from the town church in processions, but most of the celebrants' efforts go into the parades of masked figures, raffles, bingo, dances, banquets, drinking and benign bullfights that make these occasions breaks from the humdrum round of chores. And the Christmas-New Year season is a time of extended street celebration everywhere, especially in San José.

Dates are approximate, and vary from year to year. Regular events that are not legal holidays are also mentioned.

January 15	Alajuelita (southwestern metropolitan San José) Santa Cruz, Guanacaste
January 17 to 24	Palmares
February 6 and 7	Venecia de San Carlos. Food festivals, agricultural fair, dances, fireworks.
February 6 and 7	San Vito de Java
February 8	Boruca. Indigenous celebration.
February 11-22	Jacó
February 10-14	Liberia
February 25	San Isidro de El General. Cattle fair and bullfights)
February 28	Grecia
March	Cattle show at Bonanza fair grounds.
March 15-21	Puriscal
March 19	Day of the Artisan. Craft fair, downtown San José
March 25-28	Guápiles
April 23-26	Tilarán
April 26-May 2	Ciudad Quesada (San Carlos), bullfights and cattle fair.
May 7-10	Muelle de San Carlos
May 15	Day of San Isidro (St. Isidore), celebrated in all towns bearing this saint's name
May 28-30	Paraíso, Cartago
July 16	Festival of the Sea, Puntarenas
October 12	Limón Carnival
October 12	Festival of corn, Upala.
November	Coffee harvest contests.
December 8	Negritos festival, Boruca; Fireworks Day (Día de la Pólvora) elsewhere.
December 12	La YegÂita, native celebration in Nicoya, Guanacaste.

WHAT TO PACK

When packing for your visit to Costa Rica, keep in mind that the climate is moderate. For San José and the Central Valley, take the kind of clothes you would wear during the spring at home. A light sweater or jacket might be required for the evening, especially during the dry season. For early-morning excursions, you'll do best to dress in layers, perhaps a sweater over a shirt and t-shirt. Remove layers as the temperature climbs, or as you descend to lower altitudes.

For visits to either coast, you'll want lightweight clothing, preferably all-cotton, or cotton blends.

In general, informal clothing is suitable. Even in San José, you may dine at your hotel in slacks and sport shirt or blouse. At the best restaurants, however, and at formal events, such as concerts at the National Theater, a dress or jacket and tie are appropriate. Costa Ricans value a neat appearance (just look at how they dress!) and regard visitors who wear patched clothing with puzzlement.

Fashionable, full-cut shorts are acceptable daytime attire in San José. Short-shorts and cutoffs are generally not worn in the capital, except for sports or around the house.

Before you pack, consider what your trip will be like. You don't want to carry items that you'll never unpack. On the other hand, you don't want to leave behind any essentials. If you'll be at one hotel, take as many changes of clothes as you feel you'll need (as long as it all fits in a couple of suitcases), and do the laundry when you get home.

The other extreme is incessant travel, a single change of clothes in a carry-on bag, and laundry in the hotel sink every night.

A compromise is to leave a large bag at your hotel in San José, and carry a smaller bag as you travel around the country. At the very least, this leaves you less vulnerable to having all your possessions stolen.

Cosmetics, Toiletries, and Personal Items

Bring your cosmetics, toiletries, and small personal items, including:
- sunglasses
- your favorite personal kit of aspirin or substitute, sunscreen, sunburn cream, malaria pills, spare prescription glasses, mosquito repellent (most convenient in stick form), etc.

Habits, Hobbies, and Vices

According to your habits, hobbies and vices, take your:
- camera and waterproof bag, film (more than you think you'll need), batteries
- camping equipment and flashlight
- personal stereo
- duty-free cigarettes and liquor.

Other Basics

If you'll be traveling by bus and train, a travel alarm will come in handy for early departures. Hotel wake-up calls are unreliable.

Keep your luggage as light as practical, tag your bags inside and out, and pack your indispensable items in your carry-on. Remember: if you don't take it, you might not find it, or you might not want to pay the price.

PACKING CHECKLIST

Here are some suggestions for what to take. Pencil in additions that suit you, and cross out irrelevancies.

Essentials include:
• passport
• travelers checks
• tickets
• some U.S. cash in small-denomination bills

Money Belt
Protection against pickpockets and robbery is an increasing concern in Costa Rica. Take a money belt or some other concealment device if you feel comfortable wearing it.

Which Clothes?
Take lightweight all-cotton clothing, or loose-fitting, easy-care cotton blends.

Include:
• hat with ample brim. Cheap straw and cotton hats are widely available in Costa Rica, but the fit is often tight on gringos.
• a bathing suit
• a few shirts or blouses
• shorts
• comfortable walking shoes. Running shoes will suffice for most purposes. Boots can often be rented when really needed.
• socks, underclothes
• sandals or surf shoes
• at least one lightweight, long-sleeved top and slacks, in case you overexpose yourself to the sun, and for evenings, when mosquitoes might lurk.
• a light sweater or jacket for cool mornings and evenings, though a heavier one or a jacket will do at higher altitudes, such as at the peaks of volcanoes.
• a raincoat or umbrella if you travel during the rainy months (May through mid-December in San José), or along the Caribbean side of the country. Taking shelter from the rain for a few hours, however, is no special inconvenience.
• a dress-up outfit, if you think you might need it — a jacket and tie, or dress, or formal blouse and skirt.
• for forest reserves, slippery jungle walks, and back-road travel, take one set of expendable lightweight clothing, preferably with long sleeves.

Reading Material
Bring a moderate amount if your visit will center on San José, where you can trade your used books, or a pile of books for a beach holiday.

Fishing and Diving
Fishing and diving equipment are available, but the selection is sometimes limited, so you're often better off with your own gear. If you have them, take:
• mask, snorkel and fins
• regulator, buoyancy compensator, certification card, wet suit (optional)
• preferred fishing equipment (unless assured of availability)

Packing for Other Sports
Take equipment for other sports that you practice, as it is unlikely to be found easily in Costa Rica.
• a day bag for carrying purchases, sunscreen, whatever. I prefer a see-through mesh bag — it shows that you have nothing worth stealing. Fanny packs are insecure and undesirable in towns, but fine for the countryside.
• A pen or two, including a felt-tip pen (ballpoints clog up) and paper.

TRAVELING ON YOUR OWN
Can you travel in Costa Rica, book your own hotels or show up unannounced, find good food and fun things to do? Can you change your plans to stay longer in a nifty place, take off with new friends, or follow your whims?

Of course you can. After all, flexibility and changing plans can be part of the fun and enrichment of travel. And you've picked the right book to show you exactly how to do it!

Let's face it. Many travel packages for Costa Rica are outrageously overpriced, for no other reason than that the country is popular. Numerous operators of small hotels complain that their customers are gouged by travel agents. Most U.S. agencies simply re-sell the services of a Costa Rican operator, and take no responsibility if an unsatisfactory hotel or tour is substituted.

If you are going to Costa Rica at the busiest times — Christmas, New Year's, Easter — you should have hotel reservations in hand. And there are some notorious tight spots, such as Quepos and Manuel Antonio, where reservations can be meaningless and price-gouging is a continuing problem. Otherwise, there are more and more hotels opening, and you can almost always find a place to sleep with no advance notice.

Making Reservations
Of course, it's always best to try to call at least a day before your intended arrival, in order to make sure that your room is clean and ready. Most hotels and travel services have personnel who can understand basic English.

You can write, as well, but my experience is that Costa Ricans, like many Latin Americans, push written communication to the bottom of a handy pile — if your letter arrives at all. They prefer to deal with a voice or a person. A fax has a better chance of being answered than a letter, especially if your arrival with dollars is imminent.

And some hotels, for whatever reason, just do not respond to inquiries from individuals, or take forever to respond. Where you see the words "book through travel agents" as part of a hotel description in this book, a direct contact will probably be fruitless.

USING TRAVEL SPECIALISTS
Why Use a Travel Agent?

I just told you that you don't have to. Now I'll tell you why it might be wise in your particular case.

Some travel agencies and wholesalers reserve blocks of rooms for their clients. This could leave you out in the cold in the more popular parts of the country, where accommodations are in short supply.

Travel agencies have buying power, contacts, access to cheap group air fares. (But sometimes, they impose high markups and service charges.) *Sometimes* travel agents are up-to-date on the newest hotel, the latest adventure, the most knowledgeable guides. (But sometimes they know no more than you, and simply pass on requests to a contact in San José.) Through travel agents, you can join a group of like-minded persons (birders, naturalists, divers) to enhance your experience and make new friends.

For many travelers, it's worthwhile to have everything arranged in advance in order to enjoy every minute of precious vacation time.

By temperament, I'm opposed to group travel. But I have to acknowledge that some of my most memorable experiences, in Costa Rica and elsewhere, have come on group trips, and excursions that could not easily have been arranged without a travel professional.

Throughout this book I mention travel agents and specialists who can help tailor a trip or provide you with special services you just can't arrange without help (like taking a diving trip along the Pacific coast).

By all means, try a local travel agency first before you shop around at a distance. Compare prices and ask for references. Don't be afraid to take charge, and to look for a travel planner who will keep your interests in mind.

Consider itineraries that make all the arrangements for difficult-to-reach areas, and allow some flexibility elsewhere. Avoid packages that involve successive day trips from San José through the same scenery, accompanied by the same canned patter from different guides.

Here is a *partial* list of companies that specialize in travel to Costa Rica in one way or another, or that run tours to Costa Rica with some frequency in collaboration with operators in San José. I regularly add or delete travel agencies in new editions, so if you have a good or bad experience, by all means let me know.

Outdoor Excursions

Mariah Wilderness Expeditions, P.O. Box 248, Point Richmond, CA 94807, tel. 800-4-MARIAH or 510-233-2303, fax 510-233-0956. This is a white-water rafting company that grew to become a comprehensive travel planner for Costa Rica, with trips including, but not limited to, sea kayaking, mountain biking, and environment-oriented excursions. Personal counselling is available regarding mountain and rain forest lodges, beaches, and the practicalities of getting where you want to go within your time limitations and budget. Mariah has developed a number of modular itineraries, to be snapped together according to individual preferences, for as few as two persons.

Nature Tours

• **Voyagers International**, P. O. Box 915, Ithaca, NY 14851, tel. 800-633-0299 or 607-257-3091, fax 607-257-3699. Voyagers' programs, emphasizing natural history, are run by a Costa Rican travel planner who is also a biologist. Group departures are scheduled throughout the year, and include Monteverde, the Osa Peninsula, river trips, and can include rafting, all accompanied by a naturalist. Trips can also be customized, with guided and self-drive segments, or organized for groups. Ask for their detailed travel planner booklet, with capsules on destinations, and assorted practical information; or speak to their Costa Rica specialist.

• **Adventures Costa Rica**, 16 North 9th St., Bozeman, MT 59715, tel. 406-586-9942, fax 586-0995

• **McTravel Services Inc.**, 20378 Fraser Hwy., Langley, BC V3A 4G1, Canada, tel. 604-530-5855 (operated by a Canadian and a Costa Rican)

• **Go Travel**, 4930 Cìte des Neiges, Montreal, Quebec H3V 1H2

• **Multicentre Costa Rica**, 4571 St-Denis, Montréal, Québec H2J 2L4, tel. 514-847-9279, fax 847-9280. *Specialité: services en francais.*

• **Journeys**, 4011 Jackson Rd, Ann Arbor, MI 48103

• **Pioneer Tours**, Box 22063, Carmel, CA 93922

• **Blyth & Co.**, 68 Scollart St., Toronto, Ontario M5R 1G2

• **Costa Rica Experts**, 3540 N W 13th St., Gainesville, FL 32609

• **Ocean Connection**, 16728 El Camino Real, Houston, TX 77062

• **Mountain Travel**, 6420 Fairmount Ave., El Cerrito, CA 94530

• **Overseas Adventure Travel**, 349 Broadway, Cambridge, MA 02139

• **Preferred Adventures**, One West Water St., St. Paul, MN 55107, tel. 612-222-8131, fax 612-222-4221
• **Quest Nature Tours**, 920 Yonge St., Toronto, Ontario, M4W 9Z9, tel. 800-387-1483, specializes in birding trips
• **Quester's Tours and Travel**, 257 Park Ave. So., New York, NY 10010
• **Sierra Club Outings**, 730 Polk St., San Francisco, CA 94109
• **Special Expeditions**, 720 Fifth Avenue, New York, NY 10019
• **UET Travel**, 8619 Reseda Blvd., Northridge, CA 91324, tel. 818-886-0633, fax 818-993-5243
• **Wilderness Travel**, 801 Allston Way, Berkeley, CA 94710
• **Worldwide Adventures**, 920 Yonge St., Toronto, Ontario M4W 9Z9

Travel Agents In Costa Rica
In general, I don't recommend that you deal directly with travel agencies in Costa Rica from your home, mainly because there is nothing in the way of consumer protection.

However, because of the popularity of Costa Rica, some reputable agencies soon fill the blocks of room and tour space they reserve; others charge unconscionable markups, or don't take the time to take your interests and needs into account.

If you're not having luck with a local agent, consider a call to one of those listed starting on pages 180-183. **Tikal Tours** and **Costa Rica Expeditions** have good reputations, and personnel who can deal with you in English. A telephone call or fax to reserve day trips could be worth the cost.

BED AND BREAKFASTS

Bed-and-Breakfasts are now a *movement* in Costa Rica. Whereas a few operated discreetly and largely by word of mouth at the time of my last edition, there are now scores of B&Bs in San José, the Central Valley, and, to a lesser degree, throughout the provinces. They afford visitors a chance to stay in the homes of Costa Ricans and of foreign residents, and to fit into the rhythms of daily life.

If you'd like to settle in for a while, rather than rush from place to place; learn where to find a cheap glass of beer and companions with whom to spend the afternoon; find out where to buy fresh-baked buns for a dime, and who sells empanadas from her kitchen, and where the local bus stops are, then bed-and-breakfasts might be more your speed than formal hotels.

Just remember that you're staying in somebody's *home*. Your hosts may take a personal interest in you, and if that is not welcome in your own case, a more conventional hotel might be more suitable. Tours and travel services might not be available, though there are now some services that cater exclusively to the clients of B&Bs (for example, a gentleman who offers horseback excursions through the forests above Escazú, a private guide with his own van, among others). A swanky in-house restaurant, midnight room service, and comings and goings at odd hours are, of course, out of the question.

The **American Bed and Breakfast Association** operates a central clearing house and referral system, based at **Park Place**, a B&B in suburban Escazú. Call or fax them at 289200 or 234157 between 10 a.m. and 2 p.m., daily except Sunday, or write to P. O. Box 1012, Escazu, Costa Rica. To the degree that they are able, they'll place you in a suitable home-away-from-home for the duration of your visit, or for part of it. Once you enter the bed-and-breakfast network, you can pretty well be taken care of for your entire stay in the country, with referrals to lodging places and compatible people heading the same way as you are.

Bells' Home Hospitality, P. O. Box 185-1000, San José, tel. [2]254752, fax [2]245884 (in the U.S., Dept. 1432, P.O. Box 025216, Miami, FL 33102-5216) arranges stays in spare rooms in over 50 private homes in the San José area, at a rate of about $60 double, including breakfast. The agency provides detailed directions, and can arrange airport pickup. Plans are afoot to make rooms available throughout the country. Write or call for a pamphlet describing the homes and the families with which you can stay.

Costa Rica Home and Host, 2445 Park Ave., Minneapolis, MN 55404, tel. 612-871-0596, fax 871-8853 operates a similar service, with higher rates. Another way to move in with a Costa Rican family is to enroll in a language school. Most can arrange room and board with a Costa Rican family. Conditions are usually modest, and the family won't speak English — that's the whole point. This is one of the more inexpensive routes to take. See language-school listings, pages 76-77.

Or, consult ads in the *Tico Times* or *Costa Rica Today* to find a family that has a spare room.

SOURCES FOR MORE INFORMATION ABOUT COSTA RICA
Tourist Board
- **Costa Rica Tourist Board** (*Instituto Costarricense de Turismo*)Tel. 800-327-7033. Use this number to request a mailing that includes some basic flyers about Costa Rica. Or write to:
- **Instituto Costarricense de Turismo**, Apartado Postal 777-1000, San José, Costa Rica. Allow a month for a response to a written or telephone inquiry. Tel. 800-343-6332. This is the number for information for travel agents. It is answered in San José. Call [2]231733 from within Costa Rica.
- In the U.S., write or call **Costa Rica Tourist Board**, 1101 Brickell Avenue, ground floor, Miami, Florida 33131; Tel. 305-358-2150.

Maps
    For a detailed map, send a check for $5 (marked "for deposit only" or "unicamente para abonar en cuenta") to **Jiménez y Tanzi**, P.O. Box 2553-1000, San José. Ask for the *mapa de carreteras de Costa Rica*. A detailed map of Costa Rica published by **ITMB** (item 156) is available from map and travel bookstores, or may be ordered from ITMB, P. O. Box 2290, Vancouver, B.C. V6B 3W5, Canada.

Special Interests
    For fishing, horseback riding and other special-interest travel, contact one of the travel agencies listed elsewhere in this book. Travel agents who are familiar with Costa Rica are a good source of general information as well.

Embassies
• **Costa Rican Embassy**, 1825 Connecticut Ave. NW, Washington, DC 20009, tel. 202-234-2945
• **Costa Rican Embassy**, 150 Argyle St., Ottawa, Ontario, Canada, K2P 1B7, tel. 613-234-5762
• **Costa Rican Embassy**, 14 Lancaster Gate, London W2 3LH, tel. 71-723-1772

Consulates in the U.S.
• 8 South Michigan Ave., Chicago, IL 60603
• 4200 Republic Bank Tower, Dallas, TX 75201
• 2616 South Loop West, Houston, TX 77054
• 1343 West Olympic Blvd., Los Angeles, CA 90015
• 28 West Flagler St., Miami, FL 33130
• 2 Canal St., New Orleans, LA 70130
• 80 Wall St., New York, NY 10005

Books
    For additional copies of this book, send $14.95 (plus $2 shipping for each book ordered) to **Open Road Publishing**, P.O. Box 11249, Cleveland Park Station, Washington, DC 20008.

Other useful books about Costa Rica include:
• John and Mavis Biesanz, *Costa Rican Life*. New York: Columbia University Press, 1944; reprinted by Editorial Lehmann, San José, 1976.
• Richard Biesanz, et. al., *The Costa Ricans*. Englewood Cliffs: Prentice Hall, 1982; reprinted by Editorial Universidad Estatal a Distancia, San José, 1983.
Both of the above books are comprehensive studies of Costa Rican

society. The first is regarded by many as a classic; many of its observations are still valid today.

- J. P. Panet and Leah Hart, *Latin America on Bicycle*. Champlain, New York: Passport Press, 1987. Includes a chapter about a bicycle trip through Costa Rica.
- Mark Edelman and Joanne Kenan, editors, *The Costa Rica Reader*. New York: Grove Weidenfeld, 1989. Collection of articles about Costa Rican society.
- Gary Stiles and Alexander Skutch, *Birds of Costa Rica*. Ithaca, N. Y.: Cornell University Press, 1989. The authoritative, illustrated guide to Costa Rica's birds, including local terminology along with English and Latin names.
- Mario Boza, et. al., *The National Parks of Costa Rica*. Madrid: Incafo, 1981. Imperfectly rendered English version, but the color photos and information on flora and fauna are solid.

Periodicals

Costa Rica Today, an English-language weekly newspaper, is devoted to the attractions of Costa Rica. Its motto: *The beauty of it all*. Each edition has numerous fresh articles, color photos, calendars of weekly events, accommodation and restaurant ads, and an extensive classified section (and also investment promotions, which you should read with caution). *Costa Rica Today* is distributed at no charge in Costa Rica, and can be obtained by subscription abroad from Costa Rica Today 117, P. O. Box 25216, Miami, FL 33102.

The *Tico Times*, published on Fridays in San José, is one of the best English-language newspapers in Latin America. Articles cover events in Costa Rica and Central America, as well as local traditions, business, fishing, and items of human interest. The "On the Town" column reports reliably on restaurants and entertainment. The letters column is a free-for-all where the problems of the world are debated and solved. Ads for lodging and services will interest many visitors and potential visitors. An annual subscription in the United States or Canada costs about $50. Write to P.O. Box 145450, Coral Gables, FL 33114-5450. A comprehensive tourist edition is published annually in October.

(One oddity of Costa Rica: with excellent English-language publications, and a number of businesses that advertise heavily, you might get the impression that there are more and better facilities out there than actually exist.)

Videos

If you want to see the product before you go, several tourist videos of Costa Rica are available. *Costa Rica Today*, running time one hour, can be ordered by mail for $30 from **Cota International**, P. O. Box 5042, New York, NY 10185.

GETTING TO COSTA RICA

It's always a good idea to re-check entry requirements, with either a Costa Rican consulate or a reliable travel agent, before you leave home. Recent regulations:

Citizens of the United States or Canada must have a tourist card or a passport to enter Costa Rica.

Passport holders are issued 90-day visas upon arrival at the international airport. Visas for overland travel to Costa Rica should be obtained in advance at a Costa Rican consulate.

Tourist cards are issued at the check-in counter by airlines serving Costa Rica, upon presentation of a birth certificate or other substantial documentation, accompanied by a photo identification, such as a driver's license. Tourist cards cost $2 and are valid for 30 days. Monthly extensions may be obtained at the immigration department in San José (see below).

PASSPORTS SI!

Passports are preferable to tourist cards as an entry document for citizens of the United States or Canada. They allow an unquestioned stay of 90 days, and are required by most banks in order to cash a travelers check.

Travelers from countries of Western Europe can also enter Costa Rica with a passport only, as can citizens of Argentina, Australia, Brazil, Colombia, Guatemala, Iceland, Israel, Mexico, New Zealand, Japan, Panama, Romania, South Korea, and Venezuela. Permission is granted initially to stay for 30 to 90 days.

Travelers from most other countries, and all business travelers, must have a passport with a visa issued in advance. Check with your airline or a Costa Rican consulate for requirements.

All tourists may be required to demonstrate their financial resources upon arrival, as well as show a return or onward ticket.

Land borders are officially open from 6:30 a.m. to 10 p.m., with breaks from 11 a.m. to 12:30 p.m. and from 5:30 p.m. to 6:30 p.m.

ARRIVING BY AIR

Air traffic to Costa Rica is undergoing a boom, with service available from more and more cities. Major gateways for non-stop travel from the United States to Costa Rica are Miami, Orlando, New Orleans, and Houston. Service is also available, usually with intermediate stops, from Los Angeles, New York, and Dallas.

With a change of plane, you can reach San José via Mexico or Honduras. And direct flights operate between San José and San Juan, Puerto Rico; the Colombian island of San Andrés; and many cities on the South American mainland.

Fares

As any slightly experienced traveler will tell you, what counts is not what the fares are, but what fare your travel agent can get. An unrestricted round-trip fare between New York and San José can be as high as $1,260. Advance-booking and seat sales will cut the price by half or even more. Travel agencies that do a volume business negotiate lower fares. For example, Voyagers International will sell a ticket from New York for as little as $422, when you buy a tour. Cheap packages can be improvised to take advantage of low fares.

Stopovers can add to the value of your ticket. On **Sahsa**, up to two stopovers in each direction can be included at no extra cost. In effect, you can see virtually all of Central America for the price of an excursion ticket to San José. Your options include: a few days in Belize, for a visit to the offshore cayes and the archaeological sites; an excursion to the Bay Islands from San Pedro Sula; and a jaunt to Guatemala for Mayan ruins, colonial monuments, and unsurpassed handicrafts. On **Lacsa**, you can stop in Guatemala if you're traveling from New York, or in Mexico City or Guatemala on the way from Los Angeles.

Charter Flights

Charters from Canada are operated throughout the year by **Fiesta Holidays** in Toronto, **Nolitours** in Montreal, and **Fiesta West** in Vancouver, among others. Charters often depart at odd hours, but they save multiple takeoffs and landings, and the price is right. Currently, very few charters operate from the States.

Information on charter flights is available only through local travel agencies, not from the company that organizes the charter. Prices vary according to where and when you make your reservation, so check around before you pay. There are some bargains available — as little as $700 Canadian funds for your ticket plus a week at a hotel.

Most charter flights land at the international airport near San José. Flights are planned for the airport at Liberia, not far from the Pacific beaches of northwest Costa Rica.

Buy a Round-Trip Ticket

It's usually cheaper and avoids local taxes, and you might have to show an onward or return ticket to satisfy the immigration authorities in San José.

AIRLINES WITH DIRECT SERVICE TO SAN JOSÉ	
American Airlines	Miami
800-433-7300	Dallas-Fort Worth
Aero Costa Rica	Miami
800-237-6274	Orlando
Lacsa Airlines	Miami
800-225-2272	New York (stops en route)
	New Orleans
	San Francisco (stops en route)
	Los Angeles (stops en route)
Continental	Houston
800-525-0280	
United	Miami
800-241-6522	Los Angeles (stops en route)

AIRLINES WITH THROUGH SERVICE TO SAN JOSÉ	
Sahsa	Miami, New Orleans, Houston
800-327-1225	
Taca	New York, Miami, Houston
800-535-8780	
Mexicana	New York, Denver, etc.
800-531-7921	
Aviateca	Miami, New Orleans, Houston,
800-327-9832	Chicago, Los Angeles

ARRIVING BY CAR

The shortest highway distance from Brownsville, Texas, to San José, Costa Rica, is about 2,250 miles. For the vast majority of travelers, who have limited vacation time, it's simply not worthwhile to consider driving, with six borders to cross, difficult mountain roads, and fears of political turmoil and breakdowns en route.

However . . . if you're going south for the winter, if you're planning to spend time elsewhere in Central America as well, if you're camping, if you happen to be continuing onward to South America, or if your vehicle is simply indispensable, driving may be indicated. Rest assured that getting to Costa Rica is eminently possible.

Your major requirement is a vehicle in good shape. Have it checked out, tuned up and greased before you leave home. Replace cracked or withering belts and hoses, bald tires and rusting brake lines. If you're planning extensive travel off the main roads, consider taking a couple of spare tires, a gasoline can, water for you and the radiator, points, plugs, electrical tape, belts, wire, and basic tools. Otherwise, there's no reason to prepare for a safari, and the family sedan will serve you well. Be prepared to disconnect your catalytic converter south of Mexico, where unleaded gasoline is not available.

Avoid extra fees by crossing borders during regular business hours, generally from 8 a.m. to noon and from 2 p.m. to 6 p.m. It's prudent to travel during daylight hours only, to avoid stray animals and inebriated humans. Fill your tank whenever you can — gas stations can be few and far between. Plan your route to avoid transiting El Salvador — a direct crossing from Guatemala to Honduras is possible.

Essential documents for entry to any Central American country are your driver's license, vehicle registration, and passport with visa obtained in advance. Liability insurance is available in each country you cross. Coverage for damage to your own vehicle may not be available.

Vehicle permits for Costa Rica are issued at the border, are valid for 30 days, and may not be renewed. Drivers wishing to stay longer must take their vehicles out of the country for two days.

Maps of Mexico and Central America are available from your local automobile club, or at travel bookstores.

ARRIVING BY BUS

The disadvantages of bus travel all the way to Costa Rica are obvious — long hours in a sitting position, inconvenient connections, border delays, and much else. You can, however, see much along the way, and the price is right. Total fare from the U.S. border to Costa Rica is under $100, and this can be reduced by using less comfortable, slower, second-class local buses. Overland travel will require that you pick up visas in advance for all the countries you'll be transiting.

Some specifics: First-class buses, similar to those used by Greyhound, operate from all U.S. border points to Mexico City, a trip of from 10 hours to two days, depending on your crossing point. Buses of the **Cristóbal Colón** line depart Mexico City at least twice daily for the Guatemalan border, sixteen hours away, connecting with buses for Guatemala City.

Buses for Esquipulas leave you near the Honduran border. From there, travel via San Pedro Sula and Tegucigalpa to Managua. Direct buses operate onward to San José. The trip through Mexico may be shortened by following the Gulf coast route from eastern Texas, avoiding Mexico City.

ARRIVING BY PRIVATE BOAT

With a major marina a Playa Flamingo on the Pacific coast, you might well think of sailing down from California, or through the Panama Canal. If you do so, make sure you clear customs and immigration at the first port of entry: Coco or Golfito on the Pacific, Barra del Colorado on the Caribbean.

EXTENDING YOUR STAY

To stay in Costa Rica beyond the period initially authorized, you must exit the privileged world of the casual visitor. Idiosyncratic and changing regulations, whim and lineups can take a heavy toll on your time and patience.

If you are even thinking about staying longer than ninety days, it would be a good idea to get in touch with a Costa Rican consulate before you leave home, and review current regulations regarding travel with children, financial means, and anything else you or they can think of.

Currently, you may be granted a 60-day extension on a 30-day tourist card or visa, no extension at all on a 90-day visa, or an exit visa if you have already overstayed.

To extend the validity of your tourist card, present three passport-sized photos to the immigration department in La Uruca (eight blocks west of Lacsa, along the expressway — take the Alajuela bus). Be prepared to show several hundred dollars in travelers checks and your ticket home, and to pay modest fees. The extension takes several days to process.

The easiest way to remain after 90 days is to simply leave Costa Rica for three days, and then return. If you overstay your tourist visa, you'll pay fees of up to $40 for a 30-day exit visa and assorted taxes, in addition to charges for a child-support waiver (*pensiones alimenticias* stamps) purchased at the airport. Some travel agencies will take care of all this paperwork.

Longer stays, student visas, residencies and special situations usually require the intervention of a lawyer, and extensive paperwork that can take months or even years to complete. Really, it's an endorsement of the country, or a demonstration of masochism, that so many hang in there.

Pets require a veterinarian's attestation that the animal is free of parasites, distemper, hepatitis, leptospirosis and gastroenteritis, and has had a rabies vaccination. For forms, contact the **Zoonosis Department**, Ministry of Health, P. O. Box 123-1000, San José. Various stamps are required. A Costa Rican consulate can provide details.

CUSTOMS - ENTERING COSTA RICA

Visitors are allowed to enter Costa Rica with any used personal possessions that they will reasonably need, including sporting equipment. Items unfamiliar to customs inspectors, including medical articles, could be taxed heavily. The exemption for new merchandise is $100 of customs duty. New merchandise may include up to three liters of liquor (which you can purchase on arrival at the airport), one pound of tobacco, and six rolls of film.

CUSTOMS - RETURNING HOME

U.S. Customs allows an exemption of $400 per person in goods, including one quart of liquor and 200 cigarettes. Canadian residents may use their once-yearly $300 exemption, or their $100 quarterly exemption for goods brought home, with a limit of 1.1 liters of liquor and 200 cigarettes.

Costa Rica prohibits the export of pre-Columbian artifacts. In practice, there is a black market in these items, and there is limited official concern for pieces of little artistic value. One should be careful, however, not least because many artifacts are phony. Items made from protected species, such as turtles and alligators, could also get you into hot water, or at least be confiscated, when you try to get them through customs at home.

GETTING AROUND COSTA RICA

BY AIR

Costa Rica's domestic airline, **Sansa** (tel. [2]333258 in San José), operates flights to a number of outlying towns from **Juan Santamaría International Airport**. Fares are a bargain: $35 or less to any point with scheduled service. And you only have to check in at Sansa's San José office. The airline takes you out to the airport in its own van.

Sansa's flights save a lot of the wear and tear involved in overland travel. Even if you like to see things at ground level, they provide an easy lift back to San José. The drawbacks are insufficient flights to a limited number of destinations, variations from schedules, lost reservations, and, occasionally, separation of passengers from their luggage.

Latest destinations and flight frequencies are: to Quepos, daily; to Golfito and Coto 47 (near the Panamanian border), six times weekly; to Tamarindo, four times weekly; to Sámara and Palmar Sur, three times weekly. From time to time, flights are scheduled to Barra del Colorado.

Travelair, a newer airline, offers a more reliable service and more destinations — as well as higher prices. Still, no round-trip ticket on Travelair is more than $115 or so. Current destinations on Travelair are Quepos, Limón, Golfito, and Palmar Sur (all daily); and Barra del Colorado, Nosara, Carrillo and Tamarindo (two to three times weekly). Call Travelair at [2]327883 in San José.

Recent schedules are given in coverage of towns in this book.

Charter flights in small planes are also available from **Tobías Bolaños Airport** (just west of San José) to places without regularly scheduled service, such as Tortuguero National Park. Arrange such flights through travel agencies, or directly through the companies listed in the yellow pages under *Aviación*.

NO FEAR OF FLYING

When you take a local charter, you could be in for unexpected thrills. The routing to Tortuguero is usually through a dense bank of clouds — dry season or wet season, it makes no difference. To the left, obscured by mist, is the volcano Barva. Off to the right is the steaming, jagged peak of Irazú. Your pilot, relying on instruments and skill, threads his little craft through the passage between the two, always maintaining a safe altitude — you hope.

On a more cloud-free routing from San José to Corcovado National Park, the Escazú ridge looms directly in front of your window, drafts knock you almost to slamdown . . . and then, with the help of pilot body English, the earth falls way.

Down to the west, the Pacific breaks in white crests along gentle curves of beach between rocky headlands. A forested outcrop topped by clouds is Manuel Antonio National Park. The mud of the River Barú, the rocks of Punta Dominical and the winding Sierpe River follow, the last ending in a line of waves at its mouth. Ridge arms form bays and inlets around the rim of Osa, visible and disappearing as the plane skirts and then darts through greater and lesser white puffs of cloud, exits over a meandering river in a dense stand of jungle, and breaks over a circle of swamp. The last ridge is crossed almost at tree-top level, then it's over the waves and up the beach, a twist into the wind, and a poke back onto the dirt strip at Carate.

Phew.

I have no statistics on aviation safety in Costa Rica, but I am told that the larger and more powerful the plane, the more likely that you will safely climb out of the Central Valley and get to where you're going. If this does not sound encouraging, consider using air taxis only for short hops in non-mountainous areas (for example, from Golfito to the Osa Peninsula).

BY BUS

There are several tiers of bus service in Costa Rica. Depending on where you are in the country and how far you're going, getting around by bus can be pleasant and comfortable, tolerable, or — if you're not prepared — an ordeal.

Service between towns in the Central Valley is provided in large buses similar to those used on the city lines in San José. These generally have padded seats, which are closer together than those in comparable American buses, but comfortable enough for the distances involved.

Fares on suburban routes are generally fixed, no matter how far you travel. Fare cards are usually posted near the driver's seat.

Buses in the Central Valley may be boarded either at their terminals, or at bus stops, which are marked by shelters, rectangular signs, or short yellow lines painted along the edge of the road. Pay the driver, choose a seat, and enjoy the sights along the way.

Buses operating on the major highways between San José and the far points of the country are roughly comparable to Greyhound buses in the

United States. They may be older, and lack air conditioning and lavatories, but they are generally well-cared-for, and mechanically sound. Drivers of long-distance buses try to maintain the maximum legal speed, even on winding roads. Bus crews are ready for such side-effects as nausea with plastic bags (comforting). Prepare yourself with motion sickness pills if you're susceptible.

Tickets for long-distance buses may be purchased in advance, and this is recommended for weekend travel. If you try to board a long-distance bus along its route, it might or might not stop — there's no fixed rule. Try to select a waiting place where the driver will see you well in advance and have a chance to slow down. Ask a handy local for advice.

Buses operating in rural areas outside the Central Valley are of an entirely different breed. Most are similar to American school buses. Some in fact *are* old school buses, right down to the yellow paint. (Old school buses never die. They just go to Central America.) Seats are stiff, with minimal padding, designed for small people traveling short distances.

Rural buses stop frequently to let out and pick up passengers, as well as chickens, cardboard boxes full of merchandise, and whatever else has to move. Add poor roads and steep grades, and a trip of fifty kilometers could take a couple of hours. Many a passenger has to stand in a crowded aisle, for there is often no other way to go.

Country people in Costa Rica are used to conditions on buses, and may even doze off, despite the bouncing and shaking and cramped quarters. Without precautions, however, the visitor may find rural bus trips excruciating.

TIPS FOR BACKROADS BUS TRAVEL

Some tips for enjoying, or at least surviving, your trip:

Look for a place where you can stretch your legs. The seat behind the driver is usually best. If it's not available, try an aisle seat, even if this costs you some views. Get to the bus terminal early to be sure of getting a seat at all.

Sit toward the front of the bus - the shaking is always worse at the rear. By all means, go to the bathroom before you get on the bus (nobody else will tell you this), and don't drink too much coffee or any other liquid before you set out.

Rural buses will generally stop anyplace you flag them down. Pay the driver or his helper, and call out *¡parada!* to get the bus to stop.

Fares on all buses in Costa Rica are low, generally less than 2¢ (U.S.) per kilometer.

BY TAXI

It doesn't occur to most people, but taxis are a very practical way to get around the countryside in Costa Rica. Current official rates are about 70¢ for the first kilometer, 25¢ for each additional kilometer, and $3 per hour of waiting time. For trips over 12 kilometers, the driver is allowed to negotiate the charge. At the official rate, a 120-kilometer round trip from San José to Poás volcano should run less than $30, including a couple of hours of waiting. Even if you're charged more, the cost should compare favorably to that of renting a car. In addition, you'll be able to look around instead of keeping your eyes glued to the road, and can direct the driver to slow down or stop where you please.

Travel by taxi is not without its problems. Many drivers are used to overcharging tourists, sometimes by claiming that their meters don't work. Look for a driver who will agree to charge the legal rates (which your hotel can confirm), or at least not too much more.

For long-distance travel, of course, you'll want to use airplanes or comfortable buses. But taxis are a good bet for going those last few kilometers in rural areas. In the Nicoya Peninsula and other areas with poor roads, taxis are usually Jeeps or similar vehicles well suited to local conditions.

BY TRAIN

Costa Rica's world-famous **Jungle Train**, from San José to Limón, is out of operation, due to repeated landslides, though parts of the line operate in the lowlands for banana plantation tours. Currently, there is limited scheduled passenger service from Limón southward, along the Caribbean, and in the San José area at rush hours.

BY BICYCLE

Bicycle tours within Costa Rica's national parks are offered by travel agencies in San José (see page 182). The company supplies mountain bikes, though according to experienced cycle tourist and author J. P. Panet, riding a bike other than your own can be a painful experience.

J. P. Panet is co-author of *Latin America on Bicycle* (Passport Press), which includes a chapter about a bicycle trip through Costa Rica.

BY CAR

Driving your own car makes a small country significantly smaller — but not without a price. Gasoline outlays and car rental rates in Costa Rica are higher than those in the United States. Rental cars are easy marks for thieves, as well as for traffic police looking for payoffs.

Getting Your Bearings

In the Central Valley, through roads are well marked with standard rectangular signs. In the center of any town along a main highway, signs point the way toward the next towns in all directions, and usually indicate distances.

On back roads in the Central Valley, signs are generally inadequate. To complicate matters, place names are repeated. San Isidro de Coronado is just a few miles from San Isidro de Heredia. Take the wrong turn from San Isidro de Heredia, and you'll end up in Concepción de San Isidro, when you might have been looking for Concepción de San Rafael – each within a few minutes' drive.

Take heart. Everybody gets lost. But you can minimize aimless wandering by paying careful attention to driving instructions, looking at a map, and asking for directions at *every* church and crossroads as you approach your destination.

Main routes outside the Central Valley are well-marked, but secondary roads are not. Navigation is made even more difficult by the lack of accurate, up-to-date road maps for some areas. Ask directions at junctions if you have any doubts.

Theft
Never, ever, leave anything of value in an unattended vehicle, even for minutes! Thieves lurk wherever visitors roam: at volcanoes, restaurants, national parks, beaches, in "protected" hotel parking lots.

Gasoline stations
Bombas, gasoline stations, are sparse, so fill up before turning off any main route. Some gasoline stations will accept Visa or Master Card. Unleaded gasoline will soon be available.

Supplies
Supplies and refreshments are abundant along most roads in Costa Rica. There's always a *pulpería* (grocery store) where you can stop for soft drinks, cookies and other goodies, always a *soda* (diner) where you can have some basic eats if no formal *restaurante* is in view.

Road Conditions and Hazards
Though Costa Rica has had no recent wars, some of the main roads through mountainous areas, and many secondary roads, look as if they've been mined. There is generally no warning even for monumental pot-holes. On and off paved roads, much of your attention is devoted to dodging potholes, or it should be. Conditions are generally worst toward the end of the rainy season. Many unpaved roads are graded but once a year. Consider December 1 as the end of mud season for driving the dirt roads of Costa Rica.

Inquire at every opportunity about road conditions ahead (usually at gasoline stations), especially in the rainy season, and interpret the response with caution. Costa Ricans will usually tell you that a road is passable. Gringos will say that you can't make it after a heavy rain, what with swollen rivers and mud up to your axles. The truth lies somewhere in between, and depends on what you're driving.

On mountain roads, beep your horn at curves and drive at moderate speeds. The driver going up a hill has the right of way, so be prepared to pull over or back up on narrow stretches. Oncoming drivers will sometimes flash their lights to warn of a hazard ahead. Slow down.

It's never wise to drive at night on unfamiliar roads, especially in the Central Valley, where the winding right of way is used by people, some of them unsober, as well as vehicles.

Other assorted hazards include herds of cattle in the road, driven by cowboys on horses or bicycles; and slow-moving trucks. Most hazard signs use easily understood symbols, though a few use words that you might not know. (See road vocabulary in **Tico Talk** chapter).

Legal Matters

The speed limit on the open road is 75 kilometers (47 miles) an hour, and it's seriously enforced. I got my first speeding ticket ever in Costa Rica — the radar clocked me at a blazing 91 kilometers per hour on the flat, straight highway from Limón to San José. You can also get a ticket for not using your seat belt. The worst part is waiting in line at a bank to pay the fine — and pay you must, or risk being turned back at the airport.

Your local driver's license is good for 90 days in Costa Rica. Should you stay longer, you'll need a Costa Rican license.

Be sure to stop at roadside checkpoints if you're flagged down. It's usually nothing sinister. The police might be looking for contraband turtle eggs, not firearms.

But some traffic police are corrupt. A dollar or two in *coffee money* will get the cop to overlook your lack of an original registration or some other claimed infraction. It's annoying to pay, of course, but the Cheshire cat grin, seen through the rear-view mirror as you drive off, is priceless.

In the case of higher demands, confiscation of documents, or requests for payment of "fines" on the spot, get the name of the police officer, if you can. You can file a complaint, and you should, even if it's inconvenient. It's time for Costa Rica to clean up.

Repairs

Many auto parts are hard to obtain outside of San José. Try to have your car serviced and repairs made in the capital or nearby. Parts for some makes of car are simply not stocked in Costa Rica, but drivers of most

Japanese and smaller American cars should have no problems in this regard.

Car Rentals

The smallest cars — the Subaru Justy or equivalent — rent for about $25 daily plus 25¢ per kilometer, or $50, including insurance, at the unlimited mileage rate. These vehicles are comfortable only for two adults, and are worse than useless on many unpaved roads during the rainy season. A compact car that will fit four adults goes for about $56 per day (more with automatic transmission), while a four-wheel drive vehicle — almost essential for the Nicoya Peninsula, or a trip to Monteverde — comes in at about $65 a day. This doesn't include gasoline— roughly $8 for 200 kilometers of driving in a Justy, $20 or more in a Jeep.

Slightly lower rates are sometimes offered when you reserve in advance. I did this once through Budget, though upon arrival I encountered mysterious service charges (I refused to pay), bait-and-switch insurance sales ("*your mandatory insurance provides no protection, sir*"), and much wasted time — on my meter — while we attempted to come to a consensus about pre-existing damage. But I'm told that similar tactics are used by other companies. In any case, you probably won't get a price break at the moment of renting, so it doesn't hurt to call around before you leave home. Inquire too if your own insurance policy or one that comes with your credit card will cover damage to a rented car in Costa Rica. If so, try to get a statement to that effect in writing. (Such policies generally don't include liability coverage, which is sold at the usual unconscionable rates, often with deductibles that approach $1,000.)

RESERVE YOUR CAR!

I strongly urge you to reserve your rental car before you leave home through a company with a familiar name. You'll generally get a better rate than if you rent on the spot. And if a dispute arises over shady practices — not uncommon in this business — you'll have better luck if you take your complaint right to the head office than if you write letters to Costa Rica.

6. BASIC INFORMATION

Listed here, in alphabetical order by topic, are practical information and recommendations for your trip to Costa Rica.

BUSINESS HOURS

Businesses generally open at 8:30 or 9 a.m., close for a couple of hours starting at 11:30 a.m. or noon, then open for the afternoon from 1:30 or 2 p.m. until 6 p.m. On Saturdays, many businesses are open in the morning only. Continuous hours, without the midday break, are becoming more common at the larger stores in San José. In the hotter lowlands along the Atlantic and Pacific, stores open earlier, and the midday break is longer. You'll soon get used to doing your shopping before or after the break, or rest (*descanso*), which, by the way, is rarely called a siesta.

During December, as Christmas bonuses are spent, normal hours are abandoned, and many stores remain open throughout the day, and even on Sunday morning.

BUREAUCRACY

This comes first alphabetically, but I didn't want to start this chapter on an unpleasant note.

All countries have their problems – natural disasters, human rights violations, racial tensions, refugees, whatever. Costa Rica has its bureaucracy. When you put it in perspective, it seems a minor matter. To deal with it, however, is deadly.

Costa Ricans are used to runarounds and frustrations in government and commerce. Processing insurance claims, obtaining non-emergency health care, and receiving payments for officially marketed crops all can involve inexplicable delays. Seekers of licenses must peck patiently at the roosts of officialdom. Labor inspectors, hotel inspectors, transport inspectors, tax inspectors meticulously go through their motions. Queues as orderly as any in London form at bus stops, government offices, and even at the entrances to supermarkets. Standing in line is an honorable profession and source of employment in Costa Rica. Many businesses have one or more *mensajeros* (messengers) for this purpose. Their badge of office is a motorcycle helmet.

Visitors may think they are exempt from engagement with the domestic bureaucratic mentality, and in most cases they are. Some exposure, however, is inevitable. Hour-long lineups at the airport immigration counters are not unusual. See the "Money and Banking" section in this chapter for another example.

COST OF LIVING

It will be obvious from prices mentioned in this book that travel expenses in Costa Rica are somewhat — but not much — lower than in the United States, while many items cost more.

In popular areas, hotel rates are rising by as much as 25% per year. A middle-range hotel room costs from $60 to $80 for a double in San José, though you can find clean, airy rooms on the outskirts, especially in bed and breakfasts, for $35 to $50 double. The most modest hotels in San José charge about $20 double. As new rooms are opening all the time, the rate of price increase will probably slow down.

Five dollars will buy a basic, wholesome meal in San José, while a gourmet-quality repast may carry a tab of $15 or more, not including wine, which is expensive. Outside the Central Valley, fine cuisine is usually not available.

Tour prices, I'm sorry to say, are in many cases way out of whack. A day's rafting excursion from San José costs about $80, or about double what you'd pay in Alaska or on the James River in Virginia. However, travel companies are proliferating like amoebas, and prices should stabilize.

While automobile ownership and maintenance are expensive, public transport is not. The bus fare from San José to any border point is less than $10. Scheduled flights in small planes cost less than $50 to the most distant towns. Hiring a taxi costs about the same as renting a car, or less.

Foreigners who live in Costa Rica find that they save considerable amounts on services and housing, and on the heavy clothing and other items that they can live without because of the mild climate.

Heating and air conditioning are unnecessary in most well-built houses in San José. Many a comfortable home has a fireplace more for esthetic than practical reasons. Lower land taxes and insurance rates further reduce fixed costs. Electric rates are not the bargain they once were, but with fewer appliances, consumption is generally much lower than in North America. Household workers are generally paid less than $200 per month, plus health insurance and other benefits.

Houses cost roughly half what they do in the United States, sometimes less. But comparisons in this respect are imperfect. The housing market has its ups and downs in Costa Rica as in other countries, and construction methods are different. Most houses come without the appliances and built-in closets and cabinets that one expects in the States, and electrical wiring and plumbing standards are lower. However, better-quality construction is available, and I have seen some condominium units in San José that would make an American apartment dweller cry in envy.

Rental housing is reasonably priced. Two-bedroom apartments with some furnishings start at about $350 per month in middle-class neighbor-hoods, though in exclusive areas the tab can be $1,000 per month or higher.

The crunch, when it comes, is in consumer goods. Tape recorders, home computers, cameras, watches, appliances, and almost every other imported, manufactured item costs double to triple what it does in the States. Clothing of local manufacture is priced slightly higher than similar American items, and variety is limited. Cosmetics, whether locally made or imported, are expensive.

At the supermarkets, many packaged and processed items cost more than in the States, while fresh foods cost the same or less. By adjusting eating patterns, one can usually end up with a lower food bill.

Here is a rather unscientific sampling of prices for grocery and non-grocery items at a San José supermarket:

Meat, one-third less than U.S. prices, or lower; fish, one-half to same; cosmetics and diapers, double or higher; local canned foods, same to one-half more; imported canned foods, double or more; eggs, one-half higher; coffee, two-thirds less; dairy products, slightly less; beer, slightly less; fruit and vegetables in season, same to two-thirds less; Gerber baby foods, same to double. Some specific recent prices: cigarettes, $1 per pack; local brands of liquor, $3 per 750 ml bottle; imported wines, $7 and up for a bottle of drinkable French wine, slightly less for Italian or Chilean brands; Scotch whiskey, $12 and up; Spanish brandy, $20; imported American peanut butter, $5 for a 12-ounce jar; filet mignon, $2 per pound.

In general, persons who are not too attached to mechanical gadgets and pre-packaged, processed foods can maintain a comfortable standard of living for less than in the United States.

ELECTRICITY

Electrical supply is at 110 volts, alternating current, throughout Costa Rica. Sockets are of the American type, usually without provision for a grounding prong. Non-grounded American and Canadian appliances should work without adapters. However, it's always wise to ask about the voltage in your hotel before you plug anything in. In remote locations, such as fishing camps, generators may operate on a non-standard voltage.

GETTING MARRIED

According to my source, a hotelier whose spouse is a Costa Rican lawyer, getting married in Costa Rica couldn't be simpler.

If you've been previously married, you'll sign an affidavit attesting to your divorce. It will help to have a copy of your divorce papers, notarized by a Costa Rican consul. An attorney will examine your passports, make out the appropriate documents, and even perform the ceremony.

In a couple of weeks, you'll have documents ready for translation, and registration at a courthouse in your own country.

GETTING YOUR GLASSES (OR ANYTHING ELSE) FIXED

If you have a few spare moments, drop off your broken eyeglasses at any optician in San José and have the frame welded for $2 or so (the price is prohibitive in the States). Have that important document sealed in plastic (*emplasticado*) for less than a dollar by a sidewalk-based specialist. Reset the stone in a cherished ring. Repair that favorite old pair of shoes. Or the baby stroller.

Virtually all the skilled services that have disappeared in a disposable society flourish in Costa Rica. It's a treat to take advantage of them, and to get to know a side of living you might not otherwise experience here . . . or at home.

HANDICAPPED ACCESSIBILITY

There is little positive to report on the accessibility front in Costa Rica. Sidewalks in San José are as rutted and potholed as streets and highways. There are no indentations to allow easy street crossing. Hallways in hotels are usually narrow. Even in major public buildings, such as the airport terminal, there are no handicapped-accessible rest room stalls.

A few bright spots are mentioned in the text of this book. For example, Lapa Ríos, the luxurious wilderness lodge in the Osa Peninsula, provides ramp entryways to some of its units. But an able-bodied companion is a must for any first-time visit to Costa Rica by a handicapped person.

HEALTH CONCERNS

The health worries that usually accompany a trip to Latin America — mad dashes to the bathroom, general malaise as unknown microbes attack your insides, long-forgotten diseases like typhoid turning up in the best hotels — hardly apply to Costa Rica, where sanitary standards are generally high and most people are educated enough to have an idea of how disease spreads. Good sense and normal caution should be enough to see you through Costa Rica in good health.

In most cases, no special inoculations or vaccinations are required or recommended for visitors to Costa Rica. You can check current conditions by calling the Communicable Disease Center hotline in Atlanta, tel. 404-332-4555. You should, in any case, get your health affairs in order before you travel. Catch up on immunizations, such as those for tetanus and polio, and consult your doctor if any condition or suspected condition, such as an ear infection, might trouble you during air travel. Take along the medicines that you use regularly, and an extra pair of prescription glasses.

Water in San José and in most of the towns of the Central Valley is chemically treated and is probably safe to drink, though many experienced travelers avoid tap water anywhere. If you're not confident of water quality, stick to bottled sodas or beer. Suspect water is easily treated with laundry bleach (two drops per quart, let stand 30 minutes).

Limit exposure to sun if you haven't seen any for a while, and take along insect repellent for the west coast in the rainy season, and for the Caribbean at any time. Also, take it easy on alcohol until you become accustomed to the higher altitude in San José.

For extensive travel at the budget level or off the beaten track, a dose of immunoglobulin for protection against hepatitis and a typhoid booster are advisable. If you're heading to the Caribbean lowlands, where there are occasional malaria outbreaks, and will be staying in rural areas or unscreened budget accommodations, take a weekly dosage of a malaria preventative, such as Aralen.

Budget travelers should avoid fleabag hotels. Fleas and similar insects are not only unpleasant in themselves but can carry disease. If both top and bottom sheets are not clean and clean-smelling, move on.

Having an Operation

Plastic surgery is a growing non-traditional earner of foreign exchange for Costa Rica. Many a foreigner flies in to have breasts, wrinkles, or nose renovated at a fraction of the cost in the States or Europe. If you're interested, check the ads in *Guide* magazine, *Costa Rica Today*, and the *Tico Times*.

You'll also find ads for dentists (*travel to Costa Rica and return home with a beautiful smile*), acupuncturists, homeopaths, ophthalmologists, and many other practitioners, both mainstream and alternative. Some have trained at reputable universities in the United States and Latin America. You won't want to select your care strictly from an ad, so ask for references from anyone you contact, and consider consulting your doctor at home before treatment. Credit cards are often accepted for payment.

If your treatment is not covered by medical insurance at home, you might find that the price is right for treatment in Costa Rica, and all or part of your travel expenses could be tax deductible as well!

Medical Care

Short-term medical insurance is available for about $50 per month, less for students, through **International Cultural Exchange Association**, P. O. Box 687-1011Y, San José, fax [2]227867. The card issued through this program allows treatment at hospitals of the Costa Rican social security system. This card is not a substitute for comprehensive medical insurance from a company in your own country.

Recuperating and Recovering

A growing number of facilities provides counseling, treatment for drug and alcohol abuse, and post-operative convalescence in benign surroundings. The **Forest Clinic** in Escazú, tel. [2]285438, associated with a U.S. clinic, has English-language psychiatric services. **Casa de Campo**, tel. [2]295309, has similar services. The luxurious **Tara Resort Hotel**, among others, discreetly cares for patients recovering from cosmetic surgery.

I am not in a position to recommend any particular service, but you can get leads through health-care professionals in the United States, or from ads in the *Tico Times* and *Costa Rica Today*.

INVESTING IN COSTA RICA

Con men are an old story in Costa Rica. Get into a casual conversation with anybody who has lived in the country for several years, and you'll turn up at least a dozen cases of people losing a substantial part of their savings in cocoa, gold mining, a cattle ranch, or some other enterprise that was marketed to visiting marks, or in unenforceable loan contracts.

Most victims don't love Costa Rica any less for these little problems, mind you, and blame nobody but themselves. But they sure wish they hadn't signed on the dotted line.

Of course, Costa Rica has much going for it as an investment target: stable governments; an educated population; relatively low wages; well-developed domestic transport, electrical system, and telecommunications; ports on two oceans; duty-free or low-duty access to the United States; excellent sanitary conditions; and mild climate.

But there are also perils. Most business start-ups, in Costa Rica as elsewhere, go belly-up within a couple of years. Export incentives, such as tax credits, are controversial in some quarters, and could be withdrawn at any time. And shady characters operate with fewer restrictions than elsewhere.

I mention these matters only because others might conveniently omit them. Be more cautious than at home before parting with your money.

Seek counsel from a disinterested party. You will probably have no legal recourse if your money evaporates in a flurry of documents and contracts that you can't understand.

Sources of investment information (beside the fellows who advertise seminars or lurk in your hotel lobby) include:

• **Cinde** (Coalition for Investment Initiatives), P. O. Box 7170-1000, San José, tel. [2]200036, fax 204750. Offices at 992 High Ridge Rd., Stamford, CT 06905; 7200 NW 19 St., Miami, FL 33126; 221 N. La Salle St., Chicago, IL 60601; 635 Sanbourne Pl., Salinas, CA 93901; Eisenhowelaan 128, The Hague, Netherlands

• **Cenpro** (Export Promotion), P. O. Box 5418-1000, San José, tel. [2]2 17165, fax [2]235722

• **Costa Rican-American Chamber of Commerce**, P. O. Box 4946-1000, San José, tel. [2]332133, fax [2]232349

• **Cámara de Comercio de Costa Rica**, P. O. Box 1114-1000, San José

LEARNING SPANISH IN COSTA RICA

Learning Spanish will ease your way in Costa Rica, and enrich your life afterwards. Your whole living environment is your language laboratory, so chances are you'll pick things up more easily than at home.

What does it cost?

There are other countries where you can go to language school at a lower price than in Costa Rica, but many students prefer San José's low-key atmosphere and level of amenities, and the comprehensiveness of some of the programs. A four-week package of study, room, meals in a private home, and escorted trips around the country, costs $1,200 or more. Instruction in small groups for four hours daily, without excursions, will run about $900 for four weeks.

These are just general guidelines. Write, call or fax the schools listed below for more details, and ask for referrals from recent students. Some travel agencies also offer study-and-flight packages.

Language Schools

Some of the language schools in Costa Rica are:

• **Instituto Universal de Idiomas**, Apartado 651-2050, Moravia, tel. [2]570441

• **Instituto Británico**, P. O. Box 8184-1000 San José, tel. [2]250256, fax [2]531894. Teaches both English and Spanish as a second language, in San José and in Liberia, in northwestern Costa Rica

• **ICAI** (Instituto Centroamericano de Asuntos Internacionales), Apartado 10302, San José, tel. [2]338571, fax [2]215238, runs a comprehensive one- to four-week classroom and tour program, and an intensive ten-week course.

• **Centro Lingüístico Conversa**, Calle 38, Avenidas 3/5 (Apartado 17-1007), San José, tel. [2]217649, fax [2]332418. Courses are available in San José, and at a farm west of the city.
• **Forester Instituto Internacional**, Los Yoses (P. O. Box 6945-1000, San José), tel. [2]253155, fax [2]259236.
• **Lisa Tec**, P.O. Box 228-4005, San Antonio de Belén, has a quiet, suburban location.
• **ILISA**, P.O. Box 1001-2050 San Pedro, tel. [2]252495, fax [2]254665. Direct line from U.S. and Canada: 800-377-2665.
• **ICADS** (Instituto de Estudios de Desarrollo Centroamericano), P. O. Box 3-2070, San José, tel. [2]250508, fax [2]341337 or Box 025216-826, Miami FL 33102-5216, has programs that combine language study with volunteer work in Costa Rica and Nicaragua.
• **Instituto Americano de Lenguaje y Cultura**, San Pedro (P. O. Box 200-1001 San José), tel. [2]254313, fax [2]244244.
• **Instituto de la Lengua Española**, Apartado 100-2350, San José, tel. [2]277355, fax [2]270211. Fifteen-week courses.
• **Instituto Interamericano de Idiomas Intensa**, P. O. Box 8110-1000, Calle 33, Avenidas 5/7 (no. 540), Barrio Escalante, San José, tel. [2]256009
• **Centro Cultural Costarricense-Norteamericano**, Calle 37, Avenida Central, tel. [2]259433, fax [2]241480. (P.O. Box 1489-1000, San José). Associated with the U.S. government. Features computer-assisted grammar-tuning, conversation partners, possible college credits. Facilities are rated excellent by readers, fees are slightly lower than elsewhere.
• **Centro Panamericano de Idiomas**, P. O. Box 151-3007 San Joaquín, Heredia, tel. and fax [2]380561. U.S. tel. 603-469-3610, fax 469-3500. Small-town setting for study and family stays, airport pickup.
• **Costa Rican Language Academy and Latin Dance School**, P.O. Box 336-2070, San José, tel. [2]338938, fax [2]338670. *"Learn our language and lifestyle together."*
• **Escuela d'Amore**, Manuel Antonio National Park (P. O. Box 77, Quepos), tel. [6]770543. Spanish classes in a resort setting.

In addition, assorted colleges and universities in the United States offer credit courses in Spanish in Costa Rica. For more information, look at the postings at the Spanish or Romance Languages department at a large university near wherever you happen to be. **The Universidad Autónoma de Centro América**, tel. [2]255878, fax [2]252907, pre-arranges college credits in the United States for a number of its Spanish-as-a-second-language courses.

Getting By Without Spanish

One of the remarkable aspects of Costa Rica, for me, at least, is how many foreign residents do *not* speak Spanish, yet get along just splendidly. Over and over again, I've seen hotel owners, charter boat operators, and retirees speak to their employees and associates and Costa Rican spouses in English (or French or German), and get exactly what they want.

It's not that the Ticos understand every word. Most can decipher little, if any, English. But the cultural differences between North Americans and natives are far fewer than in many other Latin American nations, where even fluent Spanish might be of little use in deciphering local ways.

Ticos can usually figure out what you want, even if you can't exactly express it, and they are almost universally willing to help a foreigner out. So if you don't speak a word of Spanish, and don't think you have much chance of learning any, just don't worry about it. You'll get by.

MONEY AND BANKING

Costa Rica's unit of currency is the *colón* ("ko-LOHN"), which is named after Christopher Columbus (Colón in Spanish). Each colón is divided into 100 céntimos (which, with inflation, you will rarely see). In slang usage, the colón is sometimes called a peso.

In this book, I've quoted most prices in U.S. dollars, based on the current rate of exchange (about 125 colones to the dollar). Costa Rica's currency has an unstable recent history, and devaluations are now a routine matter. You may even find that some prices are *lower*, in U.S. dollars, than those I've indicated. However, rates for hotel rooms, tours, car rentals, and other services are fixed in dollars, and then converted to colones at the current rate. You won't get a break on these as the value of the currency shrinks.

Changing Money

Unfortunately, changing your foreign currency to colones could turn out to be your most unpleasant experience in Costa Rica. The levels of bureaucracy in Costa Rica's banks are unsurpassed. You might have to wait in line for more than an hour while somebody in front of you cashes in sheet upon sheet of winning lottery tickets, or has his loan payments calculated on antiquated adding machines and then transferred to record sheets by a teller with hunt-and-peck typing skills (and how they insist on using typewriters!)

And after waiting, you still might not get your money changed. I once had my travelers checks refused because I had no permanent address in Costa Rica. I was turned down at other banks because my brand of travelers checks was out of favor (they wouldn't say why). Some visitors are refused because they have no passports, although none is required to enter the country.

Leaving Costa Rica With Local Currency

U.S. funds may be repurchased at the airport bank before leaving Costa Rica, if available. Avoid leaving the country with extra Costa Rican money, which will be exchanged abroad at an unfavorable rate or not at all.

TIPS FOR CHANGING MONEY

With a few precautions you can avoid problems with the banks and their sadistic methods.

Some suggestions:
• Buy colones at airport exchange counters before you enter the country.
• Exchange a substantial amount on arriving at the airport in San José. The airport bank is relatively hassle-free.
• Change money at your hotel, if it performs this service. The rate, however, will be slightly less favorable than at the banks.
• Use a bank's specialized exchange office, when available. In downtown San José, the most convenient such facility, operated by Banco Mercantil, is opposite the tourist office, on Calle 5 just south of Avenida Central. Watch for pickpockets as you leave!
• If you must exchange money at a bank, get there early in the day, and get as much cash as you feel comfortable carrying. Normal banking hours are from 9 a.m. to 3 p.m.
• Use credit cards when possible (see below). As a bonus, you'll save the one-percent commission that most banks charge on travellers checks.
• Carry a passport for identification.
• Take U.S. dollars in cash or travelers checks. Other currencies, such as Canadian dollars and sterling, are difficult if not impossible to exchange. (See below.)
• Do as the Costa Ricans do, and use the black market. Actually, a better term would be "gray market," since unofficial currency transactions operate pretty much in the open, and are no longer even illegal. The street rate may not even be any better than what you'll get at a bank, but there are no lineups, and travelers checks are accepted with a minimum of fuss. Dealers generally operate near the post office in San José. How do you find them? Generally, you don't have to look for them; if you walk through the area, they will find you. Try to carry out the exchange off the street (in a hotel lobby, for example). Have some familiarity with Costa Rican currency, and put your cash away immediately in a money belt or inside pocket safe from thieves.

If this is more than you want to deal with on a vacation, credit cards are a better alternative.

Receiving Money

Money from home may be received by telegraphic or Telex transfer through a bank in San José. Make sure you know through which bank it will be sent — several have similar names. International money orders may also be sent by registered mail, but safety is not assured. The U.S. State Department, tel. 202-647-5225, can assist with money transfers. Regular money orders and personal checks are nearly impossible to cash.

Credit Cards

Visa and Master Card are widely accepted in Costa Rica, American Express to a lesser extent. You may reasonably expect to use your credit card at restaurants where a meal costs $5 or more per person, and at any large hotel that charges $25 or more for a double room. Smaller, family-run hotels and inns generally do not take credit cards, even for $100 rooms. The bank rate of exchange in effect on the date of your purchase will be applied (the card issuer may charge a commission as well).

Local contacts are: **American Express**, tel. [2]330044 (230116 after business hours); **Visa** and **Master Card**, tel. [2]532155 (Credomatic, Avenida Central, Calles 29/33); **Diners Club**, 210078.

Sterling, Marks, Francs, Canadian Dollars

If you've ignored my advice and brought along these currencies, try the services of **Compañía Financiera Londres**, on Calle Central near the corner of Avenida Central (next to La Casona), third floor. Rates will most likely be less than favorable.

Business Transactions

Goods should generally be shipped to Costa Rica against advance payment or irrevocable letter of credit.

PAYING OFF THE COPS

The traffic police are on the lookout for *you* (they know the cars that tourists drive, and the license-plate codes of rental vehicles), and will not hesitate to impose a "fine" for a phony offense, which you must pay on the spot, or risk having the vehicle impounded (so they say).

This scam has been running for years, with the tacit approval of higher-ups. North Americans find it particularly annoying and in bad taste, but keep in mind that obvious tourists in cars are subject to more life-threatening indignities in Cairo and Miami.

If you're not willing to pay a few dollars here and there, be prepared to stare down the cops; or show an official-looking document; or talk your way out of the situation ("I'm on my way to meet with the Minister of Public Security, who is a personal friend of my cousin"), or to accept a legitimate, or at least genuine, traffic ticket that you will have to pay after standing in line at a bank; or to take down the cop's name and file a complaint.

POST OFFICE

Wise residents of Costa Rica use the local mail system only when they have to. Letters from abroad are regularly opened, delayed, or lost while dishonest postal employees look for checks and valuables.

Enclosure of money, checks, or anything other than correspondence ensures that your letter will not arrive. Even registered mail provides limited protection — a $20 maximum indemnity if the letter is sent from the United States.

When possible, avoid the mails altogether, and send a fax.

The next-best choice is to use a mail drop in Miami, when available (many such addresses are given for hotels and other services in this book). These letters will be forwarded by private courier for pickup in San José.

If you have to use the mails to Costa Rica, send a post card, if your message will fit. Otherwise, use a flimsy air-mail envelope and lightweight paper, to make it obvious there's nothing inside. Good luck!

When writing to hotels, businesses or individuals in Costa Rica, use the post-office box, if known, in preference to the street address. The term "P. O. Box" (in English) is well understood, though you may of course use the Spanish equivalent, *apartado*.

Letters may be sent to you in Costa Rica in care of *lista de correos* (general delivery), Correo Central, 1000 San José (or any other city where you may be). There is a small charge for each letter picked up. Tell your correspondents to write neatly or type. Illegible foreign handwriting is responsible for many a letter going astray.

You may receive parcels at *lista de correos*, but, except for used books, there isn't much point in having anything sent. The customs duty usually exceeds the value of the merchandise. Tell the folks at home to send a money order instead.

Approximate postal rates are as follows: for light letters, up to 20 grams, via air mail, to the United States or Canada, 30¢; to Europe, 40¢. Post cards by air to the United States or Canada, 25¢; to Europe, 35¢.

PRECAUTIONS

I like to tell my friends in América del Norte that Costa Rica is like a Carmen Miranda movie: Latin America without the downside. The visitor is relatively un-harassed by peddlers and beggars, and doesn't stick out like a sore thumb, as in some neighboring countries.

But beguiled visitors can sometimes paint a picture more paradisaical than that which actually prevails. It's easy to become entranced by the pace of life, the apparent lack of urban ills, the friendliness of most of the populace.

In fact, there is probably no country in the world where novitiate visitors are more likely to throw normal caution to the winds than Costa

Rica. And there is probably no country in the hemisphere where visitors so easily fall victims to petty criminals and con men.

So let me take a moment of your time to counsel you that pickpockets lurk in crowded squares, and wherever there are tourists. Visitors' routes are well defined, and the thieves and con men know exactly where to find you.

People who are overfriendly without reason may well be overfriendly for a very bad reason. The candy or cookie shared by the friendly stranger on the bus could well be drugged.

Those barred windows are not just a Spanish tradition, as some real-estate salesmen would have it — they keep out thieves.

It isn't smart to walk in quiet or deserted parts of town at night.

Costa Rica is no cauldron of crime, but there are bad eggs, especially in San José, as in any urban area. If you don't do anything you wouldn't do in any unfamiliar place, you'll probably be safer than in most other cities.

Losing Your Luggage

If you park your car on any street in San José, it will be broken into, at night, and sometimes during the day. (Fortunately, there are few parking spaces downtown.) Hotel parking lots are not secure unless they are enclosed, with a guard on duty (report many, many readers). Even volcanoes are not secure. You can never, ever leave anything in a parked car with the expectation of seeing it again.

If your luggage rides out of sight on a bus, there's a chance you won't get it back. When using public transportation, it's better to carry hand luggage only.

RETIRING IN THE TROPICS

Before there was much in the way of tourism, before the national parks were open to visitors and before beach resorts had been developed, there was a colony of retired foreigners lured by the good life in Costa Rica: comfortable houses available for much less than in many countries; an agreeable climate in most areas year round; excellent health care; friendly and accepting people. It also helped that the retirement law granted residence with special privileges that included duty-free importation of cars and household goods.

How times have changed! Duty-free imports of vehicles and household goods are a thing of the past, and other benefits are being challenged by legislators resentful of the presence of a privileged class of foreigners. The government is downright fussy about who it allows in, and obtaining resident status can be an excruciating process.

But notable benefits are still available, and are likely to remain in place.

Under current law, foreigners may qualify for retirement residence with monthly pension income of $600, an investment income of $1000, or by making a large deposit in a Costa Rican bank or an investment in a business. They obtain all the rights (and, in some cases, hassles) of Costa Ricans, except working and voting. Income from abroad is exempt from taxes. Retirees can own businesses. And entry under the retirement law is one of the few ways to take up residence legally.

Attractions for those of you considering retirement in Costa Rica are the climate, the friendly people, and a high standard of living. Cable and satellite television with programming from the United States are widely available. Liquor, entertaining, and household help are relatively inexpensive. Except in a few parts of San José, retirees can walk around and relax in parks at all hours without fear. Newcomers fit into the daily rhythms of a village or town and get to know their neighbors after days or weeks; at home, they might remain strangers for years.

Not all retirees find Costa Rica to their liking, of course. Some find it difficult to communicate in Spanish. Trips back home are expensive. Suitable housing is lacking outside of the Central Valley and a few coastal developments, and is ever more expensive in the Central Valley. Many goods carry high prices, especially foreign liquor and appliances. Currency fluctuations and inflation make it difficult to predict future living costs. Postal service is a continuing scandal. Residents must stay in the country for at least six months every year, and renew their papers annually. And in some cases, the good life can get to be boring.

Do you really want to retire in Costa Rica? It might not be a bad idea. But understand that it's a fair-sized business, too. Many who would sell you on the idea will also take your money for legal services, seminars, property, rentals, or investments that might help you qualify for special retirement status. Before you invest your money and effort, make a few extended visits.

Assistance in obtaining retired-residence status is given by the Costa Rican Tourist Board. Information is also available from the **Asociación de Residentes de Costa Rica** (Association of Residents), P. O. Box 700-1011 San José, tel. [2]338068. And there are lawyers and agents who will assist you for a fee; try to get a recommendation from a retiree or the Residents Association.

Lifestyle Explorations, 101 Federal St., Suite 1900, Boston MA 02110, tel. 508-371-4814, fax 369-9192, specializes in familiarization trips for prospective retirees and investors to Costa Rica and several other countries. Their program includes sessions with resident foreigners.

SCHOOLING

The **University for Peace,** at Ciudad Colón, west of San José, offers masters degrees in human rights, education for peace, and communication for peace, as well as courses on natural resources. Most instruction is in Spanish, though exams may be written in English or French. For information, write to P. O. Box 199-1250, Escazú, Costa Rica.

Become a Visiting Student

Private institutions of higher education that regularly admit foreign students include:

• **National University,** P. O. Box 217-1017, San José, tel. [2]315855, fax [2]317569. U.S.-accredited.

• **Instituto Centroamericano para la Administración de Empresas,** P. O. Box 960-4050, San Pedro, tel. [2]412255, fax [2]439101. M.B.A. programs.

• **Universidad Interamericana de Costa Rica,** P. O. Box 6495-1000 San José, tel. [2]346262. Puerto Rican-accredited.

• **Universidad Internacional de las Americas,** P. O. Box 1447-1002, San José, tel. [2]335304.

• **Friends World College,** P. O. Box 8496-1000, San José, tel. [2]250289. Quaker-associated.

• **Universidad Autónoma de Centro América,** P. O. Box 7637-1000, San José, tel. [2]340701

• **ICAI,** mentioned above under language programs, periodically offers seminars and conferences that include meetings with regional politicians. In the U.S., contact **Consortium for International Education,** P. O. Box 188882, Irvine, CA 92713, tel. 714-955-1700, fax 714-955-2945.

• **ICADS** (Instituto de Estudios de Desarrollo Centroamericano), mentioned above under language study, has semester-abroad programs in ecology, women's studies, journalism, and other fields. Fees are $4000 to $5500, plus transportation.

• **The Organization for Tropical Studies,** directly and in collaboration with various universities, offers courses in tropical biology, ecology and forestry at its research stations at La Selva and Wilson Gardens. Write to P. O. Box DM, Duke Station, Durham, NC 27706 (tel. 919-684-5774) or P. O. Box 676-2050 San Pedro, Costa Rica.

• Biology programs at Monteverde are available through the **Council on International Educational Exchange,** 205 East 42 St., New York, NY 10017.

Other broad programs in humanities and the natural and social sciences are offered by American universities with campuses or offices in

Costa Rica. Generally, you must be already enrolled in the university before you can take its courses in Costa Rica.

Send the Kids to School

Various schools offer English and bi-lingual programs, following a curriculum compatible with that of school systems in the United States, Britain, and other countries. Among them:

• **The British School of Costa Rica**, Rohrmoser, P. O. Box 8184-1000 San José, tel. [2]200131, fax [2]327833.
• **Colegio Lincoln**, Moravia, tel. [2]357733.
• **Colegio Humboldt**, Rohrmoser, tel. [2]320092.
• **Colegio Metodista**, San Pedro, tel. [2]250655.
• **Costa Rica Academy**, north of San José, tel. [2]390974.
• **Country Day School**, Escazú, tel. [2]280873.
• **European School**, Heredia, tel. [2]373709.
• **International Christian School**, Barrio Escalante, tel. [2]251474.
• **Marian Baker School**, San Ramón de Tres Ríos, tel. [2]343426.

SHOPPING

Costa Rica offers visitors many rewards, but shopping is not near the top of the list.

Only a handful of indigenous crafts — pottery, hand-woven textiles and musical instruments made on a small scale for home use — can be found for sale in stores and museums.

Most of what you see at hotel shops and souvenir stores will be non-traditional handicrafts largely intended for the tourist market — things like miniature painted oxcarts, reproductions of pre-Columbian artifacts, painted wooden frogs, gourd mugs, hammocks, hand-blown glass, and items made from unusual and attractive hardwoods such as rosewood (*cocobolo*), teak, lignum vitae (*guayacán*), and heart of amaranth (*nazarena*). There's also the usual run of straw hats, t-shirts, macramé, ashtrays and the like. Local production is supplemented by more interesting imports of textiles and basketry from Guatemala, El Salvador, and Panama. You should have no trouble finding these, but just in case, I've given the names and locations of some stores in the shopping section of the San José chapter of this book.

If local crafts aren't overwhelming, don't overlook some of the non-souvenir items that are cheaper in Costa Rica than at home. Utilitarian luggage and other leatherwork can, in some cases, be a good buy. Stop into a supermarket and pick up a pound or two or three of coffee. Most brands are ground too finely for your own coffeemaker, and don't travel well in their cellophane packaging. Volio is one brand available as whole beans to grind at home, Britt is another, at a much higher price.

Tropical delicacies such as *palmito* (heart of palm) are priced reasonably (though the harvest of some species contributes to deforestation). Hot pepper sauces, chocolates, tropical fruit preserves, and much else can fill up those empty spaces in your luggage.

Once you start in at the supermarket, take a look at some general department stores *(almacenes)* and shopping centers *(centros comerciales)*. You might or might not find goods you like at prices to suit your budget, but you'll get an idea of what the Costa Ricans buy and what they have to pay.

STAYING OUT OF TROUBLE

It's not too likely that you'll get into hot water while visiting Costa Rica. But some customs and practices may differ from what you're used to. Relax and act as if you're on vacation, while keeping in mind some possible sore points.

Drugs, of course, are a touchy item, especially when used by foreigners. Penalties for possession of anything from marijuana on up are severe, so abstention or at least discretion is advised.

Costa Rica is a democracy, but quite security-conscious. Visitors may be asked for identification at any time, and jailed (yes!) if they do not have proper papers. Always carry your passport or tourist card with you, and arrange prompt replacement if either is lost or stolen.

If there are any black marks against you — traffic tickets, customs duty owed, a debt outstanding — clear them up, no matter how minor. Otherwise, you could be prevented from leaving the country.

TAXES

Almost all goods and services in Costa Rica are subject to a value-added tax *(i.v.a.)*, currently 11% and rising. Hotel rooms are subject to an additional tourism tax, bringing the total bite to 14.3%. At the airport, the exit tax is approximately $8.

TAXIS

In San José, you pay about 70¢ for the first kilometer, 25¢ for each additional kilometer — a bargain! In rural areas, additional kilometers cost slightly more. Waiting time is charged at about $3 per hour. If your trip is over 12 kilometers, you'll have to negotiate the rate with the driver.

TELEGRAMS

International telegrams are handled by **Radiográfica Costarricense**, Calle 1, Avenida 5, San José. Telegrams may be dictated by dialing 123, or transmitted through your hotel operator. In all cases, the rates are quite high — usually 50¢ per word or more. Domestic telegrams cost only a few cents per word.

TELEPHONES

Costa Rica has a modern, direct-dial telephone system, with more lines per inhabitant than almost any other nation in Latin America.

TELEPHONE NEWS

All phone numbers in Costa Rica will convert from six to seven digits in April 1994.

In most cases, an initial digit will be added. In some cases, the third digit will change.

In this book, the extra digit is indicated [in brackets].

Verify problem numbers in the telephone directory, or dial 113 for assistance. If calling from outside Costa Rica, ask your operator to connect you with directory assistance in San José.

CALLING COSTA RICA
Dialing Direct

From the U.S. or Canada, dial 011-506, followed by the local number in Costa Rica. There are no area codes.

Using operator assistance

For collect or person-to-person calls, dial 01-506, followed by the local number; or call your operator.

Dialing 1-800

Some of the toll-free numbers listed in this book will connect you directly to Costa Rica from the United States, and in some cases from Canada as well.

Be cautious! When you use this service, you'll be dealing with an overseas company. Complaints about service, or billings to your credit card, will be more difficult to resolve than if you deal with a company at home. Also, the costs of 800 service to Costa Rica are not inconsiderable, and the person at the other end may not be patient with a long-winded inquiry.

I recommend that you first try a domestic toll-free service when planning your trip.

Dialing Costa Rica Direct

1-800-252-5114 will get you in touch with a Costa Rican operator from the United States, 1-800-463-0116 from Canada. Use this service if you speak Spanish and wish to call collect or need additional local information.

CALLING HOME
Using your regular service

To reach an operator from your home telephone company, or use its credit card, dial 114 for AT&T, 162 for MCI, 163 for Sprint, 161 for Telecom Canada, 167 for British Telecom, from any private or public phone in Costa Rica. From a hotel, you'll have to ask for an outside line.

Dialing Direct

From a private phone, dial 00-1 (for North America), followed by the area code and local number.

Operator Assistance

Dial 09-1 (for North America), followed by the local number. An operator will ask for your instructions (person-to-person, collect, credit card, etc.).

Or dial 116 and give your instructions to the operator, in English, at a slightly higher charge.

Telephone Credit Cards

Telephone credit carsa from the United States, Canada, the U.K., France and Japan are accepted by the Costa Rican telephone system.

Calling From the Phone Company's Offices

In San José, go to **Radiográfica Costarricense**, Avenida 5, Calle 1. Visa, Master Card and American Express are accepted at this location.

Calling Your Hotel Operator

This will usually cost far more than any of the above.

RATES

An operator-assisted call to New York costs about $9 for three minutes, or $7 after 7 p.m.

A direct-dialed call to New York costs $2 per minute, $1.60 after 7 p.m., 80¢ from 10 p.m. to 7 a.m., and on weekends.

CALLING IN COSTA RICA

Public telephones are available in most towns, most conveniently on the main square. Usually, there's a long lineup to use them, and many are out of order.

The easiest coin phones to understand are those that require you to place your coins (5, 10 and 20 colones) on a rack, to be swallowed as needed. With others, you deposit a coin when signalled to do so. If you're slow about it, your call is cut off. Magnetic-card phones are slowly coming into use.

Rates from public phones are quite cheap — even less tha
private homes.

Many stores and hotels will allow you to use their phones for a char
of about 25¢ (U.S.) for a local call.

SERVICE NUMBERS IN COSTA RICA	
110	Collect calls within Costa Rica and operator assistance.
112	Time of day
113	Telephone number information
114	AT&T USA Direct (deposit coin at public phone)
161	Canada Direct
162	MCI to U.S.A.
163	Sprint to U.S.A.
167	British Telecom U.K. Direct
116	International long distance (operators speak English)
117	San José police
118	Fire department (*bomberos*)
127	Rural police
128	Emergency Red Cross assistance
[2]27-7150	Traffic police

CALLING FROM HOTELS

Hotels impose hefty surcharges on phone calls. It will usually be far cheaper to call home collect or charge the call to a telephone credit card, or to call a local number from a pay phone.

DIALING A WRONG NUMBER

Watch your fingers! As mentioned on page 87, an extra digit [indicated in brackets in this book] will be added in mid-1994 to every phone number in Costa Rica. If your call does not go through, re-dial with the extra digit. Verify problem numbers in the telephone directory, or dial 113 for assistance.

If calling from outside Costa Rica, ask your operator to connect you with directory assistance in San José.

TELEVISION

In addition to local and Latin American programming in Spanish, occasional programs in English are broadcast on Costa Rican television stations. San José and most of the Central Valley have cable television with

...amming in English on over a dozen channels,
...nportant sporting events, as well as Geraldo,
...the Central Valley, many hotels pick up U.S.

... (if you don't want to).

Costa Rica is on Central Standard Time, equivalent to Greenwich Mean Time less six hours.

TIPPING

As you well know, tipping is demanded when least deserved, e.g., by tour guides who are already earning a good salary and commissions. Resist the importunings, unless there has been a special kindness or service. You pay quite enough for most tours in Costa Rica.

On the other hand, hotel personnel who take you in as family are unlikely to hint for extra money, but they may well deserve an envelope with a few dollars if you've stayed a few days. A porter should get up to 50¢ per bag for carrying your luggage.

In restaurants, a 10% service charge is added, by law, to all bills, so there's no need to leave any additional amount unless service is especially good.

Taxi drivers are never tipped.

When in doubt about whether or how much to tip, remember that a tip is a reward for good service. Poor service means no tip.

WEIGHTS AND MEASURES

Costa Rica is firmly on the metric system. Gasoline, juice and milk are sold by the liter, fabrics by the meter, tomatoes by the kilo. Gone are the days when visitors were confused by a hodgepodge of yards, *varas*, *manzanas*, *fanegas*, *caballerías*, gallons, and assorted other English and old Spanish measures.

Old usages survive mainly in giving directions. People will usually say 100 *metros* (meters) to indicate a city block, but you'll sometimes hear 100 *varas*. In fact, a block is closer to 100 varas, a vara being an old Spanish yard, equivalent to 33 inches or .835 meters.

YOU'LL ENJOY COSTA RICA!

I know a retired clerical worker who regularly takes extended vacations in Costa Rica because, as he says, "it's warm, low-key, a great place to relax, and the beer is cheap."

On the other hand, I know a sophisticated travel writer who has lived in the Caribbean, been to dozens and dozens of countries, and now is an

editor at a book-packaging firm. She took her mom to Costa Rica for a few weeks at the beach, and found it to be one of her most rewarding trips, because "it's warm, low-key, a great place to relax, and the beer is cheap."
Enough said.

7. SPORTS & RECREATION

FISHING

There's great sport fishing in Costa Rica, not only along both coasts, but in mountain streams and lakes as well.

Plenty of world records have been broken, but some fishermen have gone home disappointed. You have to know when the fish are running, and where stocks have been depleted by runoffs and pesticides.

Caribbean Fishing

On the Caribbean side of Costa Rica, the most notorious species is the pesky and finicky tarpon. Tarpon are caught between January and June in rivers, lagoons and estuaries, and weigh as much as 100 pounds. Other species common to the Caribbean are snook, usually weighing over 25 pounds; the related and smaller calba, or fat snook; the bass-like machaca and guapote; mojarra, which resembles a bluegill; and shark, mackerel, mullet and jack crevalle. All are found in inland waters, even shark, though stocks are said to have declined in recent years, due to sedimentation and contamination by pesticides.

Deep-sea fishing in the Caribbean is limited by the unpredictability of storms and heavy surf at river mouths, but some lodges have large boats to get fishermen safely out during calm periods. Species found not too far from shore may include barracuda, jacks, sawfish, tuna and wahoo.

Pacific Fishing

On the Pacific side, black and blue marlins of up to 1,000 pounds are the big attractions, especially up north in the Gulf of Papagayo; along with sailfish, roosterfish, wahoo, rainbow runner, barracuda, a variety of snappers, jacks, pompano, shark, swordfish, yellowfin tuna, bonito, dorado (mahi-mahi), grouper and corvina, or sea bass. The smaller fish are found in river mouths and estuaries, the larger species out in blue water.

Inland Fishing

Inland, some of Costa Rica's mountain and lowland streams and lakes hold trout (generally on the small side), guapote, machaca and bobo (related to mullet), as well as smaller fish. Inland fishing is permitted all year in Lake Arenal and the Reventazón River; December through August elsewhere.

The most accessible fishing for trout of any size is along the Savegre River at the cabins of the Chacón family (tel. [7]711732. To find a good inland fishing spot, hang out at the bus station of a lowland town at the base of the sierra, such as Villa Neilly. Look for a guy with a fishing rod and discreetly follow him aboard his bus. Stay on for the ascent from the steaming plain, winding back and forth up the face of the mountains, splashing through rushing streams. Take note of where the fisherman gets off, then backtrack and return the next day.

Fishing equipment is in short supply, so serious anglers should bring their own gear, unless availability is confirmed in advance. Your fishing camp or resort will recommend specific types of rods, reels and line when you reserve. For tarpon fishing — the big attraction on the Caribbean coast — six- to-seven-foot rods with 12- to 20-pound line are used. Reels should hold 200 yards of line. For snook and fly fishing, 10- to 12-pound line is enough. Lighter gear is sufficient for guapote and trout in fresh water. For deep-sea fishing, everything is usually provided by the fishing camp or boat operator.

Catch and Release

Most responsible fishing operators in Costa Rica encourage you to return your catch to the sea, and bring home photos, not trophies.

Permits

A permit is required for fishing. If you book a week at a fishing camp, the management will probably take care of this detail. Otherwise, you'll have to buy a permit at the **Dirección de Pesca**, Calle 24, Avenida 2, tel. [2]552170. This may have to be further validated at other offices for either river or offshore fishing.

PEAK SEASONS AT QUEPOS (PACIFIC SOUTH)	
Sailfish	December through April
Dorado	December through May
Marlin	November through April
Snook, Tuna	May through December
Roosterfish,	
Snapper	All year
Fishing may be limited during heavy rains in October.	

PEAK SEASONS AT FLAMINGO (PACIFIC NORTH)

Marlin	April through August
Sailfish	April through August
Dorado	June through August
Tuna	December through January
Roosterfish	February through July
Snapper	May through August

PEAK SEASONS AT BARRA DEL COLORADO (CARIBBEAN COAST)

Tarpon	January through May inland, rest of year off shore
Snook	December and January in rivers, all year off shore
Jack Crevalle	All year
Tuna	All year
Bonito	All year
Barracuda	All year
Dorado	All year
Sailfish	February, March, April

San José-based Fishing Specialists
In San José, contact:
- **Sportfishing Costa Rica**, P.O. Box 115-1150 La Uruca, San José, tel. [2]333892, fax [2]236728; or 800-374-4474 U.S.-Costa Rica. This outfit sponsors an annual two-ocean fishing tournament, and operates boats at Quepos and Drake Bay.
- **Costa Rica Dreams**, P. O. Box 79-4005, San Antonio de Belén, tel. [2]393387, fax [2]393383. Fishing off Quepos and Caño Island.
- **Flamingo Bay Pacific Charters**, tel. [2]314055

In-Country Fishing Services and Lodges Specializing in Fishing
Outside San José, contact:
- **Hotel Flor de Itabo**, Playas del Coco, tel. 67[0]0011
- **Hotel El Ocotal**, Ocotal, tel. 67[0]0230
- **Bahía Pez Vela**, Ocotal, tel. 67[0]0129 (U.S. reservations, tel. 800-327-2880)
- **Blue Marlin Fishing**, Flamingo Beach, tel. 67[4]4043, fax 674165
- **Pesca Bahía Garza**, based at Villagio La Guaria Morada, Playa Garza (U.S. reservations: P. O. Box 1269, Marathon, FL 33050, tel. 305-289-1900, fax 289-1195

- **Guanamar**, Puerto Carrillo, tel. [6]536133 (P. O. Box 7-18⁸
  tel. [2]394544. U.S. reservations: tel. 800-245-8420)
- **Hotel Tango Mar**, Tambor, tel. 61[2]2798 (tel. [2]231864 in San José)
- **Hotel Oasis del Pacífico**, Playa Naranjo, tel. 61[1]1555
- **Fred Wagner**, Puntarenas, tel. 63[0]0107
- **North-South Sportfishing**, Quepos, tel. [2]275498
- **Treasure Hunt Tours**, Quepos, tel. 77[0]0345)
- **Reel 'n Reelease Sportfishing**, Dominical, tel. [6]711903
- **Río Sierpe Lodge**, Sierpe River (tel. [2]201712 in San José)
- **Sanbar Marina**, Golfito, tel. [7]750874 or 800-435-3239 from U.S
- **War Eagle Marina**, Golfito, tel. [7]750838 or [7]885083
- **Golfito Sportfishing**, Zancudo, tel. [7]750353
- **Golfito Sailfish Rancho**, Golfito (tel. [2]357766 in San José. U.S. reservations: tel. 800-531-7232
- **Los Almendros**, Zancudo, tel. [7]750515
- **Zancudo Pacific Charters**, Zancudo, tel. [7]885083
- **Parismina Tarpon Rancho**, Parismina (Calle 1, Avenidas 7/9, María José Building, tel. [2]226055; U.S. reservations tel. 800-531-7232 or 512-377-0451, or 800-862-1003 direct to San José)
- **Río Parismina Lodge**, Parismina (U.S. reservations: tel. 800-338-5688 or 210-824-4442)
- **Río Colorado Lodge**, Barra del Colorado (P. O. Box 5094-1000, San José, tel. [2]324063; U.S. reservations: tel. 800-243-9777)
- **Isla de Pesca**, near Barra del Colorado (P. O. Box 7-1880, San José, tel. [2]394544, fax [2]392405. U.S. reservations: tel. 800-245-8420)
- **Casa Mar Fishing Lodge**, Barra del Colorado (U.S. reservations: tel. 800-327-2880 or 305-664-4615, fax 305-664-3692
- **Tortuga Lodge**, Tortuguero, tel. 71[6]6861 (tel. [2]570766, fax [2]571665 in San José)
- **Silver King Lodge**, Barra del Colorado, tel. [7]880849 (U.S. reservations: tel. 800-847-3474)
- **Aventuras Tilarán**, Tilarán, tel. 69[5]5008. Lake Arenal fishing.
- **Finca Zacatales**, tel. [5]711732. Trout fishing.

ADDITIONAL INFORMATION ON FISHING

More details on these lodges are given in this book in the coverage by regions.

Arranging a Fishing Trip From the US
Agencies that book fishing trips to Costa Rica:
- **Flamingo Bay Pacific Charters**, 1112 East Las Olas Blvd., Fort Lauderdale, FL 33301, tel. 800-654-8006, fax 305-522-2637
- **World Wide Sportsman**, P. O. Drawer 787, Islamorada, FL 33036, tel. 800-327-2880 or 305-664-8833, fax 305-664-3692

- **Flamingo Bay Pacific Charters**, 1112 East Las Olas Blvd., Fort Lauderdale, FL 33301
- **PanAngling Travel**, 180 N. Michigan Ave., Chicago, IL 60601
- **Dockside Tours**, 339 Hickory Ave., Harahan, LA 70123
- **Anglers Travel Connections**, 3220 W. Sepulveda Blvd., Suite B, Torrance, CA 90505
- **Pesca Bahía Garza**, P. O. Box 1269, Marathon, FL 33050, tel. 305-289-1900, fax 289-1195

CRUISING THE GULF OF NICOYA

The yacht *Calypso* makes a daily cruise from the yacht club in Puntarenas to seven islands in the Gulf of Nicoya. This is a well-planned excursion that has been improved and refined and copied over the years. A stop is made at a deserted, palm-shaded beach for swimming, snorkeling, beachcombing, and a gourmet picnic lunch that includes fresh gulf fish. They even take a portable toilet ashore.

Fare is about $70, including overland transportation from San José, or slightly less if you're already in Puntarenas. Book the cruise through any hotel in Puntarenas, or call tel. [2]333617, fax [2]330401 in San José, or 61[0]0585 in Puntarenas. Longer runs are also available.

Several other companies offer variations on the original Calypso excursion:
- **Sea Ventures**, tel. [2]327412, fax [2]327510, operates day trips from Puntarenas into the Gulf of Nicoya, with live music on board, a buffet, and snorkeling. Scuba diving can be arranged.
- **Fantasía Islands Adventures**, P. O. Box 123-5550 Puntarenas, tel. [2]550791, fax [2]231013
- The *Costa Sol*, operated by **Grupo Costa Sol** (tel. [2]200722, fax [2]202095, tel. 800-245-8420 in the United States), may well be the largest tour boat in the gulf, a 100-foot yacht with two decks, two bars, and room for 125 passengers. Live music is provided throughout a day excursion, which includes a landing at Bahía Ballena.
- **Blue Seas First Class Cruise**, tel. [2]337274, tries to top the others with an open bar.

CRUISING THE COASTAL WATERS

The ship *Temptress* regularly carries up to 62 passengers along the Pacific coast of Costa Rica from Puntarenas. That's too small a load to offer casinos and dance bands; instead, you get the services of a biologist, video movies, board games, open-air bar and film-processing lab. All cabins are on the outside, with large rectangular windows.

Nights are spent underway, days at anchor off national parks and in secluded bays. Two shore excursions, one strenuous and one less so, are offered daily. Both are softly educational, and emphasize wildlife and Costa Rica's natural diversity.

Several routes are available: a six-night southern cruise that takes in Manuel Antonio National Park and the Osa Peninsula; a three-night southern cruise; and a four-night cruise along the Nicoya Peninsula and Tempisque River estuary. The price of $250 to $300 per person per day includes travel from San José to port, water skiing, snorkeling, kayaking, shore excursions, laundry service, and local brands of liquor and beer. There are extra charges to arrange fishing, and for diving.

Contact **Temptress Cruises**, 1600 N.W. Le Jeune Rd., Miami, FL 33126, tel. 800-336-8423, 305-871-2663z; or Cruceros del Sur, P. O. Box 5452-1000, San José, Costa Rica, tel. [2]201679, fax [2]202103.

CRUISING A TROPICAL RIVER SYSTEM

In colonial times, the San Juan River along the border of Nicaragua was a highway between the interior and the coast. In the nineteenth century, it was an invasion route, the back door to the heart of Central America, used during the conflicts between William Walker, Nicaragua, Costa Rica, and Commodore Vanderbilt. And until a couple of years ago, it was off limits to outsiders, a sometime theater of war in the Sandinista-Contra struggles.

Now you can board a bus in San José, drive past the La Paz falls between Barva and Poás volcanoes, and embark on a river boat at Puerto Viejo on the Sarapiquí. Downriver, past stands of bananas and still-uncut forest, the craft navigates the San Juan, along the northern limit of the Barra del Colorado Wildlife Refuge. Joining you at various times are toucans, crocodiles, sloths, monkeys and butterflies. The delta branch of the San Juan called the Colorado leads into Costa Rican territory, through palms and a network of man-made and jungle canals, to the Caribbean at the village of Barra del Colorado.

From this point, you can fly back to San José after a night along the beach, stay to fish for tarpon, or continue along the canal system to Tortuguero National Park.

River excursions to the Caribbean are offered by:
• **Costa Sol** (tel. [2]234560 in San José, 800-245-8420 in the United States)
• **Costa Rica Adventure Tours**, Hotel Corobicí (P. O. Box 5094-1000), tel. [2]328610, 800-243-9777 in the United States.
• **Ríos Tropicales**, tel. [2]336455; and Costa Rica Expeditions, tel. [2]220333

WATCHING THE FIREWORKS OF NATURE

Much of the backbone of Costa Rica, the mountainous spine of the country, was formed in fire and brimstone, as the molten underworld spewed up in the eruptions that formed today's volcanoes, and enriched the soil of the Central Valley.

To modern Costa Ricans, this is not ancient history, but daily life. The lakes of Poás volcano, just northwest of San José, simmer and steam and spit boiling water. Smoky Irazú, to the northeast, pours out noxious fumes, and periodically burns off the farms on its slopes.

But the most reliable performer these days is **Arenal,** the perfect volcanic cone that lies about three hours' travelling time to the northwest of San José. After a sleep of several centuries, Arenal awoke at the end of July, 1968, and in a hail of lava and ash and boulders, promptly reduced the surrounding forest, pasture, and fields to a moonscape.

And it hasn't stopped since. On most nights, clouds of iridescent gas cling to the summit. The earth rumbles, and boulders the size of a house explode a thousand feet into the air, to a resounding orchestral accompaniment of pops and crackles and booms, to bounce and shatter their way down. Lava in red, orange, and yellow spews and slithers along the slopes.

Nobody in his right mind climbs Arenal, but several lodges in the vicinity offer safe ringside seats, with a view from the porch of your room and across an intervening river valley to the nighttime show; others sponsor day or night excursions to favorite lookout points, and almost every travel agency in San José organizes volcano-watching excursions— just make sure before you go that recent activity has been reported, and that the weather has been clear. And while you're in the vicinity, take a soak in waters from one of the hot springs that bubble up from the same underworld that begat the volcanoes.

For more details, see page 428-432.

SPELUNKING - DESCEND TO THE NETHERWORLD

Concealed under the undulating dry hills of **Barra Honda National Park**, in the Nicoya Peninsula, lie dozens of caverns, most still unexplored in modern times, some plunging to depths of more than 600 feet. The surface of this ancient seabed is pocked with holes where cave roofs have collapsed, allowing access — after strenuous hikes — to the cathedrals formed over the eons by the clandestine chemistry conducted below, while the peninsula slid and lifted alongside the mainland.

Grotesque skeletal remains are merged into stalagmites or washed over with frozen calcium carbonate streams. Bats, rats, insects, and blind fish inhabit an underscape of "soda straws," "cave grapes," and stone "popcorn." Occasionally a human slithers down a rope above, but infrequently, for the great drop through nothingness discourages visits from above.

The caves of Barra Honda may be visited in the company of park rangers only. Contact the **National Park Service** at the Bolívar Park Zoo

**EXPLORING THE
NETHERWORLD**

in San José. Tours with descents into the caves are operated by **Turinsa,** Avenida 3, Calles 3/5, San José, tel. [2]219185. Do not attempt the trip on your own. The park is parched for much of the year, with little shelter, and some visitors have perished.

To the north of Lake Arenal, the **Venado Caves** underlie the Guanacaste mountain range, and are still being shaped by underground streams, rapids and cascades. Visits are arranged by hotels and travel agencies in Tilarán and Fortuna.

RAFTING THE RAPIDS

Here's the bottom line: there's plenty of water in Costa Rica's rivers, you can go rafting somewhere in the country at almost any time of year, the sights along the way — exotic macaws, flocks of monkeys, sugarcane fields, dense rain forest trailing vines into the water — are available on comparable trips nowhere else, and, maybe best of all, the water is warm.

There are runs in Costa Rica for every skill level. A trip along the **Corobicí River** in Puntarenas province — a stereotypical slow-moving tropical river — affords ample opportunity for birding and observing streamside life. It's rated class I-II — unchallenging. On the Atlantic slope, the **Reventazón River** (Class III), with plenty of rapids separated by sedate stretches, is considered world-class, but parts are suitable for beginners. The **Pacuare** (Class IV), precipitous, with difficult rapids, rushes through gorges billowing with exuberant growth. According to one rafting guide, these three are "technical" rivers — you have to make successive crucial moves in each rapid. But they're not expert runs — if you flip over, you'll be washed onward into deeper, safer water. The **General**, in the south-central Pacific region (class III-IV), with more volume than any California river, has continuous roller-coaster waves, whirlpools, gorges punctuated by waterfalls, and varying water levels. There are few bugs along the General, which can be rafted for six months of the year.

One-day beginners' trips are offered by travel agencies in San José for about $75. Week-long expeditions on several rivers, camping along the way or staying in hotels as appropriate, with some sightseeing, cost about $900. The organizers provide raft, paddles, helmet, and life jacket. Visitors should wear a bathing suit and tennis shoes, and take a change of clothing.

What to Expect on Your Raft Trip

Having encountered a rafter of rafters at my hotel on one visit to San José, I had little choice but to enroll in a beginners' trip on the Reventazón River. In true Tico fashion, we were offered beer upon arrival at the put-in point "to calm your nerves." When we started off with a splash fight, I was ready to ask for my money back. I soon changed my mind.

After basic instructions in paddling, and strapping on life jackets and buckling helmets, we were afloat. There was plenty of time to pick out birds, wave to farmers, observe the population of trees and plants that pass by too quickly along a highway, or are hidden in the forest on a hike. We took intermittent rapids paddling, soaking ourselves thoroughly in the first, leaned back in between to watch sugarcane and forest, vines dangling, debris stuck in tree branches in times of high water. A warming, misty drizzle lasted the entire run.

At a midway stopping point, our guides assembled a tropical gourmet picnic of heart of palm, sprouts, paté, cold roast beef, ham, several cheeses and fruit. It disappeared as quickly as it had materialized. Then we were off for the second act, all rapids, and furious paddling to make it through without capsizing, splashing and gasping, all thoroughly exciting, though in a playful way, for we were assured that a spill would not result in any harm. We arrived upright in any case. And in a couple of hours, after a change of clothes, a sales pitch for t-shirts, and naps in the van, we were quite out of the wild, back in San José.

Arranging a Raft Trip
From the United States
- **Mariah Wilderness Expeditions**, P.O. Box 248, Point Richmond, CA 94807, tel. 800-4-MARIAH or 510-233-2303, fax 510-233-0956
- **Voyagers International**, P. O. Box 915, Ithaca, NY 14851, tel. 800-633-0299 or 607-257-3091, fax 607-257-3699

In Costa Rica
- **Costa Rica Expeditions**, Calle Central, Avenida 3 (P. O. Box 6941-1000), tel. [2]220333, fax [2]571665
- **Ríos Tropicales**, Paseo Colón, Calles 22/24 (P. O. Box 472-1200, Pavas), tel. [2]336455
- **Tropical Pioneer**, P. O. Box 29-2070 Sabanilla, tel. [2]539132, fax [2]534687. Rafting.
- **Aventuras Naturales**, Avenida Central, Calles 33/35, tel. [2]253939, fax [2]536934. Rafting, mountain biking.
- **Costa Rica Rafting**, tel. [2]253939
- **Safaris Corobicí**, Cañas, tel. and fax 69[0]0544. Unlike most other rafting companies, Safaris Corobicí specializes in float trips on easygoing lowland rivers. Participants need not paddle.

KAYAKING COSTA RICA

River kayaking trips most often are an easy float down the Bebedero River through the marshy and jungly Palo Verde Reserve in the northwestern lowlands, or along the Sarapiquí in the northern lowlands.

More ambitious trips take you paddling from beach to beach along the rocky Pacific coast. A motorized mother ship provides security and delivers camping equipment and goodies. The wild stuff — shooting class VI rapids on the Reventazón River — isn't for casual visitors, though many competition kayakers spend the winter training in Costa Rica, and trips can be arranged on the same tamer rapids used on day rafting outings from San José.

Kayaking Specialists
Kayaking specialists include:
- **Rancho Leona**, La Virgen de Sarapiquí, tel. 71[6]6312, with trips on jungle rivers north of San José. (see page 431)
- **Ríos Tropicales**, Paseo Colón, Calles 22/24 (P. O. Box 472-1200, Pavas), tel. [2]336455. Rafting and kayaking excursions.
- **La Paloma Lodge**, at Drake Bay (P. O. Box 97-4005, San Antonio de Belén, Heredia, tel. and fax [2]39054.

Arranging a Kayaking Trip
Kayaking trips are arranged by:
- **Mariah Wilderness Expeditions**, P.O. Box 248, Point Richmond, CA 94807, tel. 800-4-MARIAH or 510-233-2303, fax 510-233-0956.
- **Laughing Heart Adventures**, P. O. Box 669, Willow Creek, CA 95573.
- **Ecosummer Expeditions**, 1516 Duranleau St., Vancouver B.C., Canada, tel. 604-669-7741, fax 669-3244 *or* 936 Peace Portal Dr., Blaine WA 98230, tel. 206-332-1000 or 800-688-8605.

RIDING BIKES

Ascend to the top of a volcano, look around, and start down! Or set out from San José . . . it's all downhill, to the east and west. Take your bike along from home, with proper precautions for packing, or rent one when you get to San José.

Costa Rica is a mountainous country, but that doesn't make it a tough go for mountain biking. Distances between overnight stopping points need never be more than 50 kilometers, unless you want a longer day. Roadside refreshment is available at shops and eateries everywhere. Buses will pick up you and your bike when you don't want to re-trace your steps, or when the ascent back to San José looks a *little* too strenuous.

Latin America on Bicycle by Jean-Pierre Panet is essential reading material for prospective cyclists in Costa Rica. Included are dozens of useful tips on everything from getting your bike on and off the plane without damage, to health tips. Included is a chapter about a cycling trip in Costa Rica.

Mountain bike rentals are available from **Costa Rica Sun Tours**, Avenida 4, Calle 36, tel. [2]553418, for $20 or so per day. (Panet recommends taking your own bike, with the saddle that you're accustomed to).

Geoventuras, P. O. Box 554-2150 Moravia, tel. [2]828590,, fax [2]828333, arranges cycling tours for groups of up to 20 persons. These trips are generally non-strenuous: a mostly downhill ride through the Orosi Valley, with hikes in the Tapantí forest reserve, and descents of volcanoes. Vans take the bikes from San José, and lunch is included. Multiple-day tours are also available.

Dos Montañas de Pacuare, Paseo Colón, Calles 22/24, tel. [2]336455, organizes one day trips in Tapantí National Park for about $70 from San José.

SURFING THE PERFECT WAVE

Surfing is not my field of expertise. But according to information supplied by the Costa Rica Tourist Board, steady winds give the northern Pacific coast good waves from early December through April. The mouth of the **Barranca River**, near Puntarenas, is known for the longest left wave in the world, but the water is filthy. **Tamarindo**, to the north, is cleaner, if more tame. Conditions are usually better at nearby **Playa Grande** ("fine beach break"), or farther up at **Roca Bruja** (Witch's Rock), in Santa Rosa National Park.

In the southern Pacific coastal region, there are said to be high waves throughout the year. Surfing tournaments are held at **Playa Hermosa**, north of Jacó, and at **Manuel Antonio**, near Quepos. **Pavones**, down near the Panamanian border, has become home to some expatriate surfers who have found the perfect wave. The best waves roll in this area from April through October.

On the Caribbean, around **Limón** and to the south, there are good waves from December through February and June through August. Caution and skill are required in this area, as high waves break over coral reefs. **Isla Uvita**, reachable by boat from Limón, sometimes has surfable waves, but the best is the **Salsa** at Puerto Viejo.

Bring your own board by all means. If you can't, one outfitter is **Mango**, tel. [2]251067, in San Pedro, east of San José. There are also surf shops with rental boards in Puntarenas, Tamarindo, Jacó, Quepos and Cahuita.

And to keep up on the very latest in Costa Rican surfing, read the column by Mark Kelly in *Costa Rica Today*.

SLEEPING OUT UNDER THE STARS

Camping is not a traditional outdoors activity in Costa Rica, not least because the outdoors are often viewed as dangerous. And imported equipment, from tents to sleeping bags to good backpacks, can be expensive.

The most obvious places in which to camp are national parks, which usually have sleeping spaces supplied with outhouses and showers.

Organized private campsites are found at Jacó. These have more in common with trailer parks than with getting back to nature.

When camping on a beach or in the countryside, always ask permission if there's anybody around, and offer to pay. You might find some unexpected hospitality. And I won't lecture you about packing out your garbage.

If you don't bring your own equipment, rental gear is available locally at **Alquileres y Toldos Fiesta** in San Pedro (one block north of Banco Anglo), tel. [2]249155. Prices are about $35 per week for a two-person tent. Other supplies are available at **Aro**, Avenida 8, Calles 11/13. Or try calling [2]338090 for an outfit that rents a package of tent, two sleeping bags and water bottle for about $10 per day.

Centro de Aventuras, Paseo Colón, Avenidas 22/24, next to the Ríos Tropicales travel agency, runs an exchange of camping equipment. Stop by, or call [2]550618. If you're on your way home, consider lightening your luggage and making your tent available to a local camper or other visitors.

GAMBLING

If it's gaming you're looking for, you'll find it in San José, and a couple of other spots around the country, in a most tame fashion.

The major game is a blackjack variation called **rummy**. In the Costa

Rican game, a two-card total of 21 is just 21, not an immediate win. And three cards in ascending order pay back triple your bet, no matter what your total. You can also fold and keep half your bet.

Rummy is everywhere. If your hotel doesn't have a casino, go next door. Tables function 24 hours at the Gran Hotel, Club Colonial and Hotel Royal Garden, in the afternoon and evening at the Holiday Inn, and at the San José Palacio, among others. And there are casinos at many beach resorts. Betting minimums range from $1 to $2.

A couple of casinos also offer a form of craps, using dominos, and a version of roulette. For now, slot machines are not available.

In the provinces, a more popular game is bingo, and you may want to join in if you spend some time in any small town.

The biggest game, the earner of imagined millions and a lifetime of ease for every Costa Rican, is the national lottery. By all means buy a ticket or a fraction of a ticket from a street vendor. You have a good chance of at least getting your money back if the last digit of your number is the same as that of the winner.

GETTING A BIRD'S EYE VIEW

Flightseeing, that staple of scenic viewing in Alaska, has come to Costa Rica. And in a country where so many vistas and topographies are packed into a small area, viewing it all from above is both practical and priceworthy.

But this kind of excursion is not for the faint of heart. Small aircraft, turbulence, and pilot capabilities make for more sudden free falls, dips, and unprogrammed bumps and tilts, and a, uh, more interesting trip, than you're likely to experience elsewhere. Fellow-passengers stare at each other, too cool to verbalize their impressions. Is the pilot really heading into that ridge? Are we going to make it over? Those trees look awfully close (Maybe you've just seen *Alive!*).

Yes, it's breathtaking.

Providers of airborne sightseeing:

- **Helicopters of Costa Rica**, south of the main post office next to Banco Lyon, tel. [2]313269, fax [2]333225
- **Saeta Taxi Aéreo**, at Tobías Bolaños Airport (P. O. Box 9-163 Pavas, tel. [2]321474, fax [2]329514) runs a point-to-point service, and offers a menu of day outings from San José, including: View of Poás volcano, one hour, $250; Overflight of Lake Arenal, 90 minutes, $380; the banana zone, two hours, $620; the Talamanca Mountains, 90 minutes, $370. These rates are for four or five passengers.
- **Aeronaves**, Tobías Bolaños Airport, tel. [2]321413, fax [2]321176
- **Aerolíneas Turísticas de América**, Tobías Bolaños Airport, tel. [2]321125, fax [2]325802
- **Taxi Aéreo Centroamericano**, Tobías Bolaños Airport, tel. [2]321317

HORSEBACK RIDING
Horses are available almost anywhere in Costa Rica. Knowledgeable folk are not put off by the small, local animals, known as *criollos* (which are bred to get a job done without consuming excess feed), though larger, more well known breeds — Arabians, Morgans — will also be found. Costa Rican horses can have problems with persons of weight, so if you're over 200 pounds, make sure you advise the agency or operator.

Riding rates can range from $5 per hour to $75 for a day outing to $150 for an overnight trip.

Among regions and lodges that offer equestrian excursions:
- **Guanacaste**: most hotels, and private operators in Monteverde; Hacienda La Pacífica, Cañas; Albergue de Tilarán and Puerto San Luis, Tilarán; Hotel Las Espuelas, Liberia; Hacienda Guachipelín; Hacienda Los Inocentes; Hotel Flor de Itabo, Playas del Coco
- **Nicoya**: Villa Serena, Junquillal; Hotel Rancho Suizo, Nosara; Hotel Oasis del Pacífico, Playa Naranjo; Hotel La Hacienda, Tambor; Hotel Tango Mar

Around San José
Horseback excursions are available from:
- **Hacienda San Miguel**, tel. [2]291094, at Rancho Redondo in the shadow of Irazú volcano. Day trips from San José through cloud forest. Beginners are accommodated. About $65 per person.
- **Irazú Horse Trekking**, tel. [2]232811. Takes riders right to the top of Irazú volcano, and to other destinations, for a price of about $80.
- **Tipical Tours**, tel. [2]338486, arranges rides through cloud forest near Cerro de la Muerte, with guaranteed quetzal sightings. About $90. Rainbow Tours, tel. [2]338228, has riding near Carara Biological Reserve, about $75; L. A. Tours, Avenida Central, Calles 5/7, tel. [2]214501, has a day outing to a farm near Orotina, on the Pacific slope, about $75.
- **Robles Tours**, tel. [2]372116, fax [2]371976, rides to Barva volcano; Magic Trails, tel. [2]538146, fax [2]539937, rides through Prusia Forest Reserve, on the slopes of Irazú.
- **Saragundí Specialty Tours**, Avenida 7, Calles Central/1 (P. O. Box 7126), San José, tel. [2]550011, fax [2]552155, has a one-day horseback and hiking tour for about $75.
- **Hotel El Tirol**, tel. [2]397371, Hotel El Cypresal, tel. [2]374466, and the other mountain hotels above Heredia also arrange riding.

Caribbean Area
- **Chimuri Lodge** and **Hotel Punta Cocles**, Puerto Viejo; various hotels in Cahuita.

RIDING THE WIND

Get set for takeoff! World-class windsurfing attracts more and more Costa Ricans and foreigners to Lake Arenal. Winds are steady out of the east at 20 to 30 knots, and water temperature is about 70 degrees Fahrenheit. The lake is 1,800 feet above sea level and 20 miles long, and waves are usually no higher than three feet.

Hotels that have equipment ready at Lake Arenal include:
• **Tilawa Viento Surf**, P. O. Box 92, Tilarán, tel. [6]695050 or 800-851-8929
• **Rock River Lodge**, tel. [2]224547, Puerto San Luis, Tilarán, tel. 69[5]5750
• **The Art of Fun**, a sports shop and tour operator, tel. and fax 69[5]5008.
• **Playa Tambor Beach Resort** (U.S. reservations tel. 800-858-0606) and several hotels at Tamarindo also have equipment.

VISITING THE NATIONAL PARKS

Costa Rica is one of the leaders in Latin America in preserving its natural treasures. More than a quarter of the country's land area is protected in some way in national parks, national monuments, nature reserves, biological reserves, and recreation areas. Park planners have attempted to protect a sample of each climate and ecosystem in the country.

While some parks are in remote locations, visitors are encouraged to enjoy all of them. Camping facilities, nature trails, visitors' centers and shelters are provided in most.

The creation of the national parks is part of a double-edged policy regarding the natural environment. Timber operations and land-clearing for farming are proceeding apace, with the encouragement or acquiescence of the government, and destroying native flora and fauna at a frightening rate. A number of parks were last-minute creations that rescued unique areas from farming or touristic development just in the nick of time. But these wild areas of reduced size, even when protected, might not be able to support viable populations of endangered plant and animal species in isolation.

The parks are beginning to be exploited for their biological riches by drug companies, among others, through the National Institute of Biodiversity, which is providing plant and insect samples to Merck Frosst, a pharmaceutical company, in return for fees that will be shared with the park system.

In most of Costa Rica's national parks, visitors will be on their own, with minimal guidance from administrators or interference from other tourists. You'll be freer than in most similar reserves to wander about at your own pace, observe wildlife, and discern the finer features of plants and geological formations. But you'll also have a greater responsibility than elsewhere both to watch out for your own safety and to tread lightly.

Visits to the national parks and reserves, except the most frequented and accessible ones (**Poás, Irazú, Cahuita, Guayabo, Carara, Manuel Antonio** and **Santa Rosa**), should be preceded by inquiries at the national parks information center in the Bolívar Park Zoo in San José, as to seasonal conditions, the current state of facilities, and access by public transportation. A detailed description of the parks and their wildlife, with excellent color photos, is Mario Boza, et. al., *The National Parks of Costa Rica.*

Park user fees, while modest, are meant to defray some of the costs of running the system. Recent fees, approximately, are: entry to park, $2; lodging, where available, $8 daily, less for students; horses, $4 per hour; camping, $3 daily; boat rental, $4 per hour; dockage, $16; caving, $4 per descent.

Most of the parks are described in the text of this book. See "National Parks" in the index.

Some Special Parks and Reserves
Parks and reserves not otherwise mentioned are:
• **Ballena Marine National Park**, located between Dominical and the Osa Peninsula, Ballena ("whale") includes coral reef, mangrove, shoals and a wide variety of shore line and marine features. As the name implies, whales frequent this reserve, most notably humpbacks, from December to May.
• **Santa Ana Recreation Area**, west of San José, slated to become the home of the National Zoo, when $5 million is found to fund the move.
• **Peñas Blancas National Wildlife Refuge**, north of Puntarenas, which, despite the name, is noted more for its flora than fauna.
• **Chompipe Mountain Municipal Reserve**, a 200-hectare section of rain and cloud forest in San Rafael de Heredia, adjacent to Braulio Carrillo National Park in the Central Valley.

8. SCUBA DIVING

INTRODUCTION

When you think of spectacular diving in Central America, you usually think of Belize or the Bay Islands of Honduras. But – surprise of surprises – Costa Rica holds its own in undersea as well as on-shore natural attractions.

Diving resorts – or resorts with diving facilities – are clustered around Playa del Coco in the northwest (Condovac, Hotel El Ocotal) and at Drake Bay in the southern Pacific coastal area. Cahuita National Park, on the Caribbean, has some coral spots, and there are wrecks to explore just to the south, near Puerto Viejo.

Northwest diving trips generally include islets a couple of miles from the mainland, and sometimes the Murciélago (*Bat*) Islands, 30 miles out. Most diving is at 30 to 40 feet, and mostly what you see is fish, but not just any fish. There are morays, jewfish, octopus, manta rays, grunts, snappers, occasionally sharks, in schools that number in the hundreds. And there are also rock formations, rather than intricate coral reef, though there are some undersea caves and coral clusters.

Water temperatures are generally from 75 to 85 degrees, somewhat lower when winds are from the north during the dry season. Wet suits are sometimes required. Visibility runs up to 80 feet, but can be limited by the same marine microorganisms that make fish so abundant, and by river runoff and silt during the rainiest times. The waters are generally clearest in the Gulf of Papagayo, where there are no river mouths.

Wall and limited reef diving are available off Caño Island, accessible from Drake Bay on the Osa Peninsula, and from Quepos. Some of the densest schools of fish will be seen in this area, among them snapper, grouper, barracuda, eels and rays, along with bright tropical species. Visibility tops out at about 70 feet. Up on the surface, sea turtles, dolphins, and whales are common sights.

MORE SCUBA DIVING INFORMATION
Look for additional diving information throughout this book in areas where scuba diving is offered.

Coco Island, farther out in the Pacific, has recently opened as a diving area, offering clear views of sperm whales, sting rays, eels, and the large game fish of the area, along with undersea pinnacles. But the real attraction is the chance to view sharks — hammerhead and white-tip, among others. Visibility is usually between 50 and 75 feet, and currents are strong.

A ten-night excursion to Coco Island on the 120-foot *Okeanos Aggressor* (a floating resort with a capacity of 18 divers), including seven dive days, costs $2,600 or more — and this does *not* include air fare to Costa Rica or any accommodations on land.

DIVE OPERATORS

Diving operators in Costa Rica include:

• **Diving Safaris**, Apartado 121-5019, Playas del Coco, tel. 67[0]0012. Based at Hotel El Ocotal (see pages 323-324), one of the most experienced diving services in Costa Rica, with new diesel-powered boats. Courses and certification upgrades, and package trips based at the hotel are available.

• **Virgin Diving**, Hotel La Costa, Playa Hermosa, Guanacaste (tel. 67[0]0472 or [2]218949) offers regular diving trips to Bat Island at $115 per person, and daily half-day dives at $55, or $75 with all equipment.

• **Mario Vargas Expeditions**, Playas del Coco, tel. 67[0]0351.

• **Rich Coast Diving**, Playas del Coco, tel. 67[0]0176, fax 67[0]0164). Offers somewhat lower rates than others in the Coco area: $45 for a two-tank dive ($65 with full equipment), $70 for a resort course.

• **Tango Mar**, near Tambor, in southern Nicoya, tel. [2]231864

• **Río Sierpe Lodge** near Drake Bay (P. O. Box 818-1200, Pavas, tel. [2]202121, fax [2]323321) has packages priced from about $160 per day of diving. Diving is also available at the Caballito del Mar Hotel at Drake Bay, tel. and fax [2]315028.

• **Flamingo Divers**, Flamingo Beach, tel. 67[4]4021, offers two-tank dives for $70 plus equipment rental, full open-water certification for about $400.

• **Viajes Tropicales Laura**, Limón, tel. [7]582410, arranges diving along the Caribbean, including wreck diving, as does Hotel Las Palmas, near Puerto Viejo, tel. [2]553939.

Among San José dive shops are:

• **Tropical Sceneries**, Calle 29, Avenidas Central/8 (P. O. Box 2047-1000, San José), tel. [2]242555, fax [2]339524. Offers one-day dive trips from San José to Herradura, near Jacó, at $125 per person, plus equipment charges; diving packages based at Río Sierpe Lodge, near Drake Bay; and longer trips to Coco Island.

- **Cruceros del Sur**, Sabana Norte, San José, tel. [2]326672. Represents *Okeanos Aggressor* to Coco Island.
- **Deep Sea Scuba**, Centro Comercial El Cruce, San Rafael de Escazú, tel. [2]326324 and [2]898191, fax [2]312145. A diving service operated by a Costa Rican with extensive experience in the States. Excursions are available on both coasts, as well as equipment rentals and service.
- **Mundo Acuático**, San Pedro, tel. [2]249729, is a dive shop that operates trips to both coasts.

Agencies that arrange diving in Costa Rica include:
- **Go Diving**, 5610 Rowland Rd., Minnetonka, MN 55343.
- **See and Sea Travel**, 50 Francisco St., San Francisco, CA 94133.
  Books trips on *Undersea Hunter* to Coco Island
- **Aggressor Fleet**, P. O. Drawer K, Morgan City, LA 70381
  Tel. 800-348-2628 or 504-385-2628, fax 384-0817.
  Operates *Okeanos Aggressor* to Coco Island.
- The cruise ship *Temptress*, mentioned above, offers diving excursions in its water sports programs.

THE OCEAN BECKONS

SCUBA SAFETY

As yet, there are no decompression chambers in Costa Rica. The nearest emergency facilities are in Belize and in Cozumel, Mexico. If you run into trouble, especially at a remote dive site such as Coco Island, immediate help will *not* be at hand.

Rather than take chances, take precautions:
• Never dive alone.
  Tell your guide when you last dived.
• Inquire about unusual conditions.
• Never dive if you don't feel alert and well.
• Never drink and dive.
• Never dive where you can't easily get out.
• Never dive while on medication, unless you first consult a doctor.
• Never feed fish while diving — you could attract sharks and barracudas.
• Never dive beyond your physical capabilities.
• Avoid diving if you have asthma, diabetes, or are subject to seizures.
• Dive with a partner you can trust; your life depends on your buddy.
• Do not touch coral or unfamiliar sea plants or fish. You could suffer painful injury.
• If confused or unsure, get out of the water.
• Inspect your diving equipment carefully.
• If unsure of your divemaster, ask for a referral from a recent client. Otherwise, look elsewhere.

The **Divers Alert Network**, an association of medical doctors based at Duke University (P. O. Box 3823, Duke University Medical Center, Durham, NC 27710, provides emergency medical referral. Call 919-684-8111.

Insurance tailored for divers is available from P.B.A., P. O. Box 907, Minneapolis, MN 55440, tel. 800-446-2671 or 612-588-2731.

9. TAKING THE KIDS!

INTRODUCTION

Do you remember when children flew for half price? Sharply reduced rates for children have pretty much bit the dust in the United States, but half-fare children's tickets are still the norm on many international routes, even when you buy a reduced-rate ticket.

If you regularly travel with your children, as I do, get out your calculator and figure your total family travel costs. You could well find that it's cheaper for all of you to go to Costa Rica than to many a domestic destination!

Is Costa Rica kid-friendly? For most kids and parents, probably yes. Health and sanitary standards are acceptable, and few people give you funny looks if you take children to restaurants, museums, or anywhere else.

And there are sights and activities for kids as well as grown-ups. As a father of three children, each of whom has individual habits, preferences, tastes and travel styles, I wouldn't dare tell you that your own child will love any particular attraction.

But there sure is a lot to choose from: the zoo in San José, and private mini-zoos elsewhere; beaches; hotel-resort complexes with kiddie-size pools and even child care; jungle boat rides and monkey-watching expeditions. Take in the attractions according to what you know of your kids. And remember that while sloth-watching along the Tortuguero canal might be initially more interesting than the safari ride at Disney World, a coloring book might be needed after a few hours.

Practicalities

Children need their own identification for immigration purposes. If there is any chance that you and your child will stay over 30 days, contact a Costa Rican consulate about applicable regulations and procedures, before you leave home.

Special health concerns for children are few. If you're going to spend time at the beach, make sure that your child gets plenty to drink, and limit exposure to the sun. In general, follow the same precautions for children as for adults (see pages 73-74).

At the beach, you'll want to keep an eye out for your kids' safety, of course. But in Costa Rica, you'll have to increase your vigilance. At most resorts, there are no lifeguards, or any provisions to assist swimmers in difficulty. Given unpredictable currents and official indifference, drownings occur on a too-regular basis. I wouldn't let my own children go more than a couple of feet from shore at any beach.

Pack clothing items similar to those for adults. As well, take a few books and toys (the latter are expensive locally), including a pail and shovel for the beach.

Traveling With Babies

Take baby wipes for quick cleanups, and take changing supplies and bottle-feeding equipment, if needed. Disposable diapers are available in Costa Rica, but cost double what they do in the States, so you might want to pack these, too. A stroller is useful in the cities, a cloth carrier at the beach. Cribs are available in most of the better hotels and you should be able to improvise in the few cases where you won't find them.

Gerber baby foods (instant cereals and strained vegetables and meat) are manufactured in Costa Rica, and are sold in pharmacies and super-markets in San José and the larger towns. Other readily available food items for babies include canned condensed milk, canned fruit juice, cheeses, fruits and powdered formulas.

With kids in tow, you'll spend considerable time in your hotel room. Be more selective than you might otherwise be. A television in the room and a swimming pool are attractive amenities for the kids, even if you don't need them for yourself.

Hotels in Costa Rica rarely charge for children up to three years old. Older children will pay a small extra-bed charge, or half the adult rate if meals are included, but policies vary widely.

10. ECO-TOURISM

ECO-TOURIST MECCA

No doubt about it, Costa Rica is the world's eco-tourism mecca. There are hundreds of bird species, thousands of plants, and insects numbering in the tens of thousands, in habitats ranging from steaming lowland jungle to cloud forest to frosty peaks. Several worlds are crowded into a land of modest size, and visitors can appreciate them all, with not a few aches and mud puddles in the process.

But is this eco-tourism?

You might well ask — and you might well think things are a bit out of kilter — when a local company can call itself Ecological Rent-a-Car.

At its best, eco-tourism is an effort to acquaint visitors with tropical life systems, while doing as little damage to them as possible, and perhaps even protecting and enhancing them. It doesn't necessarily put the whims of the visitor first.

But for most visitors, eco-tourism is a theme, the modern folklore of travel to Costa Rica that corresponds to Mayan culture in Guatemala and schnitzel in Vienna. It involves rafting trips and hikes to hot springs, but largely, it is pattering guides, bus rides, and hotels with good and bad restaurants (with or without cable television), and friendly management.

Eco-tourism can be like tourism anywhere.

And it can even leave nature in a sadder state than before.

But we're dealing with the real world here, and the inescapable fact is that outsiders want to see a part of the world still relatively unaffected by population pressures and human alterations. And Costa Rica would like to see some economic benefit from letting outsiders in.

ECO-TOUR POSSIBILITIES

Consider some typical ecotourist adventures:

1. Spend several days in a tent near a national park. You fly in by chartered plane, burning fossil fuels. The plane also brings in beer, liquor, and tinned food. A diesel generator provides power. Garbage disappears

mysteriously. Birding and turtle-watching excursions are taken in motor-ized vehicles. After a hard day getting to know nature, iced drinks are always available.

2. Fly to a luxury eco-lodge in the jungle. Locally available jungle materials — hardwoods and palm thatch — were used to construct the guest cottages, along with cement and reinforcing rods brought from San José and abroad. The kitchen serves the finest aged beef fattened in pastures that once were rain forest, the bar has an assortment of domestic and imported liquors. The lodge stands on a huge tract of formerly logged land that is being allowed and encouraged to return to forest. Elsewhere, similar large parcels have been subdivided into smallholdings.

3. You take a bus from San José, are met in a lowland village beyond Braulio Carrillo National Park, and hike for a couple of hours to a clearing, carrying all your food, cooking equipment and sleeping gear. You spend a weekend camping, birding, hiking, spotting snakes and small mammals, listening to branches crack and trees fall, and watching bromeliads and ferns renew life from the decay of the old. Mostly, you try to keep dry or get used to being rained on. Muddy and exhausted, you finally emerge from the rain forest, enlightened about the interactions of natural systems. You are one of the last to take the trip to the clearing. The land has changed hands, and will soon be planted in bananas.

4. You've been looking forward for months to visiting a national park along the southwestern Pacific coast of Costa Rica. Its pristine tropical forest, extending right to the water's edge, alive with tapirs, coatimundis, marmosets, howler monkeys and sloths, was rescued from developers who wanted to cut down the trees, shoo away the animals, and erect concrete resorts on exposed hillsides.

You arrive to find that the forest canopy is, indeed, magnificent, and alive with birds. But the park's horseshoe bays and stunning headlands and views of the glittering water and its cachet as a protected area have made it even more of a destination that the quondam developers ever intended.

Hotels and resorts and restaurants and tour agencies crowd the access road. Foul-smelling liquids seep onto the adjacent beach. Out of season, when the numbers of foreign visitors fall, area hotels boost occupancy with rock concerts, surfing competitions, and other "events" peculiar to any resort area with a marketing team. Park trails, churned to mud by incessant footsteps, are littered with cans and "disposable" diapers. The campsite has long been closed, and there is serious talk of placing the park off-limits for one or several days a week in a desperate hope that some sort of recovery might take place.

A FEW SIMPLE RULES

So what can you do to keep your depredations to a minimum?

• Leave things as you found them. Take your garbage out with you when you visit a reserve.

• Buy nothing made from endangered species of plant or animal. This can mean turning your back on coral jewelry and woodware. Ironwood (*guayacán*), purpleheart (*nazareno*), and rosewood (*cocobolo*) are endangered, among others.

• Keep nothing that you catch from the sea, unless you plan to cook it.

• Accept no "eco-tourism" label at face value.

• Ask questions about any excursion, any product, that claims to be ecological:

> Are local people employed?
> Are they being displaced from traditional ways?
> Are local resources used in a sustainable manner?

Sometimes, eco-tourism can also mean staying out of (or being barred from) overcrowded reserves. I could go on and on, but you get my point. When we visit new places, what results is not always what we anticipate, or what we want. Let's recognize the problem, and try to keep things under control.

Can you be an eco-tourist in Costa Rica? It depends on you, and on the choices you make.

ECO-TOUR MECCA

11. FOOD & DRINK

Costa Rica's food holds few surprises. Most restaurants in San José serve what they call "international cuisine," which is a combination of standard North American and European fare. *Bistec* (beef), *pollo* (chicken) and *pescado* (fish) are most often encountered on the menu, usually in forms that need little explanation. They're generally accompanied by rice and cabbage. You might as well call this Tico-style food, rather than Tico specialties.

COMIDA TÍPICA

Genuine Costa Rican specialties are generally enjoyed at home, in a very rare city restaurant that advertises its *comida típica* (native food), in simple country eateries, and as snacks. One of the most common plates in the countryside is *casado* - fish, meat or chicken married (*casado*) to rice, beans, and chopped cabbage. *Gallo pinto*, rice and beans with herbs and spices, is the staple of poor people's diets, usually served with tortillas, flat cakes made of ground, lime-soaked corn.

But you don't have to be poor to enjoy the taste of black beans and tortillas, or of *olla de carne* (a stew of beef, yucca and plantain), *chiles rellenos* (stuffed peppers), *maduros*, or *plátanos fritos* (fried plantains), *chilasquiles* (meat-filled tortillas), *pozol* (corn soup), *tamales* (corn dough with a filling of meat, rice and raisins, steamed in a banana leaf, and served at holiday times) or *tayuyas* (tortillas stuffed with cheese or beans, a Guanacastecan regional specialty). You merely have to search these dishes out, if you're not part of a Costa Rican household. The **Cocina de Leña** is one San José restaurant that challenges the prejudice against eating Costa Rica's soul food in public.

SNACKS

Traditional snack foods are easier to find. Vendors sell *pan de yuca* (yucca bread), *gallos* (tortillas with fillings), *arreglados* (bread filled with meat and vegetables), *empanadas* (stuffed pastry), and various other starchy items at markets, on trains, and at bus terminals. Other favorite snacks are tropical fruits (papayas, bananas, passionfruit, pineapple and many others) sold from carts everywhere in the country, and pipas, young juice coconuts, as well as the juice of fruits and sugarcane (*agua dulce*). *Pejivalle*, a pasty palm fruit, and palmito, heart of palm, are enjoyed as hor d'oeuvres or in salad. *Cajeta*, a heavy milk fudge, is served sometimes as dessert, as it is in other Latin countries. Hot sauces and peppers — chiles — are condiments to be added as desired, and are rarely included in a dish before serving.

THOSE ODD FRUITS AND VEGETABLES

Some of Costa Rica's vegetables and fruits will be only sketchily familiar. Rice is served at almost all meals, but a common vegetable is *chayote* (chay-YO-teh), known as *huisquil* in Guatemala, *batata* in the Dominican Republic, *chocho* in Jamaica, *christophee* in other parts, and vegetable pear in the dictionary. It's terrific when baked with butter or mashed like a potato, but when just boiled and plopped in front of you it can be, as a reader complains, "horrible in taste and texture." *Yuca* (manioc, or yucca) sometimes draws similar reactions.

Fruits can draw more pleased reactions. *Cas* and *granadilla*, full of seeds, are used to flavor fruit ices, and in preserves. The delicious *zapote* (the same as the Mexican *mamey*), brown on the outside, with a large pit and blood-red flesh, may be consumed directly, as can large mangos, but not cashew fruit (*marañón*).

When in doubt about whether you can peel and eat an unfamiliar

SNACK ON A PINEAPPLE

fruit, or whether you'll be stuck with a squishy, seedy, tart-tasting mess, buy your fruit from a sidewalk stall in San José, or at least take a good look at one, to see what's in season and what the locals do with it.

MANY CUISINES

Gourmet restaurants in San José and nearby cook tender meats to order and serve them in delicate sauces along with crisp vegetables. Chinese, German, French, Italian, Swiss and even the better "international" restaurants produce superb results with foods that are fresh and abundant throughout the year. At the less expensive eateries in San José, and in the countryside, culinary arts and sciences are, unfortunately, not widely diffused.

What you'll find can most generously be described as home-style cooking — wholesome, reasonably priced, but not finely prepared — comparable to the fare at Joe's Diner. A *bistec* (steak) will generally be a tough, nondescript slab of meat, served with some of the grease in which it was cooked. The fate of fresh seafood is often similar. Vegetables, other than rice, beans and cabbage, when they are served, will have been in the pot for too long. None of this will do you any harm, especially when you pay only three to four dollars for your meal.

Not that you won't find some pleasant surprises. At one anonymous roadside eatery near Cañas, I had the most exquisite gallo pinto, seasoned with fresh coriander and a hint of garlic, accompanied by a thin *bistec* smothered with onions. There, as elsewhere, the presence of truckers was a good sign. And at a few coastal resorts, standards are as high as in San José. But generally, when you leave the capital, lower your expectations.

Fortunately, almost every small town in Costa Rica has a Chinese restaurant, if not two or three, where *chao mein* (chow mein), chop suey and more elaborate plates tease bored palates. These restaurants are not gourmet-class, but they work interesting and edible combinations from Costa Rica's fresh vegetables and meats.

Service in Costa Rican restaurants is relaxed. You'll never be presented with a bill and ushered toward the cash register in order to make way for the next customer. The pleasures of lingering over nothing more than a pastry and a cup of coffee can still be enjoyed. If leisurely dining isn't what you have in mind, you'll have to call the waiter over to place your order, and to ask for the bill (*la cuenta*). A 13% tax and a 10% service charge will be added on. No additional tip is required.

For a basic menu vocabulary, see the **Tico Talk** chapter.

MMMM . . . ¡CAFÉ!

Costa Rica's excellent coffee, of course, is enjoyed with all meals, and is often prepared by pouring hot water through grounds held in a sock-like device. Costa Ricans claim all kinds of special properties for their brew — it won't keep you up at night, nor jangle your nerves, but will stimulate you to overall better functioning. This is only understandable chauvinism. Sometimes coffee is served with sugar already added — specify without (*sin azúcar*) if you prefer it that way. *Café con leche* (coffee with milk) is at least half milk. The concept of coffee with cream is understood only in hotels and restaurants that have a foreign clientele.

WHISKEY AND EGGS

Costa Rican eating and drinking habits in restaurants can be disorienting. As you have your morning coffee and bacon and eggs, the Tico to the left of you will be starting the day with a whiskey and a chicken sandwich. The Tico to the right of you will be cutting into a steak, accompanied by a beer. The Tico in front of you enjoys a rum and Coke while he ponders the menu. You are too polite (or dumbfounded) to turn to the Tico behind you.

I have no explanations for these customs, except to state that restaurant food is not necessarily derived from what is traditionally eaten at home. *You* were taught that eggs are eaten at breakfast. Maybe they were not. Explaining an affection for liquor is a touchy thing, but there is no doubt that Costa Ricans enjoy their booze in large quantities and at varied hours.

HOOTCH AND BEER

Much of what is consumed is *guaro*, which can be roughly translated as "hootch." Guaro is the cheapest liquor, distilled from sugarcane, and sold in bars by the shot. Sugarcane is also the base for rums of various qualities and maturities, some of them quite good. Most guaros and rums are distilled by a government-owned company, but other companies make quite drinkable vodkas and gins. Local whiskeys and liqueurs are also available, but their quality is not as high. The exception is Café Rica, a coffee liqueur, which costs more than other Costa Rican drinks. Imported alcoholic drinks are quite expensive (with the exception of whiskey, which is only moderately expensive), so if you have a favorite brand, bring a bottle or two or three with you, or shop at the duty-free store in the airport before you pass through customs. Rum and Coke (*Cuba Libre*) is Costa Rica's most popular mixed drink.

Local fruit wines are interesting for amusement, but are not taken seriously by anyone who has enjoyed wine elsewhere. Imported wines are quite a luxury. Wine drinkers will have to fork out the money (a few duty-free bottles won't go very far), or else switch to another drink for the duration.

An excellent alternative to wine is beer. Pilsen is a superb brand of beer (in my opinion), and Tropical and Bavaria (*rubia* in local slang) are almost as good. There are various others, such as Imperial (*águila*) to suit different tastes, including a local version of Heineken, that is a ringer for the real thing, but for the health warning — *tomar licor es nocivo para la salud (drinking liquor endangers health)* — which all alcoholic beverages must carry. Beer is inexpensive — as little as 50¢ in some eateries, rarely more than $1. The alcohol content is 4%.

Bars are generally the cheapest places to drink, and they serve a dividend: *bocas*. These are hor d'oeuvres that range from cheese and crackers to little sandwiches that, over enough rounds, will constitute a meal in themselves. In classier joints, you pay for the bocas.

The easiest place to buy liquor, beer or wine is at a supermarket. In small towns with no supermarkets, try the bars themselves or small general stores (*pulperías*), though the selection will be more limited. The deposit on a beer or soda bottle is usually as much as the price of what's inside.

COOKING YOUR OWN MEALS

A number of newly sprung lodging places along the beaches of Costa Rica feature mini-refrigerators, some have stoves, and a few have full kitchens that are even more elaborate than the one I cook in at home. I'm not talking modestly priced housekeeping units here. These villas can rent for well over $200 per day.

What's going on? Most new hotels in Costa Rica have been built under concessions that allow the duty-free importation of equipment and furnishings. The more extras you cram in, the higher the rate you're allowed to charge, at least theoretically. Which translates into inflated sale prices as well (many of these places double as investment schemes).

To Costa Ricans, who have traditionally decamped to the beach as families and saved a few colones by dripping their own coffee and slicing their own fruit, the concept makes perfect sense. They might even be willing to try out one of these places, if they can get an off-season rate.

For gringos, the attractions are rather reduced. In most cases, the nearest grocery shop will be miles away. The packages on the shelf will require interpretation and explanation. The steak you fetch by taxi or in a rented car will fight back.

As for traditional resort amenities — restaurants, a choice of shops, diving and fishing services — you may well have to look elsewhere.

If you want to spend hundreds of dollars for your ticket, hundreds more for your room, and then lug your groceries from San José or Toronto and cook all your meals while on vacation, that's your business. I'll go out for *gallo pinto* at the rice-and-beans place with music down the road.

12. SAN JOSÉ

INTRODUCTION

San José, the capital of Costa Rica, is many towns. At its center are steel-and-concrete towers, shops with plate-glass windows displaying the latest fashions and consumer electronic gadgetry, thoroughfares busy with traffic, and sidewalks crowded with neatly dressed businessmen and office workers. All might have been transplanted from a medium-sized Spanish city.

Just west of the main square is the bustling market area, much more Central American in character, where tinkerers, wholesalers, and vendors of food and every necessity of daily life eke out their livings from tiny shops and market stalls and street stands, where buses and delivery trucks and taxis battle to advance through the throngs and commerce overflowing the sidewalks. Here, the buildings are one- and two-story, relatively dingy, and mostly unseen by the casual observer for all the activity around them.

Farther west of downtown San José, and in some of the surrounding suburbs, are the areas of gracious living, where huddled constructions give way to spacious, ranch-style houses with green lawns, always surrounded by substantial fences. This is where California- and Florida-style living — all the amenities in a benign climate — has grafted itself onto the local scene.

And there are the working-class neighborhoods as well, once-independent villages that lodge in simple, neat and non-unpleasant tin-roofed houses, among clusters of coffee and banana trees, the thousands of people who make San José run.

Beginnings

The city was founded in 1737 as Villa Nueva de la Boca del Monte del Valle de Abra, as the expanding population of the colony of Costa Rica moved westward from Cartago, then the capital. One of dozens of farming centers in a valley of forests, pastures and little plots of subsistence crops, San José — the name of the town was shortened to that of its

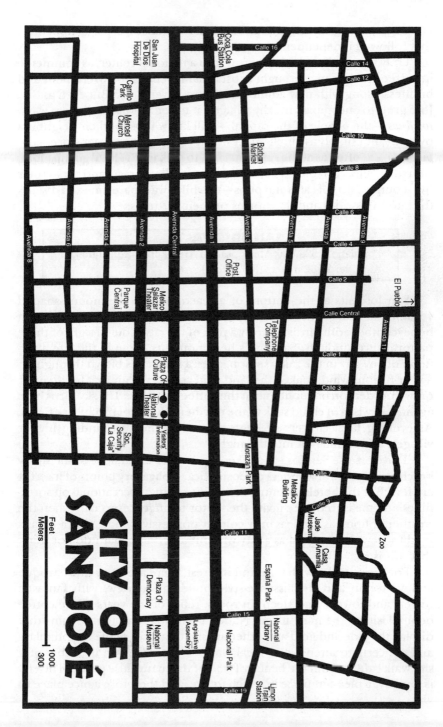

patron saint — became the capital of Costa Rica during the brief upheavals that followed independence.

Only slowly, though, did it grow into a national center, as commerce in coffee and bananas brought substantial revenues to government and business, along with new administrative requirements. But even as San José grew to encompass nearby villages, it never lost its small-town ways. *Josefinos* — the people of the capital — still know most of their neighbors by name, not simply as familiar faces. They shop at the corner store — the *pulpería* — as often as at the supermarket, to pick up the local gossip along with their eggs, coffee and beans. And they gather at *sodas* and bars— their own counterparts of cafés and pubs — to while away spare time and discuss the latest upswings and downturns of their fortunes.

SAN JOSÉ FACTS

Population: 325,000; Metropolitan Area Population: 1,000,000; Altitude: 1,182 meters (3,877 feet)

San José sits at the bottom of a teacup valley, the mound-shaped volcano Barva to the north, a ridge of hills to the south, the slopes of both honeycombed with farms. Hardly a part of the city is out of sight of these pastoral surroundings. San José's best moments come in the late afternoon of any day in the rainy season, after a storm has blown through on a near-furious wind, soaked the land, and cooled the air that for an hour or two borders on hot or humid at the coffee altitudes. The sky turns blue again, and wisps of cloud stick to the northern slopes of patchwork fields. As evening falls, clusters of lights appear in the surrounding higher villages, and twinkle on into the night.

Travelers use San José as a takeoff point for excursions to the many beaches and natural wonders of Costa Rica. Obligatory points of interest are few. But the hotels, country clubs, fine dining, recreational opportunities and measured pace invite the visitor to linger, especially when the weather at home is unpleasantly cold or oppressively hot. Costa Ricans tend to view their capital as a city without a heritage, but I do not think that this is so.

For the outsider with time and interest, there are a few fine baroque and Victorian and Renaissance-style buildings to view, with fantastic turrets and towers, and steep tin roofs, relics of the years of the coffee boom; visits to the magnificent National Theater, and to museums that display the jade and gold and other artistic treasures of the nation; plays and concerts to attend, and local ways to observe from the table of a sidewalk café or from the bench of one of the many little parks. The city is low-key, a pleasant place in which to live, and therefore a nice place to visit.

Current State of Affairs

Once you've been in San José for a few days, you'll get some sense of the character of the city — progressive and relatively prosperous, but not ostentatious; fast-paced, but not frenetic; well-mannered and neat, but friendly and not excessively formal; respectful of tradition, but with few visible reminders of the past; a national capital, a center of commerce, but manageable in size; a collection of well-off and middling and working-class neighborhoods, with few areas of grinding poverty or ostentatious luxury. One says "but" and "not quite" rather often in describing San José, and all of Costa Rica, the country that has been called the "land of the happy medium."

But despite the progress of the last century, so evident in the efficient functioning of the capital, the crowds of customers at shops and restaurants, and the dense traffic, the economic crisis of this decade, brought on by foreign debt, unstable commodity prices, and the collapse of the Central American common market, has dealt a severe blow to Costa Rica and its self-image. The nation now teeters on the brink of re-entry into the less privileged ranks of the third world. The unemployment rate has regularly been 10% or higher. Purchasing power shrank following severe devaluations of the currency early in the 1980s, and has never recovered. Fully 70% of Costa Rican families, according to official figures reported in the newspapers a few years ago, had incomes below the poverty line, then defined as $100 per month. During 1988 alone, according to central bank statistics, average salaries fell by ten percent in real terms.

Style and Fun

And yet, the hard facts are not reflected in San José's surface. The middle class struggles to maintain its style and good taste, even with limited funds. *Josefinos* are generally well groomed; their clothes are fashionable, though their wardrobes are limited. Their automobiles are small, but well maintained. Straitened elegance is the style, and it's catching. I once spotted a diplomat tooling around San José in a tiny Renault with a uniformed chauffeur.

One of the great debates into which visitors are drawn has to do with the merits of Costa Rica's women, and especially those of San José, who have acquired an extra-regional reputation for their beauty and charm. At the risk of sounding blasé, I will join the controversy and say that there are as many good-looking women in other places as well. But Ticas (and Ticos as well) are generally well groomed and well dressed, and in better shape than most Americans. And their preference for clothing that appears to have been pasted onto their bodies only enhances their fame (and form).

The liveliest time of year in San José is the month-long celebration that starts on December 1. *Chinamos*, stalls selling such seasonal goodies as apples and grapes, toys, and the makings of nativity scenes, crowd the sidewalks. Merchants open their businesses through the midday hours and even on weekends. The throngs grow larger and larger and louder and louder, and drunker and rowdier. Christmas is just a short pause in the round of parades, dancing, bonhomie, confetti-tossing, horse show, and general street partying that bursts finally at New Year's and dissolves into the traditional mass hangover. The onset of this self-indulgent orgy coincides not with any religious or civic anniversary, but with the day when the *aguinaldo*, the yearly bonus for salaried employees, is usually paid.

What-Country-Are-We-In Department

If you keep a sharp eye, you'll note pistol-packing guards not only at banks, but at hotels and major stores as well, just as in other Central American countries. Wielders of weapons are discreet, but they are there.

Who is that near the National Library, on Avenida 3, below 15 Calle, in steel helmet, with bayonet fixed? Just a soldier on sentry duty, you might think. Until you remember that this is Costa Rica and there *are* no soldiers. No, he's a civil guardsman.

If you read Spanish, you'll note that newspaper editorials freely criticize the government, and names of junketing legislators are published for the enlightenment of their constituents. Elsewhere in Latin America, the authorities of the day are treated with kid gloves. Yet freedom of the press is only available to licensed journalists.

This all might suggest that a certain country does not quite live up to its disarmed and disarming billing. Yet former President Oscar Arias, according to a reader's report in the *Tico Times*, used to show up without any entourage at his dentist, and wait his turn; and I was pleased to approach and chat with President Calderón one afternoon when, as a candidate, he strolled unguarded into a hotel where I was lurking.

ARRIVALS AND DEPARTURES

Airlines Servicing Costa Rica

Scheduled service to San José is currently provided by:

- **Lacsa**, Costa Rica's international airline, Calle 1, Avenida 5, tel. [2]310033; airport, tel. [2]416244
- **Aero Costa Rica**, San Pedro, tel. [2]534753
- **Sahsa**, Avenida 5, Calles 1/3, tel. [2]215561
- **Sansa**, the domestic airline, Calle 24, Avenidas Central/1, tel. [2]333258, fax [2]552176
- **Travelair**, the *other* domestic airline, Tobías Bolaños Airport, tel. [2]327883, fax [2]203054
- **American Airlines**, Paseo Colón, Calles 26/28, tel. [2]571266
- **Aviateca**, Calle 1, Avenida 3, tel. [2]554949
- **Continental Airlines**, Calle 19, Avenida 2, tel. [2]330266

- **Taca**, Calle 1, Avenida 3, tel. [2]221790
- **SAM** (Colombia), Avenida 7, Calles 5/7, tel. [2]333066
- **COPA** (Panama), Calle 1, Avenida 5, tel. [2]237033
- **Iberia**, Paseo Colón, Calle 40, tel. [2]213311
- **United Airlines**, Sabana Sur, tel. [2]204844

Air service to Tortuguero and other places not served by Sansa or Travelair is provided by a number of companies listed in the phone book under *Taxis Aéreos* and *Aviación*.

ARRIVING BY AIR

Juan Santamaría International Airport is located on the outskirts of Alajuela, 17 kilometers west of San José. It's a small and manageable facility serving both domestic and foreign scheduled flights.

Costa Rica's other international airport, near Liberia in the northwest, will handle charter flights of vacationers heading for the beaches.

Local charter flights use the smaller **Tobías Bolaños** airfield at Pavas, just west of San José.

When you get off the plane, you're free to shop at the duty-free stores before you pass through immigration and customs. Prices are generally lower than at U.S. airports, and of course, you won't risk breakage, so plan to take advantage. Stocks are mainly of liquor, cigarettes and perfumes, and odds and ends of other luxury goods.

Immigration and Customs

Immigration lineups are generally speedy, but if several planes touch down one after another, or a large charter load arrives, you could well stand in line for over an hour.

Next— before the cursory customs check— comes the tourist information counter. Make reservations here for a hotel in town if you don't already have one arranged, and pick up any other information you need — they're quite helpful.

Exchanging Money

To change money, look for an exchange booth. If it's not open, you'll have to go left and back inside the terminal building after you leave the customs area. Banking hours are Monday to Friday from 8 a.m. to 4 p.m. There are also informal money-changers on the sidewalk outside. It's a good idea to change a fair amount at the airport in order to avoid the long lines at banks in town.

Getting to Town By Taxi or Bus

Transport from the airport to San José is available by taxi for about

$12; and on the regular Alajuela-San José buses and microbuses that stop in front of the terminal. These run every ten to fifteen minutes, and charge less than 50¢. Luggage space on buses is limited, but the driver might allow you to put your bags in an otherwise empty seat for an extra fare.

Buses arrive at terminals scattered through central San José (see pages 129-130). Most are in areas with either no accommodations or less-than-attractive digs. Taxis in San José are inexpensive, so if you arrive after dark and are not sure of your surroundings, take one to your hotel.

DEPARTING BY AIR

All scheduled flights use **Juan Santamaría International Airport**, 17 kilometers west of San José, near Alajuela.

Getting To the Airport

Any hotel can arrange a taxi to the airport, for about $12, or you can call the airport taxi company at [2]216865.

If you can handle your luggage (you might have to pay for an extra seat), take the Alajuela microbus from Avenida 2, Calles 12/14, San José. These run almost continuously during the day.

Airport Procedures

First check in with your airline and pay the exit tax, which is currently about $8.

You can re-purchase U.S. dollars at the airport bank — if the bank is open and if the currency is available.

Airport Shops and Services

The usual assortment of overpriced airport shops solicits your last Costa Rican coins. The post office branch is open until 5 p.m. The duty-free shops, in the departure area, have good assortments of liquor, cigarettes and perfumes, and some odds and ends of other luxury goods. You can carry your purchases with you.

DEPARTING BY TRAIN AND TRAIN EXCURSIONS

Regular service to the coasts, including the **Jungle Train** to Limón, has been discontinued.

Some travel agencies organize train excursions through the Caribbean banana plantations (see below). And if you see a passenger train rumbling through San José, it's the commuter service that runs weekdays between Heredia, the Atlantic Station in San José, and the University of Costa Rica in San Pedro; or the local train from the western suburb of Pavas.

DEPARTING BY CAR

Just follow the signs! Arrows along the main thoroughfares point the way to Limón, Puntarenas, Cartago and other major towns.

DEPARTING BY BUS

Buses to various points in Costa Rica are mentioned in the coverage of towns, parks and beaches in this book. Many leave from the area of the Coca-Cola market, 16 Calle, Avenidas 1/3. For buses to other points, and to re-check schedules, inquire at the tourist office.

Service to Panama and to all Central American capitals, with connections to Mexico, is provided by **Tica Bus**, Avenida 4, Calle 9, tel. [2]218954. Currently there are departures for Panama City on daily at 8 a.m., and for Managua on Monday, Wednesday, Friday and Saturday at 7 a.m. **Sirca**, Calle 7, Avenidas 6/8, tel. [2]231464, has service to Managua on Wednesday, Friday and Sunday.

Other buses from the Coca-Cola terminal go as far as the Nicaraguan border at Peñas Blancas. **Tracopa**, Avenida 18, Calles 2/4, has three daily buses to the border of Panama at Canoas, another to David, in northern Panama.

GETTING AROUND TOWN

Avenidas in San José run from east to west, with odd-numbered avenidas north of Avenida Central, or Central Avenue, and even-numbered avenidas to the south. *Calles*, or streets, run north-south, with odd-numbered calles east of the Calle Central, even-numbered streets to the west. You'll quickly get used to this scheme as you go around the city, though you'll probably confuse your avenidas and calles at first.

The two main areas of interest are the **central business district**, around the intersection of Avenida Central and Calle Central; and the high-toned **Paseo Colón district**, to the west. Paseo Colón is a continuation of Avenida Central. From the western end of Paseo Colón to the center of the city is just over a mile, a distance easily negotiated on foot or on the many city buses that run along Colón.

North, east, west and south of the central area are the *barrios*, or neighborhoods, of the capital — Los Yoses, Sabana Sur, Bellavista, and several dozen others. Adjoining suburban municipalities, such as Guadalupe and San Pedro, comprise the *Area Metropolitana* (Metropolitan Area) with San José, and are, for practical purposes, part of a single city.

By Bus

City buses and those running to nearby suburbs provide a service roughly comparable to that in large North American cities, at a fraction of the price. The fare is usually posted near the door, and on most routes is about 10¢.

Many bus routes start at or near the Central Park. All are identified by both a number and the name of the neighborhood or suburb they serve. These are clearly posted at the stops. In addition, 20-passenger microbuses serve some of the same areas.

Buses and their stops are given for most places of interest mentioned in this chapter. For others, ask at the tourist office.

By Car

This is something you should avoid in San José, if possible. Costa Ricans are aggressive at the wheel, and their lane-changing, honking horns and screeching tires can get on your nerves. Almost all streets are one-way, making for circuitous routings through downtown—when you can move.

Alternatives to driving are plentiful. Taxis are inexpensive, bus service is adequate, and San José is a most walkable city, with places of interest clustered near each other.

If you do end up with a car in the city, note that parking is forbidden on almost all downtown streets, and the few available spaces are metered. In any case, a thief will empty your car before any cop takes notice. Park in an off-street lot, day or night.

Part of Avenida Central is a pedestrian mall. Sections are closed to traffic either permanently or for part of the day.

Renting a Car

For assorted warnings, advisories and cautions, see Chapter 6 of this book, **"Basic Information"**. Among car-rental companies operating in San José are:
• **Avis**, Sabana Norte, tel. [2]329922
• **Budge**t, Paseo Colón, Calle 30, tel. [2]233284; also at airport
• **Dollar**, Calle 38, Avenida 9, Calle Central, tel. [2]333339; and airport
• **Hertz**, Paseo Colón, Calle 38, tel. [2]235959
• **National**, Calle 36, Avenida 7, tel. [2]334044
• **Toyota Rent A Car**, Paseo Colón, Calles 30/32, tel. [2]232250
• **U-Haul**, Paseo Colón, tel. [2]221110

There are many others listed in the phone book under *Alquiler de Automóviles*, but none offer bargains.

By Taxi

Taxis are a downright cheap way to get around San José. Most trips around the city will cost less than two dollars, or less than a dollar within a neighborhood. Fares are fixed by the government, currently at 70¢ for the first kilometer, 25¢ for each additional kilometer, and $3 per hour of waiting. The tariff rises slightly at night.

Overcharging sometimes occurs, of course, and meters may be legitimately broken. Calculate the distance of your trip beforehand — figure nine blocks to the kilometer. If the meter ("*maría*") is not running, settle the price with the driver before you get in. Your hotel might be able to give you guidelines on the proper fares. Taxi drivers are not tipped.

Taxis are easily spotted — they're red (except for airport cabs, which are orange) and have roof lights. You may flag one down on the street, or have one called to your hotel.

What's In An Address?

Josefinos navigate around their city by inertial displacement from known landmarks. An ad for a certain restaurant might say that it is 200 meters west of and 150 meters north of Edificio Chile Picante. "100 meters" is another way of saying "one block" in Costa Rica (though a block is, in fact, somewhat shorter). The translation, then, is: From the Chile Picante building, go two blocks west, then one-and-a-half blocks north. This system has its charm, and is fine if you know the city, but if you're a first-time visitor, you're sunk. You'll have to seek clarification (e.g., "Where is Edificio Chile Picante?") if you get an address in this form.

Fortunately, a somewhat clearer form is generally used for addresses in the downtown area. The address of the Chalet Suizo restaurant is Avenida 1, Calles 5 y 7. This means that it's on Avenida 1 between 5 and 7 Calles. The address of the Hotel Balmoral is Avenida Central y Calle 7, meaning that it's at the corner of Avenida Central and Calle 7. In this book, I'll give such addresses as "Avenida 1, Calles 5/7," and "Avenida Central, Calle 7." Of course, you'll have to search out your target along the block indicated, but that's the way the Ticos do it.

Believe it or not, buildings also have numbers, but they're rarely posted, so an address giving a house number is of little use.

For obvious reasons, I will not always give addresses and directions in the local manner.

WHERE TO STAY

The best hotel values in San José are to found at the *upper* end of the price scale, but there are also a few good buys in the medium and budget ranges. In general, rooms are larger in the Paseo Colón area than downtown, so you might well give some thought to staying in the west end, at little sacrifice in convenience. Most of the budget hotels are downtown.

What Will You Pay?

Hotel rates have been rising by as much as 25% annually in recent years. Luxury hotels charge $125 and up for a single, $150 and up for a double, with taxes, sometimes discounted during the rainy season. A middle-range hotel room costs from $60 to $80 double in San José, though you can find clean, airy rooms on the outskirts, especially in bed and breakfasts, for $35 to $50 double. The most modest hotels in San José charge about $20 double.

As new rooms are opening all the time, the rate of price increase will probably slow down.

Do They Have Room?

Reservations are advisable at any holiday period. Take advantage of toll-free telephone numbers for this purpose, if you can. Otherwise, the airport branch of the tourist office will help you find a room in your price range when you arrive.

Can You Sleep?

San José is not a restful city by night. Traffic rolls at all hours, night watchmen blow their whistles, and celebrations, of which there are many, are marked mainly by attention-getting noises.

If you're staying at any downtown hotel, cheap or luxury, and your sleep is important to you, try to get a room that does not face the street (which often costs more). If this is not possible, then find a room elsewhere.

Are The Rooms Clean?

Housekeeping is often poor at smaller hotels, and sometimes at larger ones. You can always expect to find dust on surfaces above eye level and in carpets — unless adequate housekeeping is mentioned in my description.

Budget Note

There are lots of cheap hotels in San José, but most of them are located in noisy, undesirable areas, such as the blocks surrounding the bus terminal. Budget hotel rooms usually charge by the person, and fit no more than two to a room. If four or more compatible people are travelling together, you might do almost as well to book a moderately priced hotel, where you pay by the room, with a small charge per extra person.

The Best Hotels

To save you plowing through this section unnecessarily, let me give you some of my personal recommendations. At the luxury level, the

Cariari and Herradura are good values in country-cl[...]
of San José, and the Palacio, right on the outskirts[...]
Among higher-priced hotels, the Villa Tournón, an[...]
near Santo Domingo, are well-run and pleasant.

If you are open-ended about your travel plans, consider staying [...]
of the fine smaller hotels with personal, concierge-type service to help you
throughout your trip. The classy Santo Tomás in downtown San José, and
the Grano de Oro, in the west end, fit this description, while the Cacts
offers excellent service from Costa Ricans with international experience,
with fewer frills.

The Hotel L'Ambiance, downtown, is a fine, small hotel *de luxe*. The
Gran Vía represents good value among moderately priced hotels downtown. In a smaller hotel, some give the Don Carlos high ratings.

If you rent a car, or don't mind taking buses and taxis, the Pico
Blanco, above San José in San Antonio de Escazú, is a good value, while
the Finca Rosa Blanca (mentioned at the end of the next chapter) is a
classy and unique country inn within easy reach of the airport.

And there is practically no end of bed-and-breakfasts, some of them
quite elegant, most of them charming, located mostly in the suburbs, and
charging less than you'd pay in comparable hotel space.

If you intend to do your own cooking, and even if you don't, *apartoteles*
(apartment hotels) are also lower-priced than conventional hotels, though
without room service, shops, and other hotel amenities.

TELEPHONE NEWS AGAIN

An initial digit [indicated in brackets] will be added in mid-1994 to
every phone number in San José. If your call does not go through, re-dial
with the extra digit. Verify problem numbers in the telephone directory, or
dial 113 for assistance.

Better Hotels - West End

HOTEL CARIARI, Ciudad Cariari (P. O. Box 737-1007, Centro
Colón, San José), tel. [2]390022, fax [2]392803. 220 rooms. $125 single/
$135 double/$190 poolside/$200 and up for suites. Rates discounted
approximately 20% May to October. U. S. reservations: tel. 800-847-2568
(to Costa Rica) or 3501 W. Rolling Hills Circle, Fort Lauderdale, FL, tel.
305-476-5848. American Express, Visa, Master Card.

The Cariari is not in San José at all, but eight kilometers west of the
city, along the Cañas expressway, halfway to the airport. This is a tasteful,
modern resort and country-club complex, with a dramatic rotunda entry.
The hotel has a pool, sauna, whirlpool, and casino, as well as many shops.
For a fee, guests can use an 18-hole golf course, tennis courts, Olympic-
size swimming pool, basketball courts, and gym. Rooms have color

...isions and air conditioning, and there are car rentals and assorted ...ner amenities, including a mini-shopping center with supermarket.

Restaurants include the formal **Vitrales**, open evenings only, and **Las Tejas**, serving all meals. The **Las Maracas** bar has live music on weekends. Shuttle bus service is available to San José every two hours, at a charge. The mountain views from the extensive grounds are lovely, and I wouldn't blame anybody for spending a whole winter vacation here. The upper crust of San José society and politics frequents the facilities.

HOTEL HERRADURA, Ciudad Cariari (P.O. Box 7-1880, San José), tel. [2]390033, fax [2]392292. 234 rooms. $124-$150 single/$135-$161 double. U.S. reservations: tel. 800-245-8420. The Herradura is another large and modern hotel, constructed in Spanish-colonial style, comparable in facilities to the Cariari. Rooms are among the nicest in or near San José, and have television and air conditioning. There are two pools (one with three levels and connecting falls), outdoor whirlpools, and exercise facilities.

The **Bon Vivant** restaurant, open evenings, serves French cuisine, and is quite expensive; **Tiffany's** serves steaks, chops, and shrimp during the day, and has a daily complete dinner special for about $10; and the **Sakura** has Japanese-style food. And there are a casino, conference facilities, and even a chapel.

HOTEL CAMINO REAL, Santa Ana. This is a large hotel complex that will open in 1994. Though it hasn't proved itself in Costa Rica, Camino Reals in general have a reputation in Latin America as the hotels that get things right.

HOTEL SAN JOSÉ PALACIO, La Uruca (P. O. Box 458-1150), tel. [2]202034, fax [2]202036. 154 rooms. $126 to $138 single/$132 to $143 double, $180 and up in suites. Visa, Master Card, American Express. U.S. reservations tel. 800-858-0606. Just west of San José, towering on a hill above the Cañas expressway, the new Palacio has the nicest modern-style accommodations in the city. Standard rooms have panelling, a sofa, two queen-sized beds, mini-bar, television, wall safe, and bathroom with marble tile. Suites have a large desk and two sofas, and a balcony with city views. Junior suites have a triple-sized bed and powder room, and can be combined with a standard room. Bathrobe, loofah and shampoo provided. Two executive floors have their own express check-in area.

The pool is huge, free-form, with a planted island. There are also exercise rooms, racquetball and tennis courts, sauna, whirlpool, numerous shops, conference rooms, and, of course, a casino. One of the many nice features is that towering trees were preserved on the site, lending a tropical forest atmosphere to the grounds. Access to the hotel is only from the westbound lanes of the expressway.

Cuisine at the Palacio is Spanish, which reflects ownership by the

Barceló chain. The main restaurant serves paella, steak and fish at $10 to $15 per main course. The **Anfora** coffee shop has a $10 dinner buffet, and assorted lighter fare.

HOTEL IRAZÚ, Autopista Gen. Cañas, tel. [2]324811, fax [2]324549. 350 rooms. $88 single/$100 double, less without air conditioning. Mailing address: P. O. Box 962-1000, San José. U.S. reservations, tel. 305-871-6631 or 800-272-6654; Canada, tel. 800-463-6654. The largest hotel in San José, always lively with tour groups, the Irazú is located four kilometers west of downtown, in the municipality of La Uruca. The immediate area holds no attraction or views, but the landscaping and a U-shaped building shield guests from passing trucks.

Rooms are air-conditioned, and there are two restaurants, lighted tennis courts, pool, sauna, massage service, and numerous shops and real-estate salesmen in the bustling lobby. An hourly shuttle bus to downtown is available. Lower room rates are sometimes offered on site.

HOTEL COROBICÍ, Calle 42, Avenida 5 (P.O. Box 8-5480) tel. [2]328122, fax [2]315834. 275 rooms. $115 single/$125 double. U.S. reservations: 7955 N.W. 12th St., Miami, FL 33126, tel. 800-227-4274. A modern, cream-colored structure that towers over western San José, the Corobicí is under the same management as the Cariari.

The facilities here are very attractive, and include a large pool area, health spa, air conditioning and television, a 24-hour coffee shop as well as the Fuji, a Japanese restaurant, and a courtesy bus to downtown. Though the climate doesn't demand it, there's a huge and impressive Hyatt-style towering indoor lobby.

HOTEL EJECUTIVO NAPOLEÓN, Calle 40, Avenida 5 (P. O. Box 86340-1000 San José), tel. [2]233252, fax [2]229487. 26 units. $86 single/$97 double. Visa, American Express. A smaller hotel of executive suites, newly remodeled, catering to business travellers, with highly personalized service. Good location near Paseo Colón.

Rooms have TV and air conditioning, and there's a pool and coffee shop. Rate includes a buffet breakfast.

HOTEL PARQUE DEL LAGO, Avenida 2, Calle 40 (P. O. Box 624-1007), tel. [2]221577, fax [2]231617. 39 rooms. $108 to $132 single/$126 to $148 double, $150 to $228 in suites, $228 to $342 on V.I.P. level. U.S. reservationsw: 800-363-8869 A brand-new hotel oriented to business travellers, with assorted small in-room comforts provided: coffee maker, television, hair dryer, mini-bar, room safe, air conditioning, fax-modem connections. Buffet breakfast included in the rate, comprehensive business services (use included at V.I.P. level). No bar or restaurant.

HOTEL TORREMOLINOS, Avenida 5 bis, Calle 40, P. O. Box 2029-1000, tel. [2]225266, fax [2]553167. 73 rooms. $80 single/$95 double. In a nice residential neighborhood not far from the Paseo Colón. Travel agency, pool, bar, and moderately priced restaurant.

HOTEL GRANO DE ORO, Calle 30, Avenidas 2/4 (P. O. Box 1157-1007 Centro Colón, San José or P.O. Box 025216-36, Miami, FL 33102-5216), tel. [2]553322, fax [2]212782. 21 rooms. $66 single/$78 double standard room, $80/$90 deluxe, $122/$133 suite. A smaller hotel, this is a charming, impeccably restored and updated Victorian house and extensions, with lots of plants and shiny woodwork, courtyard with exuberant vegetation and falls, rooms with cheery floral bedspreads and modern bathrooms with gleaming brass fixtures. Housekeeping is impeccable.

I think it's overpriced, but readers have sent me rave reviews, with comments such as "beautiful furnishings," "lovely rooms," "staff terrific at arranging things (car rentals, ticket reconfirmations) without pushing themselves on visitors." Facilities include a gift ship with attractive wood pieces. Breakfast and light meals available.

Better Hotels · Downtown

HOTEL AUROLA, Calle 5, Avenida 5 (P.O. Box 7802-1000), tel. [2]337233, fax [2]551036. 200 rooms. $122 single, $133 double. U.S. reservations: 800-465-4329. Master Card, Visa, American Express. The Aurola is a San José landmark, a 17-floor aluminum-and-glass tower that mirrors the cityscape and sky. Inside are standard Holiday Inn rooms, pool, casino, underground parking, and shops. The street outside is the focal point for purse-snatching and pickpocketing in San José.

HOTEL VILLA TOURNÓN, Barrio Tournón, P.O. Box 6606-1000, tel. [2]336622, fax [2]225211. 77 rooms. $50-70 single/$65-$75 double. This is an attractive hotel, in the style of an Arizona country resort, with soaring beamed ceilings, fireplaces and huge plants in public areas, and wood floors, carpets and generally soothing furnishings in the rooms. The location—eight blocks north of Avenida Central along Calle 3, a short taxi ride from downtown — gets you out of the fumes that sometimes afflict the city center, and is convenient to the El Pueblo shopping and entertainment complex, though it can also seem like Queens Boulevard. Solar-heated pool, whirlpool, protected parking, shops, air conditioning.

HOTEL BALMORAL, Calle 7, Avenida Central (P. O. Box 3344-1000), tel. [2]225022, fax [2]217826. 121 rooms. $75 single/$80 double. U.S. reservations tel. 800-448-8355. American Express, Visa, Master Card. Rooms at this downtown hotel are good-sized, with air-conditioning and television; and there are a large lobby with ample seating, a shopping arcade, and a casino. The light, garden-style **Altamira** restaurant on the ground floor is easy on the senses.

HOTEL EUROPA, Calle Central, Avenida 5 (P.O. Box 72-1000), tel. [2]221222, fax [2]213976. 72 rooms. $45-$63 single/$57-$75 double.

Visa, American Express. U.S. reservations: tel. 800-223-6764, 212-714-2323. An early sixties hotel, with air-conditioned rooms, television, and the advantage of a small outdoor pool. Not a terrific building, the food is ordinary, and I have received some complaints about the housekeeping.

GRAN HOTEL COSTA RICA, Avenida Central, Calle 3 (P. O. Box 527-1000), tel. [2]214000, fax [2]213501. 104 rooms. $60 single/$80 double. Visa, Master Card. U.S. reservations: tel. 800-327-3573. Most Central American capitals have a once-elegant old hotel, and this is San José's. Across from the National Theater and fronting on a small park, the Hotel Costa Rica has a chandeliered rooftop dining room that still exudes some class. The tasteful public areas from a bygone era are now lively with a casino, services, and people scurrying about, but the rooms are downright threadbare and shabby. Those on the inside are quieter. You'll stay here to be in the middle of the action — the **Parisien Café** on the ground floor is unsurpassed for observing the goings-on in the center of the city.

HOTEL PRESIDENTE, Avenida Central, Calles 7/9 (P.O. Box 2922-1000), tel. [2]223022, fax [2]211205. 51 rooms. $63 single/$75 double. U.S. reservations: tel. 800-972-0515. The Presidente has especially good service among downtown hotels, and is in the process of expanding, with a 100-room section under construction. Some rooms are air-conditioned, and there are a basic restaurant, bar, a few suites, and the ever-present casino. One of the curiosities here, in a reception room, is a mural of the five-colón note, which itself is a copy of a mural in the National Theater.

Smaller Luxury Hotels

HOTEL L'AMBIANCE, Calle 13 no. 949, tel. [2]236702 fax [2]230481. U.S. Address: Interlink 179, Box 526770, Miami, FL 33152. 7 rooms. $80 single/$100 double, more in the suite. This is a classy hotel in a lovingly restored mansion just north of downtown — the manager describes it, quite accurately, as "a small *grand luxe* hotel with a commitment to excellence." All rooms are off a traditional central courtyard with fountain and miniature tropical garden, and all are individually decorated with antiques gathered from Europe, the United States and Costa Rica. Ceilings are high, floors are of wood, bathrooms are huge, with restored fixtures and tubs. A suite has a large living room, and all units have cable television. Maintenance is impeccable, but just as important is the level of personal, concierge-type service. The restaurant is intimate, excellent, and open to the public (see restaurant section, below).

LA CASA VERDE DE AMÓN, Calle 7, Avenida 9, tel. and fax [2]230969. U.S. address: Box 025216, Dept. 1701, Miami, FL 33102-5216. 8 rooms. $65 to $80, single or double. A restored Victorian house, with huge rooms and public areas, including an upstairs piano salon. Rooms have hardwood floors, wardrobes, wainscoting, area rugs, and new tiled baths. Breakfast, served in the garden, is included in the rate. Sauna available.

D'RAYA VIDA, north end of Calle 17 (P. O. Box 495-1000 San José, or P. O. Box 025216-1638, Miami, FL 33102), tel. [2]234168, fax [2]234157. 4 rooms. $70 single/$95 double. Credit cards accepted. This impeccably kept mansion is a surprise, tucked away behind gates on a dead end just northeast of downtown San José. The neighborhood is far from upper class, but security is good, and one can't put a price tag on the tranquility of the gardens, or the views afforded from a situation on the edge of a small precipice, and the at-home style of service. Public areas have chandeliers, and are decorated with paintings.

Rooms are all different, one with two large beds and private balconies, one with a bedstead carved with pineapples, a master bedroom with private bath. Business services are available, and dinners can be prepared. Airport pickup and return are included in the rate, making it easy to settle in.

Moderate Hotels - West End

COSTA RICA TENNIS CLUB, Sabana Sur (opposite Metropolitan Park), P.O. Box 4964-1000, tel. [2]321266, fax [2]323867. 27 rooms. $51 single or double. Visa, Master Card, American Express. This is a fun place in which to stay, a lively country club with many of the features of the Cariari and Herradura, but in more modest quarters. Guests have use of tennis courts, pools, sauna, bowling alley, and billiard tables, with some restrictions. The restaurant has a limited but reasonably priced menu. No shops or travel services here.

HOTEL AMBASSADOR, Paseo Colón, Calle 28 (P. O. Box 10186), tel. [2]218155, fax [2]553396. 73 rooms. $62 to $75 single/$75 to $87 double, higher in suites. Master Card, Visa, American Express. U.S. reservations, tel. 800-344-1212. Plain, good-sized rooms with minibar and television, public areas in passé peninsular taste (heavy on brooding varnished wood).

APARTOTEL LA SABANA, La Sabana (P. O. Box 8446-1000, San José), tel. [2]202422, fax [2]317386. 32 apartments and rooms. $42 double room, $54 to $90 for apartments. Visa, American Express, Master Card. A newly completed colonial-style structure, conveniently located near the Corobicí Hotel in San José's west end ("150 meters north, 50 meters west of Burger King"). All rooms have air conditioning and cable television, and on-site facilities include a pool, sauna, and washing machines. Good value for San José.

APARTOTEL CRISTINA, Sabana Norte (P. O. Box 1094-2050), tel. [2]311618, fax [2]202096. 25 units. $72 single/$78 double, credit cards accepted. Small furnished apartments with better kitchens than most such facilities, pool, garage. Not far from the Corobicí Hotel, 3 blocks north of the I.C.E. buildings across from Sabana Park.

HOTEL BOULEVARD EJECUTIVO, P. O. Box 3258-1000, San José. $52 single/$64 double ($85/$95 in suites). A modern suburban villa in Rohrmoser, the flat area west of La Sabana Park.

(The following two "apartoteles" and the ones listed after are among the best values in San José, if you don't need the shops, travel agency and room service provided by conventional hotels, and if you are not bothered by bare, harsh concrete and tile surfaces with a minimum of decoration.)

APARTOTEL CASTILLA, Calle 24, Avenidas 2/4, tel. [2]222113, fax [2]212080. 15 units. $41 single/$50 double. American Express, Visa. Somewhat worn on the outside, but the units, with one and two bedrooms, are comfortable. Near Paseo Colón.

APARTOTEL RAMGO, Sabana Sur, one block south of Metropolitan Park (P. O. Box 1441), tel. [2]323823, fax [2]323111. 16 units. From $50 single to $75 for four persons. Visa, Master Card, American Express. Plain but large apartments, each with two bedrooms, kitchen, dining room, laundry area, terrace, and cable TV, in a stark building in a residential area on the western edge of San José. Near shopping and bus to downtown. A good value for families or compatible groups.

Smaller Moderate Hotels - West End

HOTEL PETIT VICTORIA, Calle 28, Avenida 2, tel. [2]330766. 11 rooms. $55 single or double with breakfast. This is a charming (if overpriced) little hotel, a wooden house in the best old San José style, renovated with care. Entry is through a large, central hall, with a circular banquette, chandeliers, dark wood trim, and patterned tile floors. Guest rooms are off this area, behind high wooden doors and glass transoms. Each has a double bed with frilly spread, painted woodwork, and private bath with hot water. Outside, a wrought-iron fence surrounds the gardens. The name does not deceive.

Moderate Hotels - Downtown

I'm sorry to say that most downtown hotels in this category are more modest in their facilities than in their prices. Most appear to have been sliced from the same modern office cube, according to the size of the available lot, and set down in place.

All have limited public space — usually a couple of chairs and sofas in a miniature lobby — and would fit more appropriately in the crowded confines of Amsterdam. Some, indeed, have Dutch names. Don't shy away from these establishments if you want to stay in the middle of the downtown action, but in most cases, don't expect more than a modest room, either.

HOTEL ROYAL GARDEN, Calle Central, Avenida Central, P. O. Box 3493-1000, tel. [2]570022, fax [2]571517. 54 rooms. $51 single/$57 double. U. S. reservations: tel. 800-223-6764 or 212-758-4375. Exit San José, and enter the mysterious Orient through the front door of the Royal Garden. An elevator takes you to the second floor, where, at 9 a.m., Chinese music tinkles, curtains keep out all but thin shafts of daylight, and smoke floats over the blackjack tables. An unexpected milieu in Central America. Well-managed.

The restaurant features an extended *dim sum* (Chinese breakfast from carts of goodies), as well as American food. The casino functions 24 hours a day. Air-conditioned rooms have televisions, and are furnished in businesslike fashion, with plenty of Formica and vinyl surfaces. You can't get more central than this hotel. And never dull.

HOTEL PLAZA, Av. Central, Calle 2/4 (P.O. Box 2019-1000), tel. [2]571896, fax [2]222641. 40 rooms. $40 single/$52 double. Central location, restaurant and bar, carpeted rooms with television, some with balconies, others on air shafts with little light. Good closet space, and perfectly adequate, if anonymous.

HOTEL DIPLOMAT, Calle 6, Avenidas Central/2, tel. [2]218133. 25 rooms. $27 single/$38 double. A small, modern hotel. Rooms have phones, no other extras. Good value for downtown.

HOTEL AMSTEL MORAZÁN, Calle 7, Avenida 1 (P. O. Box 4192-1000), tel. [2]224622, fax [2]333329. 56 rooms. $49 to $55 single/$58 to $68 double. U.S./Canada reservations: tel. 800-327-3573, 407-367-9306. Visa, Master Card Air-conditioned rooms in various sizes, all worn and dull, though less claustrophobic than in other downtown hotels. The place is well-run, and the restaurant, of no particular genre, is popular with residents, and reasonably priced. Good location just off Morazán Park.

HOTEL AMSTEL AMÓN, Calle 5, Avenida 11 (P. O. Box 4192-1000), tel. [2]224622, fax [2]333329. 75 rooms, 15 suites. $85 and up double. U.S./Canada reservations: tel. 800-327-3573, 407-367-9306. Visa, Master Card A sister hotel of the Amstel Morazán, just about to open. Though quite new, this hotel blends into the neighborhood with low-rise construction and detailing suggestive of the turrets and arches of the old Victorian houses nearby. Conference rooms, underground parking, casino, restaurant, bar, and shops.

HOTEL DON CARLOS, Calle 9, Avenidas 7/9 (P. O. Box 1593-1000 San José or Box 025216-1686, Miami FL 33102-5216), tel. [2]216707, fax [2]550828. 25 rooms. $46-$57 single/$57-$68 double. A remodeled mansion on a quiet street, decorated with pre-Columbian art pieces, modern sculptures, plants and knick-knacks in the patios and on the sun porch. Rooms are in several sizes, from quite small to comfortable, variously with single, twin and double beds. Some are loaded with antiques. Rates include light breakfast, and other meals are available. Television room, beverage service and gym equipment available. Management puts out an extra effort, and there is a dedicated repeat clientele here, so reservations are essential. They also have apartments in a separate building east of downtown, for about $350 per week.

GRAN HOTEL DOÑA INÉS, Calle 11, Avenidas 2/6 (P. O. Box 1754-1002), tel. [2]227443, fax [2]227553. 20 rooms. $60 single/$73 double. A very nicely restored large home. Rooms have hardwood furniture, ceiling fan, television, and textured wallpaper, but are just a bit musty. Bar, meals available. There is no particular action for tourists in this fringe commercial area, but if more centrally located hotels are full, you need not hesitate to stay here.

Other "overflow" hotels in restored older houses in this area, at about $50 to $60 double, include **LA GEMA**, 12 Avenida, Calles 9/11, tel [2]263047, and **MANSIÓN BLANCA**, 9 Calle, Avenidas 10/12, tel. [2]220423.

SAN JOSE GARDEN COURT, Avenida 7, Calles 6/8 (P. O. Box 1849-1002), tel. [2]554766, fax [2]554613. 68 rooms. $38 single/$51 double/$58 triple, including breakfast. U.S. reservations, tel. 305-871-6631 or 800-272-6654; Canada, tel. 800-463-6654. Visa, American Express, Master Card. What a pity. This fairly new hotel is a good concept in the wrong place. Rooms, in a multi-story brick section, have all modern conveniences, including air conditioning, television, carpeting, and even a bathtub.

The public facilities — a pool, self-service restaurant and lounge area — are in the open or under a huge industrial-type corrugated roof that lets the wind whistle through; and there are also a travel agency, protected parking, and assorted other services. But the immediate neighborhood is San José's "Bowery", where you wouldn't want to walk at night.

HOTEL LA GRAN VÍA, Av. Central, Calles 1/3 (P. O. Box 1433-1000), tel. [2]227737, fax [2]227205. 32 rooms. $55 single/$71 double. Visa, Master Card, American Express. The usual tiny lobby, but the air-conditioned, carpeted rooms, better-sized than elsewhere downtown, are a good value. Some have balconies for watching the action on Avenida Central. The restaurant serves a set lunch for about $5.

HOTEL ALAMEDA, Avenida Central, Calle 12 (P.O. Box 680-1000), tel. [2]236333, fax [2]229673. 52 rooms. $43 single/$52 double. Visa, Master Card, American Express. If you have to be near the noisy bus station and market area, this hotel is probably your best choice, though it's expensive for where it is, and a renovation has meticulously removed all traces of the Alameda's faded fifties charm. Facilities include a full-service restaurant with a few quite reasonably priced items.

HOTEL ROYAL DUTCH, Calle 4, Avenidas Central/2, tel. [2]221414, fax [2]333927. 27 rooms. $65 single/$80 double. Visa, Master Card. Suites with carpeting, television, air conditioning, and dark old furniture. Not a great area, but you get a lot of space.

HOTEL DORAL, Avenida 4, Calles 6/8 (P. O. Box 5530-1000), tel. [2]330665, fax [2]334827. 42 rooms. $29 single/$42 double. American Express, Visa, Master Card. A recently renovated hotel on a busy street, quite nice inside, with clean, light, cheery rooms, all with television, phone and tiled bathroom.

HOTEL TALAMANCA, Avenida 2, Calles 8/10 (P.O. Box 449-1002), tel. [2]335033, fax [2]335420. 56 rooms. $25 single/$33 double. U.S. reservations: tel. 305-925-2700. Located in the noisy bus terminal and market area. Some rooms have TV, 24-hour restaurant, bar, casino.

APARTAMENTOS LAMM, Calle 15, Av. 1 (P. O. Box 2729-1000) tel. [2]214920, fax [2]214720. 19 units. $39 single/$46 double/$62 for six. Small housekeeping units, each with one bedroom, living room with sofa bed and TV, and kitchen. Some units have three bedrooms, two bathrooms, terrace, and a larger kitchen. In a central location off National Park, near the Legislative Assembly. Discounts by week and month.

APARTOTEL SAN JOSÉ, Avenida 2, Calle 17/19 (P. O. Box 4192-1000), tel. [2]224622, fax [2]333329. 12 units. $48 single/$55 double/$61 triple with one bedroom, $77 for four persons in two bedrooms. Located across from the National Museum. U. S. reservations 407-367-9306. Visa, Master Card. Similar to Apartamentos Lamm, in a more commercial area with traffic noise.

HOTEL PARK, Avenida 4, Calles 2/4, tel. [2]216944. 16 rooms. $37 for one bed, $45 for two beds. A modest hotel, run by Americans who appear to know what their clients want. Three "suites"— more attractive wood-panelled rooms out back, facing the light well — go for higher rates. This is a man's world.

Smaller Moderate Hotels - Downtown
HOTEL SANTO TOMÁS, Avenida 7, Calles 3/5, tel. [2]550488, fax [2]223950. 20 rooms, all with private bath. $42.50 and $55 single/$47.50 to $65 double, including breakfast. The Santo Tomás has matured in just a few years into one of San José's finer small hotels, impeccably kept, with a well-trained staff willing to help guests in every way possible from the moment of arrival, down to making hotel reservations throughout the country and arranging day trips and car rentals.

Guest rooms in this classic coffee planter's house, all different, have been thoroughly updated. Most have fourteen-foot ceilings, skylights, and convection ventilation, some have extensive tongue-and-groove wood-work, and all have one or two good queen-sized beds, huge dressers

(reproductions), phones, and modern tiled bathrooms, some with tubs. Art work and plants decorate guest rooms and all public areas. The patio-bar, where the buffet breakfast is served, is open to hotel guests until 10 p.m., and is one of those nooks where travellers naturally come together to exchange experiences, advice and tall tales. A cozier television nook is available upstairs. Security is excellent, laundry service available by weight.

HEMINGWAY INN, Calle 9, Avenida 9 (P. O. Box 1711-1002 San José), tel. and fax [2]225741. 9 rooms. $35 single/$55 double/$70 triple/$75 in suite, including breakfast. Guest rooms in this updated house are on the smallish side, but tastefully furnished and quite comfortable, with narrow beds, television, ceiling fan, wood floors, room safe, and a modern tiled bathroom with electrically heated shower behind a pocket door. One larger room has a canopy bed.

So what's the Hemingway connection? Rooms are variously named Steinbeck, Kerouac, etc., and, like many houses in the Amón neighborhood, this one would not be out of place in Key West. (With all this affection for Am. Lit., the owners are a Tica and a Frenchman.) Continental breakfast is served on the patio. Good value for attractive lodging near downtown.

LA AMISTAD INN, Avenida 11, Calle 15, tel. [2]211597, fax [2]211409. $25 to $35 single/$35 to $45 double. A German-operated bed-and-breakfast, in yet another restored house. Good mattresses.

HOTEL REY, Avenida 7, Calle 9 (P. O. Box 7145-1000 San José), tel. and fax [2]331769. 13 rooms. $40 single/$58 double, including breakfast. Credit cards accepted. Next to the National Insurance Institute office tower, this is a freshened-up large house. The lobby is a large, glassed-over patio, light and cheery. Carpeted rooms have two single or one large bed, television, tiled bathroom with shower, and good closet space. Free parking is provided, and the price is fair for what you get.

DOÑA MERCE BED AND BREAKFAST, 14 Avenida, Calles 13/15 (P. O. Box 3660-1000), tel. [2]231582, fax [2]331909. $35 single/$60 double. Small bed-and-breakfast operated by a retired Costa Rican couple, on a quiet street not far from downtown.

Budget Hotels

For San José, I'll call "budget" hotels that charge $40 or less double, or slightly more, if they give you good value. Budget rooms are generally small. Note that if there are more than three compatible people in your group, you can often do just as well pricewise by staying in a moderate hotel and paying a small extra-bed or extra-person charge.

HOTEL CACTS, Avenida 3 Bis, Calles 28/30 (P. O. Box 379-1005), tel. and fax [2]218616. 38 rooms. $31 single/$35 double, $50 in the newer

section, with breakfast. It's hard to call this a budget hotel when you get so much for your money: quiet location just a few blocks from Paseo Colón, cable and satelliteTV in the lobby, buffet breakfast of tropical fruits and breads included in the rate, beverage service, congeniality, even secretarial services if you need them. Rooms are simple and adequate and absolutely spotless. Family owners are around to help with everything from luggage storage to laundry trip planning and in-country reservations. Airport transportation is available, and the place is secure.

If the Cacts is full, the folks here will act as a travel agency and try to find a room elsewhere in your price range.

HOTEL RITZ and **PENSIÓN CONTINENTAL,** Calle Central, Av. 8/10 (P. O. Box 6783-1000), tel. [2]224103, fax [2]228849. 26 rooms. $10 to $23 single/$15 to $25 double. A modest, clean, Swiss-run establishment, created by joining and renovating and brightening two formerly separate establishments. The cheaper rates are for smaller rooms downstairs, sharing bathrooms. Breakfast only served, coffee on the house, reading area. Clients report they are satisfied.

HOTEL GALILEA, Av. Central, Calles 11/13, tel. [2]336925, tel. [2]231689. 23 rooms. $28 single/$35 double. Modern and plain, a few blocks from the center of town, not an attractive area, but a good value if you get a room that doesn't face the street.

PENSIÓN DE LA CUESTA, Avenida 1, Calles 11/15 (No. 1332), tel. 552896. $25 single/$35 double. You'll find a comfortable, homey atmosphere in the rooms in this venerable wooden house.

HOTEL FORTUNA, Avenida 6, Calles 2/4 (P. O. Box 7-1570), tel. [2]235344, fax [2]232743. 24 rooms. $27 single/$30 double. Visa, Master Card. Newer than most hotels in this area (c. 1958), with hot water, private bath, phones in rooms.

HOTEL BIENVENIDO, Calle 10, Avenidas 1/3 (P. O. Box 389-2000), tel. [2]211872. 44 rooms. $15 single/$19 double/$24 triple. This hotel is good news for budget travellers. A former movie theater has been renovated and recycled, with skylights and light wells making a massive building surprisingly cheery. Rooms have twin beds with attractive spreads, tile floors, central hot water in private bathrooms, open wire shelving and storage units — altogether better than what you get in some mid-range hotels. Public areas have plants, a coffee shop, ice machine, TV area, and decorative details retained from the building's former incarnation. A serious drawback is a location in the Central Market area. Get a room that does not face the street, or look elsewhere.

PETIT HOTEL, Calle 24 no. 39, tel. [2]330766. 12 rooms. $22 to $24 single, $24 to $40 double. A converted private home, with no-frills rooms far more ample and light and airy than at budget hotels downtown. Excellent location one-half block south of Paseo Colón, within walking

distance of most intercity buses. Friendly, use of kitchen permitted. The lower rates are without private bath.

POSADA TROPICAL, located across Colón from the Petit, the hotel is found behind the Mordisco restaurant and upstairs. Sleeps 34 persons in lockable louvered cabinets. No kidding. (34 times $13 per head equals $442, less cost of included breakfast. Not a bad take.)

COSTA RICA INN, Calle 9, Avenidas 1/3, P. O. Box 10282-1000, tel. [2]225203, fax [2]228385. 34 rooms. $25 single/$35 double. Visa, Master Card. Tidy and homey, on a quiet street near the city center. All rooms with private bath, and all suffering from the budget-hotel blues of San José: little light and ventilation. But there are always long-term visitors of all ages who have made this their home away from home, gathering to watch t.v. and drink coffee in the lobby. Rates slightly lower by the week.

CASA RIDGWAY, Calle 15, Avenidas 6/8, tel. [2]336168. $7 to $10 per person. Affiliated with a Quaker organization, this lodging house bills itself as "more than just a place to stay." It seeks to attract the ecologically minded, peace advocates, and those generally interested in social issues. Cooking facilities are available.

Other Budget Lodging

The above hotels are the best of the budget establishments in San José. Here are some others, which I mention without particular enthusiasm, because of what they are or where they are:

HOTEL COCORÍ, Calle 16, Avenida 3, tel. [2]330081. $15 single/ $20 double. I wouldn't want to stay in the noisy area near the bus station, but if you have to, this hotel is all right, of recent vintage, clean and secure. Rooms have private bath and hot water. There is no end of other places in which to bed down in this area, if you're not fussy.

HOTEL JOHNSON, Calle 8, Avenidas Central/2 (P. O. Box 6638), tel. [2]237633. 57 rooms. $14 to $17 single/$17 to $20 double. Your Central American businessmen hotel — dark, woody, soap operas on TV in the lobby, with families crowded around. Relatively large rooms with private bath. Bar, breakfast. Good value.

GRAN HOTEL CENTROAMERICANO, Avenida 2, Calles 6/8, tel. [2]213362. 50 rooms. $17 to $24 single/$30 double. Rank after rank of small rooms, no exterior windows, prison-like. Rooms with musty carpeting cost more.

HOTEL BOSTON, Avenida 8, Calles Central/2, tel. [2]216944. $15 double. Large, dark rooms.

A few blocks north, comparable hotels include **HOTEL CENTRAL,** Avenida 3, Calles 4/6 ($12/$15, telephone in room, private bath) and **HOTEL CAPITAL,** Calle 4, Avenidas 5/7, German-managed.

HOTEL ASIA, Calle 11, Avenidas Central/1, tel. [2]233893. $7 single/$10 double. Simple, with tiny rooms and little light, but clean. Chinese-run, as you might guess. Upstairs.

HOTEL ASTORIA, Avenida 7, Calles 7/9 (no. 749), tel [2]212174, fax [2]218497, has 12 bare but clean rooms at $12 single or double sharing bath, $24 with private bath.

Eastern San José Hotels

Eastern San José is carbon monoxide alley, where, for a good part of the day, buses, trucks and cars back up as they try to get into or out of town along Avenida Central. Nevertheless, there are some attractive accommodations in the middle- and upper-class residential districts out this way. Hotels away from Avenida Central are preferable.

TORUMA YOUTH HOSTEL, Avenida Central, Calles 31/33 (P. O. Box 1355-1002), tel. and fax [2]244085. A neoclassic tin-roofed mansion, right on Avenida Central. You stay in dormitories, and have access to laundry service, game rooms, and the special atmosphere of a younger, international crowd. Some food service. $5 or so with international youth-hostel card, breakfast included, more if you're not a hosteler. Front door open from 6 a.m. to 11 p.m. Call before you go out to check on available space. If you have an IYHF card, you'll get a discount at affiliated private accommodations throughout the country.

APARTOTEL LOS YOSES, Avenida Central, Calle 43 (P.O. Box 1597-1000), tel. [2]250033, fax [2]255595. 23 units. $46-$51 single/$54-$59 double. Visa, Master Card, American Express. Apartments in three sizes for up to six persons, with kitchen and utensils, protected parking, pool, sun area. Breakfast available. Also conference area.

HOTEL D'GALAH, P. O. Box 85-2350, tel. [2]537539. 16 units. $40 single/$48 double. Along the northern rim of the University of Costa Rica, and near the insect museum. The units here are somewhat harsh, with concrete surfaces, and there's noise from roaring buses. But the value is good, especially for families. Some units have a sleeping loft as well as a bedroom and kitchenette. A pool and sauna are promised for the near future.

HOTEL DON PACO INN, Avenida 11, Calle 33, tel. [2]349088, fax [2]349588 (800-288-2107 in U.S.). 10 rooms. $51 single/$56 double with breakfast. A small Spanish-Mediterranean style hotel in a quieter area of San José.

Hotels West of San José

HOTEL MIRADOR PICO BLANCO, P.O. Box 900-1250, Escazú, tel. [2]281908, [2]283197 (local), fax [2]395189. 25 rooms. $40 single/$46 double. U.S. reservations, tel. 916-862-1170 (Mr. Alcock). Visa, Master Card. The Pico Blanco, several white-walled buildings along a cobbled drive, is a hilltop village in itself. Flocks of scarlet macaws flutter from tree to tree. The views of the Central Valley, available from all rooms and public areas, are strictly skyscraper-quality. Decoration is both native, with tropical plants and wicker furniture, and English-pub-style, reflecting the owners. Rooms are attractive, finished with imported tile, and the mattresses are excellent. A couple of cottages are available as well, each with two bedrooms and small sitting room, at just slightly more than the room rate.

The indoor-outdoor terrace bar and restaurant, with trained German chef, are open until midnight for both guests and the general public, with musical entertainment on Friday evenings. Other facilities are a pool, several acres of gardens, and buses for spontaneous tours for guests. About 1.5 kilometers from the plaza of San Antonio de Escazú, in the hills to the southeast. The owner of this fine establishment is currently developing another lodge, on the slopes of Barva volcano.

POSADA PEGASUS, P.O. Box 370-1250 Escazú, tel. [2]284196) is more lodge-like, a large private house with porch, and a slice of the same view available from the Pico Blanco. $40 double.

TARA RESORT HOTEL, P. O. Box 1459-1250 Escazú, tel. [2]286992, fax [2]289651. 30 rooms and suites. $100 single/$155 double, more in suites. Credit cards accepted. Y'all can't miss this white antebellum mansion on a slope above San Antonio de Escazú. Drive through the white gates to the portico, and make your entrance. Beyond the high ceilings, polished hardwood and tile floors, cupola, tropical wood detailing, and chandeliers (all elegant, graceful, and impeccably maintained), are porches with million-dollar views to San José and the Central Valley.

Each suite is individually named ("Lady Ashley Suite," "Scarlet Suite," etc.) Out on the grounds are another 18 rooms in nine hexagonal cottages, and pool and tennis court. Amenities and services include courtesy airport transportation, continental breakfast, champagne on arrival, exercise room, sauna, whirlpool, satellite television, meeting facilities. Children under 12 not accepted.

Luxurious suburban garden apartments are available at **APARTOTEL MARÍA ALEXANDRA,** Calle 3, Avenida 23, San Rafael de Escazú (P. O. Box 3756-1000 San José, tel. [2]281507, fax [2]285192, 14 units, $135 triple), a block off Escazú's main street in a pleasant residential neighborhood. Units have washing machines, air conditioning, and cable television, and the complex includes a pool and sauna, bar, an excellent restaurant, and travel agency. The bus to Escazú leaves from Calle 1, Avenidas 16/18, San José.

HOTEL BOUGAINVILLEA, Santo Tomás de Santo Domingo, (P. O. Box 69-2120, San José), tel. [2]408822, fax [2]408484. 44 rooms. $70 single/$80 double. This hotel is out of the downtown core, with all comforts and impeccable service. The site is a large, elongated lot fronting on the cottage-lined main road of a suburban village set amid coffee plantations and orchards. At the street end is the three-story hotel building.

The remainder of the estate is covered with gardens, trails, pines, oxcarts and other local collectibles, and the pool and tennis courts. All rooms, with exposed beams of native woods, have two double beds, and balconies. Modern Costa Rican art hangs in the public areas. The food is quite good. The Bougainvillea is an appropriate choice if you'll be taking excursions, and have only a limited interest in San José proper.

HOTEL AMSTEL ESCAZÚ, (P. O. Box 4192-1000), tel. [2]224622, fax [2]333329. 14 rooms, 2 suites. $63 and up double, with breakfast. U.S./Canada reservations: tel. 800-327-3573, 407-367-9306. Visa, Master Card. A smallish hotel converted from a luxury private house, with pool, television lounge, bar. Air-conditioned, extensive gardens, facing one of the busiest streets in Escazú.

Bed and Breakfasts

Bed and Breakfasts are now a *movement* in San José. There are now scores of B&Bs in San José, the Central Valley, and, to a lesser degree, throughout the provinces.

Here's a sampling of bed-and-breakfasts, mostly outside the core area of San José (others are listed under downtown accommodations, above). In most cases, you'll have to take a taxi out, or arrange a pickup at a

WHAT'S UP DOC?

mutually agreed-upon landmark. Please, please, do not show up at any B&B without a reservation. Capacity is limited in every case, and because B&Bs represent such a good value, many are full or nearly full throughout the year.

THE VICTORIA INN, Moravia,tel. [2]402320, fax [2]211514 (P.O. Box 6280-1000, San José). $20 single/$30 double, suite $40 with breakfast. You can stay at this B & B without hesitation. It's a large residence, three blocks east of the town hall in Moravia, a middle-class suburb (opposite the Rincón Europeo restaurant). Two of the five guest rooms, in a separate apartment, have private baths, kitchen, a little garden and washing machine. In the main part of the house, with its huge greenhouse-style sitting area, wicker furniture, and plentiful plants and books, are additional guest rooms (two sharing baths), light and cheery, with lace spreads on the beds. Owners are helpful Tico-Americans. Essential to reserve.

PARK PLACE, P. O. Box 1012, Escazú, tel. and fax [2]289200. $35 double with breakfast. This is a modern bungalow with brick floors, basketry as decoration, wood panelling, and a high-ceilinged living room with huge glass windows. Views from the second floor are superb. There is some green space around the house, and there are trails through the forest reserve above.

The four guest rooms (two upstairs and two downstairs) each have one large bed, and a single bed may be added. Breakfast is self-serve, and other meals may be prepared by guests. Bus service right to the door is frequent from San José (sometimes a problem in the suburbs). The owner (none other than the personable Pat Bliss, one of the guiding lights of the bed-and-breakfast association) does not live on site, an arrangement that some visitors might prefer. Taxi directions: 1.5 kilometers south of Escazú church.

POSADA DEL BOSQUE, P. O. Box 669-1250 Escazú, tel. [2]281164, fax [2]286381. $49 double. This is a former plantation house in Bello Horizonte, a pretty area of old farms, pine and oak forest, and ponds, where you'll find some of the wealthiest residents of Costa Rica. The pastel yellow structure itself is not unknown to Costa Ricans—it was an arsenal for the forces of José Figueres, victor in Costa Rica's short 1948 civil war. And the owners of Posada del Bosque, Mr. and Mrs. Gilbert Aubert, aside from being Costa Rican (unusual in the B&B trade), can make their guests feel comfortable in English, Spanish, German and French.

The grounds are grassy and manicured, covered with citrus trees and Norfolk pines, and if you sit on the stone and tile terrace a while, you'll see the local horses and cattle wander in, an ox and cart straining up the road, a motmot flying into a tree. There are two play structure for kids. Inside, the seven guest rooms, more formally furnished than in most guest houses, each bear the name of a local bird species (in English and Spanish), and most have pleasing garden views. Each has a single and a double bed, huge bath, skylight, and wrought-iron sconces. The public area has a fireplace, clay tile floors, and cane ceiling. Breakfast includes mandarin juice from the garden, and yes, you can have gallo pinto and tortillas in the morning. A rowing machine and exercise bike are available to guests, and a mountain bike can be rented. Beverages are provided on a self-serve, honor bar basis.

Signs at all entrances to Bello Horizonte indicate the way to the Posada.

CASA DE FINCA 1926, Tres Ríos (P. O. Box 29-1000 San José), tel. and fax [2]256169. $75 double. As the name indicates, this was the great house of a coffee plantation, until urbanization replaced the coffee bushes with pleasant suburban bungalows on wide streets. But enter the compound of the house, stand in the formal front garden with its fountain and large trees, and you're back in those gracious days. The house itself, of stucco and wood, has tongue-and-groove wooden ceilings, encased archways, hanging plants, antique pieces, and old-style glazed tile floors. A substantial doll house recalls privileged children who once lived here.

The 11 rooms are all different, not as elegant as the public areas, but quite comfortable, with wicker furniture, and large bathrooms — some quite modern — with a shower or tub. Some units are panelled, others have interior gardens and private open-air showers. Breakfast is an assortment of fruits, juices, coffee and breads, and special plates can be prepared with advance notice. German, English and Spanish are spoken. The owners also operate Villa Serena, the intimate beach hotel at Junquillal on the Pacific.

VILLA ESCAZÚ, P. O. Box 1401-1250 Escazú, tel. and fax [2]289566. $35 single, $45 double, $60 triple. Here's a shiny house that might have been transferred from the alps, complete with panelling, stone fireplace, and cathedral ceiling. (In Escazú, the houses are *not* all alike.) Extensive gardens on the surrounding hillside, terraced down to a stream, contain flowers, pines, and 50 varieties of fruit trees — all indicators of good birding — as well as a croquet pitch. Four guest rooms each have twin or queen beds.

Full breakfast is served on a terrace, a barbecue is available, and dinners can be prepared on request. Three blocks from town church and bus stop of San Antonio de Escazú.

The Bed and Breakfast Association

The above are some of the B&Bs that I've looked at in person. But there are many more which belong to the **American Bed and Breakfast Association**. This is an organization that includes establishments with from three to ten guest rooms. Since they are private homes, rather than hotels, you won't find most of them on official lodging lists. On the other hand, members agree to adhere to certain standards, which cover cleanliness, the variety of guest towels, dishes and cutlery, and many other banal and fine points that are ignored in more standard Costa Rican lodging, so I think that you can try most of the member lodging-places without trepidation.

The Bed and Breakfast Association operates a central clearing house and referral system, based at **Park Place B&B**. Call or fax them at 289200 or 234157 between 10 a.m. and 2 p.m., daily except Sunday, or write to P. O. Box 1012, Escazú, Costa Rica. To the degree that they are able, they'll place you in a suitable home-away-from-home for the duration of your visit, or for part of it.

Once you enter the bed-and-breakfast network, you can pretty well be taken care of for your entire stay in the country, with referrals to lodging places and compatible people along your route.

Here are some additional B&Bs in the San José area. For more details, either call the B&B directly, or the Bed and Breakfast Association. Except as indicated, only English is spoken. ("Spanish spoken" usually indicates a Costa Rican rather than a foreign owner.)

CASA DE LAS TÍAS, Escazú (P. O. Box 295-1200, San José), tel. and fax [2]285517. $55 double. Credit cards accepted, free airport pickup with reservation, Spanish and French spoken.

COSTA VERDE INN, P. O. Box 89-1250, Escazú, tel. and fax [2]284080. $58 double, less from May through October. No need to call — when they have space, they send a temptress to greet incoming passengers at the airport.

CENTER FOR CREATIVE ARTS, P. O. Box 597, Santa Ana, tel. [2]828769, fax [2]826959. $25 double. Yoga, arts, and alternative health care emphasis.

PARVATI INN, P. O. Box 20-1250, Escazú, tel. [2]284011. Owners are vegetarian yoga teachers. Spanish spoken.

ROXANA'S BED AND BREAKFAST, P. O. Box 1086-1100 Tibás. $30 double.

HOMESTAYS

For more bed-and-breakfast listings, see "Country Lodging," at the end of the next chapter.

The above are "dedicated" country-style B & Bs, in which the whole household often functions around the bed-and-breakfast business.

Arrangements can also be made to stay in spare rooms in private homes, where families are living working and workaday lives, by

• consulting newspaper ads,

• by making living arrangements through a language school (in which case nobody will speak much English). This is one of the more inexpensive routes to take. See language-school listings, pages 76-77.

• by using specialized agencies. One such is **Bells' Home Hospitality**, P. O. Box 185-1000, San José, tel. [2]254752, fax [2]245884 (in the U.S., Dept. 1432, P.O. Box 025216, Miami, FL 33102-5216). Rooms are available through Bells' in over 50 private homes in the San José area, at a rate of $35 single or $50 double, including breakfast. The agency provides detailed directions, and can arrange airport pickup. Plans are afoot to make rooms available throughout the country. Write or call for a pamphlet describing the homes and the families with which you can stay. Another agency with higher rates and add-on "booking fees" is **Costa Rica Home and Host**, 2445 Park Ave., Minneapolis, MN 55404, tel. 612-871-0596, fax 871-8853.

More Choices

There are other hotels than those listed above, in outlying areas, some of them very attractive. But I think that most first-time visitors will want to stay near the central area of San José, and my listings are slanted accordingly.

For longer visits, consult the ads for guest houses and furnished apartments and houses in the Tico Times. But be warned that furnishings and facilities will often look cold and harsh to outside eyes. For starters, **PAUL VIGNEAULT** (P. O. Box 7046-1000 San José, tel. [2]263775, fax [2]264693) has a couple of houses with garages for rent in San Francisco de Dos Ríos, for about $150 per week.

Country Lodging Near San José

If you have a rental car, or don't mind travelling by taxi or local bus (neither of which is challenging or expensive in Costa Rica), there are some attractive and even superb lodging places in the Central Valley to consider. All are less than 30 minutes from the very center of San José, yet provide an atmosphere considerably removed from that of the capital. I've grouped listings of country hotels and inns at the end of the next chapter, starting on page 219.

Trailer Park

The only trailer park currently operating near San José is in San

Antonio de Belén, eight kilometers west of the city, not far from the airport. Take the San Antonio turnoff from the Cañas expressway, then continue two kilometers to the entrance, opposite the Seaboard Marine depot— there is currently no sign. This is a pleasant parking area with lots of trees, though facilities are limited. Rates are under $10 per day. Telephone 412270 or 412595.

WHERE TO EAT

Some very good food, indeed, is to be found in and near San José. Numerous restaurants specialize in Swiss, Central European, Spanish, French, Italian and Chinese cuisine, as well as steaks and seafood. There are many clean, reasonably priced luncheonettes, and a very few restaurants even serve native Costa Rican specialties.

The best chefs take advantage of the beef, fish (usually corvina, or sea bass), chicken and fresh fruits and vegetables that are abundant at all times of the year. Shrimp and lobster are usually available and are attractively served in a number of restaurants, but are no bargain — that innocent shrimp appetizer suggested by your waiter will usually run well over $10. Drinkable wines and imported liquors are quite expensive — double or triple the American price — so you might want to consider the excellent Costa Rican beers or local rums and other spirits.

Most restaurants open for lunch from 11:30 a.m. to 2:30 p.m., and for dinner from 6:30 or 7 p.m. to 10 or 10:30 p.m. Luncheonettes ("sodas") and many of the inexpensive restaurants are open throughout the day. A good hour for dinner in San José is 7:30 p.m. or so.

Some of the better dining places are open in the evenings only. But at those that serve lunch, you'll often find an all-inclusive special for about the same price as a main course alone. Look for the *almuerzo ejecutivo*.

My selection of restaurants is mostly limited to the downtown and Paseo Colón areas, near the major hotels. Also take a look at the restaurants mentioned under hotels, above.

But don't limit yourself to these. There are many more good choices, both in central San José and in the suburbs. Consult the ads and the "On the Town" column in the *Tico Times*, and the reviews in *Costa Rica Today*.

Or walk into any place that looks attractive. You generally don't have to worry about the safety of the food.

Downtown

CHALET SUIZO, Avenida 1, Calles 5/7. The Swiss Chalet is nicely atmospheric, with wainscotted walls, wooden beams, brick hearth and costumed waiters. The house steak, covered with ham and cheese, is excellent, and there are fondues, goulash, smoked pork chops, seafood items, fine French and Italian desserts, and much more. Most main courses run $5 to $7, the inclusive lunch $5.

ISLE DE FRANCE, Calle 7, Avenidas Central/2. An excellent little French restaurant. Not at all cheap for San José, but moderate as French restaurants go. A daily complete lunch goes for about $10. Generally available are paté maison, tournedos, Vichyssoise, rich soups, and sea bass and rabbit dishes, some appearing on the regular menu, others as daily specials. Most main courses are $10 and up, shrimp and lobster dishes are as high as $25. Open weekdays for lunch and dinner, Saturday for dinner only, closed Sundays.

CASINO ESPAÑOL, Calle 9, Avenidas Central/2. The gastronomic tour continues with fine Spanish cuisine. Specialties are quail in wine, tripe, Asturian fabada (stew), and paella. Elegant atmosphere and service. Entrees $6 to $10, fixed-price lunch for $5.

For more formal but still friendly Spanish food, turn the corner to **GOYA**, Calle 1, Avenidas 5/7. Rabbit in wine, beef with mushrooms, paella, $6 to $9 for a main course, tablecloths, arches and atmosphere included.

West End

LA MASIA DE TRIQUELL, Avenida 2, Calle 40. Spanish and Continental cuisine in a large old house with plenty of arches and stuccoed walls. Paella, sea bass in bearnaise sauce and steak in garlic sauce starting at about $10.

LA BASTILLE, Paseo Colón at Calle 22, is a fine French restaurant, the oldest in San José, where food preparation is painstaking. Assorted soups such as consommé with sherry, appetizers like caviar, and classic beef preparations as a main course: stroganoff, filet mignon, tenderloin provenáal in Café de Paris sauce; also sea bass in an interesting wine sauce with apples, grapes and peaches. $15 and up.

LA PIAZZETTA, Paseo Colón, Calle 40, features a long list of specialties from the regions of Italy. This means not only familiar and exotic pastas, but assorted dumplings, bean dishes, and delicately cooked steaks and fish in sauces composed variously of cheese, mushrooms and truffles. From about $12, closed Sundays.

Also serving elegant Italian cuisine, but with more familiar fare, such as lasagne and fettucine, is **EMILIA ROMAGNA**, Paseo Colón, Calle 32/34, tel. [2]332843. The setting is one of brick arches and plants, and the elegant sustenance is accompanied by breads and flavored butters (salmon and garlic-coriander, among others) prepared on-site. About $20 and up for a meal. Jazz is played every night from 8 p.m. (minimum two drinks).

BEIRUT, Avenida 1, Calle 32. Your classic neighborhood Lebanese eatery, anything but elegant, but clean and pleasant. You eat in one of several rooms in an old wooden house. Kibbeh, kabba, schawarma, kebabs and combinations thereof, for $5 and up. Lebanese food is always good. Closed Monday, lunch only on Sunday.

MACHU PICCHU, 32 Calle, Avenidas 1/3, opposite the Beirut, emphasizes Peruvian staples: seafood, potatoes, and corn. Main courses, such as sea bass in wine or with garlic sauce, picante de mariscos (a sort of seafood casserole with garlic, onion, cheese and olives — excellent!) cost $3 to $6, and can be supplemented with appetizers like stuffed potatoes or ceviche (seafood cocktail) for a dollar or two; though, as elsewhere, the giant shrimp will lighten your wallet. The decor is nautical, with nets and turtle shells, and the cooking and atmosphere are more home-style than elegant.

The GRANO DE ORO, the hotel in a restored mansion at Calle 30, Avenidas 2/4, serves light items on a glassed-in porch and out on the patio, from noon to 10 p.m., among them chicken, lasagne, quiche, "enchilada pie," and attractive salads. This is a good place to decompress from any urban hassles.

ANTOJITOS CANCUN, Paseo Colón, Calles 24/26, next to Pizza Hut, downstairs, has Tex-Mex tacos, enchiladas and burritos in assorted combinations for $2 to $6, and all the beer you need to wash it down. Kiddy seats available.

LOBSTER'S INN, Paseo Colón at Calle 24. Good seafood. Lobster and shrimp are expensive — $20 — but sea bass (corvina) is reasonable at under $10, served in a variety of ways, and there are continental main courses — beef in sauces, veal cordon bleu, chicken chasseur.

ANA, Paseo Colón, Calles 24/26. An unpretentious and inexpensive Italian restaurant serving lasagna, spaghetti, veal and non-Italian dishes for $4 and up. Pleasant surroundings, especially in the upstairs dining room.

A few blocks away, at the corner of Avenida 2 and Calle 24, PIZZERIA DA PINO serves all kinds of pizzas starting at $3, along with lasagna.

BEMBEC, just south of Colón on Calle 40, is an informal terrace-and-garden eatery and pastry shop. You sit at terrarium tables (literally - you'll see what I mean), and select from an unusually creative menu of fruit plates, salads, burritos, tacos, and items unique to the establishment. The montaditos are a hearty sandwich of beans and cheese and assorted fillings between flour tortillas, topped by meat or chicken and salad — a sort of Central American variation on a Lebanese theme, original and delicious. As little as $4 for a light meal, more for the substantial daily specials, or with a large dessert, such as peach cake.

MORDISCO, Paseo Colón, Calles 22/24 (next to the Ríos Tropicales travel agency) specializes in food that is good for you—sandwiches of hummous, chicken or tofu, salads, vegetable paté, leek pie, fresh fruit drinks, and fruity mousses. A light meal costs about $5, and the open setting is attractive, but can be noisy.

ARIRANG, at Paseo Colón and Calle 38, in the Centro Colón building, is your standard Korean family restaurant. You're served various combinations of pork or beef or chicken with vegetables, or tempura, at formica tables. It's very good, and at $4 or so for a main course, the price is right. Open 11:30 a.m. to 2:30 p.m., and 5:30 to 9:30 p.m.

SODA PINTICO, in the same building as Arirang, on the ground floor, is a rare eatery in this neighborhood that serves Costa Rican-style food, in this case in luncheonette surroundings. Order gallo pinto with eggs, tacos, enyucados, cheese-filled gallos, or the daily complete lunch. It will be hard to spend more than $3. Just make sure you arrive by 4 p.m.

Chinese eateries are less plentiful in the west end than elsewhere in San José, but you'll find a couple on Calle 32 just north of Colón. **JARDIN FELIZ** has a Szechuan-style menu, with the likes of spicy chicken and vegetables for $4 to $6.

LOS RANCHOS, near the east end of Sabana Norte (just behind Burger King — go around the block) is currently the top-rated steak house in San José. Tender beef comes in assorted cuts with jalapeño or less exotic sauces, and a salad bar; and grilled chicken and seafood are available as well. $10 and up, set lunch about $6. Open for lunch, and from 7 p.m. for dinner, continuously on Saturday, to 9 p.m. on Sunday.

SODA TAPIA, Calle 42, Avenida 2, opposite Metropolitan Park. More a café than a soda, good for sandwiches and fruit salad at the outdoor tables.

West End Fast Food

There's a **McDONALD'S** on Calle 42, a couple of blocks south of Paseo Colón. **POLLO KENTUCKY** (Kentucky Fried Chicken) has an outlet at Paseo Colón, Calles 32/34 which, whatever its culinary virtues, is a common reference point for giving directions. **PIZZA HUT** is at Paseo Colón and Calle 28. The **BURGER KING** on Sabana Norte, a block west of the Hotel Corobicí, has a large children's play area with Ikea-style plastic balls.

West End Self-Service Joints

AUTO SERVICIO COLÓN, Calle 34, Avenidas Central/1, is a bar with a self-service food counter.

SAN JOSÉ 2000 is not a restaurant, but a shopping center in suburban Uruca. If you're staying at the Hotel Irazú next door, you'll find some good alternative eating here. **LA FUENTE DE LOS MARISCOS** offers seafood at prices much lower than elsewhere in the city: shrimp from $3 to $10, depending on the size, a combination dish for $4. **EL**

TAPATÍO, a Mexican restaurant and bar, serves several kinds of *mole*, tacos and burritos for about $5, accompanied by beer and recorded jazz. And there are a Chinese restaurant and a steak house. From the Paseo Colón area, it's a short hop by taxi or the Alajuela bus to San José 2000 along the Cañas expressway.

Hotel Dining

L'AMBIANCE, Calle 13 no. 949, in a restored mansion, has the most elegant dining room of any downtown hotel, in a garden-style setting. The service is attentive. Recent lunchtime offerings included tournedos dijonnaise, fettucine primavera and mahi-mahi with saffron au beurre blanc, at a reasonable $7 to $10, and there are sandwiches as well. Add a salad and dessert, or order seafood, and the tab will climb toward $15 or $20. Phone 226702 to reserve.

The **HOTEL DON CARLOS**, Calle 9, Avenidas 7/9, serves a daily lunch amid the plants in its pleasant courtyard patio. Choose from lasagne, pasta, or a Tico-style rice-and-beans-with-something for about $5, sometimes to the accompaniment of guitar music.

At the **HOTEL LA GRAN VÍA**, Avenida Central, Calles 1/3, the restaurant is a quiet, light corner up on the third floor. The lunch of the day goes for about $4, and there are assorted complete breakfasts for $3. This is a good place to eavesdrop on long-term foreign residents as they plot their projects.

Among other hotels, the **AMSTEL** (Avenida 1, Calle 7) is notable for quality preparation and presentation, though not originality. A complete dinner goes for about $12. Lunch, for $7 or so, can include such main courses as sea bass meuniäre or a Tico-style combination plate or chicken in fruit sauce. The **HOTEL VILLA TOURNÓN**, off the downtown beaten track, also has some fans.

Probably no city in the hemisphere has as many **Chinese** eateries for its size as San José. Chinese food generally runs in the medium price range. You pay extra for rice.

One of the better Chinese restaurants is the **NUEVA CHINA**, another is **EL AVE FÉNIX**, both in San Pedro (see below).

In the downtown area, a good choice is **FULUSU**, Calle 7, Avenidas Central/2. Spicy Szechuan-style dishes, large bowls of soup and assorted appetizers and steamed dumplings are served. Any main course is large enough to share among two persons. As little as $6 for a meal.

LUNG MUN, Calle 1, Avenidas 5/7, serves Tico-style food at its lunch buffet, for about $3. A la carte American and Cantonese food runs $4 to $6 for a main course. If you have a hankering for shrimp, you can get it in your chow mein here for much less than elsewhere.

Another good downtown choice, with both western and oriental choices (including Szechuan plates), and an extended *dim sum* breakfast, is the restaurant of the **HOTEL ROYAL GARDEN**, Calle Central and Avenida Central. Lunch costs just $5.

Two good Chinese restaurants are located on Calle 11, between Avenidas 6 and 8. **TIN JO** offers Gen. Hon's chicken (with cashews, served in bird's nest), sweet and sour pork and seafood dishes, as well as more ordinary Cantonese dishes, at $5 and up for a main course, $10 and up for large shrimp. Down the street, **DON WANG**'s specialties, such as diced chicken with peanuts and hot peppers, are spicier, and prices are reasonable.

LA HACIENDA, Calle 7, Avenidas Central/2, is one of many restaurants in San José specializing in charcoal-broiled steaks and chops. Mixed grills, steaks or luncheon specials for $8 and up. **KAMAKIRI** steak house, Calle 3, Avenidas Central/1, upstairs in the arcade, is more lively, with music. **LA ESMERALDA**, Avenida 2, Calles 5/7, is a lively, clean, cathedral-like, open-to-the-street establishment with strolling Mexican musicians. Steaks from $5, set lunches for $3 or less, including a beverage.

BALCÓN DE EUROPA, Avenida 9, Calles Central/1, is more than a restaurant, it's a tradition, recently moved to this location. The establishment, extremely popular, serves Italian-style meat main courses, such as scallopine, for $7. House wine, at $1.50 a glass, is more inexpensive than just about anywhere else in San José. The daily lunch special (example: veal in wine, soup, dessert), pastas and small pizzas cost about $5. Native combination plates are offered as well. For the price, the food is more attractively served than you might expect, and you get real vegetables, not just rice.

A charming hole-in-the-wall that also serves Italian food is **SAN REMO**, Calle 2, Avenidas 3/5, with house spaghetti, lasagne, and standard Costa Rican fare, with nothing over $5, including some shrimp dishes. Capuccino, pastries and breakfast are served as well.

You could spend weeks in San José and think that native-style food didn't exist. **LA COCINA DE LEÑA** (*The Wood Stove*), in the El Pueblo shopping center north of downtown, is one of a few places where you can enjoy home cooking. Tiny tables, piles of firewood, whitewashed walls, subdued lighting, and decorations of colorful enamelware and gourd beakers all re-create the atmosphere of a dark, smoky country kitchen. The menu — printed on a paper bag — is a lesson in traditional Costa Rican cooking. Some items: *olla de carne* (meat stew), *mondongo en salsa* (ox in tomato sauce), stuffed pepper or cabbage, *chilasquiles* (tortillas filled with meat), *pozol* (corn soup), and the old standby, *gallo pinto* (rice and beans). Most entrees are served with tortillas and beans, and run $4 to $6, or you can get the complete lunch special for $5. To get here, take the Calle Blancos bus from Calle 3, Avenidas 5/7.

Also in El Pueblo are **LANCER'S STEAK HOUSE,** which offers complete, low-priced lunches; and numerous other eating and drinking spots.

PAPRIKA, Avenida Central, Calle 31, in the back of a commercial building, with Swiss and Italian specialties (goulash, veal dishes and stuffed pastries) served in a homey environment: bare wooden tables with checked napkins, decorations of stained glass. $12 and up, about $8 for the inclusive weekday lunch.

Cafés

There aren't many of these, but two are reminiscent of Europe. The Parisien Café of the **GRAN HOTEL COSTA RICA**, Calle 3 at Avenida 2, provides sidewalk seating with a view to the national theater, the Plaza de la Cultura, and the continuing activity of vendors and buskers in the adjacent small park. A fine place for extended sitting, reading, or people-watching at any hour — it's open through the night. More elegant is the café across the street in the **National Theater** itself where, at marble-topped tables, surrounded by works of art and bathed in recorded chamber music, you can enjoy a sandwich and coffee for less than $3, or a luncheon special for slightly more.

Sodas

Sodas are San José's all-purpose coffee shops and diners, where in simple, soda-shop surroundings you can enjoy anything from a cup of coffee or a drink to a sandwich or a steak. The blue-plate luncheon special usually runs $4 or less with tax and service. Similar fare and clean surroundings are available at almost any soda in San José. Among them are:

SODA CENTRAL, Avenida 1, Calles 3/5. A hole in the wall with cheap sandwiches and drinks.

SODA PALACE, Avenida 2, Calle 2, on Parque Central. Good seats for watching the main square. Mainly drinks and sandwiches. A block to the east, the soda of the Melico Salazar theater, **La Perla**, at Avenida 2, Calle Central, offers Spanish items such as paella, as well as set lunches, and is open through the night for drinks and bocas.

RISAS, Calle 1, Avenidas Central/1, is somewhere between a soda and a restaurant/bar. *Ceviche* (marinated-fish cocktail), stews and steaks for $5 and up, fishburgers and American-style (large) hamburgers in several decorations for $2.50, and even meatball heroes are served. Open 11 a.m. to midnight.

Also somewhere in-between is **SPOON**, on Avenida Central, Calles 5/7, with light lunches and heavy desserts. About $5 for lunch with lasagna, a salad or the plat du jour, or $2 for something gooey with coffee.

CONFETTI'S, Avenida Central, Calle 15, is a modern and clean restaurant-bar along soda lines, good for a drink and a rest after a tour of the National Museum.

POLLO CAMPESINO, Calle 7, Avenidas 2/4, serves chicken roasted on a spit over a coffee-wood fire, and many a resident swears by the result. $2 gets you a quarter-chicken with tortillas and pickled carrots and chiles. Salad, fries and beer are available as well. Look for the red sign, just off Avenida 2. This is a cozy, informal, crowded hole-in-the-wall with a beer-barrel bar, and you'll probably think I've sent you to the wrong place. If somebody in your party doesn't like chicken, ask for the Chinese menu.

MANOLO'S, Avenida Central, Calles Central/2, a favorite of many long-time San José residents, is open 24 hours to serve whatever you like in whatever atmosphere you choose. Proceed no further than the open-to-the-street snack joint at ground level for greasy, finger-shaped Mexican donuts (*churros*) and a cup of coffee, then hurry on your way. Or stop for more than a few minutes on the balcony one flight up, for the lunch of the day ($3), Manolo's club-like special sandwich, croissants with orange cream, breakfast combinations, or something else from the extensive but not expensive menu (even a filet mignon weighs in at under $6), with quick, coffee-shop service.

For finer tastes, ascend a short staircase to yet another dining area, large and formal and overlooking the street through large windows, where sirloin tips and other formally prepared steaks and chops go for about $10 and up.

Fast Food

McDONALD'S, familiar and reliable, is at Calle 4, Avenidas Central/ 1. In addition to Big Macs and fries, they have refreshing iced tea with lemon. Be prepared for some sticker shock. Prices are somewhat higher than in the United States, and much higher than those of comparable products with local names. Another location is at Avenida Central, Calles 3/5, opposite the Plaza of Culture.

McDonald's clones include **HARDEE'S**, Avenida Central, Calle 1.

POLLO KENTUCKY (Kentucky Fried Chicken) has outlets at Avenida 2 and Calle 6 and Calle 1/Avenida 3. The colonel's lunch runs about $4.

ARCHI'S, Avenida Central, Calles 3/5, is a cross between McD's and the Colonel, serving two pieces of chicken and a roll for about $2.

BURGER KING and **TACO BELL** have outlets on Calle 5, Avenidas Central/2, opposite the tourist office, and there's another Burger King on Avenida 1, Calles 1/3. Taco Bell often has a daily special.

Last and not so fast is **PIZZA HUT**, serving pizzas, subs and spaghetti, at Avenida 1, Calles 3/5; and Calle 4, Avenidas Central/2. Six dollars and up for a large pizza, also salad bar.

Vegetarian

This is not an easily achieved style of eating in Costa Rica. Even your beans and rice are likely to contain generous amounts of lard.

SODA VISHNU, Avenida 1, Calles 1/3, is vegetarian, with fruit and vegetable cocktails, and an Indian-flavored lunch special for $2.

NUTRISODA, Avenida 2, Calle 3, downstairs in the arcade next to the Gran Hotel Costa Rica, is vegetable-oriented.

East of downtown is **DON SOL**, 7 Avenida B, no. 1347 (go up the east side of the Casa Amarilla, then a half-block east), with a complete lunch for a couple of dollars, and a la carte salads, fruit drinks, vegetable stews and pastries.

EL EDÉN, Avenida 5, Calles Central/1, has a daily lunch for $3, including soup and dessert, more bland than the fare at its counterparts.

Inexpensive Food

There are cheap eateries all around San José, including the sodas mentioned above. Almost any modern office building has a ground-floor luncheonette where clerical workers take a quick and affordable lunch. Additional choices:

Restaurant Poás, Avenida 7, Calles 3/5, is a jungle of palms, bromeliads, ferns, begonias, corkscrew vines, and parrots, with more natural life than you'll see on a bad-luck or rainy day in the wild. Blue-plate lunch specials go for $3 or less. Some, like *casado* (meat with cabbage and rice and beans) and *olla de carne* (stew) are home-style Costa Rican classics. Breakfast and dinner are served as well.

CANDILEJAS, Avenida 4, Calles 1/3, a cut above a soda, is usually crowded with secretaries having a budget meal at café-sized tables. Choose from native-style steak, casado, and the like for $3 and up, or the daily blue-plate special for only $2. Food is simple, but tasty.

PATTIE SUPREME, on Calle 9, Avenidas 6/8, opposite the Soledad Church, serves the Afro-Caribbean counterpart of the empanada, with a filling of meat, chicken or lobster, for as little as 50 cents.

For a whole array of cheap, inelegant eateries, hasten to the **CENTRAL MARKET**, Calle 6, Avenida 1, where you can fill your stomach with cabbage, rice, beans, eggs, and/or stew for $2.

Self-Service

The point-and-shoot method of ordering is useful if you're in a hurry, or if your Spanish produces unpredictable results.

CHIPS, on Calle 5 opposite the Plaza of Culture, is a step up from most fast-food joints, with lasagna, chicken, omelettes, salads, a changing assortment of specialties, and pizza; $4 and up for lunch, less for the daily special.

GOYA, Calle 1, Avenidas 5/7, **LUNG MUN**, Calle 1, Avenidas 5/7, both mentioned above, and sometimes other restaurants, have cafeteria set-ups at lunchtime where you can fill your plate for $3 or less.

KING'S, Avenida 1, Calle 3, has chop suey and Tico-style food, at $3 for a full meal.

Snacks

POPS, Avenida Central, Calles 1/3 (and just about everywhere else in San José) has the best ice cream in Costa Rica. From 5¢ for a cone.

PASTELERÍA SCHMIDT, Avenida 2 at Calle 4, sells excellent breads and pastries, which may be eaten in, with a cup of coffee, or carried out. Another location (among many) is at Avenida Central and Calle 11.

San José's ubiquitous fruit carts sell bananas and pineapple and papaya at almost every corner. At Christmas, they offer apples and grapes, which are great and expensive delicacies. And there are many hamburger and hot dog vendors as well.

Escazú Restaurants

Farther west, and south, in suburban Escazú, is the **EL CHURRASCO** steak house (tel. [2]289332, (*150 metros al sur del Centro Comercial Blvd. Rosa*). Look for a sign pointing the way from Escazú's main street. Here you get brick surroundings and pottery decorations. Steak comes in assorted cuts and sizes, draft beer is served, and there are salads and appetizers — and music on Friday and Saturday evenings. $10 and up. Drive, or take the Escazú bus from Avenida 1, Calles 16/18, San José.

The **MARÍA ALEXANDRA** restaurant, in the "apartotel" of the same name, nearby, is also excellent. Chef Hans, of durable fame, cooked for John F. Kennedy when he came to Costa Rica. The establishment is known for its fine sauces, and if you like shrimp, this is your best bet in the area.

ABACUS, on the main street into Escazú, serves cràpes of both the main course and dessert variety, the former with anything from roast beef to vegetables; and there are Tex-Mex items and desserts. About $6 and up.

LUCAS, an informal eatery in the same part of town, has Costa Rican-style items (tacos, casado combination plates), as well as more elegantly prepared steaks and fish, and also gets a crowd for beer, wine and elaborate desserts. About $9, less for the lunch special.

San Pedro/East End

This is not an area that most visitors get to on their first trip. But you'll go out this way to be near a university crowd, or if you visit the insect museum. If you're not already planning to be in the immediate area, call first to check if the restaurant is open.

LE CHANDELIER offers the finest continental dining in San José.

Meats and poultry are served in delicate sauces, vegetables are crisp, and service and presentation are faultless. On a visit here, I had one of the specials of the evening, breasts of chicken in morel sauce, which, aside from being delicious, was easily double the portion I would expect in Manhattan or Montreal. Paté, a cheese plate, and cookies come courtesy of the house. Regular items include Caesar salad for two, three tenderloins in café de Paris sauce, and sea bass quenelle. Le Chandelier's exterior is unpretentious, but the beamed ceilings, fireplace and rough-stuccoed walls inside suggest the *campagne*; additional seating is on the terrace. You'll spend at least $20 for dinner — it's worth it — but the tab can run much, much higher. From the traffic circle in San Pedro (Calle Central at the bypass highway), go south two blocks past Burger King, then west, then take the first turn south. Call [2]253980 to reserve.

The **NUEVA CHINA,** Calle 11, Avenida Central, San Pedro, is everybody's recommended Chinese restaurant. The decor and ambience are authentically oriental, right down to the imported tile. The menu has two sections, Chinese and "international" (if you want it). Peking duck can be prepared with a day's notice, but on a walk-in basis, you can try shrimp soup, garlic-honey chicken, or chicken Szechuan. Main courses come in two sizes, and run $5 to $12. Remember to order your rice separately if you want it. And insist on spicy if you like it that way. Chinese white wine is available. My fortune cookie: "*La prisa puede llevarle a cometer errores importantes.*" To reach the Nueva China, take the San Pedro bus from Avenida 2, Calles 3/5.

A bit nearer to downtown, **EL AVE FÉNIX**, on Avenida Central on the way into San Pedro, a block east of the traffic circle, gets high marks from many connoisseurs of Chinese cuisine.

Other good restaurants out this way include **LAS MALVINAS** (tel. [2]243131), a well-known seafood house farther down Avenida Central in Curridabat. **TEQUILA WILLY'S** (tel. [2]251014) serves Tex-Mex nachos, fajitas, enchiladas and the like in a wild decor. The locale is a large blue-and-white house, about two blocks east of La Nueva China.

Food With A View

The mountains that tower to the south of San José offer views that rate as Empire State Equivalents, and the rare opportunity to appreciate, from solid ground, vistas of valleys and towns and clouds clinging to peaks, or the nighttime lightscape of lights blazing across San José, and twinkling on up hazily discerned volcanic slopes. And you can enjoy the show to the accompaniment of some unpretentiously good food.

About five kilometers past San Antonio de Escazú (see page 193), on a winch-class road that loses its pavement, is **TIQUICIA**, an adobe, peasant-style house with terrace, where meats are cooked over wood and charcoal. For less than $10 you can have a combination plate or chicken and rice, with beer (not too much!). If you're driving, turn right at the Miramontes restaurant on the way up to San Antonio, then inquire for "Tee-KEE-sya" at every turn.

Above Aserrí (see page 191), on the road to Santa María de Dota, is **MIRADOR RAM LUNA**, a somewhat more formal establishment with the appearance, at first glance, of a small hilltop estate. Inside, the large dining area is glassed-in, with ferns and broadleaf plants providing a greenhouse air. A fireplace serves to burn off any chill at the 1825-meter altitude. Here you enjoy yet another slice of Central Valley view, along with excellent steak-house fare, reasonably priced at $5 and up for a main course. The Mexican-style sirloin, and steak stuffed with cheese and ham, are both good choices. Open for lunch and dinner every day.

If you're not driving, Ram Luna is easiest to reach by taking a bus to Aserrí, then a taxi.

BARS AND CLUBS

Drinking is a pastime that most Costa Ricans feel comfortable with, and the visitor, in turn, will feel comfortable in any halfway-decent-looking bar. All are reasonably priced, with domestic drinks for $1 or less. Bocas (snacks) are served on the side, sometimes at a price in the fancier establishments. Many of the downtown bars are good places to rendez-vous with other foreigners. Among them:

ESMERALDA, Avenida 2, Calles 5/7, mentioned above as a restaurant, is popular at night for drinking to a background of mariachi music.

MARLEY'S, Avenida 1, Calles 5/7, serves chili con carne and chili dogs, Virginia ham sandwiches, and good steaks, and keeps the television tuned to crucial games. Bocas are free from 4 to 6 p.m.

TROPICAL TINY'S, Avenida 2, Calles C9/11, heavy with red brick, is also screen-oriented.

NASHVILLE SOUTH, Calle 5, Avenidas 1/3 is your light-wood, down-home bar where serious music is played, and chili con carne and fried chicken are served.

DISCO TÚNEL DEL TIEMPO, Avenida Central, Calles 7/9, is a discotheque, not a bar, probably more to local tastes than yours, but centrally located.

Around the corner, the **BIKINI CLUB**, Calle 7, Avenidas Central/1, has pretty waitresses. There are some gay bars in this area.

RESTAURANT-TABERNA POÁS, Avenida 7, Calles 3/5, a budget eatery during the day, does double duty as a dance hall at night, a perfect locale for a jungle fantasy out of *El Grande de Coca Cola*. Venture among the palms, bromeliads, ferns, begonias, corkscrew vines, and parrots, and wiggle it.

CHARLESTON BAR, Calle 9, Avenidas 2/4 (opposite the church and around the corner from the gas station), is loaded with memorabilia of bygone days in another country. The bar at the **PARK HOTEL**, Av. 4, Calles 2/4, is a gathering spot for Americans and other foreigners on extended stays. The neighborhood is just a little bit seedy, but not in a dangerous way.

DISCO SALSA 54, Calle 3, Avenidas 1/3, is just what it sounds like.

TABERNA CAYUCO, Calle 11, Avenidas 1/3, is said to show videos of X-rated movies, a genre banned from cinemas.

KEY LARGO is at Calle 7, Avenida 3, on Morazán Park is a nice, old house, and also San José's most notable prostitute pickup point. The ladies and taxis line up outside.

BAR MÉXICO, Avenida 13, Calle 16, is a bright spot in a run-down neighborhood, painted on the outside in red, white and green, well-kept with polished wood tables in the arched interior. Marinated fish and snacks are served with the drinks, but the attraction is mariachi music. Open from 3 p.m., from 11 a.m. Saturday, closed Sunday. Walk from the Coca-Cola bus terminal area, or take the Barrio México bus from Avenida 2, Calles 6/8. Next to the bar is the neighborhood church, visible from many parts of San José, huge and multidomed on a bare, concrete utility-building base. Also out this way is the art-deco **LIVERPOOL BAR**, with live music in the evening, in assorted genres.

Boobs are the subject at **JOSEPHINE'S**, Avenida 9, Calles 2/4, tel. [2]572269, one of the few non-hotel clubs that put on a live dance show for dining guests. If bouncing breasts under diaphanous disguise are what you seek, you'll find them, along with steaks, chicken, and lighter snacks. Drinks are not overpriced, and putas are not visibly on the prowl, which makes for a wholesome and relaxed air at San José's premier nightclub presentation.

EL CUARTEL DE LA BOCA DEL MONTE, tucked away on Avenida 1 between Calles 21 and 23, east of downtown, is a lively, late-hours bar and native-style eatery. There are full meals of steak, tripe, and fish, with salad, bean soup, fried plantains and yuca, for $6 on *down*; but you'll mostly come for the difficult task of keeping up with the locals at drinking. There's live music on some evenings. The name recalls an early appelation of San José.

BROMELIAS, a couple of blocks away at Avenida 3, Calle 23, is a bar in a recycled and modernized section of the huge customs shed that handled cargo coming in on the now-defunct railroad.

EL YUGO DE ORO in Cinco Esquinas, just north of downtown San José, is a favorite late-hours place for many Ticos, who enjoy the *bocas* (snacks). But what snacks! — cannelloni gratinée, beef cordon bleu, assorted seafood, barbecued tidbits, all served free with drinks or available as menu choices for $7 and up. A mariachi band often plays till midnight, and there are luncheon specials. Any taxi driver can take you for $2 or less. Call [2]572088 to check if they're open.

In the west end, **GALLERY Y BAR SHAKESPEARE**, Avenida 2, Calle 28 (next to the Teatro Olivier), usually has guitar music or some other low-key entertainment in the evening. Cover charge of a couple of dollars.

For drinking and dancing, **EL PUEBLO** shopping center, mentioned above under restaurants, has numerous bars and *boâtes*, ranging from intimate to multi-level, as well as trinket shops for an evening of browsing in a pleasant mock-colonial environment. Take the Calle Blancos bus from Avenida 3, Calles 5/7, or a taxi.

Head east to San Pedro to find a university crowd near the University of Costa Rica.

CLUB COCODRILO, on Calle Central in San Pedro is a popular hangout, with continuous movies, flashing lights, videos, and a namesake over the huge bar.

TX, several blocks to the west on the same street, shows music videos and serves original near-lethal drinks.

The **BAR BALEARES**, a block west of the Mas x Menos supermarket, sometimes has reggae music, and provides chess boards and darts on demand.

LA VILLA, just over a block south of Banco Anglo, attracts a more serious crowd to enjoy movement music of the hemisphere, and inexpensive food and snacks.

HORA ZERO, a block in the opposite direction from Banco Anglo, serves inexpensive food to the accompaniment of sixties rock.

Men will feel comfortable at **CLUB MADRID**, a pool hall with cheap drinks, a block east and almost two blocks north of the San Pedro church. And women will feel comfortable nearby at **LA TERTULIA**, a feminist gathering point. Don't confuse your gender.

SEEING THE SIGHTS

San José does not have all that much in the way of obligatory sights to see. If your time is short, limit your rounds to the high points: the **National Theater** and **Plaza of Culture**, the **National Museum**, and the **Jade Museum**. These can be seen in a half-day, or between excursions to the volcanoes and countryside around San José.

At a more leisurely pace, you can cover the itinerary below, and get to know the city better, in a couple of days or more. Most of the places mentioned are within a half-mile or so of the Central Park.

Downtown and Vicinity

The Main Square

Any walking tour of San José starts at the **Parque Central** (the Central

Park, or main square), bounded by Calles Central and 2, and Avenidas 2 and 4. Bus after city bus stops and accepts the long queues of commuters along all four edges. Horns beep incessantly and traffic slams into gear and races ahead at the change of lights on wide Avenida 2. Office buildings and advertising billboards tower overhead.

The park is an oasis in all this, a neat, gardened square where workers on their breaks and anyone with a few moments to spare will sit on benches, pass the time of day, read a book, and, perhaps, engage the visitor in conversation about such favorite themes as Costa Rican democracy, Costa Rican economic problems, Costa Rican foreign policy, and Costa Rican women. Public concerts are offered on most Sunday mornings in this musically concerned city.

Across Calle Central from the park is the **Catedral Metropolitana** (Metropolitan Cathedral), one of the many undistinguished urban churches of relatively recent vintage in Costa Rica. Cream-colored, blocky on the outside, with neo-classical pediment and columns at the entry, the Cathedral has a massive, barrel-arched interior. Much more interesting is the ecclesiastical administration building attached to the rear of the Cathedral, done in the charming and disappearing nineteenth-century San José style, with a European face — in this instance stone-cased windows and pediments straight out of Renaissance Italy — and a red tin roof.

On the north side of the square, at the corner of Calle Central, is the restored **Melico Salazar theater**, a period piece of pre-depression tropical urban architecture, with fluted Corinthian columns, balconies, and stuccoed relief sculptures in the pediments.

National Theater

A couple of blocks down Avenida 2, at the corner of Calle 3, stands the **Teatro Nacional** (National Theater), which over the years has come to embody San José and its self-image as a cultural center. And with good reason, for a more impressive public structure is to be found in no city for a thousand miles to the north or south.

The construction of the theater came about in a fit of national pique, after an opera company cancelled a performance in San José in 1890, for lack of a suitable hall. In response, a cultural tax was levied on coffee exports, and later on all imports. The appropriate experts were engaged, and the theater was completed seven years after the insult.

Though sometimes advertised as a replica of the Paris or Milan opera, the block-long National Theater is neither, and stands on its own. Columns and pediment and window arches are carved into the massive stone blocks of its majestic Italianate neo-classical facade, which is crowned with allegorical statues of Dance, Music, and Fame (copies of the

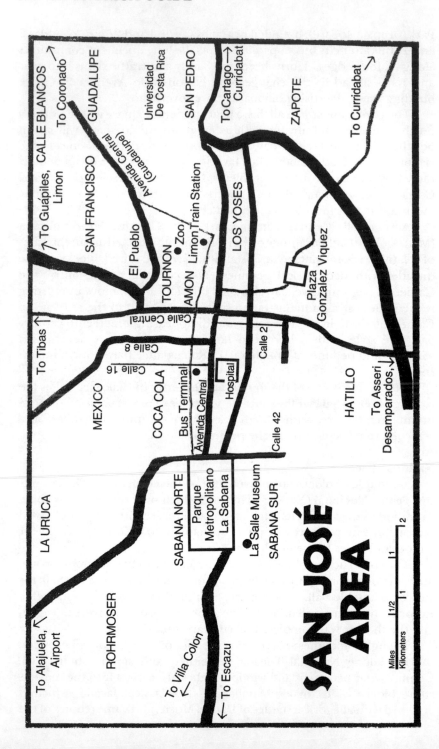

originals, which are protected from pollution elsewhere). The sides of the building are less elegant, faced with cement plaster, and the tin roofing is purely San José.

Astride the entrance to the theater stand statues of Beethoven and the Spanish dramatist Calderón de la Barca; in the vestibule are allegorical figures of Comedy and Tragedy. In the Costa Rican tradition of importing and assimilating Culture, these were executed by European masters. Belgians designed the building and fabricated its steel structural members. And Germans, Spaniards, and Italians collaborated on the architectural work and interior decoration. But Costa Rica is present as well. The sculpture called Heroes of Misery, in the vestibule, is the work of native Juan Ramón Bonilla; and the stairway paintings depict themes of Costa Rican life and commerce — coffee and banana harvest and shipment, and local fruits and flowers. The parquet flooring in much of the theater is made from native hardwoods.

Especially impressive inside the theater building are the foyer, upstairs, with its three-part ceiling painting representing Dawn, Day, and Night; the interior marble staircases; the gilt decorations throughout; and, of course, the multitiered great hall.

The National Theater is the locale of regular concerts by the national orchestra, which was transformed into a full-time professional and teaching organization in 1971, with the acquisition of a number of foreign musicians; and of performances by the youth orchestra, and native and foreign drama companies and artists. Tickets are sold in advance at the kiosk alongside the theater, for as little as $2. Admission for sightseeing costs about $1.

Opposite the entrance to the National Theater is a little park where vendors of handicrafts — model oxcarts, dolls, jewelry and leather— display their wares. Adjacent is the stately Gran Hotel Costa Rica, with its pleasant ground-floor café. There's another café in the theater itself.

Central Avenue

North of the theater, the stretch of Avenida Central for several blocks in each direction is a pedestrian mall, where vehicles are restricted or banned for part of the day. In place of cars, the avenue fills up with shoppers, along with buskers, and merchants of a hundred products and services that you weren't looking for, but which you will no doubt find useful. A great press mounted on a truck squeezes sugarcane for juice. Vendors peddle ices, and roast sweet corn, and flowers and toys and sunglasses and lottery tickets and shoe laces and fruit. Lamination of identification cards and engraving of jewelry and valuables are performed on the spot, for minimal fees.

Plaza of Culture

Along Avenida Central between Calles 3 and 5 is the **Plaza de la Cultura** (Plaza of Culture). The commercial buildings that once occupied the site were razed to create an open expanse decorated with flowers and benches, and platforms, where outdoor performances are sometimes given.

To preserve the broad vista to the adjacent National Theater, a complex of exhibit halls has been constructed *below* ground level. Foremost of the displays is the exquisite gold collection of the Banco Central de Costa Rica, with over a thousand pre-Columbian decorations, mostly from burial sites in the southern Pacific coastal region of Costa Rica. Also included are jade ornaments from Costa Rica and other countries. And there are pre-Columbian ceramics, modern art, and numismatic items as well. Currently open only from 10 a.m. to 5 p.m. Friday through Sunday.

Near the entrance to the exhibit area, at the corner of Avenida Central and Calle 5, is the information center of the **Costa Rican Tourist Board** (Instituto Costarricense de Turismo), where the personnel are quite helpful in answering questions, providing maps, schedules and brochures, and generally orienting the visitor. Hours are 9 a.m. to 5 p.m., Monday through Friday.

National Museum

Six blocks east of the Plaza of Culture, and up the hill known as the Cuesta de Moras, is the **National Museum** (Museo Nacional), housed in the old Bellavista Fortress, once the headquarters of the now-defunct army.

Of major interest in the museum is the pre-Columbian collection, one of the largest of its kind. All of the materials are shown quite logically, divided into the three major cultural zones of the country, and arranged chronologically for each. Many but not all of the exhibits are labelled in both English and Spanish, and a map helps to explain Costa Rica's importance as a meeting point of three cultural traditions.

It's fascinating to see in a few minutes the progress of pottery in the Nicoya region, over a period of more than a thousand years, from plain and primitive figurines to the exquisite polychrome vases in anthropomorphic form that were manufactured at the time of the Spanish conquest. In the Atlantic region, the figures are less sophisticated, in buff and brown, but no less beautiful. The Diquis region is represented by its own pottery styles, and by its fabled, near-perfect stone spheres, some of which are up to two-and-a-half meters in diameter. There are, as well, examples of goldwork, including pendants and pectoral discs, and jade from the northern half of Costa Rica.

The National Museum also has an extensive collection of colonial furniture; printing presses and historical imprints from the era of independence; period costumes; portraits of presidents and politicians; and a cellar of religious art, including saints in wood and plaster, vestments, and paintings executed over the period from colonial times to the present. An ethnohistory exhibit bespeaks a growing awareness by modern Costa Rica of multicultural contributions to national life. A geology exhibit illustrates tectonic plates, and explains the tremors you may feel from time to time.

Bellavista fortress itself is one of the few colonial-style structures in San José, dominating the central part of the city, massive, towered, gray and brusque on the outside, pocked by bullet holes from the 1948 civil war, but quite lovely from the inner gardened courtyard, with tile roofs, whitewashed walls, and covered passageways. All of the exhibit rooms have high, beamed ceilings. On sale at the museum shop are examples of Talamanca Indian weaving, bows and arrows, and gourd crafts, which are some of the best souvenirs available in San José. Inquire as well about museum-sponsored excursions to sight quetzals or sparking volcanoes.

The National Museum is open every day except Monday from 8:30 a.m. to 4:30 p.m. (Sunday from 9 a.m.) There is a small admission charge.

Plaza of Democracy

Across Calle 15 from the National Museum is the **Plaza of Democracy**, dedicated in 1989 to mark 100 years of popularly elected governments. Like the Plaza of Culture, this open area was created by demolishing houses and offices, replacing them with terraces and amphitheater climbing the hill, suitable for cultural activities, and, with the Legislative Assembly nearby, for political demonstrations as well. Just to the north across Avenida Central, the legislature is a cream-colored, Moorish-style building. You may go in the side door and look around, but it's all quite unprepossessing and uninteresting, except, perhaps, as an artifact of Costa Rica's rather un-Latin non-aggrandizement of its political institutions.

National Park

North of the legislature is **Parque Nacional** (National Park), one of San José's nicely landscaped shady squares. The city planners have gone in for tall trees that make for a wonderful cool shade in the middle of the day. The park's centerpiece is an allegorical statue depicting the five Central American nations in arms, driving out the American adventurer William Walker, who had installed himself as ruler of Nicaragua in 1856.

Across from the north side of the park is the **National Library** (*Biblioteca Nacional*), a modern and not particularly attractive airline-terminal sort of building, decorated with a splotchy mosaic of the sun.

There are exhibit areas inside.

A block east of the library, at Avenida 3, Calle 21, is the old, Victorian-style Limón train station, now a national monument and open to the public as the **Railroad Museum**.

Stop by to admire the impressive steam engine of the Northern Railway (as the line was called before nationalization) on a spur in front, and the collection of memorabilia inside. There are photos of old San José, as well. Hours are 9 a.m. to 3:30 p.m., 10 a.m. to 3 p.m. on weekends, with a small admission fee.

Northwest of National Park is the block-square compound that formerly housed the National Liquor Factory. Liquor is a big business in Costa Rica, in terms of the size of the country, and most of it is the business of a government-owned company. The site is being converted into a cultural center.

España Park

West of the liquor factory, between Avenidas 5 and 7, at 11 Calle, is **Parque España** (Park of Spain), also known as **Parque de la Expresión**, an enchanting little enclave of towering tropical trees transplanted from around the country. On Sundays, many of San José's artists display and sell their work here.

On the north side of Parque España, at Avenida 7 and Calle 11, is the modern office tower of the Instituto Nacional de Seguros, the government insurance monopoly. On the eleventh floor is the **Museum of Pre-Columbian Jade** *(Museo de Jade)*, open Monday through Friday from 9 a.m. to 3 p.m. The name of the museum is somewhat misleading, for the collection is comprehensive, with contemporary pottery, tools, weapons and dress of the surviving native peoples of Costa Rica; exhibits showing how jade and gold and stone were worked; and a fascinating assortment of utilitarian art, with such pieces as *metates* (grinding stones) in anthropomorphic form. Of course, there is much purely decorative art, including jade pendants and necklaces produced by cultures that have now been obliterated.

(The term *museo*, as used in this case and elsewhere in Costa Rica, can be misleading. Costa Rica's museums would be better called "collections" — small, often unithematic, visitable, and leavable, quite unlike monumental warehouses elsewhere which are impossible to appreciate on a single visit.)

The jade museum also offers from its high perch some excellent views of San José and environs — to the north and the volcanoes from the lounge, and to the south and the city center from the vestibule. The first building visible to the south is the **Edificio Metálico** (Metal Building), an unusual structure designed in France by Victor Baltard, architect of Les

Halles. Incongruous and green-painted, with rusting roof panels, the Edificio Metálico was one of the first of the pre-fabs, shipped in pieces from Europe. It's now used as a school.

Across Calle 11 from the insurance building is the attractive, Spanish-style **Casa Amarilla**, which houses Costa Rica's foreign ministry.

North of Parque España is **Barrio Amón**, one of the more traditional neighborhoods of San José. Here are large, older homes in wood, decorated with fretwork and crowned with steep tin roofs; and stuccoed brick homes with Renaissance and baroque elements, sometimes painted in pastel colors. See this tropical wedding-cake architecture while you can. Construction in San José has slowed down with the economic problems of recent years, but these buildings are sure to disappear.

The Zoo

At the northern edge of downtown is **Parque Zoológico Simón Bolívar** (Simón Bolívar Zoological Park). Follow Calle 7 north, then Avenida 11 east to the entrance. Here are turtles, monkeys, macaws, peccaries, vultures, jaguars, alligators, ducks, and much else brought from all parts of Costa Rica to a rain forest planted in the middle of the city, complete with palms, bromeliads and aromatic plants. The zoo is well worth a visit if you have even a mild interest in the wildlife of Costa Rica. Also here is an information center for the national parks where publications are on sale. Bolívar Park is open Tuesday through Friday from 8:30 a.m. to 3:30 p.m., weekends and holidays from 9 a.m. to 4:30 p.m., with a small admission charge.

South of the zoo, back in the central part of the city, is **Parque Morazán**, divided by heavily trafficked Calle 7 and Avenida 3 into four separate gardens. The nicest is the Japanese-style northeast section, with ponds, a temple-like gazebo, little bridges, and a kids' playground. The structure at the center of the park is the Temple of Music, another of San José's tributes to the finer things.

Watch your wallet or your purse in this area — pickpockets abound.

Snake Museum and Other Points of Interest

On Avenida 1, between Calles 9 and 11, is the **Serpentario** (Serpentarium), another of San José's manageable mini-museums, or collections. Here you can encounter several dozen snakes, (among them a copperhead, jumping viper, bushmaster, boa constrictor, black cobra, parrot snake, and the star of the show, a python 5.3 meters long), in circumstances benign rather than frightening, fully labelled in Spanish (with some signs in English as well) as to species and habits, and well-lit. Some are not from Costa Rica, you will be pleased to know. If you wish to contemplate and identify dangerous species before an excursion into the wild, this is the place. You'll also find frogs, toads, iguanas, and lizards, all to be viewed for one small fee. Hours are 9 a.m. to 6 p.m. every day. Look for the Fuji Film sign and take the stairs up.

Turning west, on Calle 7, Avenidas Central/1, is a collection of old photos of San José, with a $2 admission charge, which you may want to skip if your interest in local history is limited.

Farther west, on Calle 2, facing a pleasant mini-park, is the baroque palace that houses the **Central Post Office** (Correos y Telégrafos, or Cortel).

Central Market

The **Central Market** (*Mercado Central*), at Calle 6 and Avenida 1, is a block-long area housing vendors of flowers, baskets, vegetables, shoes, spices, and a few souvenirs. It's small and sedate by Central American standards, but worth a walk-through. Other markets nearby are the **Borbón**, a block north, at Calle 8 between Avenidas 3 and 5, and the **Coca-Cola** bus terminal and market (named for an old bottling plant), Calle 16 between Avenidas 1 and 3. Just as interesting as the markets is the thriving general commerce of the area, where stores, stalls and street hustlers hawk fruit, firecrackers, flypaper, firearms, and countless other articles, many of which you'd have trouble finding at home.

Carrillo Park

One last downtown reference point, bounded by Avenidas 2 and 4, and Calles 12 and 14, is **Parque Carrillo** (Carrillo Park), also known as **Parque Merced**, after the church nearby. The park is typically treed and nicely landscaped, though the neighborhood is heavily trafficked and noisy. One interesting feature, though, is the park's centerpiece, a four-foot-diameter pre-Columbian stone sphere from Palmar Sur, in the southern Diquis region. Other examples of these near-perfect forms are to be seen at the National Museum and, as originals or reproductions, on many a lawn in San José, where they are popular decorations.

Centro Commercial

North of downtown, and of interest to visitors with time to browse and shop, is the **El Pueblo Shopping Center** (*Centro Comercial*). This is a tasteful, charming collection of shops, offices and restaurants, constructed in a style reminiscent of a colonial village, with narrow lanes, wrought-iron lamps, tile roofs, whitewashed brick and stuccoed walls, and beamed ceilings. It's almost better than the real thing. Most of the action at El Pueblo takes place after dark. Take the Calle Blancos bus from Avenida 5, Calles 1/3, or a taxi.

Paseo Colón and Sabana Park

Less than a mile to the west of downtown, at the opposite end of the upscale **Paseo Colón** district, is **Parque Metropolitano** (Metropolitan Park), or **La Sabana**, once the airport for San José. A drained lake has been restored, trees have grown back, and extensive sport facilities have been erected, including a pool, gymnasium, and stadium.

On the east side of the park, facing Paseo Colón, is the former airport control tower, a Spanish-style structure now converted to the **Museo de Arte Costarricense** (Museum of Costa Rican Art). Most of the paintings reflect an appreciation of the bucolic and the archaic that contrasts with modern Costa Rican life. Frequent subjects and motifs are idealized landscapes, Indian cultures long gone from the land, and oxcarts and whitewashed adobe houses; in other words, the simple life. Of the works displayed, Francisco Amighetti's woodcuts have earned the most fame outside of Costa Rica. The museum is open every day except Monday from 10 a.m. to 5 p.m., and there is a small admission charge. Any Sabana bus from Avenida 3, Calles Central/2, or from the Central Park, will stop near the entrance.

The **Museo de Ciencias Naturales** (Natural Sciences Museum), is located near the southwest corner of La Sabana park, at Colegio La Salle, a secondary school. The collection includes thousands of stuffed birds, monkeys, and other denizens of the wild, many in mock-ups of their natural habitats. The museum is open Monday through Friday from 7 a.m. to 3 p.m., Saturday until noon, with a small admission charge. Buses from the Central Park marked "Sabana Cementerio" stop nearby.

> **Outside Downtown**

Insects and Fish

The high point of San José for visitors interested in insects will be the **Entomology Museum** *(Museo de Insectos)*, housed in the basement of the Escuela de Artes Musicales on the north side of the University of Costa Rica, in San Pedro. Take the outside steps down, on the east side of the main entry.

Most of the collection, which you can examine to the accompaniment of music filtering through the ceiling, is housed in one large room. The specialty is butterflies. Take a look at the huge blue morphos and many others, stunning even when dead, in iridescent purples, yellows and blues, colors that easily disguise them as flower petals. And there are poisonous spiders, moths, and models of tropical landscapes from several zones. Some tour guides will tell you that the sting of the peanut-head lantern fly will cause certain death unless the victim promptly engages in sexual intercourse. (You may take this as you wish.) My favorite item is the canned ants from Bucaramanga, Colombia.

Hours are from 1 p.m. to 5 p.m. Monday through Friday, and there is a small admission fee. Take a San Pedro bus near the Social Security building (**La Caja**), Avenida 2 between Calles 3 and 5. As long as you're out here, you might want to look in on the university's own nature reserve, in the middle of the ring of classroom buildings, and its botanical gardens. For more information, call [2]535323, extension 5318.

(For those who are *really* into insects, there is another **Museo de Insectos y Mariposas** [Insect and Butterfly Museum] in suburban Santo Domingo de Heredia, 300 meters west of the bridge on the River Virilla, open daily except Monday from 9 a.m. to 5 p.m., admission $5. This includes the private Whitten Collection, which the curators claim is one of the largest of its kind.)

Further west, in San Francisco de Dos Ríos, is **Mundo Sumergido** (Submerged World), an exhibition of tropical fish, featuring Caribbean fish in a re-creation of their coral reef habitat, as well as Atlantic and Pacific species. The fish are on display in the back of an aquarium shop, four blocks east and two blocks north of the Y-junction on the road into town. Call [2]275491 for information.

Butterflies

Spirogyra is an urban butterfly garden northeast of downtown San José (Calle 46 at Avenida Central, Guadalupe, "50 meters west, 150 meters south of San Francisco church"). On display are a couple of dozen of the 4000 resident Costa Rican species, in an environment of flowering plants that provide nourishment, and fruit species that butterflies call home. Hours are 8 a.m. to 4 p.m., admission about $4. Take the Guadalupe bus from Avenida 3, Calles 3/5.

Oxcart Museum

South of central San José, in the working-class suburb of Desamparados, is the **Oxcart Museum**, in a venerable house that contains as well artifacts of the old rural life-style on which Costa Ricans look so fondly. Open daily except Monday from 8 a.m. to noon and 2 to 6 p.m.

MOVIES, THEATER, & OTHER ENTERTAINMENT

Admission to first-run American and other foreign films runs about $1.50 in San José — a bargain. Most have subtitles, so you'll be able to hear the original sound track. A few are dubbed into Spanish (*hablado en español*, the ad will say). Newspapers give current attractions and sometimes the show times. Rarely, however, do they reveal the address of the theater, so look it up in the phone book under "*Cines*," or ask at your hotel desk.

Check the billboard at the **National Theater**, once repairs are

finished, for concerts, plays and recitals, some feat[u]
known artists. Tickets are bargain-priced, starting a[t]
number of active theater groups, and their performa[n]
open-air theater, are advertised in the newspaper[s]
given at the restored 1920s **Teatro Melico Salazar**, a[t]
Olivier at Avenida 2, Calle 28, near Paseo Colón, am[ong]
the Olivier theater, **Sala Garbo** exhibits art movies and classics.

On the raunchy side, supposedly staid San José has more than its
share of strip joints and raunchy bars (see "Bars and Clubs," pages 164-166). Massage parlors advertise in various publications. Be protective of
your pockets and your health.

Non-striptease musical acts are featured at the bars and night clubs
of some hotels, especially the **Irazú**, **Corobicí**, and **Cariari**. The major
downtown hotels usually have bands on weekends.

SHOPPING

For some general guidelines as to what to look for, see pages 85-86.
In this section, I'll mention some of the more interesting stores in San
José.

There are wise and worthwhile purchases to be made in San José, but
they won't necessarily be items intended for tourists. The limited
selection of domestic handicrafts includes leatherware and items made
from wood, and crocheted and macramé articles. T-shirts and similar
universal souvenirs help fill the shops, along with handicrafts from
neighboring countries.

Various leather stores have shoes, attaché cases and handbags that are
similar in quality to what you would find in the United States. Prices are
slightly lower than at home (if the stuff at home isn't on sale). Among such
shops are **Galería del Cuero**, Avenida 1, Calle 5; and Del Río, Calle 3,
Avenida 5.

La Galería, at Calle 1, Avenida Central/1, exhibits and sells paintings,
painted wood articles, and bowls of rosewood and other tropical hardwoods. The grains and fineness are exquisite, but do you really want to
spend up to $100 for a portion-sized salad bowl? Assorted woodware is
also available at **Magia**, Calle 5, Avenidas 1/3, and **Suraska**, Calle 5,
Avenidas 1/3. And there's a good selection in the shop at Calle 5, Avenida
5.

The **National Handicrafts Market** (*Mercado Nacional de Artesanías*),
Calle 11, Avenidas 2/4, is a store with handicrafts similar to what you'll
find in hotel gift shops — woodware, small cotton hats, macramé, and t-shirts. A few blocks away, **CANAPI**, an artisans' guild, Calle 11, Avenida
1, has a similar, larger store, lately with attractive bamboo furniture. Down
the block, the **Souvenir Shop**, at Calle 11, Avenidas Central/1, has

ly inexpensive wood carvings and Guatemalan handicrafts. More
rally located is **ANDA**, Calles 5/7, Avenida Central, another artisans'
utlet, with mostly wood and leather crafts.

You'll sometimes find examples of weaving by Costa Rica's indigenous population on sale at the shop of the National Museum. The shop
of the **Neotrópica Foundation**, Calle 20, Avenidas 3/5, has handicrafts
made from traditional materials.

At the public markets, such as the **Central Market**, you'll find a fair
selection of what crafts there are in Costa Rica, along with fruits and
groceries. The ornamental plants are beautiful, and cheap, but you can't
take them home. (Well, you *can*, but you better get the right procedures
from your department of agriculture before you even think about doing
so.) Tidbits of pottery, hammocks, and paintings are hawked in the little
park in front of the Gran Hotel Costa Rica, adjacent to the Plaza of
Culture.

The largest collection I've seen of wood items, dolls, leather, t-shirts,
embroidered blouses, ashtrays, pots, straw hats, jewelry, and other items
ranging from silly to superb is in the gallery of stalls called **La Casona** on
the east side of Calle Central, just north of Avenida Central. Some of the
leather is quite nice, and there are many items from Panama (*molas*),
Guatemala (weaving), and El Salvador (cloth birds) to supplement local
production.

Antiques will also be found in the Central Market area, and at some
hotels. Pre-Columbian pottery cannot be bought legally, and reproductions are getting scarce. But if you're interested, one place where you can
look at pre-Columbian effigy mortars, pottery, and colonial antiques is
through the window and inside **Familiar La Viña**, a family eatery and
imbibing spot at Avenida 7, Calles 4/6. You might even go in for a bite
and a glass of something.

EXCURSIONS FROM SAN JOSÉ

Costa Rica is small enough, and travel facilities are well enough
developed, that you can reach many far points of the country by **public
transportation** and return to your hotel in San José by nightfall. In order
to actually *see* anything, however, you'll probably want to confine your
one-day trips to the environs of San José and the Central Valley, e.g., Ojo
de Agua springs, Poás and Irazú volcanoes, Cartago and the Orosi valley,
and Alajuela and towns on the way to Sarchí. These places, and details on
how to reach them, are described in the pages immediately following this
section and in Chapter 13, "The Central Valley."

By taking a tour or renting a car, you can extend your one-day travel
range to the Pacific beaches near Puntarenas and at Jacó, and, perhaps,
the port of Limón on the Atlantic.

By chartered plane, you can also make a one-day trip out of a visit to the Tortuguero reserve on the Caribbean.

Day outings are also arranged through travel agencies for white-water rafting, volcano climbing or volcano watching, scuba diving, horseback riding, jungle exploration, cruises in the Gulf of Nicoya, kayaking, and mountain biking; and the list keeps expanding.

Numerous companies offer one-day rafting excursions from San José, mostly on the Reventazón River.

And for organized walks in Braulio Carrillo, Carara and other national parks, look up "National Parks" in the index.

For information on these adventures, look at the agency listings below, or the coverage of special interests throughout this book.

Where To Go First?

At the risk of sounding Philistine, I will state that much of the scenery near San José is essentially similar. You'll want to be selective, especially if you're on a short trip, or wish to get down to the hard work of sunning yourself on a beach, or rafting a wild river, or fishing. Choose one volcano and one scenic circuit for starters, then see the other sights as time and inclination allow.

Listed below are some nearby destinations in approximate order of interest:

• **Poás Volcano**. Impressive cloud forest, craters and views, well conceived visitors' center and exhibits. How many of your friends have ascended a real volcano? An alternative is a trip to an observation point where you can view the fireworks on Arenal Volcano at a safe distance (you can't go to the crater).

• **Orosi Valley**. Plunge into a broad, magnificent valley full of lush coffee farms, with colonial churches, lakes, and a river of rapids; stop at an unusual botanical garden on the way.

• **Aserrí** or **San Antonio de Escazú**. Short excursions by city bus, miniature versions of the Orosi circuit.

• **Alajuela**. Most pleasant of the nearby provincial capitals, on the way to Poás volcano. Excursion may be extended by meandering along the old road to Grecia, the furniture-making town of Sarchí, and Naranjo.

• **Irazú Volcano**. Views as fine as those from Poás (if you hit a clear morning), but barer at the top, with few facilities.

• **Tortuga Island**. Calypso Tours and several other companies offer one-day cruises in the Gulf of Nicoya for about $75, including the round-trip bus ride from San José. See page 183 for details.

- **Ojo de Agua**. Fine for swimming and boating. You'll be interested if your hotel in San José has no pool.
- **Cartago.** For those with reasons of religion.
- **Heredia**. Stop if you have extra time, while on the way to somewhere else.
- **Santiago Puriscal.** A scenic, mountainside-clinging ride.

Visit other towns, ascend to **Braulio Carrillo National Park**, or go horseback riding, rafting, or boating, according to your fancy and funds, before you head to the edges of Costa Rica. For travel details, read the coverage ahead.

Tours and Travel Agencies

Your own style, money supply, and your destination will determine whether you use a travel agent or group tours while in Costa Rica. Even if you're used to making your own way by bus and train, you'll find that only a tour, taxi or rented car will get you to the top of a volcano on certain days of the week, or all the way through the Orosi Valley without having to backtrack or trudge part of the way. And of course, tours are social as well as practical. You meet people and share experiences.

Travel agencies will also help you to keep up with new hotels, though you should bear in mind that they are always acting in their own interest, not yours. And whether you get a knowledgeable guide, or one who justifies his employment with endless patter, can make a big difference. Try to sort out promotion from fact by comparing notes with fellow visitors.

Beware of Tour Prices!

Prices for day-long adventures are often much higher than what you would pay in the United States. For example, a one-day rafting trip from San José, at about $80, costs quite a bit more than a similar trip in Alaska (which is not exactly a low-cost area).

Why is this so? Many excursions in Costa Rica are booked in advance, demand is heavy in season, and the clientele generally does not question pricing. In other words, they charge high prices because they *can*.

Do not hesitate to ask for a discount of 20% when you book a day trip directly with the company that runs it (after all, they won't have to pay a commission), or for a low-season discount, or for a student rate, or the seniors' discount.

Major Travel Agencies

- **American Express/TAM**, Calle 1, Avenidas Central/1, P. O. Box 1864-1000), tel. [2]330044, fax [2]228092 (night/weekends, tel. [2]230116)

- **Blanco Travel Service**, Avenida Central, Calles 7/9, tel. [2]221792
- **Costa Rican Trails**, P. O. Box 2907-1000, San José, tel. [2]224547, fax [2]213011
- **Henchoz Tours**, Calle 5, Avenidas 3/5, (P. O. Box 883-1002), tel. [2]339658, fax [2]339357
- **Intertur**, Avenida 1, Calles 3/5, tel. [2]331400. Advertises discount tours.
- **Infotur**, on Avenida 2 opposite the rear of the National Theater (P.O. Box 03 6150 San José), tel. [2]234481, fax [2]234476, makes reservations at most hotels and for rafting, car rentals, etc. They also have a garbled on-line database.
- **Tropical Pioneer**, P. O. Box 29-2070 Sabanilla, tel. [2]539132, fax [2]534687. Rafting.
- **Turismo Creativo**, 7 Calle, Avenidas Central/1 (P. O. Box 1178-1011), tel. [2]331374, fax [2]330368
- **Tursa**, lobby of Gran Hotel, tel. [2]336194
- **Swiss Travel Service**, Hotel Irazú, tel. [2]326039
- **Tikal Tours**, Avenida 2, Calle 7 (P.O. Box 6398-1000), San José, tel. [2]571480, fax [2]231916

You'll probably book where it's most convenient, generally at your hotel. Bear in mind that agencies work on commissions, and will sometimes try to sell you the most expensive trip, no matter what your interest, e.g., a flying tour to Tortuguero, instead of a more leisurely canal-boat excursion (if that's what you're after).

If you have trouble getting what you want, do not hesitate to contact a trip operator directly. You can even consider calling from abroad—most have personnel who speak English.

Specialty Tour Companies
Among more specialized travel agencies and trip operators are:
- **Ríos Tropicales**, Paseo Colón, Calles 22/24 (P. O. Box 472-1200, Pavas), tel. [2]336455, fax [2]554354. **Rafting** and **kayaking** excursions.
- **Costa Rica Adventure Tours** (Río Colorado Lodge), Hotel Corobicí (P. O. Box 5094-1000), tel. [2]328610, fax [2]315987, has packages that include jungle cruises along the Tortuguero Canal and Sarapiquí and San Juan rivers, and tarpon fishing in the Caribbean region.
- **Costa Rica Rainbow Connection**, P. O. Box 7323-1000, tel. and fax [2]407325, is a holistic network and alternative travel service, "using the tremendous potential of Costa Rica as a high-energy healing land." Workshops and power-center visits are planned, and a recent tour was on the theme "Journey through wonders and wisdom of magical Costa Rica."

- **CIPTR**, Calle 40, Avenida 4, tel. [2]552693, takes groups to **Cararareserve**, among other destinations, and employs local people to provide food and horses to participants.
- **Parismina Tarpon Rancho**, Calle 1, Avenidas 7/9 (María José Building, tel. [2]226055 or 800-862-1003 (U.S.-C.R.), fax [2]221760, offers sport fishing trips on both coasts, as well as tours to Tortuguero.
- **Costa Rica Expeditions**, Calle Central, Avenida 3 (P. O. Box 6941-1000), tel. [2]220333, fax [2]571665. Rafting; coastal and river. Fishing; birding and national park tours. Mainly a wholesaler.
- **Aventuras Naturales**, Avenida Central, Calles 33/35, tel. [2]253939, fax [2]536934. Rafting, mountain biking.
- **Geotours**, P. O. Box 469Y-1011 San José, tel. [2]341867, fax [2]536338. Specializing in tours to Braulio Carrillo, Santa Rosa, Guanacaste and Cahuita national parks, and Carara Biological Reserve.
- **Geoventuras**, P. O. Box 554-2150 Moravia, tel. [2]828590, fax [2]828333. Specializing in natural history, language study, mountain biking, volcano trips, birding. An unusual tour includes old and functioning gold mines, as well as the Monteverde reserve.
- **Horizontes**, Calle 28, Avenidas 1/3 (P. O. Box 1780-1002), tel. [2]222022, fax [2]554513. Bus and cycling trips to national parks.
- **Costa Rica Dreams**, P. O. Box 79-4005, San Antonio de Belén, tel. [2]393387, fax [2]393383. Fishing off Quepos and Caño Island.
- **Sportfishing Costa Rica**, P. O. Box 115-1150 La Uruca, tel. [2]339135, fax [2]236728, 800-374-4474 direct from U.S. Fishing along the west coast.
- **OTEC Tours** (Organización de Turismo Estudiantil Costarricense), Calle 3, Avenidas 3/5, Calles tel. [2]220866, fax[2]332321, specializes in travel for Costa Rican students. You can use their services if you're a student, a teacher, or are under 26 years of age, and provide two photos, though their prices are only marginally lower than elsewhere. Their offerings include one-day diving and equestrian trips.
- **Sertur**, Avenida 5, Calles 1/3, tel. [2]572363. In addition to the usual run of excursions, Sertur has day river trips, birding excursions to Caño Negro Wildlife Refuge (a little-visited wetlands area in the San Carlos plain), and a multi-day beach and marsh tour along the Pacific coast.
- **Cotur**, Calle 36, Paseo Colón/Avenida 1 (P. O. Box 1818-1002, San José), tel. [2]330155, fax [2]330778. Three-day, two-night tours on the Miss Caribe to Tortuguero National Park by bus and canal boat. They also have mountain and coastal fishing programs. Make sure you get a written confirmation.
- **Cruceros Mawamba**, P. O. Box 10050, tel. [2]339964, and Mitur (Hotel Ilan-Ilan), Paseo Colón, Calles 20/22 (P. O. Box 91-1150), tel. [2]552262, fax [2]551946, have Tortuguero packages similar to

Cotur's. Mitur also has an overnight trip to Lake Arenal, including a boat trip.

- **Rancho Leona**, tel. 71[6]6312, in the village of La Virgen on the Sarapiquí river, sponsors jungle kayaking excursions. See page 431 for details.
- **Jungle Trails** (Los Caminos de la Selva), Calle 38, Avenidas 5/7 (P.O. Box 5941-1000, San José, tel. [2]553486, fax [2]552782), organizes rain-forest and mountain hikes, rafting, and tree-planting excursions.
- **Saragundí Specialty Tours**, Avenida 7, Calles Central/1 (P. O. Box 7126), San José, tel. [2]550011, fax [2]552155, has a one-day horseback and hiking tour for about $75. They also arrange bungee-jumping, which they claim carries a German certification (as if you could verify this).
- **Tropical Sceneries**, P. O. Box 2047-1000, San José, tel. [2]242555, fax [2]339524, offers one-day dive trips from San José to Herradura, near Jacó, at $125 per person; diving packages based at Río Sierpe Lodge, near Drake Bay; and longer trips to Coco Island.
- **Tipical Tours**, tel. [2]338486, arranges horseback tours.
- **Robles Tours**, tel. [2]372116, fax [2]371976, rides to Barva volcano; Magic Trails, tel. [2]538146, fax [2]539937, rides through Prusia Forest Reserve, on the slopes of Irazú.
- **Rainbow Tours**, tel. [2]338228, has riding near Carara Biological Reserve, about $75; L. A. Tours, Avenida Central, Calles 5/7 (P. O. Box 492-1007), tel. [2]214501, has a day horseback outing to a farm near Orotina, on the Pacific slope, about $75.
- **Calypso Tours**, Arcadas building by the Gran Hotel (P. O. Box 6941-1000 San José), tel. [2]333617, fax [2]330401. Cruises to islands in Gulf of Nicoya and to Cocos Island; diving, and trips to Monteverde.The gulf cruise is perhaps the most highly rated day trip in Costa Rica. **Seaventures**, an associated company, takes participants sailing across the Gulf of Nicoya, and offers sail charters.
- Day trips in the Gulf of Nicoya are also offered by **Bay Island Cruises**, P. O. Box 145-1007, tel. [2]312898, fax [2]394404; and **Fantasía Island Cruise**, P. O. Box 123-5400 Puntarenas, tel. [2]550791, fax [2]231013.
- **Costa Rica Sun Tours**, Avenida 7, Calles 3/5, San José (P. O. Box 1195-1250 Escazú), tel. [2]552011, fax [2]553529. Specialties are river fishing, and stays at Tiskita Lodge near Panama and the Arenal volcano observatory.

TYPICAL TOUR OFFERINGS AND COSTS

- San José city tour, $20 and up, three hours.
- Irazú volcano and Cartago, $40, half day.
- Day trip to Arenal Volcano, $80; overnight, $160.
- Day trip to Carara Biological Reserve or Braulio Carrillo National Park or Guayabo National Monument, $70.
- Lankester Gardens and Orosi valley, $20 and up, half day, $45 full day.
- Orosi Valley and Irazú volcano, with visit to coffee farm, $50 and up, full day.
- Poás volcano, $35, half day.
- Heredia, Alajuela and Sarchí, $25 and up, half day.
- Braulio Carrillo Park and Limón: a drive-through trip, with some hiking, and explanation of flora, $75.
- "Traditional night" — basically a meal with a view for $35.
- Ride on part of the old "Jungle Train" route, $80.
- Bus to Puntarenas and boat cruise in the Gulf of Nicoya, $75.
- Trips to beach resorts, $100 per day.
- Rafting on the Reventazón River, $80.
- Jungle tours by bus to Limón, then by canal launch to Tortuguero reserve, returning by air, or boat and bus, $200 to $400.
- Monteverde reserve, two nights, $200 and up.

PRACTICAL INFORMATION (In Alphabetical Order)

Banks

You'll have no trouble finding a bank in downtown San José.   Most are open from 9 a.m. to 4 p.m., Monday through Friday. The **Banco de Costa Rica** branch at Calle 7 and Avenida 1 is open until 6 p.m., and is convenient to some of the larger hotels. **Banco Mercantil** has an exchange boutique downtown with quick service, at Calle 5 near Avenida Central, opposite the tourist office on the Plaza of Culture, open weekdays from 9 a.m. to 5:30 p.m. Watch for pickpockets outside.

For D-marks, Canadian dollars and French francs (if you've ignored my advice and brought along these currencies), try the services of **Compañía Financiera Londres**, on Calle Central near the corner of Avenida Central (next to La Casona), third floor.

Black-market money-changers, during periods when they are tolerated, congregate along Avenida Central between Calles 2 and 4, near the post office. There's usually only a small spread between the official and free market rates.

For tales of woe about changing travelers checks, see "Money and Banking" in Chapter 6, "Basic Information."

Books, Magazines, and Newspapers

For reading material in English, German and Spanish at a reasonable price, your best bet is **Book Traders**, a used-book exchange at Avenida 1,

Calles 3/5 (Omni Building), upstairs behind Pizza Hut, open 9 a.m. to 5 p.m. except Sunday. Titles are in many genres. Bring your good used paperbacks from home to trade at two-for-one, or sell at 10% of the cover price. They have another outlet in west-end Escazú, a block west of the U.S. ambassador's house, open daily to 7 p.m., Sunday to 5 p.m.

(You can find copies of this book at Book Traders, as well as, sometimes, at the Hotel Cacts.)

New books in English are sold at up to triple U.S. list price at some outlets, despite an insignificant import duty. The **Universal** department store, Avenida Central, Calles Central/1, and **Librería Lehmann**, Avenida Central, Calles 1/3, have limited selections.

For French and Italian magazines, try **Librería Francesa/Librería Italiana**, Calle 3, Avenidas 1/Central.

The *Tico Times* an excellent local newspaper in English (see page 57), as well as *Time, Newsweek*, the Miami *Herald* and other imported magazines and newspapers, are available at many hotels.

Costa Rica Today, an excellent tourist-oriented weekly, is distributed at no charge in many locations.

There are several other tourist-oriented glossy publications, which are mainly useful for clipping discount coupons.

Churches
Among places of worship in or near San José are:
• **Bahai Center**, Avenida 4, Calle 22, tel. [2]225335.
• **Shaare Zion Synagogue**, Calle 22B, Paseo Colón/Avenida 1, tel.[2]339222. Friday 5:30 p.m., Saturday 9:30 a.m. and 4:30 p.m., also daily, morning and evening.
• **B'nai Israel** reform community, tel. [2]258561. Friday at 8 p.m.
• **Church of Jesus Christ of Latter-Day Saints**, Avenida 8, Calles 33/35, tel. [2]250208.
• **Carmelite Conven**t, opposite Lamm's restaurant, San Rafael de Escazú, tel. [2]281920. Mass in English on Saturdays at 4:30 p.m.
• **International Chapel of St. Mary**, Sheraton Herradura Hotel Catholic mass in English, Sunday at 4 p.m. Tel. [2]826698.
• **Anglican Church of the Good Shepherd**, Avenida 4, Calles 3/5, tel. [2]221560. Services Sunday at 8:30 a.m. (10:30 a.m. in Spanish).
• **Union Church**, Moravia. Sunday service at 9 a.m. and 10:30 a.m. Call [2]356709 to arrange transportation.
• **International Baptist Fellowship**, one block north of Banco Anglo, San Pedro, tel. [2]598743. Sunday service at 9 a.m., and Sunday school.
• **Seventh Day Adventist**, Church of God-Living Doctrines, tel. [2]357026. Saturday at 9 a.m.
• **Escazú Christian Fellowship**, tel. [2]315444. Worship and Sunday

school at Country Day School, Sunday at 5:30 p.m.
• **Friends' Peace Center**, Av 6B at Calle 15, Sunday at 11 a.m. Tel. [2]336168

Doctors

Emergency medical attention for visitors is available at any public hospital. The most centrally located is **Hospital San Juan de Dios**, Avenida Central and Calle 16, tel. [2]220166. For a Red Cross ambulance, call [2]215818.

For treatment on a non-emergency basis, try the **Clínica Bíblica**, a church-related organization, at Calle 1, Avenidas 14/16, tel. [2]236422; the **Clínica Americana**, Avenida 14, Calles Central/1, tel. [2]221010; or the **Clínica Católica** in Guadalupe, tel. [2]255055. They have English-speaking doctors available, and provide service 24 hours.

LIKE A CARMEN MIRANDA MOVIE

I've touched on this before, but while we're on the subject of San José, it bears repeating.

I like to tell my friends in América del Norte that Costa Rica is like a Carmen Miranda movie: Latin America without the downside. The visitor is relatively un-harassed by peddlers and beggars, and doesn't stick out like a sore thumb, as in some neighboring countries.

But beguiled visitors can sometimes paint a picture more paradisaical than that which actually prevails. So let me take a moment of your time to counsel you that pickpockets lurk in crowded squares, and wherever there are tourists. If you park your car on any street in San José, it will be broken into. (Fortunately, there are few parking spaces downtown.) People who are overfriendly without reason may well be overfriendly for a very *bad* reason. Those barred windows are not just a Spanish tradition, as some real-estate salesmen would have it — they keep out thieves. It isn't smart to walk in quiet or deserted parts of town at night.

San José is no cauldron of crime, but there are bad eggs. If you don't do anything you wouldn't do in any unfamiliar place, you'll probably be safer than in most other cities.

Embassies and Consulates

Most of the addresses below are for consulates. For those not listed, look in the phone book under *Embajadas y Consulados*. Most are open mornings only.
• **Belgium**, Los Yoses (east of downtown), tel. [2]256255
• **Belize**, Guadalupe, tel. [2]539626
• **Canada**, Calle 3, Avenidas Central/1, ground level (P. O. Box 10303-1000 San José), tel. [2]553522
• **Denmark**, Paseo Colón, Calles 38/40, tel. [2]572695
• **El Salvador**, Los Yoses, tel. [2]253861

- **France**, Curridabat, tel. [2]250733
- **Germany**, Rohrmoser, tel. [2]325533
- **Guatemala**, Barrio California, tel. [2]335283
- **Honduras**, Los Yoses, tel. [2]340949
- **Italy**, Avenida 10, Calles 33/35, tel. [2]342326
- **Japan**, Rohrmoser, tel. [2]321255
- **Mexico**, Av. 7 no. 1371, tel. [2]338874
- **Netherlands**, Los Yoses, tel. [2]340949
- **Nicaragua**, Avenida Central, Calles 25/27, tel. [2]333479
- **Panama**, San Pedro, tel. [2]253401
- **Switzerland**, Centro Colón (Paseo Colón/Calle 38), tel. [2]214829
- **United Kingdom**, Paseo Colón, Calles 38/40, tel. [2]215566
- **U.S.A.**, Pavas (western suburbs), tel. [2]203939 (8 a.m. to 4:30 p.m.),203127 (evenings and weekends). Send mail to P. O. Box 10053-1000, San José. The bus for Pavas leaves from Avenida 1, Calles 16/18, San José. A train departs from the old Pacific station for Pavas at 6:30 a.m. and 12:45 and 5:45 p.m.

Laundry

You'll probably entrust your cleaning to your hotel or a neighborhood laundry. One of the few self-service laundries is **Lavamatic**, in the Cocorí shopping center (*Centro Comercial)* east of downtown. Take a San Pedro bus from Avenida 2, Calle 5, laundry in hand. Or try **Burbujas** in San Pedro, half a block west, the 25 meters south of the Más x Menos supermarket.

Libraries

For books in English, visit the library at the **Centro Cultural Costarricense Norteamericano** (U.S.-Costa Rican Cultural Center), a U.S.-sponsored institution, in eastern San José. Call [2]259433 for current hours and directions. To borrow books, you'll have to become a paying member.

The other main libraries, in case you're doing serious research, are the **University of Costa Rica library** in San Pedro, and the **National Library**, Avenida 3 and Calle 15.

Maps

Good road maps of Costa Rica and of the Central Valley are available at no charge at the tourist board's information center at the **Plaza de la Cultura**. The same maps are sold at newsstands elsewhere in the city.

Detailed topographical maps, of interest to hikers, are available at the **Universal** and **Lehmann** department stores on Avenida Central, downtown. If the maps you want are out of stock, go to the **National**

Geographic Institute of the Ministry of Public Works, Avenida 20, Calles 9/11. Hours are 8:30 a.m. to 3:30 p.m. Assorted geographic publications are also sold, in the mornings only. Take the Barrio La Cruz bus from the Central Park to the ministry, go through the gate, turn left, and look for the "Mapas" sign.

National Parks

The National Park Service has an information center in the Bolívar Park zoo. A booklet on the parks in English, with descriptions and travel advice, is on sale, though some of the information is outdated, and you should ask for current details about any park you intend to visit. Inquire also about seasonal conditions in the more remote parks. Some of the personnel speak English.

Pools

There are several public pools in the city, including one at **La Sabana Park**. The most fun, however, is **Ojo de Agua** (see pages 215-216 in Chapter 13, "The Central Valley."

Post Office

The main post office is **Correos y Telégrafos** (or **Cortel**) is at Avenida 1, Calle 2. A rate sheet is available at the counter to the left, inside the main entrance on Calle 2. Line up at the bank of windows to weigh your letters and buy stamps. Hours are 7 a.m. to 9 p.m. weekdays, Saturday from 8 a.m. to noon. General-delivery mail (*lista de correos*) is kept in the first large hall toward Avenida 1, at window 17 — there's a separate entrance. The philatelic department is through a separate door off the main lobby, and upstairs.

Supermarkets

Supermarkets are not hard to find anywhere in San José. A huge one is **Yaohan**, at the end of Paseo Colón on Calle 42, opposite the Corobicí Hotel. Like many other supermarkets, Yaohan has a selection of general merchandise — pots and pans, towels, plastic goods — in addition to food items. Inside parking is available. One centrally located general department store is **Galerías Plaza de la Cultura**, Avenida Central, Calles 5/7. There are others to the west along Avenida Central. Browse through any of these, and you'll soon find that the selection of locally made items is quite limited, while imported goods are expensive.

And, if you happen to be looking for an item of hardware, you can always stop in at **Ferretería Glazman**, Avenida 3, Calles 12/14.

Telegrams

Radiográfica Costarricense handles domestic and international telegrams. If you have access to a private phone, you can send your telegram by dialing 123. Otherwise, take your message to the telegraph office at Avenida 5, Calle 1, or send it through your hotel operator. Domestic telegrams are inexpensive — about 3¢ (U.S.) per word, 6¢ in a foreign language. Overseas telegrams are frightfully expensive.

Telephones

Public coin telephones are plentiful in San José, but they are not kept in good repair, nor are the appropriate coins — 5, 10 and 20 colones — always abundant. A good place to find working coin phones is outside the ICE building at Calle 1, Avenida 2. Some hotels have public phones in their lobbies.

In addition to other options, overseas calls can be made from the offices of **Radiográfica Costarricense**, Avenida 5, Calle 1. Visa, Master Card and American Express are accepted at this location.

For more information on using telephones, see Chapter 6, "**Basic Information.**"

Tourist Office

The visitors' information center of the **Instituto Costarricense de Turismo** (Costa Rican Tourist Board) is located at Avenida Central and Calle 5, at the entry to the underground exhibit area in the Plaza de la Cultura. Maps, hotel brochures and a sheet of bus and train schedules are available, and extensive files are maintained on special-interest areas — cultural attractions, camping, and business services, to name a few. The personnel will usually try hard to obtain information they don't have. All speak English. Hours are 9 a.m. to 5 p.m., Monday through Friday, Saturday to 1 p.m. For information by telephone, call [2]221090 or [2]216127.

Water

Tap water in San José (and in most larger towns of Costa Rica as well) is safe to drink. But if you're wary of it, for reasons of taste or chemical difference from what you're accustomed to, or are just plain cautious, stick to bottled soda water (*soda*, or *agua mineral*).

Water pressure in much of San José is quite low. The better hotels have pressure tanks and pumps, but in more modest accommodations, you may get no more than a dribble from the tap.

Walking

Being a pedestrian in San José is at times a risky business. At some intersections, traffic lights are arranged so that it is technically impossible to cross in the clear. And even where the signals appear to be with you, many a driver will slip into gear and bear down on you the moment the light changes. Be cautious and fleet of foot.

Weather
The average daily high for San José varies hardly at all from month to month — it's almost always in the mid-seventies Fahrenheit (22 to 25 Centigrade). Average nighttime lows are about 60 (15 degrees Centigrade), excellent for sleeping. Even the recorded extremes are moderate — 92 is the highest temperature ever recorded in San José, 49 the lowest (33 and 9 degrees Centigrade).

Precipitation, however, is quite variable. It rains almost every day from May to October (Costa Rica's "winter"), with monthly totals of about 10 inches, and the air gets to be uncomfortably sticky toward the middle of the day. The rains slacken off in November, and from January until the end of April, precipitation is a freakish event.

Aside from rain, there are a number of seasonal signs in lieu of sharp differences in temperature: variation in length and clarity of daylight; the flowering of poinsettia, erythrina trees, coffee plants and other species throughout the year; and alterations in the richness of the green of surrounding hills.

NEARBY TOWNS
San José is surrounded by dozens of settlements, ranging from suburbs where life is a virtual extension of the urban bustle, to bucolic hillside villages where events unfold at the pace of an oxcart, within full view of the city below. You can drive from point to point in the vicinity of San José, if you have a car available. But my preference is to hop on one of the frequent suburban buses, and to look ahead and to both sides of the road, catching glimpses of local sights and goings-on, and longer views whenever the bus stops to pick up or discharge passengers. Self-made bus tours to towns near San José literally cost pennies.

MORAVIA AND CORONADO
Moravia is a handicraft center seven kilometers northeast of downtown San José. The best-known shop is the **Caballo Blanco**, located on one corner of the main square, where thick leather belts and furniture and a few more finely manufactured items of luggage are on display. There are various other souvenir and wicker furniture shops and stands on the road into town, and a craft shopping mall, **Mercado de Artesanías Las Garzas**, a block south and a block east of city hall, with stocks of items from all over Latin America.

The crafts alone are not enough to draw a visitor to Moravia. One also comes here to sit on the large square and watch a slower, smaller-town life than that of San José. You'll note far fewer cars on the streets than in the capital, knots of people in conversation, and an indescribable something that turns out on closer examination to be an unaccustomed quiet.

The bus for Moravia leaves from Avenida 3, Calles 3/5, San José. Get off at the stop in Moravia where most other passengers debark. This is two blocks from the square. To continue your tour, walk back to the bus stop and wait for a bus marked "Coronado."

Beyond Moravia, the Coronado road rises through an area of lower-middle-class suburbs, where small and well-cared-for wood and concrete-block homes stand in clusters among coffee groves and pasture. About one kilometer before Coronado, in Dulce Nombre, is the **Instituto Clodomiro Picado** of the University of Costa Rica, where snakes are studied. Ask the bus driver to let you off nearby if you wish to visit. A few rattlers, fer de lance and coral snakes are on display. Hours are 8 a.m. to noon and 1 to 4 p.m., Monday through Friday. On Friday afternoons, you can witness the "milking" of snakes for their venom, from which antivenin is made.

After a visit to the Institute, walk or drive up the hill to **Coronado**, a sleepy, pleasant farming center with a surprisingly large and impressive tropical cement-clad, tin-roofed Gothic church. Some points in town offer good views to San José, and the direct road back to the capital is lined with substantial houses that take advantage of the vistas.

The direct bus for Coronado leaves from Calle 3, Avenidas 5/7, San José. You can walk down to Moravia in less than an hour, and be rewarded with sights more interesting than those in the two towns themselves.

ASERRI

The ride out to the village of **Aserrí** takes the visitor through the working-class suburbs of Desamparados and San Rafael, then into the crowded countryside, up and up over rolling hills, by rushing streams, and past farmhouse after small neat wooden or stuccoed farmhouse, each just in from the roadside, front yard decorated with bougainvillea, hibiscus, and poinsettia. Tiny pastures and vegetable plots pass by, islands in a sea of shiny-leafed coffee trees shaded by banana plants.

Once in Aserrí, gaze down at San José, at the bottom of the valley; take a look at the whitewashed, colonial-style church; and examine the Aserrí craft specialty, dolls of a rather simple sort. Catch the bus back down, or walk part of the way. The **MIRADOR RAM LUNA** restaurant, above Aserrí, makes a good lunch stop.

The hill town of Aserrí is only ten kilometers from San José, and 128 meters (420 feet) higher. Buses leave from Calle 2, Avenidas 6/8, San José.

SANTIAGO PURISCAL

Getting there is all the fun of this longer excursion through breathtaking, rolling countryside covered with coffee and orange trees, sugarcane, banana plants, and settlement after small settlement. Some 20 kilometers out from San José, the road ascends to country of pine and oak, and precipitous mountainside pastures where some force other than gravity appears to hold cattle to earth. To either side are sheer drops of a thousand feet and more. Each hairpin turn frames a new view of the Central Valley, increasingly far below.

At about kilometer 30, on the crest of the southern ridge, is the Guayabo reserve of the **Quitirrisi Indians**. The Quitirrisi live like other rural Costa Ricans, but they are poorer, less well educated, and have a limited command of Spanish. Their horizons are largely limited to the boundaries of their settlement. You'll notice Indians alongside the road with bundles of baskets, which are woven from vines, and sold in San José.

Buses for Santiago Puriscal leave about every 45 minutes from the Coca-Cola station, Calle 16, Avenidas 1/3. The trip takes about an hour, but one can get off around the Indian reserve and walk for a while (take a sweater), then catch a return bus.

ESCAZÚ

Escazú is the garden suburb where diplomats and wealthy industrialists have long made their homes, along with retirees with a certain amount of income or good taste. Here there are tree-lined streets; a couple of country clubs, one posh, one down-to-earth; private schools; and a stock of good housing. Absent are much of the noise and pollution that afflict parts of San José.

There is also a certain amount of the tradition that is missing elsewhere in Metropolitan San José. Escazú is the Town of Witches, where occult arts are practiced. Oxcarts are used to transport farm produce. Tile-roofed whitewashed adobe houses with blue-painted porches recall the days when this was a quiet agricultural center.

What remains of small-town Escazú is passing through the throes of gentrification. Centenary adobe houses are changing hands and being repaired and updated, with all modern conveniences. A Restaurant Row has grown up along the entry road from the Santa Ana expressway, with something in the order of 20 establishments, and all kinds of boutiques and gift shops line the main street for several kilometers out toward the American Embassy residence. Escazú is where the expanding bed-and-breakfast movement is concentrated. An upscale mall, a cousin to El Pueblo north of downtown, is under construction. Clinics, decorators, and anybody with an clientele rather than customers set up base in Escazú.

Much of the world of Escazú is accessible only with a local connection.

I was fortunate enough one day to spend some time at the **Country Club**, a world unto itself, of colonial-style buildings of endless proportions containing restaurants and lounges and bowling lanes and gyms and basketball court and sauna, not to mention Olympic pool, tennis courts, and golf on the grounds. With a local resident as your guide, you can take a peek at Manhattan. I'm not kidding — behind the hedges that line the road at a certain house, you can glimpse a painstakingly constructed model of the foreshortened island, with lighted skyscrapers, a moat representing the East and Hudson rivers, the Brooklyn, Manhattan, Williamsburg and 59th Street bridges, and even the Statue of Liberty and a private observation tower.

Wander Escazu's streets in your spare moments, in the same way you would look among the shops in Sausalito or South Beach Miami or any other trendy tourist area; or poke around in a car, since everything is quite spread out.

Buses for Escazú leave from Avenida 1, Calles 18/20, near the Coca-Cola terminal, San José.

SAN ANTONIO DE ESCAZÚ

The hill village of **San Antonio de Escazú** features a fine Ravenna-style church, and good views down to San José and across to the hump-shaped volcano Barva. Brightly painted oxcarts are in use as a practical means of moving goods in an era of expensive gasoline, and not merely to please the eye of visitors. Oxcarts and drivers (*boyeros*) are honored in a celebration in San Antonio on the second weekend in March. Rural, slow, clean, sunny, industrious and quite civilized, San Antonio appears to have been transplanted from hills somewhere above the Mediterranean.

On the peak above town is the **Reserva Forestal Pico Blanco** (Pico Blanco Forest Reserve). In fact, the reserve has been so successful in returning farms and pastures to forest, that the white rock that gives the mountain its name is no longer visible from San José. The variety of birds up here, including the motmot, is somewhat different from what you'll be led to find on most tropical birding trips.

Buses for San Antonio leave from Calle 16, Avenidas Central/1.

WHERE TO STAY

Several hotels and guest houses in San Antonio de Escazú, and below in San Rafael de Escazú, provide more tranquil surroundings than you'll find in San José. See pages 146-151 for more details. For restaurants, see page 162.

194

13. THE CENTRAL VALLEY

INTRODUCTION

In almost every way, the Central Valley is the heart and soul of Costa Rica. Most of the population lives on this twenty-by-fifty mile plateau, bordered to the north by the Poás, Barva, Irazú and Turrialba volcanoes, and to the south by an older mountain ridge. Almost all of Costa Rica's industry, most of the all-important coffee crop, and much produce for home consumption come from here. Public administration, education and power generation are centered in this mini-state.

And as if all the facts about industry and agriculture and human resources were not sufficient for one small region, the Central Valley is blessed as well with more than its share of natural beauty: great slopes carpeted with coffee trees, and broken by waterfalls, rippling streams, and rivers of rapids; pine groves and pastures on rolling hills; rocky canyons and lakes; a climate as benign and temperate as any on earth, where almost anything will grow; slumbering volcanoes, their slopes carved into farms of neat squares; and small, well-built houses everywhere. It is as close to one's idealized vision of the "country" as one is likely to get.

And yet, hardly a part of the Central Valley is really rural. Paved highways reach almost every point, giant electricity pylons step across the landscape, rivers are dammed and harnessed at every edge of the plateau. A cement factory, a knitting mill, rise amid pastures and coffee. Town gives way to fields and then to village and fields and town, each settlement with its dominating church and flowered gardens.

Nevertheless, man and nature appear for all the world to live in beauteous harmony. All of man's intrusions might have been placed with a sense of how things look, how they interrelate, and how they are kept up. It is this machine-in-the-garden aspect of the Central Valley that is especially attractive, and unique in this part of the world.

The Switzerland of Costa Rica?

The Central Valley is the part of Costa Rica that sometimes is called the Switzerland of Central America. In fact, there is nothing Swiss about the climate, or the tin-roofed houses. The bare statistics of per-capita

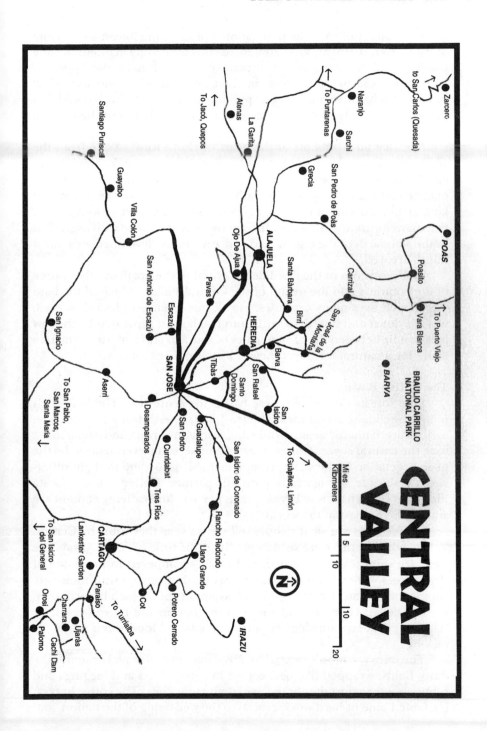

income would not earn the population a place at the lowest social rung of any Swiss settlement. Only contented cows munching in mountainside pastures present a roughly comparable vista. But in the apparent industriousness of the people, in their concentration and use of all resources at hand, in their general public orderliness, it could be said that the Swiss are somewhat reminiscent of the Costa Ricans of the Central Valley.

Not that all is sublime at the heart of Costa Rica. Aside from the economic shocks of recent times, there are natural shocks. Volcanoes erupt periodically and spew ashes, boulders and destruction. Earthquakes shake down houses and cathedrals. People, too, are not always kind to the land when they live so near one to another. A close look reveals that many a gurgling stream is off-color or slimy, and lined with trash. But by the standards of the region, and of many a more developed area, most things are well.

The volcanoes of the Cordillera Central to the north are the source of the contours and the wealth of the Central Valley. Much of the land was shaped over many centuries, as volcanic ejecta and lava showered, washed down and oozed, to settle into two basins, separated by the low hills that lie between the present cities of Cartago and San José. The lava made for a natural fertility, renewed by periodic eruptions.

The Coffee Basin

Pine forests dominated these basins for centuries. The Spaniards found the climate at altitudes of 900 to 1,500 meters ideal for subsistence agriculture, if not for wealth-producing plantation crops, and began to cut back the natural cover. Coffee trees, of course, came eventually to be the main vegetation in the valley, complemented, according to slight differences in altitude, by sugarcane, corn, and pasture. Coffee is now to Costa Rica what citrus fruit is to Israel. Yields per acre and caffeine content are among the highest in the world.

Coffee trees are what visitors will see most as they tour the Central Valley, but how these are seen depends on the time of year. Always the trees are shiny-leafed, crowded, and usually pampered in the shade of larger trees. Shortly into the rainy season, they glisten with moisture. Dozens of delicate, white-fingered blossoms erupt on each branch, then shower down. For most of the growing season the berry (*cereza*, or "cherry") is green, turning red and finally to oxblood when ready for picking.

The rains are mostly over when the armies of coffee pickers enter the dusty fields, wrapped like beekeepers in heavy shirts and leggings and rubber boots against the abrasions of dense branches. The coffee harvest is a fabled time of hard work, crucial to the well-being of the nation, and the president himself hands out awards to the best workers. Ripe berries are selected by hand, dumped from baskets to carts, and hurried to the mills where simple machines scrape off their outer hulls. The slime that coats the beans is soaked away by a day of fermenting, then the beans are spread, sun-dried during the day on concrete platforms, and mounded and covered by night. A second skin is rubbed off, the beans are sorted and polished, and a government agency supervises the orderly marketing of the crop. Harvest time is when the plantations are busiest, but throughout the year, workers plant and prune and clear and fertilize and otherwise tend the trees.

The relatively advanced development of the Central Valley makes it easy for the visitor to explore. Roads go everywhere, and on most of them, buses both comfortable and frequent. Good hotels and restaurants are not part of the valley's blessings, though there are some establishments worthy of recommendation; and no place is far from the haven of San José.

CARTAGO

Defeated in their attempts to found viable settlements in the merciless lowlands, the early Spanish settlers of Costa Rica turned their attention to the temperate uplands. In 1564, Juan Vásquez de Coronado, the Spanish governor, was able to write to the king: "I have never seen a more beautiful valley, and I laid out a city between two rivers. I named the city Cartago, because this province also bears that name."

The **Guarco Valley**, where the new head settlement was sited, had abundant water, fertile earth, and a population of a few thousand who were less hostile to Vásquez than the natives of the coast had been to his more belligerent predecessors. While the colonists did not succeed in establishing full dominion over the colony from their new highland base, nor in subjecting native peoples to labor on vast plantations of export crops, they at least were able to till subsistence crops and hold their own. In and around Cartago, which remained little more than an impoverished village for many years, was Costa Rica born and shaped.

Cartago lost its central position toward the end of the colonial period, as Costa Rica achieved a rough prosperity and settlement pushed westward in the Central Valley. The relative decline of the city was affirmed shortly after independence, when the capital was moved to San José.

Costa Rica's old capital is today not at all colonial in flavor. Virtually all structures of the pre-independence period were damaged or destroyed by a string of natural disasters: earthquakes in 1841 and 1910, and intermittent rains of ash and debris from the always-threatening volcano Irazú that looms over the city to the north.

A Religious Capital

But despite its political decline, Cartago remains a religious capital. Ten blocks east of the main square is the **Basílica de Nuestra Señora de Los Angeles** (Basilica of Our Lady of the Angels), with its six-inch-high black statue of the Virgin, the object of special devotion on August 2, and of pilgrimages throughout the year.

According to tradition, the little statue was discovered on the outskirts of Cartago on August 2, 1635, by a girl named Juana Pereira. It was twice removed and placed in a box, and each time miraculously reappeared in its original location. Yielding to divine will so clearly expressed, the ecclesiastical authorities decided to build a church where the Virgin had been found. The statuette twice was stolen from its shrine, in 1824 and 1950, but each time was returned. The original church was damaged in the 1920 earthquake, and the present basilica dates from 1926.

That is the religious background, which is considerably more impressive than the structure itself. The basilica stands out as an agglomeration of confused styles, roughly Byzantine at the front, with a motley collection of angels grafted on, domes bubbling overhead, barren, gray stone blocks forming the sides and rear. It is as if the officials of the Church realized that they had to do something for their Virgin, but, having abandoned colonial and native artistic traditions, found themselves at a loss as to how to go about it.

The interior of the basilica is no better. Vaults and columns painted in splotches of green and brown and glittering silver defocus one's attention from the altar.

The shrine of **La Negrita**, as the statue is familiarly called, is below ground level. Nearby is a room full of discarded crutches, and miniature gold and silver hands, legs, arms, and assorted other parts of the body, all testifying to the healing powers of the Virgin and of the waters that flow from the spring under her shrine.

Back at the center of Cartago are the more esthetically pleasing ruins of the **Church of the Convent** (**Iglesia del Convento**, or, more simply, **Las Ruinas**). Only the massive, moss-encrusted stone-block walls remain of this colonial structure, with their simple, pleasing, Moorish-Spanish contours. The roof fell in during the 1910 earthquake, after the structure had been damaged in previous tremors, and the church was abandoned. The walls now enclose a gardened space, where bougainvillea, pines and a lovely pond attract a variety of birds. The cobbled section of street in front of the church adds to the atmosphere.

CARTAGO FACTS

Population: 32,000; Altitude: 1,450 meters (4,756 feet);
Location: 23 kilometers from San José

ARRIVALS AND DEPARTURES

Arriving By Bus

Buses for Cartago leave from Avenida 18, Calle 5, San José, about every ten minutes from 5 a.m. to 11 p.m. These proceed northward to Avenida 6, where you can catch them on the corner.

Aside from its religious structures, Cartago is on the routes to the **Irazú volcano** and the **Orosi Valley**, and many day tours make a brief stop in town.

WHERE TO STAY AND WHERE TO EAT

Do not try to stay overnight in Cartago! All the hotels, clustered a block up from the market, across the railroad tracks, are fleabag, noisy dives of the worst sort. (I know!)

The food situation is mildly brighter. There are numerous modest *sodas* and restaurants around, including one behind the basilica, and fast-food outlets in the center of town.

IRAZÚ VOLCANO

At 3,432 meters (11,260 feet), **Irazú** is the highest volcano in Costa Rica. It is also one of the most active, and certainly the most feared, a rumbling presence, continually steaming, boiling and fuming, that has practically destroyed the city of Cartago on more than one occasion, and played continuing havoc with the lives of farmers who till the soil and raise livestock on its slopes. But paradoxically, the volcano is also a benefactor. Its ash renews the richness of the soil, even while it blocks water pipes and roads.

Irazú's most recent active cycle started with a bang on March 13, 1963, when boulders and ash began to rain down on homes and farms near the volcano's peak. Over a two-year period, rivers in the vicinity of Cartago were dammed and the city flooded; corrosive ash fell like a gray snow-storm over San José, damaging water pumps, home furnishings, and many a respiratory system. Dairy production plummeted as pastures were seared or covered over, and output of coffee and vegetables likewise fell. With help from abroad, dikes were hurriedly constructed to divert deviant waters from doing further damage, and the millions of tons of ash were swept up, and carted away. Irazú's peak assumed a new form as part of the mountain collapsed into the space vacated by magma. Even today, spurts of sulphurous smoke, steam and water are part of a continuing reformation and growth of the mountain.

The distinction of Irazú among volcanoes in the modern world is that is one of the few semi-active ones that can easily be viewed up close. A paved highway climbs right to the peak, which is protected as a national park. If you happen to ascend when the peak is free of clouds — a near impossibility during the rainy season, and an uncertain condition even in dry times — you'll be rewarded with views to both oceans, or at least to a good part of the country.

ARRIVALS AND DEPARTURES

Get an early start! Aside from the unique experience of ascending a volcano, you'll want to beat the clouds to the peak in order to get an ocean-to-ocean view.

By Bus

Public buses for Irazú leave on Saturday and Sunday at 7:30 a.m. from Avenida 2, Calles 1/3, San José (near the Gran Hotel); they make a stop in front of the ruined church in Cartago a half hour later. Fare is about $4. Call [2]519795 to check the schedule.

On other days, you can catch a bus in Cartago along side the Ruinas church for Tierra Blanca, on the volcano's slopes and hike the rest of the way — a strenuous effort in the thin air — or else look for a taxi at the end of the line.

By Car, Taxi, or Tour

Otherwise, go in a rented car, on a tour, or in a taxi from Cartago. The crater is 32 kilometers from Cartago, or 54 kilometers from San José, and the route is well marked. There's a nominal admission charge to the volcano, usually collected only at busy times.

SEEING THE SIGHTS

Visitors to Irazú should be prepared with warm clothing. A couple of sweaters will do, though a down ski jacket would not be too much. Rain gear will help even during the dry season, when wind-borne moisture will sting the skin.

The ride up Irazú proceeds slowly, through pastures and corn fields. Past the town of **Cot**, the air becomes increasingly windy and cold, and the trees more twisted. On the cool, ash-fertilized slopes, potatoes are the main crop, along with carrots and onions. And there are many dairy farms, all now recovered from the 1963-65 calamities, and awaiting the next ones.

Sites on the way up Irazú include the neat farming villages of **Potrero Cerrado** and **Tierra Blanca**, each dominated by a church; a pair of *miradores*, or lookout points, furnished with concrete picnic stools, and a rambling old white, tile-roofed sanatorium.

Past the sanatorium, a trail leads to the **Prusia Forestry Reserve** on the western slopes, an area that was replanted after it was turned into a desert in the 1963 eruption. Hiking trails, campsites, and picnicking facilities are available. Common trees are pine, alder and eucalyptus. There is also an unusual mushroom forest, where some species grow up to a foot across.

You'll find a run-down hotel about 20 kilometers out of Cartago, 12 kilometers from the crater.

At the Top

Over the last few kilometers of the ascent, the face of the mountain changes dramatically, from green pasture to oak forest laden with epiphytes at the park boundary, then to a seared, boulder-strewn primeval surface of ash and bare soil where wind-beaten ferns and shrubs maintain a tenuous hold. Around the next turn, one half expects to encounter a herd of dinosaurs poking their heads through the mist. Charred tree trunks stand as monuments to the last period of intense activity, while a few younger saplings take root for what will probably be an abbreviated life in the severe surroundings.

Once atop Irazú, you can examine a small exhibit on geysers, fumaroles, mudpots, ash, and other forms and evidence of volcanic activity. Slog through the ash and view the craters — slowly. The air at this altitude is short of oxygen, and you will be short of breath, as well as buffeted by wind and mist. The **Diego de la Haya** crater contains a lake, tinted to a rusty hue by dissolved minerals. The main, western crater, which swallowed up several earlier craters, currently shows virtually no activity or gas emissions.

There are active fumaroles on the northwestern slope. Much of this, it bears emphasizing, will not be visible because of the clouds that shroud the peak even during much of the dry season. But even when the top of Irazú is clouded over, a few minutes of exposure to the nasty environment and a glimpse of the fantasy-world landscape will be long remembered.

Avoid the area on the side of the main crater opposite the parking lot.

THE OROSI CIRCUIT

East of Cartago is the well-traveled scenic circuit through the Orosi Valley. The route covers only about 55 kilometers from Cartago, easily driven at a leisurely pace in a couple of hours. Bus travel requires some backtracking, but a trip to the halfway point will give you more than half the available pleasure.

SEEING THE SIGHTS

Orchids

About seven kilometers east of Cartago is the **Lankester Botanical Garden** (Jardín Lankester) of the University of Costa Rica. Take the Paraíso from Cartago's main square, or drive, from Cartago to the Ricalit roofing factory (on the left), then continue one-half kilometer down the side road to the south, to the entrance.

The Lankester Garden is most famed for its orchid collection (said to be showiest in March and April), the largest of its kind in the world, begun as a private effort by Charles (Carlos) Lankester, a native of England. But there is much, much more in this well-planned wonderland: bromeliads and other epiphytes, acres and acres of transplanted hardwoods, fruit trees, bamboo groves, cacti, medicinal aloe plants, dreamy and deadly nightshade, and many others. Species are identified only by Latin tags, but you'll recognize some as house plants, especially in the more jungly areas, where ponds are crossed with the aid of bridges made from vines. One large section has been left untended to grow back to native forest.

Guided walks through the gardens are offered on the half hour from 8:30 a.m. to about 2:30 p.m. daily. You can wander through at other times, but you'll be assigned an employee as a tail to make sure that you stick to the brick path and don't pick anything. Admission is about $1.

To continue your trip without a car, go back to the highway and pick up a bus marked "Orosi."

Views

A couple of kilometers past Paraíso on the road to the south is a *mirador*, or lookout point. Take advantage of it if you can for 20-mile views down into the great Orosi valley, carpeted with pasture, sugarcane, and, of course, dark green coffee forest. The **Río Grande de Orosi** snakes along at the bottom and joins lesser streams to form the **Río Reventazón** — the Foaming River. The town of **Orosi** can be picked out, along with smaller clusters of houses and ranches and coffee plantation centers on hillsides and in the lesser valleys spreading out in all directions, as clearly as if you were flying overhead. In the distance is the very end of **Lake Cachí**. This is surely one of the most spectacular views in a country of spectacular views, superior in clarity to any road map.

The lookout point is a garden with manicured pines, hedge cedars, bougainvilleas, and picnicking and play areas and shelters. Even if you're traveling by bus, it's a good place to stop with a box lunch. Or you can pick up snacks at the adjacent stand.

WHERE TO STAY

Just before the lookout point, modest accommodations are available, all affording outstanding vistas down into the Orosi valley.

The bed-and-breakfast of the Teutol family, tel. [5]747632, has three rooms with warm quilts, at about $15 per person. English, Spanish and German are all spoken fluently.

SANCHIRÍ LODGE, tel. and fax [5]733068, 800 meters off the road, charges $40 with breakfast for up to three persons in rustic woodsy cabins, each with a balcony on the edge of a precipice, and a bathroom below lined with sheet stone quarried on the site. The restaurant serves olla de carne, picadillo, mondongo, and other country specialties for about $5.

OROSI

After the lookout point, the road twists and descends into the valley, and finally straightens and runs flat along the river, through coffee groves to the garden town of Orosi, in colonial times a village where Indians were forcibly settled. Here is a lovely restored church dating from the mid-eighteenth century, with brightly whitewashed walls and red tile roof. In violation of all tradition, the main door faces eastward, rather than to the west. The church houses a small collection of religious art. There are hot springs at the edge of town, but you can safely save your swimming for later.

ARRIVALS AND DEPARTURES

Most buses to Orosi end their run near the Motel Río (see next page). Without a car, you can walk or hitch a ride toward the Cachí Dam, or backtrack to Cartago to pick up a bus to Cachí, through Ujarrás.

COFFEE TOURS

Orosi Coffee Adventure offers daily tours at the **Renex plantation** and mill tours (on the main road, past the village), at 10 a.m. and 2 p.m. The fee is $16 with lunch, $12 with a snack only, and, according to when you visit during the year, you can see the picking, washing, repeated peeling, fermenting, washing, drying, and sorting of the famous bean before packing for export.

For information, contact **Aventuras Turísticas de Orosi**, tel. [5]733030.

TAPANTÍ NATIONAL PARK

A branch road two kilometers from Orosi passes the Río Macho hydroelectric works, and winds ten kilometers up yet another beautiful valley to **Tapantí National Park**, accessible only in your own vehicle or on foot. There are nature trails a kilometer past the entry point (you pay a small fee), with plants well marked with their names, and explanations of their roles in forest life. Signs point the way to a bouldery wading area in the rushing Río Macho, which is known as a good trout stream. Three kilometers past the hiking area is a lookout point, which offers prime views to a chute of water, and down the valley, but as vistas go in Costa Rica, this one is not of national standing.

WHERE TO STAY

A youth-hostel-type shelter, with mattresses only, is available to visitors for a small fee. Call [2]334160 and ask for a radio patch to Tapantí if you wish to reserve a space.

CABINAS KIRI, just before the entry to the park and 300 meters off the access road, has four guest rooms in two cabins, at about $39 per person with three meals. You can also stop here just for a meal or drink.

PALOMO

Past the suspension bridge two kilometers from Orosi (or adjacent, by a shaky footbridge that avoids a road loop) is **Palomo**.

WHERE TO STAY

Right at the end of the bridge, without an identifying sign, is the **MOTEL RÍO** (or **Palomo Resort**), which has an oversized swimming pool overlooking the Reventazón, open to non-guests at a small charge. The pleasant, cane-ceilinged pavilion dining room is best known for its river fish, and also serves steaks. Main courses cost about $5.

You can phone or fax the motel at [5]733057 to reserve for a night in the country. The seven units are not luxurious, but they're quite large — some have kitchens — and the rush of the river by your door is soothing. At about $30 double (Visa and Master Card accepted), they're a good value, indeed. If the car gate is closed when you arrive, walk in and look for the caretaker. Dinner is served by reservation only.

CACHÍ DAM

Continuing by car (or tour bus), you'll proceed about eight kilometers past the spur for the village of **Cachí**.

Along the way is **Casa del Soñador** (House of the Dreamer), the fanciful bamboo-panelled house of woodcarver Macedonio Quesada. Statues of town gossips, worked in coffee root, stare at curious passersby from the windows. Inside is a trove of folkware and pre-Columbian pieces; adjoining is a studio used by the artist's son, Hermes.

Onward is the **Cachí Dam**, one of the larger hydroelectric projects of the Central Valley. The dam is encrusted with lilies on one side; a trickle of water spills downstream into a great chasm on the other.

THE UJARRÁS MISSION

Past the dam, a kilometer and a half to the west down a side road, at **Ujarrás**, are the remains of a Spanish mission, one of the first churches in colonial Costa Rica. According to tradition, a humble Huetar Indian fished a box from the river and carried it to Ujarrás, from where it could not be budged. When opened, it was found to contain an image of the Virgin. A church was built on the site, in about 1560.

A few years later, when the British pirates Mansfield and Morgan landed at Portete, a force was hastily organized to expel the invaders. After a prayer stop at Ujarrás, the defenders marched to the Caribbean, where they defeated the superior English force. The victory was attributed to the Virgin of Ujarrás. The church was later abandoned after a series of earthquakes and floods, and the image, now less recalcitrant, was taken to Paraíso. But the ruins, in a manicured park, remain a pleasing sight. They are the locale of an annual tribute to the Virgin in mid-March.

CHARRARA PARK

Charrara recreation area, two kilometers from the main road down a spur from the road to Ujarrás, is something like a lakeside state or provincial park, with swimming area, basketball court, changing rooms, and a restaurant. It's well-kept and pleasant enough. Closed on Mondays, there is a small admission fee.

More Views

The last stopping point on the Orosi circuit is the **Ujarrás lookout point**, high above the valley, where the highway curves back to the west, toward Paraíso (six kilometers from the Charrara turnoff) and Cartago. Take a good look before you leave the scenery behind.

WEST AND NORTH OF SAN JOSÉ

HEREDIA

Founded in 1706 at the foot of the extinct Barva volcano by migrants from Cartago, **Heredia** is a short commute from San José. One of Costa Rica's largest coffee mills is on the outskirts, the National University is located here, and there are some impressive mansions on the western side of town. But most of the population is working-class, and the central area has a down-at-the-heels air.

Orientation

Nevertheless, there are some architectural gems in Heredia. The main church on the central park, dating from 1797, is one of the few in Costa Rica that survive from the colonial period. With massive walls of stuccoed stone blocks stained brown and black and overgrown with moss, a triangular pediment, and an almost separate, squat bell tower, it is a near-perfect example of the public architectural style of the last years of Spanish rule. The low contours were meant to resist earthquakes, or at least control damage from vibrating, toppling towers and walls. The church is also one of the more atmospheric buildings in Costa Rica, without excessive restoration and sprucing up.

Set back from the north side of the park is **El Fortín**, the old Spanish fortress tower that is the symbol of Heredia. With gun slits that widen to the exterior, in defiance of standard military architecture, El Fortín stands as an unintended symbol of Costa Rica's non-belligerent nature. A number of other buildings on the square have a colonial air, with colonnades and aging tile roofs.

One last item to see in Heredia is an art deco church on the secondary square at Calle 6 and Avenida 8. It's homely, but cute in its way.

> **HEREDIA FACTS**
> Population: 32,000; Altitude: 1152 meters (3779 feet);
> Location: 11 kilometers from San José

ARRIVALS AND DEPARTURES
By Bus

While Heredia's attractions are not to everybody's taste, the town is on the way to Alajuela and the Barva and Poás volcanoes. Do stop by if you have the time. Microbuses for Heredia leave from Calle 1, Avenidas 7/9, San José. Bus service is also available from Alajuela.

WHERE TO STAY

On another road branching from the Monte de la Cruz road is **HOTEL EL TIROL**, a Tyrolean-style hotel in a private forest, where you can spend the night or stop for an excellent meal. Farther west on the slopes of Barva, on the narrow, paved road that winds from the village of San José de la Montaña down to Birrí, are three more hotels that take advantage of the broad views and fresh mountain air. These are all described at the end of this chapter.

SEEING THE SIGHTS NEAR HEREDIA

In **San Pedro de Barva** is a museum dedicated to everything that has to do with coffee. An assortment of specialized equipment is on display, some of it dating back to the last century. The museum, four blocks north of the church, is open weekdays until 3 p.m.

The bus for San Pedro de Barva leaves from Avenida 1, Calles 1/3, Heredia.

Barva, a couple of kilometers north of Heredia, is a standard Central Valley town, but for the low, thick-walled buildings with red tiled roofs that line the grassy square. It's not really colonial — the church is baroque nineteenth-century — but it's enough to make you think you're in some

FRUIT AND VEGETABLE STORE

less-advantaged part of Central America.

The bus for Barva runs from Calle 1, Avenidas 1/3, Heredia.

In **San Joaquín de las Flores**, on the way to Santa Bárbara, is **Butterfly Paradise**, one of several exhibition areas of this sort that have opened in Costa Rica in the last few years. Hours are 9 a.m. to 4 p.m. daily. For information, call 212015 or 241095.

North and east of Heredia are suburban villages and private and public forests that are a weekend resort area for the capital. Roads are poorly marked. If you're driving, stop and ask for directions at every church.

San Isidro de Heredia has a large, impressive, country-Gothic church. The village is most easily reached by a turnoff to the west from the expressway to Limón. (This is *not* San Isidro de Coronado, which is east of the highway).

Directly north of **San Rafael de Heredia**, a cedar-lined road climbs the slopes of Barva volcano, through pastures broken by streams rushing down over falls. If you have a rented car, it's pleasant to poke around the byways of the area, though some, such as that leading to the **Bosque de la Hoja Park**, are suitable only for four-wheel-drive. Near Bosque de la Hoja is a **miniature working railroad**, open on weekends.

Monte de la Cruz park, high up, offers from its concrete cross, for a small fee, magnificent views over rolling pasture and beyond a screen of pines to the city of San José and the Central Valley stretching out below. Behind are duck ponds, and above, gnarled and mossy bromeliad-laden oaks. There are picnic tables; or, you can stop at an inelegant but reasonably priced restaurant, which offers the same great vistas through its picture windows, and shelter from the continuous winds as well. Up here on the edge of the volcanic divide, rain clouds can blow through at any time of the year.

BRAULIO CARRILLO NATIONAL PARK

Farther north from Heredia is **Braulio Carrillo National Park**, which takes in the extinct **Barva** and **Cacho Negro** volcanoes. The park was established to protect the flora and fauna along the highway to Guápiles and Limón, in the Caribbean region.

Carrillo Park, which varies in altitude from 500 to 2,906 meters (9,534 feet, the peak of Barva volcano), encompasses tropical wet forest, premontane wet forest, and montane wet forest, or cloud forest. All that "wet" means that branches are laden with orchids, bromeliads and mosses, while ferns, shrubs and much else compete with trees for floor space. On the Atlantic slope are numerous waterfalls and pools. Strong winds blow through, between the Irazú and Barva volcanoes.

Common animals in Carrillo Park include foxes, coyotes, white-faced, spider and howler monkeys, ocelots, sloths and several species of poisonous snakes. More than 500 bird species have been catalogued, including the uncommon quetzal, the long-tailed symbol of liberty whose feathers were treasured in ancient Mesoamerica. Spottings of the quetzal are usually made in the forest atop Barva.

ARRIVALS AND DEPARTURES

By Car

One entry point is 20 kilometers from Heredia, reached via a road through San José de la Montaña, and the horse country and oak forest beyond. This route will take you to the crater lake atop **Barva Volcano** (see below).

The toll road to the lowlands (*Autopista a Limón*) runs right through the saddle between the Barva and Irazú volcanoes, roughly following a historic cart road that connected San José with the railhead at Carrillo, before the line from Limón to San José was completed. The eerie roadside vegetation is untouched by farmers, in contrast to readily accessible terrain everywhere else in the country. The winding highway, fog, and heavy traffic make it unwise to stop just anywhere along this route, though there are some sections of the park partially developed for visitors.

The Alto de la Palma entrance, north of Moravia, has been closed to visitors because of landslides and preservation work on the old cart road. Inquire at the park service as to current conditions.

By Bus

Buses for Guápiles will drop you at the ranger station near the entrance to the Zurquí tunnel. Departures are about every half hour from Calle 12, Avenidas 7/9, San José.

WARNING ABOUT BRAULIO CARRILLO PARK

Braulio Carrillo Park along the toll highway is a muggers' paradise. Visitors alone or in small groups are easily cornered on secluded trails. Perpetrators disappear easily into San José, not far away. Numerous visitors have been robbed at gunpoint, and their cars vandalized or stolen.

The trail from the ranger station, on the south side of the Zurquí tunnel, is relatively frequented, and probably safe (I make no guarantees). Farther on, the Botarrama trail, beyond the River Sucio, should be avoided, unless you are advised by a reliable source, or are with a fair-sized tour group.

BARVA VOLCANO

Barva (2,906 meters) presents a different aspect from the other major volcanoes of the Central Valley, Irazú and Poás. Its peak is lower than that of its neighbors, and forested. The top is reached by a trail, so it doesn't constitute an "attraction" for groups on tour buses. Views from the top are limited. But the cloud forest is fascinating, and with a start by car or by public transportation, Barva can be visited on a day outing from San José.

The narrow road through San José de la Montaña, winding up Barva's flanks through horse-grazing pastures and oak forest, is paved as far as Sacramento, and passable beyond with four-wheel drive. If you've come by car, park and lock at this point, or as far beyond Sacramento as you can go. Three kilometers beyond the end of the pavement is a ranger station, at the boundary of Braulio Carrillo Park. Official hours here are from 8 a.m. or 4 p.m.

Ascending Barva

A muddy jeep trail (used only by official vehicles) ascends from the ranger post through dense, moss-laden high cloud forest, then narrows and descends to the lake in Barva's crater. Once you reach the shore, you can continue for another 200 meters or so, via a more difficult and squishy trail, to a lookout point at a higher elevation, though it is usually fogged in. At a steady pace, you can reach the lake from the ranger station in under an hour, and return — mostly downhill — in about a half-hour.

By public transportation, take a Paso Llano bus from Heredia (5 , 6:30 or 11:30 a.m.), get off as far as it goes toward Sacramento, and start walking. From here, it's about two hours or more to the peak. Later buses go only as far as San José de la Montaña, adding still another hour to your walk, through beautiful forest and past small dairy farms, but along a paved road, and not very adventurous. Confirm bus hours, and current rules concerning camping, with the park service at the zoo in San José before you go.

The **Jungle Trails** travel agency, near the Hotel Torremolinos (tel. [2]553486), regularly organizes trips to the top of Barva.

ALAJUELA

Located just a short ride west of the capital, **Alajuela** ("a-la-HWEH-la") is Costa Rica's second city, founded late in the colonial period, in 1790. Bustling, with a climate warmer than San José's, Alajuela is an important cattle marketing and sugar-processing center, and, increasingly, a site for small manufacturing industries. The denizens of the town are famously good humored, and well they might be, for Alajuela is the most pleasant of the provincial capitals, a place where lingering around the square is the chief diversion, and a recommended one.

Alajuela's main claim to fame is as the birthplace of **Juan Santamaría**, the drummer boy who set fire to the headquarters of the American adventurer William Walker in 1857, thus helping to bring about the defeat of the filibuster forces that had taken control of Nicaragua.

> **ALAJUELA FACTS**
> Population: 46,600;Altitude: 941 meters (3,087 feet);
> Location: 23 kilometers from San José

ARRIVALS AND DEPARTURES
By Car
The city is just a short hop from San José. If you're driving, take the Cañas highway (Autopista General Cañas, or simply *la pista*). The turnoff for Alajuela is near the airport.

By Bus
Buses leave from Avenida 2, Calles 12/14, San José, every 15 minutes or so until about midnight, then every hour on the hour. The bus terminal in Alajuela is at Calle 8, Avenidas Central/1, three blocks west of the square. Microbuses leave as well from Avenida 4, Calles 2/4 for San José.

Departing
Once you've made the rounds of Alajuela, you'll have your choice of

continuing to Poás volcano, Ojo de Agua springs, a butterfly farm, a tropical zoo, and the towns of Grecia, Sarchí and Naranjo; which places are describedlater in this chapter.

WHERE TO STAY

HOTEL ALAJUELA, Calle 2, Avenidas Central/2 (P.O. Box 110, tel. 41[1]1241), a half-block from the square, $27 single/$34 double, is a fairly clean, homey, and relatively modern establishment, with 32 modest rooms. Rooms on the street side can be quite noisy. There are few decent hotels in downtown Alajuela, and only 20 rooms in this one, so call before you come. (Hint: Alajuela is only a half-hour from San José by frequent bus and microbus.)

On the edge of town, **APARTOTEL EL ERIZO** (P. O. Box 61-4050 Alajuela, tel. and fax 41[2]2840), ten blocks west of the square along Avenida 1, at the Lucky Strike sign, has 11 harshly furnished garden apartments in a stuccoed block, with cooking and laundry facilities, as well as phones and televisions. The gardens are pleasant, anyway. The rate is $60 daily, and each sleeps three or four persons.

HOSTAL VILLA REAL, tel. 41[4]4856, two blocks north and one block east of the church, is a bare-bones traditional wooden house, clean and adequate, operated as a lodging place by enthusiastic young people. There are five rooms sharing bath at $12 single/$22 double/$30 triple. Tell Flavio that I sent you.

WHERE TO EAT

There are a few enjoyable restaurants in Alajuela.

The menu of **JOEY'S**, a drinking and eating spot open to the square, decorated with garish winking light strings, interleaves French toast, hamburgers and fries, chef's salad, filet mignon and sea bass with Pittsburgh, Durango, Costa Rica, and other elements in the life of the proprietor. About $6 to $8 for a meal. Joey's doubles as a travel agency and home-away-from-home for wanderers.

MARISQUERÍA LA SIRENITA, on the south side of the main square near the church, serves inexpensive seafood. With harsh fluorescent lighting and minor nautical decor, you won't come for the atmosphere. But the sea bass in a tomato-and-herb sauce is excellent for a couple of dollars or so, and you can order shrimp by size without breaking your budget.

The **CENCERRO** (*the cowbell*), upstairs on Avenida Central, facing the park, serves charcoal-broiled steaks and fish and chicken dishes. $8 and up.

For more home-style cooking, try **LA JARRA**, at Calle 2 and Avenida 2, a block south from the square and upstairs, with many windows to catch the breeze. Scores of potted plants decorate the large room, and there are a few balcony tables. About $6 for a full meal, $3 for the daily luncheon special, sandwiches for less.

LAS COCINAS DE LEÑA, Calle 2, Avenida 6 (three blocks from the square along the same street as the Hotel Alajuela) is an unpretentious Tico-style bar and grill with Formica tables and varnished walls. Mexican and Tico snacks — *nachos, chalupas* — and grilled steaks and fish go for $4 and $5. Live music on weekends.

SEEING THE SIGHTS

The main square of Alajuela is a shady forest-garden, with mango and palm trees, where locals and not a small number of resident foreigners observe the passing of the day from stone benches. Also hanging out in the park, more literally, are a few two-toed sloths, those snail-slow creatures that look slug-ugly in photos but are cute and furry in the flesh. Assorted statuary and fountains complete the picture. Bordering the park are a number of substantial old buildings from the coffee-boom days, with massive walls, stone-trimmed windows, iron grilles, and, in one instance, corner turrets.

A statue of the **Erizo** (the *Hedgehog*, as local hero Juan Santamaría is affectionately known, for his bristly hair) may be seen a block south of the main square, on Calle 2. Torch in hand, rifle at his side, he stands ready to repeat his deed.

Facing the east side of the central park is the city's main church, an uninteresting neo-classical structure with simple lines. (For orientation purposes, Calle Central runs along the east side of the park, by the church, Avenida Central along the south.)

About five blocks east of the central park is a more attractive church, built in a Costa Rican simplified baroque style, with angels popping up around the edge of the faáade.

A block north of the square is the **Juan Santamaría Historical Museum**, housed in the solid building at the corner of Calle 2 and Avenida 3. Costa Ricans and Yanqui-bashers will examine the artifacts and battle paintings of the Walker war. Others will admire the building itself, with its wide archways, massive beams, whitewashed walls and tile roof.

William Walker continues to serve a rather useful purpose in Costa Rica, as an outlet for any resentments against Americans, who are generally liked. If you get into a conversation on the subject, be sure to condemn Walker's acts of more than a hundred years ago, which were, in fact, despicable. The man sought to re-institute slavery, held elections of doubtful validity, and found excuses to break numerous promises and betray his friends.

Hours at the museum are 2 p.m. to 9 p.m., daily except Monday.

POAS VOLCANO

Poás has several distinctions. It has one of the largest geyser-type craters in the world — 1.5 kilometers across and 300 meters deep. It contains two lakes, one in an extinct crater, one in the fuming main crater. It is in continuing activity, in the form of seeping gases and steam, as well as occasional geysers and the larger eruptions of every few years (the last in 1978). Most practically for the visitor, it is easily reached by a paved road to the peak (2,704 meters — 8,871 feet— above sea level), and the facilities atop the mountain are the best in the national park system.

Orientation

The climate atop Poás is less severe than that on Irazú; the peak is several hundred meters lower, and the steam and gases burn out a smaller area. Vegetation is therefore more abundant. But on a windy day, or when the peak is enshrouded in a dripping pea soup, the visitor will find nothing benign about the environment. Nighttime temperatures well below freezing are not uncommon.

Much of the upper part of Poás is cloud forest, the enchanted, cool, moist environment where orchids and bromeliads and vines thrive at every level, along with humble ferns and mosses on the ground. The Poás cloud forest is especially rich in mushrooms and lichens. Parts of the national park are former pastures that are being allowed to return to their natural states; these contain many oak trees. Other sections near the peak are meadow-like, or are characterized by low shrubs and gnarled and twisted trees.

Wildlife in the Poás forest is not abundant, possibly because nearby slopes are farmed intensively. Among the inhabitants are brocket deer, coatis, sloths, cougars, and the Poás squirrel, which has been found only in this vicinity. Birds include several types of hummingbirds, trogons, and the emerald toucanet among more than 70 recorded species.

With increasing volcanic activity in recent years, rains of gases, acids and ash have damaged crops in the surrounding area, and caused authorities to limit access to the park. Currently, visitors may spend no more than 30 minutes at the main crater. They are warned to leave immediately if they feel any irritation of the throat or eyes, not to picnic near the lookout, and not to drink from the park's acidic water system.

ARRIVALS AND DEPARTURES

Get an early start! Aside from the unique experience of ascending a volcano, you'll want to beat the clouds to the peak in order to get an ocean-to-ocean view. Take a good look at the volcano before you start your ascent. If the cloud cap is dense and widespread, it might be better to wait for another day.

Poás is open to visitors from 8 a.m. to 3:30 p.m. Rain gear will come in handy even in the dry season, when heavy winds whip clouds across the peak. Take a sweater or jacket as well. Temperatures can dip sharply in minutes.

Two routes are available, through Alajuela or Heredia. These converge at the little village of Poasito, high on the volcano's slopes.

Either way, the visitor ascends through coffee, cattle and horse country. I won't bother to describe in detail the increasingly dramatic and grandiose vistas that are afforded of the Central Valley and of distant volcanoes and mountain ridges as the road winds onward and upward into pine and oak altitudes, such landscapes and views having been mentioned elsewhere.

By Car

If you're driving, take the Cañas expressway to Alajuela, then follow the clearly marked road via San Pedro de Poás and Poasito. The peak is 37 kilometers from Alajuela, 59 kilometers from San José. An alternative route from San José goes through Heredia and Barva, and up to Los Cartagos and Poasito, through equally dramatic and windy landscapes as those along the Poasito road. Try both routes.

By Bus

A public bus to Poás (Tuasa, tel. [2]337477) leaves on Sundays only from 12 Calle, Avenidas 2/4, San José. Be there by 8 a.m. Fare is less than $5. This is an all-day excursion — bring a snack. The ride up takes two hours, with a twenty-minute rest stop at a café high on the volcano, near Poasito. Three hours are allowed on top before departure, more than ample time to see both accessible craters and the cloud forest.

On other days, buses are available from Alajuela to Poasito (lately at 5 a.m. and 1:30 p.m.). This still leaves you ten kilometers from the peak. You'll have to walk, hitch, or hire a taxi to finish the ascent.

By Tour or Taxi

Tours operate to Poás most days from San José, or you can hire a taxi to take you all the way at a reasonable cost.

SEEING THE SIGHTS

The substantial **Visitors Center** includes an auditorium where a half-hour slide show about the national parks is sometimes given. Orient yourself at the exhibit area before walking around, since you'll be covering a lot of territory. Aside from a model of the volcano and its craters, there are some wonderful peek-a-boo contraptions where you can try to identify animals by their tracks, samples of volcanic products, volcanic cross-sections, and descriptions of the extensive flora of Costa Rica.

The Craters of Poás

From the visitors' center, you'll probably head first to the **main crater**. Along the walkway you'll notice the plant called the *sombrilla del pobre* (poor man's parasol), which is characteristic of the open areas of Poás. The leaves grow up to two meters across, which explains the name and occasional use of the plant.

Visitors are not allowed to descend into the fuming main crater, but the views from its rim are impressive. At the bottom is a sometime lake formed by rain water, its shade of green changing according to the amount of sulfur it contains at any given time. Water level varies according to the whims and fury and fractures of the earth underneath. Intermittent geyser activity results from water seeping into fissures along the bottom of the lake, then boiling and exploding upward. More likely, you'll see gas and steam escaping from fumaroles along the lake's edge. The rim of the crater is burned and strewn with rock and ash, and only a few shrubs struggle for survival in the noxious environment.

After a visit to the active crater, climb to **Laguna Botos**, the water-filled extinct crater near the highest point on the volcano. The lake is named for an Indian tribe that once inhabited the area.

The last major attraction atop Poás is the **nature trail**, a run of about half a kilometer through a relatively undisturbed stretch of cloud forest, providing a more interesting route to the crater than the road. The signs in Spanish along the way are more poetic than informative, and some specific labels of trees and plants would be useful (says the gringo). This is the most accessible area of forest of this type in Costa Rica.

Vistas and Fog

Unfortunately, it's easier to describe many of the features of Poás than actually to see them. The top of the mountain is often clouded over, at least partially. However, the clouds shift frequently. If the main crater is obscured at first, take another look before you leave. The shroud might have lifted. The view to either coast, and northward into Nicaragua, might also open up from time to time, so keep an eye peeled.

OJO DE AGUA

A few kilometers south of Alajuela, just southeast of the international airport, are the **Ojo de Agua** springs and recreation area (not to be confused with the town of the same name, which is west of the airport). Water gushes from the earth at a rate of 200 liters per second, and most of the flow is directed into an aqueduct that supplies the city of Puntarenas, on the Pacific.

Much of the remainder is used for the amusement of the citizenry. In the tree-shaded park surrounding the springs are three pools, tennis courts, and a lake with rowboats. On weekends, this is a great place to rub elbows and much else with the locals. Go during the week if you prefer solitude, or serious swimming (or pass it up altogether if the pool at your hotel is more to your taste). Entry costs about 50¢, and changing rooms are available. There are cheap eateries both inside and outside the gates. Through no particular logic, the recreational facilities are managed by the national railroad company.

Buses operate to Ojo de Agua from Avenida 2, Calle 22, San José, hourly on the half hour during the week, and every fifteen minutes or so on weekends. There are also buses from Alajuela and Heredia.

West of Ojo de Agua, at **Guácima**, is the **Butterfly Farm**, where several dozen species of the insect are raised for live export to European exhibitions. The part open to the public is a hillside rain forest under protective netting. A dammed stream tumbles into a pond, ferns and fronds and violets and impatiens step up and around the boulders, trees tower above. And, of course, there are butterflies, several dozen species or more, according to the season, along with ants and spiders and lizards that the netting doesn't keep out, and displays of leaf-cutter ants under glass.

The butterfly exhibit opens every day at 9 a.m. Tours operate continuously (the last starts at 3:30 p.m.), terminating at a stand where t-shirts and mounted butterflies may be acquired. The earliest hours are best for watching butterflies emerge from their cocoons.

The farm also offers a "bee tour" aboard a traditional oxcart, a two-hour excursion that includes a look at hives, explanations of bee life cycles, and insights into Mayan apiculture in ancient America.

The farm is about half a kilometer south of Guácima, southwest of the international airport. Take the road around the airport, or the road westward from the Cañas expressway through San Antonio de Belén. Signs are posted at every junction. A direct bus runs intermittently from San José (currently Monday, Tuesday, Thursday).

The Butterfly Farm is open daily from 9 a.m. to 3:30 p.m. Admission is a steep $9 for the butterfly tour, $8 for the bee tour and oxcart ride, or $16 for both (this is not a misprint). Rates are lower for students and children, but most families can find better values elsewhere. Phone 48[0]0115 for information or bus directions from Alajuela. The owners speak English.

LA GARITA/DULCE NOMBRE

West of Alajuela, along the highway to Atenas, at Dulce Nombre, is the **Zoológico de Aves Tropicales** (Tropical Bird Zoo, "ZOH-oh AH-veh"), which holds an outstanding collection in a lovely landscaped setting. (In fact, the area around Dulce Nombre and La Garita is replete with beautiful gardens and plant nurseries.) Species represented include owls, honeycreepers, toucans, hawks, parrots and macaws.

Usual hours are 9 a.m. to 5 p.m. daily, admission is a couple of dollars. Stop this way if you're passing through the area, or have a special interest in tropical fauna.

ARRIVALS AND DEPARTURES
By Bus
The Atenas or La Garita bus from Alajuela passes the entrance (on the north side of the road), or you can look for a Dulce Nombre bus from the Coca-Cola terminal in San José.

By Car
By car, drive eastward for three kilometers from the Atenas exit of the expressway.

WHERE TO STAY
Several bed-and-breakfasts, largely owned by retired Americans, are located in the area around Atenas. These are described at the end of this chapter.

WHERE TO EAT
The road onward to Atenas is popular for weekend excursions. Various roadside restaurants specialize in chicken roasted over coffee wood, and barbecued meats. The **FIESTA DE MAÍZ** eatery serves *pozole*, *tamales*, *tortillas*, and everything else fashioned in whole or part from corn, the traditional staff of life of Central America — corn on the cob, corn fritters, tamales, corn soup, corn stew, corn bread. Open Fridays through Sundays only.

About four kilometers up the road from the Fiesta de Maíz toward Turrúcares is **LAS CAMPANAS**, a charming indoor/outdoor roadhouse illuminated by fixtures with macramé lamp shades, where the likes of *paté de foie*, chili con carne, sirloin in sauce, and quail are served, along with rabbit, which is not on the menu. You can be served in English, French (*Ö la canadienne*) or Spanish.

GRECIA, SARCHÍ, NARANJO
The old Pan American (or Interamerican) Highway skirts the northern rim of the Central Valley, passing through the picturesque towns of Grecia, Sarchí and Naranjo. Most traffic now speeds to the coast on the

Bernardo Soto Expressway. But the old highway affords a pleasant, slow meander through rolling countryside.

Grecia is most notable for its unusual brick-red church. The surrounding hills here at the hotter, lower end of the Central Valley are largely planted in sugarcane, and much of the output is processed in Grecia.

Beyond Grecia is **Sarchí**, the preeminent craft center of Costa Rica, where dozens of small wood workshops line the highway. Here, tropical hardwoods are made into chairs, tables, and, of course, the brightly painted oxcarts with kaleidoscopic wheels for which Costa Rica is famous. The intricate painted designs on the carts are said to be handed down from father to son. These items are strictly for the local market, but the miniature oxcarts and statuettes are suitable for carrying off. The bi-towered church of Sarchí, with its unusual number of windows, is worth a glance. Costa Rica's country churches are, in general, charming, in contrast to the dull metropolitan temples.

The last major town on the Pan American Highway, before it drops to the coast, is **Naranjo**, dominated by an attractive cream-colored baroque church with double mission-style towers.

ARRIVALS AND DEPARTURES
Arriving By Bus
Buses operate to Grecia, Sarchí and Naranjo every half-hour from Alajuela (Tuasa station). To continue to the coast, take a San Ramón bus from Naranjo to the Soto highway (*la pista*) and flag down a bus for Puntarenas or Guanacaste.

Departing By Bus
You can also continue to Ciudad Quesada (San Carlos) and onward to Lake Arenal or the northern lowlands. **San Ramón**, junction for the road to Ciudad Quesada (San Carlos), has yet another intricate church in intricate northern Italian style. Next to the main square is a museum that honors the way of life of country people, with a replica of a peasant home and old-fashioned tools.

SOUTH OF SAN JOSÉ

The road through Aserrí crests the mountains that crown the Central Valley, and twists up and down broken terrain through the towns of **San Marcos de Tarrazú, San Pablo de León Cortés, San Cristóbal Sur, San Gerardo de Dota** and **Santa María de Dota**, in a loop back toward the Pan American Highway and Cartago. With these names — Saints Mark, Paul, Christopher, Gerard and Mary — this has come to be called the *Route of the Saints*.

Santa María, reached first by the ribbon of branch road from the Pan American Highway, has an attractive square, with a monument to those who died in the 1948 civil war. Otherwise, it is just a typical Central Valley Town, picturesque not in itself, but in the breathtaking approach by which it is achieved, with successive mountain silhouettes as a backdrop.

Copey, six kilometers beyond, has a falls and small lake.

ARRIVALS AND DEPARTURES

By Bus

Buses for Santa María depart about every two hours from Avenida 16, Calles 17/21. Check with the tourist office for the latest schedules.

WHERE TO STAY

The **HOTEL DOTA**, tel. [5]741026, with bar and restaurant, $7 per person, will do as a stopping point for the night.

COUNTRY LODGING NEAR SAN JOSÉ

Attractive alternatives to city hotels are to be found in the villages and valleys and on the mountain and volcanic slopes around San José. Despite surroundings of orchards and forests, the inns and lodges of the Central Valley are only minutes from downtown San José, and a short ride from the international airport.

The valley hotels are most suitable if you have a car at your disposal; or are a repeat visitor, and know exactly what you are getting. But anyone can consider them as a base for all or part of a stay in Costa Rica. And, should you change your mind about your preferred style of accommodation, you needn't feel isolated and locked in. These hostelries will also give you a rough idea of country living in the Central Valley, in case you're considering a move. For approximate locations, see the map at the beginning of this chapter.

FINCA ROSA BLANCA COUNTRY INN, P. O. Box 37-3009, Santa Bárbara de Heredia, tel. [2]399392, fax [2]399555. Six suites, one master suite. $85 to $170 single, $115 to $200 double, $29 per additional person, plus tax. U.S. reservations: tel. 800-327-9854.

I was uncertain whether to list the Rosa Blanca as an accommodation or a point of interest. The main house, set amid orchards of citrus, macadamia and cashew trees, is a fantasy made real, a combination of Gaudiésque and Pueblo Indian elements, along with personal whimsy.

Stuccoed walls curve around a central, 40-foot chimney, pre-Columbian ceramics in its niches. Nooks abound, bedecked with collectibles and treasures from around the world. A staircase climbs skyward to the master suite with its crows-nest bedroom and terrace, and pool/tub filled by a stream coursing through a rock garden. In another suite, a scene painted in a niche continues the view through an adjacent window. The Black-and-White room has an art nouveau theme. And this is just the start.

The plantings around Rosa Blanca attract birds, which can be spotted in the foliage right outside the various levels of the main house. Views, according to cloud patterns, are variously to mountains and valleys and near and distant hamlets.

Breakfast is included in the rate, and other meals will be prepared on request. Also for rent is a cottage (*casita*) built in the style of a traditional Costa Rican country house, with three bedrooms, for $100 to $150 per day, less by the week or month. A pool will be added soon.

To get to Rosa Blanca, from the airport or Alajuela, drive through Santa Bárbara, turning north at the sign before Barrio Jesús.

MI KIVA, in the hills above Santa Bárbara, operated by the former owners of the Rosa Blanca, has a large main house in Santa Fe pueblo style, and two miniature pueblo bungalows available for rent. Contact Rosa Blanca for directions and rates.

POSADA DE LA MONTAÑA, P. O. Box 1-3017, San Isidro de Heredia, tel. and fax [2]398096. U.S. reservations, P. O. Box 308, Greenfield, MO 65661, tel. 417-637-2066. $30-40 single/$35-45 double, including breakfast, $70 and up for units with kitchenettes, lower rates for rooms sharing bath. Visa, Master Card, American Express.

On a cool, wind-swept slope, the **MOUNTAIN INN** is an American-owned bed-and-breakfast on several acres affording long views of San José, the Central Valley, and the forests stretching toward Limón between the volcanoes Irazú and Barva. The property includes coffee and fruit plantings and a huge vegetable garden, all of which attract birds. Six rooms in the main house, each with two beds, are off a huge *sala* with fireplace. Six more concrete "cabina"-style units, with outside entry and parking at the door, can be combined with kitchenettes for families or groups. Washing machines are available to guests, and horses can be hired nearby. Beverages and airport pickup available. Children and pets welcome. English, Spanish, Russian and French spoken. This is the closest accommodation to Braulio Carrillo National Park.

If driving, take the Limón Highway to the San Isidro de Heredia exit (left side), continue four kilometers to the bridge, then 1.5 kilometers north. Signs point the way. Call for bus instructions.

The hotels below are along the road between Birrí and San José de la Montaña, north of Heredia. Buses run from Heredia to San José de la Montaña. Continue by taxi, if you're not driving.

HOTEL DE MONTAÑA EL PÓRTICO, P. O. Box 289-3000, Heredia, tel. [2]276022. 16 units. $65 double, $12 per additional person. The best of the country lodges in the immediate area, with brick-and-wood units clustered around a pond, a restaurant, sauna and pool. Phone 212039 in San José to arrange transportation.

HOTEL CYPRESAL, P. O. Box 7891-1000, San José, tel. [2]374466, [2]231717 in San José, fax [2]216244. 24 rooms. $57 single/$63 double. Credit cards accepted. Also with pool, whirlpool, sauna, large restaurant. Units have kitchenettes, TV, television, some have fireplace. Horses available, also meeting facilities, along with package trips with excursions to several national parks, using the hotel as a base.

CABINAS LAS ARDILLAS, tel. [2]228134. Adjacent to the Cypresal in a pine-and-cedar park. Units, built of logs and brick, have long valley views, and there are a restaurant and play area. The rate is about $40 for a unit that will sleep a couple and two children, $75 for a much larger unit into which up to eight persons can be crowded.

Higher up, near the park at **Monte de la Cruz**, is:

HOTEL EL TIROL, P.O. Box 7812-1000, San José, tel. [2]397371, fax [2]397050. 23 units. $90 double in chalets, up to $175 double in suites, breakfast included. Visa, Master Card, American Express. The main building here is genuinely Tyrolean, in a suitable mountain landscape of conifers and meadows, and the cottages are dollhouse versions, with cutout wood trim. Each guest unit has a bedroom upstairs and a sitting area with convertible bed downstairs, and welcome electric heaters. Adjacent is a section of private forest, with hiking trails and waterfalls. Riding horses are available. Dinner is served in front of a fireplace in the main building, and is attraction enough for many visitors. Steak and seafood and rabbit main courses are offered on a French menu. A complete meal costs about $20, and is usually excellent. El Tirol reminds me of the original Trapp Family Lodge in Stowe, Vermont.

ORQUÍDEAS INN, San José de Alajuela (P. O. Box 394, Alajuela), tel. 43[9]9346, fax 43[9]9740. 18 rooms. $57 single/$68 double with breakfast. Visa, Master Card. This is a colonial-style hotel in a little estate just past the junction for Grecia on the road from Alajuela to Poás volcano. Rooms have arched openings, and furniture throughout is of white wicker. The higher rate is for a suite with hardwood floor, and a huge terrace overlooking the pool. The location is good if you'll be ascending Poás by car; road noise could be a problem. Airport pickup available.

LA PROVIDENCIA ECO-LODGE, tel. [2]317884, has four rustic no-frills cabins behind the restaurant of the same name, almost at the top of Poás volcano, for $60 double. Horseback riding is available.

TUETAL LODGE, Tuetal (P. O. Box 1346-Alajuela), tel. and fax 421804. 7 rooms. $28-$35 single/$35-$40 double. In the village of Tuetal Norte, about a $2 taxi ride from Alajuela, four blocks west and one-and-a-half blocks south of the church. Some units have a kitchen. Breakfast available at $3, and beverages. English-speaking owner. Will have pool and tennis.

POÁS VOLCANO LODGE, Vara Blanca (P. O. Box 5723-1000 San José), tel. and fax 41[9]9102. 8 rooms. $70 double, $110 in suite. A lodge with a British country flavor, built of stone, concrete, and hewn beams, surrounded by pasture, forest, and Central Valley views.

VILLA BLANCA HOTEL, San Ramón (tel. [2]284603, fax [2]284004 in San José). 36 units. $95 double in cottages, $68 in lodge rooms. This is an attractive cloud-forest country lodge on a huge cattle farm 20 kilometers northwest of San Ramón (which is along the highway to Puntarenas), including a forest reserve and trails. The main building has the flavor of a traditional hacienda great house, with open kitchen and a central fountain. Cottages are unusually attractive, with exposed beams, splashily colored rugs and spreads, rocking chairs, built-in ledges, and beehive corner fireplaces. Furnishings include refrigerators and desks. But the most notable fact about Villa Blanca is that the host is former president Rodrigo Carazo. Call for information about package stays. Day trips to the property from San José cost about $70.

Near La Garita

LA CHATELLE. P. O. Box 755-1007, tel. 48[7]7781, fax 48[7]7271. $99 in luxury unit, $80 double in standard unit, with breakfast and airport transfer. Rates lower May, June, and August through November.

Here's an idiosyncratic collection of one-unit cottages, all named for volcanoes. The "luxury" units (their term), with cone-shaped roofs reminiscent of Africa, have a queen-sized and single bed in a loft, another bed downstairs, and full kitchen; the Presidential Suite, with woody decor, has a vaulted ceiling. Standard units have brick walls, and are probably damp on rainy days. Facilities include a pool. The grounds are lush and rolling, and there is a steak-house restaurant that gets a weekend clientele. The rate includes breakfast and transfer from the airport; but a rented car would be helpful, as the owners, who include an American, are not always around to see to the needs of guests. The hotel is one kilometer south of the Fiesta del Maíz restaurant on the road to Atenas.

LA PIÑA DORADA bed-and-breakfast, Turrúcares, tel. and fax 48[7]7220. 5 rooms, $55 to $75 double.

If you follow directions (take the first left after the Fiesta de Maíz restaurant in La Garita and continue 2.8 kilometers) and show up here under your own steam, you'll think you've wandered out of your way. La Piña Dorada is just your standard Spanish-Mediterranean country estate, with vaulted central ceiling in the great house, formal library, huge *sala* with arched picture windows, hand-carved chairs, projection TV, and all the other bare necessities. The grounds, covering two acres, include citrus, banana and mango trees, a goldfish pond with falls and a palm isle, parking under cover, and a large illuminated pool squarely in front of the house.

Guest units vary in size — the largest has a huge sitting room. Comfortable furnishings include wicker chairs, and double or king-plus custom beds. Local art hangs everywhere. Despite the overwhelming facility, hospitality afforded by Mr. and Mrs. Bill Coffey is home-style and friendly. Wine is served at cost, breakfast is huge, with sausage or bacon. Here's your chance to live like the rich and famous for a few days, or for a few weeks, while you see Costa Rica.

By taxi, it's just 15 minutes from the airport to La Piña Dorada.

BED AND BREAKFAST

Here are some additional B&Bs in the Central Valley. For more information, either call the B&B directly, or the Bed and Breakfast Association in Escazú, near San José, tel. [2]289200 or [2]234157. Except as indicated, only English is spoken. ("Spanish spoken" usually indicates a Costa Rican rather than a foreign owner.)

West of San José and the International Airport
ANA'S PLACE, P. O. Box 66, Atenas, tel. 46[5]5019. $45 double, kids and pets welcome, Spanish spoken.

FINCA MIRADOR, P. O. Box 110, Grecia, tel. 44[6]6260. $30 double, airport pickup at extra charge.

COUNTRY INN LA GUÁCIMA, P.O. Box 807-4050 Alajuela, tel. 48[0]0179, fax [2]218245. $60 double, kids and pets welcome. Southwest of the airport.

VILLA TRANQUILIDAD, Atenas (P.O. Box 28-4013 Alajuela), tel. 46[5]5460. $35 double, free airport pickup. Dutch and German spoken.

East of San José
BELLO MONTE, San Ramón de Tres Ríos (P. O. Box 8-5630, 1000 San José), tel. and fax [2]343879. $40 to $50 double. Kids and pets welcome, Spanish, French, German spoken.

Heredia and North of San José
FINCA WA DA DA, P. O. Box 465-3000 Heredia, tel. and fax [2]398284. $35 double. In the middle of a coffee farm.

LOS JARDINES, P. O. Box 64-3011, Barva de Heredia, tel. [2]601904. $32 double. Children welcome.

14. THE OTHER COSTA RICA

Outside the Central Valley is another country, a Costa Rica that in many parts is as underdeveloped as any in Central America. Some of the differences from the highlands will be immediately apparent to the visitor. The population is generally sparse, and good roads are sparser. Houses are often ramshackle affairs, and the neat, flowered gardens around San José give way to dirt yards where chickens scratch for tidbits. The climate, of course, is generally hotter, and usually more humid.

More traditional Latin ways hold sway, in forms both attractive and difficult for the visitor to accept. Events unfold at times at a mañana pace, and schedules are an imperfectly understood concept. Warmth and hospitality are the norm, and the visitor can easily feel at home in any town where he lingers.

Other changes from the highlands are not visible, or slower to manifest themselves. The social-security system provides limited coverage outside the Central Valley, where there are fewer salaried employees. Electricity and drinkable water have not yet reached many smaller settlements. Large banana and palm plantations, cotton farms and cattle ranches take up more of the land than small family homesteads.

Modernization, quite simply, is generally less than in the Central Valley, and much more uneven. There are pleasant, clean, bustling lowland towns such as Liberia; idyllic, nearly isolated national parks; and serene beach settlements. And there are places where, at first glance, the major elements of life appear to be liquor, litter and loud music.

Once you leave the main lowland routes, a flexible schedule is a must, unless you make ironclad arrangements through a travel agency. Expect simpler food and less-than-top-notch service, barer hotel rooms and lower standards of hygiene. There are beach and mountain resorts where these cautions don't apply, but in general, more tolerance and understanding are required. Remember to phone ahead for reservations when possible, and to reconfirm schedules off the main routes, where bus service is limited.

15. THE WILD EAST

INTRODUCTION

North and east of the mountainous backbone of Costa Rica is the triangle-shaped Caribbean coastal region, a vast area of dense tropical forest. No time of year, no remote corner of the Atlantic slope, is ever dry. Clouds blow in from the sea throughout the year. Those that don't drench the area directly shed their water against the central mountains, from where it flows back to the Caribbean in numerous rivers, and often overflows onto the low-lying, poorly drained land. Rainfall at Limón, in the center of the coastal strip, reaches 150 inches in many years, and near the Nicaraguan border, approaches 200 inches.

Despite the thick layer of plants in the lowlands, the soil is poor. Enriching ash blows only westward from the volcanoes of the highlands, and constant rain leaches nutrients.

The tribes that lived in this area before the Conquest were the least settled of Costa Rica, relying on hunting and gathering for their food, as well as on corn plots that had to be frequently relocated as the earth was exhausted. The Caribbean was the locale of the first attempts by the Spaniards to conquer and settle Costa Rica. But jungle heat, endless rain, insects, poisonous tree sap, snakes, dense vegetation, yellow fever, malaria, dysentery, and a hostile population were only some of the obstacles to establishing a plantation agriculture in the region.

In the nineteenth century, as Costa Rica began to export large quantities of coffee, it became clear that a direct, all-year transport route to the Caribbean was needed. In an epic undertaking, and at a cost of thousands of lives, a railroad was completed from the port of Limón to San José in 1890. Long before that date, however, a new export crop was being carried on the route: bananas. Costa Rica was the first nation to supply the world with the fruit, and within a few years, the crop was second only to coffee in earnings. But Panama disease ravished the plantations in the 1930s, and operations were relocated to the Pacific lowlands. Later, cacao, rubber and abaca (manila hemp) were planted, but none proved as profitable as bananas.

The Wild East Today

Spurred by new road and canal construction, settlements are today spreading through much of the formerly empty Caribbean region. Forests are being cut down and converted to pasture, or tilled for crops. And the once-moribund banana industry is reviving, with disease-resistant varieties.

The environment in much of the Caribbean region is still largely uncomfortable, in parts threatening to human existence. Why, then, would anybody venture there, except out of necessity?

Here's why: the trip to Limón is an interesting descent from highlands to jungle through varied zones of vegetation. The Caribbean coastline is one nearly continuous sweep of white beach, most of it deserted. Wildlife treasures abound, including green turtles in their protected nesting area at Tortuguero. Fishing, especially for tarpon, is world-class. The blacks who form a large part of the lowland population are a fascinating culture, quite different from other Costa Ricans. And also, there is nothing menacing in those parts of the Caribbean lowlands where the visitor is likely to tread.

New Road, Old Road, Railroad

Two major routes lead to the Caribbean area:
• The "new" highway to Limón and the beaches, via Braulio Carrillo National Park. By car or bus, you can reach the coast from San José in under three hours on this route.
• The meandering, up-and-down "old" highway, via Cartago and Turrialba. Travel time is about double, but the scenery is varied, and there are more interesting stopping points along the way.

Until recently, the **Jungle Train** also ran from San José to Limón, more or less parallel to the old road, with branch lines into parts of the lowlands. The line closed following landslides in 1990 and 1991. A lowland section remains in operation along the Caribbean coast, and parts of the system are used by tours.

Each of these routes has set the stage for a new level of development of this once-forbidding area. I'll cover them, and the sites and sights along the way, in historical order.

The Jungle Train

Any mention of the railroad line to the Caribbean requires a preliminary excursion into Costa Rican history. Primitive trails descended the Atlantic slope to navigable lowland rivers from at least early in the colonial period, and probably before, but these were often made impassable by rain, and Costa Rica's limited international trade was channeled through the Pacific port of Puntarenas. As early as 1820, an improved route to the

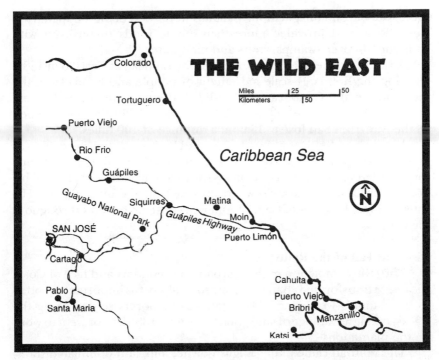

Caribbean was proposed. But no way was found to construct an all-season road, and Costa Rica's ever-expanding coffee exports continued to reach Europe only after a long detour around the tip of South America.

In 1871, the Costa Rican government contracted with Henry Meiggs, an American who had built railroads in the Andes, to construct a line from Limón to San José. The work came under the supervision of a nephew of Meiggs, Minor C. Keith.

Workers were recruited, mostly from New Orleans, and financing was arranged, but the project appeared doomed from the beginning. Floods washed out sections of track almost as soon as they were laid. Nearly 600 of the first 700 workers were soon dead of malaria. The first 25 miles of track cost 4,000 lives, mostly new Chinese recruits who succumbed to yellow fever. Keith himself lost three brothers and an uncle, but pushed on nevertheless, contracting workers from Italy and around the Caribbean. Those who survived were mostly West Indian.

Keith's credit was exhausted before the tracks had progressed far, but his men labored on for months without pay, partly out of personal loyalty, partly because there were few alternatives. Finally, Keith sought temporary revenue by planting banana shoots, brought from Panama, along completed sections of track. Native strains of the fruit already grew in the area, but were inedible, and left to rot. The desperate scheme was successful beyond imagination. Bananas were soon being shipped from Costa Rica, and provided more than ample funds to push on with construction over swamps, rivers and mountains.

A road was opened from San José to the railhead at Carrillo in 1882, allowing the first large-scale movement of people and goods from the highlands to the Caribbean. Landslides, floods, cave-ins, and illness continued to plague the builders, but by the end of 1890, the line was open all the way from San José to Limón, a distance of 100 miles.

Meanwhile, Keith continued to expand his banana business. He was granted vast tracts of land and a 99-year lease on the railroad in exchange for completing its construction on his own account. He consolidated his holdings in Costa Rica and elsewhere into the United Fruit Company. His International Railways of Central America constructed lines throughout the isthmus.

Rise and Fall of the Railroad

With the completion of the railroad, the economy and face of Costa Rica were transformed. Bananas came to be almost as important as coffee to the nation's well-being. Many Jamaican laborers settled along the tracks, taking advantage of land grants under an 1884 law, or went to work on the plantations.

The railroad came under English ownership, and dominated transport in the Caribbean region until the 1970s, when an all-weather road to Limón was completed. With containerization of ocean cargo and the increasing use of trucks, and with buses providing more rapid passenger service, the line, nationalized in 1972, became a chronic money-loser. Traffic declined to just one daily passenger train in each direction between San José and Limón, before landslides put an end to through traffic.

> **TAKE THE OLD TRAIN**
> Inquire at the tourist office or a travel agency about the availability of excursions along the old rail line. Currently, **TAM Tours** (tel. [2]222642) operates a train on a lowland portion of the line, with a stop at a banana warehouse.

The Old Road

The road from San José to Turrialba descends along one tributary valley of the Reventazón, climbs, and descends to the next, seeming to take the path of greatest resistance in abhorrence of bottom lands subject to washouts.

Cervantes, 21 kilometers from Cartago, is perhaps best known to Costa Ricans for its food products, especially pickled Jalapeño peppers.

Just past the village, a branch road climbs to **Pacayas**, on the slopes of Irazú volcano, then loops along the slopes of Turrialba volcano. Smaller farming and coffee-processing centers, **Naranjo** and **Juan Viñas**, lie along the main road.

TURRIALBA

Located where the Central Valley starts to slope down toward the Atlantic jungles, Turrialba is lower, warmer, more languid, and less tidy than towns nearer to San José. Turrialba marks the approximate limit of coffee cultivation. The valley of the Reventazón and its tributaries in this area typically are pastured or planted in sugarcane along their lower, flatter reaches, and covered with coffee bushes on higher slopes.

> **TURRIALBA FACTS**
> Population: 32,000; Altitude: 625 meters (2,050 feet);
> Location: 64 kilometers from San José

ARRIVALS AND DEPARTURES
Arriving By Buses
Buses for Turrialba leave from Avenida 6, Calle 13, San José, about every hour from 7 a.m. to 9 p.m. The trip takes less than two hours.

WHERE TO STAY
HOTEL WAGELIA, tel. 56[1]1596. 18 rooms. $40 single/$58 double, or $57/$73 with air conditioning, TV, refrigerator. An attractive, modern hotel, very clean, with rooms around a courtyard landscaped with palm trees and boulders. Two blocks from the bus station, on the way to San José. The hotel arranges trips to Turrialba volcano, CATIE, and Guayabo National Monument.

Lesser hotels include **LAROCHE**, on the entry street into town, tel. 56[1]1624, and the **PENSIÓN CHELITA** across the street, tel. 56[0]0214, both with rooms for less than $7 per person; and the **CENTRAL, CHAMANGA** and **INTERAMERICANO**. The latter has a few rooms with private bath.

Near Turrialba
TURRIALTICO, tel. 56[1]1111, 8 kilometers from Turrialba on the Limón road, is a woodsy lodge and restaurant with a view. The lodging rate in the 12 rooms is about $25 for up to three persons, under a tin roof (great in downpours!) and off a large sitting area open to the sky. Seating in the restaurant is at tables fashioned from oxcart wheels in an open area under the guest rooms. Cooking is native-style, on a wood stove, and the fare includes steaks, casados, and tortillas stuffed with beans and cheese. Most items cost $4 or less.

POCHOTEL (tel. 56[0]0111, fax 56[6]6222, P. O. Box 121-7150), two kilometers from a turnoff nine kilometers from Turrialba, is harder to reach, but has better views to Turrialba and the installations of CATIE. The menu is native-style, with corn or tripe soup, gallos, casados, and grilled beef and chicken for $2 to $5 per item. There are six rooms here as well as a trailer, going for $20 double, $5 per extra person. Visa and Master Card accepted.

ALBERGUE DE MONTAÑA RANCHO NATURALISTA is a lodge that offers rain forest birding. Call [2]397138 for information.

CASA TURIRE, P. O. Box 303-1750 Turrialba, tel. [5]731111, fax [5]731075. $98 double, $130 to $200 in suites. Add $20 for breakfast and dinner. Take a deep breath, straighten your posture, and prepare for your grand entry to Casa Turire ("tu-REE-ray"). At the end of a kilometer-long palm-lined drive looms a huge three-story tan concrete form wrapped with verandas, making architectural reference to vernacular agrarian structures.

Inside is pure elegance. French doors and large windows frame great lawns and misty mountains, fans whir softly overhead, patterned tile echoes footsteps, a cozy corner bar opens into a grand atrium.

Proceed up a stairway to view a junior suite with its wooden floor, stencilled walls, area rugs, private terrace, armchairs, television concealed in custom-built cabinet, lights in sconces, mini-bar, lockable security box, and large bathroom with tub and hair dryer. Pause at the window, and gaze down to the eight-shaped pool and whirlpool, and terrace. Move on to a standard room, with most of the same amenities, on a slightly reduced scale. Continue and try on the *piéce de resistance*, the master suite, with sitting room, refrigerator, upstairs bedroom, air conditioning, and two full bathrooms, one with a whirlpool, and views through an oversized window to whomever advances onto the grounds of the estate.

Take your *restauration* in the dining room, always elegantly set with crystal, serving a daily continental menu, usually with a choice of two main courses; relax in the game room, with dominoes and other sedate, non-computerized pastimes; take a horseback outing to inspect production in the fields of coffee, sugarcane and macadamia on the domain; or ride a mountain bicycle, play golf, or join a rafting trip.

Obviously, if you have a few dollars to spare, and maybe even if you don't, you will take the opportunity to spend at least a night at Casa Turire, and you will make no excuses for doing so.

"Plantation hotel" only begins to suggest what Casa Turire is. To reach Casa Turire, take the turnoff just after the bridge on the highway south from Turrialba. Continue alongside the Reventazón River and follow the signs four kilometers to the entry.

Children are not allowed through the gates.

SEEING THE SIGHTS

Turrialba is basically an agricultural center of no great attraction. But those with a special interest in agriculture or archaeology might want to make a stop. Many rafting groups also pause here before or after riding the Reventazón.

To go **rafting** here, it's best to make arrangements through a specialized agency in San José.

Four kilometers east of town, on the road to Limón, is **CATIE**, the **Tropical Agronomic Research and Education Center**. Native plant diversity and the range of altitudes and environments on CATIE's more than 2000 acres of land afford a wealth of opportunities for testing plant and animal strains, and developing more efficient ways of cultivating traditional crops. The library on tropical agriculture is recognized as the best of its kind anywhere. CATIE's staff comes from many countries. Guided tours may be arranged by phoning 566431 three days ahead, or through travel agencies in San José. Or you can just drop in and look at the rather lovely and attractively landscaped estate around the main building. Take a local bus from Turrialba, or a taxi for about $3.

GUAYABO NATIONAL MONUMENT

About 20 kilometers north of Turrialba, on the slopes of the Turrialba volcano, is **Guayabo National Monument**. Although Costa Rica is especially rich in pre-Columbian antiquities, its early inhabitants lived nomadic existences, or concentrated in villages and towns built of highly perishable materials.

There are no great native ceremonial centers that survive to this day, as they do in Honduras, Guatemala, El Salvador, and Mexico, or at least they have not yet been discovered. Which is why the Guayabo complex, with its constructions of natural and hewn stone, is considered important by Costa Ricans.

The Guayabo site includes paved walkways, walls, and circular stone constructions, or mounds, that might have been foundations for conical houses of a South American sort, with sides of saplings covered with palm thatch. The largest mound has a stairway oriented to the volcano Turrialba, and volcanic ash found in pottery here indicates that the mountain might have figured in ceremonies or cures.

Subterranean and surface aqueducts, terminating in rectangular stone storage tanks (also signs of South American cultural influence), are still serviceable. These run from some of the hundred or so springs (which first drew people to settle here), and were stepped to slow the flow of water.

Other finds are fluted points, scrapers and knives which show stylistic influences from both north and south; tombs (which have been opened only by grave-robbers); and carved stone tables, grave markers and blocks of undetermined purpose (petroglyphs), which might have been altars. Some of the markings on the stone objects are obviously persons or gods; in some cases jaguars and alligators can be recognized; but most are non-representational, and remain a mystery to modern viewers. From the size of tombs, the height of the inhabitants can be estimated—160 cm. for men, 150 cm. for women.

Archeologists estimate that Guayabo was occupied before the time of Christ, and that the population reached as much as 15,000. It was abandoned for undetermined reasons well before the Spanish first came to Costa Rica. In the absence of historical records, activities at the site remain a mystery, though it appears that Guayabo was some sort of administrative-commercial-ceremonial center. It is on a natural route from the highlands to the Caribbean. And paved causeways lead from the center to smaller sites with similar characteristics up to nine kilometers distant.

ARRIVALS AND DEPARTURES
By Car or Taxi
Access to Guayabo is by a winding road in poor condition. The last few kilometers are unpaved. Your best bet, if you're not driving, is to hire a taxi in Turrialba for the round trip.

By Bus
Buses that pass not far from the site currently leave Turrialba Monday and Friday at 11 a.m., and return on the same days at 1 p.m.

SEEING THE SIGHTS
In addition to the 20-hectare archeological site, Guayabo comprises a 217-hectare natural zone of premontane rain forest dense with vines and epiphytes, and alive with birds and animals. About 160 bird species have been recorded. Residents include sloths, raccoons, coatis, and many others. The astounding aspect is that most of this life has regenerated or been attracted in just the 25 years that the former pasture has been protected. The natural attractions will be for many the main reason for visiting.

Guayabo is open daily from 8 a.m. to 3 p.m. In order to protect the site from foot traffic in delicate areas, as well as from looters, visitors may enter the archeological zone only on a guided walk, which is arranged on demand. The fee is about $2. Guides speak only Spanish, but are good communicators, and will show an English fact sheet, as required, to get across the main points.

The guided walk, which lasts about an hour, takes visitors for about

1000 meters through forest, and another few hundred meters through the cleared archaeological site. The trails are excellent, gravelled or stepped as required, with various marked points of interest and resting spots. Notable species are pointed out, including a tree that catches birds with its sticky sap; the *guarumo*, swarming with ants that keep it clean; and a tree whose fibers are used by natives to make fishing nets. A lookout point provides a panorama of the archaeological site. The trail leads onward by the stone structures, but you're forbidden to scramble over them.

A second nature trail, with no signposts, may be visited without guides. A roadside observation point past the entrance affords views to a few spots of primary forest and the Guayabo River canyon (when not fogged in). Other facilities here include a picnic area, campsite, and a room with artifacts, including stone zoomorphs, grinding stones, and displays that contrast Guayabo monochrome pottery with other styles found in Costa Rica.

WHERE TO STAY

HOTEL LA CALZADA, almost adjacent to Guayabo, has five double rooms, sharing bathroom, for about $21 double, Visa accepted. Call 560465 or fax 560427 to leave a message, or write P. O. Box 260-7150 Turrialba.

This is a pretty spot with a pond (where you can fish for tilapia), long-distance views over pastures, and trees and plants identified by signs and tags. Tico-style meals are available as well if you're just visiting Guayabo for the day.

EXCURSIONS FROM TURRIALBA

Farther north is the semi-active **Turrialba Volcano**, which rises to an altitude of 3,339 meters (10,955 feet). Access for climbing the volcano is usually from the village of Santa Cruz, north of the town of Turrialba, or from the picturesque village of Pacayas, which may be reached by bus from San José or Cartago.

One last excursion from Turrialba is to **Moravia de Chirripó**, 30 kilometers away in the mountains to the east. In the region are small settlements of Talamanca Indians, who after centuries of isolation are coming into contact with the mainstream culture of Costa Rica. Inquire in Turrialba for buses or trucks headed to Moravia.

EXCURSIONS ON THE ROAD TO LIMÓN

The quick way to Limón is on the highway through **Braulio Carrillo National Park**. Buses cover the 100 miles from San José in under three hours. The misty environment and the other-worldly vegetation are intriguing, though of necessity the trip unfolds at too rapid a pace.

From San José, a divided expressway ascends the slopes of the **Barva Volcano**, into highland tropical forest. Just 21 kilometers out of the capital, now on a two-lane road, you dart out of the Central Valley, into the eerie Zurquí tunnel, the only highway tunnel in Costa Rica, unlit but by headlights, the roadway — marked by reflectors along the center line — visible only intermittently as clouds from the far end probe and slide through.

Beyond is the enchanted high forest of Braulio Carrillo National Park. The road curves, ascends and drops and ascends again, through near-permanent mist revealing at times moss-, epiphyte- and orchid-laden trees, and shiny-leafed plants at ground level. All vehicles travel cautiously, from the lack of visibility, or from the thin air.

About 35 kilometers from San José is a roadside parking area, with lookout point and trail. It's one of the few access points to the interior of the park along this route. But visitors should not stray from within sight of the road, except in large groups. Muggings occur on a regular basis.

Farther, on the descent toward the lowlands, is a wide spot by a bridge, from which one can observe the orange-brown waters of the Río Sucio (*Dirty River*), laden with minerals from the volcano Irazú, merging with the clear Hondura River flowing from lower slopes.

Fifty kilometers from San José, where the highway comes off the volcano and onto the plain of Guápiles, is the junction for a side road to Puerto Viejo de Sarapiquí (see page 433-434).

From this point, the run to Limón is flat and nearly straight. Major towns along the way are **Guápiles**, of little tourist interest, and **Guácimo**.

About four miles outside Guácimo is **Costa Flores**, a flower farm and botanical garden in development. Giant heliconias are grown here for export to the world, and escorted tours are available. If you're driving by, take a quick detour and see how things are going.

LIMÓN

Limón, Costa Rica's main Caribbean port, opened to banana traffic in 1880, but its place in national history is more venerable. Christopher Columbus landed offshore, at Uvita Island, in 1502. The first Spanish attempts at settlement were made in the area. Intermittently through the colonial period, encounters with the British and Dutch, both commercial and bellicose, took place at Portete, just a few kilometers to the north.

The port city of Limón that grew with the railway was as much a part of the British West Indies as of Costa Rica. Blacks from Jamaica and other islands constituted most of the population, and English was the only language that mattered in business. Immigrant workers kept their British passports, sent their children to school in English, read Jamaican newspapers, and went to the movies to see British films. Limón and the banana

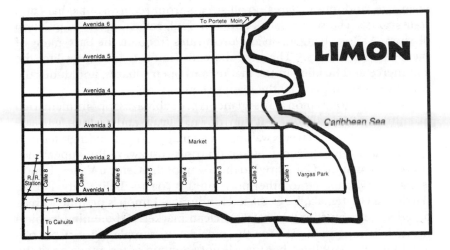

lands were separated from Costa Rica not only by language and culture, but also by a law that forbade blacks from crossing the Central Valley or overnighting there.

This separate society began to break down in the 1930s, when the banana industry was uprooted by Panama disease, and relocated to the Pacific lowlands. After the civil war of 1949, blacks were granted full citizenship, and in small numbers began to migrate to the Central Valley. Meanwhile, more and more Costa Ricans of the overcrowded plateau looked for opportunities in the warm country to the east. Most black children were educated in Spanish after 1949, and the use of English has been declining since.

Limón today is a mixed Hispanic and Afro-Caribbean city, but more and more, the Hispanic predominates. The local Creole patois, permeated with Spanish words, is the language of the older generation. Blacks are discouraged from using what Hispanic Costa Ricans consider "bad" English, though many can still speak a rather elegant and formal Caribbean dialect. English has no official status, and is studied only in secondary school.

Nevertheless, Afro-Caribbean ways hold on. Columbus Day is celebrated in Limón as it is throughout Latin America, but with a fervor and style that correspond to Carnival in the islands. Home cooking, heavy on fish, tripe, rice, coconut, and stews with cow's feet, is less than familiar to other Costa Ricans. Religion is a vibrant part of the lives of the black population, and not the formality that it is to the broad class of Hispanic Costa Ricans.

People rise early in Limón to beat the heat, go about their business, then take a long break until the worst of the sun is gone. Businesses stay open late, and music blares on all streets from record shops, bars and restaurants. The sounds are Latin and Soul, reflecting the population division. Sailors, hangers-on and prostitutes frequent the bars, many of them open 24 hours. The best show in Limón is the street life, the commerce and hustling in the market and open squares, and under the concrete overhangs on all the main streets.

To the visitor, Limón at first glance is probably a disappointment, rich in culture and tradition, but run down. Fruit and sodden garbage sometimes rot in the streets waiting for a tardy pickup, buildings decay in the salt air, ironwork balconies and tin roofs rust away. But appearance is a relative matter. Compared to the towns of the Central Valley, Limón is shabby. Compared to other ports on this coast — Belize City, Puerto Barrios in Guatemala, La Ceiba in Honduras — Limón is pristine with its paved streets, functioning sewers, a clean market. Of teeming tropical ports, it is a good choice for the outsider to sample. But if people-watching in a throbbing, hot town is not your cup of tea, move on to the beaches and parks to the north or south.

> ### LIMÓN FACTS
> Population: 55,000; Altitude: 3 meters;
> Location: 68 kilometers from San José

ARRIVALS AND DEPARTURES
Arriving By Bus
Buses for Limón leave every hour from 5 a.m. to 7 p.m. from Avenida 3, Calles 19/21, San José.

Arriving By Air
The airstrip is three kilometers south of town, along the sea. **Travelair** (tel. [7]327883) has a flight on Mondays, Wednesdays and Fridays from San José, fare $88 round trip.

Departing By Bus
Cahuita and Puerto Vargas can be reached on day excursions from Limón, though they're more fun if you stay for a day or two.

From Limón, rickety, usually crowded buses leave from Avenida 4, Calles 3/4 at 5 a.m., 10 a.m., 1 p.m. and 4 p.m., arriving at Cahuita in about an hour, and at the junction for Puerto Viejo about 30 minutes later. There are buses at 6 a.m. and 2 p.m. that go right into Puerto Viejo and on to Manzanillo. Get to the station early to find a seat.

The public bus for Playa Bonita, Portete and Moín runs every hour from Calle 4, Avenidas 3/4 in Limón.

Return buses for San José leave every hour from 5 a.m. to 7 p.m. from Avenida 2, Calle 2.

Departing By Taxi
A taxi from Limón to Cahuita costs about $25.

Departing By Train
The train to the banana-producing Estrella Valley, south of Limón, leaves Monday through Friday at 4 a.m. and 3 p.m. Return trains from the end of the line at Ley River are at 5:50 a.m. and 4:50 p.m. This train will get you close to the Hitoy Cerere Biological Reserve. Or, you could ride only as far as Penshurst, and continue southward to Cahuita by bus on the coastal highway.

Departing By Air
Travelair (tel. [2]327883) has a flight to San José on Mondays, Wednesdays and Fridays, fare $88 round trip.

GETTING AROUND TOWN
Avenida 2 is Limón's main street, running east from the railway passenger station to Vargas Park, near the waterfront. There is no odd-even segregation of *avenidas* and *calles*, as in San José. The freight line of the railroad, running to the docks, bounds Limón to the south, along Avenida 1. Street numbers are posted, but some of the signs are in the wrong place. Locals use their own tags — Avenida 2 is the Market Street.

WHERE TO STAY
It isn't a good idea to arrive in Limón on a weekend without a reservation. The best hotels are on the northern edge of town, or farther out at Portete.

HOTEL MARIBU CARIBE, Portete road, tel. [7]584010. 24 units. $68 single/$85 double. The newest hotel near Limón, on a rise along the water, with commanding views. Guest rooms, relatively small, are in unusual round cottages with high thatched roofs. All are air conditioned. Amenities include a double pool, air conditioning, and television. Restaurant and bar, tour service.

HOTEL MATAMA, Portete (P. O. Box 686-7300 Limón), tel. [7]581123, fax [7]584499. 16 units. $52 single/$70 double/$17 additional person. These are attractive bungalows sleeping up to eight, well finished with details in tropical woods, in a nicely lush hillside setting. Some units have little interior gardens in the bathrooms. There are kids' and adults' pools, and an attractive open restaurant.

More inexpensive accommodations near the above hotels are mentioned below, under Playa Bonita and Portete.

HOTEL ACÓN, Calle 3, Avenida 3, P. O. Box 528-7300, tel. [7]581010. 39 rooms. $27 single/$36 double. Best in the center of town, despite plain, bare rooms and washbasins that drain into the showers. Clean and air-conditioned.

HOTEL INTERNACIONAL, Avenida 5, Calles 2/3 (P. O. Box 288), tel. [7]580423. 25 rooms. $15 single/$20 double with fan, $18/$30 with air conditioning. New and cheery, replacing a hotel that collapsed in the 1991 earthquake. Try to get a room with outside windows, rather than one of the cubicles toward the center of the building. Protected parking is included in the rate.

HOTEL MIAMI, Avenida 2, Calles 4/5, tel. [7]580490. 32 rooms. $16 single/$25 double, less with fan only. Bare rooms right on the main street, but, with air conditioning, one of the better buys in Limón.

HOTEL PARK, Avenida 3, Calles 1/2, tel. [7]580476. 14 rooms. $15 to $19 single/$20 to $23 double. Once Limón's grande dame, with restaurant, bar, good view of the port, and an aura of faded glory. Adequate, if you can do without air conditioning. Rooms without sea view cost less. Not too clean.

HOTEL TETE, Calle 4, Avenida 3, tel. [7]581122. 14 rooms. $15 single/$25 double. In the center of the action, opposite Limón's market, but clean.

HOTEL LINCOLN, Avenida 5, Calles 2/3, tel.580074. $6 per person. Plain, fans available.

HOTEL CARIARI, Calle 2, Avenidas 2/3, tel. [7]581395. 7 rooms. $5 per person. Bare, hot. If you can get by the toilet down the hall, the second-floor balcony offers good people-watching opportunities.

There are other cheapies on the same block as the Cariari. Inexpensive lodgings can also be found on Calle 4, opposite the market.

Other lodgings are available around **Playa Bonita**, five kilometers north of Limón, and in **Moín**, the terminus of the Tortuguero Canal. These are mentioned below.

WHERE TO EAT

With the sea nearby, lobster and shrimp cost slightly less in Limón than in San José. Another specialty is Jamaican-style cooking, but unfortunately, it's a home phenomenon that only rarely makes its way to restaurant menus.

In general, you can eat wholesomely and heartily in Limón, but not always exquisitely.

LIFEBUOY (yes, that's the name), Avenida 3, Calles 2/3, opposite the Hotel Acón, is a McDonald's-style walk-up-and-order place with not only cheeseburgers and fried chicken, but also Caribbean-style rice and beans, and fresh fruit drinks. $4 and less for a meal.

MARES, a bar and restaurant, is sort of pleasant, opposite the market on Avenida 2, Calles/3/4, and open to the sidewalk on one side — and to a supermarket on the other. Sit on wicker chairs, watch the street action or the shoppers (depending on which way you're facing), and consume standard Tico fare of burgers, spaghetti, or beef. About $6 for a full meal.

The dining room of the Hotel Acón is air-conditioned and comfortable. The menu has the usual assortment of chicken, beef and fish main courses for $6 or so, American breakfasts for $4.

The **SPRINGFIELD**, along the water at the northern edge of town, is justly popular with residents and visitors. Inexpensive Caribbean-style offerings include rice and beans with turtle, and you can get assorted steak and fish plates, and even shrimp for under $10. The place is cool, clean, dark, and is livelier the later it gets.

LA FUENTE, Calle 3, Avenidas 3/4, is cleaner than the run of restaurants here. About $6 for a meal.

If none of these places attracts you, you can get roast chicken to take out, with a stack of tortillas, at Avenida 2, Calles 6/7. For the cheapest meals, try rubbing elbows with the locals at the eateries inside the market buildings.

The **AMERICAN BAR** is an open-to-the-street place at Calle 1 and Avenida 2, opposite Vargas Park. Sailors and available women and persons on extended visits and even a few locals hang out here, more for the booze than the food. And you'll have no trouble finding additional drinking spots in Limón.

SEEING THE SIGHTS

The favorite place for sitting down in Limón is **Vargas Park**, a square of jungle at Avenida 2 and Calle 1, facing the sea. Giant hardwoods struggle against the odds with strangler figs, huge palms shoot toward the sky, vines and bromeliads compete for space and moisture, birds dart and flit through the tangle. There are supposed to be monkeys and three-toed sloths up there somewhere in the canopy, and perhaps you'll be luckier than me and spy them.

Across from the park is Limón's perfect tropical-port city hall, with its cream-colored stucco, open arcades and breezeways, balconies, and louvered windows. Limón's older architecture is well suited to the climate. Thick walls moderate the extremes of temperature, concrete overhangs block the sun and keep people dry when it rains, as it does drenchingly often.

The market, on Avenida 2 between Calles 3 and 4, is ever lively, set back in a large building in its own little park. Stop in and admire the papaya and passionfruit, as well as the more mundane but no less impressive one-pound carrots. The streets around the market are Limón's social center, where purveyors of food and games of chance set up shop during the Columbus Day celebrations and for the month preceding Christmas. The Columbus Day "carnival" season features floats, street bands, dancing and masquerades, and everything else that one expects to find in the islands at Mardi Gras.

Along the southern rim of Limón (Avenida 1) are the railroad tracks and the piers where bananas are loaded aboard ship. Despite the long journey to markets all over the world, bananas are delicate. In hot weather, the large leaves of the plant collapse to shelter the fruit. In dry spells, pores contract to conserve water. On the plantations, colored ribbons identify plants of the same age, to be harvested together. Once the stems with their "hands" (rows) of "fingers" (individual fruits) are cut from the plant, natural defenses are gone, and the fruit is rushed from the field to cooled ship's hold in 18 hours. The plants are chopped down after harvest, but new plants grow up from suckers and bear fruit in nine to fourteen months.

Growing and shipping bananas is an industrial-style operation. The fruit is loaded into cargo containers right after cutting, minimizing damage from excessive handling. With advanced cultivation techniques, Costa Rica's banana fields have the highest yields in Latin America. But they also use heavy doses of insecticides, which are contained by plastic bags wrapped around the fruit, but eventually seep into waterways. And discarded blue plastic from plantations is a visible pollutant of lowland waterways.

It is the Latins in Limón who stay up late and party. The bars open at 8 a.m. and soon people are bending elbows. Blacks, religious Protestants most of them, go family-style to the numerous and substantial churches.

Try to catch and understand snatches of Limón English. Many a word is different from what you know, and the rhythms and speech patterns further obscure what is said. Most confusing is that many of the words are not English at all, but Spanish, notably numbers. Most of Limón's blacks can also speak a more standard form of English that you'll find intelligible in direct conversation.

Limón is located on a rocky point, and is one of the few places along Costa Rica's Caribbean coast without a beach. There's a government-sponsored pool in town, but most visitors will prefer the nearby beaches.

EXCURSION TO TORTUGUERO NATIONAL PARK

You can also get to **Tortuguero National Park** and back in a day, though, again, an overnight stay is preferable. Package visits to Tortuguero are most easily arranged from San José. See page 182 for more details on your options. In Limón, **Tortuguero Odysseys** (tel. [7]581940 or

[7]580824), **Caribbean Magic** (tel. [7]581210), **Mawamba tours** (tel. [7]584915), **Viajes Tropicales Laura** (tel. [7]582410) and the **Hotel Maribu** all offer excursions to Tortuguero, ranging upward from $60 for a day trip.

NORTH OF LIMÓN

PLAYA BONITA, PORTETE, AND MOÍN

Several beaches north of Limón are play areas for people from the area and for weekenders from San José. **Playa Bonita** is a public park about four kilometers from Limón, with an absolutely idyllic bay, plenty of lush jungle vegetation as a backdrop, and a beach that attracts quite a share of debris. Facilities are limited — a few picnic tables and a children's play area.

Portete, a little cove full of fishing boats, adjoins Playa Bonita to the north. You can sit at one of the many little stands that serve food, and watch as lobster traps are prepared, or just stare at the sea or the jungle and coconut trees. The shore is rocky and littered, and the water is none too clean.

Moín ("moy-IHN"), seven kilometers from Limón, reached by a spur from the highway or by the coast road from Limón, is hardly a town at all, but rather a transport center. All of Costa Rica's oil supplies are off-loaded here, and stored in huge tanks, and cargo containers are shifted between trucks and ships. More interestingly, Moín is also the passenger and freight terminal for the Tortuguero Canal (see next page).

Ask permission in Moín to enter the compound of **Japdeva**, the government agency in charge of economic development in the area, to take a look at river port operations. Coconuts, bamboo, cacao, and bananas are unloaded from canal boats, and consumer goods, largely bottled sodas, are loaded for the return run. From the terminal, you can see the waterway, thick with water lilies, its banks lined with vine-entangled trees, dissolving in the distance into swamps.

Beyond Moín, across a narrow bridge, a rough road runs northward between rows of palms, the Tortuguero Canal on one side, waves on the other. There are only occasional houses, a plywood factory, and, four kilometers out, the public Cocolito pool in landscaped gardens (on the inland side, across the railroad tracks), which has been closed recently. The beach is deserted, and the drive is nicer in this stretch than the ride on the oil-slicked canal. The end of the road is at the mouth of the Matina River, about 20 kilometers from Limón.

WHERE TO STAY

Near Playa Bonita and Portete are a number of beach houses, and a few places offering accommodations to transients. Bare beach *cabinas*, just south of Playa Bonita park, little more than cubicles, are available starting from $10 double.

CABINAS COCORÍ (tel. [7]582930) are a slight cut above the others, concrete units with cooking facilities, the better ones upstairs with views. The rate is $45 for up to five persons, less in the off season. The **Hotel Matama**, mentioned above, is in this area.

HOTEL MOÍN-CARIBE (tel. [7]582436), in Moín on a hill overlooking the oil tanks of the port, has 14 double rooms for $25 single/$40 double with private bathroom. About half of the rooms are air-conditioned (but with no windows), and there are balconies with pleasant views, if you look in the right direction. They have a restaurant and bar, and this is the nearest hotel to the boat for Tortuguero.

SEEING THE SIGHTS
Tortuguero Canal

The **Canal de Tortuguero**, a 160-kilometer stretch of natural rivers, lagoons and estuaries, and connecting man-made waterways, runs from Moín almost to the Nicaraguan border. The canal is the main "highway" of the northern coastal region. Cargo and passengers move on narrow, tuglike, 30-foot-long launches.

To ride on the canal, you have a number of choices, not all of them convenient. See pages 244-246 for details. Most likely, you'll take a tour boat, which allows you to take everything in at a slo-o-o-w pace.

Near Limón, the canal is muddy, slicked with oil, crowded with parked *cayucos* (canoe-like boats), lined with garbage dumps, and congested with vegetation. The railroad line parallels the waterway for 15 kilometers, a dirt road follows on the Caribbean side, to the mouth of the Matina River. A log dump identifies a plywood factory. Grassy banks alternate with mangrove and strips of shacks on blocks, and clusters of thatched huts, little cacao trees in their yards. Knots of women wash clothes. Fishermen and farmers get around by dugouts that serve all the purposes of pickup trucks elsewhere. Yellow signs point the way to destinations down secondary canals and waterways. Pastures and banana fields stretch inland behind the high banks. Cargo boats labor along. Here and there, a beautiful beach is visible through cleared sections on the bar.

After **Matina** village, the semi-industrial strip is left behind. Settlement is more intermittent, the water clears, wildlife and vegetation are more abundant. Vines trail among the water hyacinths, palms stand on the banks. Signs identify man-made sections of the waterway (*canal artificial*), no more than 50 feet across. Farming along the banks is in intermittent, disordered, cleared and fenced patches. As wildlife comes into view, your boat slows down. A sloth clutches the branch of a leafless tree. Troops of howler monkeys roar as they tail-dance from branch to branch.

Parismina, 48 kilometers from Moín, at a passage through the bar, is the site of a small settlement and several tarpon fishing camps. An existing fishing facility is being converted to a naturalist lodge. For information, call 800-862-1003 (direct to Costa Rica)

TORTUGUERO NATIONAL PARK

Several hours and 55 kilometers out of Moín (80 kilometers north of Limón), the cleared fields suddenly give way to what first appear to be green cliffs towering above the canal and lining the rivers that stretch inland. A closer examination reveals that they are unbroken stands of trees, many over 100 feet tall. The oil slick is totally gone by this time, and the surface reflects the green world above. A sign and checkpoint announce that you have entered **Tortuguero National Park**.

If some of what has come before has been tiresome or disappointing, what follows will almost certainly fulfill your fantasies of the jungle. More pseudo-cliffs of trees poke back along the Sierpe River. Trees canopy the waterway, and trail vines. Pastel-colored toucans and macaws, monkeys swinging through the trees, sloths hanging from branches, alligators taking the sun, turtles lounging on logs, and, perhaps, some of the coatis, jaguars and ocelots that roam the forest will come into view, if the frequent, heavy rainfalls do not inhibit your sightings. The screams of monkeys and whistles of birds pierce the air.

ARRIVALS AND DEPARTURES

Getting to Tortuguero and staying in the park are not easy unless you arrange a package trip through a tour company. There is no regularly scheduled air or boat service.

By Air

The landing strip, four kilometers north of the village, is currently served by chartered flights operated in conjunction with lodging-and-tour packages. On your own, you can have an air taxi service drop you at the park and pick you up a few days later.

By Boat

Traffic on the canal is sparse and irregular, and without advance arrangements through a travel agency, you can't count on anything. When locals can't find a boat, they simply walk along the beach — six hours to Parismina, twelve or more to Tortuguero — and count on friendly dugout owners to take them across intervening estuaries.

The traditional route to the park, by canal boat from Moín, just north of Limón, has been choked with vegetation, and is impassable from time to time. When the Caribbean is calm, boat operators take open water as far as Matina, but this can be dangerous, as storms blow in without warning. Another way is to take a car or taxi along the canal-side road as far as Matina and hire a boat there.

Operators of trips from Moín include the reliable Mr. Alfred Brown-Robinson of **Tortuguero Odysseys** (tel. [7]581940 or [7]580824), who runs a round trip in twelve-passenger boats. Departure from Moín is at 8 a.m., travel time is about three hours. Cost is $60, not including tours in the park.

The riverboat *Francesca*, tel. [2]260986 in San José, operates a 26-foot fiber glass boat with 150 horses of power from Moín to Tortuguero, zipping through the least interesting parts of the canal, and slowing down for troops of monkeys and other canalside inhabitants. The boat is narrow enough to permit easy viewing by all passengers. Trips are booked with a minimum of four passengers, at $60 each.

Caribbean Magic, P. O. Box 2482-1000, San José, tel. [2]581210, has a $60 one-day trip to Tortuguero from Moín. Or make arrangements for a day trip through the **Hotel Maribu Caribe** or one of the other hotels north of Limón.

Some boat owners offer cheaper service from the Moín canal terminal (they congregate by the signs that read *Se hacen viajes a los canales*), but be cautious about using their services. I've received complaints from visitors who wasted their time stuck in the lilies. To inquire about government boat service (unreliable and recently suspended), phone [7]581106.

Booking a Tour

In the case of Tortuguero, it's worth it to book travel and sleeping in a single package. But beware! Overbooking and trip cancellations can be a problem, and the cheapest service is not always your best choice.

Most tour operators bypass Moín, and take visitors down the Pacuare or another lowland river that empties into the Caribbean. (As well as taking you through the park, this route allows you to see close-up how bananas are cultivated right to the water's edge, where the native vegetation has been cut and the riverbank is collapsing, where bits of blue plastic used to contain insecticide float in the water and out to sea to choke fish.)

Cotur, Calle 36, Paseo Colón/Avenida 1 (P. O. Box 1818-1002, San José), tel. [2]330155, fax [2]330778, has a three-day, two-night package trip from San José that includes a bus ride, travel to Tortuguero on a canal boat, all meals, accommodations at the Jungle Lodge, and a half-day tour of the park. The price is about $200 per person. Departures are usually on Tuesday and Friday, but there are extra trips when demand warrants.

Similar trips are offered aboard the *Mawamba* (highly rated by

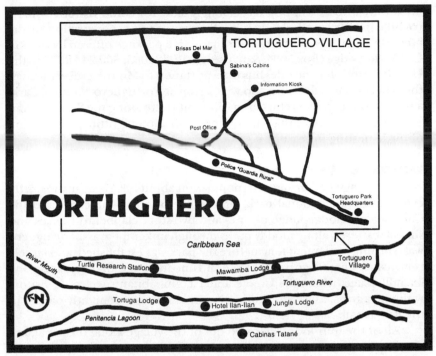

readers), a larger, more enclosed boat. The price is lower on the Mawamba tour if you stay at the basic Sabina's Cabins instead of Mawamba Lodge. Call [2]339964 in San José to arrange your travel, or [7]581564 in Limón. The *Mawamba* is also available for charter by smaller groups. **Mitur**, P. O. Box 91-1150, San José, tel. [2]552262, fax [2]551946, has a virtually identical program, based at the Hotel Ilan Ilan. Parismina Tarpon Rancho (see below, under fishing), near the southern end of the park, is also a base for some turtle-watching trips.

Costa Rica Expeditions (tel. [2]570766, fax [2]571665) charges more than other companies, but its trips are generally more reliable. A one-night visit to Tortuguero (no park tour included) costs $200 per person, or $300 per person if there are only two passengers, with air transportation one way and return by boat and bus; a trip with air transportation both ways, and a tour through the park, costs $240 per person (or $360 with only two passengers); a two-night trip with air travel one way costs $300 per person or more, again with extra charges for park tours.

The riverboat *Francesca*, tel. [2]260986 in San José (see above) offers a $160 two-night package trip, using the Manatí Lodge.

The tour boat ride along the canal is usually slow, deliberately so, to allow and encourage you to spy and hear howler monkeys, sloths, and birds that frolic and lurk along the way. But retracing a route that is jungle-lined only in part can be excruciatingly slow for some visitors; while a round-trip by plane lacks the air of adventure of a penetration of the jungle by river. One attractive alternative is a package offered by the **Río Colorado Lodge** (Box 5094, San José, tel. [2]324063, 800-243-9777 in the United States) that includes bus transportation to Moín, a cruise through the canal to Barra del Colorado with a stop at Tortuguero National Park, a night's lodging, and return by a different route along the San Juan and Sarapiquí rivers. (Note that this tour does not allow nighttime observation of turtle nesting in season).

WHERE TO STAY

The village of **Tortuguero** (population about 300) is near the northern limit of the national park, on the bar between the canal and the Caribbean, a hodgepodge of one- and two-story clapboard houses and shacks scattered along muddy paths through unkempt grass. Tortuguero was a fishing settlement long before the park was established, and largely remains so. The village has a remote and unconcerned air, but it's also one friendly place, where the Creole and Tico inhabitants welcome visitors with open arms, as well as flowing liquor and music at nightly parties in the dance hall.

All of the tour lodges, located out of the village along the canal, are cheery places where, if you have any luck, you'll be thrown together with a group of congenial people with whom you can share tall tales late into the night, in screened dining rooms and on porches, while you wonder just what those noises out there are.

What You Get for Your Money

Rates at local lodging places are usually expressed as a package that includes transportation and meals. Prices have more than doubled for Tortuguero trips in the last few years. This expresses not simply price gouging (of which there is a certain amount) and a limited number of places in which to stay, but also the fact that a lot of the supplies required for tourists — toilet paper, long-life milk, vegetables — are bulky or heavy and travel by air charter in the absence of scheduled boats.

In any case, to avoid unpleasant surprises, *inquire about the price of anything that's not included in your package*, especially drinks at the bar — many guests are furious when presented with the bill at checkout.

Canal-Side Lodges

The **TORTUGA LODGE** (25 rooms, all with private bath), operated by Costa Rica Expeditions, is more than three kilometers north of Tortuguero village, just across the canal from the airstrip. The few second-story rooms, with balconies trimmed with bamboo and cane, are the most desirable. All rooms have passageways outside, and plenty of chairs and rockers where you can sit and chat with fellow jungle club members, while you regard the gardenias and ferns and parrots on the grassy grounds.

The dining room is a thatched pavilion with reed mats on the ceiling and rough-hewn trees as pillars, and, with dart board, it doubles as a bar outside meal hours.

Motor boats with guides are available for fishing or exploring the waterways of the park, at $30 per hour and up, and excursion to Tortuguero Hill and to see turtle nesting in season (June to October) are available for $11 per person and up. To get to Tortuguero village on your own, have one of the hotel's launches take you across to the airstrip. It's then a one-hour walk along the beach.

The rate for a room and fixed-menu meals at Tortuga Lodge, if you're not on a package, is about $100 single/$147 double, about half-price for children under ten. Contact **Costa Rica Expeditions**, San José, tel. [2]570766, fax [2]571665 for information, or tel. 71[6]6861 direct to the lodge.

MAWAMBA LODGE, one kilometer north of the village of Tortuguero, has about 16 rooms in basic screened cement and wooden cottages. The compound is less tidy and attractive than that of other canal-side lodges. The principal advantage here is that Tortuguero village and park headquarters are accessible via the beach, about a 15-minute walk, which liberates you somewhat from depending on the hotel for transport and optional excursions. Call [2]339964 in San José for details.

The **JUNGLE LODGE**, one kilometer from the park, is a neat complex of red-roofed elevated buildings on the bank opposite the village — look for the windmill. The waterlogged clearing is planted with tough grass, broken by coconut palms, tropical plants and fronds, and provided with dry walkways and rough-hewn log benches. The 14 rooms are good-sized, comfortable but not luxurious. All are panelled with dark wood, hold three beds, and have fans and private showers. Everything is kept quite clean. The bar is of bamboo and hardwood, with a thatched canopy, and drinks are priced lower than elsewhere. The lodge in general is well-run and nicely worked in. A couple of trails lead under huge, buttress-trunked trees to the river bank opposite. Contact Cotur (see Miss Caribe, above) if you would like to stay here without a tour. The rate is about $45 single, $60 double.

The **HOTEL ILAN-ILAN**, operated in conjunction with the Mitur excursion, has comparable canal-side facilities to those at the Jungle Lodge, but in rather plain concrete block units.

MANATÍ LODGE, tel. [7]881828, north of the village near the turtle research station, is smaller than most other canal-side lodges, with a thatch-roofed wharf, attractive grounds, and rooms in three wooden structures. A two-night stay, in conjunction with the riverboat Francesca, costs about $200 per person.

In the Village

There are also rooms for rent in the village of Tortuguero. At **SABINA'S CABINAS** (tel. 71[8]8099), clapboard units spread out on a trim and tidy grassy seafront property, with ginger plants and palms, the rate is about $5 per person, or $20 double with private toilet facilities, or more if the traffic will bear it.

BRISAS DEL MAR has less attractive cabinas at a lower price, and a bar and dance floor. The no-frills **CABINAS MERYSCAR**, along a lane that leads from the information kiosk south toward the beach, has cubicles going for $6 per person or less, and serves cheap meals. And there are other, similar establishments facing the waves.

The advantage in staying at Sabina's or one of the nearby spots is that you can hike to the beach or through part of the park on your own, or more easily hire a local guide or dugout. At the canal lodges, you are a captive of your tour program.

It's also possible to **camp** in the park, but the best rain protection is essential.

WHERE TO EAT

Food, if you're not on a package, is available at several places around the village. The attractive no-frills **PANCANÁ** restaurant, currently Canadian-run and the best alternative to hotel food, serves lasagne, chili con carne, and rice and beans with fish for about $6, and good sandwiches. Most tables are on a patio. From the park information kiosk, head south and take a turn from the lane that leads toward the beach.

MISS JUNIE, north of the village center, will serve home-style rice and beans with fish or meat and salad for about $5, on two hours' notice.

SEEING THE SIGHTS

Turtle Haven

Tortuguero National Park is most famed for the nesting sea turtles that give their name to both the park and the adjacent town. Every year from June to November, turtles waddle ashore at night, climb past the high-tide line, excavate cavities in the sand and lay their eggs, then crawl off, exhausted. Only fifty years ago, the waves of turtles were so dense that one turtle would often dig out the eggs of another in the process of making its nest. The eggs were gathered by locals almost as soon as they were deposited, and enjoyed great popularity not only as a food, but because of their alleged aphrodisiac powers. The turtles, too, were often overturned and disemboweled for their meat and shell.

Tortuguero is one of the few remaining nesting places of the green Atlantic turtle, a species that reaches a meter in length and 200 kilograms in weight. Other species that nest at the beach are the hawksbill, loggerhead, and the huge leatherback, which weighs up to 700 kilograms. Each turtle comes home to Tortuguero every two to four years, and returns several times in the season, usually at intervals of twelve days, to nest again.

TURTLE TIMETABLES	
Peak Nesting Seasons at Tortuguero	
Green:	July ·September
Leatherback:	May and June

Turtle Hazards

Even with human enemies partially under control in the park, the turtle eggs, slightly smaller than those of hens, face numerous perils. Raccoons, coatis and coyotes dig them out and eat them up. The hatchlings that emerge two months after laying face a run for the sea made perilous by crabs and lizards, and birds that swoop down and pluck off tasty morsels of leg or head. Only a small fraction of hatchlings reaches the sea, and fewer still make it to adulthood. The odds are being improved somewhat by programs that see to the safe transfer of hatchlings to the water.

But protection of the eggs is only a partial solution to the multiple threats to turtles, and to their survival as a species. Fibropapilloma, a cancer that attacks green, Ridley and loggerhead turtles, is on the increase worldwide. (The Turtle Hospital in Marathon, Florida, is making important advances in understanding the disease and how it is transmitted.) Pollution of the seas kills turtles slowly and horribly. Heavy oil glues jaws shut, and plastic blocks digestive systems. Turtles that ingest junk starve over a period of six or seven months, as their fat layer is consumed.

Protected Fauna and Flora

The park is also an important conservation area for other plant and animal species, as much of the tropical forest nearby is cut down. Freshwater turtles, manatees and alligators are found in canals, as well as sport fish, and sharks that reach up to three meters in length.

Forest animals include the jaguar, tapir, anteater, ocelot, white-faced, howler and spider monkeys, kinkajou, cougar, collared peccary, white-lipped peccary and coatimundi. You'll probably hear these rather than see them in the dense vegetation. Over 300 bird species have been reported, including the endangered green macaw, Central American curassow, and yellowtailed oriole. Most easily sighted are the large birds that frequent the waterways, such as anhingas, flamingos and kingfishers.

All of Tortuguero is wet — rainfall averages 5,000 millimeters (200 inches) per year — but there are several vegetation zones. Morning glory vines, coconut palms and shrubs characterize the sandy beach area, while other sectors are covered with swampy forest that bridges the waterways. In the forest on higher, less saturated ground, orchids and bromeliads live at all levels and take their nourishment from the air, and "exotic" house plant species, such as dieffenbachia, flourish. Tortuga Hill, a 390-foot rise, is the highest point all along the Caribbean coast of Costa Rica.

TORTUGUERO DO'S AND DONT'S

If you can arrange it, you'll come to Tortuguero during nesting season, June to November. Strict rules are enforced to protect turtles from poachers and over-curious visitors. Among them:

1. Walk on the beach only when allowed. Inquire of park rangers or at your hotel.

2. Do not shine flashlights on turtles. Lights distract and disorient them. (Lights are usually not needed to see turtle tracks.)

3. Do not touch an overturned turtle. Some have been flipped by researchers.

4. Do not take any action on your own if something appears untoward. Report the problem to a researcher or ranger.

What to Bring

Inclusive tours generally include a morning's cruise on the canals for bird and animal sightings; and a walk along trails through the section of the park south of Tortuguero village.

For either, you'll do well to pack along rafting shoes or similar footwear that will stay on your feet as you tramp through the sucking mud. Shorts are indicated, rather than long pants. Insect repellent is a necessity. Field glasses will greatly enhance any visit to Tortuguero, even if you're not a devout birder. Monkeys and birds abound, though the abundant vegetation can get in the way of seeing whatever is out there.

Hiking

Two **trails** lead through the rain forest from park headquarters. The longer, **Gavilán**, takes about 40 minutes to cover, slopping through puddles and mudholes. Guides will point out little poisonous snakes darting past, and tree snakes that you might mistake for leaves. Look, but don't touch. Some of the plants are irritating or poisonous.

Cruising the Canals

Birders and observers of wildlife in general will perhaps appreciate more a cruise through the park's canals. (A half-day excursion is included with most packages.) From the water, you'll have a better chance of spotting cormorants, egrets, herons, anhingas, sandpipers, and man-of-war, as well as roaring howler monkeys, white-faced monkeys, fresh-water otters, assorted trees, and those wonderful, iridescent blue morpho butterflies. Most guides employed by the lodges are familiar with nomenclature in English as well as standard Spanish and local usage.

Local guides with non-powered canoe-like boats (some are modified Colemans) may be hired in the village, near park headquarters, at a rate of about $3 per person per hour, or $2 per person per hour if you paddle yourself. Rates may be slightly negotiable, but most village guides are *not* adept at spotting or naming animals.

Consider going out on your own, after taking the excursion included in your package. Head inland to the smaller canals, where the vegetation bridges overhead, and the motors of fishing boats are too faint to be heard above the rustlings of coatis on the forest floor and the whistlings of birds at every level above.

Stay out of the water when you take out a boat, and don't swim along the beach. The sand is great for walking and beachcombing, but sharks are sighted regularly. The black sand is also well littered with plastic and glass, a reflection more of the currents (the same ones that help the turtles to shore) than of anyone's sloppiness. Posts along the beach indicate distance from a point just north of the turtle research station and airstrip, in increments of one-eighth mile.

OTHER FACILITIES

Tumbledown, disorderly, relaxed Tortuguero is gradually going upscale. Several tourist-oriented businesses have opened shop in new, brightly painted concrete-block houses with neat gardens and clipped grass. One is the **Paraíso Tropical gift shop**, north of the town center, with the usual selection of t-shirts and post cards.

North of the village, adjacent to the airstrip, is the **green house**, headquarters for turtle research. There are no public facilities, and visitors are not welcome.

Right in the village is an **information kiosk**, with historical and social information about the people of the region, as well as vegetation and, most notably, the waves of turtle-laying.

South of the village is the **park administration building**, reached by trails through squishy terrain. Rainy and dry season mean nothing in Tortuguero. The ground can be saturated at any time of year, and planks and stumps are little help. Exhibits at the administration building show monkey craniums, among other items. Camping and fishing permits are available here.

BARRA DEL COLORADO

The Tortuguero Canal terminates at the settlement of **Barra del Colorado**, which sits astride the mouth of the Colorado River, a delta branch of the San Juan River that borders Nicaragua. Barra prospered in the forties as a lumber center and depot for cargo coming downriver from Nicaragua. But as woodcutting and river trade declined, so did Barra's fortunes. The population is now down to a few hundred, many of Nicaraguan descent.

Barra serves today as a sport fishing center. But it also has its attractions as an out-of-the-way place with a friendly populace, where one can stay on the edge of the wild in relative comfort. Flora and fauna in the surrounding area are protected, at least nominally, in the Barra del Colorado National Wildlife Refuge.

The wide San Juan lies entirely in Nicaragua, but Costa Rica enjoys full rights to use the river. More than a hundred years ago, Cornelius Vanderbilt established a combination riverboat-ferry-stage coach service that used the San Juan as part of a passenger route across Nicaragua, connecting with steamers from both coasts of the States. The service was disrupted during William Walker's takeover in Nicaragua, and as part of the post-war settlement, Costa Rica pushed its border north to the banks of the river. Panama thereafter dominated interoceanic transport, though the San Juan has been proposed from time to time as part of a new canal.

The most famous navigators hereabouts nowadays are the sharks that move between Lake Nicaragua, upstream on the San Juan, and the Caribbean. Sharks frequent the coast down to Tortuguero as well, feeding on the abundant fish and making swimming one of the less peaceful diversions available.

ARRIVALS AND DEPARTURES
By Air
Travelair (tel. [2]327883) has a daily flight from San José, fare $88 round trip.

By Boat
Small cargo boats operate up the San Juan and Sarapiquí rivers to Puerto Viejo, which is tied by road with San José. Or you can travel this route with more certainty on the package boat trip operated by the **Río Colorado Lodge** through Tortuguero.

Private boats may be hired for jungle cruises in the vicinity, or for trips to Tortuguero Park.

WHERE TO STAY

RÍO COLORADO LODGE, 12 rooms. Package price $300 per person daily minimum per day of fishing with meals, use of boats, and guides; or $75 single/$100 double without fishing. San José office: Hotel Corobicí, P. O. Box 5094-1000, tel. [2]324063. U.S. reservations: 12301 N. Oregon Av., Tampa, FL 33612, tel. 800-243-9777 or 813-931-4849. Simple but comfortable screened cabins, whirlpool, satellite TV.

This is mainly a fishing lodge, but the management also organizes excursions through the Tortuguero Canal and welcomes non-sportsmen to beachcomb and relax on the edge of the jungle. A mini-zoo on the grounds hold animals from the area. Open all year, within walking distance of the airstrip.

SPORTS AND RECREATION ALONG THE CARIBBEAN

Caribbean Fishing

Although remote, the Caribbean coast of Costa Rica is world famous for sport fishing. Tarpon, or *sábalo*, is the most notable (or notorious) species, most easily found in rivers and lagoons from January to June, with March and April the best months (though tarpon habits are unpredictable, and some claim June and July are best). Tarpon generally weigh from 60 to 100 pounds. A world-record 182-pound tarpon was caught from the Tortuga Lodge in 1987.

Second to the tarpon as a sport fish is snook (*róbalo*), generally caught from mid-August to mid-October, and averaging over 25 pounds. Other species are snapper (*pargo*), machaca, guapote, bass, mojarra, king mackerel, grouper, catfish, sawfish, and jacks, which generally run under five pounds.

Almost all the fishing along the coast is in fresh-water river estuaries and lagoons, which at times are converted into furious cauldrons of spawning fish. At the right times, not having a good catch is virtually impossible. However, fishing is said to have declined in recent years in inland waterways, due to sedimentation and contamination by pesticides.

Fishing in the open waters of the Caribbean is a risky business, due to the unpredictability of winds and storms, and heavy surf at estuaries, but some lodges have large boats to get fishermen out, or will fish in open water during the limited calm periods.

Fishing Camps

In addition to the Río Colorado Lodge, the following fishing camps are located along the Caribbean:

PARISMINA TARPON RANCHO, near Parismina (40 kilometers north of Limón), tel. 71[2]2583. 10 rooms, from approximately $250 per person per day of fishing. San José address: P.O. Box 5712, tel. [2]357766;

U.S. reservations: P. O. Box 290190, San Antonio, TX 78280, tel. 800-531-7232 or 512-377-0451, fax 377-0454, 800-862-1003 direct to San José.

Rebuilt after the 1991 hurricane, Tarpon Rancho will soon "split" into a nature-oriented lodge at the current location, and a newer fishing lodge between the Parismina River and the Caribbean. Rooms are in wooden cottages. Fishing is from 16-foot aluminum skiffs. An unusual feature here is *King Kong*, a mother ship that carries skiffs through dangerous surf at estuary outlets to safer waters beyond. Open January through November. Rate includes open bar, accommodations in San José, and transport to and from lodge.

Lodge policy is: "We have a tremendous record for catch and release, and we are very proud that our guests are participating with us in this program."

RÍO PARISMINA LODGE, From $285 per day of fishing, including transfer from San José. U.S. reservations: P.O. Box 46009, San Antonio, TX 78246, tel. 800-338-5688 or 210-824-4442, fax 210-824-0151. One of the newest of the Caribbean fishing lodges, located opposite Parismina village. You'll find a few more amenities here than at other coastal fishing camps, including a pool and Jacuzzi. Wood-panelled rooms, clustered four to a building, have ceiling fans, are on a jungle estate. Fishing craft here are 21 feet long with 125-hp outboards, which the operators claim reduces the danger of crossing rough surf at river mouths. Food is said to be good, equipment is well maintained, and most drinks are included in the package price. Closed July and part of December.

ISLA DE PESCA, near Barra del Colorado. 12 units, approximately $250 per day, all-inclusive. In San José: P. O. Box 7-1880, tel. [2]394544, fax [2]392405. U.S. reservations: tel. 800-245-8420. Simple A-frame cottages, with full bathrooms. Fishing is from 16-foot skiffs. Rates include the flight from San José to Barra, as well as use of boat and guides, and meals.

Isla de Pesca is also the jungle base for a river safari along the Tortuguero Canal, and the San Juan and Colorado rivers. Rates range from $150 to $300 per person for a one- or two-day trip.

TORTUGA LODGE, mentioned above under Tortuguero. Packages with fishing from a skiff run $350 for the first day, $189 each additional day, with room, meals, guide, basic fishing equipment, and transport from San José. Add $160 per day if you're alone. Call Costa Rica Expeditions, tel. [2]570766, for information.

CASA MAR FISHING LODGE, Barra del Colorado. 12 rooms. $300 per day and up. U.S. reservations: P. O. Drawer 787, Islamorada, FL 33036, tel. 800-327-2880 or 305-664-4615, fax 305-664-3692. Unlike some other fishing lodges, Casa Mar has full-time electricity. Guests stay in screened wooden cottages, each with two rooms. Package rate includes meals, boat, guide service, transport from San José, and bar consumption. Open January through mid-May and September through October.

SILVER KING LODGE, tel. [7]880849, fax [7]881403, 800-847-3474 in U.S. From $350 per day of fishing inclusive. One of the newest fishing operations, Silver King has about 20 nineteen-foot boats equipped with depth finders and fish locators. They're authorized to take anglers over to lakes and rivers in nearby Nicaragua, which, for obvious reasons, have been little exploited in recent years. Facilities are a bit more finished than at other lodges, with ceiling fans, tiled bathrooms, and large beds.

One-upmanship report: rates at Silver King Lodge include not only meals and boats and guides, *and* open bar, *but also* laundry service, *and* if you call their 800 number, they'll send you an excellent video of lodge facilities and on-site fishing action.

Contact any of the fishing lodges, or their U.S. representatives, for a fat packet of information that will give you ample details about the quality of cooking, guides, boats, camp furnishings, and fishing grounds, along with ample endorsements, all of which will demonstrate, beyond reasonable doubt, why it is the premier fishing resort on the Caribbean. This is no fish story.

River Exploration

Several tour operators offer rafting trips down the lower, wider, and slower stretches of the Parismina and Reventazón rivers. Contact **Ríos Tropicales** or **Costa Rica Expeditions** (see Chapter 12, "San José") to arrange travel.

THE TALAMANCA COAST REGION

The coast to the south of Limón, as to the north, is a nearly continuous stretch of sandy, idyllic, usually deserted beach. There are a few differences, however. Rainfall is lower to the south, and the terrain is generally better drained. This gives the landscape a less jungly nature, and makes it more habitable. It also makes things easier for the visitor, though you will be inevitably rained upon.

Transport to the south is better developed as well. A paved road runs down the coast to Puerto Viejo, a branch road reaches Sixaola on the Panamanian border, and rail lines and spurs serve the banana operations of the area. The region is still relatively sparsely settled, however, with many kilometers between settlements, and few places where a visitor may stop for the night. Inland rise the Talamanca mountains that lend their name to this region.

South from Limón, the main road generally hugs the coast. Visitors may take a bus and get off at any point that looks attractive for swimming and sunning at deserted beaches. Landward, scrub vegetation alternates with cattle pastures and coconut plantations.

Aviarios del Caribe Rainforest Preserve

About 30 kilometers from Limón is **Aviarios del Caribe**, a private reserve of regenerating rainforest on the mainland and an adjacent 150-hectare island in the delta of the Estrella River. Visitors can take a leisurely canoe tour for about $25 per person, including beverages and fruit, and running commentary on wildlife, in English. This trip will be especially interesting to birders — the local list was recently at 255 species and counting, and the site is on migration paths for many species. Being right on the water allows a better view than you might get by hiking through the adjacent forest.

There is also wildlife to be seen: alligators and sharks are occasionally sighted; and flora: if conditions are not superb for birding, you can go ashore at a farm where ginger and flowers are grown for export.

Facilities at the site include a well-manicured little estate, lawns bedecked with heliconia and ginger; a main building with large library and common room upstairs, open to the air for birding while you eat, with displays of frogs and butterflies, and a pet sloth named Buttercup; five large guest rooms downstairs, with a bed-and-breakfast rate of $35 to $40 single/$50 to $60 double; a refreshment area and sheltered dock — excellent for civilized observation of the wild — and bathrooms with hot showers available to day visitors. An adjacent section of forest can be explored on trails. Canoes can be hired by the hour, and fishing can be arranged.

For information, write to P. O. Box 569, Limón, or fax [7]584459.

Southward, the main highway starts to run back a couple of kilometers from the sea. A branch road goes up the valley of the Estrella River, where a revival of banana cultivation is under way.

HITOY CERERE BIOLOGICAL RESERVE

Beyond, in the slopes of the Talamanca mountains, is the forest of the **Hitoy Cerere Biological Reserve**, challenging to visit because of ceaseless rains, but for the same reason especially rich in varieties of plant and animal life. Accommodations at the ranger station can sometimes be arranged through the National Park Service in San José.

You can travel this route by **bus**, or by **train** from Limón (weekday departures at 4 a.m. and 3 p.m.) to Ley River. Or, if you only want to get a flavor of the banana-era railroad, ride as far as Penshurst, and continue southward to Cahuita by bus.

CAHUITA NATIONAL PARK

Cahuita National Park has beaches as beautiful as any on the

Caribbean. Just offshore is a living coral reef, the most accessible in Costa Rica, where brightly colored fish feed and breed. In the marshes and forests of the park, animal and bird life are abundant.

The coral reef, which consists of the remains of small animals called polyps, lies up to half a kilometer from shore, and from one to seven meters under the surface. With diving equipment, you can see the formations — brain, elkhorn, star and dozens of other corals — as well as the fish, sponges, crabs and snails that are attracted to feed and live on the reef. At two points on the reef's western side, cannonballs, anchors, cannon and bricks have been found, giving evidence that a Spanish galleon (or more than one) sank in these waters.

In the reef-protected shallows of Cahuita, sargasso and other grasses flourish, along with conch and ghost crabs. Dead trunks of trees lie just under the water, penetrated by seawood borers, the termites of the sea.

Beyond the reef at the south end of the park, Cahuita's lovely beach, beaten by huge waves, backed by coconut palms, is a nesting site for green, Hawksbill and leatherback turtles. The gentle sweep of the bay is quite unusual on this coast. In some sections, little pools form at low tide, temporarily isolating fish.

Inland, Cahuita's protected area includes extensive areas of marsh.

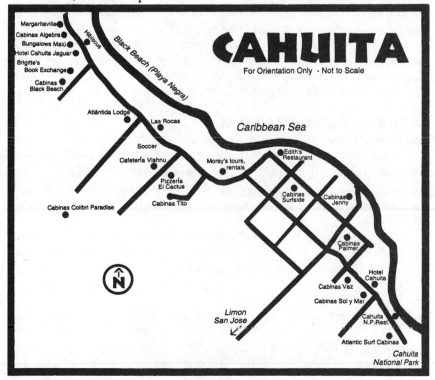

The Perezoso (Sloth) River that flows to the sea in the park is dark brown in color, said to be an effect of the high tannin concentration, which also reputedly keeps a cap on the local mosquito population. The forests are alive with howler monkeys, white-faced monkeys, three-toed sloths, anteaters, and collared peccaries. Raccoons and coatis are often seen along the nature trail, which penetrates the damp world of ferns and bromeliads and huge jungle trees.

The town of **Cahuita**, 45 kilometers from Limón, at the northern end of the park, has sandy streets, widely separated houses, a friendly assortment of people, and a range of hotels and eating places.

The southern entrance to the park is about six kilometers farther on, at **Puerto Vargas** (Vargas Harbour), which is a bay, not a village. Here the park administration, nature trail and camping facilities are located.

There are no banks, no car-rental agencies, no fishing lodges (as yet), no significant action.

Cahuita is a live-and-let-live place where one can stay for a while without any particular justification. The small population includes Creoles who speak Spanish at the shops and unintelligible English among themselves; Germans, French and Americans on extended stays, spending their days surfing or performing exercises to the background of a pounding surf; and nights stringing necklaces or visiting with Albert and the hospitality of the armchair at his beach shack; notable transients, such as the Amerindian from Surinam who spends his days whittling a bow and arrow with a machete; Hispanic Costa Ricans, of course; and the Bribri Indian from the bush of the Talamanca mountains who works at one of the hotels and deals with guests in impeccable Californian.

ARRIVALS AND DEPARTURES

Arriving By Bus

From San José, comfortable, direct buses for Sixaola (without a stop in Limón) depart from Avenida 11, Calles Central/1 (tel. [2]210524), at 6 a.m., 2:30 p.m. and 4 p.m., passing both entrances to Cahuita Park. The trip through Braulio Carrillo National Park and the humid coastal plain takes about four hours.

From Limón, rickety, usually crowded buses leave from Avenida 4, Calles 3/4 at 5 a.m., 10 a.m., 1 p.m. and 4 p.m., arriving at Cahuita in about an hour. Get to the station early to find a seat.

Arriving By Taxi

A taxi from Limón to Cahuita costs under $25.

Departing By Bus

Departures from Sixaola for Limón are at 5 a.m., 8 a.m., 10 a.m., and

3 p.m.; from Sixaola for San José at 5 a.m., 8 a.m. and 2:30 p.m. These buses pass Cahuita about 25 minutes out of Sixaola.

Buses for San José pass Cahuita at approximately 7 and 10 a.m. and 4 p.m. For Limón, buses pass at approximately 6:30 and 10 a.m. and 1:30 and 3 p.m. Buses southward, to Puerto Viejo, pass at about 7 a.m., 3:30 p.m. and 5 p.m.

WHERE TO STAY

Most hotels can be reached by dialing [7]581515 and asking for the appropriate extension. Or, ask the operator for the hotel by name. Reservations can also be made by faxing **Cahuita Tours**, [7]580652.

HOTEL JAGUAR, tel. [7]581515, ext. 238 (P. O. Box 7046-1000 San José, tel. [2]263775, fax [2]264693). 45 rooms. $30 single/$55 double with breakfast and dinner, $75 double in deluxe rooms. Visa, Master Card.

The Jaguar sets the standard for Cahuita. Guest rooms, in several buildings well-spaced on informal grounds, are extraordinarily large, with high ceilings, clerestory windows, white stuccoed walls, red tile floors, wooden louvers, and generous wooden trim. Covered passageways are punctuated with squares of garden. A number of the design features effectively aid passive cooling without air conditioning. Unusually for this area, hot water supply is ample.

There are trails through the property, 17 acres with fruit trees and exuberant and unruly vegetation. Caimans hang out in a creek, and pacas and agoutis scurry through the brush. Treks to the Talamanca mountains and river fishing and boating excursions can be arranged. There is a guard to keep an eye on cars at night. The owners, a Canadian and a Tica, have extensive hotel experience. Cuisine is excellent, and with two meals included in the rate, the Jaguar is a bargain. Located at Black Beach. (For more Black Beach listings, see following page.)

Central Cahuita

HOTEL CAHUITA, tel. [7]581515, extension 201. 10 units. $17 per person. Best of a few small hotels in the center of the village (a relative matter). Harsh, motel-style rooms are off a pleasant courtyard, and most can sleep up to six persons. Small pool. A section of hotel rooms is currently being renovated.

CABINAS VAZ, tel. [7]581515, extension 218. $18 single/$22 double. Similar to the Hotel Cahuita, without the arches in the dining area.

SURFSIDE CABINAS, tel. [7]581515, extension 246 (P. O. Box 360, Limón). 15 units. $18 single/$22 double with breakfast. Substantial concrete row units, a few blocks from the park entrance, on the way to Black Beach (Playa Negra). Protected parking.

CABINAS JENNY, tel. [7]581515, extension 15. 10 rooms. $26 to

$35. A two-story, cream stuccoed building in an excellent location overlooking the sea. The higher rate is for the upstairs rooms with balcony over the ocean, and cross ventilation.

Black Beach

Black Beach, a kilometer from the center of Cahuita, where the following accommodations are located, is more isolated, not that any part of Cahuita is urban.

ATLÁNTIDA LODGE, extension 213 (fax [2]289467 in San José). 30 units. $40 single/$45 double/$50 triple with breakfast. Visa, Master Card, American Express. Atlántida Lodge is a compound that has steadily expanded and improved its facilities over the years, without losing the informality characteristic of Cahuita.

Pale yellow stuccoed bungalows with thatched roofs are set among the palms and grass and fruit trees of spacious grounds. Hammocks hang from the trees, quiet pets roam the length of their chains, and toucans reside in their own screened enclosure. All units have screen doors and windows, porch with bamboo railing, lamps fashioned from gourds, ceiling fan, beds with thick foam mattresses, and a basic tiled bathroom with shower and hot water. A buffet breakfast of fruits and breads is included in the rate. Other meals can be prepared on request, and nothing could be more enchanting than dining in the gazebo as subdued lights sparkle on the grounds and mysterious noises filter out of the forest. Also available: free shuttle to the bus stop, and transportation from San José. A pool is to be completed shortly. The signs are in English, but you can gab on in French and other languages with owner Jean Harvey.

CABINAS TITO, ext. 286. 10 units. $30 double. Of accommodations that are operated by local people, these are the most attractive. Separate wood-panelled cabins with porch are in a quiet area where the palm trees and plants have been left in place to attract birds.

COLIBRÍ PARADISE, tel. extension 263. 3 units. $40 each. Comfortable little one-room cottages, each sleeping up to four, painted a cheery white and blue, with stove, refrigerator and hot shower. Take the path from the beach road, or enter by car from the highway. A good buy.

CABINAS BLACK BEACH (extension 251) has four woodsy units with private baths in a large garden for $15 single/$20 double. Four more units are permanently under construction. Visa and Master Card.

BUNGALOWS MALÚ, on a large, grassy lot, are attractive octagonal rock-and-wood units covered with thatch and informally furnished with items like a bamboo-trimmed mirror. One unit has two bedrooms, the others one large room, all have a small refrigerator. The rate is about $35 double/$40 triple/$45 for four persons.

CABINAS Y CHALET HIBISCUS, one of the few lodging places in

Cahuita fronting directly on the sea, has two attractive but small bungalows with mosquito canopy and tiled bathroom going for $45 double, and two houses that sleep up to six persons for $80 and $100 respectively. The beach is coral rock, but there's a pool on-site and the grounds are attractive.

CABINAS ALGEBRA, a couple of kilometers from town, has a few simple rooms in a lush tropical garden, for $25 to $35 for up to four persons, best if you have a car.

Other lodging places include **CABINAS PALMER** (tel. ext. 243, 8 units, $22 double), with rooms that are adequate enough, with bathroom, but right next to the street; **CABINAS SAFARI**, just across the street; **CABINAS SOL Y MAR** (tel. ext. 237), with eight concrete units right in the center of town, for $20 double upstairs, $16 downstairs; and **CABINAS ATLANTIC SURF**, one block inland from the park entry, with woodsy construction and porches — pleasant, but too bad about the location.

Other Places to Stay

And there are many, many, many other cabinas available past Moray's along the lanes that lead back from Black Beach, some with owners from your own hometown, most with just two or three rental units. If you plan to stay a while — and why not? — check in anywhere, drop your luggage, and spend a pleasant few hours walking around, exploring the lanes and nooks and crannies of Black Beach, inspecting accommodations, and striking a deal.

Camping is currently available at Vishnu, on one of the lanes leading up from Black Beach; and in Cahuita National Park at the southern entry point, Puerto Vargas.

Roadside stopping-places on the way to Cahuita:

CLUB CAMPESTRE CAHUITA, tel. [7]551676 ([2]234254 in San José, fax [2]215005, P. O. Box 214-1150 La Uruca). 24 kilometers south of Limón. 20 rooms. $50 for a unit that sleeps up to six. Visa, MasterCard. A Tico family-style resort and campground on a palm-shaded lot, recently rebuilt, with kids' and adult pools. Rooms have fans. The thatched-roof restaurant is pleasant, serves a variety of seafood at moderate prices, and even has a surprising list of imported wines.

CABINAS LEMAIRE, tel. [7]582859, 26 kilometers from Limón. $23 double. Opposite a deserted beach. Bar, pool, and bare rooms.

WHERE TO EAT

The cuisine of the **HOTEL JAGUAR** would get high ratings in San José, so you will be surprised to find such excellent fare in this little place. The style is continental, with an emphasis on elaborate sauces made with local spices and the best meats, and inclusive of native vegetables. The

262 COSTA RICA GUIDE

menu changes daily, and features such items as sirloin in peanut sauce; medallions of beef in two sauces; shrimp in herb sauce; fish steamed in banana leaf with chutney; dorado (mahi-mahi) in herbs; lobster; moussaka; and even, at times, chile con carne.

The setting is the open-air patio under a traditional Caribbean house, a sort of takeoff on unpretentious fine dining in the French countryside. Perhaps best of all is the price. Most items, even shrimp, go for about $10 *including* salad, vegetable and coffee. Complete breakfasts go for about $4. But hold your horses ... at busy times, the single dinner seating, at 7:30 p.m., may be reserved for hotel guests, so check first.

LAS ROCAS, at Black Beach, not far past Moray's, has the most pleasant atmosphere of any dining spot in Cahuita, in a glassed-in room looking out to palms, the beach and the sea. It's also the most formal place, with tile floor, panelled bar and ceiling fans. You won't spend more than $8 for steak or fish.

CABINAS BLACK BEACH serves lasagna, among other items, in a pleasant bar and restaurant. The restaurant at the **HOTEL CAHUITA** is popular, with lunch and dinner for $6 and up. Right next to the entrance to the park, the restaurant under the great thatched roof (behind the concrete building) serves good *casados* (meat or fish or chicken with rice, beans and cabbage) for $5, and assorted steaks, fish, Italian items, and sandwiches; and there is another restaurant under the concrete rotunda across the way, with a basic menu of fish and steak, from about $5.

Way out at the north end of Black Beach, **MARGARITAVILLE**, a Canadian-U.S. family venture, is a house where a fixed-menu meal is served in the evening for about $7. It might be cabbage rolls or stroganoff or something else you won't usually find in Cahuita. Sit on stools on the porch as the kids help out, and stay on afterwards to finish things off with margaritas, of course, and music.

EDITH'S RESTAURANT is locally famed as a bastion of Creole specialties — coconut flavored fish in banana leaf, fry cake with chicken, curried snapper, herbal teas and the like — served on an expanding porch of Miss Edith's house. But take a good look at other people's plates before you order. Much of what comes out of the kitchen will appear to unaccustomed palates as starchy, overcooked, and inedible.

And there are assorted eating shops tucked along the lanes near Black Beach, among them **CAFETERIA VISHNU** (not vegetarian) and **PIZZE-RIA EL CACTUS**.

WHERE TO DRINK

Of drinking spots, **LLOYD'S BAR** is the one with the fewest hassles (if you don't want hassles), and the only one that reserves the right of admission.

SPORTS AND RECREATION

Moray's, near the rural guard post (at the turn to Black Beach), tel. [7]581515, ext. 216, is one of several places that arrange boat trips, snorkeling, horseback rides, and jungle and mountain walks, with most trips running about $25 for a half-day. The slopes of the Talamanca range begin just a kilometer inland. One little house on the main street has souvenirs, of a sort.

The **Hotel Cahuita**, the **Cahuita Jaguar**, and several others rent out bikes, snorkeling equipment, and boogie boards.

Mr. Alan Foley, who operates out of a window at the Hotel Jaguar, can arrange an outing to the **Bri-Bri Indian reserve**, south of Cahuita and inland. For $25 a person, it's something like spending an afternoon visiting relatives, except that the family that takes you in and provides lunch lives in a compound of thatch-roofed houses and makes baskets and carved gourd jugs. Mr. Foley also can arrange a tour of a banana plantation, snorkeling at various points along the coast, and canoeing on the Sixaola River through Bri-Bri lands. Ask him as well about low-cost fishing from small boats with hand lines — not elegant, but at about $60 for two persons, it beats by far what you'd pay at one of the fishing lodges north of Limón.

Viajes Tropicales Laura, tel. 581515, extension 244, can arrange trips up to **Tortuguero** and back, without the necessity of your going to Limón to organize things.

Brigitte's Cabinas, up the lane before the Jaguar Hotel, has half-day horseback trips to the mountains behind Cahuita, for about $30.

If you plan to snorkel, you'll find the water clearest from February through April, when it rains the least.

The park is usually nearly deserted (where do all these people go?), except on weekends and at holiday periods, which should be avoided.

PUERTO VIEJO

Fifteen kilometers south of Cahuita, **Puerto Viejo** (Old Harbor) is a mixed Tico, Creole and Indian community, about a kilometer-and-a-half off the paved road. Though larger than Cahuita, Puerto Viejo is hardly bustling. A derelict barge just offshore sprouts a tree.

Aside from a laid-back village that moves to a reggae beat, the attractions of Puerto Viejo are the mostly deserted beaches to the south, the Bri-Bri Indian reserve just inland, sparsely inhabited mountains that can be explored on foot or horseback, and the Gandoca Manzanillo wildlife refuge, along with a model low-impact eco-tourism program that aims to introduce visitors to the Talamanca region through local folks.

ARRIVALS AND DEPARTURES

Arriving By Bus

A direct bus for Puerto Viejo leaves San José (Avenida 11, Calles Central/1) at 3 p.m., and there are other buses at 6 a.m., 2:30 p.m. and 4 p.m. that pass the junction on the highway outside of town.

From Limón, there are buses at 6 a.m. and 2 p.m. that go right into Puerto Viejo and on to Manzanillo, from Avenida 4, Calles 3/4. Other buses to the junction leave at 5 a.m., 10 a.m., 1 p.m. and 4 p.m.

You'll have to hitch or walk in, unless you've arranged transport in advance through one of the hotels.

Departing By Bus

Direct return buses to San José leave at 7 a.m. from the center of Puerto Viejo, and at about 5:30 a.m., 8:30 a.m. and 3 p.m. from the highway junction. Buses pass at about 6 a.m., 1 p.m. and 4:30 p.m. for Limón.

WHERE TO STAY

Puerto Viejo and the area to the south are booming with newly opened accommodations. Most are run by families or groups with sound ideas about introducing visitors to the natural treasures of the region without despoiling them. But since the lodges ("cabinas") are small and spread out, and communications are limited to a couple of phones, it is difficult to reserve space, or to find a bed on busy weekends or at holiday periods.

You can attempt to reserve by phoning or faxing [7]580854 (at the Manuel León store), indicating the hotel you're interested in, and requesting a reply. English is widely understood in this area. A couple of pricier hotels have San José contact numbers.

ATEC, the local eco-tourism association, based at an office opposite Soda Tamara in Puerto Viejo, has in the works a coordinating system for the various cabinas. For now, they publish *Welcome to Coastal Talamanca*, a directory of accommodations and facilities. It is also a primer on the way of life in the Talamanca region. ATEC and local businesses also have a map-folder of Puerto Viejo to help in locating hotels and services. For ATEC's eco-tours in the back country, see below.

A few hundred kilometers before Puerto Viejo

CABINAS BLACK SANDS, about 400 meters north of where the road meets the beach. A Bribri Indian-style stilt building here is partitioned into three rooms, with a common cooking facility, porch, and separate shower and outside toilet. Unpretentious, to be sure, but don't let the rusticity fool you. There is electricity, the place is clean, and the

American managers are quite hospitable. *This is one of the few lodging places in the immediate area that is right by the beach.* The rate is $17 double, or $42 for the whole cottage.

CHIMURI LODGE is not far from the beaten track, but is an entity to itself. Follow a track for several hundred meters from a sign on the road, then ascend through jungle, alive with birds and animals and creeping vegetation, on steps and slabs of tree trunk, toward sunlight and a clearing. Here you come upon four A-frame thatched cottages on stilts, furnished simply, with porches. The rate is $20 single/$26 double, with use of a communal kitchen. Bathrooms are also shared.

Access to local ways is facilitated by the owners, a Bribri native Costa Rican from the interior and his Austrian wife. Jungle walks and horseback rides of about six hours can be arranged for $35 per person, including provisions, or for shorter periods. Boots are provided for hiking. Mountain bikes can be rented, and the excursions are available to non-guests as well. There are also trails through the reserve and farm on which the lodge is located. Dealing with outsiders and keeping the integrity of your own culture can be a touchy business, so be patient.

EL PIZOTE LODGE, tel. and fax [7]581938, tel. [2]291428 in San José. 16 units. On a turn from the road into Puerto Viejo (just after the bridge), *"Coati Lodge"* offers accommodations of several types, all constructed above ground level on the edge of a park-like clearing. Rooms have good mattresses, fans, and lamps and other homey little bits of furnishings. Some share bathrooms, at about $45 double. Attractive individual cottages, at about $75 double, have a tile-floored bathroom with a screened shower looking right into the forest. These are well spread out and offer plenty of privacy. Family units sleep up to six persons for $130. Meals are served, at about $6 for breakfast, $12 for a hearty dinner.

Nature trails run through the adjoining uncleared forest. The sense of the place, with fine woods used in construction, and carefully tended grounds, is that of an upscale jungle resort, rather than a seaside hotel. It is, indeed, a hike to the beach, which at its nearest point is a thin, shadeless strip out beyond the main road.

Puerto Viejo

The white-and-yellow clapboard **PENSIÓN AGARICIA**, at the edge of town, is the most attractive of lodging places right in Puerto Viejo, clean and hung with plants, with sea view from the porch. The five small rooms, upstairs over the eating area, share baths, and go for about $25 single/$30 double. Room 4 has cross ventilation. German is spoken.

CABINAS JACARANDA are attractive, woodsy rooms a couple of blocks from the sea, past the Coral Café, by the Garden restaurant. The rate is about $16 double, or $25 with private bath.

HOTEL PURA VIDA, facing the soccer field, is an airy, Caribbean-style two-story building with large, cool rooms with tile floors. Toilets are shared, but there is a sink in every room, and at $20 double, it's a good value.

The **HOTEL MARITZA** (tel. [7]583844), **CABINAS RITZ** and **HOTEL PUERTO VIEJO** near the center of the village all have plain, basic rooms, shared bath, and rates of under $8 per person. The Maritza also has a row of newer cabinas on a rear lot for about $25 double. **CABINAS STANFORD** and **CABINAS MANUEL** have units with individual toilet and shower for about $10 per person. And various persons around town have rooms to let.

KISKADEE is a trek from town, up the path behind the goal of the soccer field, through cooler forest, to a wooden lodge in a clearing. For about $5 per person in a common room, everyone gets along and nobody snores.

WHERE TO EAT

SODA TÁMARA, a block back from the water, is a general store and eatery with a few tables inside, and an attractive dining area under the thatched roof outside. Food with a Caribbean flavor is served rapidly, attractively, and at low, low prices. Rice and beans with meat or fish, casado, or fish with plantains, topped off with bread pudding or patty, will cost $4 or less. They also have sandwiches and fresh fruit drinks, and pasteurized dairy products.

CAFÉ CORAL, a block and a half from the water (turn right after the Pensión Agaricia) has a long breakfast session on the porch until noon, with pancakes, omelettes and fresh breads, then re-opens at 6:30 p.m. to serve pizza. The **HOTEL PUERTO VIEJO** has lately had Mexican-style food, and there is a Chinese eatery.

THE GARDEN, an oversized gazebo up the street from Café Coral, is operated by a four-star chef from Trinidad via Toronto. It was closed up when I looked in during the off-season, but the word is that the food is quite good, if pricey for Puerto Viejo.

NIGHTLIFE AND SPORTS

Activities in Puerto Viejo include listening to reggae music, and watching dugouts being hacked from giant logs. There are two "discos" — bars with dance areas — called **Stanford's** and **Bambú**, just south of the village, by the dump.

Boogie and surfboards are available for rent at various points around town. Surfing is best from December through March — the Salsa Brava wave, just past the center of town, is considered a world-class challenge.

EXCURSIONS
Eco-Info and Adventures

ATEC, the local eco-tourism organization, based at an office opposite Soda Tamara, can fill you in on where you'll find trails and mangroves and coral in places like the **Gandoca-Manzanillo Wildlife Refuge**, and where you won't; and where an overgrown cacao farm will make for a rewarding flora-hunting excursion.

ATEC will also set you up with local guides for snorkeling, fishing for snapper from a dugout, trekking up through the rain forest of Rest-and-Be-Thankful Hill, herb- and bush medicine-hunting, expeditions into the Kekîldi Indian reservation, monkey- and toucan-spotting, meals in village homes, and a horseback ride to the hill settlement of San Rafael (among other adventures);, but be prepared to wait for up to two days to get your trip organized — communication is quite poor, and messages usually have to be hand-carried.

Half-day trips generally run about $15 per person, full-day trips $25, boat trips $80. Students get a discount. More difficult overnight trips can also be arranged, if you have camping equipment.

And if you're indecisive about where to stay, a map outside the ATEC office indicates all the small, mostly locally owned lodging places in town and stretching toward Manzanillo (which should make you even more indecisive).

ATEC is a non-profit organization, and a model of what low-impact tourism can be. You can write to ATEC, Pto. Viejo de Talamanca, Limón, or fax them at [7]537524. Be patient in waiting for a reply.

Jungle walks and horseback rides can be arranged through some hotels, most notably **Cabinas Chimuri**, the owner of which is authorized to take visitors into the Kekoldi indigenous reserve to the south.

MANZANILLO

A newly cut dirt road runs through the forest along the sea to **Manzanillo**, 12 kilometers south of Puerto Viejo. The area is hardly populated for now — there are scattered vacation houses, including those of a couple of ex-presidents — and magnificent trees grow right to the edge of the road and arch overhead. Streams are crossed on rattling and somewhat unsure plank bridges. A spur road will eventually loop back to the paved highway.

This area is being developed for tourism, so go and see it now, before all the trees are cut down. Though much of the land is included in the Gandoca Manzanillo Wildlife Refuge, most of the holdings are private, and conservation regulations are spottily enforced.

ARRIVALS AND DEPARTURES
By Bus

Buses run from Puerto Viejo to Manzanillo at about 7 a.m. and 3:30 p.m. The same buses leave Limón at 6 a.m. and 2:30 p.m. At other times, you can often pick up a ride on a passing pickup truck.

WHERE TO STAY NEARBY

For various reasons (restrictions on building, where the road runs, low-lying terrain), most lodging places are along the road, on the wrong side from the beach, and have more in common with jungle lodges than with traditional beach resorts. There's nothing wrong with this, as long as you know what you'll be getting. Though the lonely trails through jungle to the shore can, at times, present a security problem. Never walk to the beach alone.

Inquire locally, or with a travel agent in San José, as to new accommodations that might be available in this area, or drive along and look.

ESCAPE CARIBEÑO, 500 meters after the discos of Puerto Viejo, is a set of substantial brick and stuccoed bungalows in a garden, with tiled floors, refrigerators, and hammocks on the porch. The rate is $30 double, $50 for up to six persons. Under Belgian and Costa Rican management.

HOTEL PICASSO, on the beach side of the road, is a two-story wooden house with rooms over the eating area, as well as three freestanding rooms and some precious seafront and breeze off the water. Hammocks hang on the informal grounds. The rate is $30 to $40 double with breakfast.

VILLAS DEL CARIBE, 12 units. Tel. [2]332200, fax [2]212801. U.S. reservations: 800-231-7422. $120 double, $140 for four, $170 for 6. This is a row of two-story apartments, each with sea-view terrace and balcony, barbecue, outdoor shower, kitchen, bathroom with indoor garden, and either one or two bedrooms. Missing are a pool, restaurant, and other entertainments and facilities that one would reasonably expect in a resort in this price range. There's also nothing much nearby, so a car would be useful. Otherwise, if you want to lug your groceries from San José or Toronto and cook all your meals while on vacation, that's your business. About three kilometers from Puerto Viejo.

MARACU, next along the road, has several rooms above an eating facility, at $35 double.

HOTEL PUNTA COCLES, 6 kilometers south of Puerto Viejo. (P. O. Box 11020-1000 San José, tel. [2]243926, fax [2]340014). 60 rooms. $70 single/$80 double/$160 for five. $30 for three meals. American Express, Visa, Master Card.

Another jungle lodge, of tan bungalows on low-rise stilts, each with two guest rooms. Standard rooms have high ceilings, two skinny beds, fan

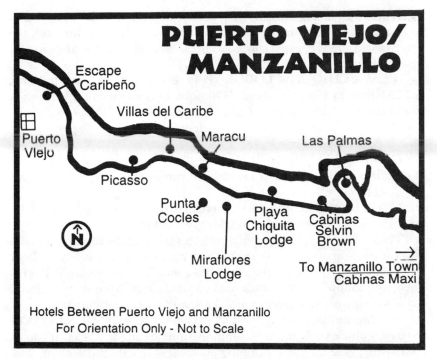

PUERTO VIEJO/ MANZANILLO

Escape Caribeño

Villas del Caribe

Puerto Viejo

Maracu

Las Palmas

Picasso

Punta Cocles

Playa Chiquita Lodge

Cabinas Selvin Brown

Miraflores Lodge

→
To Manzanillo Town
Cabinas Maxi

Hotels Between Puerto Viejo and Manzanillo
For Orientation Only - Not to Scale

and air-conditioning, lots of windows, and a motel-style tiled bathroom with central hot water. Larger rooms have fold-out beds, and cooking facilities.

The various structures are connected by a thatch-covered path, welcome in drenching rains. There are also a pool with a large wooden deck, and restaurant. Bicycles, snorkeling equipment and horses can be arranged. The place is quite nice, but if you're here for the sun and sand, bear in mind that it's a 200-meter walk to the beach, across the road and through the woods, and you might not be getting what you think you're paying for.

MIRAFLORES LODGE, Playa Chiquita (P. O. Box 7271-1000 San José), tel. [2]335127, fax [2]335390. 8 rooms, 4 with private bath. $30 to $40 single/$$40 to $50 double/$60 in suite, with breakfast. This is a personalized, comfortable and relaxed jungle bed-and-breakfast, about half a kilometer from the beach, in the middle of a flower plantation on the slopes of the Talamanca range. Heliconias, ginger, bananas and orchids are all around outside — and inside as well. Attractive, informal rooms are airy and screened, and have bamboo and wicker furniture, and either twin or a king-sized bed. Some share bathrooms, others are larger suites with private facilities. The central upstairs common room is open to the forest canopy, and ideal for wildlife observation while you sit, sup, and schmooze. Bicycles and water sports equipment available. Owned by an American from Panama, located on the inland side of the road, the lodge is said to serve especially good breakfasts. Offbeat outings can be arranged.

PLAYA CHIQUITA LODGE, (P. O. Box 7043-1000, San José, fax 800-234-1838 in U.S., $40 single/$70 double) is a row of unsubstantial rooms on stilts with porch in front, similar to some of the accommodations at Tortuguero. Restaurant, inadequate walkways, expensive for what it is. Sea side of road.

CABINAS SELVIN, on the sea side of the road, is a village-like kind of huddle of bare rooms and a restaurant run by cheerful people. About $10 double.

HOTEL LAS PALMAS, (P. O. Box 6942-1000 San José, tel. [2]553939, fax [2]553737). 60 rooms. $60 single/$70 double.

The rooms here are quite small, but this is one of the few hotels in the area within sight of the sea, facing the water across a grassy-sandy lot. Pool and atrium bar. Turn off the main road nine kilometers from Puerto Viejo, and follow the sand track for two kilometers. Note that this hotel has some construction-permit problems, and faces condemnation.

At **Manzanillo**, a fishing post of just a few houses, **CABINAS MAXÍ** has basic cubicles, and more accommodations are in the works. If you're not driving, take food and camping equipment in case the accommodation at Manzanillo is full.

EXCURSIONS

Gandoca-Manzanillo National Wildlife Refuge protects a reef area offshore of Manzanillo, as well as mangroves, swamps, palms, and beaches where turtles lay their eggs. Nearly 400 bird species have been identified here, and leatherback turtles nest every year in May and June.

Guiding services in the refuge, and advice on what to look for, are available from ATEC, the ecotourism service in Puerto Viejo.

Past the turn for Puerto Viejo, the main highway winds and climbs and dips through lush forest to **Bribri**, 65 kilometers from Limón, on the banks of the Sixaola River. Bribri includes in its population a number of indigenous Costa Ricans.

Inland from the town of Bribri and Puerto Viejo are reserves established to protect the ways of the Bribri and Cabécar indigenous groups. Outsiders are generally not allowed to enter these areas without permission from the native governing councils.

RURAL DWELLINGS

A Taste of Panama

Sixaola is the formal crossing point to the isolated northwest region of Panama, reached by a road that winds from Bribri through the hills along the bordering Sixaola River (said to be excellent for fishing). No roads continue to the rest of Panama from this area, though flights are available to David, and onward to Panama City.

You can explore the border country and even cross over in a rather informal way without going very far from the end of the paved road. Continue four kilometers from Bribri to Chase, along the road to the interior. Just uphill past the village, at the sign indicating the Bribri reserve, turn left and down to the river bank, where you'll see a thatched shelter.

All around are misted hills, sparsely dotted with country dwellings. With luck, you'll find someone with a motorized dugout who can run you up through the rapids of the mountain-bordered river. Otherwise, for a tip of 50¢ or so, you can be paddled and poled across in a dugout to the beach on the opposite bank. There, climb up to two duty-free shops with the oddest assortment of raisins, canned peanuts, and Panamanian beer, as well as a few potentially useful items such as t-shirts and suntan lotion.

In this space and time warp, the operators of the business are Palestinians from Chicago who play Middle Eastern music on loudspeakers, prices are in colones, there is no sign of the neighboring republic's authority, and electricity arrives via a cable from the Costa Rican side; but I can assure you that it is, indeed, Panama. No roads lead out— the goods arrive by boat — though it's possible to hire a horse for onward travel.

16. THE PACIFIC NORTH

INTRODUCTION/PACIFIC COSTA RICA

Pacific Costa Rica covers a vast sweep of territory along the wide side of the country, from Nicaragua down to the Panamanian border. Overlooking a complicated, varied terrain are the volcanoes and mountain peaks of the Guanacaste, Tilarán, and Talamanca mountain ranges, which largely block the rains that blow across Costa Rica from the Caribbean. Winds from the Pacific blow rain clouds ashore from May through October, while the rest of the year is dry.

But there are exceptions to this general picture. The Guanacaste lowlands of the northeast, hemmed in by coastal mountains, are subject to periodic droughts. In the south, on the other hand, near Golfito, the coastal mountains act as a watershed, and it rains throughout the year. In general, rainfall, humidity and discomfort increase toward the south. The daytime temperature throughout the area is generally in the nineties Fahrenheit (32 to 37 Centigrade).

The central part of the coastal region is a narrow plain, broken by rivers that drip down over rocky beds from the highlands in the dry season and rush down in torrents during the rainy months. Farther to the north, the plain widens into the savanna of Guanacaste, a former forest area that lost its natural cover as it was turned into farm and grazing land. A rocky fringe borders the sparsely populated Nicoya peninsula, in the north, along the sea. Barely settled at all is the Osa Peninsula, in the southern part of the region.

Travel to the main towns in the northern part of the Pacific coastal region — Puntarenas, Cañas, Liberia — is made easy by an excellent highway and frequent bus service. Most of the main attractions — notably the best beaches — are off this route, however, and are reached by plane, or with difficulty on poor roads.

PUNTARENAS

Puntarenas is a one mile-long sandspit (which is what its name means), sticking out into the Gulf of Nicoya, a narrow, muddy estuary on side, clear water on the other. Opened to shipping in 1814, the port was for many years Costa Rica's only outlet to world commerce. The coffee crop moved down to the coast from the highlands on oxcarts with a legendary breed of driver, rough and ready, but scrupulously honest.

Today, the major shipping terminal is nearby at the modern port of Caldera. But Puntarenas is still one of the larger cities in the country. Trains and trucks arrive with goods, and the streets are choked with commerce.

The location of Puntarenas would appear strategic for the visitor. Ferries provide the easiest access to some of the nicer beaches on the Nicoya peninsula. Cruises touch the many islands in the Gulf of Nicoya. Puntarenas is the nearest Pacific point to San José.

Unfortunately, though, some of the city is a dump. I don't mean only that the beach is contaminated for its whole great length along the south side of town. The central part of the city is composed of dismal, rotting and rusting, ramshackle structures, cheap flophouses, and bar after bar oozing drunks. A stench often permeates the humid, dense air.

Beyond the commercial center, the sights are more pleasant. There are some nice residences and hotels near the western tip of town and back toward the mainland, and a substantial yacht club. The headquarters of the port, at the main pier, are in a lovely old building. On Calle 7, there is a marvelous tan, crazy-stone church, looking quite English. Eating in the open-air diners along the beach and mixing with the crowds that come down for the day from San José can be pleasant. But you didn't come all the way from home to linger here. Costa Rica has much nicer seaside places to offer.

PUNTARENAS FACTS
Population: 43,000; Altitude: 3 meters
Location: 112 kilometers from San José

ARRIVALS AND DEPARTURES
Arriving By Bus
Buses for Puntarenas leave from Calle 12, Avenida 9, San José, every hour from 6 a.m. to 6 p.m. The trip takes about two hours.

Arriving By Car
The main automobile route to the coast from San José is via the Cañas Expressway, past the airport, funnelling onto a winding, narrow road past San Ramón. Total driving time is about two hours. An improved highway through Santa Ana and Orotina to the coast is planned.

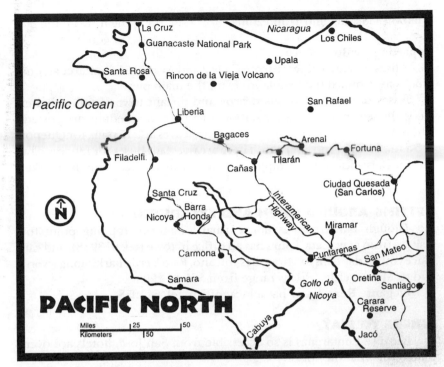

La Cruz
Nicaragua
Los Chiles
Guanacaste National Park
Upala
Santa Rosa
Rincon de la Vieja Volcano
San Rafael
Pacific Ocean
Liberia
Bagaces
Arenal
Fortuna
Filadelfi
Tilarán
Cañas
Ciudad Quesada
(San Carlos)
Santa Cruz
Barra
Miramar
Nicoya
Honda
Carmona
Puntarenas
San Mateo
Samara
Oretina
Santiago
Golfo de
Nicoya
Carara
Reserve
Interamerican Highway

PACIFIC NORTH

Miles | 25 | 50
Kilometers | 50

Cabuya
Jacó

Departing By Boat or Ferry

The main reason for a foreign visitor to go to Puntarenas is to leave promptly for one of the nicer places along the coast. Many are accessible by boat, either directly or in combination with car or bus travel.

A passenger-and-automobile ferry operates daily between Puntarenas and Playa Naranjo, on the Nicoya Peninsula. Sailings from Puntarenas are at 4, 7 and 10:30 a.m. and 1:30 and 4:30 p.m.; from Playa Naranjo at 5:15 and 8:30 a.m., noon, and 3 and 6 p.m. Phone 61[1]1069 to check schedules. *Arrive well before scheduled departure time, park, and line up for your ticket.* The crossing takes a little over an hour. Buses for Nicoya meet the ferry.

The Playa Naranjo ferry provides a shortcut to the southern part of the Nicoya peninsula. Buses going to the town of Nicoya meet the ferry, but public transport to other places is hard to find. Playa Naranjo is a dock and little else, but lodging is available just a few hundred meters down the road (see pages 344-345).

A passenger-and-car ferry also leaves for Paquera, also in the Nicoya Peninsula and south of Playa Naranjo, daily at 6 a.m. and 3 p.m. This is a newly upgraded service, so check at the tourist office in San José or hotels in Puntarenas for departure point and recent schedules. Buses and taxis provide onward connecting transportation from Paquera toward

Tambor, Cóbano, and Montezuma.

Departing By Bus

Buses for San José leave from Calle 2 and Avenida 4, Puntarenas, one block east (toward the mainland) from the main pier.

Buses depart for various nearby and distant towns from a shelter along the sea opposite the bus station for San José. Schedules are posted. The bus for Santa Elena, near Monteverde, leaves at 2:15 p.m., for Quepos at 5 a.m., 11 a.m., and 2:30 p.m. There are five daily buses for Liberia. The bus for Barranca, at the armpit of the peninsula, leaves from the market in Puntarenas.

GETTING AROUND TOWN AND EXCURSIONS

Though Puntarenas is not a usual long-term stopping point for visitors from afar, **Cata Tours** has an office in town (tel. 613948), and can place you on day trips to Miravalles volcano, Palo Verde Park, along rivers, and to Monteverde. Prices range from $65 to $90.

Elegante Rent A Car has a local office, tel. 611958.

WHERE TO STAY

Because Puntarenas is so accessible from San José, hotels are over-priced for what they offer:

HOTEL TIOGA, Paseo de los Turistas (Avenida 4, beach side), Calle 17, ten blocks west of the large pier), P. O. Box 96-5400, tel. 61[0]0271. 46 rooms. $32 to $47 single/$40 to $60 double. Nice rooms, many with views to the sea, well-maintained, air-conditioned. Best of the downtown lodgings. There's a pool, and a moderately priced restaurant. Rates include full breakfast in the fourth-floor dining-room-with-a-view. Higher rates are for rooms with hot water and balconies.

HOTEL CAYUGA, Calle 4, Avenidas Central/1 (one block north of the microwave tower), P. O. Box 306-5400, tel. 61[0]0344, fax 61[1]1280. 31 rooms. $12 to $20 single/$15 to $28 double. Located near the center of town, which is unfortunate, because this is the best hotel buy in Puntarenas, clean, modern, with a fair restaurant and air conditioning.

HOTEL RÍO, P. O. Box 54-5400, tel. 61[0]0331. 15 rooms. $10 single/$14 double, more with private bath. A modern hotel a half-block west of the market, downtown. The new rooms here have fans and private baths. Boat services available. Best deal for budget travelers.

HOTEL LAS HAMACAS, Paseo de los Turistas (Avenida 4), Calles 7/9, tel. 61[0]0398. 25 rooms. $15/$25. Quite visible, a compound facing the beach, but a last choice among the centrally located hotels, with hospital-type rooms and no hot water.

CASA ALBERTA (6 rooms, tel. and fax 63[0]0107, $250 by the

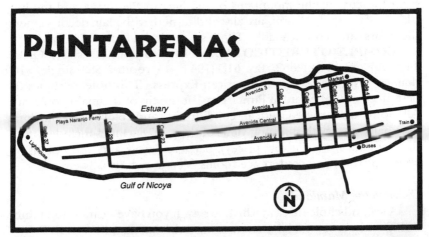

week with meals) is a small hotel catering to seniors, located in the eastern part of Puntarenas, near the mainland. Hearty food is Austrian and Canadian, and fishing charters can be arranged here.

Various *cabinas* (simple rooms with few facilities) are also available at locations along the beach, at prices of about $8 per person and up:

OASIS DEL PACÍFICO (tel. 61[0]0209), at 7 Calle on the sea, has 17 basic rooms going for $26 to $44 double, a pool which is available for day use, fast food, dancing, and an owner from France. Cooking facilities are available in some units. A half block from the bus station, the **HOTEL IMPERIAL** is a clean old wooden building that faces the water and offers rooms with shared baths for under $10 per person. And there are loads of other cheap hotels.

La Punta

The area at the tip of the peninsula is quite pleasant, unlike most of the rest of Puntarenas. If you arrive on the late ferry or are planning to embark in the morning, these hotels are good bets:

HOTEL LA PUNTA, P.O. Box 228, tel. 61[0]0696. 20 rooms, 1 suite. $16 single/$27 double. Visa, Master Card. A tan, two-story plantation-style building, unpretentious, clean, and cheery, just one block from the ferry for Playa Naranjo. Tiled pool, whirlpool, table tennis, bicycles for rent, communal TV. The open-air restaurant with juice bar is reasonably priced, at $4 or so for breakfast, $6 for lunch with fish. Look for the south-seas style second-floor veranda. English spoken.

HOTEL LAS BRISAS, Calle 31, tel. 61[2]2120. 20 rooms, $33-$15 single/$57-$67 double. Of recent construction, clean and airy. The higher rates are for larger rooms with tubs, and balconies with views away from the city, to the mountains of the Nicoya Peninsula and the hilly islands of the gulf. All units are air-conditioned, with plain decor, cement-tile floors, and Formica table. There's a pool and basic restaurant.

COMPLEJO TURÍSTICO YADRÁN, Paseo de los Turistas (P.O. Box 14-5000), tel. 61[2]2662, fax 61[1]1944. 43 rooms. $83 single/$100 double. Visa, Master Card, American Express. This hotel occupies the best piece of real estate in Puntarenas, at the tip of the main boulevard. All rooms are carpeted, with air conditioning and color television. Some have balconies, with stunning views of the gulf. Facilities include a third-floor restaurant (relatively pricey), bar, children's and adult pools, bicycles for rent, and conference rooms. Very quiet, usually empty.

Closer to the Mainland

A second-choice area in which to stay, if you have a car or don't mind taking taxis, is several kilometers toward the mainland:

HOTEL PORTO BELLO, Avenida 1, Calles 72/74, P. O. Box 108-5400, tel. [2]321248, 61[1]1322, fax 61[0]0036. 35 rooms. $63 single/$80 double, less out of season. Visa, Master Card, American Express. Attractive Mediterranean-style construction, bordering the estuary. Stuccoed, villa-style rooms with arches and outside buttresses have air-conditioning, television, large beds, unattractive furniture, and back doors that open onto lush gardens and the two pools.

HOTEL COLONIAL, adjacent to the Yacht Club, Calle 72, P. O. Box 368-5400, tel. 61[1]1833. 44 rooms. $40 single/$58 double. Colonial-style compound, adequate air-conditioned white rooms with two large beds. Two pools and playground, good value. The hotel borders the estuary and mangroves, which are good for birding.

San Ysidro

Out at the eastern end of Puntarenas, at San Ysidro, are a number of compounds that attract the family trade from San José. One of the better of the lot is **CABINAS SAN ISIDRO**, but these are still barracks-like rows of housekeeping units.

Barranca

These hotels are located near the somewhat off-color Barranca River just south of Puntarenas, about a kilometer along the coastal highway from the junction with the highway for San José. Aside from Doña Ana park and beach, there are no facilities of interest to visitors in the immediate area.

HOTEL FIESTA, P. O. Box 155-4005, tel. 63[0]0185 ([2]394266 fax [2]390217 in San José). 144 rooms and 36 suites. $90 single or double, up to $350 in suites, children stay free. U.S. reservations: 1-800-424-6423.

This is the most modern hotel in the Puntarenas area, a white concrete structure on three levels surrounding a garden with one of the two pools. The bathrooms are large, otherwise the rooms are utilitarian, with pink highlights. Rooms on the lower level have garden terraces. An odd air-conditioning system has one unit for every two rooms.

The Fiesta is oriented away from the wide beach. The huge bar is built in the shape of a boat, and shares a high thatched pavilion with the restaurant, adjacent to a second, larger pool with an island. Breakfast is usually served buffet style, lunch and dinner are $10 and up. It's a long taxi ride to alternative eating spots. Facilities include tennis courts, disco, casino, exercise room and sauna, car rental, water-sports equipment. Heavy security. This hotel attracts mostly tour groups, at a discount from the high posted rates.

CASA CANADIENSE (P.O. Box 125, Puntarenas, tel. and fax 63[0]0287) is a friendly Canadian- and French-operated beachfront guest accommodation, about half a kilometer west of the Fiesta along a side road. The five units range from single bedrooms to two-bedrooms-with-kitchen (they supply the coffee, but no breakfast). Rates are from $30 to $45 double, up to $55 for four. On-site are a pool, Ping Pong, darts, and rainy-day games.

HOTEL RÍO MAR, tel. 63[0]0158. 50 rooms. $17 single/$22 double/ up to $75 for large units. An older hotel in a relaxing riverside setting, with a children's pool only, across the road from the water. Family-oriented, with some rooms sleeping up to eight persons. This is a good stopping place if you're driving and don't want to go into Puntarenas.

CABINAS SURFARI (tel. 63[0]0776), opposite the Río Mar on the beach, offers low-priced camping in the spot of your choice under the palms on extensive grounds. There are also inexpensive cabinas, large and bare, which are slowly being rescued from a state of ruin, but the sea and open environment are forgiving if you come at mid-week. The name reflects the clientele.

WHERE TO EAT

The best food, like the best lodging, is toward the tip of the peninsula. **LA CARAVELLE**, on Paseo de los Turistas between Calles 19 and 21, is a French restaurant, with nautical displays and wood panelling inside, and a *terrasse* for outdoor eating. As formal a place as you'll find in Puntarenas, it offers the expected pepper steak, steak-frites and sea bass for $10 or so per person, shrimp and lobster for more, and Chilean wine by the glass for only $2. Open for lunch and dinner, closed Monday and Tuesday.

Next door, the **BIERSTUBE**, with high ceilings and heavy beams, accommodates up to 200 would-be Bavarians, inside and at sidewalk tables.

Elsewhere, the restaurants of the **HOTEL LA PUNTA** and the **HOTEL LAS BRISAS**, near the car ferry for Playa Naranjo, offer good value and pleasant outdoor eating areas.

Downtown, you'll find the most fun, and the freshest fish, at the open-air eating places along the beach, near the main pier.

SPORTS AND RECREATION

Being a place where the sea and boats have always been important, Puntarenas celebrates with particular enthusiasm the **Festival of the Virgin of the Sea**, on the Saturday before or after July 16. Boats are festooned with decorations and pass in review. Dances, parades, beauty contests, fireworks and drunkenness are part of the goings on.

Swimming

Since the beach at Puntarenas isn't inviting, you might want to look for other swimming opportunities. The boats mentioned below will take you to some nice beaches on the Nicoya Peninsula for overnight stays. Nearer to Puntarenas, the best swimming is at **Doña Ana beach**, a public park with ample jungly shade and picnic areas and a restaurant, on a rocky inlet along the road to Caldera and points south. The Mata Limón bus from Puntarenas passes the entrance.

Cruises

The yacht *Calypso* makes a daily cruise from the yacht club to seven islands in the Gulf of Nicoya. Fare is about $70, including overland transportation from San José, or slightly less if you're already in Puntarenas.

This is a well-planned excursion that has been improved and refined and copied over the years. A stop is made at a deserted, palm-shaded beach for swimming, snorkeling, beachcombing, and a gourmet picnic lunch that includes fresh gulf fish. They even take a portable toilet ashore. Book the cruise through any hotel in Puntarenas, or call tel. [2]333617, fax [2]330401 in San José, or [6]610585 in Puntarenas. Longer cruises are also available.

Cruises along similar lines are offered by **Fantasía Island Cruise**, tel. [2]550791, **Bay Island Cruises**, tel. [2]312898; **Blue Seas First Class Cruise**, tel. [2]337274; and **Sea Ventures**, tel. [2]329832, fax [2]327510.

Arrangements can also be made to visit the islands in the Gulf of Nicoya. On **Chira**, the largest, near the northern end of the gulf, cattle are raised and salt is extracted from sea water. **Guayabo**, **Negritos** and **Los Pájaros** islands are biological reserves, noted for their abundance of seabirds. **Guayabo** is an important nesting site for brown pelicans, and peregrine falcons are known to hibernate there. **Cedros** and several smaller islands have no restaurants, hotels or any other facilities, and few inhabitants, but are excellent locales for birding. **San Lucas** island, halfway across the gulf, was formerly a prison colony, and is now being developed as a tourist destination. A regular boat service has sometimes operated on Sunday mornings.

Fishing and Water Skiing

To hire a boat for touring, or for fishing or water skiing, try Fred Wagner at **Casa Alberta**, tel. 63[0]0107; or **Taximar**, with an office at the **Hotel Rio**, tel. 61[1]1143 and 01[0]0991.

NORTH FROM PUNTARENAS

The main coastal highway runs north through the rolling plain inland from Puntarenas, passing through Cañas, and then over flat country to Bagaces and Liberia. None of these places is of much interest to visitors. But off the road, and accessible from it, are some of the natural wonders for which Costa Rica is known.

MONTEVERDE(CLOUD FOREST RESERVE)/SANTA ELENA

High on the ridge above the coastal plain are the town of **Santa Elena**, and the adjacent farming colony and cloud-forest reserve of **Monteverde**. Costa Rica is rich in montane tropical rain forest of the type included in the Monteverde reserve — the forest atop the volcano Poás is one example, and is much more accessible.

The slow ascent to Monteverde offers spectacular views, the rolling, pastured countryside is idyllic and even spiritually uplifting, and the reserve is large. The inns in the area invite the visitor to linger and explore the forest, or relax in the fresh mountain air.

The Monteverde farming colony was founded on April 19, 1951, by Quakers from Alabama, some of whom had been imprisoned for refusing to serve in the U.S. armed forces. There were only oxcart trails into the area at the time, and the trucks and tractors of the settlers had to be winched up the mountains.

Land was laboriously cleared, and the colony eventually found some prosperity in dairy farming. Monteverde cheeses now have a solid share of the Costa Rican market. Over the years, some of the original families moved on, while non-Quakers bought land in the area. Monteverde is now a mixed, largely English-speaking community.

Conservation Pioneers

The original settlers set aside 2,500 hectares of land to protect native plant life, even as it was being destroyed by clearing in other parts of the colony. A private foundation, the **Tropical Science Center**, now administers the **Monteverde Cloud Forest Reserve**. Government protection has been afforded to the rare species found at Monteverde, including the golden toad (*sapo dorado*), which is known to live only in rain pools in the vicinity.

The area of the reserve has been expanded to 10,000 hectares (22,000 acres) by the purchase of adjacent lands, some of which had been farmed but are now being allowed to return to their natural state. Another 5,000 hectares comprise the **Children's Tropical Forest** *(Bosque Eterno de los Niños)*. These protected areas now form the core of the 110,000-hectare **Arenal Regional Conservation Unit**, stretching along the Pacific backbone of Costa Rica.

ARRIVALS AND DEPARTURES
Arriving By Bus

A bus operates to Monteverde from Calle 14 (extension of Calle 12), Avenidas 9/11, San José, departing Monday through Thursday at 2:30 p.m., Saturday and Sunday at 6:30 a.m. Telephone 61[1]1152 in Monteverde, [2]223854 in San José to check the schedule. Currently, the Sunday departure from San José is omitted in the rainy season. The trip takes about five hours.

Pacific Transfer runs a bus called the *Silver Bullet Express* with reserved seats and snacks, with seats for $40 one way, $70 round trip from San José. Call [2]272180 (fax [2]281015) for schedules and pickup points.

From Puntarenas, a bus departs daily for Santa Elena, six kilometers from the reserve, at 2:15 p.m. (from Calle 2, along the beach). Buses are of the uncomfortable school-bus type that serve the back roads of Costa Rica. If you miss the direct bus from San José, connect with this bus in Puntarenas (leave San José no later than 11 a.m.) or at the Lagarto junction, kilometer post 149 on the Pan American highway. (Take a bus from the Coca-Cola terminal area, 16 Calle, Avenidas 1/3, heading toward Cañas or Liberia, leaving no later than 11:30 a.m. The Santa Elena bus passes Lagarto at about 3 p.m.)

From Tilarán, near Lake Arenal, one daily bus departs for Santa Elena is at noon.

From the junction on the Pan American Highway, it's a two-hour ascent by bus on a bumpy, unpaved road to Santa Elena, with spectacular views, on a clear evening, of the sunset and orange-tinged sky over the Nicoya Peninsula, below and in the distance. When visibility is limited, you'll have to settle for views of the nearby landscape, as it changes from rolling hills covered with citrus and mango trees to steep grazing lands on the slopes of the mountain ridge, patches of oak and evergreen forest, and many a cool, misty valley with scattered clusters of farmhouses.

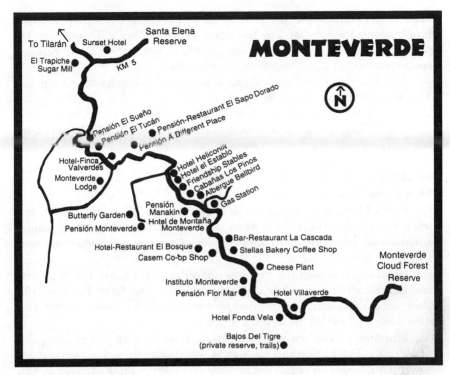

Arriving By Car

Travel by car will cut as much as a day from a round trip to Monteverde, and facilitate getting back and forth between the reserve and scattered hotels and restaurants. Follow the Pan American Highway (Route 1) to the junction at kilometer 149. The last 32 kilometers of dirt road will usually take at least an hour and a half to cover, and in the rainy season may be passable only with four-wheel-drive. There is currently a controversial plan to pave the route.

You can also reach the reserve by the little-travelled route that follows the crest of the mountain range from Tilarán, near Lake Arenal (see page 296).

Arriving By Tour

Most travel agencies in San José offer tours to Monteverde. Transportation can be arranged as well through some of the hotels mentioned below.

Departing By Bus

The bus for San José departs from the cheese plant Monday through Thursday at 6:30 a.m., Friday through Sunday at 3 p.m. Telephone 61[1]1152 in Monteverde to check the schedule. Currently, the Saturday departure is omitted in the rainy season. Passengers are picked up at hotels along the way, and at the bank in Santa Elena. Tickets can be purchased in advance at the San José bus station or at El Bosque restaurant and at some hotels in Monteverde.

The bus for Puntarenas departs at 6 a.m. from Santa Elena; for Tilarán, near Lake Arenal, at 7 a.m.

A bus leaves from Santa Elena for Tilarán at 7 a.m.

From Tilarán, near Lake Arenal, one daily bus departs for Santa Elena is at noon.

WHERE TO STAY
First Considerations
Santa Elena is a pleasant little town, about 1500 meters above sea level, though the dramatic, broken landscape all around, strong winds, and the cool, misty air make it seem higher. There are numerous bars, and also a few lodging places.

However, you might as well stay nearer to the reserve. The pensions and hotels mentioned below are listed in order from Santa Elena uphill, along or on byways from the road to the reserve. A couple of establishments are well off the beaten track.

The direct bus from San José passes those lodging places along the main road. The bus from Puntarenas terminates in Santa Elena, from where you'll have to walk (if you have the energy after arriving in the evening), or hire a car to take you to your hotel.

Best Hotel Buys
Lodging has mushroomed in the Santa Elena-Monteverde corridor, roughly tripling the number of available beds in the space of just a few years. After looking over all the accommodations recently, I decided that **Hotel El Bosque** had the best value/price ratio, and when I stayed there, I wasn't disappointed. **Hotel Finca Valverdes** and **Hotel El Establo** also seem to be quite good for the price. In fact, with all the competition for your custom in Monteverde, there are good buys in middle-range lodging almost anywhere you look.

For budget value, the Spartan **Pensión Monteverde** is hard to beat if you have wheels (it's off the main road a piece), and I still like the **Pensión Flor Mar**, where I first stayed some years back.

Bear in mind that if you're travelling by bus, you could face an early start on the day you leave, and you might want to stay near a pickup point (see departure schedules above). Traffic is sparse, so don't count on being able to hitch a ride after the bus goes.

And with all the new rooms available, Monteverde can be a busy place during the dry season, so call ahead to reserve a space, if you can. If you write, direct your mail to P. O. Box 10165-1000, San José, unless another address is indicated.

PENSIÓN EL SUEÑO (tel. 61[3]3656), charges about $5 per person with shared bath, or $9 with private bath, serves meals, and can procure horses.

PENSIÓN EL TUCÁN (tel. 61[1]1007) charges about $7 per person with shared bath in second-floor rooms that are better than others in town, or about $9 with private bath. There's an eatery downstairs.

And there are various other *cabinas* in the area with similar low rate.

HOTEL-FINCA VALVERDE'S (tel. and fax 62[2]2557, 10 rooms, $30 single/$38 double, $8 per additional person, credit cards accepted) is a guest ranch, just off the road and not far from Santa Elena, but with a remote air, as the installations are set well back on a large property of forest and pasture. Woody rooms are in cabins elevated on stilts. All come with a balcony, tubs and a loft, and can sleep up to four persons. There's also a restaurant. Horses can be hired for riding on the trails here, at about $5 per hour. And with all the foot traffic in the Monteverde reserve, you chances of seeing sloths and armadillos and quetzals and toucans just might be better on a private property such as this.

PENSIÓN A DIFFERENT PLACE is a plain block structure with economy rooms at about $5 per person — and that includes breakfast!

EL SAPO DORADO (tel. and fax 61[2]2952, 10 rooms. $50 single/ $60 double/$12 per extra person) offers accommodations in woodsy cottages each with two guest units, called "suites" with some justification. They have two large beds, porch, private bathroom, card table, rocking chair, and fireplace. English and German spoken, good restaurant (see below).

PENSIÓN MONTEVERDE (MONTEVERDE INN), (10 rooms, about $10 per person, or $25 with three meals) offers million-dollar views at guest-house prices. The large, rustic and clean if Spartan bedrooms are in several farm buildings off the main visitors' route. Most have private bath, the showers are hot. One kilometer past Santa Elena, go right for 400 meters, then left another 500 meters. You'll need your own vehicle, or a willingness to settle in, and then hike out when necessary. Horses are available for rent at about $5 per hour.

HOTEL HELICONIA, tel. 61[1]1009, fax 61[3]3507. 22 rooms. $55 and up double. A rustic, chalet-style building, a kilometer up from Santa Elena. Downstairs rooms have tile floors. Upstairs rooms, with more panelling, are pleasanter, but walls are thin and some bathrooms have large un-curtained windows. Add about $6 for each meal taken at the hotel. Horses and boots are available.

HOTEL EL ESTABLO, tel. 61[2]2854 ([2]250569 in San José), fax 61[3]3855. 20 rooms. $40 single/$50 double. One of the nicer of the new hotels in Monteverde, a collection of several small tiers of rooms with balconies and walkways and public lounge areas with fireplace, all enclosed by walls of windows, lending an outdoor ambience to the indoors. Rooms are wood-panelled, with carpeting, good mattresses, and nicely finished detailing. Large family rooms are available. The restaurant serves only beer and wine to accompany meals (about $20 for breakfast, lunch and dinner) in keeping with the family atmosphere. Transport from San José can be arranged.

PENSIÓN MANAKÍN (tel. 61[2]2854, 6 rooms, $20 double with bath or $5 per person sharing bath), has panelled rooms almost as nice as those at pricier places, but the grounds are bare. Breakfast is available at an extra charge.

CABAÑAS LOS PINOS (tel. 61[0]0905, 6 units) is a set of cabins spaced amid pines (obviously). The tariff is $45 double/$70 for four persons/$100 for six.

HOTEL DE MONTAÑA MONTEVERDE, tel. 61[1]1846. 30 rooms. $40 single/$55 double/$62 in family room. In San José: P. O. Box 70, tel. [2]333890, fax [2]226184. American Express, Visa, Master Card. Located about 1.5 kilometers from Santa Elena, the Hotel de Montaña is cozy and rustic, with hardwood-panelled rooms, and beds covered with thick woolen blankets. There are acres of adjoining farm and woods available to guests for exploration, and spectacular views down toward the Pacific.

Horses are available for rent, and boots are lent for hiking through the reserve. Amenities include Jacuzzi and sauna (at an extra fee). Transportation to the hotel can be arranged through the San José telephone number.

ALBERGUE BELLBIRD (tel. 61[2]2652, 9 rooms) is a large, plain house with balcony surrounded by a parking lot. Rooms are small and attractive. Those with private bathroom go for $25 double. With shared facilities, the rate is $12 single/$20 double. Restaurant on site, horses and hikes arranged.

HOTEL BELMAR, tel. 61[1]1001, fax 61[3]3551. 32 rooms. $45 single/$55 double. The Belmar consists of towering three-story chalet-style buildings which, though not in an indigenous contemporary architectural idiom, suits the high forest surroundings. Rooms are not as large as elsewhere, but beautiful panoramas are afforded from the private balconies, all the way to the Gulf of Nicoya. Attentive service by the owners. Boots, horseback trips and transportation to the reserve are available. They'll also pick you up in San José on request. Set meals cost about $8 each, $5 for breakfast. Turn left off the road to the reserve about 1.6 kilometers out of Santa Elena, then continue 300 meters to the hotel.

HOTEL EL BOSQUE, tel. and fax 61[2]2559. 21 rooms. $20 single/$28 double/$34 triple. The rooms here are well off the road from the restaurant of the same name, in seven lowland-ranch-style buildings of stuccoed block and timber, set in a wide semicircle on attractive grounds with pines and gardens. All rooms have private bathroom with hot shower, cathedral ceilings, and good mattresses. They're not only a good buy, but if you stay here you get a 15 percent discount in the restaurant.

The hotel property includes nine hectares with trails, some through primary forest. Camping area available. About three-and-a-half kilometers from the reserve.

PENSIÓN FLOR MAR, tel. 61[0]0909. 6 rooms. $22 per person with three meals, $25 with private bath. Three kilometers from Santa Elena and three from the reserve, the Flor Mar is a rustic place that reminds me of a summer camp. Basic and friendly. You sleep on bunks, and can have a room all to yourself if they're not too busy. The food is sometimes vegetarian, and hearty, and they'll pack a lunch to carry to the reserve if you so desire. This is probably the only place in Costa Rica that serves imitation coffee.

FONDA VELA HOTEL, tel. and fax 61[2]2551 (tel. [2]571413, fax [2]571416 in San José). 29 rooms. $53 single/$63 double. Rooms in this hotel, all with private bath, are in several chalet-style buildings spaced along the slopes of a former dairy farm; most are light, cheery and oversized, with large windows affording long views to the lowlands. The establishment also has its own stables with more than a dozen horses (for hire at $8 per hour); a nature trail through mixed forest; several ponds; and a craft shop. Meals are served by candlelight. Meeting room available. Four kilometers from Santa Elena, closest hotel to the reserve.

HOTEL VILLAVERDE, tel. 61[3]3555, has 5 simple cabins for rent at $15 per person, or $30 with three meals. Visa and Master Card accepted.

MONTEVERDE LODGE, tel. 61[1]1157 (P. O. Box 6941, San José, tel. [2]570766, fax [2]571665). 27 rooms. $76 single/$89 double/$103 triple. Visa, American Express, Master Card. This is one of the most substantial hotels in Santa Elena, a jumble of clapboard siding, Plexiglas bubbles, triangular mini-pediments, humdrum brick-and-reinforced concrete interior, and high-tech steel-and-glass greenhouse that would suit the Musée Pompidou — altogether an architectural stomach ache.

But the rooms are the best-equipped in the area, wood-panelled, with terrazzo floors, desk, good mattresses, full tiled bathroom, and outset windows. Features include a whirlpool in view of the lobby. And, whatever the esthetics, the design is intended to bring the outdoors indoors while keeping out the elements, which purpose is accomplished; and the operator, Costa Rica Expeditions, is environmentally conscientious.

Inclusive packages are offered. Example: two nights, three days with meals, transportation from San José and one day in the reserve, about

$300 per person. Fixed-menu meals are served (add $35 daily), cribs available at no charge. Children under ten pay half or less for meals, room.

SUNSET HOTEL, tel. 61[3]3558, off the road leading to the Santa Elena Reserve, has three rooms with heavy wooden furniture at $18 per person with breakfast. The price is right, and the location is good if you have a car and want to be in a quiet spot. German is spoken, as well as English, and the cooking is good.

Bunks are available right at the **Monteverde Reserve** if you make advance reservations (see page 290).

Camping

Camping is available at the **HOTEL EL BOSQUE**, and might be individually arranged with some of the other hotels.

WHERE TO EAT

If you find good food at your hotel, don't look any farther! Most visitors flop back to their rooms and showers after a day of trudging, and outside eateries have not developed to the same degree as hotels, though there are a few choices.

The **SAPO DORADO** tavern and lodge is on a rise about a kilometer toward the reserve from Santa Elena, affording views to the Gulf of Nicoya from its terrace. Pizzas, soups, beef, tuna steak, pastas, and cheesecake are the fare, subject to daily rotation and announcement on the chalkboard. They always have a vegetarian offering, and try to limit fat content. **EL BOSQUE** (The Forest), a restaurant 2.2 kilometers out of Santa Elena, charges lower prices than you'll pay in most of the hotels of the area, in a large room with many windows to afford a view of the greenery and mist all around. Casados and similar standard Tico fare goes for about $6. If you order anything with a fancy name, you're asking for trouble.

The **FONDA VELA HOTEL** has a pleasant candle-lit dining room set with cloth napkins and wine glasses, and with good food. Breakfast or lunch $5 to $6, dinner about $10. And there are various diners in Santa Elena, and a couple of unpretentious coffee shops along the road to the reserve, none particularly distinguished. **LA CASCADA**, on a rise above the road, has glass walls for forest viewing while you eat, and a menu of steaks served with loud music (just what you came to Monteverde for).

WAITING TO ENTER MONTEVERDE

From time to time, the number of visitors allowed into the reserve may be limited, in order to protect the fragile trails. Current policy is to admit no more than 100 persons into the reserve at any time. Since the hotels in the area can accommodate many times this number of persons, it is almost inevitable that you will have to wait to enter during the dry season.

SEEING THE SIGHTS
One Enchanting Cloud Forest!

The Monteverde cloud forest is created by winds, particular temperature and moisture conditions, and mountainous topography, which combine during the dry season to hold a steady cloud cover along the continental divide.

During the rainy season, of course, the forest receives its full share of precipitation from storms blowing up from the coast. The rains, and the moisture in the air, nourish trees and plants rooted in the ground, as well as many plants that live at the upper levels of the forest, and take their nutrients directly from the mist and dust that pass through the air.

Exotic Flora and Fauna

The result is an enchanted, fairy-tale environment, where trees are laden with orchids, bromeliads, mosses and ferns that obscure their branches, where the moisture and mild temperatures and sunlight filtered by the forest canopy encourage the exuberance of begonias, heliconias, philodendron and many other tropical plants in every available space on the ground.

Leaves are gigantic, vines penetrate everywhere, flowers blow through the air from the tree canopy. The forest is almost visibly growing and changing, throbbing and vibrating with life at all levels. Hummingbirds feed on nectar, frogs use pools of rainwater trapped in bromeliads to rear their young, worms and tree roots alike mine decaying matter whether it lies on the ground or in the crook of a branch. The air resounds with a crack as an epiphyte-laden branch drops to the ground, to rot and return to life by feeding the creatures and plants all around.

More than 2,000 plant species have been catalogued at Monteverde, including more than 500 kinds of trees, 300 orchids, and 200 ferns. Within the 10,000-hectare reserve there is a variety in the forest habitat. Parts are relatively dry, with little undergrowth, others are swampy. There are areas of dwarf trees, and gradations from premontane to rain and cloud forest.

And, of course, there is more to the forest than the trees and lesser plants. Of over 400 bird species, the most notable is the quetzal, with its long arc of tail feathers. It nests in the trunks of dead trees. Other visually spectacular species include the three-wattled bellbird, the great green macaw, the bare-necked umbrellabird, and the ornate hawk-eagle. Assorted trogons in addition to the quetzal inhabit the reserve, along with more than 30 varieties of hummingbird. About 500 kinds of butterfly are found. Among the more than 100 mammalian species are howler, white-faced and spider monkeys; coatis and their cousins, raccoons; and pumas, ocelots, jaguars, tapirs, and kinkajous. Some of these may be seen scurrying for cover as you walk through their territory.

The two-inch golden toad, a symbol of the natural treasures that may turn up in protected areas, once bred by the thousands in puddles in the reserve during May and June, but has been seen rarely in recent years.

Hours and Facilities

The reserve is open to the public from 7 a.m. to 4 p.m. every day. Sign in, and pay your entry fee (currently about $10, less for students). Give the person at the reception desk an idea of your route so that somebody can look for you if you don't return.

On sale at the entrance are bird and plant lists, as well as a guide for the nature trail (which is marked only with numbers). Boots can be rented, when conditions require them.

Currently, no tent camping is permitted in the reserve. Fewer than a dozen beds are available in a couple of basic rooms for about $5 per person, and these are often quickly taken. Call 61[2]2655 to try to reserve a space.

Guided walks in English or Spanish can be arranged at the reserve entry. These last about three hours, and cost $25 per person. Currently, scheduled departures are at 7, 7:30, 8, 8:30 and 9 a.m. The earlier the better, before the arrival of large numbers of visitors chases off the animals.

Slide shows are also given in a building in the reception area, at 4:30 p.m. daily, and there is a small gift shop.

Walking or Hiking the Reserve

Trails are well marked, and it would be difficult to lose your way. There is some mud (more squishy leaf rot than shoe-sucking ooze) and damp terrain, but thoughtful planners have placed plank bridges and stump steps wherever they are needed. Leon Bean's Maine hunting shoe would be the ideal footwear for a walk in these woods, but otherwise, any sturdy walking shoe and an eye to where you step are all that are needed. If you're not prepared, most hotels will rent rubber boots for a dollar or so.

Elevations vary from about 1,500 to 1,700 meters. Most of the steeper grades are near the entrance, so don't be discouraged.

You'll be handed a map when you pay your fee. Any of several routes is possible, for walks of a few hours to a few days. While you're supposed to come to look at the forest and animals, the long-distance views are also magnificent, especially from the point called **La Ventana** (The Window, or Opening).

However, you will be very lucky indeed if you see an ocean. This is, after all, a cloud forest, and the clouds are often there.

One last bit of advice before you take off on your walk is to go slowly. Stop every once in a while and take a 360-degree look at the moss- and bromeliad-laden canopy, and at the lower levels of the forest. If you only walk at a steady pace — in other words, if you hike — your eyes will be necessarily glued to the trail in order to keep your footing, and you'll miss the whole show overhead.

OTHER SIGHTS NEAR MONTEVERDE
SANTA ELENA RESERVE

About five kilometers up and up from Santa Elena on a serious washboard road, through several river beds, is the second front of rainforest conservation in the Monteverde area, the Santa Elena Reserve.

Santa Elena is strictly a junior partner to Monteverde, covering only 310 hectares, to Monteverde's 10,000, and receiving visitors who number in the dozens on a busy day.

But Santa Elena has several distinctions and differences that make it a worthwhile detour, if you have a four-wheel-drive vehicle or are willing to hike up. It affords vistas toward Arenal volcano, which can't be seen from Monteverde; it has more mixed flocks of birds, though fewer quetzals; its forest is of a different composition, including about 20 percent secondary, and dwarf forest; it is at a higher elevation; and it gets a hefty 5,000 millimeters a year of precipitation.

Common and not-so-common animals at the Santa Elena Reserve include jaguars and smaller cats, several poisonous snakes, peccaries, howler monkeys, tayras, and sloths. Prominent birds are tinamous, toucanets and linnets.

Several trails run through the reserve, one of them crossing the continental divide. **Youth Challenge** (*Reto de la Juventud*) trail offers views to Arenal volcano on clear days. **Portón Pesado** trail crosses through recovering forest, with a greater variety of birds and vegetation than elsewhere. **Caño Negro** trail passes through a variety of forest types.

Hours and Facilities

Hours at the Santa Elena Reserve are from 7 a.m. to 4 p.m., admission about $6, less for students. Boots can be rented, and refreshments are available. The administration, by the secondary school in Santa Elena (which uses any profits toward environmental education), is totally separate from that of Monteverde. Student crafts, including embroidery and painting, are available at the reception center.

SEEING THE SIGHTS

The Butterfly Garden, on a side road a couple of kilometers from Santa Elena, is a series of greenhouses and flyways where forty species of butterflies native to the Monteverde area are raised and displayed for visitors, along with specimens of local flora and mounted butterflies.

A tour enlightens visitors about butterfly life cycles and the plants with which they live and interact.

This display is roughly comparable to other butterfly exhibits in Costa Rica, but at $5 per person, the entry fee is much more reasonable.

Bajo del Tigre is a trail through a small, separately administered conservation area, at a lower level than that of the Monteverde reserve, so vegetation differs.

San Gerardo de Abajo, over the continental divide and about three hours away by horse, is the site of another biological station, administered by Costa Rican farmers and part of the biological corridor that includes the Monteverde and Santa Elena reserves. Arrangements can be made to stay overnight (call 61[2]2757 to arrange it all), within view of Arenal volcano and Lake Arenal.

Another destination is **Cañitas**, on the mountain route to Tilarán (see below), a country town just like Santa Elena — except that it sees few visitors. The **Los Tornos** gold mine is also within trotting distance.

El Trapiche is an old-fashioned sugar mill, about four kilometers from Santa Elena on the back road to Tilarán, where you can see cane being pressed for its juice, which is boiled and dried into hard brown blocks. It's also a t-shirt shop, of course. Currently, cane is pressed only on Tuesdays, Thursdays and Saturdays. Nearby is an **Ecopark**, in reality a private house and mini-zoo where captured deer and tepezcuintles (pacas) are kept to amuse visitors at an admission fee of a couple of dollars.

The very last site to see in Monteverde is the **cheese factory**. Visitors may look in on the operations, which are unspectacular.

The Monteverde community as a whole attracts much curiosity, in the same way that the Amish do in Pennsylvania. It is, after all, unusual to find an English-speaking, North American-descended farming colony dispersed over these beautiful mountains. Once reticent to share their ways with outsiders, the descendants of the original settlers have gradually moved into the hospitality trade; and, over the years, Santa Elena and Monteverde have become more and more Costa Rican in majority and character.

PRACTICAL INFORMATION

A bank operates in Santa Elena.

Riding horses can be rented at Pensión El Tucán and Pensión El Sueño, in town, at about $5 per hour, and at Valverde's, Monteverde Inn, Hotel Heliconia, Hotel de Montaña Monteverde, Fonda Vela, and several other hotels, as well as at Friendship Stables.

A gas station is located about two kilometers up the road to the reserve.

CASEM, a cooperative crafts store next to the Bosque restaurant, offers cards and place mats and shirts embroidered with toucans and quetzals. They have a coffee roaster.

LAS JUNTAS AND THE GOLD MINES

At kilometer 164 on the Interamerican Highway, a branch road leads north for six kilometers through hills covered with pasture and seasonally dry forest to **Las Juntas** (or **Las Juntas de Abangares**). Now a pleasant-enough agricultural center, Las Juntas is a town with a past. It lies at the center of a gold-mining region that was exploited at the end of the last century by Minor Keith, among other entrepreneurs. Workers and scoundrels came from every continent to seek and gamble away fortunes. The cemetery was said to be an especially busy place on paydays. Ore was carried from the mountains on cableways and by railroad. Power was provided by what was at the time the largest hydroelectric plant in the country.

On the square of Las Juntas, you'll find the **María Cristina** (named for the wife of Minor Keith), a reduced-scale but quite real locomotive that once hauled ore for the Abangares Gold Fields Company. All around are neat houses with colorful flower gardens. Some of the inhabitants of nearby hamlets with names like Berlín and Boston claim to be descended from the foreign workers who once flocked to this zone. Small-scale mining still goes on, but the boom days are long past.

An unpaved road continues up and down along a river to **La Sierra**, five kilometers past Las Juntas, where there is a small eco-museum, an open-air collection of old mining equipment, a playground, and a hut with photos of old mining installations. If you're driving, park at the village and *walk* the last few hundred meters. Hours are from 6 a.m. to 5 p.m.

The road into the mountains above Las Juntas provides an alternative and little-travelled route toward Monteverde, below the peak known as **La Mujer Dormida** (Sleeping Woman), through pastures and forest, past crystalline streams, and scattered — very scattered — houses.

At kilometer 168 is the junction for a road that goes to the town of **Nicoya** and the Nicoya peninsula, via a ferry crossing of the Tempisque River (approximate operating hours 6 a.m. to 7 p.m.). Along the way is **Barra Honda National Park**, with its many caves (see pages 315-316).

CAÑAS

At kilometer 188 is the farming center of **Cañas** (altitude 90 meters). Good accommodations are available, along with easy access to Tilarán and Lake Arenal (see below), Palo Verde National Park, and the lazy lowland rivers of the vicinity.

ARRIVALS AND DEPARTURES
Arriving By Bus
Buses for Cañas depart five times daily from Calle 16, Avenidas 1/ 3, San José.

WHERE TO STAY
HACIENDA LA PACÍFICA, P.O. Box 8-5700 Cañas, tel. 69[0]0050. 28 rooms and cottages. $45 single/$68 double. Visa, Master Card, American Express. Five kilometers north of Cañas, along the highway, the attractive La Pacífica offers three different types of units, ranging from modest to quite comfortable (though without air conditioning) in cottages widely spaced on shady lawns.

La Pacífica is a self-styled *Centro Ecológico* (Ecological Center), a model farm where environmentally sound methods are used to raise cattle and crops. All of the hacienda, covering about 16 square kilometers of cultivated fields, pasture and windbreaks, is open to visitors for exploration, along roads, trails, on foot or on horseback (for a modest fee with guide).

About two kilometers from the hotel is the dairy; five kilometers away is the hundred-year-old ranch house. Near the guest accommodations, trees in groves are handily labelled — tamarind, cocobolo, hog plum, and many others. Swimming is available in both a pool and a lake. Birds squawk, goats whinny, and roosters crow. It's all quite lovely. But also, trucks roar and an occasional small plane drones. But for the latter noises, I could recommend La Pacífica as a vacation destination in itself; and rates are a trifle high just for sleeping. Your best bet might be to stop by for lunch and a look around. The food is good — mixed grills, chops and cordon bleu for $8 and up — served in a pavilion bordered by cages of macaws, a fish pond, and leafy plants and ferns.

HOTEL EL CORRAL, tel. 69[0]0222. 12 rooms. $15 single/$28 double. Visa, Master Card. Right on the highway, a plain, two-story tan building with clean, adequate rooms, air-conditioned. Inexpensive restaurant with odd decor (stuffed deer head, wrought-iron fixtures, reproduction of Old Master, etc.).

Also in Cañas, **CABINAS COROBICÍ** (tel. 69[0]0241), six blocks east of the highway, is basic but friendly, with rooms for about $5 per person.

WHERE TO EAT
LA PACÍFICA presents a good table (see above), and is worth a stop. Nearby on the highway, and adjacent to the rapids of the Corobicí River, are two roadside restaurants: the **RINCÓN COROBICÍ**, with steaks, fish and souvenirs; and the less formal **EL GUAPINOL**.

SPORTS AND RECREATION
Float Trips

Safaris Corobicí, tel. and fax 69[0]0544, located next to La Pacífica on the highway, runs float trips on the Corobicí, a tropical river that lazes through marsh, mangrove and pasture to Palo Verde National Park. No paddling is required; you sit back and watch for egrets, toucans, monkeys, herons and alligators from your privileged perch. Prices range from $35 for a two-hour trip to $60 for a half-day motorized trip to the Tempisque River, with lunch. If you wish, you can also take part in reforestation by planting a tree on any trip.

Motor Boat Trips

Transportes Palo Verde, at Hotel El Corral, tel. 69[1]1091, operates motorized river trips through Palo Verde park and the salt-water estuary to the Tempisque River, at similar prices. Children under 14 go half price on all these trips, which are, in fact, eminently suited for kids, in contrast to white-water excursions on other rivers in Costa Rica.

Bicycle Trips

Bicycle trips down from Lake Arenal are also available from **Safaris Corobicí**, tel. and fax 69[0]0544.

The Zoo

Just down a side road from Safaris Corobicí is a **mini-zoo** with peccaries and other small forest mammals in a barnyard setting.

TILARAN, LAKE ARENAL

Tilarán (altitude 564 meters), 22 kilometers from Cañas through foothills of the Tilarán range dotted with cylindrical hydroelectric stations, is picturesque, warm, slow-paced, clean, and lightly trafficked, a ringer for a hill town in the Portuguese Algarve. Tilarán is developing as a center for adventures on and around Lake Arenal.

Four kilometers beyond Tilarán, the branch road approaches fjord-like, man-made **Lake Arenal**, the perfect Arenal volcano at its south end, islands sprinkling its waters. Much of the land surrounding the lake comprises **Arenal National Park**, currently in a state of development and expansion.

The lake is said to be good for sport fishing: guapote, a bass-like fish, and machaca populate its waters. And a constant breeze makes it a world-class windsurfing destination. Volcano-watching, hiking and general "ecotourism" are also attracting more and more Costa Ricans and foreigners to Lake Arenal, and some new accommodations have appeared in Tilarán and above the lake to serve them.

Under Arenal's surface are the remains of twelve pre-Columbian settlements, which were encountered with the aid of American satellite photographs and radar tracking. They appear to have been incinerated during an eruption of Arenal several thousand years ago, in the manner of Pompei. This archaeological curiosity was submerged during the construction of the Arenal hydroelectric project and the filling of the lake.

ARRIVALS AND DEPARTURES
Arriving By Bus

Buses for Tilarán leave from Calle 14, Avenidas 9/11, San José, at 7:30 a.m., 12:45, 3:45 and 6:30 p.m. The trip takes about three hours. From Ciudad Quesada (San Carlos), buses depart for Tilarán at 6:30 and 9:30 a.m., and 1 and 3 p.m., passing through Fortuna.

Arriving By Tour

The Mitur travel agency in San José (tel. [2]552031) has a two-day, one-night trip to Lake Arenal, via San Carlos, that includes time on the lake in a boat; and other agencies offer comparable outings.

Departing By Bus

From Tilarán, buses depart for San José at 7 and 7:45 a.m. and 2 and 5 p.m.; for Arenal, across the lake, at 10 a.m. and 4 p.m. and 10 p.m.; for Cañas at 5, 6:20, 7:30 and 10 a.m. and 3:30 p.m.; for Monteverde at noon; for Puntarenas at 6 a.m. and 1 p.m.; and for San Carlos (Ciudad Quesada) at 7 a.m. and 12:30 p.m.

Departing By Car

By car, you can attempt the road past Nuevo Arenal toward Arenal volcano, but unless you have four-wheel drive, you might have to turn back.

A typically rutted Costa Rican country road winds along the crest of the Tilarán mountain range toward Santa Elena and Monteverde. With a sturdy vehicle, it takes two hours or less to negotiate the 50 kilometers to the reserve.

The first seven kilometers are paved, to Quebrada Grande. Beyond, the road climbs to La Florida, and deteriorates to a rock bed running through windblown, pastured hills, and little family farms. Old-style milk cans are left for collection at the gates. Various side roads lead off to dead ends, or down to Las Juntas de Abangares. If you're at the wheel, ask directions at every fork, for Nubes, and then for Santa Elena.

GETTING AROUND THE LAKE

The right fork at the lake approach takes you six kilometers to

Tronadora, where there are some basic cabinas with lake access.

The main road runs northwest, then circles the waters through the highlands above. There are no shoulders on which to pull off to admire the view, and few access points to the tempting water below.

The town of **Arenal** (or Nuevo Arenal), altitude 620 meters, 29 kilometers beyond the junction at the lake approach, at the end of the pavement, is a neat assemblage of concrete bungalows. "Old" Arenal lies somewhere below, in the lake. **Fortuna**, with a stretch of poor road in between, is 73 kilometers distant, past Arenal volcano.

A few buses a day ply this route all the way to Ciudad Quesada (San Carlos).

WHERE TO STAY

CABINAS EL SUEÑO, tel. 69[5]5347. 12 rooms. $15 single/$25 double. Visa, Master Card. A block from the square, and pleasant enough, with carpeted rooms, upstairs courtyard and fountain. **Soda El Parque**, underneath, serves basic meals at low prices.

CABINAS LAGO LINDO, tel. 69[5]5977, near El Sueño, are the bargain place in which to stay in Tilarán, six airy rooms with linoleum floors and slim beds, at $7 per person, or $20 double with private bath.

CABINAS MARY, tel. 69[5]5479, on the square, has rooms with bath for $7 per person, or $5 per person sharing toilet facilities.

And there are other lodging places with rooms for about $5 per person.

WHERE TO STAY/SPORTS AND RECREATION

THE SPOT/EL LUGAR tourist center, tel. 69[5]5711, makes arrangements for fishing and water sports, and has mountain bikes to rent. They have 16 rooms for $25 single/$45 double with hot water and fan. The lobby opens up to a pleasant garden behind a commercial building; the adjacent **CATALA** restaurant is the most formal dining area in town.

THE ART OF FUN/AVENTURAS TILARÁN (tel. and fax 69[5]5008) is a sports shop that arranges windsurfing, horseback rides, cave tours, river tubing, lake fishing, and boat rides. These mostly cost $50 or under for the day. Overnight biking and camping trips can also be ordered up. Windsurfers and mountain bikes are available by the hour or day, and lessons can be arranged in several languages. They can have rooms to rent in several houses around Lake Arenal at about $15 per person, bed and breakfast.

Two hotels nearer to the lake that also cater to windsurfers are **ROCK RIVER LODGE** and **TILAWA VIENTO SURF** (see below).

Lodges and Sport Centers Around Lake Arenal

These facilities, along or (more usually) above the lake, can be reached most easily from Tilarán if you have a car.

Other hotels and lodges near the eastern end of the lake (see page 300) are usually reached via San Carlos because of the execrable condition of the road in between.

PUERTO SAN LUIS (P. O. Box 02-5710, Tilarán), tel. 69[5]5750, fax 69[5]5950. 20 units. $34 single/$62 double. Master Card, Visa. This is an informal recreational resort, on a rolling lakeside plot, one of the few accommodations with direct access to the water. Cabina rooms are well-equipped, if not well-decorated, with carpeting, television, double bed, mini-refrigerator, and tiled bath. The restaurant offers local fish and Tico country food, with few items above $4. But you come here for the sporting life: horses ($5 per hour), water skiing and fishing ($25 per hour), and windsurfing ($50). Excursions are also arranged to the Venado caves north of the lake, and by boat around the lake or to Arenal volcano.

To reach Puerto San Luis, take the right fork as you approach the lake from Tilarán, and continue for about two kilometers through the village.

HOTEL TILAWA VIENTO SURF, P. O. Box 92, Tilarán, tel. 69[5]5050 or 800-851-8929 direct to Costa Rica, fax 69[5]5766. 28 rooms. $52 single/$66 double/$81 triple with breakfast. The Tilawa, modeled after the Palace of Knossos on Crete, caters to windsurfers and others who don't mind staying in a setting of splendor. Comfortable guest rooms are decorated with Guatemalan spreads, and have orthopedic beds. Bathrooms have both tubs and showers. Junior suites at a slight higher rate have cooking facilities. All rooms overlook the lake, and afford splendid views to your choice of four volcanoes, gardens and fountains.

The Minoan theme is carried throughout, from the stencils on bedroom floors to frescoes in the bar and restaurant (glassed-in to provide superb views even in the rain). There are also a tennis court, and a large pool, dramatically situated above the lake, the only one within miles. Non-guests may swim with a minimum consumption at the bar.

But the specialty at Tilawa is outfitting guests for riding the wind on Lake Arenal. Rigs are ready at a separate lakeside launching area (and access to the lake is difficult except at the few spots with permits), and lessons are available. Just specify your board length when you reserve, and bring along your favorite helmet and shorty wet suit. Daily rates are $35 to $40 for a board. Canoes are available for similar rates, there are mountain bikes and Hobie Cats, and fishing can be arranged.

XILOE (tel. [6]599806, fax [6]599882), at the western bend of Lake Arenal 16 kilometers from Tilarán, has five wooden cabins for rent at $40 double, $55 for four.

Equus, adjacent to Xiloe, has horses for rent at about $10 per hour.

ROCK RIVER LODGE (P. O. Box 2907-1000 San José, tel. [2]224547, fax [2]213011). 11 units. $40 double, $12 per additional person. The six bedrooms here each come with a double bed and upper and lower bunks, in a woody building on a hill overlooking Lake Arenal from the north, about 18 kilometers from Tilarán. Another five individual bungalows with kitchenettes rent for about $50 double. Separate from the guest areas is a substantial rustic lodge-dining room with stone fireplace, where hearty windsurfer fare is served — fettucine in a meat-cream-celery sauce, chicken dumplings, and the like — at about $10 for a full meal, and they swear by their desserts.

Windsurfer rentals are arranged at about $45 per day.

MIRADOR LOS LAGOS, tel. 695484 (P. O. Box 31, Tilarán). 7 units. $40 for up to four persons. What a pretty spot this is . . . cottage units on a slope looking down to a fishing pond, rolling farmland and pasture, and the winding waters of Lake Arenal. Rooms are country-plain and neat, with double beds and hot water. In the wooden main house, a pool table is available to guests.

The terrace restaurant offers inexpensive meals of lake fish, chicken, and Costa Rican specialties. About 20 kilometers from Tilarán. Horses are available for rent for about $6 per hour, and tours are arranged to caves and springs.

ECO-ADVENTURE LODGE (P. O. Box 60, Tilarán, tel. [2]214209 in San José), near Lake Cote, north of Lake Arenal, is three kilometers down a side road from a point 23 kilometers from Tilarán. Rates in 25 rooms with private bath are $46 single/$55 double, in 12 cabanas, $56/$75. Additional charges are $25 for three meals, and $100 per person for transportation from San José. Horses, mountain bikes and windsurfers are available for rent. Call the San José number before you visit.

ALBERGUE ALTURAS DE ARENAL (tel. [2]226455, fax [2]228372, P. O. Box 166-1007, San José), four kilometers west of Nuevo Arenal, has the flavor of rural Costa Rica in a stuccoed, tile-roofed building with a sheltered dining terrace decorated with oxen yokes and other Tico country paraphernalia. Rooms are simple and carpeted, renting for $31 double with breakfast.

CHALET NICHOLAS (P. O. Box 72-5710 Tilarán, tel. and fax 69[5]5387 in Tilarán for messages) is an American-owned cozy "first-class guest house" (as the sign says) at kilometer post 48, two kilometers west of Nuevo Arenal, a chalet with magnificent views from the front porch down to Lake Arenal. And when the clouds lift, Arenal volcano comes into view. Two bedrooms sharing a bathroom, and an upstairs loft with private bath, are available for $39 double. These have either one large or two single beds. Birding is good among the surrounding fruit trees, and several species are kept in a large cage on-site. They also have their own riding horses ($15 for a spin) and video player, and can arrange fishing. Owners John and Catherine Nicholas are retired New Yorkers.

Several other B&Bs are sprouting along this road:
The **SWISS BED AND BREAKFAST**, just east of Nuevo Arenal, is open intermittently when the gate is not chained.
LA CEIBA BOAT, BED AND BREAKFAST (P. O. Box 9, Tilarán, fax. 69[5]5387), up a steep side road from the unpaved lakeside road, has four clean, comfortable guest rooms with hot water in a bungalow with lake view, renting at $20 per person. The giant ceiba tree that gives the place its name towers over the garden, and there is adjacent primary forest with trails. This is a restful spot, cool and pleasant. There's a Ping Pong table, sailboat for up to four persons available for rent, beach access; lunch and dinner cooked on request. English, Spanish, German spoken.

SIGHTS TO SEE
ARENAL BOTANICAL GARDEN, on a hillside about 4 kilometers east of Nuevo Arenal, has about 1200 species of plants on permanent display, most prominent among them cloud-forest plants such as brome-liads and heliconias. And, of course, butterflies and birds are attracted to such surroundings. Admission is about $4 per person when the gate is unlocked. For information, call 69[5]5266, extension 273, in English.

WHERE TO EAT
For fine dining in Tilarán, you better bring along your own food. Otherwise, the **CATALA RESTAURANT** in The Spot Hotel has a formal atmosphere and standard menu. **CABINAS MARY** and **CABINAS EL SUEÑO** also have plain dining rooms.
But if you have a car and want pleasant views with your food, by all means continue to one of the hotels around the lake, mentioned above.

NORTHWARD FROM CAÑAS
Back on the Inter-American Highway, at **Bagaces** (kilometer 215), is the junction for the Miravalles thermoelectric generating project, 27 kilometers to the northeast on the Miravalles volcano.
MIRAVALLES VOLCANO LODGE, 30 kilometers from Bagaces at the end of a road onto the volcano, is a ranch house on a farm where heart of palm is produced. Package ranch vacations run about $300 for two nights and three days, including walks to fumaroles. Call **Natural Expeditions**, tel. [2]272920, if you're interested in visiting.

PALO VERDE
Southwest of Cañas, near the mouth of the Tempisque River, is **Palo**

Verde National Park, a reserve of seasonally dry tropical forest of the type which once covered much of this area. Birds flock to Palo Verde, and so do birders: the leafless state of the trees during the dry season makes it easy for the latter to view the former. At least 300 species have been recorded at Palo Verde, including an occasional jabiru, scarlet macaws, and wood storks, roseate spoonbills, blue-winged teals, and black-bellied tree ducks numbering in the thousands and even the tens of thousands. There are hiking trails and observation points.

ARRIVALS AND DEPARTURES

Uno, an agency that specializes in trips to Palo Verde, can be reached at tel. [6]537589, fax [6]536713. Cost of a day outing is about $100.

Otherwise, look into the boat and raft excursions of Safaris Corobicí and Transportes Palo Verde (see page 295).

Palo Verde is best reached by way of the Lomas Barbudal Reserve. Other access routes cross private property. Inquire at the National Parks Service in San José before visiting.

SEEING THE SIGHTS: AREA RESERVES

Less developed for visitors is the adjacent wetland Lomas Barbudal Biological Reserve, a refuge for migrating waterfowl, including herons, egrets, ducks and grebes. The station for the reserve is reached by taking an unpaved road from the kilometer 221 marker on the Pan American Highway, negotiable in a sedan in the dry season. Six kilometers out, the terrain drops off sharply, from bare flatlands with scattered trees to a river bottom that remains moist throughout the year, alive with bird songs and dense with trees and bushes. If you arrive by car, continue to the second parking area, adjacent to the station, if road conditions look promising. Here bird lists and t-shirts are on sale, and there are exhibits of butterflies and other fauna. There are trails from this point, and a picnic area nearby.

At the mouth of the Tempisque River is the Rafael Lucas Rodríguez Caballero Wildlife Refuge (*Refugio de Vida Silvestre*), which encompasses a variety of habitats ranging from dry forest to marsh to lagoons to pasture and evergreen groves, where peccaries, deer, white-faced monkeys, waterfowl and crocodiles can be observed, among others. The Rodríguez Caballero Refuge may be reached by raft and motorboat from the La Pacífica ranch and hotel along the Pan American Highway. For information about the wildlife refuge, contact the Wildlife Department (*Departamento de Vida Silvestre*) of the Ministry of Natural Resources, Energy and Mines, Calle 9, Avenidas 11/13, San José, tel. 338112, or the national parks information center in the San José zoo.

In the refuge is the Palo Verde Biological Station of the Organization for Tropical Studies, where research facilities are available and outside visitors may stay for about $50 daily, with meals provided, if space is available. The fee for a day visit is $15. Contact the **Organization for Tropical Studies**, P. O. Box 676, 2050 San Pedro, tel. 406696, fax 406783; or P. O. Box DM, Durham, NC 27706 U.S.A., tel. 919-684-5774.

(As you can tell from this flurry of names and places, conserving the wonders of nature can be a matter of complex jurisdictions.)

LIBERIA

Liberia, the major city of northwestern Costa Rica, is a bustling place with wide, clean streets, relatively good accommodations, and a pleasant, dry climate. All lowland towns should be like Liberia. Strangely, modern Liberia is one of the oldest cities of Costa Rica, founded in 1769, when the area was part of Nicaragua, then a more prosperous and populated colony than Costa Rica. **La Agonía**, dating from the last century, is one of the senior churches of the country.

Liberia is the capital of **Guanacaste**, a province with a separate tradition and a separate history from the rest of Costa Rica. By Spanish fiat, the area was detached from Nicaragua in 1814 in order to give Costa Rica a population sufficient for representation in the Cortes (parliament) at Cadiz. A vote in Nicoya in 1820 confirmed the transfer, at a time when Nicaragua was racked by civil wars. That early exercise in self-determination is celebrated on July 25 every year. Nicaragua for many years protested the loss of the territory, but finally gave up its claims in the Cañas-Jérez treaty of 1858.

The province takes its name from the *guanacaste* (earpod) tree that provides shade on vast, flat grasslands. In a country short on folklore, Guanacaste provides tradition and color for all of Costa Rica. The *punto guanacasteco* is the national dance. Music played on the *marimba*, a xylophone-type instrument used by pre-Columbian Indians of Guanacaste, with sounding boxes made from wood or gourds, arouses nostalgic feelings in San José, though it has no roots there.

The culture of Guanacaste is largely Mestizo, or mixed Indian and Spanish. The Chorotega Indians of this area had strong ties to the peoples to the north, in Mexico and coastal Central America, before the arrival of the Spanish. Even today, there are pockets of Chorotega life in the Nicoya peninsula, where old farming practices, such as the use of the digging stick, and traditional forms of burnished pottery, are maintained. Mostly, however, the Chorotega heritage can be seen in Guanacastecan faces that are browner than those in other parts of Costa Rica.

Large areas of drought-prone Guanacaste have been made productive for rice and cotton cultivation with the construction of irrigation systems. A sparse population produces surpluses of fruit, corn, and beans as well.

But for most Costa Ricans, Guanacaste signifies vast herds of cattle munching away on the grasslands. The folkloric figures par excellence of the area are *bramaderos*, Costa Rica's poor man's cowboys, mounted on horses with elaborately decorated saddles, and *boyeros*, tenders of oxen.

LIBERIA FACTS
Population: 21,500; Altitude: 150 meters (492 feet);
Location: 236 kilometers from San José

ARRIVALS AND DEPARTURES
Arriving By Bus
Buses for Liberia leave from Calle 14, Avenidas 1/3, San José, every day at 7, 9 and 11:30 a.m., and 1, 4, 6 and 8 p.m. Most are modern units, and cover the route in about four hours. There are additional buses from Avenida 3, Calles 18/20.

Departing By Bus
Liberia is the transportation crossroads of northwestern Costa Rica.

From the bus terminal, a block from the highway, and three blocks north and four blocks west of the square, buses leave for San José about every two hours from 4:30 a.m. to 8 p.m. Other buses for San José depart from the Pulmitán terminal a block away.

Other departures are:

For La Cruz, passing the entry to Santa Rosa National Park, about every two hours from 5:30 a.m. to 8 p.m. (some of these buses continue to the Nicaraguan border at Peñas Blancas); for El Coco beach at 5:30 and 8:15 a.m., and 12:30, 2, 4:30 and 6:15 p.m.; for Playa Hermosa and Playa Panamá at 11:30 a.m. and 7 p.m.; to Santa Cruz and Nicoya, every hour throughout the day; for Cañas Dulces, 6 a.m., noon and 4:30 p.m.; for Puntarenas, five daily buses.

Current schedules are clearly posted.

Arriving and Departing By Air
The Liberia airport is located about 10 kilometers out, on the road to Nicoya. International charter flights are slated to begin using this facility shortly.

WHERE TO STAY
HOTEL EL BRAMADERO, P. O. Box 70-5000, tel. 66[0]0371. 24 rooms. $27 single/$39 double with air conditioning, $19/$28 with fan. A modest motel with rooms arranged around a courtyard and pool, and a large pavilion restaurant, the Bramadero has seen better days. Located at the turn from the highway into town. Travel services and car rental available.

NUEVO HOTEL BOYEROS, P.O. Box 85, tel. 66[0]0722, fax 66[2]2529. 62 rooms. $41 single/$57 double. Visa, Master Card, American Express. Also located at the turn into town. Modern, with air conditioning, pools for kids and adults, and attractive leafy landscaping. Bands sometimes perform on weekends – inquire beforehand if you need a good night's sleep.

HOTEL LA SIESTA, Calle 4, Avenidas 4/6, P. O. Box 15-5000, tel. 66[0]0678, fax 66[2]2532. 24 rooms. $41 single/$56 double. Visa, Master Card, American Express. Clean hotel, with small pool and air conditioning, enclosed parking, and inexpensive restaurant. From the Central Park, walk one block toward the highway on Avenida Central, then two blocks to the left. Safe-deposit box available.

HOTEL LAS ESPUELAS, tel. 66[0]0144 (P. O. Box 1056-1007 Centro Colón, San José, tel. [2]339955, fax [2]331787). 40 rooms. $47 single/$60 double. Visa, American Express, Master Card. Best in the area, a hacienda-style building with palm-shaded grounds, courtyard filled with birds and flowers, a good, reasonably priced restaurant with kids' menu, quiet central air conditioning (highly unusual), pool, and meeting facilities. Located on the highway, about a kilometer south of the turn into town.

Las Espuelas has several package trips from San José that include excursions to beaches, to a cattle ranch (with horseback riding, $150 overnight), and to Santa Rosa National Park.

HOTEL EL SITIO (P. O. Box 471-1000 San José), tel. 66[1]1211. 52 rooms. $45 double with fan, $65 with air conditioning.

On the road toward Nicoya, an airy, open, modern ranch-style complex with two pools, simple dining. Higher rates are with air conditioning. Rental cars available.

Budget Lodging

For cheaper, no-frills lodging, the HOTEL GUANACASTE (tel. 66[0]0085), half a block in from the highway, near the Hotel Bramadero, will do in a pinch. Cubicles in assorted sizes go for $20 or less double, most with private toilet.

HOTEL LIBERIA (tel. 66[0]0161), PENSIÓN MARGARITA (tel. 66[0]0468), and PENSIÓN GOLFITO (tel. 66[0]0963) all have rooms for $6 per person or less.

WHERE TO EAT

Most of the above have hotels have restaurants and bars.

The POKOPÍ restaurant, opposite the Hotel El Sitio on the Nicoya road, is a small steak and seafood house, with such items as chicken in wine sauce, pepper sirloin tips (excellent!), charcoal-broiled steak with all the trimmings, salads, pizza, and the unexpected sea bass a la Goldberg (in white sauce with mushrooms), for $6 and up. They also have children's plates and sandwiches for $3 or less. It's worth planning to arrive here for lunch or dinner. Open from 11 a.m. to 10 p.m., later on weekdays. Attached is the Kuru disco.

SODA GABI, on Avenida Central about two blocks past the square (opposite the highway) serves breakfast and lunch. LAS TINAJAS, on the square, has hamburgers, milk shakes and fried chicken.

Restaurant JAUJA, on the road into town, has open-air tables and a menu that includes fruit drinks and several Mexican items.

And there are assorted Chinese restaurants with names like CHUNG SAN and CANTON.

HOTEL LA SIESTA, two blocks south of the square, has an inexpensive no-frills no-hassle restaurant, with beef and fish main courses for $5 or less, and even shrimp for under $10.

SEEING THE SIGHTS

The museum/visitors' center is located in one of the oldest houses in Liberia, three blocks south and one block east from the square. Stop in, and ask any questions you might have. This facility is operated by a locally based organization, and provides up-to-date information on lodging, excursions, conditions at nearby volcanoes, and the like. They have detailed sectional maps of northwestern Costa Rica available for consultation. And on display are saddles, brands, and other implements and artifacts of the ranching life. If you're interested, ask for directions to some of the other old houses in town. For phone inquiries, dial 66[1]1606. Hours are 9 a.m. to noon and 1 to 6 p.m., Sunday to 1 p.m., closed Monday, open holidays.

The major point of interest in Liberia is La Agonía, the church at the end of Avenida Central that provides a taste of the old Costa Rica. It's a simple, low-slung building of stuccoed adobe and rubble, with just six amphora providing decorative elements along the pediment — altogether colonial in style, though records show that construction of the church started well after independence, in 1852, when Liberia was a remote outpost known as the town of Guanacaste. The front door is *usually* open from 3 to 4 p.m.

Not too far away is the house of a local character who, in manner of fellows in rural New England, collects glorious junk and exhibits it on his porch — saw blades, oxcart wheels, great wooden mortars and pestles, a Detroit Tigers batting helmet. Don't even think about buying. And on Avenida 4, a giant guanacaste tree has been left to live out its natural life nearly in the middle of a not-so-busy intersection. Three cheers!

EXCURSIONS

Several travel agencies arrange excursions from Liberia. The **Hotel Las Espuelas** (see above) has inclusive tours from San José. **Guanacaste Tours** (P.O. Box 55-5000 Liberia, tel. 66[0]0306, fax 660307) runs day trips to beaches and parks. **Punto Norte** (tel. 66[1]1313, fax 66[1]1736, P. O. Box 26-5000 Liberia) is based at **Hotel El Sitio**. They run trips to national parks and coastal wildlife reserves, ranch trips, and arrange boat trips, diving and fishing; and an investment tour that gives you partial reimbursement if you take the plunge.

RINCON DE LA VIEJA NATIONAL PARK

The Rincón de la Vieja volcano northeast of Liberia, one of five in the Guanacaste range, rises to an altitude of 1,995 meters (6,216 feet). Slopes steaming with mud pots, hot springs and geysers; heavy rainfall and resultant lush vegetation; abundant mammalian wildlife (white-faced monkeys, collared peccaries, and especially coatimundis) and a variety of birds all create a rare combination of sights and experiences for the visitor to the volcano and the surrounding forest.

Nine craters lie within the park boundaries, including the dormant crater of Santa María volcano (1,910 meters), a cold lake surrounded by dense vegetation. All but the main crater of Rincón de la Vieja are inactive.

The ascent of Rincón de la Vieja on this route is completed in two stages. First comes a walk of two to three hours from park headquarters to the Las Pailas area, where mud bubbles and shoots into the air. From there, the climb to the summit takes six to seven hours. Severe winds, suddenly dropping temperatures, fog, rain, and loose, rocky volcanic debris underfoot can make the going difficult and the rewards elusive. A morning ascent during the driest months (December to May) is recommended for the best views at the summit. But even if the peak is obscured, the clouds may blow away if you sit and wait.

Camping is permitted, and is recommended in order to get an early start toward the summit from the mudpot area.

ARRIVALS AND DEPARTURES
By Car or Foot

The road from Liberia to the southern access to the park, about 25 kilometers distant, crosses the city dump and a chalky, uninhabited plain with sparse growth of seasonally dry forest. There are no regular buses and there is usually no traffic, but the park service in San José might be able to help with transportation if it already has a vehicle going out. Contact the park service in any case before visiting (at the zoo in San José), or the tourist office in Liberia. You can also hike, which is somewhat of a ritual among Costa Rican outdoor enthusiasts, but it's an exposed and dusty routing in the dry season.

If you drive this way, you'll make it through the last few kilometers only with a four-wheel-drive vehicle.

WHERE TO STAY

About 17 kilometers out of Liberia, a spur track leads to **RINCONCITO LODGE**, where rudimentary lodging is available for $10 per person. Meals are about $6 each, and horses and guides are available at about $7 per person in a group for volcano trips. Call 66[0]0636 to arrange transportation, at about $40 for a small group.

An alternative course is to head to Curubandé, off the Inter-American Highway north of Liberia, and stay the night at one of the lodges along another route to the volcano.

HACIENDA-LODGE GUACHIPELÍN (P. O. Box 636, Alajuela, tel. 41[6]6545, fax 42[1]1910, or tel. 66[2]2429 at the lodge), 18 kilometers from the highway and 6 kilometers past Curubandé, is a cattle ranch out of the old days, a once self-contained fiefdom where the *hacendado*'s word was law. Bunk beds in a venerable wooden ranch house cost $15 per night, and there are private rooms for $40 and $45, plus $20 for three meals. Horses are available for hire, as at many country lodging places, but, unusually, Hacienda Guachipelín also gives riding lessons. Transportation can be arranged from Liberia on request.

At **RINCÓN DE LA VIEJA MOUNTAIN LODGE**, along the same road past Curubandé (P. O. Box 114-5000 Liberia, tel. 68[5]5422, fax 66[0]0473), double rooms are available for $36 to $40, plus another $30 for three meals. A bus operates at 2 p.m. from Liberia to Curubandé (return bus at 5 a.m.), or the ranch can arrange to pick you up for $10 (they have a car coming to Liberia several times a week).

You can continue the next day to explore the volcano either on horseback or on foot. It's about a five-hour walk to the main crater. Tours are available for $70 to $85 per person, with professional guides well versed in the flora and fauna of the volcano, to mudpots, fumaroles, sulphur pools, fresh-water springs and lagoons. The ranch also runs a river tubing excursion, arranges meetings with local people and ridealongs with the cowboys, and can send you for a soaking in a natural hot spring with mud that is said to be curative. Call to inquire about package rates.

In Liberia, you can arrange a day trip to the volcano and lodge (about $80) through the **Hotel Bramadero**.

BUENA VISTA LODGE (tel. 66[5]5147, fax 66[0]0090, $35 to $55 double in dorms or rooms), on a farm about 20 kilometers off the main highway via a rough road through Cañas Dulces, also offers horseback excursions to the park, as well as a spring-fed spa.

SANTA ROSA NATIONAL PARK

Located 36 kilometers north of Liberia, **Santa Rosa National Park** was established in 1971 as a historical monument. The natural treasures of the park, which were originally included only incidentally, are now the main attraction for the foreign visitor.

The Santa Rosa hacienda was the scene of one of Costa Rica's most glorious military episodes — an episode that lasted the approximately fourteen minutes it took for a Costa Rican force to defeat the invading army of William Walker on March 20, 1856. Walker's army — and much of the opposing Costa Rican army as well — was finished off not long afterward in a cholera epidemic. The original great house of the Santa Rosa hacienda still stands as a monument to the victory. Santa Rosa's location near the Nicaraguan border made it the scene of later intrigues and battles as well, during an insurrection in 1919, and, most notably, during a 1955 invasion by political exiles.

Among the many natural features of the park are an extensive protected area of deciduous dry tropical forest; and Nancite beach, where hundreds of thousands of Pacific Ridley turtles nest from August until December every year.

ARRIVALS AND DEPARTURES

The junction for the access road to Santa Rosa is at kilometer 269 on the Pan American (Inter-American) Highway. If you're not driving, you'll have to hitch or, more likely, walk the seven kilometers from the highway to the hacienda building and administration center.

Arriving By Bus

Buses leave Liberia for La Cruz and/or Peñas Blancas about every two hours from 5:30 a.m. to 8 p.m., passing the junction. From San José, buses for La Cruz depart from Calle 14, Avenidas 3/5 (tel. [2]231968) at 5 a.m. and 7:45 a.m. and 4:15 p.m. Time to the junction is about five hours.

Departing By Bus

Return departures from Peñas Blancas are at 11 a.m. and 3:30 p.m. From Liberia, buses leave for La Cruz and Peñas Blancas about every two hours.

SEEING THE SIGHTS

Partly because of its historical importance, the park is quite well run, and is one of the most visited in the national park system. Best time to visit Santa Rosa is in the dry season, when thirsty animals congregate around the permanent water holes and streams, making for easy viewing. During the rainy season, when few visitors appear, markers along the nature trail may be down.

Facilities at or near the park center include a historical museum in the old great house of the hacienda, seven kilometers from the Pan American Highway, and a nature trail nearby. The campsite, about a kilometer away, back toward the park entry, then down a side road, near the administration building, is basic, with showers and latrines, as well as many picnic tables. It's muddy in the rainy season (when I have spotted snakes), and there are no shelters. There's a small fee to camp, in addition to the admission fee to the park.

The *casona*, or great house of the Santa Rosa hacienda, is a large, whitewashed building with aged tile roof and wooden verandas. Part of the casona might date from the colonial period, though the age of the building is indeterminate. Houses of this sort were continually repaired, remodeled and expanded during their useful lives. The stone corrals around the house are almost certainly a few hundred years old, and were in use until the hacienda was nationalized. Great wooden mortars and pestles lie in the shade of the eaves. In the clearing in front of the casona is a huge guanacaste tree, witness to past battles.

Park Trails

Along the kilometer-long nature trail, signs point out features of plants, such as seasonal loss of leaves, which are adapted to the scarcity of water for much of the year; rock formations; and plants that survive the periodic fires of the dry lands. Typical dry-forest vegetation includes oaks, wild cherry, mahogany and the calabash, or gourd tree, the acacia bush, the ficus tree (*higuerón*, or *amate*), and the gumbo limbo, also called the naked Indian from the rich, reddish-brown color of its bark. Less exotic, "decorative" vegetation is also present, such as the hibiscus.

Several additional trails can be explored. The **Indio Desnudo** trail goes through a recovering dry forest. Animal sightings are said to be good along the **Los Patos** trail along which, near waterholes during the dry season, one can sit at a prudent and non-interfering distance and watch raccoons, coatis, spider monkeys, tapirs, agoutis, deer and assorted birds take their turns at the trough. Other wildlife that is more or less easily spotted in the dry season includes white-faced and howler monkeys, ocelots, jaguars, coyotes, armadillos, iguanas, collared and white-lipped peccaries, and rabbits. As well, more than 250 bird species have been recorded.

Much of the savanna of the central part of Santa Rosa was created through clearing of the native forest. The grass periodically burns off, either through accidental fires or controlled fires set by park personnel. Efforts are being made to regenerate the forest in these areas. Typically for Costa Rica, there are several habitats in the park beside seasonally dry forest. More moist areas contain abundant hardwoods that never lose their leaves. Gallery forest sweeps over the park's waterways. Near the coast are mangrove swamps, with dense populations of crabs, and high, sandy beach.

Beaches, Turtles, and Canyons

Nancite Beach is one of two known nesting areas in Central America for the **Pacific Ridley Sea Turtle**. During the rainy season, the turtles crawl up onto the beach, first by the dozens, then the hundreds, then the thousands, to shove each other aside like so many commuters fighting for space, dig nests, and lay eggs before departing for the open sea. Green and leatherback turtles nest at the beach as well, but in smaller numbers than the Ridleys. With humans and other predators scooping up eggs when park employees aren't looking, and vultures and frigate birds diving down for bits of hatchlings, less than one percent of the eggs make it to the sea as young turtles. Crabs and sharks lie in wait to further deplete their numbers.

Access to Nancite is controlled, in order to protect the turtle eggs. Inquire at park headquarters before heading for the beach, by trail or in a four-wheel-drive vehicle.

Naranjo, a larger beach than Nancite, is an excellent locale for bird watching. You can camp here along the shifting estuary. The **Mirador Valle de Naranjo** trail affords a view of Naranjo Beach, as well as of the **Peña Bruja** outcrop.

Cuajiniquil ("kwa-hih-nih-KIHL") **Canyon**, at the northern edge of the park, contains a series of waterfalls, as well as numerous palms and ferns in its moist environment. **Platanar Lake**, covering a hectare, is four kilometers north of the great house and administrative area, and attracts varied waterfowl as well as mammals during the dry season.

North of the main section of Santa Rosa Park is the **Murciélago Annex**, a rugged, seaside strip of scrub forest and rocky outcrops where jaguars and mountain lions roam. Notable in this section of the park is **Poza El General**, a year-round waterhole, which can be reached by trail.

The Murciélago section was expropriated by the Costa Rican government from former Nicaraguan president Anastasio Somoza. Access is via the Pan American Highway to the turnoff for Cuajiniquil village, 30 kilometers north of the junction for the main section of Santa Rosa Park. The entrance to the park annex is eight kilometers past Cuajiniquil.

There are also several isolated beaches near Cuajiniquil, both within and without the park. **Playa Blanca** is especially pretty. You can sometimes hire boats to poke around the inlets or to take you to the Murciélago ("bat") Islands, about 25 minutes out to sea.

Junquillal Bay Recreation Area (*Area Recreativa Bahía Junquillal*) including turtle nesting sites, dry forest and mangroves, is currently being developed for visitors, with campsites and trails.

Access to the Park Annex

Roads lead to various bays and Playa Blanca. You'll need a four-wheel-drive vehicle to penetrate very far into the park annex, otherwise you can rent horses in Cuajiniquil, or hike.

Buses operate at 5 a.m. and noon from La Cruz, 20 kilometers south from the Nicaraguan border on the Pan American Highway (see below), to Cuajiniquil (you can board one of these at the highway junction), and sometimes directly from Liberia (recently at 3 p.m.; inquire at the tourist office there, or the bus station).

There are a couple of inexpensive rooms available for rent above the **CUAJINIQUIL** restaurant. Call the public phone, 669030, to inquire about availability. Farther on, the **COOPEJUSA** ("Ko-o-peh-HOO-sah") restaurant serves meals and offers horseback rides on a cattle ranch, as well as beach access.

GUANACASTE NATIONAL PARK

Guanacaste National Park, one of the newest in Costa Rica, east of Cuajiniquil and the main highway, covers more than 800 square kilometers (over 300 square miles), and takes in some of the remaining uncleared dry tropical forest of Costa Rica, as well as the Orosí and Cacao volcanoes. Lake Nicaragua can be seen from the slopes of Orosí. Guanacaste is a park in the process of becoming and visitors' facilities are still being developed.

Much of the protected area consists of former pasture that is being encouraged to regenerate from existing nuclei of primary forest, mostly on volcanic slopes. Farmers whose land was incorporated into the reserve have been given salaries to protect resident animals instead of hunting them, as they once did. There are archeological sites in the park as well, where ancient Indian petroglyphs have been discovered; and sections where moist forest and dry forest intermingle. Evergreen forest on the high slopes is similar to what once covered Costa Rica's Central Valley.

The main entry point is opposite the entry for Santa Rosa National Park. You should make inquiries at Santa Rosa, or at the San José zoo, before visiting. There are three biological stations in the park: **Cacao**, on the slopes of Cacao volcano, in cloud forest; **Maritza**, on the slopes of Orosí, in transitional wet-humid forest; and **Pitilla**, in lowland rain forest on the eastern slopes of the park. Visits to these are arranged through scientific organizations or tour companies.

From a lookout point in La Cruz, **Isla Bolaños Wildlife Refuge** is visible offshore. The 99-acre island, covered by dry forest, is a nesting site for brown pelicans, American oyster-catchers, frigate birds (the only known nesting site of the latter two species in Costa Rica), and other seabirds. The public is banned from the island, but may approach in boats, which can be hired locally.

WHERE TO STAY

HACIENDA LOS INOCENTES (tel. 669190), a guest ranch, is east of the Inter-American Highway along a road that branches about five kilometers below La Cruz. 13 rooms are available, and there is a pool. Telephone [2]395484 in San José, fax [2]378282 for information about rooms and horses. The basic rate is about $55 per person with meals.

Peñas Blancas, 311 kilometers (194 miles) from San José on the Pan American Highway, is the small town located on the border with Nicaragua.

If you plan to visit Nicaragua, it's advisable to first obtain a visa in San José, if needed (Canadians, among others, currently require one). The border is open from 6:30 a.m. to 11 a.m., 12:30 p.m. to 5:30 p.m., and 6:30 p.m. to 10 p.m.

In addition to the buses mentioned above, there are direct buses from San José right to Managua (see page129).

THE NICOYA PENINSULA

The Nicoya Peninsula is separated from the rest of Costa Rica by the Gulf of Nicoya, as well as by Indian heritage, and a colonial past as part of Nicaragua. Sparsely populated, with poor roads, Nicoya enjoys a relatively dry climate, due to the barrier of hills and low mountains along the coast. Those same mountains create a series of sun-drenched beaches with rugged, dramatic backdrops (more on these later). Inland are some of the oldest towns in Costa Rica, as well as mountain-trimmed plains where cowboys rope stray horses and calves (often right on the road you're trying to negotiate), and fields of sorghum, sugarcane and irrigated rice ripen in the sun. In parts of Nicoya, as in few other areas of Costa Rica, steep hillside plots of corn are laboriously cultivated with hand tools, using methods that have not changed in hundreds of years.

There are several routes into Nicoya: by ferry from Puntarenas to Playa Naranjo or Paquera; by the road that branches from the Pan American Highway at kilometer 168, crossing the Tempisque River by ferry; and by the main highway south from Liberia to Belén, Santa Cruz and the town of Nicoya.

SANTA CRUZ

Santa Cruz is a sleepy, clean, pleasant, sunny and hot town, with a ruinous bell tower surviving from a colonial church. Several stores here sell pottery made in Nicoya's particular style, brown-colored and often with tripod bases, much of it made by Chorotega Indians in **Guaitil**, a craft center near Santa Bárbara, about ten kilometers to the east. The town comes alive for its annual fiesta, culminating on January 15.

For most visitors, Santa Cruz is a stopping point on the way to some of the Pacific beaches.

SANTA CRUZ FACTS	
Population:	approximately 7,000
Location:	56 kilometers from Liberia

ARRIVALS AND DEPARTURES

Arriving By Bus

From San José, buses for Santa Cruz leave from Calle 16, Avenidas 1/3, at 7:30 a.m. and 2, 4 and 5:30 p.m. Telephone **Tralapa**, [2]217202, to confirm the schedule. The **Alfaro** company (Calle 14, Avenidas 3/5, San José) has additional service. And there are hourly buses from Liberia.

Departing By Bus

Tralapa buses for San José leave at 4:30, 6:30 and 8:30 a.m. and 1 p.m. Telephone Tralapa, [2]217202, to confirm the schedule.

Buses leave at 10:30 a.m. and 3:45 p.m. for Tamarindo; for Paraíso, four kilometers from Junquillal beach, at 10:15 a.m. and 2:30 p.m. from the bus stop two blocks west of and one block north of the church; for Potrero, passing Brasilito and Flamingo, from the town square at 10:30 a.m. and 2:30 and 6 p.m.

WHERE TO STAY

HOTEL DIRIÁ, tel. 68[0]0080 (P.O. Box 4211, San José). 36 rooms. $26 single/$47 double. A roadside establishment on the edge of town, unprepossessing on the outside, with functional, air-conditioned rooms arranged around a courtyard, garden and pools. The dance hall next door might not be an advantage on weekends.

HOTEL SHARATOGA, tel. 68[0]0011 (P. O. Box 33, San José, tel. 336664). 40 rooms. $19 single/$26 double. A lesser hotel, located a few blocks in from the highway, half a block from the square. Air-conditioned rooms, mini-swimming pool, restaurant, and sparsely furnished rooms. This is a family-style hotel, in the Costa Rican sense. A marimba band plays on weekends.

WHERE TO EAT

There are several Chinese restaurants, those saviors of the traveler's stomach in Costa Rica, and assorted places for snacks. Best-known for home cooking, though, is **COOPETORTILLA** ("koh-oh-peh-tor-TEE-ya"), housed in a cavernous tin shed three blocks south of the church on the square. Casados, gallo pinto, and tortillas cooked over wood fires are served for just a couple of dollars.

NICOYA

Nicoya, the major town of the peninsula, is a commercial and cattle center, its single point of interest being an attractive, whitewashed, tin-roofed colonial church, one of the oldest in Costa Rica.

NICOYA FACTS	
Population:	approximately 11,000
Location:	78 kilometers from Liberia

ARRIVALS AND DEPARTURES

Arriving By Bus

Buses leave for Nicoya from Calle 14, Avenidas 3/5, San José, at 6, 8, and 10 a.m., and 1, 2:30, 3, 4:30 and 5:30 p.m., operating via Liberia or the Tempisque ferry. And there are hourly buses from Liberia.

Departing By Bus

Buses for San José leave from the Nicoya bus station, south of the square, at 4:30, 7:30 and 9 a.m., noon, and 2:30 and 4 p.m. The trip takes five hours.

Buses depart for Playa Naranjo at 5 a.m. and 1 p.m., meeting the ferry for Puntarenas.; to Nosara beach at 10 a.m. and 1 p.m.; and to Sámara and Carrillo beaches at 3 p.m. (on Saturday and Sunday at 7 a.m. as well). Schedules may vary in the rainy season.

WHERE TO STAY AND EAT

HOTEL CURIMÉ, P. O. Box 51, tel. 68[5]5238. 20 rooms. $56 per unit, sleeping from one to four persons. No credit cards.

Half a kilometer south of the main square, just off the Sámara road, the Curimé is a large, palm-shaded and altogether pleasant compound of hacienda-style bungalows. Pool and children's play areas. The restaurant is a pleasant terrace overlooking the pool, with many potted plants, but is unexpectedly expensive

In town, lodging places include the plain and adequate **HOTEL LAS TINAJAS** (tel. 68[5]5081, $10 single/$14 double); and the **HOTEL JENNY**, a block south of the square (tel. 68[5]5245, $16/$21 in air-conditioned concrete rooms). And there are several lesser places.

Several Chinese restaurants on the square serve square meals for $5 and up.

BARRA HONDA NATIONAL PARK

About 14 kilometers northeast of Nicoya, off the road that leads to the Tempisque River and the Pan American Highway, is **Barra Honda National Park**, with its extensive limestone caverns, and peaks offering long-distance views out over the Gulf of Nicoya.

Barra Honda mountain, once thought to be a volcano, rises 300 meters above the surrounding plain, and is pocked by holes where the roofs of underlying caves have collapsed. The caves were formed — and are still being formed — by the rapid erosion and chemical decomposition of layers of limestone sediment that once lay on the bed of a prehistoric sea. A geological fault line runs roughly along the nearby Tempisque River; the former seabed was steadily lifted as the Nicoya Peninsula slid alongside the mainland.

There are more than two dozen caves in Barra Honda, some of them still hardly explored. Most are entered by vertical drops, and the difficulty of entrance might account for their excellent state of preservation. Various caves have stalactites, stalagmites, "soda straws," cave grapes, "popcorn," "fried eggs," and numerous other formations.

Pozo Hediondo, once thought to be a crater, reeks with bat guano, though the bat population of the other caves is low. Other denizens of the dark are rats, insects, birds, and blind fish. **Nicoa Cave** contains skeletal human remains, some grotesquely meshed with stalagmites or covered with layers of calcium carbonate. Visitors may enter the caves with the permission and supervision of park rangers.

Facilities in Barra Honda Park include trails, latrines, drinking water, and a campsite. The bluffs are high, and will require quite a lot of exertion to ascend. Park headquarters are in the town of Barra Honda, four kilometers west of the highway from Nicoya to the Tempisque River. It's another six kilometers to the center of the park.

ARRIVALS AND DEPARTURES

By Tour

If you're interested in descending into the caves, contact the National Park Service at the Bolívar Park Zoo in San José. A park ranger must accompany you. Tours with descents into the caves are operated by Turinsa, Avenida 3, Calles 3/5, San José, tel. [2]219185.

Departing By Bus

Alfaro buses depart at 2:30 p.m. from Calle 14, Avenidas 3/5, San José, for Hojancha, passing the turn for Barra Honda at dusk in the dry season. More feasibly, travel first to the town of Nicoya, then take a morning bus heading by the turnoff for the park, 15 kilometers from Nicoya. A bus at 10:30 a.m. goes to the town of Barra Honda; other buses reach Santa Ana, about two kilometers from the park.

Departing By Ferry
Vehicles cross the Tempisque River on the direct road from Nicoya to San José on a ferry. Service is continuous, from 6 a.m. to 7 p.m. (to 9 p.m. on Sunday, Monday and Friday). At busy times, the ferry might make several trips until you get aboard. Fare is about $3 for a car and driver. Snack stands will feed you while you wait.

NEARBY SIGHTS AND LODGING
Near the caves, **Las Delicias** (*Delights*) is a cooperative project to involve local people with tourists, and vice-versa. Three cottages are available at about $15 per person per day, campsites for just a few dollars, and meals are served. Call 68[5]5580, a public phone nearby, to reserve.

EAST OF NICOYA
East from the town of Nicoya, the main highway runs for 75 kilometers (the last 40 unpaved) to the ferry slip at Playa Naranjo (see page 344), through sugarcane and rice fields, and pastures broken by clumps of trees, and bordered by windbreaks. The plain is edged by mountains and random, lumpy hills, but at a few high spots along the way, tantalizing glimpses of the Gulf of Nicoya are available. The distance is covered in four hours by slow (and dusty) bus, in half that time by car.

Carmona (Nandayure canton) is the major town along the way.

Jicaral has one of Costa Rica's impressive country churches, but one of the few found outside the Central Valley, a large, modern, bi-towered structure executed in reinforced concrete in a folksy Romanesque style.

Farther on are **salt pans**, where the road runs along the water.

BEACHES, BEACHES, BEACHES

First, the good news. Along the coast of the Nicoya Peninsula are dozens of beaches, each set in its own sweep of bay, bordered by rocky promontories and hills and coconut palms and lush tropical foliage, drenched in sun, with views to glittering blue sea broken here and there by huge rocks and by islets. Some of the beaches are virtually deserted, others have luxury hotels where most of one's needs are anticipated and attended. Commercial exploitation is limited, so far, to a few enclaves. There are no coral jewelry salesmen to hound sunbathers, few noisy discos or beachwear shops, and rarely are there crowds.

Now, the bad news (or hard facts). The nicest beaches in Nicoya are difficult to reach. Most of the roads to the coast are dusty and rutted, or muddy and occasionally impassable, depending on the time of year. Buses reach some of the coastal villages only once a day, after crunching, thumping, seemingly interminable (but only 30-kilometer-long) rides and numerous river fordings from Santa Cruz or Nicoya, and deliver passengers with a new coat of fine, reddish-brown grit. A few beaches are served by bus with less than daily frequency, and some not at all. Getting from one beach to another is often difficult, if not impossible. The motto of public transport in Nicoya may as well be "you can't get there from here."

The alternative to bus travel is to rent a car (an expensive proposition in Costa Rica, where a four-wheel-drive car might be indispensable), and brave the roads on your own. If you can find your way, that is. Some roads shown on maps of Nicoya exist only in the minds of hopeful cartographers, or are not generally passable.

Beyond the problems of access, Costa Rica's Pacific beaches have far fewer facilities than one might expect from the publicity about them, *except* in a few heavily trafficked centers. And many of the accommodations are *cabinas*, budget-priced rooms with cold water only. There is only a limited stock of rooms in the middle range.

What to Expect

What you'll find at any beach is unpredictable (unless you read this book carefully before you go). Restaurants at the beaches offer little variety, but a few hotels have good chefs, and the food scene is generally improving. **Tamarindo** is a notable bright spot. There is little opportunity for shopping and browsing, except at **Jacó Beach** and **Manuel Antonio**, in the southern coastal region. Car-rental agencies, dive shops, or many of the amenities one associates with a beach resort are found only at **Playas del Coco** and **Flamingo Beach** in the north, and Jacó and Manuel Antonio in the south. Food stocks in stores — where there are stores — can be limited to a few basics, even if cooking facilities are available in your villa.

But the bad news might also be good news. So many of the Nicoya beaches are nearly deserted and unspoiled precisely because they are hard to reach. If your intention really is to swim and take the sun and read and enjoy some special company without any distractions, then there are few better places to go than the less accessible beaches of Nicoya. As overnight destinations during a week of hopping around Costa Rica, forget them. But for a few days at a time at least, most are fairly wonderful.

To make your beach excursion easier, consider renting a car, even if you normally use public transportation. Fill up on gas at every opportunity — filling stations are sparse. Or else hire a taxi to take you, say, from the town of Nicoya or Santa Cruz to one of the beaches. Some beach hotels and travel agencies will also make transportation arrangements, and air service is available to several centers.

Consider carefully where you will stay. If you're going at a leisurely pace, you can always book into one of the cabinas in a beach village and switch the next morning if you're not satisfied. But if you've invested a certain amount of money in a short vacation, many of the available accommodations just won't fill the bill, especially when the rain is pouring down and the streets have turned to mud. Some of the secluded resorts around the peninsula are beautiful, impressive properties. But because of their isolation, you're at the mercy of your hosts, should there be some spanner in the works — a chef on vacation, a non-functioning air-conditioner, whatever.

Call ahead, when you can, to reserve a room, and to allow your hosts to lay in supplies — a difficult task at beaches. Reservations are essential on weekends. You could well arrive after a difficult trip, only to find that all the cabinas have been taken by hordes of local *excursionistas* travelling on chartered buses.

Reconfirm bus departure times at the tourist office in San José. If you're driving, especially in the rainy season, inquire about road conditions. Key bridges might be washed out, swollen rivers could be unfordable in the small car you've rented. If you're backpacking and camping out— tempting on deserted stretches of coast — take supplies from San José or some other large town. If there are children in your group, take a variety of snacks (a good idea for adults, too). And take a supply of cash — you'll find few banks to exchange travellers checks. Try to avoid arriving after dark. In general, don't count on finding anything out there that you haven't been told is there.

REAL ESTATE OPPORTUNITIES

Land and villa sales to foreigners constitute one of the more visible economic activities in parts of Nicoya, and the visitor to Costa Rica is sure to come across some compatriot who is harvesting baskets of cash at least in his dreams in the land business. (There are also the coconut business, the mango business, the shrimp business, the jojoba business, the macadamia business and others in which your buddies from home will deal you in on "secure" future profits for a substantial investment now, but those are other stories.) Various hotels in Nicoya exist at least partly to encourage the romance between visitor and house lot (or condominium, or time-sharing unit).

There is no reason to get a creepy feeling about real estate activities in Nicoya — the climate, the views and much else are attractive. But one should bear in mind that promised amenities, such as electricity, running water, transportation and shopping, might not materialize during your lifetime.

NICOYA COAST BEACH RESORTS
Here's a rundown, from north to south:

PLAYAS DEL COCO

The beach here is in a dramatic setting on a large horseshoe bay with great rocks offshore, sailboats gliding around, and dozens of fishing boats tied up or on their way in to or out from shore. But this is one of the Pacific points most easily reached from San José, and it shows. The little town and the central part of the beach are dirty, though there's less litter the farther you walk from the center.

ARRIVALS AND DEPARTURES

Playas del Coco (or simply **Coco**) is the center of a mega-beach area that includes **Ocotal**, to the south, and **Playa Hermosa** and **Playa Panamá**, to the north. Public transport to nearby beaches is limited, so many passengers arrive to Coco by public transportation and are picked up, or continue by taxi.

Arriving By Bus

Buses leave Liberia for Coco approximately at for El Coco beach at 5:30 and 8:15 a.m., and 12:30, 2, 4:30 and 6:15 p.m. Service may be curtailed in the rainy season.

One bus a day leaves from Calle 14, Avenidas 1/3, San José, at 10 a.m. for El Coco; the trip takes just under five hours.

Arriving By Car

To drive to Playa Hermosa or Playa del Coco, take the main Nicoya highway and turn off at the Tamarindo restaurant, 20 kilometers from Liberia. El Coco is 15 kilometers onward.

Departing By Taxi or Foot

To reach the nearby beaches of Ocotal or Playa Hermosa, if your hotel isn't arranging transport, it's easiest to take a taxi or hitch.

Departing By Bus

A bus leaves for San José at about 8:30 a.m., and there are six daily buses for Liberia in the dry season.

To continue by bus to beach towns to the south, take the Liberia bus as far as the junction at the Tamarindo restaurant, and flag down a bus going your way.

WHERE TO STAY

HOTEL FLOR DE ITABO, P. O. Box 32, tel. 67[0]0292, fax 67[0]0003.

22 rooms, 5 suites. $60 single/$65 double, $45 in bungalows slightly less in low season. American Express, Visa, Master Card.

This attractive hotel, well managed by European owners, is not on the beach — in this case an advantage. The large, beamed, tile-floored restaurant (reasonably priced) looks out through archways to the huge adults' pool and children's pool, lawns shaded by coconut palms, and jungly gardens beyond. Rooms are comfortable, with carved hardwood bedsteads, air conditioning, and satellite television. Suites, at $95 daily, have cooking facilities.

Boats are available for **deep-sea fishing** at $450 to $560 per day, or $30 per hour on a 21-footer; and, unusually for Pacific coastal hotels, **river fishing** as well. And horseback riding and trips to Rincón de la Vieja are offered. Private transportation from San José can be arranged, along with car rental. It's all quite nice if your stay will be centered on your hotel. But consider: if you have to go a kilometer from the beach to find pleasant surroundings, is this where you want to be? Maybe so. English, German, Italian and French are spoken.

HOTEL COCO PALMS, P. O. Box 188-5019, tel. 67[0]0367, fax 67[0]0117. Twenty rooms. $60 to $70 double. Visa, Master Card. This hotel, one block from the beach next to the soccer field, has just been totally renovated under its new German management. All rooms are air conditioned, with attractive wicker furniture. Facilities include a central thatched roundhouse restaurant, pool, and casino. Unfortunately, some rooms have only views of parked cars outside picture windows.

At the beach, accommodations are of the popular sort, without hot water, and with neighbors close on. The **HOTEL CASINO PLAYAS DEL COCO** offers the best of the available *cabina*-type rooms with sea view and private bath for $25 double, or $40 in a unit that will sleep a family. If you're stuck in back, the rate is slightly lower. The price drops from July through November.

There are similar places to stay, such as **CABINAS EL COCO** next door, which also has a few better rooms, and **CABINAS LUNA TICA**, to the left as you face the beach; and lesser ones, with prices down to $10 per person, or $5 in the rainy season, none of which I can particularly recommend. Private houses toward the ends of the beach are rented out from time to time. And there are some housekeeping units on roads off the beach, at about $25 per day.

WHERE TO EAT

The **DON HUMO ("MR. SMOKE") ROTISSERIE** restaurant, where the road leads off toward Ocotal, is the most modern and formal eating place in town. There is excellent chicken roasted over a wood fire, as well as fish and kebabs. The operators, who speak English, can also arrange for deep-sea fishing.

PIZZERIA PRONTO, on the entry road a couple of blocks from the beach, is one of several pizza joints.

Assorted stands sell fried fish, and there are several bars. Or try the **HOTEL FLOR DE ITABO** for a sit-down meal away from the crowds.

SPORTS AND RECREATION
Diving
There are several **dive shops** in the Coco area:
- **Diving Safaris**, at the Hotel Ocotal (see below) is the oldest operation of its kind in the area.
- **Virgin Diving** (tel. 670472) at La Costa Hotel and Villas, up the coast at Playa Hermosa, offers half-day, two tank dives for $55, or $75 with equipment. They also give open-water courses for $300 and an introduction to scuba for $95.
- **Rich Coast Diving** (tel. 670176, fax 670164), on the main road into Playas del Coco, near the beach, offers somewhat lower rates than others in the area: $45 for a two-tank dive ($65 with full equipment), $70 for a resort course.

Fishing
Various hotels and shops rent fishing gear and boats. The **Mareas** shop organizes fishing at under $40 an hour — not bad.

NORTH OF PLAYAS DEL COCO
PLAYA HERMOSA
Hermosa is a more serene place than Coco, with a few houses scattered along the low ridge that backs the water.

ARRIVALS AND DEPARTURES
Arriving By Bus
A bus for Playa Hermosa and Playa Panamá leaves from Calle 12, Avenida 7, San José, at 3:30 p.m. There are also daily buses from Liberia, about 35 kilometers away, at 11:30 a.m. and 7 p.m. Or take a bus to El Coco, then a taxi for seven kilometers to Playa Hermosa.

Arriving By Car
If driving, turn off the road to El Coco at the La Costa sign, about ten kilometers after the Tamarindo restaurant.

Departing By Bus
Buses depart Playa Hermosa at 5 a.m. for San José; and at approxi-

mately 6 a.m. and 4 p.m. for Liberia.

WHERE TO STAY

CABINAS PLAYA HERMOSA, tel. 67[0]0136. 20 units. $23 single/ $40 double/up to $55 for five. This is a compound pleasantly landscaped with cactus, giant aloe and hibiscus, at the end of a winding 500-meter spur road. All rooms, in whitewashed brick buildings that bear a patina of age, have fans and private bath. The beach in front is the most attractive in the area. Quiet, compared to the honky-tonk style of hotels at El Coco, with no shops, outside restaurants or diversions other than those at the hotel, not that you need them. The owner is Italian, and home-made pasta, steak bolognese and other surprising fare emerge from a sparkling tiled kitchen, at $6 or so for a main course.

HOTEL EL VELERO, tel. and fax 67[0]0310. 12 rooms. $36 single/ $40 double. A substantial and attractive beachfront Mediterranean-style villa and compact compound with pool and, sometimes, loud music. Rooms have two low double beds with good mattresses, red tile floors, two ceiling fans, dressing table and wardrobe. French spoken.

There are also some cheaper and far less attractive cabinas nearby. **LOS CORALES**, several blocks from the beach (tel. [2]570259), is a time-sharing development with twelve air-conditioned cabinas that sleep up to six. The rate is about $100 on weekends, less during the week. Grounds are rough and rocky, but there are a pool and play areas.

HOTEL AND VILLAS LA COSTA, tel. 67[0]0267 (P.O. Box 55-1001, San José, tel. [2]218949), fax 670011. 100 villas and 54 hotel rooms. $114 double ($90 in low season), $20 per additional person. Three kilometers onward from the central part of Playa Hermosa, La Costa is a vacation village with amenities and activities that include windsurfing, water-skiing, fishing and diving facilities, sailing, tennis courts, a nice sandy beach, and pool. Rooms in the hotel, high on a hillside overlooking the sea, have two double beds, tub, hair dryer, and central air conditioning. Villas, arranged in camp-style rows down the hill, have a bedroom and living room, kitchenette, and terrace.

PLAYA PANAMA

Two kilometers past La Costa, **Playa Panamá** is a sweep of beach that looks out on the great sheltered Gulf of Papagallo, almost surrounded by green carpeted hills. Deserted but for a few shacks, it must be something like the Acapulco of 70 years ago. And another Acapulco is what it might one day become, for there are ambitious and controversial plans to establish a vacation city here.

LUSH COASTAL SCENE

For now, most residents have been moved out, and you can arrive under your own steam, with supplies, and swim and picnic in magnificent solitude . . . for how long, I don't know.

SOUTH OF EL COCO

PLAYA OCOTAL

Three kilometers south of El Coco, **Ocotal** is reached by an unpaved road, rutted and difficult to negotiate in the rainy season. But there are rewards, if you're interested in a secluded hotel, deep-sea fishing, or diving.

ARRIVALS AND DEPARTURES

Access to Ocotal is by car or taxi from Playas del Coco.

WHERE TO STAY

HOTEL EL OCOTAL, tel. 67[0]0230, fax 67[0]0083 (P.O. Box 1, Playa del Coco). 43 units. $100 single/$125 double/$240 in suite. Slightly lower April through November. American Express, Visa, Master Card. This hotel is in a bare but dramatic clifftop setting colored with frangipani and bougainvillea, overlooking multiple coves and inlets with black-sand beaches and rocky islets offshore. Some rooms are in a row looking seaward, with walls of glass. More attractive are individual villas with two larger rooms in each, parquet floors, and a better bathroom. Ten new units are at beach level, next to the diving shop and the third swimming pool. (Management will not confirm the type of room you will have.) All rooms are air-conditioned, with television, coffee-maker, and mini-refrigerator.

Facilities include tennis courts, pool, riding horses, and equipment for fishing and water skiing. Deep-sea fishing programs, using 32- and 42-foot boats, are available at $600 to $750 daily per boat. Despite its isolation, the hotel's restaurant is reasonably priced. Security measures are quite evident.

VILLA CASA BLANCA, P. O. Box 176-5019, Playas del Coco, tel. and fax 67[0]0448. 12 units. $51 single/$57 double with breakfast. This inn is a welcome ray among the anonymous lodging places of the vicinity, a Mediterranean villa (or "white house," as the name would have it) set back from and overlooking the sea. The interior is open and lofty, with varnished wood ceilings and warm tile floors; the management is North American and friendly; and the rooms, all with private baths and wood trim, have individually selected furnishings and decorations, including canopy beds in some. All rooms have overhead fans, and some are air-conditioned. Two condominium units are also available at about $100 daily.

The charm continues outside, where entry is by a bridge over the pool and on through the bougainvilleas and past the outdoor breakfast pavilion. Fishing, horseback riding and pickup in Playas del Coco can be arranged.

VISTAS DEL OCOTAL (tel. [2]553284 in San José, 514-381-3382 in Montreal) are row condominium units consisting of a bedroom, sleeping loft and cooking area, located in the flat terrain below the Ocotal Hotel. The property has a pool. The rate is $96 for up to three persons, $110 for six. These would be cramped with six, and maybe even with three persons. Plans call for the addition of a bar and disco, pool, and tennis courts.

BAHÍA PEZ VELA, tel. 67[0]0129, P. O. Box 7758 San José; or c/o World Wide Sportsman, P. O. Drawer 787, Islamorada, FL 33036, tel. 800-327-2880 or 305-664-4615. Fishing packages from about $325 per day.

Located at Playa Negra, another beautiful little black sand cove about two kilometers past Ocotal via a concrete road, Bahía Pez Vela was the first of the west-coast fishing resorts in Costa Rica. Specialties are sailfish, roosterfish and dorado.

Not everything at Ocotal is private. If you take a right turn at the gate house, the public road continues to Ocotal beach, where you will find no hotels, one bar, tamarind-shaded sand, and the quiet that was missing at El Coco.

SPORTS AND RECREATION
Diving
Diving Safaris, based at Ocotal, schedules a scuba dive every day of the year at 9 a.m. The staff includes PADI instructors and divemasters. With two new diesel-powered boats and a pontoon boat, Diving Safaris regularly takes visitors out to the Bat and Catalina islands. Courses and certification upgrades are available, as well as week-long packages. Make arrangements at the Hotel Ocotal; or write to **Diving Safaris**, Apartado 121 5010, Playas del Coco, Costa Rica, tel. 67[0]0012.

Swimming
At **Belén**, 40 kilometers from Liberia on the main Nicoya highway, a branch road heads for the sea at Brasilito, 32 kilometers away, and onward to the beaches of Flamingo and Potrero, to the north. The route to Brasilito and Flamingo is paved; other beaches are reached by branch dirt roads.

Follow the Playa Flamingo signs from Belén if you're driving.

BRASILITO
The road reaches the water at Brasilito, where a wide, sandy beach lines a typical horseshoe bay. There are some basic cabinas here and a couple of fish restaurants. **Conchal Beach**, almost adjacent, can be reached on foot, or with a four-wheel-drive vehicle.

ARRIVALS AND DEPARTURES
Use the same buses as for Flamingo (see next page).

WHERE TO STAY
CABINAS CONCHAL (tel. 67[4]4257), about 500 meters before the beach on the entry road, under French management, is a better value than most other lodging places in the immediate area, at $26 single/$31 double. Guest rooms are individual stuccoed cabins around a gravel courtyard with dry-forest trees, simple but with good beds.

HOTEL BRASILITO, right in the village, has two rows of basic rooms atop each other, overpriced at $30 single/$50 double.

HOTEL VILLAS PACÍFICA, tel. 68[0]0573, P. O. Box 10-5150 Santa Cruz. 5 rooms. $150 double/$230 for five persons. A kilometer past Brasilito, and another kilometer along a side road, this hotel is atop a hillock in a large estate. The condominium guest units are plantation-style, with tile roofs, two bedrooms, kitchen and living room. Public areas have soaring ceilings.

Villas Pacífica is billed as a fishing lodge — fishing packages run about $2000 per week — though the boats are parked a couple of kilometers away at the Flamingo marina. The pool is large, and the sea views from the terraces are excellent. The restaurant is fairly pricey, but so are most things in this area, and the food is good in any case.

PLAYA FLAMINGO

Four kilometers onward from the turn for Villas Pacífica is **Flamingo Beach**, a stunning horseshoe of white sand in the web of a hand-shaped promontory, bordered by cliffs and a large hill.

What distinguishes Flamingo is what man has added to nature: a marina which, though small, is the most complete in the region.

For all the money that has been poured into the attractive facilities at Flamingo, there's no town, and little shade. If you're not into fishing, sunbathing and real-estate pitches, and don't have a car to circulate to other locales, Flamingo can get old rather quickly. Flamingo has the air of a town looking for the next rich sucker to come along.

ARRIVALS AND DEPARTURES

Arriving By Bus

From San José, buses depart daily at 8 a.m. (direct) and 10:30 a.m. (connecting) from Avenida 3, Calles 18/20; return trip at 2 p.m. Phone [2]217202 to reserve. Buses for Brasilito, Flamingo and Potrero leave daily from Santa Cruz at 4 a.m., 10:30 a.m., and 2:30 p.m. The run to Potrero takes about two hours. Verify this schedule at the tourist office before leaving San José.

Express bus service is provided three times weekly from San José, fare $30 each way (about five times the fare on the public bus). Departure is in the morning from the Herradura and Cariari hotels, returning in the evening. Call [2]391584 or [2]392921 to reserve.

Arriving By Air

By air, charter a seaplane to take you right to the marina from Pavas airport outside San José. The fare is about $450 each way for five passengers. Call the Flamingo marina, tel. 67[4]4203, to make arrangements. Otherwise, fly to Tamarindo (see page 331), then take a taxi, if you haven't arranged to be picked up by your hotel.

Arriving By Boat

I'm told that the approach to the slips at Flamingo is through water that is quite shallow for sailboats. If you plan to dock at Flamingo, clear customs and immigration first at Playas del Coco (if approaching from the north), otherwise you'll be sent back.

Departing by Bus or Air from Flamingo, Brasilito, and Potrero
Buses for Santa Cruz depart from Potrero depart at 5 a.m., 2 p.m. and 4 p.m., passing through Flamingo and Brasilito. The run to Potrero takes about two hours. Verify this schedule at the tourist office before leaving San José. The return bus to San José leaves at 2 p.m. Or, you can book the express bus back from Flamingo (see above), or a flight from Tamarindo.

WHERE TO STAY

HOTEL PLAYA FLAMINGO (90 rooms) and **PRESIDENTIAL SUITES** (23 condos, 120 rooms), tel. 67[4]4010, fax 67[4]4060 (P. O. Box 692-4050 Alajuela, tel. [2]391584, fax [2]390257). $110 single/$120 double. Suites from $180 double, $205 for four persons. Visa, American Express, Master Card. The sprawling main hotel here, at water level, is all first-class, except for the need to cross a road to reach the beach. Rooms are large and comfortable, air-conditioned, with televisions, and most have terraces.

On the hilltop overlooking the Flamingo Beach Hotel, condos and rooms in the Presidential Suites are indifferently furnished, but have complete kitchens and two bedrooms, and offer more sweeping views from multi-story towers. Between the two sections, there are three pools, including one for children, and two bars. The restaurant is attractive, with no surprises on the menu. (assorted spaghetti, brochettes, stroganoff, a few kids' choices). Car rentals, casino.

Flamingo Marina Resort, tel. 67[4]4141, fax 67[4]4035 (tel. [2]218093 in San José). 35 rooms. $110 double/$185 in suite. Visa, Master Card, American Express. This low-slung tan concrete building overlooks the Flamingo marina. All rooms have sea-view terraces, and the standard rooms are nice enough, with one double bed, a smaller bed, television, air-conditioning, mini-refrigerator, and standard motel-style bathroom. But the suites are *different*, with a large, shaded terrace that includes a kitchenette with tiled island, and private whirlpool. Bar, restaurant, large pool, children's pool, tennis.

VILLAS FLAMINGO, tel. 67[4]4215, [2]390737 in San José. 24 units. $115 double to $171 for six. This is the first accommodation along the road into Flamingo, where the road bends along the sea, and currently the best value. Two rows of two-level apartments are set back across a grassy and treed area from the beach. Each modern unit has two bedrooms, three bathrooms, several sleep sofas, fans (no air-conditioning), and upstairs terrace. There is a pool on the property, but no hotel services are available. Rates are slightly lower by the week, and the monthly rate is about $1,800.

WHERE TO EAT

Just down the road from the Hotel Playa Flamingo is **MARIE'S RESTAURANT**, an attractive, informal, open-air bistro. Complete breakfasts are served for $5, as well as lasagne, cordon bleu, Mexican combinations, and seafood items for $7 and up, tacos and sandwiches for less.

Up at the pinnacle of Flamingo, **MAR Y SOL** offers a continental menu with sea view. About $15 and up, call 67[4]4151 to reserve.

TIO'S BAR, on the way into Flamingo, is also a restaurant, recreation center and general hangout, with golf driving range, tennis court and pickup softball games.

Over on the mainland, two kilometers from the center of Flamingo, **HAL'S AMERICAN** serves roast chicken, pizza and pasta with sea view under a thatched roof. You can play mini-golf before, while, or after you eat. Call 67[4]4057 for delivery to your room.

A few basic food items are available at the **Marina Trading Post**.

SPORTS AND RECREATION

The **Quicksilver Dive Shop** at Flamingo, tel. 67[4]4010, offers windsurfers, mountain bikes and boogie boards for rent. They'll take you diving.

Flamingo Divers, tel. 67[4]4021, offers two-tank dives for $70 plus equipment rental, full open-water certification for about $400.

The **Marina Trading Post** has information about privately owned beach and hillside houses available for rent, at up to $300 per night. Catamaran rentals can be arranged as well.

Deep-sea fishing in the Flamingo area, at $250 to over $1000 per day, is available from:

• **Flamingo Bay Pacific Charters** (tel. [2]314055 in San José; or 1112 East Las Olas Blvd., Fort Lauderdale, FL 33301, tel. 800-654-8006, fax 305-522-2637), with packages from $300 per day of fishing, including room, meals, and transport from San José.

• **Blue Marlin Fishing**. Stop in at their office in Flamingo, or call 67[4]4043, fax 67[4]4165.

• **Sportfishing Costa Rica** (P.O. Box 115-1150 La Uruca, tel. [2]333892 in San José, 800-374-4474 U.S.-Costa Rica direct).

NIGHTLIFE

Restaurants and shops of interest to visitors are sparse in the Flamingo area. A rental car is almost a necessity for any variety in dining, food shopping, beaches, etc.

Amberes is a bar-casino-disco up the hill in the Presidential suites where you can while away your time as your colones trickle away.

PLAYA POTRERO
WHERE TO STAY
Around the sweep of bay from Flamingo are:

BAHÍA FLAMINGO, tel. and fax 68[0]0976, a compound of beachside cottages with a small pool, currently being remodeled.

CABINAS CRISTINA, 200 meters back from the beach in a pasture, has four basic housekeeping units with hard beds, cooktop and refrigerator for $30 double. Telephone 68[0]0997.

There's also a simple eatery in the area of these lodging places, but no other facilities. The village of Playa Potrero — a soccer field, general store and several houses — is three kilometers onward.

PLAYA PAN DE AZÚCAR (SUGAR BEACH)
A dirt road winds up into the hills beyond the village of Playa Potrero and down to solitary **Playa Pan de Azúcar**.

WHERE TO STAY
HOTEL SUGAR BEACH, tel. 680959 (P. O. Box 66-5150 Santa Cruz). 10 rooms. $68 double with fan, $90 double with air conditioning. This hotel's brochure calls its beach the most beautiful in Costa Rica. With a gentle hillside and gray sand, trees growing down almost to the water, and streams meandering through, I can't take issue with the claim. Four rooms are in an elevated round house, the others in ranch units with front porches facing the bay and offshore islands.

Food is served under a great rotunda. Breakfast $3 to $4, main courses at lunch and dinner from $6. A pet iguana scurries around the grounds, and monkeys and macaws share the hillside with guests. Horses are available, and a dive shop is planned. There's nobody out here but you and the people at the hotel. With advance notice, you can arrange a pickup at Tamarindo airstrip, or at Perla's Cantina in Playa Potrero, where the bus from Santa Cruz ends its run.

PLAYA CONCHAL
Conchal ("shell") **Beach**, at the village of Puerto Viejo, is almost adjacent to Brasilito, reached by an unpaved road that branches at Huacas, or by a jeep trail along the coast from Brasilito. There are some shells, as the name implies, which tend to pile up at the northern end; but more driftwood and assorted beach litter. Conchal is wide, little-frequented, relatively enclosed by ridges, with rocks offshore. Aside from one resort hotel, there are a few inexpensive cabina units, rental apartments, a snack bar, and fishing boats available for excursions.

WHERE TO STAY

HOTEL CONDOR CLUB, Puerto Viejo (P. O. Box 102-2300 Curridabat), tel. 68[0]0920, fax 68[0]0944. 40 rooms. $90 single or double. Visa, Master Card, American Express. This is a little hilltop village of rock-and-steel-and-glass buildings, more than a kilometer back from the ocean. (The hotel maintains a separate beachside pool and snack bar — an odd arrangement.) Guest rooms are in several six-sided bungalows that don't have a terrace or much of a view, but are fairly well furnished with assorted single, double or triple-sized beds, a small television, and standard tiled bathroom.

PLAYA GRANDE

South of Conchal, Playa Grande ("Great Beach") is broad and open, bordered by extensive mangroves, and noted for leatherback turtle nesting (November through March) at **Las Baulas de Guanacaste National Park**, which takes in the strip of beach. There are controversial development plans that could see the scrub that borders the beach divided into house lots. For now, there are one hotel, solitude, and many dirt roads leading nowhere.

Playa Grande is reached by a road that branches at Matapalo, past Huacas.

WHERE TO STAY

HOTEL LAS TORTUGAS (P. O. Box 184, Santa Cruz), tel. 68[0]0765. 11 rooms. $70 single or double, lower May through September. In San José, Tikal tours, tel. [2]232811.

At the south end of Playa Grande, Las Tortugas is an overgrown concrete beach house. The large, slate-floored rooms are air-conditioned, with plenty of wood trim but little decoration. The owners are conservationists, and offer canoe trips and boat tours of the river estuary.

There is one other accommodation in the area, **Cabinas Playa Grande**, about a kilometer back from the beach, with six cabinas going for about $25 double.

PLAYA TAMARINDO

Tamarindo is a wide, mostly empty beach curving around a miles-long bay, with rocks and little sandy islands offshore. Pelicans float overhead and dive into the waters, skiffs bob up and down in the gentle surf. The setting is nearly perfect. And yet, many who know the Nicoya beaches say that Tamarindo is spoiled. Which is a measure of what some of the other beaches are like.

There is something of a village at Tamarindo, with a few houses spread out along the last stretch of road, and a couple of hotels. More development is on the way — the subdividers have arrived, billboards advertise house lots for sale, and dozens of vacation houses have been erected to the south. But the village remains fairly peaceful and low-key. The tamarinds that give the beach its name are the trees with the dangling seed pods, and fingery, brush-like leaves. Birding is excellent in the nearby mangroves and tidal pools.

ARRIVALS AND DEPARTURES

Arriving By Bus

A direct bus for Tamarindo leaves from Calle 14, Avenidas 3/5, San José, daily at 3:30 p.m.; phone [2]217202 to reserve. Another bus leaves from Avenida 3, Calles 18/20 at 4 p.m. The trip takes about five hours. From Santa Cruz, a bus for Tamarindo leaves the main square at 3:30 p.m. The **Hotel Tamarindo Diriá** has a direct air-conditioned bus three times a week for $50 round trip (versus $10 for the public bus).

Arriving By Air

There is daily air service from San José as well, on **Sansa** airlines, tel. [2]335330. Fare is under $40 each way, and inexpensive packages with hotel are available. **Travelair** (tel. [2]327883) flies most days of the week to Tamarindo from San José, fare $114 round trip.

Arriving By Car

If you're driving from San José, the preferred route to Tamarindo is the road that forks from the main Nicoya highway at Belén. Continue through Huacas (instead of turning for Flamingo) to the junction for the dirt road to Tamarindo. Total distance is 38 kilometers from Belén. Tamarindo can also be reached by road from Santa Cruz, unpaved for part of the way.

Departing By Bus

A return bus for San José leaves at about 5:45 a.m., and there is usually another bus at about noon. Or inquire at the Tamarindo Diriá for the express bus.

Departing By Air

Some Travelair and Sansa flights touch down in Nosara or Sámara on the way back to San José.

WHERE TO STAY

HOTEL EL JARDÍN DEL EDÉN, tel. 67[4]4111 direct to hotel; tel. [2]202096, fax [2]249763in San José. 18 rooms and 2 apartments. $80 to $100 single/$97 to $125 double ($140 in apartment); $15 per additional adult, $10 per child. Rates include breakfast. This is the nicest small hotel to have opened recently along the Pacific, a hilltop Mediterranean villa that is pleasant both to regard and to inhabit. Each room is different in size and shape. Most have terraces, some have private flower-bordered sandy gardens, all have ocean and sunset views, some are reached through winding passages that suggest medieval intrigue. Bedspreads are cheery, showers are oversized and lined with Talavera tile, lighting is dazzling or subdued according to your requirements, there are both air conditioning and ceiling fan, and a minibar-refrigerator stocks beverages at unusually fair prices. Apartments have a separate bedroom and a Mexican-tiled kitchen, and built-in wardrobes. Even the service sinks in the corridors are disguised to fit the decor.

As for the grounds and facilities . . . there are fountains, there are terraces and gardens, a pool with bar and Jacuzzi and larger free-form pool in succession down the hillside, and stone-flagged walkways. The bar-restaurant is a lovely area, with thatched roof supported on posts fashioned from tree trunks, tables inset with glazed tiles, and a rough red-tile floor. And of course there are chaises longues and thatched umbrellas, and rock gardens and planters. The included buffet breakfast consists of fresh breads, fruits, juices, eggs prepared to order, and lots more. The restaurant changes its offerings daily to take advantage of available fresh ingredients.

I don't usually go into the backgrounds of the owners, but in this case, the *chef de cuisine-dessinateur* from France and one-time public-relations specialist from Italy know exactly what they're doing, and they personally supervise operations to see that it's all done right. The Jardín del Edén — Garden of Eden — is about 400 meters back from the main road in Tamarindo.

HOTEL PUEBLO DORADO, tel. and fax [2]225741. (P. O. Box 1711-1002, San José). 22 rooms. $75 single/$89 double. American Express, Visa, Master Card. Across the road from the beach, a sleek *art modern* concrete hotel with all the essentials: air-conditioning, medium-sized pool, bar and restaurant, t-shirt-and-tanning-lotion shop, and guest rooms on two levels with tile floors and minimal but attractive furnishings. English and French spoken, limited but reasonably priced menu.

HOTEL PASATIEMPO, fax 68[0]0776. 10 bungalows. $80 double. On the way into the Tamarindo Bay development, the new Pasatiempo consists of attractive cottages surrounding a pool. Each has tile floor, high ceiling, overhead fan, one or two beds, and bathroom with vanity and large shower. A short walk from the beach. The restaurant is currently frequented by the owners of other hotels in Tamarindo.

HOTEL EL MILAGRO, P. O. Box 145-5150 Santa Cruz, tel. 67[4]4042, fax 41[8]8494. 21 rooms. $46 single or double with breakfast. Visa, Master

Card. The individual cottages of this hotel crowd the hillside behind the restaurant of the same name, in two rows, but they're nice enough, even if they don't have views. Each has a semi-circular porch, a sliding door that opens almost the whole width of the unit, either two beds or a large bed with trundle bed, high ceiling with fan. Pool; Dutch and English spoken.

CABINAS ZULLYMAR, tel. [2]264732. 27 rooms. $26 to $50 double/ $32 to $57 triple. At the end of the road, rooms with private bath, around a shady courtyard. Curiosities in an otherwise simple place are the hardwood doors on the older rooms, carved with pre-Columbian motifs. All rooms have fans, and newer units have hot water and refrigerators, the higher-priced ones with very high ceilings, better bathrooms and refrigerators. Across the road from the Zullymar is its former Bar, El Tercer Mundo (Third-World Bar). Why they changed that wonderful name, I'll never know. Good, plain food is served, mostly beef and fish, at $4 to $5 for a main course.

CABINAS POZO AZUL, tel. 68[0]0147. 27 units. $30 to $40 per cabina, $20 to $32 in the low season (June, and August through November). Despite the "cabina" tag, these are housekeeping units, with refrigerator and stove, on a hillock at the entry to town. They're relatively new, most are air-conditioned, and there's a large pool. Standard units have two beds, larger ones have three beds and a separate kitchen. A good buy. A few units with fan only go for lower rates.

CABINAS MARIELOS (tel. 414843 in Alajuela) has just five plain units with one or two beds, going for $25 to $35 double depending on the season. They also have a house that sleeps 12, for $75. The grounds are pleasant.

Past the village, the Tamarindo Bay residential development is sprouting numerous substantial vacation homes.

Near the entry, the 33 identical tan cabinas of **TAMARINDO BAY RESORT CLUB** (tel. 68[0]0883, [2]234289 in San José) rent for $106, $66 in the rainy season. The grounds are rocky, and the units, which sleep five, have industrial carpeting, fiberboard walls, a living room, and sleeping space for five in two bedrooms. The kitchens are fully equipped, however, and there are a pool and bar. If you don't expect much, you won't be disappointed.

HOTEL TAMARINDO DIRIÁ, tel. 68[0]0474 (P. O. Box 4211-1000, tel. [2]330530, fax [2]553355 in San José). 60 rooms. $80 to $114 single/ $90 to $114 double, higher in suites. American Express, Visa, Master Card. The senior hotel at Tamarindo has attractive, mature grounds landscaped with lush tropical trees and colorful shrubs, and a pool. The air-conditioned rooms are on the small side, with televisions (with satellite programming), and worn Spanish-colonial furniture and flamingo bedspreads that could bear updating. Attractive restaurant, with a few unusual plates such as paella and steak "Gordon blue." Water skiing and fishing are available.

HOTEL DOLY ($27 double), formerly a flophouse, has upgraded to a set of concrete-block rooms with an eatery below. The advantage, if any, is that it's on the beach side of the road.

WHERE TO EAT

With a resident French-speaking population that requires gratifying food, Tamarindo is the culinary capital of Pacific Costa Rica. Lucky you.

JOHAN'S BELGIAN BAKERY is a surprise eating spot, with no pretense at all, serving fresh croissants, rye bread, waffles piled with fruit, sandwiches, cookies, and gourmet pizza to eat in or take out. For about $3, you can have a light meal, accompanied with fresh juice, in the shady compound in back, overlooking a tidal inlet, while you watch the sea birds, and ducks and roosters wandering about. Hours are 6 a.m. to 5:30 p.m.

LOCO RANCHO, next to Johan's, is an informal open-air bar and eatery with rock music, bamboo dividers, and assorted sandwiches, pastas, pizzas and salads. $8 and under for everything.

At the opposite end of the spectrum is **EL MILAGRO**, where the dining is formal inside and on the terrace of a tan bungalow, to the accompaniment of light music, with views through archways to the sea. Red snapper, dorado and steak-and shrimp combinations are served at $10 and up, less at lunch.

Check out the restaurant of the **JARDÍN DEL EDÉN**, the hotel on the hill above town. One of the owners is a French chef by training, with a commitment to using only fresh ingredients. When I last spoke to him, he was planning *prix-fixe* meals with a different theme for each night of the week — Costa Rican, Mexican, Spanish, seafood, and French (with wine included in the last case, of course, for about $15 to $20). A recent evening menu offered Hawaiian salad, pasta with fresh basil, and green-pepper steak. How could you go wrong?

The **COCONUT CAFÉ**, owned by the people from Johan's, is perfect for a long fantasy evening, an open bar under a thatched roof, with palms, and cushioned rattan furniture in seemingly random groupings. The menu is creative and changes daily. Recently included were couscous, pepper steak, Thai chicken and red chicken curry. Figure $15 as a minimum. Open at 6 p.m.

The **FIESTA DEL MAR** restaurant, under the huge thatched roof where the road ends in the village, is where, for $6 to $20, you can get a whole fish or lobster, casado, steak, chicken, or, sometimes, *talluza*, a Guanacastecan specialty made with ground corn, ham, fish, lobster, cheese, chicken, and whatever else is around the kitchen.

NACHO'S, near the end of the road into town, serves fast food and ice cream. And the **SUNRISE CAFÉ**, at the very end of the road, serves breakfast, supplanted in the evening by the attached **NOGUI BAR** with offerings of drinks and light dinner.

And in the Tamarindo Bay development, a kilometer from town and the beach, is the **BAR-RESTAURANT STELLA**, serving Italian nouvelle cuisine in the open under a soaring roof. Dorado in papaya sauce or linguine in mixed seafood sauce go for about $10, if you can get past the owner's guard dogs.

Also out this way, the restaurant of the **HOTEL PASATIEMPO** currently has a very good chef, and is a favorite after-hours gathering spot for proprietors of *other* hotels. $10 and up for the day's fish or filet in sauce.

RANCHO MEXICANO, a roadhouse about a kilometer before town on the way in, serves tacos, stuffed chiles, and a combination plate for $10 and under.

You can also find a few rice-and-bean places, but not as many as you might reasonably expect in a Costa Rican beach village.

SPORTS AND RECREATION

Fishing at Tamarindo, and windsurfing and water skiing and swamp trips, are available from **Papagayo Excursions**, tel. 68[0]0859. Their trips can be booked at the Hotel Tamarindo Diriá gift shop.

A less expensive fishing alternative is to look for the fellow who sells burgers and snacks out of a trailer at the end of the road (if he's still around). He can take up to five people fishing in an outboard for about $40 per hour, with extra charges to rent rods and reels.

Iguana Surf, under the thatched cupola right after the Tamarindo Bay Resort, rents out surfboards, kayaks and boats, and there are also rentals at the Pueblo Dorado hotel.

Flamingo Divers offers its services from a shop opposite the Coconut Café.

Several other tour shops around town can arrange for boat trips through the estuary to spot birds in the mangroves, or to Tamarindo National Wildlife Refuge (see below) or Playa Grande, just up the coast, to spot nesting turtles.

Tamarindo National Wildlife Refuge, south of the village of Tamarindo, is a turtle nesting area that also includes a variety of mangrove types. Birding trips through the waterways of the reserve and turtle-watching trips in the nesting season (November through April) are available from local operators. Typical species are egrets, frigatebirds, pelicans, gulls, spoonbills, and Muscovy ducks.

Car Rentals - Check in at **Johan's Belgian Bakery**.

PLAYA JUNQUILLAL

Hardly anybody lives here. The beach is empty, clean and beautiful, on a two-kilometer-wide bay trimmed by rocky outcrops, bordered by a wide strip of tall grass. Like a number of other Nicoya beaches, Junquillal ("hoon-ki-YAL") is a favorite nesting site for sea turtles.

ARRIVALS AND DEPARTURES

By Bus

Buses for Junquillal leave from Avenida 3, Calles 18/20, San José, at 2 p.m. Phone [2]217202 to check the schedule. Service may be seasonal.

A hotel shuttle bus, $50 round trip, currently operates Saturdays, Tuesdays and Thursdays from San José, returning the following day at 2 p.m. Call Exotur, [2]272180, to reserve.

Other buses leave Santa Cruz (recently at 10:15 a.m. and 2:30 p.m.) for Paraíso, four kilometers from Junquillal. Otherwise, take a taxi to Junquillal from Santa Cruz, or from the Tamarindo airport.

By Car

The road from Santa Cruz, 34 kilometers away, is paved for 18 kilometers to the village of 27 de Abril.

WHERE TO STAY

VILLA SERENA, tel. and fax 68[0]0737, P. O. Box 17-5150, Santa Cruz. 10 rooms. $135 per couple with meals, slightly less in the rainy season. If rooms are available, singles are accommodated. Visa, Master Card, American Express.

Not right on the beach, but an intimate estate a few steps away, with large, comfortable rooms. Everything is in good taste; classical music usually plays in the background. Facilities include a library, riding horses, game room, and dune buggy. Rooms in the main house have terraces facing the ocean; others are individual cottages on the grounds. Fishing trips and excursions to mangrove areas can be arranged. The long-time owner used to say: *"Ours is a small hotel where a stay is more like a visit to a friend's house than to an indifferent hotel. People who don't enjoy Villa Serena don't enjoy anything and should not travel, period."* The new owners are less demanding of their guests, but maintain the same high standards. English, German and Italian spoken.

HOTEL ANTUMALAL, tel. 68[0]0506, P. O. Box 49-5150 Santa Cruz. 23 cottages. $85 single/$107 double. Visa, Master Card. A tasteful cluster of colonial-style buildings on a hill overlooking the sea. Pool with bar, tennis court, lovely thatched dining pavilion. Friendly management. The food is good. Located about 500 meters beyond Villa Serena.

There are some other cabinas at Junquillal which, *when open*, cost about $15 per person. However, don't arrive and expect to find cheap accommodations, unless you have a car and can retreat.

HOTEL IGUANAZUL (P. O. Box 1130-5150 Santa Cruz), tel. 68[0]0783. 24 rooms. $70 double, lower May through September. In San José: tel. 272180. Four kilometers from Paraíso, via a track that forks from the Junquillal road, the Iguanazul is all alone on grassy-pebbly grounds along the beach. High-ceilinged, ranch-style rooms, grouped six to a stuccoed cottage, have red brick floors, fan, and bathroom with Mexican-tiled vanity and shower. The pool is large. Amusements include volleyball, snorkeling, rental videos, horses for hire. You'll drive here, or they'll bring you from San José on their own bus at a charge of $20 each way.

Seven kilometers along another road from Paraíso is:

LAGARTILLO BEACH HOTEL, 6 rooms. $55 double. In San José, Primavera building, Avenida Central Calles 5/7, tel. [2]571420, fax [2]215717. Poof! You drive along a narrow, sandy track, over hill and dale, through cattle pastures and second-growth dry forest, and this hotel appears in the middle of nowhere. If you want to be away from everything, this is your place.

Rooms are nice enough, with rough furniture, along the lines of what you'd find in a soft-adventure lodge — bunks in some cases. The restaurant-bar is open to the air, with moderately priced meals. It's 200 meters or so through jungle to the beach, which you can hear but not see from your room. Bicycles and boogie boards, fishing and horses available.

BEACHES SOUTH OF NICOYA

An road runs up and down from Nicoya, through pastures and occasional corn fields closed off by wire strung to living poro fence posts, south to the Pacific at Sámara.

Paving is to be completed by 1994. The branch route northward to Nosara may be barely passable toward the end of the rainy season, when trucks carrying the rice harvest from the interior of the peninsula churn up the road.

SÁMARA

Sámara has a long, gray beach, wide at low tide, littered with driftwood, bordered by promontories. Islands and rocks and a coral reef break the waves along the long entrance to the bay, making this beach relatively safe for swimming.

There are numerous vacation homes in the area, but Sámara is also something of a fishing and farming village. On a morning stroll, you might see a pig being carved up, agricultural laborers on their way to their duties, boats being prepared for the day's passage.

Aside from a few hotels, Sámara has more facilities than most small villages on the Nicoya coast. There's even a well-stocked (especially with liquor) convenience store.

More Development, with a big D, is in progress. The road to Cangreja, the adjacent settlement across the river, has been cut by the construction of an airstrip, forcing a long detour, and bulldozers have pulverized a large swath of village in preparation for future construction.

ARRIVALS AND DEPARTURES FOR SÁMARA AND CARILLO

Arriving By Bus

A bus leaves for Sámara and Carrillo at noon from Calle 14, Avenidas 3/5, San José. Buses leave Nicoya for Sámara and Carrillo at 3 p.m., on Saturday and Sunday at 7 a.m. as well.

Arriving By Air

Sansa airlines (tel. [2]335330) operates flights from San José three times a week. Fare is about $75 round trip, and inexpensive packages with hotel room are sometimes available. **Travelair** (tel. [2]327883) flies Thursdays and Sundays to and from San José, fare $100 round trip.

Arriving By Car

Sámara is 36 kilometers from Nicoya by the recently paved road.

Departing By Bus

A bus leaves for San José at 4:30 a.m., another for Nicoya at 6 a.m., and at about 1 p.m. on weekends.

Departing By Air

Sansa airlines and **Travelair** fly back to San José.

Departing By Car

If you're driving, the direct road up the coast fords several rivers. It's a safer bet to backtrack toward Nicoya, as far as the gas station at the junction for the inland road to Nosara.

WHERE TO STAY

None of these hotels are right on the beach, but the village is small and it's only a short walk from anywhere to the water. Rates in Sámara have always seemed to me to be pricier than they should be in a small and pleasant beach village. But numerous rooms have been added to the town's accommodations recently, and more are on the way. Don't hesitate to ask for a discount from the posted rate.

HOTEL SÁMARA BEACH, tel. [2]339398. 20 rooms. $74 double with air conditioning, $63 with fan ($63 or $51 in rainy season). Visa, Master Card. A two-story Spanish-colonial-style building in a compound, operated by present-day Spaniards, with a peninsular restaurant attached. Rooms have wicker furnishings, one large and one narrow bed, and a bathroom with bidet and tub.

HOTEL BRISAS DEL PACÍFICO, tel. 68[0]0876, fax [2]552380 (P. O. Box 129-6100, Ciudad Colón). 24 rooms. $65 single/$75 double. Visa, Master Card, American Express. About one kilometer south of the village, on a hillside overlooking the sea. Pool, and nicely landscaped grounds. German-run, altogether attractive. Limited daily menu of German specialties.

HOTEL MARBELLA, tel. and fax [2]339980. 14 rooms. $46 single/$50 double. Master Card, Visa. Several blocks back from the beach, the Marbella is a stuccoed building with economy-level resort facilities: a pool in a pebbly courtyard, and rooms with basic furniture, ceiling fan, hot water, and small terraces with town views. Pleasant and unpretentious. Breakfast is available. German-run. Rental cars available.

AUBERGE CASA DEL MAR is a bed-and-breakfast, one block from the main street on the way toward Carrillo. Seven airy, spotless rooms, each with sink, are available at $40 single/$46 double ($25/$35 in rainy season) with the personal attention of owners from Chicoutimi. Showers are shared. To reserve in North America, call 418-695-2737 in Jonquiére, Québec, in French, or fax 418-547-2328 in English.

VILLAS PLAYA SÁMARA. Tel. [2]330223, fax [2]217222 in San José. 73 rooms and villas. From $108 double. American Express, Visa. North American reservations, tel. 418-687-3211. Two kilometers south of Sámara, this is a resort of hotel rooms and individual housekeeping units built in something like the style of a traditional Costa Rican *rancho*, with white walls, tile roofs, and rough wooden posts. They have from one to three bedrooms and small kitchen.

Unlike most other compounds of this type, this one has comprehensive on-site services and facilities, including a large pool and children's pool, whirlpool, restaurant and bar, and assorted games and amusements that include tennis, shuffleboard, bicycles, badminton, water skiing and volleyball. Among the options is a meal plan with service on your own terrace. The grounds are rather bare but will probably mellow with time. All this comes at a price: the rate in villas is $142 in a one-bedroom unit, $210 with two bedrooms, $273 with three bedrooms — expensive, and currently being discounted. Add $30 for three meals, $18 for children.

There are also some welcome new cabinas in the budget range. **CABINAS ARENAS,** at one of the intersections in the village, are new, concrete rooms with fan, good value at about $9 per person, though dark.

Some of the other budget accommodations are dismal, and lacking more than one sheet on the bed. **HOTEL-RESTAURANT PLAYA SÁMARA** (also known as **Los Almendros**), at the center, might be okay but for the late night disco. You get a room with private bath here for $8, $5 in the mud season.

At other lodging places in Sámara, and nearby at Cangreja (adjacent by walking through the river, or riding around the airstrip), there's sometimes a long walk to the john. The **HOTEL YURY**, tel. 680022, is probably the best of the cluster of lodging places in Cangreja, at $6 per person with private bath.

Camping is available at the **COCOS** campground toward the south end of the village.

WHERE TO EAT

The restaurant of the **HOTEL SÁMARA BEACH**, under a conical thatched roof, serves paella for about $12 per person, as well as pizza and spaghetti.

Otherwise, stick to the offerings at your hotel, or try one of the bars.

CARRILLO

Carrillo is a village on another huge bay, eight kilometers southeast of Sámara.

WHERE TO STAY/SPORTS AND RECREATION

There are also basic cabinas here, and:

GUANAMAR, tel. [6]536133 (P. O. Box 7-1880, San José, tel. 394544, fax 392405). 24 units. $140 double, $290 in bungalow for eight. Fishing packages from about $350 per day of fishing. U.S. reservations: tel. 800-245-8420.

Guanamar is a hilltop compound overlooking the village, with multiple decks and elevated walkways surrounding the pool and running treehouse-fashion up and down between the thatched bar and restaurant and the various levels of accommodations. Rooms are carpeted, with televisions, and have porches. Fishing boats can be chartered for $400 to $700 a day. Guanamar started as a fishing camp and grew. Horses are available.

SUNSET INN, $100 for three/$10 per additional person, less in rainy season. Reservations: TAM Travel in San José or tel. 671270. A low-key, clifftop cluster of cottages, halfway between Sámara and Carrillo. Rooms have two double beds, tile floors, ceiling fans, nice bathrooms, carved bedsteads, and televisions with satellite programming. There will eventually be 21 units, and a pool. Views take in the village of Carrillo and sweep toward Sámara. The rate includes breakfast, which is served in the house of owner Wayne Winter.

Carrillo Sport Fishing is based at this hotel. Facilities are available to videotape fishing excursions. A seven-day package, including three days of fishing, meals, and transport from San José, costs upwards of $1000 per person.

NORTHWEST OF SÁMARA

PLAYA GARZA

Playa Garza is a fishing village about 14 kilometers from Sámara.

WHERE TO STAY

VILLAGIO LA GUARIA MORADA, tel. 68[0]0784 (P. O. Box 860, Centro Colón, San José, tel. [2]224073). 30 bungalows. $113 single/$140 double, lower in rainy season.

Villagio La Guaria Morada is one of the most attractive resorts on the coast, a lush spot of bougainvilleas and palms and lawns and patios, alive with birds, along a bay all to itself. Individual guest bungalows are out of the ordinary, with red tile floors, bamboo-lined ceilings, and beams formed from rough tree trunks. Ceiling fans assist the sea breeze. Facilities include a volleyball court, large pool, casino, seaside disco, and pavilion bar and restaurant. Meals run $10 and up, cuisine is largely continental. Though Villagio is self-contained, like many other resorts on the peninsula, the village of Garza is within walking distance.

Adjacent to Villagio is **Playa Rosada**, a beach of light-pink sand, said to be a good spot for diving at low tide.

PESCA BAHÍA GARZA, based at Villagio La Guaria Morada, offers **fishing** packages that include meals, lodging, and transfers from San José, from about $325 per day of fishing. In the U.S., contact **Pesca Bahía Garza**, 2279 Overseas P. O. Box 1269, Marathon, FL 33050, tel. 305-289-1900, fax 289-1195.

Ostional National Wildlife Refuge, near Nosara, is noted for a long beach where sea turtles nest. There's also an extensive marsh where the Nosara River meets the sea, good for birding. The entry point is about six kilometers past Garza.

PLAYA NOSARA

Past the reserve entrance, the road winds up from the coast through virgin and second-growth forest. Roads wind off to residences set on lots amid the trees, in a decidedly un-Costa Rican manner. A Spanish-style condominium pops out of the landscape, multi-storied and unexpected.

This is Nosara, the favorite spot of many a retired foreigner who has settled down to life by the sea. It's not that the beach is superior to those elsewhere on the peninsula — it's just one of the spectacular seaside spots of Costa Rica — only that hustlers of building lots staked out land here first and did a better job of selling in San José. Despite difficult access by road for part of the year, the community has matured to a sedate status, and is emulated by real-estate developments that came later.

The Costa Rican village of Nosara is about five kilometers inland, a cattle and farming center with a paved airstrip that offers an express route to downtown except for the half-hour daily when a plane might land. There are some cheap cabina accommodations, but no reason to stay there. The mixed Costa Rican-and-foreign beach settlement is spread out in suburban American style along unmarked roads through the hills and flat land that border the water. Use of a car is an assumption.

ARRIVALS AND DEPARTURES
Arriving By Bus
Buses run once a day from Nicoya at 1 p.m., and from San José (Calle 14, Avenidas 5/7) at 6:30 a.m. In the rainy season, departure times may vary.

Arriving By Air
Sansa airlines (tel. [2]335330) operates flights from San José three times a week. Fare is about $75 round trip, and inexpensive packages with hotel room are sometimes available. **Travelair** (tel. [2]327883) flies Tuesdays and Saturdays to and from San José, fare $100 round trip.

Arriving By Car
Everything in Nosara is spread out, and you're well advised to arrive with your own vehicle unless you'll be satisfied to stay in one place, or you know exactly where you're going. The road to Nosara, 55 kilometers from Nicoya, forks from the Sámara road about five kilometers before Sámara. In the dry season, it's a pleasant jungly drive along a route canopied by tall trees decked with drooping vines and air plants. In the rainy season, it's not always passable.

Departing By Bus
Buses leave for Nicoya at 6 a.m., for San José at 1 p.m. In the rainy season, departure times may vary.

Departing By Air
Arriving **Sansa** and **Travelair** flights continue back to San José.

WHERE TO STAY
HOTEL PLAYAS DE NOSARA, P. O. Box 4-5257, tel. and fax 68[0]0495. 16 rooms. $57 single/$75 double ($46/$55 in rainy season). Located on a bluff above the beach. Grounds are attractive, with palms

and a fantasy of plants. An elevated observatory offers spectacular 345-degree views to the beach, and up and down the rocky coast. Rooms have high ceilings, fan, varnished brick floor, one double and one single bed, balcony, and an adequate bathroom. Bar, restaurant, pool.

HOTEL VILLA TAYPE, P. O. Box 68-5233, tel. and fax 68[0]0856. 16 rooms. $39 single/$46 double. Master Card, Visa, American Express. Located along a side road just north of the Ostional reserve, Villa Taype is a new, white hotel in several wings around the pool, and it should be attractive enough once the palm trees have a chance to grow. Plain rooms have beds with good mattresses, tile floors, adequate bathroom, good cross-ventilation, and private terraces, and either air-conditioning or fan. The beach is a two-minute walk away, and there are tennis courts and a pleasant bar-restaurant. Five bungalows are available as well, each with its own hammock house, at $63 double/$92 for four.

RANCHO SUIZO LODGE, P. O. Box 14-5233, Nosara. 10 rooms. $30 single/$40 double. Reservations in San José, tel. [2]550011, fax [2]552155. South Seas-style units on a large lot. (The "Swiss Hut" of the name refers to the owners, not the architecture.) Each attractive room has a double bed, wicker furniture, tiled floor, wood trim. Hiking, horseback riding, birding, snorkeling and turtle-watching excursions can be arranged, and there are table-tennis, whirlpool, hammock house and badminton on site. The restaurant is along the lines of a huge, screened birdhouse. This hotel is in flat terrain just a short walk from the beach.

PENSIÓN ESTANCIA NOSARA, tel. and fax 68[0]0378. 8 rooms. $46 single/$53 double. A family farm a couple of kilometers inland. Rooms are all-new, with cooking facilities, basic beds, adequate bathrooms. The attractions are monkeys on the large grounds, pool, tennis court, and horses available for hire.

WHERE TO EAT

At beach level, **OLGA'S**, an informal bar and open-air restaurant, serves a nourishing meal with a whole fish for about $6.

PASCHOLI, also known as **RENATE'S**, in a house encroached by palms and ferns and hibiscus near the Villa Taype hotel, serves pepper steak and an assortment of German specialties, including roast pork and pork ribs with sauerkraut, for about $7 and up. On some Saturdays, dinner may be by reservation only.

CAFÉ ALMOST PARADISE, on the road that ascends the hill toward the Hotel Playas de Nosara, is a shaded deck with widely spaced boards that allow a cooling breeze while you regard the breathtaking views to forest and beach. Pastas, fish in lemon butter and a Sunday brunch are offered, for $10 and under.

SOUTHERN NICOYA

Opposite Puntarenas are the dramatic bays and inlets and sandy and rocky beaches of the very end of the Nicoya Peninsula.

Despite the proximity of San José in a straight line, limited ferry service, poor public transportation, unpaved roads and the fact that this is a dead end have, until recently, made the area relatively little-traveled. Of course, these are ideal conditions for those who wish to make discoveries away from the crowd at their own pace.

But things are changing, and fast. A controversial 400-room all-inclusive beach resort has recently opened at Playa Tambor, and five hotels of the Spanish Meliá chain are planned for this coast within the next few years.

The two gateways to this area, from Puntarenas, are the ferry ports of Playa Naranjo and Paquera.

PLAYA NARANJO

There's no sandy beach here, despite the name of the town ("Orange Tree Beach"). In fact, there's hardly a town at all, only a ferry slip. There are, however, very attractive accommodations down the road from the dock.

ARRIVALS AND DEPARTURES
Arriving By Ferry

The car-and-passenger ferry sails from Puntarenas at 4, 7 and 10:30 a.m. and 1:30 and 4:30 p.m. Phone 61[1]1069 to check schedules. Arrive well before scheduled departure time, park, and line up for your ticket. The crossing takes a little over an hour. Buses for Nicoya, 75 kilometers and three hours away, meet the ferry.

Departing By Ferry

The car-and-passenger ferry leaves Playa Naranjo for Puntarenas at 5:15 and 8:30 a.m., noon, and 3 and 6 p.m. *Arrive well before scheduled departure time, park, and line up for your ticket.*

Departing By Car From the Ferry Landing

If you're driving south from the ferry landing, fill your gas tank before proceeding. The road, winding up and down hillsides from bay to bay, is unpaved, except for certain steep stretches, and for the section between Paquera and Tambor.

WHERE TO STAY

If rooms are available, each of these hotels will usually send a vehicle out to look for passengers at the dock. In its own way, each represents one of the best values on the Nicoya Peninsula.

CABINAS-BAR MAQUINAY, tel. 61[1]1763. 8 rooms. $22 single/ $26 double. This is a cheery, informal roadhouse (no late loud music!) with pool, run by a Belgian expatriate, a couple of kilometers from the ferry on the Nicoya road. Not a bad place to hang out between ferry crossings, or to stay the night.

HOTEL DE PASO, tel. 61[2]2610 (P. O. Box 232-2120 San José, tel. 333214). 14 rooms. $17 to $26 single/$22 to $44 double, $70 in family unit. Also east of the ferry, a small and attractive colonial-style hotel with tile roof and stuccoed walls. Rooms are small, but nicely done, with old-style plaster, along a long passageway facing the pool. A few rooms, at the lowest rate, share bathroom; others have air-conditioning and television. A full lunch or dinner in the restaurant costs $6 to $7.

HOTEL OASIS DEL PACÍFICO, tel. and fax 61[1]1555 (P. O. Box 200-5400, Puntarenas). 36 rooms. $52 single/$70 double/$102 triple. Visa, Master Card, American Express. This is one of the older hotels in the Nicoya peninsula, on 12 acres of lush, landscaped grounds with a South Seas air. Facilities include tennis courts, adult and children's pools, playground, a wide stretch of pebbly beach, and a large screened restaurant-bar. Each room has its own terrace with hammock. You'll sometimes hear or see roaring howler monkeys, macaws and deer. Yachts are welcome, and non-guests may use all facilities for a daily charge of about $5.

Deep-sea fishing for dorado and tuna is available from a new dock at about $250 per day, including a case of beer and sandwiches. Rowboats and motorboats also available.

PLAYA GIGANTE

Playa Gigante is the first large inlet south and east of the ferry landing, at a dramatic bay with a prominent headland to the north; but then, all bays in these parts are dramatic. The road south crosses cattle-grazing and melon-growing country, relatively dry and dusty for much of the year.

WHERE TO STAY

HOTEL BAHÍA GIGANTE, tel. 61[2]2442. 12 units ($50 single or double), and several condominiums ($75 and up).

Eight kilometers from the ferry landing, and not near any town, this hotel has motel-style cottage units in the flats near the road, and hilltop condominium units affording superb views. Meals are served in a dining pavilion with high-peaked thatched roof.

Offshore in Gigante Bay is **ISLA GITANA**, a set of cabanas, restaurant, pool and chandlery that can be reached by boat. Call 61[2]2994 to arrange pickup at Playa Naranjo or Paquera.

PAQUERA

Paquera, 24 kilometers from Playa Naranjo, is a beach town and ferry terminal.

ARRIVALS AND DEPARTURES
By Car/Ferry
The dock for the new car-and-passenger ferry from Puntarenas is at Puerto Paquera, a couple of kilometers from the center of the village. For schedules from Puntarenas, check with the tourist office in San José. There should be at least two daily sailings in each direction.

By Bus
Buses take passengers onward to Tambor, Cóbano, and Montezuma. For other destinations, you'll have to drive, take a country taxi, or walk.

WHERE TO STAY
RESTAURANT-BAR-CABINAS GINAMA (tel. 61[1]1444, ext. 119) has basic rooms at about $12 double, and a restaurant with tablecloths.
Farther on, **CABINAS ROSITA** (tel. 61[1]1444, ext. 206), just off the road, has rooms for about $18 double.
ZORBA'S PLACE, 400 meters off the main road at Playa Pochote, right on the sea, is a bare-bones beachfront compound with a few rooms for rent at $25 double, and Greek salad, keftedakia and fried fish. If you want to get away from the development that affects southern Nicoya beaches, stop here.

SEEING THE SIGHTS
Curú National Wildlife Reserve takes in a section of sea and shore north of Tambor, including both forest and beach. White-tailed deer, snakes, and small forest animals such as pacas, opossum and raccoons populate the woods; hawks, egrets, motmots and woodpeckers are common; and sea turtles occasionally nest on the beach. As with most other reserves (as opposed to parks), the land is private property. Phone 61[2]2392 *in advance* for permission to enter.

BAHÍA BALLENA

At kilometer 41, you reach **Bahía Ballena** (*Whale Bay*).

WHERE TO STAY
PLAYA TAMBOR BEACH RESORT. 402 rooms. U.S. reservations, tel. 800-858-0606, or through travel agents. $100 to $120 per person daily

(children $35) inclusive. Playa Tambor is Costa Rica's world-class all-inclusive beach resort, a village of low-lying thatched and concrete buildings that stretch over just part of a property that covers thousands of hectares. There are vast, open lawns, but also many trees and flowers and shrubs.

Rooms are in several garden-style clapboard-sided wings, entered from outside terraces and stairways. Each is air-conditioned, has a cheery pastel decor, and comes with two large beds with good mattresses, television, phone, mini-bar, louvered closet, safe-deposit box, muted textured wallpaper, a marble bathroom with tub, and private balcony or terrace bordered by a trellis.

Most common facilities are roofed over and open to the air, from the vast, cathedral-like lobby, to the main restaurant with its soaring thatch; and when the wind is up, everything roars! The pool, in the form of an overgrown amoeba, meanders on and on, under a water polo net to two bars. The beach is long and shaded by almond trees. Facilities also include more intimate bars, a theater, and tennis and basketball courts, as well as windsurfers, sailboats, and ocean kayaks, most of which can be used at no extra charge.

Optional activities are scheduled daily, including aerobics, water gymnastics, volleyball games, tropical dance lessons, and limbo parties. There are also a kids' club, beauty salon, infirmary, gift shop and newsstand, and travel agency.

All meals, snacks, local brands of drinks and wine with meals and a nightly show are also included. Most food is served buffet-style, with a nightly theme, though a la carte dining in the Rancho (a pueblo-style structure with a mismatched thatched roof) is an option. Only tours (half-day fishing, $250), horseback rides, laundry and transport from San José carry a surcharge.

TAMBOR

Tambor is a charming little beach town, another favorite place of retired foreigners, given its relative proximity to San José. Access is by car from Playa Naranjo, bus from Paquera, or small plane.

ARRIVALS AND DEPARTURES

Air taxis are available to the airstrip at Playa Tambor.

WHERE TO STAY

The **HOTEL DOS LAGARTOS** (tel. 61[1]1122, ext. 236), on a palm-shaded lot near the beach, has rooms at $15 single/ $20 double with private bath. **Cristina's Restaurant** is a pleasant eating spot in the open area under a Caribbean-style building.

HOTEL TANGO MAR, tel. 61[2]2798 (P. O. Box 3877 San José, tel. [2]231864, fax [2]552697 or Dept. 823, P. O. Box 025216, Miami, FL 33102-5216). 30 rooms. $137 to $149 single/$149 to $162 double in hotel rooms, up to $300 in beach houses. Visa, American Express, Master Card.

This is a country club with guest accommodations and beach lots for sale, reached by a two-kilometer spur road in poor condition. Guests stay in a range of units on lush grounds at the base of a hill by the sea. There is no air conditioning, but hotel rooms come with either one or two beds, bar, television, and balcony, and there are individual houses. On-site are a pool and tennis courts (bring your own racket). Amusements-for-a-fee include water skiing, all-terrain-vehicles, sailing, 10-hole golf course ($25 greens fees), horses ($15 per hour), mountain bikes, surfboards, and deep sea fishing. Children over four pay full price.

SPORTS AND RECREATION

There are also a campground, and a couple of folks who will supply snorkeling equipment and arrange boat trips to Tortuga Island (at less than you'll pay for day trips from San José); but nothing else.

Bahía Ballena Yacht Club, south of Tambor and reached by a side road after the first bridge, has permanent anchorage in a wide, calm bay, and services for yachties. The cavernous pier restaurant is straight out of the Florida Keys, but the food is basic Tico country fare with fancy foreign names.

Sailboat trips to **Herradura**, across the Gulf of Nicoya, near Jacó, have recently been available on a regular basis (departing Saturday, Sunday and Monday at 8 a.m., returning the same day). The return departure on the same days is at 1 p.m. Call **Veleros del Sur**, 61[1]1320 or 64[3]3242, for information.

At the very end of the Nicoya Peninsula are the **Cabo Blanco Reserve**, and the beaches of Montezuma.

MONTEZUMA

Reached by a difficult thread of road that winds from cliff down to shore, **Montezuma**, 65 kilometers from Playa Naranjo, is a little beauty spot, a lush concentration of greenery near the relatively rainy point of the Nicoya Peninsula, on a bay and beach punctuated by mounds of rocks. Unlike other, spread-out beach towns, Montezuma clusters around its attractive clapboard cottage church, at the foot of a ridge, its house lots decorated with bougainvilleas and other showy plants.

Montezuma attracts a long-term, youthful crowd of visitors, which, due to the end-of-the-road aspect, relative isolation, and lack of middle- and upper-range accommodations, lends the town a Woodstock-on-the-Gulf air. The transplants take a constructive interest in local affairs, keeping the beach clean (sometimes a losing battle against the weekend hordes) and contributing toward upkeep of facilities in the best communal fashion.

ARRIVALS AND DEPARTURES

If you're not driving, you can get there via bus, taxi, or a combination of the two from Paquera, where the ferry from Puntarenas docks (see page 346). Travel time from Puntarenas totals three to four hours. Taxis also provide alternative service to and from the car ferry at Playa Naranjo.

WHERE TO STAY

Several new middle-range hotels have opened recently in Montezuma, relieving a chronic room shortage, and also somewhat gentrifying the air of the village. Accommodations are insufficient for the demand, and often full throughout the year.

Most lodging spots have no phone, making it difficult to reserve space. Without a bed waiting, it would be a good idea to arrive with a sleeping bag, or your own transportation.

Campers are usually tolerated, though with no public sanitation facilities, the environment can be unappealing.

HOTEL LOS MANGOS, tel. 61[1]1122, ext. 259. $60 double in bungalows, $30 to $40 in hotel rooms. Montezuma's newest hotel extends over a hillside mango orchard south of the village center. Individual octagonal cottages with peaked ceilings are rustic and woody. Each has a porch, and copious amounts of hot water (a rarity in Costa Rica!). There is also a section of renovated rooms with tiled showers and porches in a building nearer to the road.

The pavilion dining area and circular bar overlook the orchard, the hillside, the sea, *everything*. And the pools (the only ones within quite a stretch, with water treated by an ozone process, rather than chlorine) are unique. A children's splashing area empties over boulders and down a falls to a huge adults' pool. There are also a Jacuzzi, and behind the property, a stand of virgin forest. Laundry service and hired horses are available. Guests are personally hosted by Nikos and Costas, Polish-speaking Greek brothers.

CABINAS EL JARDÍN, tel. and fax 61[2]2320. From $20 to $40 single. These are little peak-roofed houses on stilts, in forest clearings on a hillside right above the center of the village. The front office is also a travel agency.

AMOR DE MAR (tel. ext. 262, $36 double/$43 triple) is the most pleasant of smaller lodging places, a seafront house with carefully tended lawns. Rooms are panelled, cheery, with overhead fans — just what a guest house should be. Meals are served in a covered, open area facing the water.

HOTEL AURORA is a substantial concrete house with rooms at $30 double. Next door, **HOTEL MONTEZUMA PACIFIC** is a delightful two-story stuccoed house with porches, gaily painted, with rooms for about $20 double, some sharing bath.

The little **HOTEL MONTEZUMA** (tel. 61[1]1122, ext. 258) is a pleasant stopping-point, with modest facilities and modest tariffs (about $18 double with fan, private bath). **CABINAS MAR Y CIELO**, and others near the center of town, have rooms for $15 double and up.

CABINAS KAREN is owned by Karen Morgenson, who pioneered Cabo Blanco reserve and maintains a smaller reserve of her own, out of town, where limited guest accommodations are also available.

CABINAS LAS ARENAS and other cabinas and pensiones, at about $20 double, are located either along the seafront track to the south.

WHERE TO EAT

HOTEL LOS MANGOS has a large, thatch-roofed outdoor eatery next to its pool, serving Italian food.

Right in the village, the **SANO BANANO** is the major gathering spot, signboard, and information-exchange center, a pavilion emphasizing natural foods and fruit shakes. Meals of eggplant parmigiana and similar unexpected fare cost $5 and up, and they can arrange stays in beach cabins with outdoor showers, from $35.

SPORTS AND RECREATION

Horses are usually available for rent in town.

A rough road leads south from Montezuma along the water. From a bridge not far from town, you can follow a river up to a dramatic falls. But don't do any climbing — it's quite slippery on the rocks.

CABO BLANCO RESERVE AND VICINITY

Located at the southeastern point of the Nicoya Peninsula, the Cabo Blanco Absolute Nature reserve is not as absolute as its name implies. Visitors are allowed into about half of the protected area to watch the birds (especially pelicans, frigate birds and various others that frequent the shore), as well as howler monkeys, porcupines, abundant crabs, and the creatures that become trapped in tidal pools.

The woods here in the rainiest part of Nicoya are classified as moist tropical forest, and have many more evergreens than those in the northern part of the peninsula. The shore is rocky, and beaches are therefore few and small. Off the very tip of the peninsula is Cabo Blanco island, a rock that is white with encrusted guano during the dry season.

Access to the reserve is only by car or on foot, usually from Montezuma, where guided visits are often organized. If possible, get in touch with the

National Park Service before you go. Hours are from 8 a.m. to 4 p.m.

Cabuya, the village near Cabo Blanco reserve, has rooms and meals available at **CABINAS ANCLA DE ORO** (tel. 61[3]3234). The rate is about $10 per person per day. Horses and boats can be hired.

Playa Santa Teresa, northwest of Cabo Blanco, has a little-frequented beach, and the **CABINAS MALPAÍS**, with double rooms for about $25.

Playa Coyote is one of a number isolated beaches along the southwest face of the Nicoya Peninsula, between Cabo Blanco and Carrillo. You can find a basic room for the night at **RANCHO LUMA CLARA** (tel. 07[1]1236) for about $5 per person, and country-style meals for a few dollars, but if everything is full, you'll have to get out your hammock and sleeping bag, or get into your Jeep and head onward. A bus for San Francisco, four kilometers inland, leaves San José at 3:30 p.m. (Calle 12, Avenidas 7/9).

Other beaches are plentiful all around the rim of Nicoya, some with basic lodging, some accessible only by seasonally passable dirt roads, some uninhabited but for wild creatures. Go and find them!

17. THE PACIFIC SOUTH

INTRODUCTION

The southern Pacific beaches of Costa Rica are every bit as inviting and pleasing to the eye as those along the Nicoya Peninsula, though they differ in character. Most are more open and sweeping and exposed, with fewer bordering outcrops of rocks. The farther south you go, the more humid and rainy is the climate, and the more lush and exuberant the vegetation that runs up to the sand. The mugginess is always relieved and attenuated, however, by breezes blowing off the water.

There is one fact about the southern beaches that is often not mentioned in polite company: they are dangerous for swimming. Large volumes of water flow toward shore across a deceptively smooth, broad front of waves, then recede in fast-flowing, unpredictable streams. These rip currents drive bathers out to sea from waist-high waters, and cause drownings on a regular basis. Those who suddenly find themselves far from shore should swim across the current to escape its pull, then head on in. If you are not a good swimmer, stay close to shore.

Beach hotels are concentrated at Jacó and at Manuel Antonio (near Quepos), but there are numerous little-frequented beaches as well where cabinas and similar basic accommodations are available. You can poke around and explore for some of these paradisaical hideaways if you decide to rent a car in San José. By bus, such meanderings would be more difficult. There is only infrequent service along the road south of Jacó, the humidity is uncomfortably high just inland from the coast, the lesser beaches would have to be reached by jaunts of a kilometer or two along side roads, and you'll find it difficult to move on if you don't like what you see (or the facilities that you don't see) at the water's edge.

To reach the south coast by car from San José, follow the turnoff to Atenas from the highway to Puntarenas. After a potholed, winding stretch, the road is generally good past Orotina. The asphalt ends before Quepos. Beyond, the road is poor, with limited bus service.

SOUTH FROM PUNTARENAS

The new road from Puntarenas south toward Orotina is a well-surfaced, controlled-access, two-lane-wide, California-standard coastal highway.

Mata de Limón, one of the first towns out of Puntarenas, is a picturesque gathering of vacation houses around a mangrove inlet. There are some eating places, and it's pleasant to observe the birds, and stroll across the footbridge. The train from San José stops here. You could get off, look around, and continue by local bus to Puntarenas.

Caldera, a few kilometers on, is a modern container port, through which much of Costa Rica's Pacific commerce now moves. Beyond, the highway continues through the coastal foothills roughly following the railroad line. Near Orotina, it joins the road from San José via Atenas.

CARARA BIOLOGICAL RESERVE

Carara is a tropical forest area in the central Pacific coastal region. All around are fields devoted to pasture and rice cultivation. But most of Carara Biological Reserve was virgin forest when its 2,100 hectares (4,700 acres) were separated by the government from an agrarian settlement project in 1978.

The climate along the coast just south of Puntarenas is relatively dry and hot; farther on, rainfall is heavier. Carara is in a transitional area, and with its varied elevations contains a variety of vegetation types, from cool evergreens to the broad-leafed, vine- and epiphyte-laden trees that are the

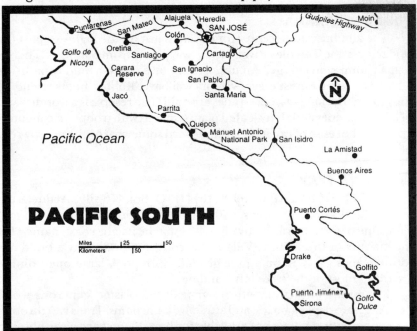

kings of everyone's imagined jungle. There are rushing streams and sedentary lagoons, and even some archaeological remains from pre-Columbian times. The undergrowth is relatively less dense and tangled than in other forests, so getting around and seeing the vegetation and wildlife are slightly easier.

Resident birds at Carara include vultures, ducks, guans and toucans, and, most notably, great flocks of scarlet macaws. Jaguars, ocelots and margays are occasionally spotted. More common are monkeys (squirrel, white-faced, howler and spider), sloths, coatis, agoutis, crocodiles, blue morpho butterflies and assorted ants.

ARRIVALS AND DEPARTURES
By Bus
Buses for Jacó and Quepos (see following pages) pass the entrance to Carara, and on a weekday, when these are not crowded, you can get off for a visit, then hop on another bus to continue your journey.

By Tour
For a more intensive acquaintance with the reserve, you'll have to come on a guided tour arranged through one of the agencies mentioned in the San José chapter. **Geotours** (tel. [2]341867) specializes in the reserve.

TOURING CARARA
The administration center for Carara is just off the highway, past the bridge over the Tárcoles River on the way down from San José. There's a small admission charge. An unposted nature trail — a muddy path — is all the access that most casual visitors will have. Rubber boots would be the gear in the rainy season. Grades are mild. The reserve is a wonderland of tall trees, vines and shiny-leafed plants, shared with troops of leaf-cutter ants. But the sense of isolation is diminished somewhat by the nearby roar of traffic.

WHERE TO STAY
HOTEL VILLA LAPAS, tel. 881611 (P. O. Box 476-4005 Alajuela, tel. and fax [2]394104). 30 rooms. $70 single or double, $59 in rainy season. Visa. One of the more attractive hotels along the Pacific coast, named for the macaws of the vicinity, Villa Lapas consists of ranch-style buildings with tile roofs, spread on ample grounds with pool, large open dining area, and most of the trees left standing.

Rooms are attractive, with rough-textured plaster, generous wood detailing, safe-deposit boxes, and attractive bathrooms. Trails run through the property, and horses are available for hire. If you have a car, this is a good base for visiting the beaches of the area. Turn inland one kilometer south of the Carara reserve.

Near Carara

Tárcoles, past Carara, is a sleepy village one kilometer off the highway, where it begins to run close to the sea. There's a rocky beach, exuberant vegetation, and some attractive tidal inlets; but mostly, Tárcoles is undeveloped for tourism.

About 600 yards past the village center is the basic **HOTEL EL PARQUE**, where rooms are available for $10 or so for anywhere from one to four persons. Past Tárcoles, at **Punta Leona** (which is a geographical expression rather than a town) is the 92-room **HOTEL PUNTA LEONA**, a private club with a swimming pool that wanders among the palms. Foreigners may use the facilities for a daily fee of about $10, or stay over for $82 double. In San José, call [2]313131, fax [2]320791 to inquire. Scuba instruction available.

Country Lodging Down the Pacific Coast

HACIENDA DOÑA MARTA ($66 double, tel. [6]536514), near Orotina, is an old cattle ranch with six new guest units, and trails through pastures and forest. Pool, riding horses available. Reservations: P. O. Box 23-3009 Heredia, tel. [2]399392, fax [2]399555.

DUNDEE RANCH (11 rooms, P. O. Box 7812-1000 San Jose, tel. [2]397371, fax [2]397050, $87 double with breakfast) is a working cattle ranch under the same management as the Chalet Tirol, near San José. A section of the property is set aside as a forest reserve, where monkeys, coatis and other mammals can be spotted without difficulty. And there is a crocodile pond, hence the name. Riding horses, tractor rides and jungle boat trips available. Rooms are air-conditioned.

HERRADURA, four kilometers off the road, features an attractive private campsite with showers and cooksites. The charge is about $2 per person. There are also some inexpensive cabinas. Otherwise, development is limited here, too. A cattle corral occupies the prime piece of real estate, and the wide curve of driftwood-littered beach is lined by palms, a few vacation houses, and pastures. Best to drop by if travelling by car, or if you have plenty of time.

Sailboat trips to **Tambor**, across the Gulf of Nicoya, near Jacó, have recently been available on a regular basis (departing Saturday, Sunday and Monday at 1 p.m.). Call **Veleros del Sur**, 61[1]1320 or 64[3]3242, for information.

PLAYA JACÓ

Jacó ("ha-KO") has what other beach places in Costa Rica are missing:

streets, and life. It is a pleasant community, where you can stroll and look in stores, shop for groceries, choose from a selection of restaurants and snack bars, and buy a souvenir at some place other than the captive boutique of your hotel. Vacation houses are scattered on coconut-palm-shaded lots, surrounded by wild grass and carefully manicured gardens. Accommodations range from basic to expensive, and there are definitely places in between. There's also a certain measure of Tico tackiness — a disco dominates the entry road. All of which is not to say that Jacó is cosmopolitan. Rice fields still reach most of the long length of the main street that loops off the highway.

Jacó is the nearest of the beach resorts to San José (if you don't count Puntarenas), three hours away by public bus, less by car, or a half-hour hop by chartered plane. The beach at Jacó is typical of this section of coast — wide, long, curving to promontories, littered with driftwood, palm-fringed in parts, vegetation creeping over some small dunes. There is also a certain accumulation of trash — diapers, bottles, juice cartons — in the most frequented sections, but the beach is large enough that most of it is inoffensive. Surfers have made Jacó their home away from home. And there are natural attractions, as well. Sea turtles lay their eggs most nights from July to December at Playa Hermosa, three kilometers to the south.

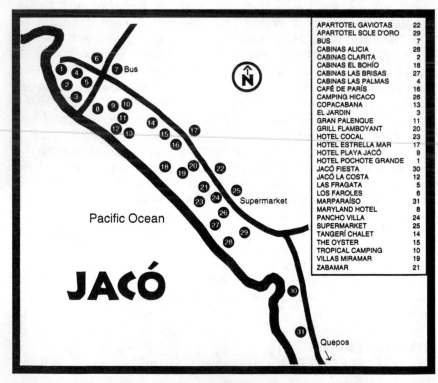

APARTOTEL GAVIOTAS	22
APARTOTEL SOLE D'ORO	29
BUS	7
CABINAS ALICIA	28
CABINAS CLARITA	2
CABINAS EL BOHÍO	18
CABINAS LAS BRISAS	27
CABINAS LAS PALMAS	4
CAFÉ DE PARÍS	16
CAMPING HICACO	26
COPACABANA	13
EL JARDIN	3
GRAN PALENQUE	11
GRILL FLAMBOYANT	20
HOTEL COCAL	23
HOTEL ESTRELLA MAR	17
HOTEL PLAYA JACÓ	9
HOTEL POCHOTE GRANDE	1
JACÓ FIESTA	30
JACÓ LA COSTA	12
LAS FRAGATA	5
LOS FAROLES	6
MARPARAÍSO	31
MARYLAND HOTEL	8
PANCHO VILLA	24
SUPERMARKET	25
TANGERÍ CHALET	14
THE OYSTER	15
TROPICAL CAMPING	10
VILLAS MIRAMAR	19
ZABAMAR	21

Pacific Ocean

Supermarket

JACÓ

Quepos

ARRIVALS AND DEPARTURES

By Bus

Bus departures from the Coca-Cola station, Calle 16, Avenidas 1/3, San José, are at 7:15 and 10:30 a.m., and 3:30 p.m. Call **Transportes Jacó**, 41[5]5890, to confirm the schedule. The **Jacó Beach Hotel** runs its own bus for groups. **Pacific Transfer** runs a bus called the *Silver Bullet Express* with reserved seats and snacks for $23 one way, $35 round trip from San José. Call [2]272180 (fax [2]281015) for schedules and pickup points.

By Air

Chartered small planes use the airstrip alongside the entry road.

Departing By Bus

Bus departures from Jacó for San José are at 5 and 11 a.m. and 3 p.m. Or take the **Pacific Transfer** express bus (tel. [2]272180).

The San José bus can drop you at Carara Reserve, or at the highway junction for Herradura and other smaller beachside villages nearby. Southbound buses generally do not enter Jacó — you'll have to head out to the highway and flag one down.

WHERE TO STAY

EL JARDÍN, tel. 64[3]3050, fax 64[3]3010. 7 rooms. $54 single/$61 double. Visa, Master Card. Rooms — small but attractive, with varnished woodwork, desks, stuccoed walls and tiled floors, and fans — are set in a compact, nicely landscaped compound with a pool. French-speaking owners. Continue along the entry road to Jacó, without turning onto the main street, and you'll end up at El Jardín.

HOTEL POCHOTE GRANDE, P. O. Box 42, tel. 64[3]3236 (fax [2]204979 in San José). 24 rooms. $61 single/$90 double. An attractive Spanish-style, two-story hotel in a quiet garden compound. Rooms have plain furnishings, high ceilings, tiled bathroom, mini-refrigerator, and terrace. Pool. Usually booked solid in the dry season. German spoken.

CABINAS LAS PALMAS, P. O. Box 5, tel. 64[3]3005. 23 units. $30 to $48 single/$37 to $60 double/$70 to $90 for six. A homey compound edged with rows of rooms, ranging from old and musty with beds and bathroom only, to newer with kitchen and washing patio. Ukrainian (Toronto dialect), English and German spoken.

HOTEL JACÓ BEACH, tel. 64[3]3032. (P. O. Box 962-1000 San José, tel. [2]201441). 130 rooms and suites. $88 single/$100 double. U.S. reservations, tel. 305-871-6631 or 800-272-6654; Canada, tel. 800-463-6654 The main hotel building, a newer building and cottages are spread out on extensive grounds — kids have lots of space to run around. Rooms are large, and all are air-conditioned, some have refrigerator and TV.

Amenities include a pool for adults and one for kids, tennis courts, casino, travel service, pool tables, and other games. The disco can be noisy. Most of the facilities are showing signs of wear, and food choices are quite limited for a large resort hotel. Transportation arrangements can be made through the Hotel Irazú in San José.

HOTEL COPACABANA, P. O. Box 150, tel. and fax 64[3]3131. 28 rooms $50 single/$62 double, $85 in suite, lower from May to November. Reservations in British Columbia: tel. 604-731-2665, fax 604-682-2766. A new, two-story hotel Canadian-operated, with the advantage of a beachside location and pool. Caters mainly to charter groups. Some units have air-conditioning or cooking facilities.

HOTEL COCAL, tel. 64[3]3067. 26 rooms. $33 to $39 single/$49 to $56 double. Low-slung, Spanish-style, with most rooms off arched passageways around the two pools in the courtyard. A few rooms face the water, at the higher rates. The architecture, and the use of fans even in outdoor areas, keep this hotel much cooler than most others. Very attractive dining area overlooking the beach. Reserve through Hotel Galilea in San José.

TANGERÍ CHALET, tel. 64[3]3001 or 420977, P.O. Box 622-4050 Alajuela. 28 units. $54 double in hotel rooms, up to $90 in cottages. There are attractive cottages, set well apart from each other on manicured grounds, sleeping up to six persons; and more standard hotel rooms. Pool.

VILLAS ESTRELLAMAR, P. O. Box 33, tel. 64[3]3102, fax 64[3]3453. 20 units. $57 double, less in low season. Visa, Master Card. Large and attractive stuccoed bungalows in a park-like setting around an 18-meter pool. Each unit has two double beds, a terrace, a kitchen with refrigerator, tiled bathroom, laundry area, and terrace. Thatched-roof bar, French spoken, good value.

APARTOTEL GAVIOTAS, tel. 64[3]3092. 12 units. $80 per unit in dry season. These modern suites with cooking facilities sleep up to six persons on a combination of beds and sofa-beds. Small pool. Rates may be as low as $27 double during May-June and August-November.

HOTEL JACOFIESTA, P. O. Box 38, tel. 64[3]3147, fax 64[3]3148. 84 rooms. $80 for one to four persons in housekeeping units, $66 in standard rooms. This is a well-thought-out and well-run establishment, of recent construction. One U-shaped section of cabina (studio) units, with pantile roof, blue-and-white painted stucco and rough wooden posts supporting an outside passageway, mimics the style of old-fashioned Costa Rican country houses. The section of hotel rooms, in three two-story buildings set around the pool, carries similar themes more subtly.

The studio units have assorted standard and roll-out beds, a very large bathroom, tiled kitchen, and laundry terrace that can double as a private sun area. Standard rooms, with two double beds, come with a refrigerator. All rooms are air conditioned and have televisions with satellite programming. Facilities include several pools, tennis court, pedal boats, and restaurant. Off-season rates may be available. All in all a very good value.

CHALET SANTA ANA, tel. 64[3]3233. 8 units. $33 to $44, less out of season. Studio units in a stucco and brick building on a well-tended lot, across from the Jacofiesta. Lower-priced units sleep three, higher-priced units sleep up to five and have cooking facilities.

MARPARAÍSO HOTEL AND CLUB, P. O. Box 6699, San José, tel. [2]216544. 25 rooms. $60 double. In a residential area next to the roads department depot, down at the southeast end of town. The beach is nice, anyway. Mostly a club for Ticos. Children's and adult pools.

VILLAS MIRAMAR, tel. 64[3]3003. 9 units. $40 double/$56 for four/$70 for six. Master Card, Visa. Colonial-style cottages with kitchenettes on extensive grounds. Good value.

APARTOTEL SOLE D'ORO, tel. 64[3]3172, charges $80 in high season for an apartment with room for four persons, about half that in low season.

CABINAS LAS FRAGATAS, 12 units. $26 double, $38 for four. Clean rooms set back from the restaurant of the same name.

CABINAS EL BOHÍO. There are about ten nice, newer units here with kitchen, in a good location near the water. The official rate is about $45, but they'll discount them except at the busiest times. There's a pool on the somewhat overgrown grounds.

CABINAS ZABAMAR, tel. 64[3]3174. 9 units. $27 double/$42 for four. Plain rooms around a pool and gravelly courtyard. Restaurant.

Cheap Lodging

The run of *cabinas* is generally better than elsewhere along the coast. **CABINAS ALICE**, $30 double, with front terrace and near the beach, are good for the price. **CABINAS CLARITA**, next to El Jardín, has rooms for $20 double with private bath, and also lockers and showers available for day trippers.

At **CABINAS LAS BRISAS**, Jack Phillips welcomes surfers. The 10 seafront units, varying from bare to comfortable, go for $15 to $25 double. Try to get a room in the roundhouse. (Las Brisas is scheduled to give way to a new hotel in the near future.)

And there are assorted other rooms in Jacó for $10 or less single. In some of the cabinas, you'll get a cooktop.

TROPICAL CAMPING is an extensive, coconut-palm-shaded area (watch where you pitch your tent), with basic sanitary facilities. Dry season only, $2 per person. **THE MARRIOTT** (a ripoff of the name), near El Jardín, also has camping on a large, grassy lot, as well as plain rooms for $15 double, with shared bath. And there are several other tent sites.

Nearby
HACIENDA LILIPOZA, P. O. Box 15, tel. and fax 64[3]3062. 20 rooms. $140 single/$215 double with meals. This hotel is altogether an odd concept, an attractive, luxury ranch-style establishment in a beach area, but on the wrong side of the highway and well removed from the water. Rooms are in two tiers along an arcade, each has two double beds, television, phone, air conditioning. Pool and tennis court. Located 600 meters inland from the highway at the south end of Jacó.
TERRAZA DEL PACÍFICO, P. O. Box 168, tel. 643222, fax 643424. 43 rooms. $68 single/$85 double. Five kilometers south of Jacó, along a beach. A standard white resort, Italian-managed, with grassy grounds, pool, casino, restaurant. Rooms are attractive, with red tile floors, and television, air-conditioning, safe-deposit box, telephone. This is a charter-class hotel, booked by tour groups. Guests can only easily use the services made available by the management.

WHERE TO EAT

LAS FRAGATAS, right at the first intersection in Jacó, has open-air dining with tablecloths, on a terrace surrounded by potted plants and ferns. About $6 and up for fish and beef variously prepared, and beverages made from fresh fruits. The house fish (sea bass stuffed with ham, cheese and shrimp) is good.

Just across from Las Fragatas is LOS FAROLES, another open-air eatery, Canadian-run, with pizza and pasta.

Modest and pleasant is LE CAFÉ DE PARIS, a storefront-and-*terrasse* facing the main street, with patisserie, salads, fresh-squeezed juices, croque monsieur, and burger and frites. About $4 to $6 for a light meal, or you can just have a coffee and pastry and hang out.

The ZABAMAR has a menu of continental fare that changes daily, but includes the like of chicken in wine or fish cooked to order. $8 to $12, open at 6 p.m.

The GRILLE FLAMBOYANT is currently the spot in Jacó for those who want a formal evening. Tables are available both inside, looking through windowed archways, and on a terrace. The fare is continental — steak in sauce mâitre d'hotel, fish meuniére — at $8 and up.

The GRAN PALENQUE, a large thatched enclosure near the Hotel Jacó Beach, has seafood and paella, and, mostly, sunset views. The OYSTER is a large, thatch-roofed pavilion along the main street, serving seafood at $10 to $25 per meal.

PANCHO VILLA'S Mexican eatery serves enchiladas and tacos, and steaks and lobster and a castle of shrimp, for $6 to $20.

And there are many, many other eateries, mostly burger and snack joints, and seafood restaurants, as well as a Chinese restaurant, which are inexpensive for fish, not so for shrimp.

SPORTS AND RECREATION

The folks at Los Faroles restaurant will help make arrangements for fishing.

Bicycles are rented at the hardware store and various other locations for about $1 an hour . . . not a bad idea in this spread-out town.

PRACTICAL INFORMATION

A bank is available for changing travelers checks.

Stores include a "supermarket" (a large convenience store), and a bakery. The gas station is at the south end of town.

Manglar Rent A Car, **Elegante Rent A Car**, **Budget**, and assorted other car-rental outfits have agencies at Jacó, mostly on the main street.

You'll find a self-service laundry on the main street near Villas Miramar.

DOWN THE COAST FROM JACÓ

Esterillos Este, down the coast from Jacó, has a long, deserted, open beach — beautiful, but not terribly safe for swimming.

HOTEL EL DELFÍN, Playa Esterillos, tel. and fax 711640 (P. O. Box 37, Parrita, tel. [2]235546 in San José). $65 single/$85 double. American Express, Visa, Master Card. Located at the end of the dirt (or mud) spur from the coastal highway, on a long, long beach, a concrete rectangular-solid-and-cylinder construction, looking somewhat like a Lego creation under the palms. If you want to be all alone with modern conveniences, you've reached your goal. Rooms have ocean-view terraces, fans, tile floors, plain furnishings. Pool, Ping Pong, bicycles, small library. Adequate restaurant under the rotunda. Inclusive packages are available with transport from San José, otherwise a car is recommended.

There are also some *cabinas* on the way to the Delfín, but nothing much else out here.

Past Esterillos, the coastal highway passes through mile after mile of what were once neatly laid-out banana plantations, with clusters of precise two-story worker housing. These have now been supplanted by equally neat plantations of oil palms. All this order is near the town called — what else? — **La Palma**. Outside of the plantations, tropical exuberance and disorder are more evident. Brown rivers ooze through mangrove and mud flats, and are negotiated by narrow, planked trestles. The broad- and shiny-leafed plants characteristic of the humid tropics grow to ferocious dimensions.

Towns are littered and ramshackle, and are few and far between. Iguanas dart across the road, and snakes slither out of the bushes. Sweat lubricates everything. The landscape is fascinating to look at, but there are few attractive stopping places, until the area of Quepos. If you have a car, you can look in at some of the beaches beyond the palms. The friendly and basic **CABINAS LA RUTA DEL SOL** are at Playa Palma, off the highway between Esterillos and Parrita.

The coastal highway is currently paved to Damas. The gravel surface beyond is well maintained to Quepos.

QUEPOS/MANUEL ANTONIO NATIONAL PARK

Once a banana shipping center, Quepos ("KEH-pos") saw its fortunes decline with those of the plantations nearby. The town is now languid and shabby, with a strip of dingy sand. Who would guess that the nicest beaches in Costa Rica are just over the ridge? Read on.

QUEPOS FACTS
Population: about15,000; Location: 144 kilometers from San José

Seven kilometers beyond Quepos are the perfect beaches of **Manuel Antonio National Park,** each an arc of sand curving around a bay strewn with islands of rock, and shaded by green bordering forests. All are backdropped by dramatic cliffs. **Manuel Antonio** beach is one of the few places in Costa Rica where unspoiled primary forest grows right to the high-tide mark, allowing visitors to bathe at times in the shade.

South Espadilla is the northernmost of the park's beaches, followed by calmer Manuel Antonio beach, offshore of which are some coral spots. **Third Beach** has tidal pools where brightly colored fish and eels are intermittently stranded. Last is **Puerto Escondido,** access to which is made difficult by the bordering rocky promontory.

Some of the most frequently observed animals at Manuel Antonio are marmosets — the smallest of Costa Rican monkeys — white-faced and howler monkeys, raccoons, pacas, opossums, and two-and three-toed sloths. Easily sighted seabirds includes frigate birds, pelicans, terns, and brown boobies. A network of trails winds along the sea, and all through the forest.

ARRIVALS AND DEPARTURES
By Bus

Direct buses for Manuel Antonio depart from the Coca-Cola terminal

in San José (Calle 16, Avenidas 1/3) at 6 a.m., noon and 6 p.m. Sl
buses that terminate in Quepos depart at 7 and 10 a.m. and 2 and 4 p.n
The trip on the direct bus takes more than four hours, and can be nausea-
inducing on the run down to the coast. On weekends, it's best to buy your
ticket in advance at the bus company office inside the Coca-Cola market.

Pacific Transfer runs a bus called the *Silver Bullet Express* with
reserved seats and snacks for $35 one way, $60 round trip from San José.
Call [2]272180 (fax [2]281015) for schedules and pickup points.

Buses also operate along the coast to Quepos from Puntarenas, to the
north; and from San Isidro de El General and Dominical, to the south.

A local bus for Manuel Antonio National Park departs about every
two hours from the south end of Quepos, next to the cinema along the
seafront. On weekends in the busy season, service is continuous.

By Air

Sansa, the domestic airline (tel. [2]335330), usually has at least two
daily flights from San José to Quepos. Fare is about $35 round trip, and
inexpensive packages with hotel room are sometimes available. **Travelair**
(tel. [2]327883) has two flights on most days of the week to Quepos from
San José, fare $60 round trip.

Departing By Bus

Direct buses leave Manuel Antonio for San José at 6 a.m., noon and
5 p.m.; slower buses from Quepos at 5 and 8 a.m., and 2 and 4 p.m. For
the **Pacific Transfer** express bus, call [2]272180 in San José.

Buses leave for Puntarenas at 4:30 a.m. and 3 p.m.; for Puriscal at 5
a.m. and noon; for Dominical and San Isidro de El General at 5:30 a.m.
and 1:30 p.m.

Departing By Air

Sansa (tel. [2]335330) and **Travelair** (tel. [2]327883) usually have at
least two daily flights to San José. With advance notice, Sansa will pick you
up and take you to the airport in Quepos for a nominal charge.
Reconfirmation of your return flight is essential.

WHERE TO STAY
The Good and the Bad

While Manuel Antonio itself was rescued from developers, in 1972,
a variety of facilities crowds the edge of the park and continues up the
bordering ridge, making this the easiest national park at which to stay.

But popularity has brought rough spots.

Most hotels are over-priced for what they have to offer, even at the
officially approved rates, and price-gouging is notorious in more than a

N

QUEPOS TOWN

- ● Hotel Kamuk
- Bus Station ●
- ● Mar Blues Bar
- El Gran Escape Restaurant
- ● Hotel Ceciliano
- Cabinas Tauro
- Cabinas Dollar
- ● Hotel Quepos
- Nota n Dreams

Arcada Restaurant	1
Barba Roja Restaurant	16
Bungalows El Salto	6
Cabinas Espadilla	33
Cabinas Los Almendros	34
Cabinas Manuel Antonio	36
Cabinas Pisces	39
Cabinas Ramirez	38
Convenience Store	9
Hotel Arboleda	29
Hotel Bahias	10
Hotel Costa Verde	28
Hotel Del Mar	30
Hotel Divisamar	18
Hotel El Colibri	26
Hotel El Dorado Mojado	21
Hotel El Lirio	7
Hotel La Colina	12
Hotel La Mariposa	19
Hotel La Quinta	27
Hotel Los Charruas	14
Hotel Los Mogotes	25
Hotel Mimo's	4
Hotel Mirador Del Pacifico	3
Hotel Plinio	2
Hotel Villa Bosque	32
Hotel-Restaurant Byblos	22
Karolas Restaurant	17
Mar y Sombra Restaurant	37
Restaurant Manuel Antonio	35
Restaurant Sukia	23
Rios Tropicales Travel Agency	13
Uruguayan Steak House	14
Valle Verde Hotel	8
Vela Bar	31
Villa Oso	15
Villa Teca	11
Villas Makanda	20
Villas Nicolas	24
Villas Sula Bya Ba	5

QUEPOS TOWN

Lighthouse

Horses

MANUEL ANTONIO NATIONAL PARK

QUEPOS

For Orientation Only - Not to Scale

couple of establishments. Singles will usually have to pay the double rate. Even guaranteed reservations might not be honored if a fellow tourist beats you to the reception desk with cash in hand. And the proliferation of intimate hostelries with no more than six rooms can mean going up and down from hotel to hotel by car, taxi or — heaven forbid — on foot in order to find an empty room.

Then there are attitude problems. The owners of one otherwise pleasant hotel leave a polite note to the effect that they are not to be bothered unless prospective guests are willing to take a room, sight unseen.

Then there are facilities problems. Though there is a veneer of good taste at many hostelries, maintenance is often spotty, and construction shoddy. In a multi-floor hotel, you will surely hear the goings-on above you.

Then there's the noise. Many rooms are right by the road, and cars beep from bar to bar late into the night.

Then there's the park. Manuel Antonio National Park was created to forestall the conversion of a forested area into a resort. The park begat hotels, and the hotels begat travel services and bars and pretentious food, which begat visitors, who inundated the park and chased away (for much of the dry season, anyway) the animals that were to be saved.

Then there's Quepos. Wherever the money is going that comes into the area, it's not being used to repair the axle-busting streets.

But . . . the rocky headlands, the ocean views, the avian concerts, the enveloping mystery of the tropical forest . . . they're all still there, and no amount of bad taste and poor management has managed to diminish them. So, by all means, spend a day or two at Manuel Antonio and see what all the fuss is about.

If possible, try to arrive with a reservation in hand for at least one night, preferably with the price guaranteed in writing. If you arrive without a booking, try calling several hotels from a public phone in Quepos. You should have no trouble being understood. Various owners and personnel speak English, Spanish, French, Magyar and German.

Not being right at beach level isn't necessarily a disadvantage: views are better from high up, a public bus passes regularly, and most hotels provide a shuttle service. Each of these hotels has its individual character, and most are small and provide a pleasant environment for relaxation and amusement.

HOTEL PLINIO, P. O. Box 71, Quepos, tel. 77[0]0055. 6 rooms, 1 cabin. $50 single/$68 double, lower May through June and August through November. Visa, Master Card, American Express with surcharge. The Plinio is a roadhouse built into a hillside, with extensive woodwork, high thatched roof, and great balconies hung with hammocks

— it looks like a big tree dwelling. Friendly owners, and good food. Rooms are near the popular bar and restaurant, but this is not a raucous all-night place. The rate includes a buffet breakfast. One kilometer out of Quepos.

HOTEL MIRADOR DEL PACÍFICO, P. O. Box 164-6350, tel. and fax 77[0]0119. 20 rooms. $63 single/$74 double with breakfast. This hotel runs everywhere up a hillside, in three two-story buildings with porches, some reached with the aid of a funicular, or by bridges that fly across declivities in treehouse manner. Rooms have a rough stucco finish, two large beds, and ceiling fan, and are a good enough value for this area. There are two restaurants, one at the very top of the hotel's private mountain, with sea view, and steak and fish for about $15 for a full meal. German spoken.

MIMO'S HOTEL, tel. and fax 77[0]0054. Six rooms. $74 double with fan, $91 with air conditioning. A cheery pink two-story roadside hotel. Rooms are huge, with large bed and sofa bed, and kitchenette, and lots of light.

HOTEL BAHÍAS, P. O. Box 186-6350, tel. 77[0]0350, fax 77[0]0171. 10 rooms. $57 single/$75 double/$85 triple with breakfast. Visa, Master Card, American Express. A charming small hotel in Costa Rican country style. All rooms are air-conditioned, attractive with tile floors and rattan furniture. The larger ones, at a slightly higher price, have both a tub in the bathroom and a Jacuzzi right in the bedroom, under a skylight, with a garden hanging overhead. Informal grounds, small pool.

HOTEL VILLA TECA, P. O. Box 180-6350, tel. and fax 77[0]0279. 40 rooms. $114 double ($90 in rainy season). A compound of mustard- and orange-painted bungalows, with two guest rooms in each, nice enough, with air conditioning, and pool and restaurant on site. But there are no views, the beds are slim twins or one double, and there is no justification for the price charged.

LA COLINA, P. O. Box 191, Quepos, tel. 77[0]0231. Fiv e rooms. $35 single/$45 double including continental breakfast. A modest, homey hillside bungalow. Good value, French spoken. If you were me, you'd head here first.

COMPLEJO TURÍSTICO EL SALTO, P. O. Box 119, Quepos, tel. 77[0]0130. Six rooms. $58 single/$75 double. This is one of several "private reserves" that have materialized near Manuel Antonio National Park, as at Monteverde, to take pressure off the fragile park environment, or simply to get in on the dollar action. At El Salto, aside from the undeveloped lots that comprise the protected area, there are hilltop rooms with private bath and ceiling fans, and majestic views to Quepos and the inland mountains, but not to seaward. The entry road is quite poor.

HOTEL EL LIRIO, P. O. Box 123, Quepos, tel. 77[0]0403. 9 rooms. $75 double ($40 May through September). An intimate lodging place.

The rooms here are in a two-story concrete bungalow and extension, on grounds shaded by huge trees (which lodge a collection of 150 orchids). Each room has fans, tiled bath, sea views, and such nice touches as dhurries on the floor and mosquito canopy over the bed (more for decoration than from necessity). Pool and light meals.

VALLE VERDE, tel. 77[0]0040 ([2]333015 in San José, fax 613-744-2691 in Ottawa), has five apartments to rent at $35 to $57, according to size. The largest has four beds. **Catanzaro Lodge**, being developed by the same management, has small cottages each with two large beds, television, terrace. Pool on site, whirlpool, bikes and riding horses available. The price will be about $100 daily.

HOTEL LOS CHARRÚAS, tel. 77[0]0409. $90 single or double, $57 in rainy season. 6 rooms. A little white colonial-style motel strip. All rooms with bar-refrigerator, one large bed and bunk beds, and magnificent sea views, but quite close to the road, and hardly worth the money.

Not far away, **VILLA OSO**, tel. 77[0]0233, has five units, also close to the road, at $52 double, or $80 to $97 in an apartment.

HOTEL LA MARIPOSA, tel. 77[0]0355, fax 77[0]0050, P.O. Box 4, Quepos. 10 rooms. $140 single/$208 double/$345 for four including two meals and service charge. U.S. reservations: tel. 800-223-6510. The nearly legendary Mariposa is one of the more tasteful hotels in Costa Rica, an intimate, luxury establishment in a dramatic clifftop setting. Each Mediterranean-style cottage is on two levels, with separate bedroom, beamed ceilings, deck, and unusual bathroom with interior garden. The views to the horseshoe beaches below and islets offshore are spectacular, from both the terraces and the small pool. Rates include light breakfast and full dinner with fixed menu (occasionally held up, according to reader reports, while the waiter tries to sell a horseback or boat tour). Children and credit cards are not accepted, reservations are essential. Three-and-a-half kilometers out of Quepos.

HOTEL DIVISAMAR, tel. 77[0]0371, fax 77[0]0525. P. O. Box 82-6350, Quepos. 24 rooms. $82 to $110 double/$92 to $120 triple (25 percent lower in rainy season). Pleasant rooms in a family-run complex of concrete buildings sprawling over a small valley. Nice touches include Delft-style tiles, central hot water (most hotels here have only one lukewarm tap), and air-conditioning in all rooms. Meals available in dry season only. Pool, protected parking, ice machine, backgammon and other games, television room, and space for meetings. Airport pickup on request. A trail leads down to the beach, or you can get a lift from the owners.

VILLAS MAKANDA, P. O. Box 29, Quepos, tel. and fax 77[0]0442. 7 units. $115 and up. Credit cards accepted. Well off the main road, these are several unusually designed buildings on a forest plot sloping to the sea, with suites that interconnect in maze-like fashion. All have screened walls fully open to ocean views, enclosed gardens in Japanese and other styles, hot water, full kitchen or kitchenette, hammock hooks, and ceiling fans; and assorted individual features such as canopy beds or custom tile floor. Rates range from $115 up to $190 for the larger suite with extra bedroom, about 30 percent less during the off-season. There is a pool, and the forest holds toucans, monkeys and other animals that are not found in the park when the traffic is heavy.

Along the same side road are **CABINAS BIESANZ**, tel. 77[0]0490, with eight hillside, weathered, camp-style units with full kitchen, going for $70 double, $100 for up to six persons. A motorized platform climbs the hill for those with difficulty walking.

EL DORADO MOJADO, P. O. Box 238-6350, tel. and fax 77[0]0368. 8 units. $125 with breakfast in villas, $75 in rooms; $75 and $50 in rainy season.   This is an attractive hillside complex, modern in style and unusually well designed. The villas have large windows, like greenhouses, but with generous overhang to shade the interiors. Inside, the lower level holds a kitchen (refrigerator stocked with drinks), sitting area, interior garden, and safe-deposit box. Upstairs are beds with Zacualpa covers, concealed lighting, built-in cabinetry, and good bathroom. Non-slip concrete bridges connect the villas, and there are a pool and barbecue. All units are air-conditioned, the villas sleep three or four persons, smaller rooms two persons.

HOTEL BYBLOS, P. O. Box 112, Quepos, tel. 77[0]0411, fax 77[0]0009. 20 units. $120 double. The main attraction here is the French restaurant, but aside from gastronomy, there are rooms in little forest bungalows, an on-site waterfall, a pool, and a 55-foot yacht. Some readers have complained about maintenance and housekeeping.

VILLAS NICOLAS, tel. and fax 77[0]0538, P. O. Box 26, Quepos. 12 units/19 rooms. $81 single/$93 double, to $175 for four, lower from May through November. No credit cards. These are ocean-view, Mediterranean-style condominium units in the semi-manicured hillside jungly setting common to hotels at Manuel Antonio. Water cascades down from the whirlpool into a large swimming pool, with a stone and wooden deck. Each unit has one or two bedrooms rented individually or in combination, Spanish-style furnishings, kitchen, tiled floors, archways, and white walls with generous wood trim. The larger "villas" are on two levels, and most have ample terraces, and cooking facilities.

VILLAS EL PARQUE, tel. 77[0]0096, are 16 ocean-view hillside condominiums with hammock terraces, available at $81 single/$93 double. Most have two bedrooms, and there are a bar, pools, and laundry facilities. If nobody's in, check at the office of Villas Nicolas next door.

HOTEL MOGOTES, P. O. Box 120, Quepos, tel. and fax 77[0]0582.

12 rooms. $7 to $90 single/$68 to $125 double with breakfast. Visa, Master Card. Cheery rooms close to the road, some upstairs with view, some without. Units have one double and one single bed, and a modern bathroom, in a house that once belonged to Jim Croce. Pool on-site.

EL COLIBRÍ, P. O. Box 94, Quepos, tel. 77[0]0432. 10 units. $75 double, less in rainy season. Gilles and Pierre offer good taste in their compound — rooms with tiled floors, varnished beams, louvered doors, and cooking facilities. The hilltop Mediterranean-style units, back from the road, across the gardens (where something is always in bloom) are the nicest, with porches and hammocks. Sea views are good from the second floor of the main building. One charming little guest unit has the bedroom on a screened upper level. A pool is under construction. Children under ten should look elsewhere. 4.2 kilometers from Quepos.

LA QUINTA, P.O. Box 76, Quepos, tel. 77[0]0434. 5 units. $65 to $75 double. This is an intimate hilltop hotel, with extensive grounds and magnificent sea views, a somewhat less pretentious version of the Mariposa. Mediterranean-style cottages all have three beds, tiled showers, terra cotta floors, and small refrigerator and hot plate. An "overflow" unit is less desirable. The personable owners, a French-Hungarian couple, are on-site to see to guests' needs. Pool. Breakfast and beverages available. 4.5 kilometers from Quepos. (The owners and I buy our sheets at the same store. They can explain.)

HOTEL COSTA VERDE, tel. 77[0]0584, fax 77[0]0560 (P. O. Box 6944-1000, San José, tel. [2]237946, fax [2]239446). 28 units. $70 each. These are bedroom-kitchenette combinations, screened and woody and attractive, atop a hill well off the road. Additional units are in a separate location downhill.

HOTEL ARBOLEDA, P. O. Box 55-6350, tel. 77[0]0092, fax 77[0]0414 ([2]351169 in San José). 35 units. $90 or more double. This hotel occupies its own section of rain forest, extending down to the water, with units at various levels. Rates are reported to fluctuate.

VILLAS DE LA SELVA (tel. and fax [2]534890) is adjacent to the Arboleda. The rate is $75 in each of two studio apartments, $100 double, $160 for up to eight persons in the three two-room ocean-view villas, each with terrace, kitchenette, barbecue, television.

APARTOTEL KARAHÉ, P. O. Box 100-6350, Quepos, tel. 77[0]0170, fax 77[0]0152. 32 units. $80 daily. Visa, American Express, Master Card. Pleasant, rock-walled cottages, each accommodating three persons, with refrigerators but no cooking facilities. Good sea views. Additional rooms, and a pool, are across the road near the beach. The restaurant, on a huge porch, serves chops and chicken cooked in the open. On the hillside just before the beach, seven kilometers from Quepos.

HOTEL DEL MAR, 3 rooms, $30 double. Simple rooms, good value.

CABINAS PISCES, near the bottom of the road from Quepos, has six rooms on a grassy lot, at $33 double.

At the beach

Starting where the road comes down to the beach (and where the bus leaves passengers), there is a series of cabinas, basic, cold-water units with few services. You might think it would be to your advantage to stay nearer the entrance to the park. But noise levels, lack of security at some hotels, harsh concrete rooms and suspect disposal systems (try not to inhale) could change your mind.

All the cabinas, spread among the palms, are close enough to each other that you can look them over before selecting one to settle into for a while. All are likely to be full or nearly full on weekends, and deserted on weekdays. Some of the facilities near the beach have been illegally built within 50 meters of the high-tide mark, and face condemnation.

Those cabinas nearest the bus stop go for $8 per person, sometimes more, sometimes less, depending on the season and the number of beds in the room. The more substantial **RESTAURANT MANUEL ANTONIO**, tel. 77[0]0212, has a few rooms upstairs.

The best accommodations in this area are on a road that winds back from the beach.

CABINAS ESPADILLA has 20 units with cooking areas for $28 single/$35 double, more with a separate kitchen. The rate drops substantially during the rainy season, except in July.

The **VELA BAR** (P. O. Box 13, Quepos, tel. 77[0]0413) has seven attractive rooms for $28 single/$40 double, $10 additional with air conditioning.

Next door is **VILLA BOSQUE** (tel. 77[0]0463, fax 77[0]0401), a new hotel with 13 frilly rooms, the nicest in this less-than-top-notch area. The rate is $80 double with air conditioning, $70 with fan. They have a restaurant and parking with 24-hour guard, and the service is friendly.

LOS ALMENDROS rents motel-style units on well-cared-for grounds for $35 to $50 for one to three persons.

There's also a private camping spot in this area, but it is exposed and not secure.

One other place with concrete rooms, **CABINAS PEDRO MIGUEL**, tel. 77[0]0035, is located a kilometer out of Quepos. $10 to $20 double.

HOTEL KAMUK, P. O. Box 18, tel. 77[0]0379, fax 77[0]0171. 28 rooms. $57 single or double. If you stay right in town, either by choice or because everything on the way to the park is taken, this brand-new three-story seafront hotel is several cuts above everything else. The halls are bright and airy with skylights and light wells, and the rooms are better than those in most of the resorts, with carpeting, two large beds, air conditioning, wallpaper and generally pleasing decor, phone, television, and terrace. No pool or spectacular views, unfortunately, but a good value for this area.

Aside from the Kamuk, there are several modest hotels where you can get a reasonably priced room if everything on the way to the park is filled, or too expensive for your budget. The **HOTEL VIÑA DEL MAR** looks out on the muddy beach, which is the best view downtown. The seafront grounds are pleasant, but the rooms are just cubicles with attached toilet and shower. $15 and up for a double. The places back toward the bus station all charge less, and give you less.

On the edge of town toward the road to Manuel Antonio, the **HOTEL QUEPOS**, tel. 77[0]0274, has cubicles and a family atmosphere for $20 double, or $25 with private bath. The **HOTEL CECILIANO**, tel. 77[0]0192, at $35 double with private bath, is somewhat better, and can provide parking in the courtyard. **CABINAS EL TAURO** and **CABINAS DOLLAR** charge somewhat less, and are adequate.

Nearby
PUEBLO REAL, tel. and fax 77[0]0536 (P. O. Box 1136-1200 Pavas, tel. [2]322211, fax [2]320587). 28 apartments. $148 per unit, $114 in rainy season. At the estuary of the Damas River, several kilometers north of Quepos, Pueblo Real is a resort development, with condominium units available for rent. Each is air-conditioned and has two bedrooms, one with bathroom and dressing room en suite (there is a second bathroom as well), balcony, and full American-style kitchen.

The furnishings are attractive (these are not standard Costa Rican apartments), and at 90 square meters, they are large. On site are a pool, large whirlpool, and two tennis courts. Plans call for a golf course, country club and marina. If you have a car, these apartments are some of the best values in the area, especially for two couples (there is plenty of privacy) or families.

WHERE TO EAT
Read the menu carefully if you stop into any restaurant on the road to Manuel Antonio. Despite modest appearances and even more modest offerings in a few cases, some of the prices are shockers.

EL BYBLOS, the French hostelry, easily has the most dramatic dining environment south of San José, a tremendous porch with towering roof, hung with basket lamps, entered by a hardwood stairway over the fountain and pool, looking out over a jungle valley. This is a formal restaurant, and I don't just mean that they have real tablecloths. Main courses include tournedos, lamb in assorted preparations, dorado *en citron vert*, and other continental fare. A full meal will appetizer and dessert will cost $20, more if you select an appropriate wine and *digestif*.

The **HOTEL PLINIO**, one kilometer out of Quepos, has a bar and restaurant with good German and Italian food. The bread is home-baked, the salads are crisp, and I can recommend the lasagne. There are also pizzas and steaks. $7 and up for a main course. If you're not staying at the Plinio, it's worthwhile to go over for a drink and a meal.

The **BARBA ROJA** bar, opposite the Divisamar, commands the same magnificent sea and cliff views available from the Hotel Mariposa. There are assorted daily specials for $8 and up, burgers for a couple of dollars, and rock music.

The **URUGUAYAN STEAK HOUSE** is a large indoor-outdoor eating area with *fogata* where the meat is genuinely charred in pampa fashion. Steaks and kebabs go for $10 to $14, and some unusual items like red (*sic*) salmon are on the menu at a higher price.

Various other eateries offer pricey French or continental food. **LA BRISE**, near the entry to La Quinta, has a light, white, gardeny, all-windows decor, and such fare as pepper steak, supràme de poulet and fettucine pistou at $10 and up for the main course alone. **LA ARCADA**, Italian-style and one of the first restaurants on the road to the park, is another relatively pricey joint, at $8 for ravioli, $15 for a fish-and-beef kebab.

KAROLA'S Restaurant, down in a valley off the main road, is an open-air but intimate bar and dining area, overlooking a forest. Current menu items include sirloin steak, seafood platter, tuna steak, and macadamia pie to finish off. $10 and up. Locals rave about the food.

BAHIA'S BAR AND GRILL, by the hotel of the same name, is a bamboo-encased restaurant with terrace outside, specializing in red meat— sirloin, steak in garlic sauce and kebabs for $10 and up.

SUKIA'S, opposite the Byblos Hotel, widely advertised around town, is a bar that serves Spanish-style *tapas* (snacks) with drinks, adequate seafood, and sandwiches and salads at lunch.

Of several eateries at beach level, the most popular is the large, open-air **MAR Y SOMBRA**, located where the road from Quepos meets the beach. A whole fried fish goes for $4 and up, depending on the size, and there are huge tropical fruit plates, breakfasts (from 6 a.m.), the usual rice-and-bean combos, and beef and pork main courses for $4 to $6.

In Quepos itself, you'll find numerous places in which to eat inexpensively in clean surroundings. **EL GRAN ESCAPE**, on the main street, serves Tico food in a large room with lamps dangling from the ceiling and posters decorating the walls. Breakfast or a full meal of casado can cost under $5. Wine available. Popular with visitors looking for food without pretense. **MAR BLUES**, on a side street by the Hotel Kamuk, has large hamburger platters with fries, daily specials, breakfasts, and drinks of all sorts. **GEORGE'S AMERICAN**, on the way toward Manuel Antonio, is on a corner and open to the street, serving burgers, Mexican *antijotos*, and seafood in preparations that change daily. At the **NAHOMI** pool (see below), along the water south of town, the terrace restaurant serves sandwiches, fish, and Costa Rican specialties in pleasant surroundings at surprisingly low prices — as little as $7 for a meal with a small steak.

VISITING MANUEL ANTONIO PARK

Despite the sometimes frenzied activity at Espadilla beach, things turn peaceful as soon as you cross a stream (wading in the rainy season) and enter the park. Check the depth by watching others cross. Visiting hours are from 8 a.m. to 4 p.m. If you plan to swim, leave your camera and valuables at your hotel desk.

Take a good look at the map posted at the entrance, and plan your route — trails are not well-marked. Take note of the illustrated signs warning of the *manzanillo de playa*, a tree with poisonous, apple-like fruits, and sap that irritates the skin.

The trails at Manuel Antonio wind through the forest, up to clifftops, and down to beaches — depending on which nomenclature you use, there are from three to five beaches, those farthest from the entrance being usually deserted. But their availability for swimming depends on the time of day — at high tide, they simply disappear, and you have to get up and hike.

Along the trails, bromeliads decorate tree limbs, and the leaf rubbish underfoot is teeming with life. Crabs scurry when you take a step. Iguanas scramble from your presence. White-faced monkeys go about their business, having seen the likes of you before.

Whatever your sightings of these, or of parrots, squirrels, iguanas, coatis, agoutis, or, more rarely, peccaries, you are sure to run into several pairs of *amantes costarricenses*. Be discreet.

AROUND MANUEL ANTONIO & QUEPOS

The less expensive accommodations at beach level at Manuel Antonio attract a lively, mostly young crowd. Many of the visitors are foreigners on extended travels. The beach is known as a good place to hang out for a while, trade information, recoup, and re-group.

The concentration of facilities and beauty also make this an event center. A three-day Festival of the Sea takes place in January. Surfing contests, rock concerts and conventions are scheduled at other times. You'll want to check what's on tap (the tourist office in San José will probably know) in order to get in on the action, or avoid it, depending on your sensitivities.

Caution is advisable when swimming here. Red Cross personnel are on hand at busy times, but otherwise, there are no provisions for beach safety, and the currents are notoriously tricky. Stay out of water deeper than your waist.

I am told by a reliable source that the mayor of Quepos took considerable offense when, in an earlier edition, I called his city "squalid, rotting, and garbage-strewn." The lack of attention to public decoration was laid to slow adjustment to self-management of affairs, following the reduction of banana company operations. Quepos is still far from pristine —"charmingly scuzzy" is what one American magazine writer called it — but it is not squalid, nor is it garbage-strewn these days. The waters off the beach in town, however, are contaminated by raw sewage, and should be avoided.

SITES AROUND QUEPOS

If you continue straight after entering Quepos, past the left turn for Manuel Antonio, and go down toward the docks, then take a half left, you can climb the hill to the old **banana company** residential compound, a suburb of pleasant, uniform, tan clapboard bungalows with red tin roofs, set behind fences on well-manicured grounds shaded by huge palms. There are sport and community centers, including one of the largest swimming pools around, and views that rival those available from the resort hotels of the area. The houses are owned by Standard Fruit, and populated by Costa Rican managers, not gringos. It's all quite a contrast to the town below. By the way, the roads are private, and you're not supposed to enter the compound, but foreigners who can't read the signs are not chased away.

Down below the fruit company homes, if you continue along the shore and around the bend about a half-kilometer from town, you'll come to **Paradero Turístico Nahomi**, which is a sort of public-resort-complex-without-hotel, a series of concrete-and-stone terraces on a rocky point of land almost surrounded by water. Here you'll find an inexpensive and pleasant shaded outdoor restaurant, open from 11 a.m.; and two **pools** and dressing rooms, which you can use from 9 a.m. on for a small fee. The surroundings are palms and plants, and except for some nearby ware-houses, the scene is as pleasant as you'll find in the area.

Slightly off the tourist track is foggy **Londres** ("London"), a farming village which you can reach on a driving or mountain-bike excursion through scenery more hilly and interesting than what you see as you travel down the coastal highway. To head to London, take the turn north, about four kilometers past the first entry to Quepos, near the airstrip. A dirt road meanders through palms, pastured hills, and sugar-cane plantings. About ten kilometers on is a steel suspension bridge, more impressive than those right on the highway, over a river that rushes over boulders even in the dry season. And just beyond is Londres proper, an out-of-the-old-days hamlet populated by barefoot peasants of no pretense, with whom, if you choose, you can raise elbows with a refreshment at the Club Social Londinense.

SPORTS AND RECREATION AROUND QUEPOS
Rafting

Ríos Tropicales, the rafting-and-kayaking travel agency, has a local office on the road to the park, tel. 77[0]0574.

Amigos del Mar (tel. 77[0]0082), with an office in Quepos, runs full-day white-water rafting trips for $60-$70, as well as more restful float trips.

Note that the rivers on this slope of the sierra are *not* runnable all year, so look for this kind of adventure during the rainy season, from about May through October. And, since the Naranjo River, used for many expeditions, is just a few kilometers from Quepos, the prices are absurdly out of line. Ask for a reduction, or save your rafting for a trip to one of the more reliable rivers on the eastern slope of the continental divide, organized from San José.

Diving

Amigos del Mar operates dive trips at about $65, and an introductory course for $100, full certification for $300. The Quepos area is not particularly noted for diving, but if you're going to be here anyway ...

Fishing

Sportfishing Costa Rica (P.O. Box 115-1150 La Uruca, tel. [2]339135 in San José, 77[0]0505 in Quepos, 800-374-4474 U.S.-Costa Rica direct), on the road that runs along the water south of town, and Costa Rica Dreams (P. O. Box 79-4005 San Antonio de Belén, tel. 77[0]0593 in Quepos), offer deep sea fishing. Longer fishing or naturalist trips are available to Drake Bay on the Osa Peninsula, Corcovado National Park, and Caño Island. Sportfishing Costa Rica has its own hotel, the DORADO MOJADO, with kitchenette units and clubhouse, and shuttle to Quepos.

At Costa Rica Dreams, the rate is $450 to $650 per day for up to four persons for deep-sea fishing, depending on the boat, including sandwiches, tackle, services of the captain, and refreshments. They recommend December through April for sailfish, November through April for marlin, December through May for dorado, May through December for snook and tuna, and all year for roosterfish and snapper. Fishing may be limited in October, the rainiest time. Costa Rican Dreams also has an open-cockpit boat for fly fishermen, at $500 per day. Half-day rentals are also available.

Sportfishing Costa Rica has boats in the area from December through

May, when winds are strong in other fishing grounds. Full-day rates are similar to those of Costa Rica Dreams.

Treasure Hunt Tours (P. O. Box 187, Quepos, tel. 77[0]0345) has boats for inshore fishing. Inquire at La Buena Nota or at your hotel.

All sportfishing operations counsel you to release your catch. In any case, there's no easy way to bring your trophy home.

Sightseeing from a Boat

One goal of day-trippers from Manuel Antonio is **Isla de Damas**, which, despite the name, is no island, but a peninsula, ten kilometers up the coast from Quepos. The floating restaurant-bar **Tortuga** serves meals of fresh fish at about $6. To get aboard, turn off the coastal highway at the Pepsi-Tortuga sign. The estuary is one kilometer onward. Little motor-boats will take you out to the Tortuga, or you can hire them by the hour to cruise through jungle-lined channels.

This is a beautiful, fascinating area, off the usual visitors' track, with secluded vacation homes and fishermen's shacks along the water. You can get here by taxi, or Erick at the Hotel Divisamar will put a group together for a trip in his van. Several tour operators charge about $65 for a boat ride through the Damas estuary, with lunch at the floating restaurant, but you can do it yourself for about a fourth (or maybe a fifth) of that price.

Costa Rica Dreams (tel. 77[0]0593) operates a half-day tour that might be a better value. For $200, up to four passengers are carried to various coastal points, including rookeries of frigatebirds and boobies. Departures are at 8 a.m. and 1 p.m., and beverages and fruit are included.

Horseback Riding

Stable Eqqus (tel. 77[0]0355), among others, has riding horses available. Inquire at the Hotel La Mariposa.

Gambling

The casino is at the **Hotel Kamuk** in Quepos.

PRACTICAL INFORMATION

Some of Manuel Antonio's touristic development has spilled down into Quepos, in the form of a few shops and services for tourists. One beachwear outlet, **La Buena Nota** (tel. 77[0]0345), at the entrance to Quepos, has used books, and owners who are said to be helpful to disoriented tourists. Among other facilities are a bank, and, at the highway junction, a gas station. **Elegante Rent A Car** has an agency, tel. 77[0]0115. And there are various other travel services (see below)

Various small businesses have horses for hire, scuba and snorkeling equipment; beach chairs, surfboards and umbrellas to rent, and offer boat tours of Damas Island, or dinner cruises.

SOUTH OF QUEPOS

During the rainy season, inquire about road conditions before traveling south from Quepos (if the highway hasn't been paved by the time you visit). As you proceed — by car, or, more certainly, by bus — the ridge of the continental divide in the **Talamanca Mountains**, with the highest peaks in Costa Rica, watches over from just thirty kilometers inland. Higher rainfall is evidenced by broader leaves, more gigantic plants, and swollen rivers, some of which, near Hatillo, you will have to ford, even in the dry season. The vast palm plantation continues. Huge oil-processing plants send up a burned-sweet smell. Every small plantation town has its bus shelters, church, company stores, rows of neat, identical housing (some models quite above the usual local standard), cantina, and Alcoholics Anonymous chapter, with its sign prominently posted.

At **Hatillo** and **Matapalo**, there are basic cabina lodging facilities, which you can look in on if you're driving.

DOMINICAL AREA

About 50 kilometers south of Quepos, Dominical is hardly a town, just a few houses, a saloon, and some inexpensive cabinas and newer hotels. Dominical's advantage, compared to other little-frequented seaside villages, is the convenience of its accommodations to the highway. The beach is beautiful, a couple of eateries serve hamburgers and fish, and there are boating and other water sports available.

ARRIVALS AND DEPARTURES
By Bus

Buses leave from Quepos for Dominical at 5:30 a.m. and 1:30 p.m.; from San Isidro de El General at 7 a.m. and 1 p.m. and 3 p.m.

WHERE TO STAY AND WHERE TO EAT
In Dominical

CABINAS RÍO LINDO (12 rooms, $48 double) is a new, motel-style accommodation where the spur from the highway enters town. Rooms are light, attractive and clean, and the open-air dining area has a comprehensive menu.

Near the bridge in town, **CABINAS WILLY** is an unpretentious getaway, a set of six riverside cabinas on a large, shaded lot, a short walk from the beach. Construction of some units is country-style, with posts of rough tree trunks, exposed beams, and plenty of wood trim. These go for about

$20 double. Larger rooms with hot water, sleeping three, rent for $25. Owner Willy Dale is an American, and can make arrangements for sailing, canoeing and rafting. Communication is via answering machine, tel. [7]711903, or fax, 71[0]0735. Inquire here as well about a cliffside luxury villa down the coast, available for about $1000 a week.

JUNGLE JIM'S (tel. [7]710866) feature a bar and restaurant with satellite television tuned to sporting events. Rooms upstairs are about $30 double.

ROCA VERDE BAR AND CABINAS (tel. [7]711414) has rooms for $10 per person. On the beach, CABINAS NAYARIT (tel. [7]712878) charges $30 double with fan, and has houses for rent. CABINAS SAN CLEMENTE, $20 double, is surfer-friendly.

At Barú

HACIENDA BARÚ is a plantation just across the bridge from Dominical that offers excursions that highlight the natural attractions of the area. Guided walks take visitors through and across beach, riverbank, orchards, mangroves, lowland and hill primary rain forest, and commercial plantations for fees of from $25 to $55 for two, according to length, from a few hours to all day, more with an overnight at a screened jungle shelter (superb for wildlife viewing).

You're guaranteed sightings of 17 species of animal (a frivolous offer — you're likely to see many more). Limited guest accommodations are available at $35 double. There are also horseback trips. Additional cabina units are planned. For information on Hacienda Barú, and recommendations to surfing and camping sites and guest ranches, speak to somebody at the gas station (*Bomba El Ceibo*), which is about one kilometer up the coast from the Dominical bridge. Or contact **Naturística**, P. O. Box 215-8000 San Isidro de El General, tel. [7]711903 (message), fax [7]710441.

South of Dominical

HOTEL-CABINAS PUNTA DOMINICAL, P.O. Box 196-8000, San Isidro de El General, tel. [7]710866 (tel. [2]255328 in San José). $30 single/$40 double, $68 for up to six persons. These are cliff-top cottages out of the South Seas — near-tree houses on stilts — amid lush greenery, four kilometers south of the village of Dominical. All units have ample screens and slats to let the breeze blow through, and two double beds as well as bunks.

The point of land atop which the cottages sit is surrounded on three sides by water, and your view is up and down the coast, over rocky flats and to wide-open water. Even if you're not staying the night, the breezy, open restaurant here is economy-priced, with no main course except shrimp priced over $6. Call for a reservation before you arrive. Access is by turning off the highway toward the beach, then going up the hill.

CABANAS ESCONDIDAS (P. O. Box 364, San Isidro de El General, tel. 72[2]2904, fax [7]710735) are informal cabins on a tract that includes 80 acres of standing rain forest, as well as tropical gardens. Arrangements can be made for fishing, horseback riding and hiking — and tai chi classes and massages. Rates are $35 double with breakfast, and other meals can be prepared. The owners speak English. Ten kilometers south of the bridge at Dominical.

FINCA BRIAN Y MILENA is what you might call a hill farm, an hour by horse from Dominical, planted with fruit trees and spice plants. Two guest cabins are available, at $60 double, or less for longer stays. Write to P. O. Box 2-8000, San Isidro de El General, or phone [7]711903.

BELLA VISTA LODGE ($30 double, tel. [7]711903), with four rooms, is a ranch guest house inland from and overlooking the sea from a thousand feet up. As at remote island camps, power comes from generators and solar cells. Meals are available for a minimal charge, along with horseback tours to little-visited waterfalls and springs, for up to $35. The owners will fetch guests in Dominical for a few dollars.

SOUTHEAST OF DOMINICAL, an improved gravel road follows the shore to Uvita, 16 kilometers away. Just inland are the **Emerald Pools**, a stepped series of falls ideal for a dip. You can look for them on your own, or hire a guide for a few dollars at the Soda Cocotico. The **Santo Cristo Falls**, reachable by horse with the assistance of one of the lodging places in the area.

CABINAS LOS LAURELES in Uvita has rooms for about $30 double.

Onward is **Playa Ballena** (*Whale Beach*). A local development association plans eventually to build hotels and a marina in this area without stamping out wildlife.

Ballena Marine National Park includes coral reef, mangrove, shoals and a wide variety of shoreline and marine features. As the name implies, whales frequent this reserve, most notably humpbacks, from December to May.

Inland from Dominical, a newly paved road winds up from the bananas and palms of the coastal strip, through ranch country, to the coffee altitudes, and mountainside pastures grazed by temperate breeds of cattle, at about 1600 meters, than down again to **San Isidro**, at the foot of Mount Chirripó, in a fresher, more arid valley, just 35 kilometers away.

SPORTS AND RECREATION

Reel 'n Reelease Sportfishing, tel. and fax [7]711903, operates inshore and deep-sea fishing trips, diving excursions, and wildlife sighting expeditions to **Caño Island** and **Violín Island**. A day's outing for two costs about $400.

DOWN TOWARD PANAMA

The southern Pacific slope of Costa Rica was, until the 1950s, isolated from the rest of the country. No highway crossed the Talamanca mountain range from the Central Valley, and all communication with the region was by a roundabout coastal route that was mostly untraveled. What population there was concentrated in the banana regions around Golfito, which were tied by narrow-gauge railroad with Panama, and by steamship with the banana-consuming world.

With improved highway links, the inland valley of the General River has become one of the fastest-growing areas of Costa Rica. Many farmers have migrated to this frontier region from the overcrowded lands of the Central Valley, with the encouragement and assistance of the government. The warm climate suits the valley to sugarcane and corn production, as well as cattle grazing.

The Mountain Route

The Pan American Highway runs south from San José, up into the Talamanca range and along the continental divide. The trip this way is an ear-popping ascent through apple country and moss- and epiphyte-laden forest, past swatches of mountain made bare by landslides, up to the windblown landscape of stunted bushes, struggling tufts of grass and feather-duster vegetation of the frigid tropics, known as *páramo*.

At **El Empalme**, the junction for the road to Santa María de Dota (see page 219) provides a good alternative meander back to San José, if you've already taken this route one way.

The highest point on the whole Inter-American (Pan American) Highway, 3,355 meters above sea level, is near **Cerro Buena Vista** ("Good-View Peak"), also known, less optimistically, as **Cerro de la Muerte** ("Peak of Death"). Both names are apt. When clouds are not clinging to the heights, the ride along the ridge affords views down to both the Pacific Ocean and the Caribbean. The second, more common name derives from the frigid climate, said to have killed many an oxcart driver.

WHERE TO STAY
Mountain Lodges South of San José

GENESIS II is a lodge in a private forest reserve off the Inter-American Highway, one of the closest facilities of its type to San José, though it has the air of being far more remote. The principal attraction here is excellent birding without distractions. Over 200 species are on the local list, including the quetzal, a variety of hummingbirds, and species

reported nowhere else in Costa Rica. Squirrels, butterflies and mg.. _
vegetation (mosses, ferns, bromeliads) are also of interest. The property,
with several trails and swimming spots, borders the **Río Macho Forest
Reserve** that protects the San José watershed.

Accommodations are along the lines of what you might find in old-
style New England country places — homey, adequate, unluxurious, with
shared bathrooms. Smoking inside is prohibited.

To reach Genesis II, drive or take the San Isidro bus to the yellow
church at Cantón del Guarco, 800 meters past kilometer 58. The reserve
is about three kilometers away on a difficult road. The rate is about $55
per person daily with meals and airport pickup. One-day and multi-day
trips are available. A volunteer reforestation program also operates here.

For details, contact Steve Friedman, P. O. Box 655-7050 Cartago, fax
51[0]0070.

Nearby
ALBERGUE DE MONTAÑA TAPANTÍ (Tapantí Mountain Lodge,
tel. [2]320436, P. O. Box 986-1250 Escazú), kilometer 62 at Macho Gaff,
is a more formal chalet-style roadhouse with cabins on open, wind-blown
lawns planted with flowers. Six simple, tidy rooms with wood floors have
basic beds and bunks, and electric heaters, and rent for $82 double. The
lodge is a base for trout-fishing, birding, horseback, and flora-observation
excursions in the páramo, arranged at prices of $12 to $60 per person.

At kilometer 80 on the Pan American highway is the junction for the
road to San Gerardo de Dota, a hair-raising ribbon that winds along and
down cliffs, sprinkled with asphalt in the steepest parts. If the cloud-forest-
and-meadow scenery along the way does not take your breath away, the
road certainly will. Nine kilometers from the highway is **SAVEGRE
LODGE** on Finca Zacatales, the ranch and trout-fishing camp of the
Chacón family. Most fishing camps in Costa Rica are on the coasts, this
being one notable exception. Accommodations are in five cabins, some
with fireplaces. Package day trips, including meals, equipment and
guides, are available through San José travel agencies for about $65.

The overnight rate, if you're on your own, is about $45 with meals.
Telephone 711732 to reserve, and to arrange to be met at the highway
junction (no bus comes out this way). A couple of fishing rods may be
available, if you're lucky. But you needn't come here just to fish—the trout
are said to be small in any case. The ranch is in the cool country, above
8000 feet, and if you've been to the peak of Irazú volcano, the vegetation
along the Savegre River will look familiar: leafy trees decorated with
orchids and bromeliads, and firs. Though not as dramatic as the scenery
along the strenuous route to the top of Chirripó, there is some of the same
feeling in the air.

Birders take note: according to some biologists, the concentration of quetzals in this area is the greatest in the world; Efraín Chacón has a line on where the birds are currently nesting, and can give visitors a good chance of sighting one.

Elsewhere along the main highway, you'll find basic, cold rooms at the **GEORGINA** restaurant at Villa Mills, but few other places at which to stop until you get to San Isidro.

SAN ISIDRO DE EL GENERAL

San Isidro is the major town of the south, a transportation and farming center at the head of the valley of the General River. The area always had a scattered Indian population, but San Isidro was founded only in 1897.

There's little of historical interest in San Isidro — most of the town was built in the last forty years, after the opening of the Pan American Highway. But the place is pleasant enough. A grotesque pink-and-white concrete cathedral overlooks a neat park of large palms. The views upward, to the Talamanca mountains, are impressive. And there are quite decent, and decently priced, hotels and restaurants for the visitor who is passing through on the way to the beach, a national park, to Panama, or to a rafting excursion on the General River. An annual cattle show and fair takes place at the beginning of February.

SAN ISIDRO FACTS
Population: About 37,000; Altitude: 702 meters;
Location: 136 kilometers from San José

ARRIVALS AND DEPARTURES

Arriving By Bus

Buses and microbuses for San Isidro operate from Calle 16, Avenidas 1/3, San José, approximately every hour from 4:30 a.m. to 5:30 p.m. Three companies on the same block alternate departures. The trip takes about three hours.

Departing By Bus

Buses and microbuses for San José depart from near the Hotel Amaneli, approximately every hour from 4:30 a.m. to 5:30 p.m.

San Isidro makes a good stopping point for southbound bus travellers, since so much traffic funnels through town. Buses for Dominical and Quepos leave at 7 a.m. and 1:30 p.m. from a block-and-a-half south of the church on the square; for Puerto Jiménez on the Osa Peninsula at 5:45 a.m. and noon from a block south of the hotel Amaneli; for San Gerardo de Rivas and access to Chirripó National Park (see below) at 5 a.m. and 2 p.m. from the main square near the Soda Nevada.

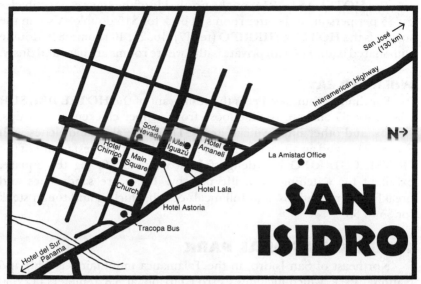

Tracopa buses for Ciudad Neily near Panama leave at 4:45 and 7:30 a.m. and noon and 3 p.m.; for San Vito de Java at 9 and 11:30 a.m. and 2 and 5:30 p.m.; for David in northern Panama at 10 a.m. and 3 p.m. (These are only partial listings.)

WHERE TO STAY

HOTEL DEL SUR, Palmares, tel. [7]710233, fax [7]710527, 60 rooms. $22 single/$30 double. Cabinas (cottage units) sleep up to five persons for $40 to $60. Visa, American Express. Five kilometers south of San Isidro along the main highway is the sprawling Hotel del Sur, with huge main pool and children's pool, basketball and tennis courts, carefully tended gardens, and even a pond. Rooms, unfortunately, are worn and institutional, with threadbare carpets, chipped tubs, and windows looking out on passageways; but the value is good, and everybody is eager to please. The restaurant offers a varied menu, and there's a gift shop. Cottage units have refrigerators. This is your preferred stopping point if travelling by car.

In San Isidro itself is the almost-new and shining **HOTEL IGUAZÚ** (tel. [7]712571, 21 rooms, $10 single, $14 double). With private bath, and located just a block from the square, it's a good deal, and worth a phone call to reserve. Other in-town hotels cater more to travelling salesmen than vacationers. The **HOTEL AMANELI** (tel. [7]710352, 40 rooms, $7 per person) is the tan concrete structure that you first see when you come down the mountain from San José. It's clean enough, and rooms have private bath.

The **HOTEL ASTORIA**, on the north side of the square, has cubicles for $5 per person, and better rooms in back for $15 double. Also on the square is the **HOTEL CHIRRIPÓ** (tel. [7]710529, 40 rooms, $10 double with shared bath, $14 with private bath), where rooms are bare and dusty.

WHERE TO EAT

For dining, your best bet is the restaurant of the **HOTEL DEL SUR** where, for $5 and up, you'll choose from pepper chicken, sirloin tips, kebabs, and other unprovincial items. There are also sandwiches with French fries, and an afternoon happy hour. In town, the restaurant of the **HOTEL CHIRRIPÓ** is a delightful Tico terrasse facing the square, excellent for watching town life pass by. There are sandwiches and breakfast combinations, and full meals of fish, chicken and tough steak for $5 to $6.

CHIRRIPO NATIONAL PARK

Northeast of San Isidro, in the Talamanca mountains, is **Chirripó National Park**, which includes Cerro Chirripó, at 3,820 meters (12,530 feet) the highest mountain peak in Costa Rica. The habitat of the park ranges from rocky, frigid heights and glacial lakes to the stunted, windblown *páramo* of the harsh altitudes of the tropics, to oak and evergreen forest, highland meadows, and cloud forest. Wildlife at Chirripó is not as varied as at some of the lowland reserves, but includes pumas, mountain goats, rabbits, and tapirs, among others. Quetzals can be sighted at lower altitudes.

There are several trails to Chirripó peak. The ascent generally takes two days. The usual route is through **El Termómetro** (The Thermometer), a climb where the visitor measures if he has what it takes to continue; then up cliffs and across valleys and plains to **Valle de los Crestones**, where shelters are available, with wood stoves and basic washing facilities.

With an early start on the second day, a climber can beat the clouds to the peak of Chirripó, four kilometers distant. Those who make it to the top are rewarded with views not only of two oceans, but of the chain of mountain and volcanic peaks marching to the northwest toward San José, and valleys and lakes along the way. An alternate way down, on the third day, is by way of **Sabana de los Leones**, with its concentration of birds and cold streams.

Before going to the park, verify current conditions and bus schedules with the National Park Service at the zoo in San José, or call [2]334070. February, March and April are the best months for a visit, with the least rainfall. December and January are also relatively dry, but colder. Water, warm clothing, and hiking boots are requisites — this is not a park for casual drop-ins. Horses are available to assist hikers with their gear.

ARRIVALS AND DEPARTURES
By Bus or Car

Access to Chirripó Park is via bus at 5 a.m. or 2 p.m. from San Isidro to the village of San Gerardo de Rivas, where park headquarters are located, or by four-wheel-drive vehicle through San Gerardo de Rivas to the park entrance, which is 15 kilometers from San Isidro.

WHERE TO STAY

Accommodations in San Gerardo are available at the *cabinas* of the **ELIZONDO FAMILY** (public phone [7]710433, extension 106), with private bathrooms, and meals can be prepared.

NEARBY SIGHTS

South of San Isidro are coffee plantations, and at lower altitudes, great rolling spreads of pineapple. To the northeast looms the ridge of the Talamanca range, hardly inhabited, and set aside as a reserve.

LA AMISTAD INTERNATIONAL PARK

La Amistad International Park stretches onward into Panama — an expression of hope for the future, since there is a certain amount of tension along the border. With the establishment of this huge park, adjacent to Chirripó, Costa Rica doubled its protected lands. Most of La Amistad remains unexplored, and there are hardly any services for visitors.

The **Helechales** (Fern) section of the park is reached through Buenos Aires and Potrero Grande, east of San Isidro de El General. The **Escuadra** section is north of San Vito de Java. Inquire about current conditions at the park service in San José, which will provide current bus schedules from San Isidro.

WHERE TO STAY

One lodge with access to the park, **LA AMISTAD** (6 rooms, $$74 single or double), in Las Tablas, has a three-day package for $425 that includes food and transportation from San José. Currently there are ten rooms, which will expand to 60 in the future. Call 77[3]3193 for information, or [2]338228 in San José, or 407-274-402 in Delray Beach, Florida, or write to P. O. Box 774-1000 San José.

ON FROM LA AMISTAD

After traversing the General Valley, the Inter-American Highway follows the canyon of the Río Grande de Térraba, through dry country, sparsely settled. This stretch is subject to rock slides. Be cautious if you're driving. A branch road follows the Coto Brus river toward San Vito (see page 417), passing branch roads that lead to some sections of La Amistad Park. Visitor facilities are limited.

At kilometer 97 (from San Isidro) is the junction for **Boruca**, eight kilometers to the northwest, populated by indigenous peoples whose ancestors were relocated, under Spanish orders, from the slopes of the Talamanca range. A mission was set up here in 1626. One of the most notable Boruca activities was their practice of birth control, through means unknown to outsiders. The traditional fiesta of the Borucas, is celebrated on February 8. Another celebration, los negritos ("little blacks") takes place on December 8, when men in blackface dance in honor of the Virgin Mary.

Farther along, where the road turns into the dripping hot lowlands, is **Palmar Norte** (260 kilometers from San José, 130 kilometers from San Isidro), a characterless highway town. Across the bridge and to the south is the more languid and pleasant half of the settlement, **Palmar Sur** (South Palmar). Here you'll espy an old coal-burning locomotive from banana days parked on a siding, a children's slide and jungle gym, and several odd stone spheres, up to the height of a small man, that hold places of honor in the shaded main square and at various points in town. These are *las bolas grandes*, the nearly perfectly spherical stone balls, ranging up to 2.5 meters in diameter, found on banana lands in the nearby Diquis Valley.

Among the mysteries of the bolas: they are made of granite, but there is no naturally occurring granite nearby; it is harder to carve larger spheres accurately, yet the larger ones are more perfect than smaller ones; few stone balls are nearly equal in size, which indicates that a template was probably not used in their manufacture; no datable artifacts have been discovered with the stone balls, which makes analysis and interpretation difficult. One suggestion is that the balls were used as burial-ground markers, but there is little credible evidence to support this idea. Stone balls from the area may be seen as well as at the national museum and in Carrillo Park in San José.

Tree Farms

South of Palmar, along the main highway, and in much of this region, you'll note neat stands of deciduous trees in all stages of growth. These are on former banana and pasture lands, leased by Stone Consolidated, the forestry and paper conglomerate (locally known as *"Ston"*). The *gmelina arborea* species can be harvested for its pulp in as little as six years, and while the trees are growing, the infrastructure is being prepared to cut and ship the wood. The long-term effects of this monoculture are yet to be seen.

ARRIVALS AND DEPARTURES

By Air

A **Sansa** airlines (tel. [2]335330) flight from San José lands at Palmar Sur three days a week in the morning and continues to Golfito. **Travelair** (tel. [2]327883) has a daily flight, fare $100 round trip.

By Bus

Buses on the Golfito and Panama runs pass through several times a day. Palmar Sur is a transfer point for visitors heading to the lodges around Drake Bay (see below). Embarkation is at a dock on the Sierpe River, about 15 kilometers south of town.

WHERE TO STAY

CABINAS TICO ALEMÁN, tel. [7]756232, next to the gas station in Palmar Norte, provide basic rooms at about $10 per person. **HOTEL CASA AMARILLA**, tel. [7]756251, by the soccer field, has cheaper rooms.

DRAKE BAY AND THE OSA PENINSULA

The Osa Peninsula, south of the Diquis Valley, is a wild and fabled area where a rough-and-ready breed of solitary prospectors until a few years ago panned the streams and tunneled the hills for gold. These men from many countries stayed in the wild for months, crossing paths with monkeys, snakes and mountain lions, and, more recently, teams of workers for large mining companies, equipped with heavy machinery.

Much of the peninsula remains virtually trackless and uninhabited, which, of course, is the attraction for visitors of a naturalist bent.

The peninsula is becoming a field of conflict between old-style businessmen and developers who seek to exploit the peninsula's treasures, on the one hand; and public and private missions to preserve and enhance Costa Rica's natural treasures.

Gold panners have been tossed out of the area that now includes **Corcovado National Park**. Public and private efforts encourage tree planting and sustainable agriculture.

Eco-entrepreneurs, disappointed with the rollout of tourism in pristine areas elsewhere in Costa Rica, have created lodges and a tent camp to bring visitors into the heart of the rain forest, while preserving it and even encouraging pasture and tilled fields to return to their natural state.

Ranged on the other side are investors in wood-pulp-processing plants, the effluent of which will obscure Osa's spectacular sunsets, and large-scale resorts with familiar brand names, currently in the planning and construction stages.

ARRIVALS AND DEPARTURES FOR OSA

By Car or Bus

An unpaved road heads to the northeast (*Golfo Dulce*) side of the Osa Peninsula, from a point on the Pan American highway 155 kilometers from San Isidro, terminating at Puerto Jiménez, 77 kilometers onward. Buses from San Isidro de El General follow this route.

By Boat

On the northwest face of the peninsula, the main area with facilities for visitors is Drake Bay, which can be reached by boat.

In between lies Corcovado National Park. Puerto Jiménez is the usual starting point for park visits, but hikers set out from the Drake Bay side as well.

By the Sierpe River

For most modern travellers, the route to Drake Bay is along the Sierpe River, winding southwest from the banana plantations and cattle pastures of the Diquis Valley, is the route to Drake Bay, lazy, wide, bordered by steaming forested hills, fern-laden trees, mangroves, and mud flats. The waters are tidal (mangrove roots dangle in the air when the tide is out), a house pokes out of the canopy here and there. But mostly, when you come down this way, there are only you, your fellow passengers, and the birds.

The river is greeted with a line of breakers at its mouth and rocks obstruct the passage to the south; but the channel has shifted to a more gentle routing than in years past, and the powerful craft used to ferry passengers to Drake Bay traverse without incident. If you hire a boat on your own, avoid small skiffs with 15-horsepower motors, and verify that the operator has experience in making the trip.

Sierpe, the town, is a river port at the end of the 16-kilometer unpaved road from Palmar Sur and its airstrip.

WHERE TO STAY IN OSA

Overnight lodging is available at the unexpectedly substantial riverside **HOTEL EL PARGO** ($17 double downstairs with fan, $23 double upstairs with air conditioning). Rooms are comfortable, with a single and double bed and mini-refrigerator. The hotel has a snack bar and its own dock. Elsewhere in town are a pizza parlor and bar. To contact anyone in Sierpe for reservations or any other reason, call the public phone, [7]758111, and leave a message in English with Sonia.

For mangrove tours and to arrange diving and fishing (if you're not staying downriver), ask for Chino at Pandón de Sierpe, under the tin open-sided shed.

Riverside Lodging
RÍO SIERPE LODGE, P. O. Box 818-1200 Pavas, tel. [2]201712, fax [2]323321. 11 rooms. About $65 per person per day including meals and transport from Palmar Sur. Diving packages from $140 per day including equipment, meals, transport from San José; fishing and naturalist packages also available. The riverfront Río Sierpe Lodge is a base for naturalists, fishermen and divers. The oldest tourist facility in the area, it was taken over a couple of years ago by outgoing American entrepreneur Mike Stiles.

The atmosphere is that of a venerable fishing camp, with a long, thatch-rooted dock to receive passengers, cement-floors, bamboo-sided central dining and gathering area lined with bookshelves, and basic rooms, either attached to the main building or in outbuildings. The lodge is isolated from any village or entertainments other than what is on-site. Power comes from a generator, or marine batteries.

Birding in the vicinity of the lodge is excellent; fruit trees and transplanted forest species also attract anteaters, agoutis, coatis and tepezcuintles; and an air boat takes visitors to the best vantage points. All the avian species of lowland southwestern Costa Rica can be sighted. A trip to Violín island, just north of the river mouth, is included in stays of a few days, for sightings of birds, mammals and marine life; though there's no telling what you'll see while chatting on the dock: crocodiles come by to visit, and manta rays and sea turtles flow upriver with the tides.

The only compressor in the area is at the lodge, and diving trips are offered to **Isla del Caño** (about $55 per person) and other points. Fishing in the river is usually good for snook, machaca, snapper, grouper and roosterfish. Offshore and out to sea are wahoo, marlin, dorado and tuna. Diving and ocean trips run on a 46-foot yacht. Also near the lodge are ancient burial grounds where ancient pottery has been unearthed.

Pickup points (arranged when reserving in San José) can be Quepos, Dominical, the river port of Sierpe, or the Palmar Sur airstrip.

Drake Bay
The northwest side of the Osa largely escapes the Pacific breakers that crash broadside against the exposed southeast face of the peninsula; the calmer waters and river estuaries here have attracted excursionists ranging from modern cruise passengers back in time to Sir Francis Drake, who left his name (locally pronounced as DRA-keh), and perhaps some treasure, at a wide, sheltered crescent where the River Agujitas empties into the sea. Spanish pieces of eight are said to wash up with some frequency, but modern visitors are usually more oriented toward natural treasures: sea turtles nest on the beach in June and July, whales can be spotted offshore in December, and dolphins sport throughout the year.

There is a wide stretch of tidal beach right before the village of Agujitas; beyond the bay, to the south, the forest grows to the high tide mark.

ARRIVALS AND DEPARTURES FOR DRAKE BAY

By Boat

One of the factors that keeps Drake Bay relatively unspoiled is that it's difficult to reach. There is no public transportation, and you can get in and out most easily with the cooperation of one of the hotels. Usually, this means booking a stay of a few days. But you can also call one of the hotels, or its contact in San José, to arrange a rendezvous with a boat that is already scheduled to bring in guests. Hotel owners cooperate on transportation matters, so you should find who's going on your first call. All personnel can talk to you in English.

By Air to Palmar Sur

Some hotels include transfer from the Palmar Sur airstrip in their rates, some add it on, and some change their policy from season to season. Verify the situation when you book. Alternative transport may be available by boat from other points than Sierpe. Air taxis can also be arranged.

WHERE TO STAY IN DRAKE BAY

A cluster of four hotels is situated at the mouth of the Agujitas River, within a few minutes' walk of each other, variously on a hilltop, a hillside, or at beach level; more basic accommodation can be found in the village.

Most lodging places rely on a generator for electricity. The lights go off when the bar closes; candles are lit if you're up any later.

LA PALOMA LODGE, P. O. Box 97-4005, San Antonio de Belén, Heredia, tel. and fax [2]39054, [2]392801 (radio to lodge). 5 rooms and 3 ranchos (cottage units). $63 per person with meals, $80 for confirmed space in ranchos. $30 for round-trip transfer from Sierpe. La Paloma occupies a seaside hilltop with some of the best vantage points in the area. Rooms are in several informally constructed buildings spread out over the lawns and under palms and native trees that have been left in place. Basic guest rooms in a row building are wood-panelled, with a screened clerestory in the high ceiling to catch the breeze. Each room has a sea-view hammock on a common porch with dividers. Furnishings are limited.

The best units are the ranchos, large, screened, cliff-edge cottages with balconies and hammocks, as well as a sleeping loft. These sleep four persons comfortably. The center of activity is the large, thatch-roofed, open-sided pavilion, with dining tables, porches, easy chairs, low conversation tables, and books and magazines. A new chef is reported to have won approval of guests.

In addition to diving and snorkelling arrange┊
sea kayaks. Access to La Paloma is by steps up from a┊
River. A pretty, shaded beach of volcanic stone is a s┊

EL COCALITO, P. O. Box 63, Palmar Norte, tel┊
([2]224103 in San José, tel. 519-782-4592 in Canada┊
person with meals. This lodge is down at the next cove┊
on a well-shaded plot. Four of the units, built of rough pl┊ ample
screened openings, are at beach level, the others are above the homey
restaurant, which is at the rear of the property and affords a view out over
the gardens and seaward. The latter have bunks, bamboo dividers and
chests, and cheery fabrics — overall, the impression is of a treehouse.

DRAKE BAY WILDERNESS CAMP, P. O. Box 98-8150, Palmar
Norte, tel. and fax [7]712436. 19 units, including 12 cabins with private
bath. $69 per person with meals, $48 in tents, children half price. No
credit cards. Most established of the Drake Bay lodges, Wilderness Camp
occupies a park-like, rolling setting on the point between the Río Agujitas
and the sea, overlooking volcanic outcrops and a rocky beach. The name
is something of a misnomer — there's no roughing it here, and the
informal dining room, with thatch roof over tin, has the only hotel-class
kitchen in the area.

Individual cabins, well spaced among the fruit trees on the property,
are built of wood and concrete block, with generous screening and
overhead fans. Most have a sea view. Tent units on platforms have real
beds and electric lamps. A separate bar pavilion offers sea views with your
drinks. Air tanks are kept ready on site for divers. The folks here are proud
of making most things themselves, from the fresh bread and desserts to
the concrete benches.

North of the River

EL CABALLITO DEL MAR, tel. and fax [2]315028. 7 units. $86 per
person with meals ($112 with single supplement). U.S. address: Box
025216, Dept. 8, Miami, FL 33102-5216. It's a bit of a climb up the hillside
to the attractive panelled and stucco individual guest units here, each with
high-peaked thatched roof, varnished wooden floors, shower with designer tiles, and plentcous sea breezes. The unusual architecture continues in an octagonal bar structure. El Caballito offers more privacy than
its neighbors.

In Agujitas

LOS JINETES DE OSA, up the beach from El Caballito del Mar, is an
unpretentious house with four rooms with bunk beds to rent. Bath
facilities are shared. The $25 daily rate includes three meals. The owner,
Pedro, who moved down from the capital some years ago, is a resource

. information. Call [2]536909 in San José to reserve a space here. ι can also arrange to share a boat out from Sierpe at $15 or so per person, minimum four passengers.

ALBERGUE CECILIA is farther on at beach level. $20 gets a bed and three meals. Cecilia also has horses available for rent (which can get you across the peninsula to the road to Puerto Jiménez), and a hillside saloon with commanding views. To reserve at Cecilia's (or to contact anyone else without a number), call [7]712336, the number of the public phone in Agujitas.

SEEING THE SIGHTS

To cross the Río Agujitas from Wilderness Camp, La Paloma and El Cocalito, follow the path upriver a few meters, to a suspension cable bridge, three planks wide, that swings and bounces as you cross. Pause midway, your back toward the sea, and look upstream, to the boulders in the riverbed, to the ferny and feathery vegetation arching overhead, shafts of light shooting down to green eddy pools. Listen to the background roars of howler monkeys in afternoon bitching matches, and you will be as close to Tarzan country as you can be anywhere these days. Now turn and look to sailboats anchored in the green lagoon, and magically, you are in Polynesia.

Beyond the bridge and up the bay is the native area of **Agujitas**, not a concentrated settlement, but a collection of wooden country houses scattered along a deeper curve of tidal beach than is to be found elsewhere on this stretch of coast, and back on the succession of furry ridges. Pastures border the bay, and streams inch into the tidal flats. The hills are spotted with occasional clearings, and weed-like wet-forest growth.

The health center looks like a shack out of a western movie. A one-room schoolhouse bears the grand name Centro Educativo Drake. One little *pulpería*, fronted by gardens, has the public phone. There are, in all, perhaps a dozen houses of concrete block, a soccer field, and cows wandering onto the beach; and except for the masters of the cows, there are usually no people in sight.

Except on a Saturday night, that is, when country people turn up from lonely farms in the interior of the peninsula, stop and cook over open fires, spend an evening at the saloon, and then, at midnight, decamp for a trip of several hours over horse trails to their beds.

No vehicle roads lead to Drake Bay, and no cars yet have been delivered aboard boats; nor are there trucks, or tractors pulling stumps or tilling fields. What doesn't move by boat moves on horseback, and the gait of the townspeople is bowlegged and straight out of the saddle. It is possible to rent a horse and poke around the interior of the peninsula, and even to get to the other side, and the road that leads to Puerto

Jiménez; though if you are inexperienced or out of pr
better to explore the trails on foot. You can even hike
trail that follows the Sierpe River from opposite the t
excursion that takes a couple of days, usually with an ov
schoolhouse along the way; though such local fauna as
and snakes (mainly in the rainy season) could impede your passage.

SPORTS AND RECREATION

Aside from reading and relaxing and getting away from it all, and sunbathing, and swimming in the sea and the Agujitas River, most hotels offer horseback riding ($50-$55 for the day), snorkeling trips at San Josecito and other beaches to the south, excursions to Caño Island ($40-$55 per person with snorkeling, $90 to $110 with scuba diving, including equipment), and to Corcovado National Park. A day of deep-sea fishing for marlin, sails and dorado runs about $250 to $300.

SOUTH OF DRAKE BAY

Beyond the hotels at Drake Bay, to the south, runs a trail that sometimes follows the beach, sometimes climbs inland through second growth and primary forest, skirting rock outcroppings, passing through rain forest greenery on a path that is occasionally challenging, mostly just pleasant, and certainly less frequented than certain stretches of trail in nearby Corcovado National Park. Houses and other constructions are appearing on this shore. At low tide, the trail may be ignored in favor of the route over the sand, and through streams that gurgle out of the forest.

About two kilometers south of Drake Bay is a recently opened tent camp for use by sport fishermen. For information, contact **Sportfishing Costa Rica** (P.O. Box 115-1150 La Uruca, tel. [2]201115 in San José, 77[0]0505 in Quepos).

MARENCO "BIOLOGICAL STATION" (tel. [2]211594, fax [2]551340, book through travel agents), just north of Corcovado National Park, is a hilltop lodge about ten minutes by boat or an hour on foot from Drake Bay, with its own airstrip and boat dock, and extensive swath of Osa landscape that includes coastal swamp, beach, and trails. Individual wood-panelled rooms are up a cliff from the sea. Attractive furnishings include leather rocking chairs. Semi-private balconies afford views to rolling lawns and formidable gardens of native trees and exotica. Larger bungalow units are on stilts.

A resident biologist accompanies guests on rain-forest walks on trails on the lodge's own reserve, and through Corcovado National Park and to the nearby Claro River. Package rates range upward from $200 per person per day, less if you arrive on your own.

Farther from the park, north of the Térraba River and directly west

.umar Norte, accommodations are available at **LAS VENTANAS DE** .SA, a cliff-top, rain-forest lodge and wildlife refuge at the northwest edge of the Peninsula, named for the "windows" formed by waves beating against seaside cliffs. Facilities are limited, but include a swimming pool, and space for 14 in rooms with ceiling fans in several hacienda-style buildings. Meals are catered by a chef from San José. The package price of about $1000 per person (plus a one-time lifetime club membership fee of $500) includes air transport from San José, five nights of lodging, meals, guided birding and beach trips, and laundry. For information, contact Natural History Tours, P. O. Box 1089, Lake Helen, Florida 32744, tel. 904-228-3356, fax 904-228-0181.

CAÑO ISLAND

Caño Island (Isla del Caño), 20 kilometers off the Osa Peninsula, was once used as a burial ground by coastal tribes. Numerous artifacts have been found, most notably small stone spheres. The variety of materials used in other objects suggests that long-distance maritime trade flourished before the Spaniards arrived. Sir Francis Drake is said to have buried treasure on the island, but no finds have been acknowledged.

Measuring about a mile by two miles, Caño appears from a distance like a head with a butch haircut. The mixed hardwood forest is mostly edged by cliffs that plunge several hundred feet into the water on the periphery. Numerous creeks run out to this edge, and these might have led to the name of the island ("creek," or "spring"). Over the years, the island has been farmed from time to time, and some locals claim that it was once used by employees of the United Fruit Company as a place to throw wild parties.

Caño Island, with its high forest, is now a biological reserve though plant variety is somewhat more limited than on the mainland.

SEEING THE SIGHTS

Caño Island is a popular destination for day trips offered by all the hotels and lodges at Drake Bay and around the Osa Peninsula. **No overnight facilities are available.** Most visits center on the small beach at the ranger station. There is no dock, but rock jetties protect the anchorage. A day fee of about a dollar is collected. Offshore there are spots of coral, but the main attractions are the schools of fish — snapper, grouper, catfish and smaller species — wafting back and forth with the tides. Farther out are eels and, most unusually, schools of as many as 500 octopi. Boulders offshore are a hazard to snorkelers who don't look where they're going. The seabed off the island is a marine reserve, but beyond the protected area, fishing for sails is excellent.

Ashore, a trail leads up from the ranger station and almost circles the island, with branches leading to a lighthouse, a *mirador* (lookout point) a falls, and a spot where *bolas*, or stone spheres, were discovered. Along the way are the abandoned pits of treasure hunters. Most of the stone spheres and golden artifacts have long since been removed. Though sightings of birds and mammals are sure to be fewer than in Corcovado National Park on the mainland nearby, the less daring among us will find a certain allure in this particular tropical forest. There are no packs of peccaries, and the resident snakes are non-poisonous.

CORCOVADO NATIONAL PARK

Corcovado National Park, in the southern part of Osa, includes vast stretches of the only virgin lowland rain forest in Central America. Among the natural treasures of Corcovado are trees of 500 species (including one kapok, or silk-cotton, that is said to be the largest tree in Costa Rica); numerous endangered mammals, among them cougars, jaguars, ocelots, margays, jaguarundis and brocket deer; eagles and macaws; assorted monkeys; snakes; tapirs; and peccaries, which may be the most destructive and dangerous species in the park. Vegetation zones range from mountain rain forest down to beach, and fresh-water and mangrove swamps. At **La Llorona**, a river empties in a waterfall directly into the ocean.

SEEING THE SIGHTS

You don't just drop into Corcovado. With its remote location, Corcovado attracts mainly scientific researchers, and visitors on all-inclusive packages with boats, buses and oxcarts organized beforehand. There are extensive trails along the beach and in the forested interior, however, as well as campsites. You can do Corcovado on your own if you're prepared with camping equipment, rain protection, high boots, snakebite kit, food, water containers and purification means, and repellent against the sandflies that infest the beaches. For walking along the beaches and up the beds of rivers, old sneakers, rafting sandals or surf shoes will come in handy.

The starting point for independent visits is usually the Corcovado Park office in Puerto Jiménez (see page 400), which you can reach by bus from San Isidro de El General or Villa Neily, or ferry or light plane from Golfito. If you give a routing, you can arrange for camping space and meals at the ranger stations along the way.

Check with the park service in San José before any visit to Corcovado, or at least with the park office in Puerto Jiménez (tel. [7]785036). Allow for contretemps — chartered planes that don't show up to airlift you out, never-ending downpours, bogged-down buses, etc.

396 COSTA RICA GUIDE

Admission to the park costs about $2. Meals are currently available at ranger stations at $4 for breakfast, $6 for lunch or dinner; though there is no guarantee that vittles will be available if you just drop in. Advise park headquarters in Puerto Jiménez of your scheduled whereabouts, when possible.

The **La Leona** sector of the park is entered from Carate (see below), where Corcovado Lodge Tent Camp is located. Camping space and meals are available at the ranger station, situated just above the beach, where a stream marks the park boundary. There is regular foot traffic through here, as the walk along the beach through the park can be the easiest and safest route.

There are no sheltered bays along this stretch of coast, and the breakers are often over ten feet high. Sharks frequent the waters off the entire face of the peninsula (in case you doubt it, look at the skulls that decorate lodges and the general store in Carate). Swimming should be ruled out, except for a wade near shore. Sharks also swim into the rivers of Corcovado when the water is over a meter deep.

Ridges of high jungle run parallel to the beach of pebbles and black sand, split from each other by meandering rivers. Birding is excellent from any vantage point along the beach, (viewing along interior trails in the park may be limited by the close foliage and lack of windows). The **Madrigal River**, about two kilometers from La Leona station, is marked by a boulder beach, where broad waves crash against the gentle curve of coast.

Some hikers take a diversion up the Madrigal River, walking in the mostly shallow riverbed. The water is clear, with boulders and gravel underfoot. Trees canopy the stream, trailing vines into the water. Orange butterflies and kingfishers appear from the cliffs to either side. Park guards recommend that hikers go only as far as the first deep pools. Beyond them are treacherous rapids and rock walls (tough to scale in a cloudburst), and, sometimes, illicit gold panners, who might not take kindly to tourists.

Beyond the Madrigal River to the northwest, rocky islets offshore mark a continuation of ridges and headlands, and jungle cliffs march up the coast in succession.

Carate, about a kilometer past the eastern edge of Corcovado Park, is a *pulpería* (general store), a dirt landing strip, and a rusting sluice that remains from the days when gold panning was legal. This is the end of the dirt road around the edge of Osa from Puerto Jiménez, and some camper vehicles make it this far and use the beach as a base for exploring the park.

If you're coming out of the park here, you can currently find a ride on Mondays, Wednesdays and Saturdays at 11 a.m. in a car operated by **Transportes Carate-Jiménez**. From Puerto Jiménez, departures are at 7:30 a.m. on the same days.

Hiking Trails

There are two major trails through Corcovado Park.

The first trail runs from the **Carate** and **La Leona** ranger station at the eastern end of the park, along the beaches and through bordering cliffs to San Pedrillo at the western end. Carate (see below) may be reached by three-times weekly bus or on foot from Puerto Jiménez, or by chartered small plane.

Drake Bay, 50 kilometers from Carate, is the logical terminus of this route, though you can take a detour up the Madrigal River, or take the second major trail inland. Allow two days to hike through the park along the coast from Carate. Unless you're informed of current tides, you'll wait at river mouths until the waters are low and you can wade across.

Another trail runs roughly north-south from the **Los Patos** ranger station to the beach at La Sirena station.

To hike this trail from the north, take an outbound bus from Puerto Jiménez toward San José or Villa Neily and get off at La Palma. Estimated walking time is about four hours to Los Patos, and another four hours or more to La Sirena. It's about a day's hike along the beach from there to La Leona station, and a day's hike back to Puerto Jiménez (or you can wait for the three-times-weekly transport).

CORCOVADO PARK TIPS

Walkers regularly transit the park on their own, and most make it through without incident. This doesn't mean that a solo trip is absolutely safe. Do you know what to do if you encounter a group of peccaries? Are they more dangerous if they're moving or if they're stationary and feeding? Are you equipped to deal with snake bites? How about sharks in rivers? You are probably okay if you stick to the beach, but a walk through the interior of the park is best attempted with a qualified guide.

WHERE TO STAY IN CARATE

CORCOVADO LODGE TENT CAMP. Reservations: **Costa Rica Expeditions**, P.O. Box 6941, San José, tel. [2]570766, fax [2]571665. Package rate from $225 with air travel from San José and meals, one night's lodging. Additional nights $50 single/$80 double with meals. A more formal lodge will eventually be built on the site of Corcovado Lodge Tent Camp, but I don't think it could ever come close to the sense of adventure and romance of the current facility.

This is modern adventure tourism. Guests walk from the Carate airstrip, while luggage and Cokes and beer are transported on a donkey cart with pneumatic tires, led by a teenaged, nature-boy native guide in muscle shirt, shorts and mud boots, who is as much a part of the scenery as the green cliffs overhead, where scarlet macaws flit in and out of the palms and a huge wild fig engages in life-and-death struggle with a strangler fig — except that the *arriero* maintains contact with base via the VHF radio strapped to his waist. A major mishap in this neck of the country is a collision of the donkey cart with a rock, sending a case of beer over the side, to pop and foam into the sand.

The custom-built tents at Corcovado Lodge, screened and with rain flaps, are erected close to each other on a ledge about fifteen feet above the beach. Each is on a platform at sitting height above an individual porch, oriented toward the beach and sunset, and no furniture is provided other than two beds of foam on boards and sapling legs. In front, hammocks are set in the palms. The surf roars below into the night, fades as if turned down, then pounds again. Electrical lighting is limited; the sun plummets after 6 p.m., and reappears at about 5:45 a.m.

Set, plentiful meals are served in a hillside dining pavilion, and there are a couple of toilet-shower houses on the way up. Behind the lodge, a trail leads up the hillside. Spottings may include scarlet macaws, spider monkeys, and the tiny green poison-arrow frog, among others.

Horseback excursions are available from Corcovado Lodge at an extra charge. Several excursions into the park are recommended, but most packages do not include any guided walks or hikes.

Do You Want to Take This Boat?

The *Guacamaya*, a pontoon boat designed to take visitors from Corcovado Lodge beyond the huge beach breakers without capsizing, and onward to Caño Island, has no straps to keep passengers from slamming into the deck, no protection from the sun, and no shelter from lashing salt spray.

No amount of warning can prepare passengers for the ride up a ten-foot swell and the body-crunching flat slam into the first dip. As the lodge itself notes, the *Guacamaya* is not for everyone. Less eventful excursions to Caño Island are available from safe anchorages in Drake Bay.

PUERTO JIMÉNEZ

The main settlement on the Osa Peninsula, Puerto Jiménez lies across the Golfo Dulce (Sweet Gulf) from Golfito.

Jiménez has a rough-and-tumble heritage, from the days when varmints from around the world passed through on their way to pan for gold in the interior. As one old hand describes the denizens of those not-so-old days, "First they undressed you as you got off the boat, then they figured how much money you had, then they figured out whether it was worth robbing you by the time you got to the end of the street."

Nowadays, things are more settled, and Puerto Jiménez is to be

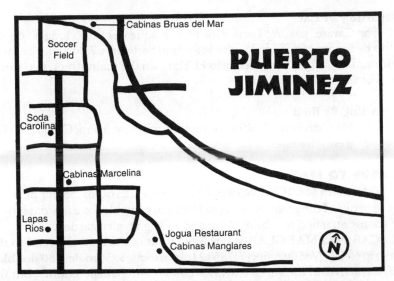

appreciated for the access it affords to Corcovado National Park, for its bay setting, under palms, by small boats and peaceful waters, and for morning views of the misty ridges marching back beyond the Golfo Dulce.

ARRIVALS AND DEPARTURES

Arriving By Bus

Buses leave San Isidro de El General for Puerto Jiménez at 5:30 a.m. and noon. From Ciudad Neily (to the south, near Panama), buses leave for Jiménez at 7 a.m. and 2 p.m. These buses will pick up passengers at points along the way.

Arriving By Boat

From Golfito, across the water, there is scheduled boat service to Puerto Jiménez (about $3) most mornings at 11:30 a.m., Sundays at 9:30 a.m. Call [7]750472 for the latest schedule.

Arriving By Air

Aeronaves de Costa Rica tel. [7]750278, intermittently runs a scheduled air service, or you can hire a small plane for the trip whenever you're ready to go.

Departing By Bus

Buses leave Jiménez for San Isidro at 3 a.m. and 11 a.m.; for Ciudad Neily, passing the junction for Golfito, at 5 a.m. and 2 p.m.

All outbound buses La Palma, from where you can walk to and through Corcovado National Park.

Departing By Car

For Carate, passing Lapa Ríos and Bosque del Cabo lodges, departures by car are Mondays, Wednesdays and Saturdays 7:30 a.m. For more information, ask at Mini Mercado El Tigre on the main street, two stores up from Soda La Carolina.

Departing By Boat

The boat leaves for Golfito, across the water, at 5 a.m. Call [7]750472 for the latest schedule.

WHERE TO STAY

CABINAS MARCELINAS (tel. [7]785007, 12 rooms, $5 per person), on a corner of the main street, is perfectly acceptable for a few days, rows of rooms attached to a bungalow, and facing an airy garden.

CABINAS MANGLAR, a few blocks out of town on the road to the airstrip (tel. [7]785002, fax [7]785121, 10 rooms, $25 single, $30 double), has attractive on the surface, with archways and panelled doors, but the rooms are plain, with fan only, and hard beds. The plantings on the grounds attract birds, and there is a bar and restaurant on site.

CABINAS BRISAS DEL MAR (tel. [7]785012, 10 units, $6 per person) is a pink building diagonally across the soccer field from the center of town, with a row of modest rooms (with bath and fan) looking right out to sea. You can swim outside your room, and the dock whence the ferry departs for Golfito is in view a block away.

For the cheapest lodging, you can apply labor in a tree nursery toward your room rent at DORMITORIO COCKLEDOODLEDOO.

WHERE TO EAT

For food, LA CAROLINA, open to the street, is the hangout of preference for the moment, with casado, fish, and meat plates for $4 or less, and sandwiches. The JOGUA restaurant has a Cantonese menu, as well as Tico fried chicken. Various bars and dance halls go in and out of fashion. Heck, it's a frontier town.

PRACTICAL INFORMATION

Caeta, a flying service at the airstrip, can drop you at Carate or Sirena, for access to Corcovado National Park, or at Drake Bay, and considering the roads and roundabout routes, it's not a bad idea to get together and book a plane.

And horses, a viable alternative in these parts, are available for hire at various points around town.

Before visiting Corcovado National Park, check in at the Parques Nacionales (National Parks) office, tel. [7]785036.

Corcovado Tours (tel. [7]785002, fax [7]785121), based at Cabinas Manglar, arranges trips through the park, as well as horseback riding, boat trips in the gulf, visits to the Guaymí Indian reserve, and even gold panning.

SOUTH OF PUERTO JIMÉNEZ

The lush, rolling landscape south of Puerto Jiménez is cattle country, sprinkled with surviving and second-growth forest, ponds where ducks and geese putter about, and plots of fast-growing pulp trees where cleared and burned off forest produced luxuriant pasture and abundant crops only until the ashes and humus were exhausted and the hard clay below had nothing more to yield. The bumpy road south fords assorted rivers and streams; bridges are being installed, in some cases by the U.S. Army Corps of Engineers, and National Guard units. The farms and pastures soon diminish in numbers and extent, for there are only limited accessible markets.

Behind the tranquility rages a struggle, repeated in other parts of Costa Rica, over the fate of the land. Unsuited for farming without expensive and perhaps unsustainable chemical inputs, it can be divided and subdivided into plots that have to be farmed ever more intensively, at lower and lower yield, as the native cover retreats and finally disappears — a Haitian scenario. Or it can be encouraged to return to forest, as livelihoods are made through alternative means, including tourism, and the selective harvesting of plant and wood and animal products, while eons-old biological patterns are maintained.

WHERE TO STAY SOUTH OF PUERTO JIMÉNEZ

LAPA RÍOS, P. O. Box 100, Puerto Jiménez, tel. [7]785130. 14 bungalows. $115 per person with meals and transfers. In the jungle near the southern tip of the Osa Peninsula, atop a hill that commands the vicinity, a thatched roof of epic proportions marks Lapa Ríos, the most luxurious tropical-forest lodge in Costa Rica.

Within rises another remarkable structure, a great interior treehouse, its several platforms, attained by a handcrafted cantilevered circular staircase, affording vistas through breaches in the thatch to dense forest stands, cliffs, beaches, and Punta Banco on the far side of the gulf. Below, awed diners converse in whispers, over the finest cuisine in a remote area, and perhaps some of the best anywhere outside San José.

All this, and much more, is Lapa Ríos, a personal dream — and devil — of John and Karen Lewis. Both ex-Peace Corps volunteers, they have given it all up and bet the bank on regenerating several hundred hectares of rain forest, with which the hotel is legally and permanently intertwined.

Guest units at Lapa Ríos — each a suite — have huge view decks, thatched roofs, screens and bamboo shades, and private garden with shower. One has a ramp for disabled accessibility. They are built on several parts of the property, some close to the sea, some high up, all within hearing and viewing range of squirrel monkeys, toucans, and the macaws that lend their name to the resort. The pool is cleaned by an ion filter, rather than chlorine.

Beyond the magnificence and comfort of the site, with its trails through forests to falls, natural pools and beaches, there are tours in and around the peninsula on offer, along with boat trips to Caño Island.

Transport to the lodge is arranged when booking.

BOSQUE DEL CABO WILDERNESS LODGE, 6 cottages. $80 single/$120 double with meals. Reserve through Costa Rican Trails, P. O. Box 2907-1000, San José, tel. [2]224547, fax [2]213011. In Puerto Jiménez, inquire at Mini Mercado El Tigre. Bosque del Cabo is a comfortable lodge *in* the wilderness, near Cape Matapalo, 1.5 kilometers off the track that twists and meanders around the Osa Peninsula. Ample bungalows set on the cliff edge beyond manicured lawns and gardens offer stunning views to window rocks and deserted beaches. Varnished local woods are used entirely in construction and panelling. There are louvers on all sides, an outdoor shower in a private garden, more than sufficient shelving, mosquito netting over the beds, sapling posts to support the porches. One cottage is divided for use by families. Dining is in a central open thatched-roof structure, and, befitting the Italian-Costa Rican heritage of the lady of the manor, includes home-made pasta.

Activities here include hikes, including one to a falls with three pools; a walk down to the beach, birding, and horseback riding (about $20); though this is a superb site for reading, meditating, and being left alone.

Much of the lodge property is regenerating forest, with some plantings by the owners, Phil and Barbara Spiers. They are also making practical arrangements to stop the smuggling of fledgling macaws out of the peninsula.

ISLA DEL COCO (COCOS ISLAND)

The world's largest uninhabited island, **Cocos** covers 24 square kilometers 500 kilometers southwest of the Costa Rican mainland. Abundant rainfall (there are hundreds of falls, some visible from seaward), wild pigs, goats, and, of course, coconuts, made Cocos a watering and provisioning outpost for ships in the colonial period. During the independence upheavals in Spanish America, the aristocracy of Peru entrusted its treasures to Captain James Thompson, who absconded and reputedly buried his loot on Cocos Island. Treasure-seekers have periodically sought the cache, but all deny success (at least publicly).

Cocos Island is now a national park and is the home of three species of bird — the Cocos Island finch, the Cocos Island cuckoo, and Ridgeway's papamoscas — found nowhere else, as well as the chupapiedra (rock-sucker), a fish with a sucking disk that allows it to ascend waterfalls.

But biodiversity is relatively limited on Cocos. What mostly draws visitors these days is the teeming life along the underwater reefs around the island. Sharks are especially abundant. Cocos Island is an increasingly popular destination for diving boats. Cliff-bordered and of volcanic origin, Cocos provides only two anchorages for ships, at Chatham Bay and Wafer Bay, with a steep muddy trail between the two. Otherwise, riverbeds are the main pathways to the interior.

ARRIVALS AND DEPARTURES
By Boat or Float Plane

Sorry, folks, you can't just catch the scheduled boat! Contact a diving service (see page 409 and Chapter 8, "Scuba Diving") to arrange a trip to Cocos on a live-aboard dive boat. Or call **Coco Island Airways** (tel. [2]324373) in San José to inquire about a day trip out on a float plane.

GOLFITO AREA

GOLFITO

Golfito, on the *Golfo Dulce* (Sweet Gulf), is the last major town in the south, an old banana port surrounded by lands that receive abundant rainfall all year.

Just a few blocks wide, Golfito stretches for several kilometers in a strip along the water, at the foot of the green, rain-forested ridge that encloses the peaceful inlet (*golfito*, or "little gulf") that gives the town its name. Past the lively, ramshackle central area is a neighborhood of uniform clapboard houses and former banana company installations on tree-shaded lawns, now used for governmental and university offices.

The plug was pulled on Golfito in 1985, when United Fruit abandoned its banana operations in the face of labor unrest and rising taxes. Tourism and a sport fishing industry are slowly developing in the surrounding area. There are attractive beaches and jungle coves a short boat commute from the port. Surfing down the gulf is legendary. But Golfito itself remains an acquired taste.

ARRIVALS AND DEPARTURES
Arriving By Bus

Tracopa company, tel. [2]237685, operates buses at least three times daily to Golfito (currently at 7 a.m., 11 a.m. and 3 p.m.) from Avenida 18, Calles 2/4, San José. The trip takes about nine hours. Other buses pass Río Claro junction on the Pan American Highway, 188 kilometers from San Isidro.

Arriving By Air

Sansa airlines (tel. [2]335330) flights to Golfito operate from San José once or twice daily, six days a week. The fare is about $55 round trip, and inexpensive packages with hotel room are sometimes available. **Travelair** (tel. [2]327883, [7]750210 in Golfito, near the airport) has a daily flight, fare $114 round trip.

Departing By Boat

Currently, there is scheduled boat service from the downtown dock to Puerto Jiménez (about $3, one hour) most mornings at 11:30 a.m., Sundays at 9:30 a.m. Return boats leave from Puerto Jiménez at 5 a.m. Call [7]750472 for the latest schedule. Scheduled service to Zancudo (see below) and Pavones is ephemeral.

Taxi boats leave for various destinations from the municipal dock downtown, and from a beach about a kilometer to the north, near the old railroad station and opposite the tourist office. **Sanbar Marina** also has taxi rates, some of them higher, some lower than those of town operators. One operator whose services I've used is José "Chepe" Atencio, whose boat the *Zodiac* lands at the city dock. Fare to Zancudo is about $25 each way for a safe load of up to four passengers. A run across the water to Playa Cacao costs about $2. Or check at Luis Brenes' restaurant for somebody already headed your way who will take you for less. Be prepared to take your shoes off to cross the tidal mud when you embark.

Departing By Bus

The **Tracopa** company runs at least three daily buses to San José. Buses depart from the old railroad station twelve times a day for Paso Canoas on the border of Panama, picking up passengers on the way through town, starting at 5:30 a.m.

Departing By Air

Sansa airlines operates flights to San José once or twice daily, six days a week. Sansa's office in Golfito is downtown, opposite El Uno hotel and eatery. **Travelair** (tel. [7]750210 in Golfito, near the airport) has a daily flight to San José. **Aero Costa Sol** (tel. [7]750607, by the airport) and **Aeronaves** (tel. [7]720278) operate air taxi services that will get you over to the Osa Peninsula in a few minutes.

WHERE TO STAY

One hangover from its days as a rough-and-tumble banana port is that in the recent past, most of the hotels in Golfito were dives, where a couple could disport at an hourly rate. With government projects under way to diversify the local economy and attract visitors, dozens of new lodging places have opened. Most of them are *still* dives. There are a few exceptions, but take a good look at your room before you drop your luggage.

The best rooms in Golfito will be found at either extreme of town: the south end, where the highway enters; or the north end, by the airport. If you're looking for a cheap room, head to the north end, toward the free port, rather than downtown. Just continue past where the bus makes its last stop. Once you settle in anywhere, you can go back and forth easily enough on the single local bus route (fare 20¢) that runs from one end of town to the other, passing by or near every hotel and restaurant.

If you don't want to stay in Golfito, you can head right out to Playa Cacao, a few minutes' ride across the bay; or to one of the beaches down the bay, or to one of the attractive and secluded lodging places to the north, such as Punta Encanto.

South End

HOTEL LAS GAVIOTAS, at Playa Tortuga, P. O. Box 12-8201, tel. [7]750062, fax [7]750544. 14 units. $30 double with fan, $40 with air conditioning. A hotel and yacht club at the best location in Golfito, where the entry road winds down to the water. Rooms are simple, attractive, high-ceilinged, with red tile floors, tiled vanities and showers, fans, and large front porches facing the water. Larger units have cooking facilities. The lovely palm-shaded compound, with pool, looks out to small boats anchored in Golfito's beautiful bay, closed almost entirely by hills. The price is quite low for what you get.

Despite the name, Playa Tortuga (Turtle Beach) is no beach, just a sidewalk.

HOTEL EL GRAN CEIBO, tel. [7]750403, 8 rooms. $20 double, $30 triple. A basic motel, but rooms have high ceilings, and the location is better than downtown, especially if you have a car.

Downtown (Pueblo Civil)

There is nothing — nothing! — to attract you to any of the downtown hotels, except for location near a couple of inexpensive restaurants, and the boat for Puerto Jiménez. All of the following are easily found within a few blocks of each other at the center of town.

The **HOTEL GOLFITO**, on the bay side of the main street (12 rooms, $10 single/$15 double), has bare rooms, but a couple at the end of the building catch the sea breeze. You have to pay a deposit for a towel.

The **COSTA RICA SURF** (P.O. Box 7, tel. [7]750034) rents cubicles for $5 per person, or $14 double with toilet. **EL UNO**, next to the boat dock, is a $2 dive, and serves Chinese food in the bar downstairs.

CASA DE HUÉSPEDES EL TUCÁN (tel. [7]750553) is newer than other establishments, but the bare rooms are still airless. The **DELFINA**, tel. [7]750043, just south of the town center, has clean cubicles for $5 to $15 double, and even a couple of rooms with air-conditioning, for about $25 double.

North End (Pueblo Americano)

Many of the stately and attractive banana company houses at the north end of Golfito have been cut up into guest rooms. Some are as airless as anything downtown, others have some redeeming value. If you're wandering around this area in search of a room, do not judge a lodging place by its exterior. There are also a couple of newer establishments built from the ground up.

HOTEL DEL CERRO, P. O. Box 52, tel. [7]750006, fax [7]750551. 20 rooms. $12 to $15 single/$16 to $20 double. On the way to the railroad station from the center of town, upstairs, opposite the port dock. The cheaper rooms have no windows, others get some breeze.

In the American Zone, you'll find these lodging places, most of them the rough equivalent of old-style "tourist rooms" that you used to find in private homes in American family resort areas.

CABINAS MARLIN (tel. [7]750191) has tiny rooms at about $5 per person, but it's on one of the first streets in the American Zone, with trees, and sure looks good if you've just come from downtown. Nearby with similar rates is **CASA DE HUÉSPEDES FELICIA**. Another block up and two blocks in is **CABINAS ADILIO**, with lower rates.

CABINAS PRINCESA DEL GOLFO (tel. [7]750243, $12 single/$14 double), in a bungalow with pleasant gardens, has five plain concrete rooms with private bath, and represents a good value. **CABINAS EL MANGLAR** and **CABINAS CASA BLANCA** (tel. [7]750124) are more guest rooms at $5, the latter in an attractive white clapboard house with grassy grounds. There are several comparable places along the streets here.

HOTEL COSTA SUR, tel. [7]750087, fax [7]750832. 24 rooms. $24 single or double with fan to $60 for five with air conditioning. This is another older house, with a new concrete section wrapping around. Nice touches on the outside include red tile walkways, but the newer rooms are plain and have minimal furnishings. Four rooms in the original house have high ceilings. The restaurant serves casados, chops and fish. Parking available.

HOTEL SIERRA, P. O. Box 37, tel. [7]750666, fax [7]750087 (or P. O. Box 5304-1000 San José, tel. [2]339693, fax [2]339715). 72 rooms. $60 single/$83 double/$12 per extra person. Credit cards. The Sierra is *the* hotel in Golfito, a tan-and-orange concrete-and-steel structure that resembles a bottling plant on the outside and a multi-level high-tech industrial treehouse in the lobby and dining areas. Beyond, it is pleasant enough; two of its three wings border the two pools.

Rooms are up to international resort standards, with pastel tile floors and bedspreads, quiet air-conditioning units, television, fan, telephone, and attractive large bathrooms. Wooden walkways fly between the upper floors of the various wings, caimans inhabit the ponds, and thirst is slaked at a thatch-roofed bar. Mountain bikes are available for rent. Restaurant main courses run about $8 to $11.

WHERE TO EAT

THE SANBAR MARINA's dining barge, moored at Sanbar Marina about a kilometer south of the town center, is a welcome addition to Golfito. Freshly painted metal surfaces are draped with fishing nets, and views are to the sailboats anchored around the harbor (or the game on TV). The fare is informal, ranging from fish and chips to assorted fishburgers and other sandwiches, with most items well under $5. This is also a good drinking spot. If you don't find the barge, it's probably out on charter for a private party. Try again.

Downtown, the **PEQUEÑO RESTAURANTE DE LUIS BRENES**, the place with the yellow awning, is a popular gathering spot. Hang around for a while, and you'll pick up all the current information about Golfito, and meet anyone who's anyone, locally. Also, the food is safe and good, strictly Costa Rican fare: complete meals with casado for as little as $3, inexpensive sandwiches, and breakfast for a couple of dollars. Mr. Brenes speaks English, and is patient and helpful.

Down the street, **POLLO FRITO RANCHERO** serves fried chicken on a terrace in a fast-food ambience, with breeze.

SAMOA DEL SUR (tel. [7]750233, fax [7]750573) is a restaurant/ bar/entertainment complex with a French and continental menu. The specialties are paella and Samoa fish, a seafood mixed grill and lobster armoricaine, all in the $20 range and enough for two; or you can have anything from steak au poivre or sirloin maitre d'hotel ($7) down to hamburgers and sandwiches for $2 to $3. This is one of the few places in the provinces where presentation of food is attractive. Dine under a huge thatched umbrella roof, open to the sea breeze and decorated with plants. What could be nicer?

The second-floor restaurant of the Costa Rica Surf hotel, **EL BALCÓN**, has pizza, and there are assorted Chinese eateries. The open-air dining area of the **HOTEL LAS GAVIOTAS**, with its aquarium, has the best view to the bay and its gentle waves, and the food is excellent for the price. Most fish courses, attractively served, are under $6, chicken and steak cost slightly more, a full breakfast about $4.

At the old railroad station toward the north end of town, the

MARISCOS DEL SUR eatery has shrimp and fish plates for $3 to $6 — the shrimp is a bargain for Costa Rica.

Farther on, in the American Zone, you'll find some of the more pleasant eating and drinking spots. The **ALAMEDAS** restaurant, cool and shady, in and around and under a white house, is decorated with plants, trellises, and wrought-iron fixtures. The menu offerings are standard fish, chicken cacciatore, hamburgers and club sandwiches, at $4 or less. **LA CAZUELITA** is a clean spot with standard Tico fare for $4 and less, and a good place to hang out over a beer or two or three.

Along the road into Golfito from the Pan American Highway, the **RÍO DE JANEIRO**, a steak and spaghetti house, and the open-air **RANCHO GRANDE**, are accessible by car or taxi.

NIGHTLIFE

And there are lots of bars in Golfito, lots of bars. **Eurekita** . . . **Palenque Los Bruncas** . . . The **Club Latino Disco** just after the old railroad station . . . The list goes on.

SEEING THE SIGHTS

With the exit of the banana business, Golfito settled in to a continuing economic depression. But, run-down as much of it is (and was, even in the boom days) it never lost the cheeriness of tropical seaside places.

The infrastructure from the old days — bank branches, roads, railroad, a harbor — has turned Golfito into the land of the future in lower Pacific Costa Rica. Entrepreneurs have started up fishing camps, and hotels, and, in a very few cases, non-conventional commerce.

But the biggest move in Golfito's recent history has been its designation as a non-quite-duty-free port, where Ticos can purchase imported goods at lower prices than in San José, provided they spend the night.

This marriage of convenience between shoppers and accommodations implies as much mutual pleasure as exists in nuptials concocted for immigration purposes. Standards are inverted. Beauty and youth fetch neither attention nor business, implying as they do a tariff that might divert resources from purchases. But that old crone of a hotel turns heads, as long as it issues a receipt for customs officers.

The warehouse-shopping center is at the far edge of town from the entry side. Visitors from abroad will not find this section interesting, except for observing such local customs as standing in line.

It is not that downtown Golfito is without attractive aspects. The cemetery, opposite War Eagle Marina, has the nicest tangled seaside landscaping, and a rusting gazebo at its center. And just south of the center of town, along the water, is an unexpectedly charming and attractive little neighborhood, with a cared-for church, spacious lawns of scruffy grass, new houses under construction, and a siding with a steam locomotive and coal car to take you back to the old days; all of which is part of a movie set.

Back in the real city, sidewalks terminate with no warning at the precipice of drainage ditches. Watch your step.

Above Golfito, an arc of wooded hills comprises the **Golfito National Wildlife Refuge**, protecting the town watershed. Facilities are limited, but hiking is feasible in the least rainy period, from January through March. Orchids and endangered tropical hardwoods are present, along with a variety of birds, most evident during rainy periods. Access is by a road that zigzags up the cliff from the soccer field, on the way between the Gaviotas hotel and downtown.

What Golfito lacks, among other things, is a decent beach, though there is a small, non-maintained swimming area near the Samoa del Sur complex. But beaches aplenty there are out of town, for swimmers and surfers.

PRACTICAL INFORMATION

For official information, the tourist office is in the **Wachong Building**, which is opposite the sea just south of the old railroad station. Hours are 8:30 a.m. to 4 p.m. Monday through Friday, tel. [7]750006. They're helpful.

For unofficial information, sit quietly at the **Pequeño Restaurante** downtown and keep your ears open.

Another gathering point is the second-floor **El Balcón Restaurant** of the Costa Rica Surf Hotel. American Legion Post 12 meets here the first Tuesday of every month at 10:30 a.m., and, informally, members hold a continuous session.

SPORTS AND RECREATION

Fishing and Diving

Several marinas cater to sport fishermen and can sometimes arrange diving.

Sanbar Marina, tel. [7]750874, on the way into town, books trips to Caño Island, Cocos Island and to Panama on the *Phoenix* and on smaller boats. They claim to have excellent food. The *Phoenix* has a crew of six for six guests. Rates start at $400 per person per day, for a package that includes air transport from San José. They can also fix you up for beach parties, jet boating, and water skiing. For reservations in the U.S., contact PanAngling Travel, tel. 312-263-0328, fax 312-263-5246. Or phone 800-435-3239 direct to Costa Rica.

Nearer to town is **War Eagle Marina**, tel. [7]750838 or 885083 (or VHF16/11), tel. 714-632-5285 fax 632-1027 in Texas, has a 53-foot

Hatteras available for day charters at over $1000 a poke, and shorter craft going for as little as $350 per day.

Golfito Sportfishing, P. O. Box 73, Golfito, tel. [7]750353, fax [7]750373, is based at Zancudo across the bay, and advertises offshore fishing at $350 to $550 per day, depending on the boat. Multi-day packages with transportation from San José are available.

Golfito Sailfish Rancho, a resort devoted entirely to sportfishing, is a couple of bays north of Golfito.

Fishing and other trips, and riding horses, can also be booked through Mr. Ron Kalman, who has an office opposite the Costa Rica Surf Hotel (P. O. Box 44, tel. [7]750449, fax [7]750373).

According to Golfito Sailfish Rancho, local fishing is best for sailfish from mid-November to mid-May; black marlin and blue marlin from mid-May to mid-October; dorado from mid-November to mid-February; yellowfin tuna from mid-May to mid-October; wahoo, all year; roosterfish, mid-May through mid-November; and Pacific dog-tooth snapper from January through April.

NEAR GOLFITO

Many visitors come to Golfito in order to leave right away, for fishing trips, or to surf at beaches along the Golfo Dulce to the southeast. The latter are reached by chartered boat, or buses over poor roads.

Across the water from Golfito is **Puntarenitas** (Little Puntarenas) island, where boats can anchor and allow passengers to hike or stop for refreshments.

PLAYA CACAO

You can espy **Playa Cacao** (Cacao Beach) if you look out from downtown Golfito across the bay, past the long pier, to a stretch of sand littered with wrecks nestled in a corner of the bay under a sweep of hill; and you can reach it in minutes by a $2 boat taxi from downtown or from near the old railroad station. (A road also runs from the free zone out through the garbage dump and around a mountain, a distance of about seven kilometers.)

Playa Cacao is popular as a day beach and drinking spot for Golfiteños. The breeze is constant, and the water is calm, and cleaner for swimming than right in Golfito, with a hefty average tide of eight feet.

WHERE TO STAY

A couple of places offer accommodations in a more pleasant setting than Golfito's.

At the end of town toward open water, you'll find **CENTRO TURÍSTICO PLAYA CACAO**, a Tico-style beach place under the palms with bar, and rooms with bath for about $15 double. Toward town a bit is Captain Tom's untidy estate, where his tin-roofed charming dive of a shipwreck, now known as the **HOTEL BARCO QUEBRADO**, remains where it was beached several decades ago. Patched in bamboo, sitting on a rock foundation, it has a couple of rooms available, without indoor plumbing, for about $5 per person. If you don't stay here, you can still chat with one-legged Captain Tom in his open-air museum of clutter, under a tin roof hung with snakeskins, plants and carved birds, surrounded by rusting marine gear.

CABINAS PALMAS (P. O. Box 98, Golfito, tel. [7]750357, fax [7]750373) is the accommodation of choice at Playa Cacao, a collection of six whitewashed octagonal cottages with thatched roofs, on shaded, grassy grounds. Eccentrically rustic, they have tile floors and baths, awning windows framed in saplings, mosquito netting, built-in planters, all kinds of nooks and shelves, curtains as room dividers, and from two to five beds. The rate is just $35 double. Call to reserve, and hurry over by taxi boat once you get to Golfito.

Mr. and Mrs. Staley, the owners (an American and a Tica), don't offer regular meals at the moment (a restaurant is being built); they arrange a picnic from time to time, and three of the units have cooking facilities. They also provide fast boat service to Zancudo and other locations on the gulf, and have a collection of pottery unearthed during construction.

North of Golfito

PUNTA ENCANTO, P. O. Box 28, Golfito, tel. [7]750220, fax [7]750373. Six rooms. $99 single/$130 double with three meals. Transfer from Golfito included with three-day stay. In the U.S., call 800-543-0397. Punta Encanto is at San Josecito beach, in a cove about seven kilometers north of Golfito, and several worlds away. There are no roads and no settlements in sight. The all-wood two-story building is set back from the sea past a shallow bowl of lawn and trees, decorated with steel sculptures of a praying mantis and dragon, an ideal situation for watching the sunset behind the hazy ridges of the Osa Peninsula, progressing by the minute from umber to gold to blue, ending in crimson bands before splashdown.

Distinguishing points of Punta Encanto include detailings, and the complete furnishings of the rooms in an attractive country manner (many lodges in the area have a bare, just-finished air); and the personal attention of the owners, Jackie and Dick Knowles, or of their managers, Graham and Margarita (the latter an excellent cook). There's also a large barbecue at the beach, which is sandy in some parts, rocky and pebbly in others. Long operated as a low key fishing lodge, Punta Encanto is now open to all. Fishing can be arranged, and there are coral spots nearby for snorkeling, dolphin watching from the shore in the morning, and canoe trips, horses and jungle walks available.

Also in this area is **Casa Orquídea**, a private botanical garden with dozens of species of fruit trees, palms, heliconias, and orchids. Open Sunday through Thursday from 7 to 10 a.m. The owners collect a fee of $5 from visitors. Local boat operators can take you over. One guest cabin is available for long-term use.

Up the coast in the next bay, at Playa Cativo, is **RAINBOW ADVENTURES**, with just a few lodge rooms, a canopy-level penthouse, and cottages, going for up to about $130 double, including meals, beer, and laundry service. To stay here, you have to buttonhole the manager when he comes in to Luis Brenes' restaurant in Golfito most mornings; otherwise, try calling 503-690-7750 in Portland, Oregon.

CABINAS CAÑA BLANCA (fax 750373, P. O. Box 34, Golfito) has just two very private, ocean-view guest units with refrigerators and cooktops, at $70 a day double, minimum stay three days. Bring your own groceries. Coastal and river tours are available.

PALM TREE-LINED BEACH

And slightly closer to Golfito is:

GOLFITO SAILFISH RANCHO, 10 rooms. From $300 per day of fishing. San José address: P.O. Box 5712, tel. [2]357766. U.S. reservations: P. O. Box 290190, San Antonio, TX 78280, tel. 800-531-7232 or 512-377-0451, fax 377-0454. This fishing operation, north of Golfito, is owned by the same people as Parismina Tarpon Rancho, and the policies are similar: open bar, meals and laundry included in the package.

Sailfish Ranch is a substantial resort as well, with soaring tile roofs, ceilings and beams of precious hardwoods, concrete walls, stone-paved paths, sea-view terraces, extensive gardens, and a jungle hillside as a backdrop. A stay here can be combined with Parismina Tarpon Rancho for two-ocean fishing.

ZANCUDO

Think of **Zancudo** as a tropic isle. A beach village south of Golfito, Zancudo can be reached overland if you have a sturdy vehicle and no schedule, or if the bus is running on the day you go. But most of the connections are by water.

"Zancudo" (san-KU-do) is the Spanish word for a particularly vexatious mosquito; though you will usually not be bothered if there is any kind of breeze. The settlement sprawls along five kilometers or so of beach, and at most of the lodging places, you'll see sand, breakers, mangrove, coconut palms, and maybe another building down the way a bit, if at all. Surfers have come here for years, and now there is just enough in the way of amenities to make Zancudo the right place for anyone who requires a beach without Big Tourism.

ARRIVALS AND DEPARTURES

Arriving By Bus or Taxi

A bus sometimes leaves for Zancudo and Pavones from Golfito daily at 2 p.m. Check first if it's going all the way or will terminate ten kilometers from the beaches. A taxi costs about $50.

Arriving By Car and Ferry

If you're driving to Playa Zancudo from Golfito, take the road back toward the Pan American Highway, then turn right onto the unpaved road about halfway along, at the El Rodeo saloon. About 18 kilometers from the junction is a flat-bottom jungle cable ferry over the Coto River (great photo opportunity). Operating hours are from 5 a.m. to 8 p.m., the fare under $2. Beyond the ferry, the road is unpaved, and in parts is best negotiated with four-wheel-drive and high clearance, or not at all. Take every right turn through the jungle and scrub farms, and you'll get to Zancudo in under two hours when conditions are good.

Arriving By Boat

To reach Zancudo by boat (or to arrange fishing), inquire at the docks or Luis Brenes' restaurant in Golfito. Since Zancudo sprawls for several kilometers along the gulf, and traffic is sparse, you should tell your boat driver where you want to land: at the center of the village, or farther south along the beach near Cabinas Los Cocos or the Hotel Sol y Mar.

At low tide, passenger boats swing out into the open waters of the gulf, past deserted beaches, run past rain forest and cliffs that reach to the water's edge, and circle around sand bars at the mouth of the Coto Colorado River to the beach. At high tide, a shorter routing is available via "La Trocha," the old banana-shipping canals that cut through the peninsula opposite Golfito. This is a more reassuring route, given the surf that breaks on Zancudo beach and the meagerness of some of the craft, across an emerald estuary, through mangrove-lined waters, past sitting pelicans, fishing herons, soaring gulls, trees arching overhead, and mangroves rising as high as trees in a North American forest, sending new branches like skeletal hands down toward the water.

Departing By Boat

From the village, you can often get aboard a return boat for Golfito at the dock on the inland side; or ask for Mauricio nearby at the general store with the sign for a public phone, or at your hotel.

WHERE TO STAY AND WHERE TO EAT

From south to north, the accommodations and facilities at Zancudo are these:

Four kilometers from Zancudo Point and the Coto Colorado River are various accommodations operated by Rainer Kremer, who speaks in a patois of German, English and Spanish, never stands still, and appears to have stepped out of the movie *"Fitzcarraldo."* His informal **TRANQUILO RESTAURANT**, ever expanding, sits across the road from the beach, amid pens of turtles and ducks, facing a private mangrove jungle. Expect to find the unexpected: chicken in walnut sauce, garlic fish, Linzensuppe, at $5 to $10 for a meal. Upstairs is **FIN DEL MUNDO**, four guest rooms mit verandah und hammock, about to be enveloped by strangler figs, at $10 per person.

Down the beach are **CABINAS LA VISTA**, unpainted two-room beach houses on stilts with railings of varnished mangrove, available for about $10 per person nightly. A hammock tower out front allows for serene observation. Rainer and partner Duncan also have horses for rent at about $8 per hour, and claim that surfing out front is the best at Zancudo.

HOTEL SOL Y MAR (P. O. Box 88, Golfito), tel. [7]750353, has four designer units in the palms, geodesic domes with tin roofs. Owners are Bob and Monika Hara, who speak English and German. The restaurant here serves Tico and American food—eggs, sandwiches, steamed vegetable, chef's salad — at $4 per item or less.

CABINAS LOS COCOS, run by long-time beach resident Susan

England and Andrew Robertson, has two cheery doll-house clapboard cottages (another architectural story, being relocated United Fruit Company houses), in an informal tropical garden with friendly parrots. Each unit has a refrigerator and stove, mosquito netting over the beds, and decks with table and chairs, and can sleep three, at $30 per day. The owners also have a silkscreen printing operation, and arrange boat excursions to the orchid gardens and to other beaches. They can be reached through the phone at the Hotel Sol y Mar, which is about 100 meters away.

North of Cabinas Los Cocos, the two kilometers to the point are slightly more densely built. The Hotel-Restaurant-Bar **PITIER**, also known as **FROYLAN'S**, tel. [7]773006, is a Tico family-style compound. $10 per person gets a room with fan and private bathroom. Nearby, **EL COQUITO** is a similar place with a big thatch-roofed bar, subject to weekend invasions of loud music. Plain family-size rooms with bath and fan go for about $15 each.

Past this point are the buildings that make up the center of the village: a two-room schoolhouse, and a couple of general stores (*pulperías*) with basic supplies. A dive shop is scheduled to be installed here.

Roy's **LOS ALMENDROS** (P. O. Box 41, Golfito, 10 rooms, $15 single/$25 double, tel. [7]750515) is a neat, fishing-camp kind of establishment, of substantial, cement-board, motel-style rooms facing seaward on palm-shaded lawns. Each has a bath and overhead fans. Meals and beverages are served to residents and walk-ins. You can also rent a 22-foot fishing boat at $250 for the day, with radio, sonar, meals and the rest.

Zancudo Pacific Charters, down the road, tel. [7]885083, will also be in operation soon with a fishing service. Call before entering.

CABINAS RÍO MAR, down near the point, consists of an old yellow-painted railroad work car, and a set of six plain railroad-style guest units with bath and fan. About $8 per person, and more basic than other places.

MOVING SOUTH

Pavones, south of Zancudo, is still mainly a surfers' beach, rocky in parts, with basic rooms available, and the perfect wave. The surrounding area has seen disputes between landowners and squatters (*precaristas*), at times violent. **PAVONES SURF LODGE** (P. O. Box 778-1000 San José, tel 222224, fax [2]222271), caters to surfers, and offers riding horses and boat trips.

Farther on is **TISKITA LODGE** ($93 single/$133 double with meals), six cottages on a fruit farm at Punta Banco, at the entrance to the Golfo Dulce. Birding is said to be excellent both in the lodge area and on trails through undisturbed rain forest, and English-language descriptions of marine and forest life in the area are provided. Reserve through a travel agent or call [2]553418 in San José.

CASA PUNTA BANCO is a private home about a kilometer from Tiskita, also within picking range of exotic fruits, and boating range of some of the most renowned surfing in the world. There are all of six bedrooms and a total of ten beds. The owners have put together booklets on tide pools on the property, the lowland rain forest, and the surrounding area of Costa Rica. Weekly rent is $700 double, $50 per additional person, and servants are available. For information, contact Deborah Jean or Joe DeLoach, **Continental Associates**, 202 W. Fifth Ave., Royal Oak, MI 48067, tel. 313-545-8900, fax 313-545-0536; or call Warren Gallo in Golfito (P. O. Box 5) at [7]750666, fax [7]75-0087.

CIUDAD NEILY

Ciudad Neily is a substantial town just off the Pan American Highway, 17 kilometers before the border. A few hotels here, such as the **MUSUCO**, $10 per person, will give you shelter for the night if you're headed onward.

ARRIVALS AND DEPARTURES
By Bus

Buses for San Vito de Java, in the mountains above Neily, leave from the terminal by the market at 6 and 11 a.m., and 1 and 3 p.m. Only the 1 p.m. bus passes the Wilson Botanical Garden. Many buses go to Golfito and to the border of Panama, and there are departures for Puerto Jiménez in the Osa Peninsula at 7 a.m. and 2 p.m.

ASCENDING FROM NEILY

From Ciudad Neily, a poor branch road, currently being reconstructed, ascends on a zig-zag route into the coastal mountain range, affording magnificent downward views along the way, and weekend fishing opportunities in gurgling streams for residents of the hot country. Above the first steep grades, the hills are planted to coffee, and on the slopes toward Panama, pasture for cattle. The landscape and climate are much like those of the Central Valley near San José, but farming units are neither large estates nor smallholdings, and many a family farm has that emblem of the rural middle-class, a Japanese pickup truck, parked in the front yard.

If you drive this way, or go by bus, consider taking the detour through **Cañas Gordas**, a little-visited border outpost.

SAN VITO DE JAVA

San Vito is a hilltop town, with the charm of streets that wind to a peak at its center, rather than running foursquare over flat terrain, and every turning reveals a new view of mountains and mist and pasture in the surroundings. The spring-like climate and mostly uncultivated fertile soil of the time attracted Italian immigrants after the Second World War, and in turn, native Costa Ricans were drawn to this new pole of development. The Dante Alighieri Cultural Center maintains the old ties.

Most of the faces in San Vito are obviously Costa Rican. But there are fair-skinned, fair-haired persons in any knot that gathers on the square. Their word of leave-taking is "*ciao*" when they take leave of each other. And some of the swept-up hair styles reminiscent of the Andrews Sisters, formal shoes with high heels, and ruffled dresses, could transport one to a prosperous hill town in Italy 40 years ago. But then a barefoot Indian woman in long skirt passes by, in town from Panama to shop and sell, and you remember where you are.

Aside from the Wilson Botanical Garden nearby (see below), the major attraction to visitors and potential residents is the relatively cool climate. After you've sat and chatted with the locals on the square, take a walk down to the Parque Ecológico, the "eco-park" on the way to the Tracopa bus stop, where trails lead across bridges and glades and down the hollows, and various species are labeled.

ARRIVALS AND DEPARTURES
By Bus
Buses for San Vito leave from Calle 14, Avenidas 5/7, San José, at 6:15, 8:15 and 11 a.m. and 2:45 p.m. These follow the direct route up the valley of the Coto Brus River.

By Car
By car, the easiest approach is via a road that follows the Coto Brus River, branching from the Interamerican Highway 90 kilometers east of San Isidro de El General.

WHERE TO STAY AND WHERE TO EAT
HOTEL EL CEIBO (tel. 77[3]3025, reservations at [2]551280) has 30 rooms, for $9 to $12 single/$16 to $24 double, and, while surroundings are plain, the water is hot and the ample grounds sloping down from the town square give the impression of a mountain resort.

There's no reason to look elsewhere, but a couple of blocks from the square on the Sabalito road are the bare concrete HOTEL PITIER and the basic CABINAS LAS MIRLAS, the latter with parking. Various other cheap hotels near the center of town are frontier centers were migrants from the Central Valley might plant themselves for a few nights.

Dining is a pleasant surprise in San Vito. The huge dining room of the

HOTEL EL CEIBO, with skylight and archways and checked tablecloths and fireplace, offers lasagne, scallopine and filet mignon, each for $4 or less, and a selection of wines. High chairs are available.

PIZZERÍA MAMMA MIA, a half block up from the square, has pizza, to be sure, from plain to super, but much more: scallopine, saltimbocca and various salads for $4 or less, and a pleasant environment with posters of Italy on the walls. The saltimbocca is made with Kraft cheese, but it's better than expected in the provinces, and the restaurant is always crowded, for good reason.

THE WILSON BOTANICAL GARDEN

The **Wilson Botanical Garden** is six kilometers south of San Vito de Java. Now owned by the Organization for Tropical Studies, which also operates La Selva and several other research stations in Costa Rica, the garden was started by Robert Wilson in 1962, with the purchase of the Las Cruces plantation.

The gardens are largely used for research and teaching; and to preserve threatened species for future reforestation programs; but visitors with an interest in natural history are welcome. Among the riches are about 2,000 plant species, 80 mammalian species, 200 bird species, and 3,000 kinds of moths and butterflies.

ARRIVALS AND DEPARTURES
By Bus

Tracopa buses depart from a station one block from the square on the Sabalito road, four times a day for San José (first bus 5 a.m., last bus 3 p.m.). The run takes six hours. Buses leave for San Isidro de El General, three hours away, at 6:30 a.m. and 1:30 p.m. Buses depart from San Vito's square for Ciudad Neily at 5:30 a.m., 11 a.m., 2 p.m., the last bus passing the Wilson Botanical Garden.

SEEING THE SIGHTS

Eight hectares of the 140-hectare site are planted gardens, and most of the rest is premontane rain forest. These make for a more manageable introduction to the flora of Costa Rica than is possible in a huge national park, though there are also exotic species from other continents that make for interesting comparisons. Views of the surrounding countryside from the garden — pasture and secondary and primary forest, and wisps and layers of cloud — are more rewarding than if you're hurrying through by road.

Ten interconnecting trails each emphasize a different characteristic plant type, such as heliconias, bromeliads, ferns, orchids, conifers, and bamboos. Estimated walking times range from a half-hour to three hours on each. An alternative routing, marked by yellow posts, takes in sections of the various trails and is probably gives the best overview for a non-specialist. A couple of hours on it should be enough for most visitors.

The entry fee to the garden is about $3, and descriptive booklets emphasizing trees, plants or the garden in general are available for another $3 each. The booklet describing the self-guided tour, in English, is well worth acquiring. Hours are 8 a.m. to 4 p.m. From San Vito, only one bus a day passes the garden, but you can take a taxi, or walk. It's mostly downhill.

Overnight accommodations and meals can also be arranged for about $60 to $80 per person. To reserve and confirm rates, contact the **Organization for Tropical Studies** (P. O. Box 676, 2050 San Pedro, tel. [2]406696, fax [2]406783; or P. O. Box DM, Durham, NC 27706 U.S.A., tel. 919-684-5774). The direct phone number at the Wilson Garden is 77[3]3278.

PASO CANOAS

Paso Canoas, 347 kilometers from San José, is the town on the border with Panama. Stores do a flourishing business with cross-border shoppers, but accommodations in the area are limited. A **Sansa** airlines flight (tel. [2]335330) operates from San José to Coto 47, not far away, six days a week. **Tracopa**, Avenida 18, Calles 2/4, San José, tel. [2]237685, has four buses a day to the border, and other companies have service rights to Panama City (see page 129).

18. AROUND THE VOLCANOES, OR ALL OF COSTA RICA IN ONE DAY

INTRODUCTION

North of San José, over and beyond the volcanoes Irazú and Poás, is an area that includes gently rolling pastured hillsides often shrouded in fog; high montane tropical forest barely touched by human settlement and exploitation; hot springs gurgling up from the interior of the earth; jungle dripping with heat and wet; homesteads hacked out of the forest by modern pioneers; and banana lands that have been cultivated for more than 100 years. All this is within just 60 kilometers of San José in a straight line.

But until recently, mountains, rivers, jungle, and traditional trade routes that ran elsewhere, kept most of this triangle off the beaten track for visitors and Costa Ricans alike. Now, with the completion of a few strategic stretches of highway, it's possible to make a circular trip through this varied area in a matter of hours, even by bus. But for the lack of beaches, it's almost like seeing all of Costa Rica, and every era of its development, in just one day.

The route described below takes you clockwise from San José. But this is just one possible itinerary. You can spin off from San Carlos toward the northwest, past the sparking volcano Arenal, and down to the Pacific coastal lowlands; take a shortcut northward over the saddle between Poás and Irazú volcanoes; or continue to Limón and the Caribbean instead of returning to your starting point.

By bus or car from San José, head to the west, along the Cañas and Soto expressways, in the direction of Puntarenas. The old Pan American Highway, parallel to the newer road, passes through the towns of Alajuela,

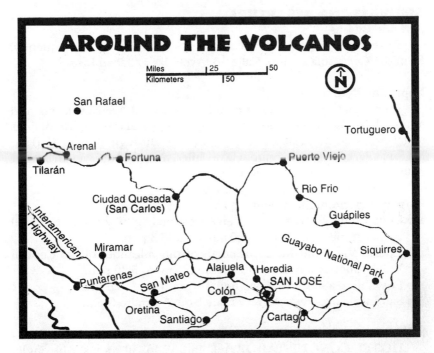

Grecia and Sarchí (see pages 217-218). At Naranjo, a sinuous branch road turns northward, up and out of the Central Valley, across the relatively low stretch of hills between the Tilarán and Central volcanic mountain ranges.

ZARCERO

Two-and-a-half hours from San José by bus, **Zarcero** has yet another of the Central Valley's cottage-style churches, with red tin roof and two six-sided bell towers. The main square is adorned with hedges trimmed into fanciful shapes of animals, curiosities that you can see from the bus as you pass through.

SAN CARLOS

About 48 kilometers north of Naranjo, and 95 kilometers from San José, is **Ciudad Quesada**, which most Costa Ricans call **San Carlos**, a bustling trading center for the surrounding prosperous area of meat and dairy production. San Carlos in itself does not count as a tourist attraction. But it's on the way to everywhere, and getting here, on a winding road through fog-shrouded, pastured hills, is a scenic meander. From the attractive, treed main square, you can see the countryside on most sides.

ARRIVALS AND DEPARTURES
Arriving By Bus
Buses for Zarcero and San Carlos leave hourly, or more frequently, from the Coca-Cola station, Calle 16, Avenidas 1/3, San José.

Departing By Bus
From San Carlos, you can go on by bus toward Arenal volcano, and around Lake Arenal; deep into the low-lying tropical forest north of Poás and Irazú volcanoes, and back to San José through Braulio Carrillo National Park; or even to remote Los Chiles, near the Nicaraguan border at the eastern end of Lake Nicaragua.

Some schedules, as recently posted:
• to Fortuna, 6 a.m., 6:30, and 9:30 a.m., 1, 3, 3:30 and 6 p.m.
• to Arenal and Tilarán, near the Pan American Highway, via Lake Arenal and Fortuna, at 6:30 and 9:30 a.m., 1 and 3 p.m..
• to Puerto Viejo and Río Frío, north of the volcanoes of the Central Valley, about every two hours from 5 a.m. to 5:30 p.m.
• to Los Chiles, about every two hours from 5 a.m. to 5 p.m.
• to San José, buses depart every hour from 5 a.m. to 5 p.m.

WHERE TO STAY
HOTEL CONQUISTADOR, tel. 46[0]0546. 30 rooms. $14 single; $20 double. A pleasant, colonial-style building. Rooms are plain, with private bath, good for the price. Protected parking. On the edge of town, along the street that leads toward San José.

The **HOTEL CENTRAL** (tel. 46[0]0766, 49 rooms, $16 to $24 single/ $30 to $33 double), on the square, is a concrete, unadorned building with plain rooms that will do for the night. And there are other, lesser hostelries.

Southwest of San Carlos
VALLE ESCONDIDO LODGE (P. O. Box 452-1150 La Uruca, tel. [2]310906, fax [2]329591). This new lodge is situated in a stand of primary forest, off the road that leads from San Ramón to La Tigra. Riding horses, mountain bikes and hiking trails are on-site. Most visits are arranged as a two-night package from San José, including hikes, talks, and a viewing of Arenal volcano, at about $400 per person.

North and West of San Carlos
A paved branch road runs northward through mostly flat, hot, sugarcane and citrus country, to **Los Chiles**, near Caño Negro Wildlife Reserve and the border with Nicaragua. You need not stop at the border. You can keep going all the way to the shores of Lake Nicaragua, and across it toward Managua.

LA QUINTA LODGE, 18 kilometers from Ciudad Quesada on the road to Los Chiles, is a roadside family-style stopping place with pool, snack bar open weekends, hammocks, basketball court, and guest facilities in a large house and cottages. The rate in bunks in the cottages is about $14 per person up to eight persons accommodated in each. In the house, a large family room goes for about $40. The River San Carlos, alive with tarpon, runs alongside the property, and you're welcome to drop a line down the steep bank (strictly catch-and-release). Caimans sometimes stop and sun themselves on the rocks. Call 46[4]0731 in Ciudad Quesada to reserve.

TILAJARI RESORT, Muelle de San Carlos (P. O. Box 81, Ciudad Quesada), tel. and fax 46[1]1083. 54 rooms. $70 single/$80 double. Visa, Master Card. Amid the sugarcane fields of the vicinity, along the San Carlos River, Tilajari is a full-fledged country club in facilities and appearance, except that the golf links haven't yet been installed on the acres of lawn. But you will find racquet ball, lighted tennis courts, a large pool and kids' pool, sauna, and a restaurant with a shaded terrace overlooking the River San Carlos.

Rooms are in pantile-roofed villas, and are on the plain side, with quiet central air conditioning. Suites, for only slightly more than the regular room rate, have a loft, separate bedroom, and television and refrigerator. These are more substantial facilities than anywhere else in the area, but the nicest part is the river that winds through the property, along which you might chance upon a crocodile taking a break. Riding horses are available, and trips to Arenal volcano and Caño Negro reserve, jungle walks and boating are arranged. About 21 kilometers from Ciudad Quesada.

RÍO SAN CARLOS LODGE, P. O. Box 354-4400 Boca de Arenal (tel. 46[0]0766, fax 46[0]0391, $63 single/$80 double with breakfast) is a lovely country house with wood-panelled rooms (one with tub inset in the floor), arched windows overlooking the San Carlos River, swimming pool, and views of Arenal volcano. The grounds are covered by trees and cultivated flowering plants. An attractive stopping point, indeed, 9 kilometers north of the junction at Muelle, but the sugar mill across the road could be a distraction at harvest times.

TOWARD NICARAGUA

To the north, the lands that roll on toward Nicaragua have being opened to settlement by new roads, constructed as part of development schemes that have led to the destruction of forests and animal life.

CAÑO NEGRO NATIONAL WILDLIFE REFUGE

Caño Negro National Wildlife Refuge was set aside to save some of the native bird species. Lake Caño Negro, frequented by migratory birds, covers 800 hectares in the rainy season, but dries up to a fraction of that size from February through May. Rare species here include the Nicaraguan grackle. There are also anhingas, ibis, northern jacana, roseate spoonbills, rare jabiru storks, and cormorants. Puma, jaguar, ocelots, and monkeys (spider, white-faced and howler) are found in the dry parts of the reserve.

ARRIVALS AND DEPARTURES

By Car or Boat

Caño Negro is located southeast of the village of Los Chiles, which can be reached by paved road. A dirt road continues southwest past the lake, and onward toward Upala. In rainy times, the lake may be accessible only by boating up the Río Frío and Patos River from Los Chiles.

By Tour

Sertur, in San José, is one of the travel agencies that operates excursions to Caño Negro. Basic camping facilities are available.

By Bus

Buses run from Ciudad Quesada (San Carlos) to Los Chiles about every two hours from 5 a.m. to 5 p.m. One or two buses a day run between Los Chiles and Upala, passing the refuge; or, it's a walk or taxi ride of about 15 kilometers.

Ujuminica, located south of Caño Negro, is a private farm that raises crocodiles and caimans for sale and for release into the wild, and has sleeping facilities for visitors. River trips to the farm can be arranged. For information, call 46[2]2004 and ask for Norman. Currently, a tour operates to Ujuminica on Wednesdays. Call Costa Rica Adventours, [2]225266.

Another road continues to the northwest, toward San Rafael de Guatuso. At a remote cattle farm on the slopes of Tenorio Volcano, is MAGIL FOREST LODGE, with ten rooms sleeping three or four persons each, private bathrooms, and bar. Getting here is a tropical adventure, off the paved road and over a cable bridge. The rate is about $120 double with meals. A typical package trip, about $500 for three nights from San José, includes meals and lodging, a visit to caves, birding and orchid-hunting walks, horseback trips to mountain lookouts, a boat ride on the Celeste River and one through the Caño Negro reserve, and a visit to an Indian reserve. Currently, departures are Mondays and Saturdays at 8 a.m. For information, write to P. O. Box 3404-1000, San José (Avenida 10, Calle 14), or call [2]212825, fax [2]336837.

Contact the lodge to arrange transport by helicopter or by four-wheel-drive vehicle from San José or from an airstrip in the region.

TO ARENAL VOLCANO

The main route from San Carlos for visitors is to the northwest. A good paved road winds and curves downward, then runs through humid, cattle-grazing lowlands, toward Arenal volcano, the Tilarán mountain range, and Arenal lake and dam.

Currently, a section of road after the dam is unpaved, and passable during the rainy season only by bus or in a four-wheel-drive vehicle.

Beyond this difficult stretch are several water sports facilities on Lake Arenal, the town of Tilarán, and the Pan American Highway at Cañas.

FORTUNA

Fortuna, 45 kilometers from San Carlos, is a pleasant and neatly laid out farming center. But its attractions lie in what is nearby: Arenal volcano; the hot springs at Tabacón; an impressive falls on the Fortuna River; caves; and fishing in Lake Arenal.

ARRIVALS AND DEPARTURES

By Air

Mr. César Romero, former crop duster and proprietor of Hotel Rancho Corcovado, will shortly inaugurate an air service to Fortuna (to an airstrip adjacent to his hotel, naturally), taking passengers from San José in just fifteen minutes or so. Call 47[9]9090 for information.

By Bus

The alternative is a winding bus ride of several hours from the capital. Take one of the Ciudad Quesada (San Carlos) buses that leave the Coca-Cola terminal (Avenida 1, Calle 16) in San José every hour. In Ciudad Quesada, connect with buses that leave for Fortuna at 6, 6:30, and 9:30 a.m., and 1, 3, 3:30 and 6 p.m.

By Tour

Arenal is full of tour shops, both attached to the various lodging places and freestanding. One guide to whom I've received several recommendations by satisfied clients is Gabino, who operates from an office on the main road near the church.

Currently, the rates for excursions look to me to be a bargain: at the **Hotel Fortuna**, a volcano night tour, or a day trip to the volcano with a stop at hot springs, goes for $10 per person.

You can go on your own, of course. But prices are so reasonable, that you should probably take your first trip with somebody who knows the terrain.

WHERE TO STAY

HOTEL RANCHO CORCOVADO, tel. and fax 47[9]9090. 30 rooms. $45 double, $15 per extra person. Weekly packages available. Located about eight kilometers east of Fortuna at a hamlet called Tanque (TAN-keh), Rancho Corcovado is a modern roadside lodging place with clean, tile-floored rooms, each with two or three beds with good mattresses, bedside lamps, and overhead fans, and, as they say here, a very good attention from the family headed by César Romero. There are two small TV lounges, and childrens' and adult pools. The veranda restaurant and bar at the rear overlook a river and pond where caimans pass the day, and howler monkeys and assorted other small mammals frequent the site. A tennis court is under construction.

LAS CABAÑITAS, tel. 47[9]9091, recently under construction on the eastern outskirts of Fortuna, will have 30 Swiss-appearing cottages of wood and stone with tile roofs, a restaurant, pool, and second-story lookout for volcano observation.

CABINAS EL TUCÁN, tel. 47[9]9048, is a great value for no-frills lodging if you're travelling by car: six plain, neat, clean rooms in two cottages, at about $10 per person, sharing bath. From the eastern entry to town, turn right, right again, and go 300 meters through a cow pasture, to where you can lodge just as if your were in the middle of the *campo*.

HOTEL SAN BOSCO (27 rooms, tel. 47[9]9050, fax 47[9]9178), two blocks off the main street, is the most substantial lodging place right in town. The newer section has large rooms with accoutrements such as shower doors, which raise the price, if not the comfort, to $30 single/$40 double; while the older part is good enough, with little extras like headboards on the beds, at $14 single/$24 double. And there is a third-floor observation platform for viewing Arenal's fireworks on clear nights.

HOTEL FORTUNA (13 rooms, tel. 47[9]9197), to the left side entering town from the east, has new, clean rooms with tile floors at $10 per person with private bath, $5 per person sharing bath. Good value.

HOTEL CENTRAL, tel. 47[9]9004, on the main street, is a neat wooden building with restaurant attached, with rooms for $6 per person or less. Like everyone else, they'll help with arrangements for horseback riding and volcano trips.

ALBERGUE BURÍO (Burío Inn, P. O. Box 1234-1250 Escazú, tel. 47[9]9076, or [2]280267 in San José, 8 rooms, $18 per person) enfolds a gardened alleyway opposite the plaza. That's a modest situation, indeed, but management counts for everything here. The owners know *everything* about the area and can arrange cave and volcano trips and fishing ($30 per hour on Lake Arenal, $300 for a group on the Río San Juan in Nicaragua). Rooms have private bath and are clean and modestly attractive, with stuccoed and panelled walls and overhead fan, and a single and a bunk bed. Breakfast is included in the rate.

HOTEL LAS COLINAS (tel. and fax 47[9]9107, 21 rooms, $14 single/$25 double), half a block off the main street from the Hotel Central, has plain rooms with private bath. They also run their own Arenal volcano and cave tours. Credit cards accepted.

And there at least half a dozen other hotels and cabinas in town. **CABINAS CARMELA**, on the main road opposite the church (tel. 47[9]9010), has an enclosed parking area, and rooms for $15 single/$20 double.

Out of Town

Out of town to the east, toward the volcano are:

FINCA DE CITO, one kilometer past Fortuna, with camping space in a pasture.

LA VACA MUCA (tel. 47[9]9186), farther down the road, has basic rooms.

JUNGLA Y SENDEROS LOS LAGOS, 3 kilometers from Fortuna, has trails through rolling pasture, available to the public for $2 per person, and a campground next to a cattle pen and rushing stream, with a $3 fee attached. **CASA DE CAMPO**, a kilometer down the road, also has camping.

CENTRO CAMPERO LAS PALMAS, tel. 47[9]9106, just farther on, also has camping space, as well as plain rooms with private bath at $15 per person.

WHERE TO EAT

LA CHOZA DEL LAUREL (Hut of the Bay Tree), west of the church on the main road, is a folksy eating spot with long wooden tables set up under a rough-shingled roof, set with home-style pottery ware. You'll be ushered into the kitchen to serve yourself from pots of rice and beans, chicken and rice, tamales, and other simmering country specialties, and charged according to what you consume, from $3 to $6. Fruit drinks and herbal beverages are also served. You won't do better for wholesome fare, and you can arrive as early as you wish for breakfast.

Elsewhere, **RANCHO LA CASCADA**, on one corner of the square, serves a standard assortment of "international" chicken, steak and fish main courses for $5 to $7 under a high thatched roof. **EL JARDÍN**, on the main street opposite the square, also offers plain food in soda-shop surroundings.

SEEING THE SIGHTS

Wildlife viewing and contact with nature in Costa Rica can be pricey experiences top-heavy with tour buses, chartered planes, guides, pre-arranged hotels and meals, markups according to what the traffic will bear, and non-refundable deposits.

Fortuna is the alternative, a low-cost, no-frills adventure center, where travelers can arrive on their own and find knowledgeable locals to take them on horseback trips, volcano viewing hikes and caving excursions, up into cloud forest, or out to fish, for as little as $15 per person per outing, or even less. Aside from the lack of a beach and pretentious dining (which perhaps you can do without), Fortuna is a complete and cheery resort where you don't have to feel as if everyone has their hands in your pockets.

Reserves and Volcanoes

You will probably have come to Fortuna to get a closer look at Arenal volcano (see below), but while you're here, numerous other adventures are available within easy reach of your hotel base. The most distant is Caño Negro Reserve, about an hour's drive north. Other easily reached destinations are the Venado caves, just north of Lake Arenal; Lake Arenal itself, for fishing (but there are few points where you can get right down to the water); and the surrounding countryside for horseback riding and walking and birding. With some guidance, you can set out by foot for Monteverde, about 20 kilometers and several mountain ridges away.

The **Fortuna River Falls** (Catarata Río Fortuna) are about 5.5 kilometers from town, from a turn from the main road by the church. Follow the washboard road for 1.4 kilometers through rolling pastures, then turn right and continue another 4 kilometers. If you reach a bridge on the first road, you've gone too far. A short path leads to a viewpoint from which you can appreciate a narrow chute that plunges from the forest into the valley below. It would be a long walk out this way, but it makes for a pleasant horseback excursion or motoring detour.

Tabacón, 12 kilometers past Fortuna, where the road drops into a lush river valley, is the site of several hot springs gushing out from near the base of Arenal volcano.

TABACÓN RESORT, once a low-priced getaway, has been rebuilt into a colonial-style country club and spa with a fee of about $12 for day use of the pool, water slides and restaurant. A hotel is under construction. Across the road and down a short path, you can enjoy no-frills bathing in steaming pools along the river for about $2.

ARENAL VOLCANO

Mount Arenal (1,633 meters), which overlooks much of the San Carlos plain and the northern Pacific lowlands, has the distinction of being the volcano in Costa Rica that most *looks* like a volcano, with its characteristic conical shape. It also acts like one, having erupted spectacularly in 1968 and spewed ashes over a wide area.

And it hasn't stopped since. On most nights, clouds of iridescent gas cling to the summit. The earth rumbles, and boulders the size of a house explode a thousand feet into the air, to a resounding orchestral accompaniment of pops and crackles and booms, and arc and fall a thousand feet back to the crater, to bounce and shatter their way down. Lava in red and orange and yellow spews and slithers along the slopes.

Nobody in his right mind climbs Arenal. Several people who have attempted to do so in recent years, including at least one tourist, have been killed. But there is no peril in observing the fireworks from a safe vantage point in the valley below, or even hiking on the *lower* part of the slopes.

Several lodges in Fortuna or closer to Arenal offer safe ringside seats, with a view from the porch of your room and across an intervening river valley to the nighttime show; others sponsor day or night excursions to favorite lookout points, and almost every travel agency in San José organizes volcano-watching excursions — just make sure before you go that recent activity has been reported, and that the weather has been clear.

Several travel agencies in San José operate day-long volcano-watching excursions to Arenal, with stops in Sarchí and at hot springs, at about $85.

About 60 kilometers from San Carlos, the road drops to beautiful, mountain-girt Lake Arenal (see pages 295-300), crossing the earthen dam that separates the lake from its natural drainage, the Arenal River.

WHERE TO STAY

ARENAL OBSERVATORY (tel. [2]552011, fax [2]553529, $60 per person, book through travel agencies) is a research station and set of cabins that offer ringside views of the fireworks on the volcano — at a safe distance of about two-and-a-half kilometers, separated by the valley of the Agua Caliente river. Canoes available, fishing arranged.This facility may be closed at times to the public; or inaccessible except with four-wheel-drive vehicle. Taxi fare from Fortuna is $25 or more.

At kilometer 61, a rough branch road leads over hills for two kilometers to **POSADA ARENAL (ARENAL LODGE)**, tel. 46[1]1881 (P. O. Box 1139-1250, Escazú), tel. [2]282588, fax [2]282798). 11 rooms. $63 to $86 single/$74 to $97 double, $97/$114 in suite. Visa, Master Card, American Express. Arenal Lodge is a ringer for a white summer cottage that you might find near a lake in New England. Mostly, it's a fishing lodge, and boats with guides for lake fishing are available at $150 per day for two. They'll also arrange tarpon fishing near the Nicaraguan border, and lake, hot springs and volcano-watching expeditions, and horseback riding. The suite is a huge room with dark wood panelling, large tub, and a privileged view of Arenal volcano from its private balcony and through floor-to-ceiling windows.

Though it can be continuously rainy in this area, there is a large patio hung with plants and birds in cages, sheltered by translucent roofing, and with a fireplace to chase away chills. Geese run around on the grassy hills, under the palms. Billiard table available. December and January are the rainiest times here, when Caribbean clouds reach this area. Call the lodge before you visit for current fishing and volcano-viewing conditions (in English).

HOTEL LOS HÉROES (P. O. Box 6083-1000 San José). 12 rooms. $80 to $110 double. This is not an imitation of a Swiss chalet, it *is* a Swiss chalet (or several of them, actually), perched on a hillside farm above Lake Arenal, about 10 kilometers past the dam, dedicated to Juan Santamaría and Arnold von Winkelried. Rooms have wall-to-wall carpeting, and plenty of hot water. The restaurant at Los Héroes serves fondue, of course (about $10), and has the most extensive wine list in the area.

At kilometer 17, from the dam, an unpaved road leads northward to the village of **Venado**, near which are caves that are open for viewing. Past kilometer 20, the road deteriorates to a rocky and muddy bed, requiring extreme respect for water-filled potholes. The fifteen kilometers or so to the village of Nuevo Arenal, where the pavement resumes, take well over an hour to negotiate, even in a vehicle with high clearance.

There are several additional lodging places between this point and Tilarán, on the south side of the lake. See pages 295-300 for more detail.

Continuing Around the Volcanoes

The paved road that runs east from San Carlos gradually descends through an area combed with hot springs. Nine kilometers away and just north of the highway is:

EL TUCANO COUNTRY CLUB, Agua Caliente de San Carlos, tel. [4]461822, fax 461692 (P. O. Box 114-1017, San José 2000, office at Paseo Colón, Calles 24/26, tel. and fax 219095). 40 rooms. $64 single/$77 double/$89 triple. El Tucano is a tropical spa and rain-forest country club, on an absolutely lovely estate of colonial-style buildings, with tennis and volleyball courts and carefully tended gardens, at an elevation of 950 meters. There is no other place like it in Costa Rica. The grounds are traversed by a river of warm mineral water (said to be curative for arthritis and degenerative diseases), which feeds the medicinal Jacuzzi. There are also saunas, three swimming pools (including one for children), a miniature golf course, horses ($5 per hour), nature trails, and a casino, which guests are encouraged to patronize.

Meals are served in a huge dining room, decorated with woven mats and paintings of toucans, to the soothing accompaniment of the rushing stream just beyond the lattice. Food is largely Italian-style, and well prepared, and prices are moderate, at about $7 for most main courses.

Anybody can dine at El Tucano, and non-guests may use the facilities for a small fee. Round-trip transportation from San José costs $120 for up to six persons. If you're driving, look for the large white gate on the north side of the road to Puerto Viejo.

More Places to Stay and Play

At La Virgen, **RANCHO LEONA** offers jungle **kayak tours**, one for beginners, with lazy paddling, and bird- and animal-watching; and an outing with a reforestation theme: participants plant seedlings in denuded and eroding areas. Trips start at $80, and can include staying as a guest in bunkrooms in the home of the operators, which has assorted porches and nooks and crannies, and exquisite stained-glass and other hand-crafted details, and a hot tub overlooking the river where you can soak after a long day and talk to the frogs. Or, for slightly more, you can stay at accommodations nearby. Transport from San José, and whitewater trips, and excursions to little-known falls and the Caño Negro reserve, can be arranged to order — many kayaks are available. Telephone 71[6]6312 to reach Rancho Leona directly. English is spoken.

The roadside **RANCHO LEONA** restaurant (look for the cupola), offers home-style soups, sandwiches, salads, eggplant Parmesan, granola, home-baked bread and fresh fruit drinks, all made from scratch. The open dining area features toadstool seats, and polished hardwood tables with inlaid chessboards and kayak designs. This is not your usual roadside stopping point.

Next door, **CABINAS TÍA ROSITA**, tel. 71[6]6475, takes the overflow from Rancho Leona.

At **Bajos de Chilamate**, a couple of kilometers from Chilamate, is **ISLAS DEL RÍO** (tel. 71[6]6898, [2]330366, fax [2]339671 in San José, 30 rooms, $57 single/$98 double with meals, slightly less in shared-bath rooms), a woodsy lodge and concrete outbuildings buildings on landscaped grounds amid 13 hectares of primary and regenerating forest along the Sarapiquí River, part of the reserve corridor that extends northward from Braulio Carrillo National Park. Rooms in the main lodge, with its terrace overlooking the river, are large, with hot water and fans, and some have tubs.

A trail protected by a thatched roof leads to the river and the islands for which the project is named, and you can wade through, or cross in a metal basket attached to a cable. Common mammals here are sloths, anteaters, and nutrias, and birding is good, especially for aquatic species.

Meals are served in the open, overlooking the river. Horses are for rent for $10 for a couple of hours. Rafting trips (class II and II) can be arranged, along with boat trips and excursions to La Selva. Sleeping facilities are planned for four nearby forest areas of different types, at lower rates than in the main lodge.

Beyond La Virgen, near the farthest point that you can go from San José on this road, is:

SELVA VERDE LODGE, Chilamate, tel. 71[6]6459. 50 rooms. $80 single/$130 double in River Lodge; $130 double to $184 for four persons in bungalows, including meals and taxes. U.S. reservations: 3540 NW 13 St., Gainesville, FL 32609, tel. 800-858-0999, fax 904-371-3710. Located on a 500-acre farm and private reserve, with both well-manicured gardens and wild areas. Buildings are joined by a long, thatch-covered passage.

The River Lodge, with most guest rooms, consists of several buildings on posts, connected by elevated walkways, projecting guests *into* the forest canopy. Rooms in this section have private bathrooms. A new combination dining room and bar overlooks the river. Across the road from the check-in area, and up a hillside, are five secluded bungalows, with space for up to four persons.

Aside from birding and jungle walks and horseback rides on the lodge properties and in nearby reserves, Selva Verde is a good base for river fishing and rafting. All kinds of trekking, cycling and rafting excursions can be arranged through the Florida office. Reservations are essential. You can also drop in and use the trails as a day visitor for a fee of about $5. A facility with shared baths accommodates groups, and conference facilities are available.

SEEING AREA SIGHTS

Just east of El Tucano, at **Marina de San Carlos**, is a small *Zoológico* (Zoo), opposite the gas station, where boas, parrots, jaguars, spider and white-faced monkeys, coyotes, raccoons, ocelots, jaguars, macaws, toucans, and a rare albino peccary, among others, are kept in an informal barnyard setting.

The Marina zoo started as the hobby of a local woman who took in wounded squirrels and other small animals. It has now been formalized, but not too much so, and it makes for a fun place to wander around as a break from your journey.

In addition to the animals in chicken-wire enclosures, the property has a small pond and dam, and a nature trail through an adjacent forest area. An admission fee of a couple of dollars is collected.

From Marina, the paved road continues over hill and down dale, gradually heading into lower country. Each town is a cluster of clapboard or tongue-and-groove houses, on concrete foundations, with red tin roofs, modest and neat. There are a couple of more substantial dwellings with carport, and, in the case of **Venecia**, a sprawling, tan, tin-sided church with red roof, surrounded by well-kept gardens.

About five kilometers to the north of Venecia are the ruins of **Cutris**, a pre-Columbian city that shows signs of having been well ordered, with wide streets. The road from Venecia comes to within two kilometers of the site, which has not been restored and has no visitors' facilities.

Past **Río Cuarto**, at **San Miguel**, the road from San Carlos joins another road from San José via Heredia, through the saddle between the Barva and Poás volcanoes. Along the way are the dramatic **La Paz** falls, at Vara Blanca, just after the Poás turnoff. According to a report in *Costa Rica Today*, the travellers' newspaper, the 4,500-foot drop of water through rocks and vegetation, and the effect of sunshine, naturally produce ionized air that is said to relieve stress and promote well-being.

Gradually, to the north of San Miguel, the towns become less neat, with much recent, ramshackle construction right along the road, and vigorous, disorderly vegetation. The wrinkles of the land become fewer, and finally fade, and groves of orange trees appear among the flat pastures. Barva volcano, often shrouded in mist or downpours, looms to the south.

This is the **San Carlos Plain** which, despite its proximity to the Central Valley, is a frontier area, where a waterlogged terrain and assorted pests and illness until recently obstructed settlement. Even now, hardly a road penetrates the jungle, and rivers are still important transport routes. The San Juan River forms the northern border of the region with Nicaragua, but it is hardly a barrier. People and goods circulate freely and without formality between the two countries along the many waterways, much to the consternation of political authorities. And in troubled recent times, some of the movement has been far from innocent.

PUERTO VIEJO DE SARAPIQUI

Seventy kilometers from San Carlos or Heredia, Puerto Viejo was, until a few years ago, the end of the road, whence one traveled onward only by light cargo boat on the Sarapiquí River, toward the San Juan River and Barra del Colorado on the Caribbean. Before peace broke out in Nicaragua, much of this area was effectively off limits to outsiders; but it has a colorful history as the fluvial highway to the interior used by William Walker and other adventurers and filibusterers of the last century.

A road extension now provides a way through to the south and east, though you might still be able to negotiate your way aboard a river boat, and make a round trip back to San José via the Tortuguero reserve and Limón. Patience and a flexible schedule would be absolute requirements for such a journey, as floods and fancy play havoc with promised departures. A surer way to float the river is on a rafting excursion organized in San José, or an inclusive trip along the Sarapiquí to Tortuguero (see pages 182-183).

ARRIVALS AND DEPARTURES
Arriving By Bus
Buses operate to Puerto Viejo from Avenida 11, Calles Central/1, San José, daily at 6:30, 9, 10 (express) and 11 a.m. and 1, 3:30 (express), 4 and 5:30 p.m. Other buses taking the longer route via Heredia depart at 6 a.m., noon and 3 p.m.

Departing By Bus
Buses depart for San José at 4:30, 6:30, 8 (express) and 10:30 a.m., and 2, 3 (express) and 4:30 p.m. Slower buses via Heredia depart at 7:30 a.m. and 4:30 p.m.

Departing By Boat
Be at the dock (next to the car-repair lot) to catch the 11:30 a.m. boat down the Sarapiquí to the San Juan River on the border with Nicaragua, calling on the way at jungle river outposts. Fare is about $4 per person, You can sleep at the basic **ORO VERDE STATION** (call [2]349507 in San José for information) and catch the boat at dawn to return upriver.

To keep moving in one direction, you can also charter a boat here. The fare for four people to Barra del Colorado is about $200, and for slightly more, you can get to Tortuguero National Park.

WHERE TO STAY
Here at what was a short time ago the end of the line (unless you planned to continue downriver to fight in Nicaragua), visitors' accommodations are sprouting, and by the time you pass through, travel shops should be in place to provide excursions on the Sarapiquí River from town, in addition to those offered by nearby hotels.

HOTEL MI LINDO SARAPIQUÍ, tel. [7]766074. 6 rooms. $13 per person. On the entry street into Puerto Viejo, small, new rooms with overhead fans, perfectly adequate.

HOTEL EL BAMBÚ, tel. 76[6]6005. 9 rooms. $45 single or double with breakfast, credit cards accepted. A substantial white concrete building across the street from Mi Lindo Sarapiquí, more attractive in the lobby (wicker furniture, plants) than in the rooms, but you get large windows, television and fan.

Lesser accommodations for under $10 per person include **CABINAS MONTEVERDE**, next to El Bambú; and **HOTEL GONAR**, near the dock.

Near Puerto Viejo
EL GAVILÁN LODGE (P. O. Box 445-2010 San José, tel. [2]349507, fax [2]536556). Twelve rooms. $46 single/$57 double. El Gavilán is just north of Puerto Viejo on a turn from the road to Guápiles, between the Sarapiquí and Sucio rivers. Eight of the rooms are adjacent to the farmhouse, crowded with three beds, with basic bathrooms. Four better rooms are in an outbuilding. Bathing is available in river and whirlpool. Guests should bring their own alcoholic beverages.

El Gavilán operates day trips from San José in its own van. Birding, boating, horseback riding, jungle walks, and fishing and kayaking are either included, with transportation and meals, in the fee of about $85, or can be arranged. The owner-operators are a German and a Costa Rican.

LA SELVA BIOLOGICAL STATION

Just south of Puerto Viejo is **La Selva Biological Station**, operated by the Organization for Tropical Studies, which takes in 1,508 hectares (3,700 acres) of lowland rain forest, most of it never disturbed by agriculture. Unlike most other parks and sanctuaries, La Selva is reserved mainly for scientific investigation. Its natural diversity is notable even in Costa Rica, with 2,000 different plant species, of the 12,000 in the country.

Most parts of La Selva can be reached by an extensive, well-marked trail system, along which trees are labeled. An arboretum holds most native species — over a thousand.

La Selva is accessible by river from Puerto Viejo, or by road — the entry is one kilometer from an unmarked turnoff about 30 kilometers from the junction with the Guápiles highway. Low-lying, concrete, institutional-style buildings are clustered in a clearing. The research center is reached by a steel cable suspension footbridge that dangles over the green, jungle-lined Puerto Viejo River.

Living facilities range from dormitories to rooms for two with shared bath. Researchers whose work is approved by the Organization for Tropical Studies are given priority. Outsiders pay about $90 daily for room and board. In response to growing interest in La Selva, a network of self-guided trails, and programs for guided visits, are being developed. Currently, you'll be allowed in for a day visit for $17, which includes a guide booklet to help you find your way on the trails.

For information on staying at the reserve, or day trips, contact the **Organization for Tropical Studies**, P. O. Box 676, 2050 San Pedro, tel. [2]406696, fax [2]406783; or P. O. Box DM, Durham, NC 27706 U.S.A., tel. 919-684-5774. Dial 71[6]6987 to reach La Selva directly. The station provides round-trip transportation three times a week from San José, and several daily trips into Puerto Viejo.

Caution: If you plan to walk any trails at La Selva, wear high boots as protection against snakebites, and never step or sit anywhere without looking first for snakes and stinging ants.

WHERE TO STAY

ECOALBERGUE SARAPIQUÍ (tel. 76[6]6122) is a run-down farmhouse adjacent to La Selva. There are four no-frills rooms with no other furniture than bunk beds. Bathrooms are shared, and the rate for all this is about $15 per person. Meals cost an additional $5 to $7 each. Horses can be hired, and there is a nice beach for river swimming. Call first, or you might find it closed.

Past **Puerto Viejo**, a good road heads southeast around Barva volcano. Much of the land to both sides is already cleared in a rather untidy fashion. Cattle are grazing, and corn is growing. You see signs at intermittent mud tracks that lead to clusters of shacks, announcing that so-and-so many farmers have benefitted from a distribution of land. And you understand the pressure to provide landless people with the means to make their own living, and the political payoffs therefrom, which in no way compare to the domestic benefits available from a policy of conserving the rain forest for future generations. At one point along the road, there is an outpost of the *Comando Atlántico del Batallón Relámpago* (Atlantic Commando of the Lightning Battalion), in helmets and camouflage fatigues, ready to control any subversive activities in this strategic area. Pinch yourself, and remember that these are not soldiers — more blur of the distinction between army and civil guard.

Near Las Horquetas

RARA AVIS, P. O. Box 8105, 1000 San José, tel. and fax [2]530844. This 1,500-acre reserve, on the site of a former prison colony, is oriented toward visitors who want to experience the rain forest with all its rough and muddy edges. Arrival from Las Horquetas, 15 kilometers distant, is by a jarring tractor cart ride over a barely passable track paved in part with rough logs. Mud boots are required for walking the trails, and formidable rain gear. Sleeping facilities are bunkrooms, though rooms with private bath are also available at a facility a sloppy hike away from the dropoff point. Numerous visitors are enthusiastic about the experience, but some complain that it's Devil's Island.

Activities at Rara Avis are birding, swimming in jungle streams and at the base of a towering waterfall, and guided hikes to learn about the complex interactions of plants and animals. Scientific investigations are sometimes in progress and there are programs to raise butterflies and export decorative plants.

The rate for accommodations is about $50 per person with meals, or $85 single/$155 double/$185 triple in rooms with private bath. From San José, add about $50 for a taxi to Las Horquetas (from where the tractor leaves at 9 a.m.), or take the 7 a.m. Río Frío bus. Reserve through travel agencies in the United States or by phone in Costa Rica, and verify that qualified guides will be on-site.

RÍO FRÍO

Southeast of Puerto Viejo, **Río Frío** is another small settlement, with basic accommodations, and a Chinese restaurant (not at all bad, surprisingly). If you come this way from San Carlos, you'll have some time between buses to stroll around, and examine town life: the latest Mexican soap operas, baseball, and news from Chicago brought to local eateries through satellite television; shop attendants engaging more in conversation than commerce; strangers on their way to scientific investigations; tractors pulling carts of produce along muddy lanes.

Beyond Río Frío are more dirt roads — and train tracks! Suddenly, you are no longer on the frontier, but in the former jungle penetrated by the railroad before it reached San José. There are great banana processing plants, with signs urging Standard Fruit workers to more productivity; banana tramways making their way through the vast fields, on bamboo supports; and papaya plantations. Places have names like Finca Seis, Finca Siete, Finca Ocho (Farm Six, Farm Seven, Farm Eight — romantic) and general-issue tan concrete-block housing.

Where the banana plants do not come up to and lean into the road, eerie, tall, ferny bamboo stands lie to either side. Bananas on tramways and railroads have an easier go of it than people: it is not hard to lose your way in this world until itself, where one rutted, narrow, bumpy road branches from another much like it, without any signs.

The twelve kilometers from Río Frío to the junction with the paved highway to San José take nearly an hour to negotiate. (Paving of this road is in progress.) Then it's an easy ride back to the capital, through the high rain forest of Carrillo Park (see pages 208-209), or to Limón on the Caribbean coast.

WHERE TO STAY

MORPHO LODGE (P. O. Box 3153-1000 San José, tel. [2]219132, fax [2]572273) operates a camp-style lodge facility on a 400-hectare tract on the eastern edge of Braulio Carrillo National Park, where continuing projects include organic farming, research, and forestry management. Trails of varying lengths cut through the property, where sightings of raccoons, coatis, deer and toucans are common.

Transportation of groups is by public bus (for Guápiles, from Calle

12, Avenidas 7/9, to the River Corinto), and the fee of about $15 includes guide orientation and allows you to share an upstairs sleeping room in a rustic building.

You cook for yourself (you bring your own food and sheet) or hike out to a restaurant, and aside from a potential grunginess, you can experience birding, trails, mud, foliage, and coatimundi-sighting similar to that appreciated by the folks in the $95 rooms down the way. Day visits can also be arranged. Stop in at the San José office, Avenida 7, Calles 7/9 (white-and-gray building), no. 9 and 10. A 10-room lodge is under construction.

A FEW BUTTONS SHORT

19. TICO TALK

Here are some basic Costa Rican and Spanish words for various situations, which you might want to become familiar with *before* you need them:

FOOD AND DRINK

almuerzo: lunch
arroz: rice
atún: tuna
avena: oatmeal
batido (en agua, leche): beverage of liquified fresh fruit (and water, milk)
birra: beer (slang)
birrear: to drink bear (slang
bistec: beef
bocas: hor d'oeuvres
café: coffee
cajeta: fudge
calamar: squid
camarón: shrimp
carne: meat (usually beef)
casado: combination plate of a main food item with rice, beans, cabbage
cena: dinner
cerveza: beer
ceviche: marinated fish cocktail
chimichurri: sauce for grilled meats, made with fresh coriander or parsley
chilasquiles: meat-filled tortillas
chile relleno: stuffed pepper
chorizo: sausage
churrasco: charcoal-broiled meat
chuleta (de cerdo): (pork) chop
coco: coconut
corvina: sea bass
cruda: draft beer
desayuno: breakfast
dorado: dolphinfish (mahi-mahi)
emparedado, sandwich: sandwich
ensalada: salad
filete: filet
fresa: strawberry
fresco: fruit drink
frijol: bean
frito: fried
fruta: fruit
gallo, gallo pinto: rice and beans with herbs and spices
guaro: sugarcane liquor

helado: ice cream
huevos: eggs
jamón: ham
jugo (de naranja): (orange) juice
langosta: lobster
leche: milk
lomito: sirloin
mantequilla: butter
mermelada: marmalade
milanesa: breaded (veal or beef)
naranja: orange
natilla: cream
olla de carne: meat stew
omelete: omelet
pan: bread
pastel: cake
pescado: fish
piña: pineapple
a la plancha: grilled
plátanos, maduros: plantains
papa (frita, al horno, puré): potato (French-fried, baked, mashed)
piña: pineapple
pipa: juice coconut
plato típico: native-style plate
pollo: chicken
pozol: corn soup
queso: cheese
refresco (gaseoso, natural): beverage (bottled soda, fresh-fruit)
ron: rum
sandía: watermelon
sopa: soup
sudada: stewed, as *carne sudada*, stewed beef
tamales: filled corn dough
tayuya: stuffed tortilla
té: tea
tocineta: bacon
tortillas: corn (or wheat-flour) flat-bread
tostadas: toast
vino: wine

GEOGRAPHIC TERMS

bahía: bay
cantón: county, canton
caño: creek
cerro: hill, peak
ciudad: city
finca: farm
golfo: gulf
hacienda: ranch
isla: island

lago, laguna: lake
parque nacional: national park
playa: beach
punto: point
refugio: refuge
reserva: reserve
río: river
villa: town
volcán: volcano

ON THE ROAD AND AT SEA

¡alto!: stop!
bomba: gasoline (petrol) station
bote: small boat, skiff
camino: road
carretera: highway
ceda el paso: yield (usually at bridge)
curva adelante: curve ahead
derrumbes: landslides
estacionamiento: parking
intersección adelante: intersection ahead
lastre (camino de): rough, unpaved road

mantenga su derecha: keep right
no adelantar: no passing
panga: motorboat
parada: bus stop
peatones: pedestrians
puente en curva: bridge at curve
tránsito entrando: trafffic entering
trepidadores: bumps in the road — slow down!
velocidad máxima: speed limit

SOME RECURRENT WORDS THAT MIGHT NOT BE IN YOUR SPANISH VOCABULARY:

Cabinas: Usually basic, cold-water beach accommodations. But cabinas can also be middle-range motel-style units. The common denominator is an outside or courtyard entrance to the room.
Campo: Space (as on a bus)
Cien metros: One block
Faja: Belt. In other countries, a faja is a sash. Not that you need a belt, or a sash, for that matter; this is just by way of illustrating that the Costa Rican language is in some ways stuck in the past.
Fila: Line; Haga fila: line up
Huaquero: Grave robber, looter
Hueco: Pothole
Macho: American, or big shot; literally, "male." But the term doesn't connote men exclusively. The North American ex-wife of an ex-president is known as La Macha.
Mi Amor: My love. Don't take it to heart if that smashing lady at the ticket counter or that incredible hunk calls you mi amor. It's a common form of address, like the cockney luv.
No se aceptan excursionistas: Busloads of holiday-makers not welcome (a good sign at any beach hotel)
Okey: Okay, you're welcome.
Pachanga: Party
Palenque: Thatched shelter (equivalent to the Mexican palapa)
Por dicha: Luckily; that's great
Pulpería: Corner Store
¡Pura Vida!: Great! ¡Lo máximo!
Salón: Saloon
Soda: A basic luncheonette
Tico: Costa Rican
Típico: Native-style, Costa Rican-style, as comida típica, a native-style meal.
Tiquicia: Costa Rica
Torta: Boo-boo, error
Verdulería: Fruit and vegetable store

INDEX

446 COSTA RICA GUIDE

DEAR READER,

By this point, you know that I speak my mind. Now it's your turn.

If you've discovered a hotel or restaurant and would like to share it with others, drop me a line. If you've had a bad experience with any service used by visitors — whether I've mentioned it or not — I want to know about that, too. Thanks for writing.

Sincerely,

Paul Glassman

OPEN ROAD PUBLISHING
P.O.Box11249, Cleveland Park Station, Washington, DC 20008
